W9-BWO-855

the Book, the Ring, & the Poet

Books by William Irvine

THE BOOK, THE RING, AND THE POET
APES, ANGELS AND VICTORIANS
THE UNIVERSE OF G.B.S.
WALTER BAGEHOT

Books by Park Honan

THE BOOK, THE RING, AND THE POET
BROWNING'S CHARACTERS:
A STUDY IN POETIC TECHNIQUE

the Book, the Ring, & the Poet

A Biography of Robert Browning

William Irvine & Park Honan

McGraw-Hill Book Company
New York St. Louis San Francisco
Düsseldorf Mexico Toronto

123456789BPBP79876543

Grateful acknowledgment is made to John Murray for permission to quote from the published letters of Robert Browning and Elizabeth Barrett Browning, as listed in the Cue Titles at the end of this volume. In addition, acknowledgment is made to the Estate of Thurman L. Hood for permission to quote from *Letters of Robert Browning Collected by Thomas J. Wise*, edited by Thurman L. Hood, Yale University Press, copyright 1933 and renewed 1961 by Thurman L. Hood; and to the University of Illinois, for permission to quote from *Letters of the Brownings to George Barrett*, edited by Paul Landis with the assistance of Ronald E. Freeman, © 1958 by the Board of Trustees of the University of Illinois.

Library of Congress Cataloging in Publication Data

Irvine, William, 1906-1964
The Book, the ring, and the poet.

1. Browning, Robert, 1812-1889. I. Honan, Park, joint author. II. Title.
PR4231.17 821'.8 [B] 72-12604
ISBN 0-07-032045-4

Preface

The complexity of Robert Browning's mind and character and the continuing vitality and importance of his poetry have inspired many special studies. Indebtedness to a wealth of these—and to Browning's inadvertent perspicacity in marrying a confirmed letter-writer—will be apparent throughout this biography. Much previously unused or overlooked material figures here as well.

William Irvine had been at work on this biography for many years, and at the time of his death he had written Chapters 1 through 21.

Park Honan was then asked to co-author the book and has worked five years. Apart from editing the earlier chapters, he has researched and written Chapters 22 through 27 entirely, and contributed substantial sections to Chapters 10 and 17.

Irvine and Honan had found themselves in intellectual sympathy considerably before the latter's work began. It is to be hoped that a close, consecutive examination of evidence, conducted in turn by the two biographers, has resulted in a vivid and just narrative as well as in a truer, fuller account of Browning, his marriage, his life, his friends, his era. Browning's poetic development is scrutinized, and one of the major purposes of the book is to illuminate his poetry biographically, with some emphasis on his notable contributions to impressionism and to the technique of the dramatic monologue.

William Irvine was Professor of English at Stanford University. His scholarship in the field of nineteenth-century literature has its base in a broad knowledge of the intellectual, social and political currents of the Victorian age. The subjects of his previous biographies—*Walter Bagehot, The Universe of G.B.S.* and *Apes, Angels and Victorians*—were not only important writers but important men of their times, Bagehot in economics and politics, Shaw in social ideas and liberal reform, Darwin and Huxley in science and culture. (Irvine's work on the present book was much facilitated by Grants in Aid from the American Council of Learned Societies and the Henry E. Huntington Library, and by two Guggenheim Fellowships.)

Park Honan has written among other works on the Victorians *Browning's Characters: A Study in Poetic Technique* and two essays preliminary to a life of Matthew Arnold. (Honan's research and writing for the present biography owe greatly to three grants from Brown University during his years there as assistant and associate professor, as well as to a Guggenheim Fellowship.) He is Senior Lecturer in English at the University of Birmingham in England.

The two biographers benefited from other aid. Much indebtedness is indicated in the list of cue titles on pages 587 and 588 of this book. The Armstrong Browning Library at Baylor, Balliol College at Oxford, the Folger Shakespeare Library, the Harvard College Library, the Huntington Library, the Library of the London School of Economics, the New York Public Library, the Humanities Research Center at the University of Texas at Austin, University College London Library, and the Beinecke Rare Book Room and Manuscript Library at Yale permitted quotation from unpublished letters. Mr. John Murray permitted quotation from unpublished documents in the aforementioned archives and in the British Museum, as well as from published Browning letters that are still in his copyright.

Mrs. Belinda Norman-Butler allowed both authors to consult letters in her private collection. The late Sir John Murray permitted William Irvine to consult unpublished material; Count Rucellai and the Marchese Nannina Fossi Rucellai allowed him to read and to quote from unpublished letters, and their family recollections of Browning were illuminating. C. M. Hancher and William S. Peterson permitted Park Honan to read and to quote from unpublished writing; Thomas J. Collins sent him copies of the then-unpublished letters from Browning to the Tennysons.

Victorian Poetry permitted the use of two articles which originally appeared in that journal—William Irvine's "Four Monologues in Browning's *Men and Women*" and Park Honan's "The Murder Poem for Elizabeth."

A great measure of thanks is expressed to Charlotte Stearns Irvine, who has provided editorial assistance and suggestions throughout, as well as research on Elizabeth Barrett Browning.

Many librarians and archivists provided generous assistance, and Park Honan mentions in particular for their valuable aid Jack W. Herring, Lois Murray Smith, and Veva Wood at the Armstrong Browning Library; E. V. Quinn at Balliol College; and Marjorie G. Wynne at the Beinecke Rare Book Room and Manuscript Library. Park Honan owes much to the critical stimulus of Norman Maclean and Lawrence A. Ragan; and to Elsie Duncan-Jones, Roma A. King, Jr., and David Lodge for their detailed criticisms of his chapters. He expresses thanks to the owners of the châlet La Saisiaz in the Haute-Savoie; to Marcel Colin for photographs and guidance at Ste. Marie and Le Croisic in Britanny; and to François Mouret and Norman Williams for research assistance at Venice and at Asolo. His writing in this biography owes in many ways to his wife Jeannette, as well as to the suggestions and encouragement of his mother and William H. Honan, his brother. He recalls Miss Mabel Purefoy FitzGerald's kindness in talking to him on two occasions about her friends of the late 1880s, Robert Browning and Mrs. Orr.

For information or other valuable help the following persons are to be very cordially thanked: Richard D. Altick, Elaine Baly, John Gilbert, Gertrude Reese Hudson, Philip Kelley, Robert Langbaum, A. G. R. Petti, Maisie Ward Sheed, T. J. B. Spencer, R. S. Stewart, Paul Turner, William Whitla, and Joe Womack. The work benefited in its final stages from the editorial suggestions of Berenice Hoffman.

Contents

the Book, the Ring, & the Poet

CHAPTER 1

Childhood

1812-24

It is not surprising that many Victorians were extremely serious and extremely illogical. The trouble was, in part, that some of their windows they never opened. The air in their houses was heavy and stagnant with conscientious affection and appropriative piety. There was so seldom any breeze of reason and detachment, of comedy and laughter, blowing through their solemn dining rooms and overfurnished parlors. Father and Mother were taken so very seriously, both by themselves and their children. Behind Father and Mother stood, on ascending levels, the schoolmaster, the congregation, the minister, the pocketbook, the Bible; much else, up to the Deity.

The trouble was also historical. Even as the Victorian period began, science was undermining conventional religion, and romanticism had recently undermined nearly everything else—and made revolt significant and attractive into the bargain. If an energetic and gifted young man felt driven to defy his parents, he was provided by the *Zeitgeist* with impressive intellectual reasons for doing so—except that he then found himself defying faith and tradition as well.

Robert Browning has usually been thought of as exuberant and happy in youth, confident and successful in maturity, robust and vigorous always—in fact, he seemed robust and vigorous to a fault. People began to wonder. In Browning's lifetime Henry James observed that he lived in two air-tight compartments—the one all energy and social noise, the other all poetry and privacy. More recently, Richard Altick, Betty Miller and others have shown that he kept fighting the battles and seeking the happiness of childhood far into maturity.[1] Yet his childhood was in many ways unconventionally happy and his parents unconventionally sympathetic.

For a genuine ancestral crime, one must go back to Robert Browning the grandfather, a capable, self-righteous, consistent man, who begot many children by two wives, rose with conviction to the post of Principal of the Bank Stock Office in the Bank of England, read *Tom Jones* and the Bible inflexibly once a year, and in old age feared the proximity of a future poet to his gouty foot.[2] Such a man was only too likely to have a sensitive and apologetic eldest son and to treat him with a narrow and ruthless rectitude. Before the age of twenty, Robert the second was offered a position on a West Indies sugar plantation to which, through his deceased mother, he was a possible heir. Though he was about as likely as Charles Lamb to accommodate himself to the institution of slavery, his father sent him off at once. Young Mr. Browning tried to live with his duties and his conscience. But he "conceived such a hatred to the slave-system . . . that he relinquished every prospect,—supported himself, while there, in some other capacity, and came back . . . to his father's profound astonishment and rage."[3] He now had some thoughts of becoming a painter. At length, faced with his father's refusal of support, he submitted to a clerkship in the Bank of England, where he labored purgatorially for a lifetime. He consoled himself with a happy marriage and a library of six thousand volumes. One observes that he was not quite at ease with the demands of ordinary life. Many years later, Elizabeth Barrett Browning, accustomed to the spectacle of a more formidable kind of parenthood, was astonished to meet "an elderly gentleman who submitted to having his face washed and his hair brushed for him by a briskly impatient daughter."[4] He was never able to talk about his West Indies experiences. "If you question him about it," his son explained to Elizabeth, "he shuts his eyes involuntarily and shows exactly the same marks of loathing that may be noticed while a piece of cruelty is mentioned . . . and the *word* 'blood,' even, makes him change colour."[5]

Meek men are seldom impressive, yet Mr. Browning impressed many. Whatever his eccentricities, he was not so suppressed as to lack the hearty, dramatic Browning manner, or the Browning capacity for enjoyment. Within his retired sphere, he showed much of his father's energy, and anticipated—in lesser degree—nearly all of his son's gifts. He was widely acquainted with several literatures—not only French, Spanish, and Italian, but Latin, Greek, and Hebrew—in their original languages. He lovingly and copiously enriched his books with notes, cross-references, charts, and chronological tables. He had, according to Rossetti, "a real genius for drawing."[6] His Pied Piper of Hamelin in verse is a startling parallel to his son's famous poem, in style and also in the baroque, rather violently humorous turn of imagination.[7] "With a touch of ambition, even a spice of vanity," his son wrote many years later, "he would assuredly have won a reputation in more ways than one." But he was the sort of man "who would have stared to hear himself mentioned as remarkable."[8] In short, having long since given up all artistic ambition on his own account, he was ready to live the more vividly in the ambition of a son. If he lacked the self-confidence to be a poet in his own right, he was in many ways peculiarly qualified to be the father of a poet.

In 1811 he married Sarah Anna Wiedemann, a lady of Scottish-German extraction, at Camberwell, where the two took a cottage in Southampton Street. The future poet was born May 7, 1812; and his sister Sarianna, January 7, 1814.

From the cradle Robert Browning the poet was a noisy, conspicuous infant. There are reports that his mother could keep him quiet only by telling him stories while she held him (perhaps forcibly) on her knee; that he extemporized verses while toddling round and round the dining-room table; that he drew wonderfully at two; that he could read and write at five; that at five-and-a-half he read Ossian and wrote Ossian imitations; and that at a slightly later age, he was removed from a neighboring school, by popular demand of the other children's mothers, because of excessive brilliance. Looking back on those childhood years, he described himself as having been "passionately religious" and connected his piety with his mother.[9]

In the story of the Browning family Mrs. Sarah Anna Browning seems to be an invisible force chiefly known by her extraordinary effects. Nobody thought to describe either her character or her appearance except Robert's boyhood friend Alfred Domett, who recalled apologetically that she had "the *squarest* head & forehead I almost ever saw in a human being, putting me in mind...of a tea-chest or tea-caddy."[10] Everybody else dismisses her with a few negatives or a few superlatives. Carlyle pronounced her "the true type of a Scottish gentlewoman," and after her death her son sometimes spoke of her, with "tremulous emotion," as "a divine woman."[11] Of those who knew her only by report, Mrs. Orr asserts that she was essentially matter-of-fact and inartistic; Griffin, that she was an accomplished musician; and Sharp, that she was intellectually inclined and fond of the romantic poets. Apparently these are attempts to deduce, as Cuvier did Megatherium, an entire and intelligible lady from a single bone of anecdote or fact. Everybody agrees that Mrs. Browning was a woman in delicate health, of quiet manners and deep feeling, with apparently formidable powers of making herself indispensable by efficient ministration and tender solicitude. She was devoutly religious and ardently musical. When finished with the practical concerns of the day, she liked to play the piano softly in the twilight. One suspects that on such occasions she gave herself up to religious reverie.

One important person for Mrs. Browning was the Reverend George Clayton. From girlhood to the end of her life, she attended his chapel in York Street, Walworth. Since many of Mr. Clayton's sermons survive, one may gain from them some idea of Mrs. Browning's theology. Described as combining "the characters of a saint, a dancing master, and an orthodox eighteenth-century theologian in about equal proportions,"[12] Mr. Clayton writes with considerable polish, some learning, and noticeable psychological acumen. He is no narrow sectarian, but speaks of the Church of England with respect and of the Church of Rome with a pitying, condescending tolerance not unlike that in the poems of Robert Browning. Though apparently a Calvinist, he is reassuringly gentle and indulgent. "If I were to reason upon first principles," he observes with British caution, "I should find it extremely difficult to account for the introduction of moral evil in the world."[13] He says almost nothing of election or predestination and, within the limits of honesty, is tactful about hellfire and eternal damnation. On the other hand, he insists on original sin, the constant threat of sudden death, and, above all, the necessity of faith to salvation.

About the last point, as the wife of a man who read Voltaire and Mandeville and the mother of a boy who seemed likely to read everything, Mrs. Browning must have worried a good deal. Yet she endured the six-thousand-volume library. She even kept house with it uncomplainingly in a modest cottage. As time went on, she tolerated poetry in her son as she tolerated erudition in her husband; indeed, she rejoiced in his poetry and abetted him in it. But she never lost sight of a heavenly accounting. Mr. Browning joined the chapel in 1820, went regularly, and died, according to his son, "an unhesitating believer in Christianity."[14] He was just the kind of man to be converted through sheer good nature and tractability, and his wife, one suspects, just the kind of woman to be irresistible in her utter conviction and consequent tender, suffering solicitude for his eternal welfare. After all, she had much to suffer in any case from her neuralgia and anemia.

In dealing with her son, Mrs. Browning did not always conquer by solicitude alone. In the last extremity, like Mr. Clayton, she could mention hellfire. When Robert fell into an arrogant habit of calling people "fools," she pointed out as a good Christian that "'whoso calleth his brother "fool" is in danger &c. for he hath committed murder in his heart already.'" "In short," her son concluded to Elizabeth Barrett, "I stood there a convicted *murderer*...to which I was forced penitently to agree."[15] Robert was attracted to his mother by fear as well as by love.

Her combination of principle and tenderness, of deep feeling and awful indispensability, produced a passionate response—probably not unmixed with anxiety—in her children. Sarianna remained permanently devoted, "giving up all society (for which her accomplishments peculiarly fitted her) and refusing to marry...all, that her invalid mother might not miss a comfort she could offer."[16] Robert, if less unselfishly devoted, was equally responsive and, for all his turbulent boldness, probably more dependent. Betty Miller has given an admirable catalogue of the symptoms. Even into his thirties, his mother bought his clothes, packed his carpet bags, bestowed the good-night kiss, slept in the adjoining room with her door ajar, and produced by her illness sympathetic illness in him.[17] No doubt these apron strings were very puzzling and at times intolerably constricting. Apparently Robert never rebelled against the maternal love and usefulness, but for several years he rebelled vigorously against the maternal theology.

From the age of eight or nine until he was fourteen, Robert went to school at Peckham, first as a boarder to the Misses Ready and then to the Reverend Thomas Ready. Both schools were chosen for their excellence and—no doubt—their piety. That of the Misses Ready was remarkable for periodical hair-brushing accompanied by psalm-singing, the zeal and tortures of which Robert mimicked so drolly that even his mother was forced to laugh. These educational ventures appear to have wasted everyone's time. Mr. Ready was ingratiated by flattering verses, then plagued by petty sabotage.[18] John Domett, an older brother of Alfred, distinctly remembered

> young Browning, in a pinafore of brown holland such as small boys used to wear in those days, for he was always neat in his dress—and how they used to pit him against much older and bigger boys in a "chaffing" match, to amuse themselves with the "little bright-eyed fellow's" readiness and acuteness at retort and repartee.[19]

In 1873 Browning told Alfred Domett that he had learned nothing at Mr. Ready's school. Poor Mr. Ready—so obviously less gifted and less learned than Browning senior—may have had little to teach that had not already been more pleasantly absorbed at home.

> My Father was a scholar and knew Greek.
> When I was five years old, I asked him once
> "What do you read about?"
> "The siege of Troy."
> "What is a siege and what is Troy?"
> Whereat
> He piled up chairs and tables for a town,
> Set me a-top for Priam, called our cat
> —Helen, enticed away from home (he said)
> By wicked Paris, who couched somewhere close
> Under the footstool, being cowardly,
> But whom—since she was worth the pains, poor puss—
> Towzer and Tray,—our dogs, the Atreidai,—sought
> By taking Troy to get possession of
> —Always when great Achilles ceased to sulk,
> (My pony in the stable)—forth would prance
> And put to flight Hector—our page-boy's self.[20]

Robert could not but admire such a father as much as he admired himself. And indeed, his father's deft and sympathetic teaching spoiled him for other schoolmasters. He made Latin declensions memorable by turning them into grotesque rhymes, and softened Homer's Greek by beginning with Pope's English, encouraging Robert to get that *Iliad* by heart before mastering the original, as he did at the age of twelve.

Camberwell was a microcosm of Browning's mature physical and intellectual world. It offered the child what Italy offered the man: books and pictures, city and country. The Browning cottage was lined from front to back door with a thick interior epidermis of books, in which the family lived as in a kind of stomach or intestine. A woman might exist imperviously at that time in such an environment but, obviously, a boy must read or die. Robert read—and with the inexhaustible, all-retentive impetuosity of childhood. He later declared he "could forget nothing—but names and the date of the battle of Waterloo."[21]

What he read chiefly were epics, tragedies, treatises on painting and music, dictionaries of biography, and voluminous collections of tales and miscellaneous lore. He spent a lifetime turning encyclopedias into poetry. From the *Biographie universelle* he got ammunition for *Paracelsus*, and *King Victor and King Charles*, the idea of *The Return of the Druses*, and the story—at least in brief—of *Sordello*. From Nathaniel Wanley's *Wonders of the Little World*, he got materials which range, according to Griffin and Minchin,[22] from *Paracelsus* in 1835 to *Asolando* in 1889. From Daniello Bartoli's *Simboli*,[23] which he read in Italian and apparently with some of the scandalized condescension that a nonconformist feels for a Jesuit historian, he obtained descriptive details for "The Bishop Orders His Tomb," as well as abundant information about the Athenian theater for *Balaustion's Adventure* and *Aristophanes' Apology*.[24]

More strictly within the field of literature, Robert read, according to Mrs. Orr,[25] Quarles' *Emblems*, Defoe's *Crusoe*, Mandeville's *Bees*, Walpole's *Letters*, "all the works of Voltaire," Junius, many of the Elizabethans, Milton, Pope, Christopher Smart, and of course Byron.

Some of Browning's best poetry depicts with authoritative familiarity the private aesthetic worlds of accomplished painters and musicians. He was one of the first and most successful to render into verse the point of view, the techniques, and even the terminology of other media, making the reader see "the shapes of things, their colours, lights and shades,"[26] or hear "those lesser thirds so plaintive, sixths diminished, sigh on sigh,"[27] without benefit of brush, canvas, piano, or musical composition. Much of the technical knowledge necessary for such poetry he acquired in childhood.

For Browning music was the purest and the profoundest of the arts. As the most subjective, the most provocative of reverie and of "inspirations" from the unknown; as the most passionate and intuitive in content, the most direct and intense in appeal, the most idealistically insubstantial and poignantly ephemeral in medium, it was the peculiar instrument of truth, which was emotion, and of soul, which was the unconscious.[28] In short, music was the sacred art, the "finger of God"[29] writing upon eternity.

Significantly, as DeVane points out,[30] religion and music, both superlative conveyors of emotion, were the two spheres which Robert shared with his mother. Once, when she was playing at dusk, as she often did, he stole downstairs from his bed to listen, and, when she stopped, threw himself into her arms sobbing, "Play, play!" Another intense early recollection was of her playing Charles Avison's *Grand March in C Major*. In later years he found the *March* bare and primitive compared to the modulated grandeurs and starlit sighs of *Tannhäuser*.

Yet, such the might
Of quietude's immutability,
That somehow coldness gathered warmth, well nigh
Quickened—which could not be!—grew burning-bright
With fife-shriek, cymbal-clash and trumpet-blare,
To drum-accentuation: pacing turned
Striding, and striding grew gigantic, spurned
At last the narrow space 'twixt earth and air,
So shook me back into my sober self.[31]

And he woke to find his childhood starting up before him, with memories of his old music teachers, of Avison himself, of the heroic figures Avison suggested—Pym and Strafford, Roundheads and Cavaliers—of what music had meant to him, and therefore religion, and doubtless of the person who stood behind both: his mother, whom apparently he could not mention in the poem.

Robert seems to have spent more time, and his parents more money, on music than any other study.[32] He had one special instructor for French, but for music he had two, Abel, distinguished for technique, and for theory John Relfe, musician to George III and author of *The Principles of Harmony* and of *Lucidus Ordo*, "an attempt to divest thorough-bass and composition of their intricacies." In his "Parleying with Charles Avison," Browning recalls with obvious pride

Great John Relfe,
Master of mine, learned, redoubtable.

From Relfe, Browning obtained a grasp of theory which enabled him later to set several songs to music, to think seriously of composing an opera, and to write knowledgably in his poems of composers and musicians, and particularly of Abt Vogler, upon whose books Relfe's system was partly based.[33] And of course he found, in his father's library, books on music which he later turned to account. From Avison's *Essay on Musical Expression,* he got a view of English music in Handel's day; and, probably from a French memoir of Claude le Jeune, the idea so frequently expressed in his poems that a musical fashion, once superseded, never recovers its power over the imagination and the emotions.[34]

As music fed Robert's appetite for the intense and suggestive, so painting fed that for the vivid and graphic. And here again he needed only the desire and capacity to learn. Within and just beyond his doorstep he was luxuriously provided with all the means of casual and informal instruction—admirable art books in his father's library, in his father himself a provocative instructor, and just two miles away in the Dulwich Gallery, a public collection of European masters then unique in England. Mr. Browning seems very early to have exercised his remarkable ability to arouse and guide enthusiasm and to coach patiently. Under the picture of a "certain cottage and rocks in lead pencil and black currant-juice" appears in his handwriting: "R. B. aetat. two years and three months."[35] At two years, most children nowadays are just beginning to relieve their unconscious tensions in swirls of violent color. Robert was soon clever at pen and ink caricatures, doubtless in the grotesque style of his father. He was also soon familiar with the half-hour walk across green meadows, past stiles and hedges, cottages and village ponds, to Dulwich Gallery.

There was "something affecting and monastic," Hazlitt felt in those days, about Dulwich College, "simple and retired" as it stood, "just on the verge of the metropolis, and in the midst of modern improvements."[36] The gallery attached to the college he found rather too large and dimly lit, and its 350 paintings in some cases placed too high and too many on a wall. Nevertheless, like all galleries of great collections, it was "a palace of thought—another universe, built of air, of shadows, of colours." On its canvases "time stands still, and the dead reappear." There was the Dutch school, from the headachy realism of Brouwer's *Interior of an Ale-house* to the "gorgeous obscurity" of *Jacob's Dream,* then thought to be by Rembrandt. There were the French and Spanish: Watteau, whose very trees had an elegant "drawing-room air with them"; Poussin, whose animals were so dignified and whose gods were so precisely, vividly real; Velasquez with his "easy lightness" of portraiture and Murillo with his wonderful peasant boys and girls—"the sun tinted the young gipsey's complexion, and not the painter." Among the Italians, there were Rosa, Giorgione, Titian; Guercino, later so much admired by Browning; Guido, with his Saint Sebastian so impressive and passionate; da Vinci and Andrea del Sarto, who might equal Raphael but for something lacking, a "more timid and laboured" execution; Maratta, who, as The Other Half-Rome records, "paints virgins so"[37]—and who paints Pompilia waiting for her death.

Exploring and traversing these kingdoms of the outward and the inward eye, Robert did not—despite their close relationship and their common ground in realism and the grotesque—share his father's taste for Brouwer and the "Dutch boors."[38] He seems to have preferred a less satiric, warmer, and more romantic realism, and perhaps most of all, an elevated and passionate piety. Lauding Dulwich Gallery to Elizabeth in 1846, he singled out "those two Guidos, the wonderful Rembrandt of Jacob's vision, such a Watteau, the triumphant three Murillo pictures, a Giorgione music-lesson group, all the Poussins with the 'Armida' and 'Jupiter's nursing'."[39]

More than any personal influence, however vivid, what had formed his ideas about painting—and therefore in part his taste—was actually a very technical five-hundred-page treatise. This "prodigious book"[40] was the long-popular *Het Groot Schilderboek* (1707), translated into English as *The Art of Painting in All Its Branches*, which the Dutch artist Gerard de Lairesse had dictated to his sons after he became blind. To the realism of such contemporaries as Brouwer and Moller, Lairesse opposed the classicism of Raphael and Correggio, and the neoclassicism of Le Brun and Poussin. His particular model was Poussin, who could tell a story as no one else could and with all the correct embellishments of tombs, temples, statues, and satyrs. No doubt Robert liked the stories, and for a time he may have swallowed the embellishments—in Poussin. In the three Lairesse paintings at Dulwich, with their skies full of flying shapes and their earth well stocked with classical monsters, embellishment proved excessive. But the great book itself he continued to treasure. The paternal library also included Pilkington's *Dictionary of Painters* and Vasari's *Lives*, which Robert read at this time and re-read later in composing his dramatic monologues. Yet at sixty-two he wrote in the old Lairesse: "I read this book more often and with greater delight when I was a child than any other: and still remember the main of it most gratefully."[41]

"The main of it," so far as Robert was concerned, dealt with landscape. What Lairesse aimed at, the tombs and temples once cleared away, was the picturesque of nature: "woods with vistas . . .; rocks, rivers and water falls,"[42] with an emphasis on variety of design, color, and interest. Certain effects are suitable to certain actions or events: sunshine to jovial occurrences and histories, clouds to councils and pleadings, torchlight to deaths and lamentations. Daybreak is appropriate for battles, morning for sacrifice, afternoon for "bacchanals and licentious actions." Again, an ugly repulsive landscape contains rugged ground, sharp hills, "muddy brooks," crooked and knotty trees, "lean cattle," and deformed men.[43] From Lairesse Robert learned to observe details and compose them into landscapes. He learned that the physical elements of nature have psychological equivalents for the beholder which become in the representations of the painter—or the poet—a language to express emotions and even ideas. In using this language he had, as the greater man, deeper and wider meanings to convey than did Lairesse, but he conveyed them more or less in Lairesse's idiom to the end of his career. Their landscapes are strikingly similar. Browning's military actions tend to occur at dawn, his tragedies by torchlight. *Pauline* and many other poems are beautiful with trees and vistas, "Childe Roland" and many others ugly and repulsive with sharp hills, muddy brooks, and deformed men.

Through the spectacles fashioned by Lairesse—as well of course as by his father, the Dulwich painters, and the English poets—Robert looked at the reality which was Camberwell and its environs. In those days Camberwell was not an ugly nor even an altogether prosaic object. What is now a grimy wilderness of brick and pavement haunted with the whirr and rattle of cars and trucks was then a quiet village beginning to change into a less sightly, more bustling sub-urb. Nevertheless, coaches still sounded their horns at the "Ele-phant and Castle." Gypsies still camped on Camberwell green. There were trees in cottage gardens and nightingales to sing in them. Within easy walking distance, there were islands of solitude like Dulwich wood, where nature corresponded to the descriptions of poets.

While at Mr. Ready's school, Robert stole out one night to Camberwell hilltop and from there, under three tall elms whispering down Wordsworthian admonitions of guilt and sin, he gazed with awe on London lit up with newly installed gas lamps. That astral vision of distant beauty was to articulate itself into the daylight intelligibility of domes and towers. It was to move disenchantingly, even threaten-ingly nearer, to unfold into the noisy, inexhaustible immediacies of thoroughfares and squares. The city was to be always a spectacle, never a daily obligation such as his father knew. Yet it invaded Robert's imagination as it invaded Camberwell itself, so that he looked even on nature with a burgher's eye. For him a country hedge was as full of strange and unlovely creatures as a third-rate boarding-house was for Balzac.

Of the infinite variety of urban and rural life on the outskirts of a great city, Robert was a rapt and curious observer. And his memory was as long as his eyes and ears were sharp. One Guy Fawkes' Day he heard a woman singing a ballad whose refrain was, "Following the queen of the gypsies, O!" Some twenty years later, the haunting nostalgia of the refrain was elucidated into the elaborate romantic narrative of "The Flight of the Duchess."[44]

At this time, Robert Browning's promised to be another prodigious

Victorian education. In cultivation of the arts and the artistic consciousness, it was superlative and even un-Victorian. In general reading and classical scholarship, it was formidable. But in mental and practical discipline, in the development of objectivity and openness of mind, it seemed likely to be deficient. Browning could recognize the facts of Latin grammar, but could he recognize the facts of life or of divergent opinion? Was York Street Christianity to be illuminated by universal knowledge, or was universal knowledge to be cut to the pattern of York Street Christianity? In short, was Robert's education to be a genuine enlargement of mind, or was it to be simply a very brilliant and glittering pile of sand in which a very gorgeous ostrich head was to be buried? The important years were those from fourteen to nineteen, during which he was to be critically confronted with other people and other people's ideas. The story of those years is complex, but the facts are few.

CHAPTER 2

To Shelley's School

1824-29

The Victorian era—so auspicious to the visiting card and the decent black coat, so safe for virtue, middle-class initiative, and vested capital both spiritual and material—was narrowly bounded by Napoleon and the French Revolution on the one side and on the other by socialism and Bernard Shaw. The interval between lasted at most sixty years—scarcely time enough for a healthy and intelligent poet to live and die with correct ideas. When in 1824 Robert arrived somewhat precociously at the age of intellectual curiosity and looked out beyond the proprieties of Camberwell Parish on the English scene, the first fine abstract Gallic frenzy of convention-smashing and utopia-building had given way to a sober British obstinacy about particular reforms and particular rights. The revolution was subsiding into prose, and so were the revolutionary poets. Wordsworth was freeing himself from the weight of chance desires by writing heavy ecclesiastical sonnets. Coleridge was burying pantheism and pantisocracy under a mountain of orthodox little sermons which he was soon to publish as *Aids to Reflection.* But a fresh generation of poets had managed to be revolutionary (or at least poetical) in spite of revolutionary failure. Keats was then a recent literary scandal, and Shelley, a recent moral one. Both were dead, yet hardly discovered. And early in the same year of 1824, Byron terminated his wicked, idealistic, sumptuously poetic career at the outset of his Greek adventure—producing shivers of horror and adoration in virtuous adults and epidemics of Byronism in literary adolescents.

Such an event could not be overlooked. At twelve, Robert made a tentative gesture toward the contemporary world by attempting to conquer it: he wrote an entire volume of Byronic verse, which he modestly called *Incondita.* Apparently his parents were impressed rather than alarmed, and tried seriously to have the manuscript published. Even after her son and husband had quite given up, Mrs. Browning continued to show and recommend it—to, among others, Miss Sarah Flower, who may have invited her confidence by a similar temperament and passion for music. Impressed in her turn by Robert's verses, Miss Flower copied and sent two poems to her friend the Reverend William Johnson Fox, an orator, writer, and Unitarian minister of growing fame. "Which verses," wrote Browning afterward with the gratitude of a neglected poet, "he praised not a little; which praise comforted me not a little."[1] The only fault which Fox detected was "too great splendour of language and too little wealth of thought."

Browning himself confirms that his verses were essentially musical. How musical, how good, or how Byronic they were, one can only conjecture from hearsay and the two specimens accidentally preserved with Miss Flower's letter.[2] Everything else—in his fastidious zeal to edit the artistic personality he presented to the world—Browning later carefully recovered and carefully destroyed.

The two surviving compositions are strikingly precocious. "The Dance of Death"—a dramatic lyric in rather skillful tetrameter couplets—suggests Scott's "William and Helen" and the graveyard school as much as Byron, and Browning himself more than anybody else. Fever, Pestilence, Ague, Madness, and Consumption describe their ghastly depredations with a lyric gusto and realism which make "Caliban" seem relatively moderate and restrained. "The First Born of Egypt," a blank-verse treatment of the Biblical episode, is certainly full of Byron's personification, rhetoric, and pomposity. But it also contains hints of Browning's later realism, even to the impressions of a man in the street. A surviving title, "The Death of Harold," further suggests the influence of Byron.

And he did not close his Byron at the age of twelve. There was in Browning a romantic snobbery and boyish conventionalism that responded strongly and permanently to Byron. Twenty years after this time, Robert confided to Elizabeth, "I always retained my first feeling for Byron in many respects. . . . I would at any time have gone to Finchley to see a curl of his hair or one of his gloves, I am sure—while Heaven knows that I could not get up enthusiasm enough to cross the room if at the other end of it all Wordsworth, Coleridge and Southey were condensed into the little China bottle yonder, after the Rosicrucian fashion."[3] The curl and gloves are significant. In the personality he assumed before the world, Browning superimposed on the poet the gentleman, the man of the world, even the dandy:

beginning as an expurgated Byron in yellow gloves and shoulder cape and moderating into a very correct Victorian in irreproachable cravats and resplendent waistcoats. As a young man, he zealously took lessons in riding, boxing, and fencing—the latter two, perhaps, in hopeful preparation for future insults. Even in the teeth of Elizabeth's humanitarian protests, he maintained that a gentleman should defend his honor. The raciness, the confident air of being *au fait,* the easy tolerance and frankness of the man of the world also entered deeply into his poetic style. In the disguise of philosophic monsters and decadent bishops he delighted as much as Byron himself in dredging mud and calling spades.

Robert had thus encountered one revolutionary without suffering obvious moral damage. The next was to present a more subtle danger. In 1826, his cousin James Silverthorne presented him with Shelley's *Miscellaneous Poems.*[4] This little book, pirated by Benbow from Mrs. Shelley's edition of the *Posthumous Poems,* contained all of Shelley's best lyrics and shorter pieces except "The Cloud" and the "West Wind." At fourteen, Robert had already traveled a good deal in the realms of gold. With considerable calm he had read Milton, Shakespeare, Pope's Homer. But here he found not only his own world and time, but his own thoughts and feelings, even his own dreams and experiences, expressed with quite breathtaking and unfamiliar freshness and beauty. So he felt about his discovery, and with justice; for psychologically, Shelley is strikingly like the youthful Browning—what Jung would call the introverted feeling type, who is deeply preoccupied with the vivid, vehement flow of his own inward images and who instinctively recognizes in them prophetic truth for the contemporary world.[5]

Who was this incomparable *alter ego*? What other of Robert's future works had he already written? After some fruitless inquiry, Robert learned from the editor of the *Literary Gazette* that Shelley's works could be obtained from Charles Ollier of Vere Street. He asked for them as a birthday present.[6] Ironically, it was Mrs. Browning who placed in her son's hands the works of a notorious atheist. At the same time she brought him three volumes of Keats, including "Endymion" and "Lamia."

Robert's copy of the *Miscellaneous Poems* may still be examined at the Victoria and Albert Museum. The book was read as passionately as it was written. Shelley's familiar lyrics look out from thick brambles and hedges of fierce and excited penstrokes. Under the title "Hymn of Apollo," the comment "Splendid" diagonals upward in Robert's bold, fastidious hand. Other comments have been painfully rubbed, scratched, and snipped from the page, leaving eloquently ominous blanks and lacunae. Professor Pottle surmises that the *Queen Mab,* more heretical in content and therefore more scandalous in the marks of approbation, was beyond even the most desperate exercise of scissors and fingernails.[7] It was not to be found in Browning's library at the time of his death. With what mixed emotions of nostalgic regret and schoolmasterly impatience he accomplished this somewhat clandestine censorship may be gathered from his inscription in the flyleaf of the surviving volume:

> This book was given to me, probably as soon as published, by my cousin, J.S. The foolish markings and still more foolish scribblings show the impression made on a boy by this first specimen of Shelley's poetry. Robert Browning, June 2, 1878. "O World, O Life, O Time."[8]

No doubt earthquakes, avalanches, and deluges all have long and quiet preparations. Quiet causes had been quietly increasing tensions in Robert's interior. His father was apparently an industrious reader of subversive books. Of late Robert himself had been reading Voltaire. For some time he had felt an increasing impulse to astonish stupidity and shatter decorum. He had spent a great many tedious hours sitting rigidly in chapels and churches and breathing the close, damp air of rectitude and solemnity. With what a superb, horrifying, exhilarating, liberating bang Shelley must have exploded in that atmosphere!

How wicked and exciting to read Voltaire! But how infinitely more wicked and exciting to read a fascinating young English poet who had also not only read Voltaire, but actually believed him, and who with astonishing vehemence and intensity had translated him, together with a whole library of revolutionaries, into contemporary verse.

Shelley taught Robert a good many things, but chiefly to be in earnest about ideas and to conceive the poet as a thinker and a prophet. Here, following on Byron, was another example of lyrical self-consciousness, of poignant self-revelation and self-exhibition. Byron had given a picture of the poetic genius as a meditative, egocentric knight-errant and as a gay, skeptical man of the world. Now Shelley presented him variously as a lyric spirit, a humanitarian savior, an uninhibited lover, and, perhaps even more congenially and impressively, as a youthful and perfervid Faust—part necromancer, part metaphysician, part heretic, and part revolutionary—who devoured libraries and exhausted philosophies, who saw through the past at a glance and realized the future in a song, who developed shocking, well-reasoned opinions on every subject, and who sailed in meditative boats on suicidal intellectual voyages of prophetic imagery toward the deepest secrets of the world. What a wealth of things to be and to write about! *Queen Mab* made Robert an atheist and a vegetarian. "Alastor" and "Epipsychidion" provided him with models for *Pauline*. And Shelley, self-delineated, contributed much to the two principal characters of *Paracelsus*. Finally, Shelley's characteristic phrases and imagery, as Professor Pottle demonstrates, are frequently echoed throughout Browning's early poetry.[9]

Judged by its effects, *Queen Mab* had the most powerful impact on the hitherto quite exemplary young member of Mr. Clayton's congregation. It is not a successful poem, but it is a very exciting failure. Apparently under cover of explaining the universe, a fairy queen delivers to a disembodied spirit with singular inappropriateness an interminable lecture on contemporary politics, revolution, pantheism, platonism, the hideousness of conventional religion, and the poisonous venality of commerce. There is in all this a vehemence and impetuosity of feeling, an intensity and abundance of ideas, a gusto in hatred and denunciation that bursts through the triteness and crudity of the form and comes home powerfully to the reader. Moreover, the splendid poetic windstorm of *Queen Mab* itself plays over an incessant earthquake of footnotes, which—in their frequent terseness, their verve of satirical caricature, their concrete and rational hospitality to merely terrestrial topics—make one wish that Shelley had in later years got a little more of his prose into his poetry.

Here were the edifice and the workshop that created the edifice, the wonders on the stage, and below stage the even more wonderful machinery that produced the wonders. Robert must have recognized with a fresh thrill of corroboration a poet who read encyclopedias. Here was the horrifying footnote on love, bristling with such statements as: "Love is free: to promise for ever to love the same woman is not less absurd than to promise to believe the same creed: such a vow, in both cases, excludes us from all inquiry." Here was the even more horrifying footnote on the redemption, devastating with such ridicule as:

> . . . four thousand years after these events (the human race in the meanwhile having gone unredeemed to perdition), God engendered with the betrothed wife of a carpenter in Judea (whose virginity was nevertheless uninjured), and begat a son, whose name was Jesus

> Christ; and who was crucified and died, in order that no more men might be devoted to hell-fire, He bearing the burthen of His Father's displeasure by proxy.

Here was a prodigious footnote on God, actually the author's early "Necessity of Atheism," in which he enters elaborately on the principles of logic and evidence to demonstrate, rather incidentally, that one cannot possibly believe in a creative Deity, though still perfectly free (for reasons unmentioned) to accept "a pervading spirit co-eternal with the universe." Just the sort of solemnly cautious and skeptical disquisition to produce, in a speculative young man, the most passionate and reckless belief. Here finally was an exalted and eloquent footnote on the eating of vegetables, in which, with an impressive display of logic and medical evidence, Shelley proves that by abstaining from meat man might eliminate disease, prolong his life, regenerate his moral nature, abolish commerce, and inaugurate an agricultural paradise.

> I address myself . . . [concluded Shelley, enlisting the religious faculty itself in the service of irreligion] to the young enthusiast, the ardent devotee of truth and virtue, the pure and passionate moralist, yet unvitiated by the contagion of the world. He will embrace a pure system, from its abstract truth, its beauty, its simplicity, and its promise of wide-extended benefit; unless custom has turned poison into food, he will hate the brutal pleasures of the chase by instinct.[10]

Robert read with horror, but he read—and rose from the footnotes of *Queen Mab* an atheist and a vegetarian.

Having got thoroughly into the mood of the horrendous footnotes, he astonished Mrs. Browning as cheerfully as Shelley had astonished the Bishop of Oxford, "and gratuitously proclaimed himself," says Mrs. Orr, "everything that he was, and some things that he was not."[11] Mrs. Orr adds, with decorous understatement, that his behavior "distressed his mother." At fourteen or fifteen, vegetarianism was bad enough—a constant source of worry about physical health and a daily reminder of spiritual disease. But the spiritual disease itself! "Now atheism, whether speculative or practical," declares the Reverend George Clayton, "is a most accursed form of misery."[12] And Robert's atheism was both speculative and practical. He not only thought damnable thoughts in private, but did damnable things in public. By his very manner of sitting in chapel, he managed to imply a low opinion of the Reverend Mr. Clayton's sermons so plainly as to draw a stern rebuke from that worthy and moderate man. Nor was Robert's predicament the less grave because he seemed at the moment very happy. Essentially, one gathers, his protest was directed against a household dominated by a strong-minded mother, against the ignominious sighs of a father who escaped—almost daily—into the details of forgotten historical murders and other bloodthirsty atrocities, but who remained nonetheless a thoroughly submissive male. The new diet is significant. Yet Robert rejected his mother's world without sacrificing her attentions or her presence. His new sense of liberty and self-dependence had been won at virtually no cost to himself.

What was to be done? Perhaps nothing, and perhaps Mrs. Browning was wise enough to do little more—otherwise he might have been driven into more drastic revolt and more permanent emancipation. Yet there is in *Pauline* a poignant note of bereavement, of grief at the loss of an ineligible idea like grief at the loss of an ineligible young lady, which suggests that Mrs. Browning eventually spoke out.

Inevitably, during this crisis, he shone with a somewhat beclouded effulgence in the firmament of Hanover Cottage; and as that firmament now seemed rather cramped and inadequate for an expanding light, he traveled into wider and fairer skies. "He had outgrown his social surroundings," his sister Sarianna explains quite simply. "They were absolutely good, but they were narrow; . . . he chafed under them."[13] In short, he began to call on the Flower sisters, to roam abroad with his cousins the Silverthornes, and to search out ambitious young men such as Alfred Domett and Joseph Arnould, both members of solid Camberwell families.

What youthful bohemianism Robert allowed himself is chiefly connected with his cousins, who were said to be very musical and very wild. When Jim, the eldest, died at an early age, Robert addressed to him the poem "May and Death," in which he refers, somewhat reticently, to

a pair of friends
Who, arm in arm, deserve the warm
Moon-births and the long evening-ends.

Altogether, Robert's bohemianism seems to have consisted largely in making genial rambles at a late hour, in following gypsy caravans—

not too closely—and in thinking Shelley's thoughts while wearing Byron's clothes.

Many forces were impelling him to seek independence. He was soon to have the means of obtaining it. His father had deeply desired and been denied a university education. Naturally, he wanted such an education for Robert. But where could he obtain it? Oxford and Cambridge were impossible because, as a Dissenter—and the husband of a stronger Dissenter—Mr. Browning could not ask his son to subscribe on oath to the Thirty-nine Articles. Providentially, a group of men so diversely eminent as Jeremy Bentham and the Duke of Norfolk proposed in 1825 to found in London a university which was to be at once nonsectarian and comparatively inexpensive, happily adapted to a strict conscience and a modest pocketbook. Though Robert was only thirteen at the time, Mr. Browning contributed £100 to the project and thereby, as one of the original "proprietors," obtained the right of free education for his nominee. On April 22, 1828, just three weeks after the first student had been entered in the books of University College, Mr. Browning wrote Thomas Coates, applying "as a parent anxious for the welfare of an only Son," for Robert's admission. "He so earnestly desires," continued Mr. Browning, "I would interest myself in procuring his admittance, that I should feel myself wanting as a Parent, were I to neglect any step to procure what he deems so essential to his future happiness."[14] Robert was accepted as Entry No. 16.

When, though still wingless, domeless, and unporticoed, University College opened its doors to students in October, Robert had taken lodgings with a Mr. Hughes in the leafy quiet of Bedford Square and registered for classes in German, Greek, and Latin. He was now approaching seventeen. But a new life in a new university very rapidly ceased to be "essential to his happiness." Within a week he withdrew from Bedford Square and, within a few months, from the college itself. On May 4, 1829, Mr. Browning wrote Leonard Horner, the Warden, a very brief letter:

Dear Sir,

I am very sorry to communicate my son's determination to withdraw from the London University (an event as painful as it was unexpected) but I must at the same time assure you that I am entirely satisfied with every thing that has been done on your part, and make my grateful acknowledgments for the kind and affectionate treatment with which you have always behaved to him.

I am,
Dear Sir,
Your obliged & humble Servt.
R Browning Junr.[15]

Robert had experienced no academic failure. He was apparently respected by his teachers and admired by fellow students. What had happened was quite simple. For one thing, he was homesick. His mother's diet he could forgo, but again not, apparently, his mother herself. Moreover, he seems to have been aghast at the humdrum and artificiality of university life. To discover Shelley is much more exciting than to listen to a professor, and to walk in a wood among the incomparable beauties of nature, far more poetic than to sit in a class among perfectly ordinary students. Fascinating hours with private tutors are not a good preparation for tense, dreary hours over public examinations, and an interminable vista of assignments is absolutely appalling to a young man in a hurry to write epics and tragedies. In short, Robert simply did not like schools, whether big or little.

Betty Miller has shown how much the hero of Browning's *Paracelsus* illuminates the fiasco at University College.[16] That highly poetic student of medicine expresses the fiercest scorn for those who sedulously listen for truth in lecture rooms. Festus—voicing almost unmistakably the mild reproaches of Mr. Browning[17]—reminds him of the time, not long since,

when, to crown your dearest wish,
With a tumultuous heart, you left with me
Our childhood's home to join the favoured few
Whom, here, Trithemius condescends to teach
A portion of his lore: and not one youth
Of those so favoured, whom you now despise,
Came earnest as you came, resolved, like you,
To grasp all, and retain all, and deserve
By patient toil a wide renown like his.[18]

At seventeen a clever boy is apt to think he can succeed in all the professions simultaneously. Robert had thought of being a poet, a painter, a clergyman, and particularly a barrister. Apparently his father favored the law, and his friends Domett and Arnould had already decided for it. But now the learned professions were closed to him. The future was soberly narrowing into one or two glittering possibilities. Indeed, having fled the contemptible and tedious mediocrity of the classroom, he had almost no alternative but to become a great poet. Accordingly, an instinctive act was rationalized into a basic, though perhaps inevitable, decision. Robert looked inward, took inventory of his talents and his acquisitions, tested the temper of his inspiration, and, giving up all idea of lucrative work, resolved to live at home and devote himself to poetry:

> I ran o'er the seven little grassy fields,
> Startling the flocks of nameless birds, to tell
> Poor Festus, leaping all the while for joy,
> To leave all trouble for my future plans,
> Since I had just determined to become
> The greatest and most glorious man on earth.[19]

Whatever their misgivings, the Brownings accepted this decision. On his own initiative, Mr. Browning rejected for his son the virtual offer of a position in the Bank of England. Even so, neither Robert nor his parents could have believed that the situation was what it had been. Unfortunately, a young future poet sitting impecuniously at home is not positively distinguishable from an ordinary young man sitting impecuniously at home. Robert did what he could to make the attitude impressive. To prepare for his profession—perhaps also to expiate his academic debacle—he read Johnson's dictionary from cover to cover. And yet, in moral and theological rebellion, as a believing atheist and a practicing vegetarian, he must have found his position more difficult than ever. He was soon to discover that vegetarianism was damaging to his chest, and a little later that atheism was damaging to his soul. Perhaps he found he could not have his mother without her heaven too.

Robert had escaped the loneliness of a tiresome competition with students whom he scorned—to face the subtler loneliness of a less imminent, more difficult competition with the poets whom he worshipped. He lived in a vacuum of possibilities, with all his masterpieces to write and nothing visible to write them with but a pen, a bottle of ink, and some very blank paper. Even the sustaining association of the past two years with the Flower sisters came to a prolonged hiatus at just this time. On the subject of atheism, Robert had learned to expect from his mother, instead of the customary receptive comfort of feminine understanding, constricted theological argument in a particularly disconcerting form. For understanding he had, not long after his conversion, turned to Eliza and Sarah Flower, who were ready, as enlightened Unitarians, to argue with him as an atheist and, as admirers of his *Incondita*, to accept him as a poet. They were his close friends through the most important crisis of his life, and were at a later period to introduce to him a considerable section of the tight little Victorian world of genius. Like Robert, they were the precocious offspring of an erudite parent.

In an age of principles and extremes, Benjamin Flower had been a rather ambiguous example of the revolutionary journalist. He was a hot-headed advocate of republicanism, but felt that republicanism should stay on the continent. He was a voluminous and intemperate defender of unitarianism, but only on the most conservative theological grounds. True, he had been in France in 1791, and, as outspoken editor of *The Cambridge Intelligencer*, he had been in Newgate in 1799. There Miss Eliza Gould—who had paid for her loyalty to *The Intelligencer* with her post as schoolmistress of South Moulton—visited him in his cell. They could not do less than fall in love and were married soon after his release from prison. Mr. Flower removed to Harlow in Essex, edited *The Political Register*, became the father of two daughters, and, after his wife's death in 1810, earnestly but rather absentmindedly faced the task of rearing them single-handed.

In her prim, bold little novel *Five Years of Youth; or, Sense and Sentiment*, Harriet Martineau gives a picture of the two girls ardently growing up in awful ignorance of the lesser feminine proprieties—dreaming about Italian liberty with dirty faces, scrambling up trees and plunging into poetry, getting Latin in their heads and holes in their stockings. The younger sister is made somewhat direly to illustrate the perils of imagination, which threatens to sap "all energy of character, all vigour of body as well as mind"[20]—in order that the elder may the more refulgently demonstrate the advantages of good sense and a "silent, perpetual self-denial" which enable her to carry her father through a brief imprisonment in France and, incidentally, to become as neat and proper as she had always been virtuous and clever. Actually, these young ladies were not translatable into the idiom of Harriet Martineau, scarcely, as their later lives were to show, into that of George Eliot or the Brontës. Both were highly gifted, fervently religious, speculatively unconventional, and somewhat overwrought. Early intimations of tuberculosis put them in a desperate haste about this world and the next.

In the black and white of Miss Martineau's didacticism, however, they appear at least in outline. Certainly one's abiding impression of

Sarah is that of abstracted quiescence interrupted by sudden earthquakes of impulse. She describes herself as "affectionate, frank, unworldly—no animal spirits, what would be called dull, unless when excited by any favourite subject or thing, and then feeling like a runaway horse. Fond of politics, and what may be called prosing about social morals. Person very thin, very deaf (making me very stupid) and five feet two and a half."[21] Elaborately conscious of herself, she was also impressionably, sometimes absurdly, conscious of others. The runaway horse of her fantasy could be started not only by "favourite subjects" but by interesting people—particularly by intriguing unknowns and attractive men. The pseudonym "Junius Redivivus," appearing after the articles of a fellow contributor to *The Monthly Repository,* piqued her into beginning a correspondence. The spectacle of a young lad of eighteen "preaching his first sermon," with "flushing face, quivering lips, and tremulous voice,"[22] prevented her from even thinking of sleep till after midnight. Believing—or half believing—herself to have none of the qualifications, she quite naturally aspired, by compensation, to be an actress. Several years after the time when Robert first knew her she won some early recognition. Macready declared that she displayed "more poetical conception, more imagination, and more genius than Malibran, Grisi, and Pasta combined."[23] But a stage career was plainly beyond her strength. Sarah consoled herself by composing hymns, and eventually achieved a rather anonymous immortality as the authoress of *Nearer, My God, to Thee.*

In a drawing by Mrs. Bridell-Fox, Eliza Flower appears as a slender, sweet-looking young woman with considerable nose, straight features, and flowing dramatic ringlets. The lips are parted, the eyes uplifted. Richard Garnett says that she was spontaneous, simple, and transparent, and hints that she talked rather too much in the interest of her friends. He also informs us that she was intimately known as "Ariel," a name only too suggestive of the voluble and rather incoherent sentimentality one detects in her letters and those of her circle.[24] But whether she talked little or much, there can be no doubt—as Harriet Martineau makes clear in *Five Years of Youth*—of her capacity for delicate and intelligent sympathy, her "devotion to the welfare of everybody about her."[25] Eliza had very early to act as a mother to her younger sister, and probably as housekeeper and secretary to her father. Life continued to offer her responsibilities, and she found a measure of happiness in accepting them. Miss Martineau's heroine had "romantic notions about the monastic life."[26]

The real Eliza Flower had romantic notions about a good many things, but particularly about genius. "What is to be done about this horrible death monster?" she writes, apparently to a friend similarly threatened with fatal disease. "To tell you all I have, and am still (not exactly suffering so much as) not enjoyed and not enjoying as I otherwise should be, and ever since I heard the words *Malibran is dead,* would be almost to make you think me weak or affected." And she concludes, "The circumstance that while the Catholic service, crucifix, tapers and all, was being performed over her, the Cathedral bell was tolling, bring tears that do one good and are a comfort—she, an actress—a catholic—a many years mistress—ah—Genius."[27] Elizabeth Barrett herself was not more fascinated by the inspired artist.

Eliza Flower sighed about other people's genius, but not, apparently, about her own. A marked talent, or genius—and that of a spontaneous and singularly unself-conscious sort—she undoubtedly possessed for music. As a child, she astonished the Harlow village organist with her compositions. As a girl, she was famous among neighbors and tradespeople for her singing, which on fine days poured forth by the hour from the balcony of her father's house. She had neither the time nor the ambition to acquire great technical knowledge, nor to develop the single-minded concentration necessary to high attainment; yet, composing in the intervals of humbler and more altruistic labors, from 1831 until her death in 1846, she published a series of works—notably *Hymns and Anthems*—which earned her considerable fame and a modest place in the history of English music.

The Flowers in 1827 had moved permanently to Dalston, near Hackney, in North London. Here—between the ages of fifteen and seventeen—Robert Browning came to hear music, read poetry, and talk atheism. In the best tradition of contemporary religious romance Sarah—who was about twenty-two when he paid his first call—undertook to reclaim him for Christianity. The result appears in a letter which she wrote to the Reverend W. J. Fox in November, 1827, from Harlow, where, apparently, she had taken temporary refuge:

> I would fain go to my Bible as I used to, but I cannot. The cloud has come over me gradually, and I did not discover the darkness in which my soul was shrouded until, in seeking to give light to others, my own gloomy state became too settled to admit of doubt. It was in answering Robert Browning that my mind refused to bring forward argument, turned recreant, and sided with the enemy. . . . I dare not apply to Papa. I dare not let him have a glimpse at the infatuation that possesses me.[28]

The word "infatuation" suggests that Robert himself proved as dangerous as his atheism. At least, she had found his role in the actual playing more impressive than her own.

Robert shared youth, poetry, the theater, and much else with Sarah Flower. But as a very fastidious young man, he could not have failed to observe those qualities in her character which she herself thought ludicrous. How disconcerting, so easily to disturb the faith of a pious young lady! To be a woman, in Browning's book, was to be strong-minded. On the other hand, there was no faintly ludicrous impressionability, no involuntary atheism, about Eliza Flower. Moreover, she was a musician and could re-enact, with fascinating new significances, most valued and intimate scenes of his relationship with his mother. That "frail and spiritual young woman, dark-eyed and dark-ringleted," must, as Mrs. Miller says, have answered every need for worship and adoration in "the immature schoolboy who sat and watched her, as 'with heart, soul, voice, finger, frame, seeming all but borne upward by the strain, as on wings to heaven,' she played or sang for him the hymns and anthems of her own composition."[29] All the available evidence, as well as tradition in the Flower family[30] and in Browning biography, indicate it was Eliza rather than her sister who caused Robert so many times to walk the ten miles to Dalston.

The friendship produced a copious record, particularly on Browning's side. All his loud rebellion and secret misgivings, his boisterous infidelity and latent Congregationalism, his boundless ambition and haunting self-doubt he poured out on the fragile and already overburdened Eliza, not only in colloquy and monologue but in letters and poems. How disagreeable to learn, in grave and reticent middle age, of her "vice of keeping every such contemptible thing,"[31] and to be pursued by the fear of some hateful memoir, some "horrible raking up of the correspondence."[32] Hardly a trace of that correspondence has survived his maneuvering to regain and destroy it all.

But perhaps some idea of the relationship may be gained from *Pauline,* whose hero resembles Robert so much that the heroine, though by no means unmistakably Eliza, may resemble her considerably. Pauline is to be a combination of lover, mother, and guardian angel. She is to be worshipped and caressed, but even more she is to soothe, protect, inspire to faith and purity, and above all listen with inexhaustible patience to the interminable self-explanations of the hero. The poem opens:

> Pauline, mine own, bend o'er me—thy soft breast
> Shall pant to mine—bend o'er me—thy sweet eyes,

And loosened hair and breathing lips, and arms
Drawing me to thee—these build up a screen
To shut me in with thee, and from all fear;
So that I might unlock the sleepless brood
Of fancies from my soul, their lurking-place,
Nor doubt that each would pass, ne'er to return
To one so watched, so loved and so secured.[33]

"No thought or hope" is to be shut from her.

No vague wish unexplained, no wandering aim
Sent back to bind on fancy's wings and seek
Some strange fair world where it might be a law.[34]

He is as good as his word. For 1,031 lines Pauline must hear herself adored and her lover expounded without being able to get in an iamb edgewise, or indeed to do anything but append, in French, a lengthy footnote in which, apparently, she apologizes for his brevity and attempts to clarify the order of his ideas.

Of course no real woman could be reduced to a silence so ideally total. On music, and particularly her own music, Eliza could speak with more authority than on Robert Browning, and there is reason to believe that the conversation was sometimes two-sided. And Eliza had another subject, indeed, another extraordinary man, to talk about. Eliza was as full of William Fox as Robert was full of himself. If she and Fox did not know they were in love, they were soon to know it. Quite inevitably, as Browning wrote Horne in 1848, "she gave me his opinions at second hand."[35] Fox's ideas—and the man who thought them—were to become very important to Robert. The ideas were perhaps most remarkable in terms of the man's personal history and spiritual evolution.

Fox was a man of brilliant gifts and eager intelligence. His life was a rather ironical adventure in freedom and optimism. The son of a Calvinist-philosophical radical weaver, he grew up in the deadly earnest, restless, hungry intellectualism of Nonconformist Norwich. As a boy, he worked at the loom while his mother read him novels, often a volume a day. At thirteen, he became a bank messenger, saved his money, bought books, devoured English drama, digested Locke, studied Latin and mathematics, wrote verse, and listened to the spiritual adventures of a prosperous grocer who had married five times, begot four children, and professed fifteen religions. At twenty, having discovered his call to the ministry while walking with a pretty girl in the fields, he entered the Calvinistic academy at Homerton, quickly developed rational doubts as to the Trinity, read night and day on the question as though under a spell, feeling that he must go on, yet that he was going wrong, "toiling to arrive at the abandonment of heaven and diligently working out . . . [his] own damnation"[36] until at twenty-three he found himself, deeply bewildered and divided, the pastor of a miniature congregation at Fareham. And now, with much incidental caution and compromise, he began that bold, rather swift voyage toward secularism in which he gave up step by step the Trinity, original sin, the Atonement and preexistence of Christ, hell and eternal punishment, the supreme authority of the Bible, and—ultimately—ordination itself. About halfway in this absorbing, soul-wracking progress, Fox fell in love—not head over heels, but, as several times before, with one eye shrewdly, apprehensively open. Apparently, he could describe the young lady's virtues at best in negatives: "She is not destitute of feeling, delicacy, talent, information or goodness. Yet not particularly sensible, refined, clever, intelligent, or capable of any very exalted virtue."[37] But she was pretty and well-formed and he was lonely, eager to love and be loved. Hesitating, delaying, upbraiding himself for his folly, he drifted into marriage. His wife did not forgive him for the little prudence he had shown. By 1829, he found himself a well-known writer, the leading Unitarian orator, pastor of the large congregation at South Place, the husband of a cold and extravagant woman, the father of three children—the first a deaf mute—and in love with Eliza Flower.

Eliza returned his love. Why, he was rather pathetically at a loss to explain. In a letter to her he enumerates his virtues—none of them what she particularly admires. Henry Linton suggests the answer. When he walked out of church after one of Fox's sermons, he felt as though his feet were raised six inches off the pavement. Fourteen years younger than Fox, looking out of a narrow experience with a wide, eager vision, Eliza seems to have experienced the permanent levitation of love and wonder at the oratorical gift and the power over great assemblies, the large knowledge and the inquiring mind, the bold quest on perilous seas of doctrine. She also felt the need and the loneliness of an unhappy man.

Something of this love Robert sensed, perhaps, as he walked in the garden at Dalston with Eliza. Certainly the ideas she expounded must have seemed a little tame after Shelley. And yet, doctrinally, Fox was very little more (or less) than Shelley with his collar turned backward.

Both held that evil was at most temporary. Both looked forward to a progress toward perfection, to an infinite felicity in some form. Shelley's atheism was not incompatible with belief in a benevolent, all-pervading Spirit. Fox believed in a God of love. Both were hostile to conventions and institutions. Both maintained that men are basically good and that to be effectually good they need first of all to be free and equal. "There is a natural alliance," said Fox, "between error and slavery, truth and liberty."[38] In short, both men were deeply indebted to the Enlightenment. That side of Shelley which exulted boyishly in the boldness of skepticism and the excitement of flux and change was attracted to Hume and D'Holbach. Fox was no less imbued with Benthamism: Christianity is "eminently simple, intelligible, and reasonable";[39] controversy, the free competition of ideas, will lead inevitably to Christian truth. Shelley held that poetry would regenerate the world; Fox, that Christ's teachings would do so. Indeed, he was sometimes as confident of the goodness of man and the efficacy of the gospels as many of his contemporaries were of the omnipotence of the steam engine and the vastness of Britain's coal resources. The two men differ most sharply on morals. As a Christian, Fox seems to have thought in terms of dualism and discipline, while Shelley as a romantic thought in terms of unity and impulse. Yet Shelley occasionally described with approval the warfare in man between the higher and lower natures, while Fox constantly emphasized love and enthusiasm as effective motives to virtue.

What, if anything, was the effect of Eliza's explanations on Robert? Presumably, to Christianize his romanticism and romanticize his Christianity, to soften the opposition between his filial orthodoxy and his unfilial heresy, and thus to keep the door open for a recantation of the more violent aspects of Shelley's doctrine.

In 1829 Benjamin Flower died. By the terms of his will Eliza and Sarah became the wards of W. J. Fox and went to live in his house at Stamford Grove West. Robert saw them no more until 1833. Why he did not is quite unknown. He may have been reluctant to intrude on a strange household—or on a friendship whose romantic nature he may have sensed.

CHAPTER 3

Crisis and Confession
1829-33

The four years from 1829 to 1833 are among the most significant and the least understood in Browning's life. By the end of this period he had apparently renounced a good deal of Shelley and once more accepted if not the Reverend Mr. Clayton, at least a good deal of the Reverend Mr. Clayton's Christianity. The crisis itself is veiled in discreet obscurity. We learn that he continued his rambles with the Silverthornes and cultivated his friendships with Domett and Arnould, that he admired Laman Blanchard's *Lyric Offerings* and heard Dr. Blundell's medical lectures at Guy's Hospital, thus preparing himself for an interest in the physician Paracelsus, that he ceased regular attendance at chapel before he was eighteen, but sought out certain celebrated preachers like the Reverends Thomas Jones and Henry Melvill. The latter—a handsome, bold-featured, aristocratic gentleman—preached the evangelical version of the established creed with Carlylean eloquence and splendor, specializing in astronomical metaphors and cosmic vistas of spiritual perspectives, yet reasoning with perfect confidence on the most ungeological texts of the Bible and referring with ceremonial courtesy to angels and archangels as though they were earls and dukes. Apparently, Robert did not see anything comical in Canon Melvill, though he was quick to be amused, or rather bored, by less eloquent men. In March 1833 he wrote in a letter to Fox:

> Impromptu on hearing a sermon by the Rev. T[homas] R[eady]—
> pronounced "heavy"—
> A *heavy* sermon!—sure the error's great,
> For not a word Tom uttered *had its weight*.[1]

By 1833, one infers, he could accept a good deal of evangelical doctrine without being able to endure hearing very much of it expounded by his former schoolmaster.

Yet his return to a more conventional faith does not pass quite unrecorded. *Pauline* reflects, though it does not explain, the event. It is also the first fruit of a very remarkable poetic dedication. On an October afternoon of 1832 Robert walked the ten miles between Camberwell and Richmond, to see Edmund Kean play Richard III. Robert was then twenty. On that evening two careers—one hopelessly bohemian and very nearly over, the other irreproachably respectable and scarcely begun—were to intersect. Kean had starved and worn his youth out brooding his way with demonic energy into Shakespeare's more magnificent criminals and evoking them, with terrifying vividness, for the complacent and unterrified amusement of provincial tradespeople. For ten years, in nightly alternation, he had lived melodious, symmetrical, superhuman villainies on the boards of Drury Lane and plotted mean, ineffectual, inebriate villainies in an Adelphi pothouse, having, perhaps in both characters, become for the stage what Byron was to poetry and Napoleon to war and empire. When Browning saw him, the restless, agile little man with hypnotic black eyes had been reduced by drink and tuberculosis to a feeble, white-faced, hollow-voiced specter who obviously intended to make the stage his death bed. His Richard was a parade of decrepitude punctuated by moments of magical power. "He whispers," says Talfourd, "when he should shout; creeps and totters about the stage when he should spring or rush forward."[2] The last act, once his best, had inevitably become his weakest. Once he had fought on Bosworth Field "like one drunk with wounds."[3] Now, even as he dealt the death blow, Richmond surreptitiously grasped his victim's hand and "let him gently down, lest he should be injured by the fall."[4] And yet his last look at Richmond was fearful. Still the attitude in which he stood "with his hands stretched out," after his sword was taken from him, had "a preternatural and terrific grandeur, as if his will could not be disarmed, and the very phantoms of his despair had a withering power."[5]

Perhaps Kean's very debility—the real tragedy beside the acted tragedy—made his performance peculiarly moving to a complicated young man. Perhaps Browning had peculiar reasons for being moved. He had, one suspects, but recently abjured the pleasures of atheism. The sense of loss, of contraction into unexciting common sense, may have made him eager for a fresh dedication. At any rate, gazing down at that listless wreck still capable of producing gasps and exclamations from the rustling and peopled darkness, Robert received a profound intimation of the power of art, and especially of dramatic and theatrical art. The long, midnight walk back across London was a dark, sinister journey into the future. His own attack on the public was to be as vastly ambitious and deviously contrived as Richard's assault on the throne. In the famous copy of *Pauline* which he later gave to John Forster, he describes the plan he conceived—as he noted in his own copy—on the evening of Kean's performance:

> The following Poem was written in pursuance of a foolish plan which occupied me mightily for a time, and which had for its object the enabling me to assume & realize I know not how many different characters;—meanwhile the world was never to guess that "Brown, Smith, Jones & Robinson" (as the spelling books have it) the respective authors of this poem, the other novel, such an opera, such a speech, etc. etc. were no other than one and the same individual. The present abortion was the first work of the *Poet* of the batch, who would have been more legitimately *myself* than most of the others; but I surrounded him with all manner of (to my then notion) poetical accessories, and had planned quite a delightful life for him.[6]

In short, Browning's artistic life was to flourish in elaborate disguise. Each poem, play, or opera was to be at once itself and a kind of dramatic monologue—the work of an author whose identity was to be as carefully constructed as that of a fictitious victim in an espionage novel. The passage suggests there was something melodramatic and conspiratorial, as well as something idiosyncratic and compulsive, in Browning's later dramatic impersonality. It also portends one of his most persistent conflicts: that between the desire for fame and the desire for privacy, the desire to communicate and instruct and the desire, perhaps, to astonish and baffle.

Walking in the dense shadows and hectic October colors of Dulwich Wood, Robert began at once to put his plot into execution. *Pauline* remained a secret to everybody but Sarianna, who herself kept secret from her brother the copies she made of favorite passages, in fear of the constantly threatening oblivion of the hearth flames. The poem survived to be completed; the family was apprised of its existence; and Robert's Aunt Silverthorne, apparently without having read it, offered to pay the expense of publication. For £30, Saunders and Otley undertook both printing and advertising, and in March of 1833 *Pauline; A Fragment of a Confession* came anonymously before the world.

Undoubtedly—as Browning maintained in his 1868 preface to the poem—*Pauline* is "dramatic in principle." There are characters, setting, monologue, crisis, and action. The progression of thought is not logical nor even very chronological, but associative and dramatic. Like Landor in his *Imaginary Conversations*, Browning is already fascinated by the dramatic possibilities of the moving point of view:

> Deeper in!
> Shut thy soft eyes—now look—still deeper in!
> This is the very heart of the woods all round
> Mountain-like heaped above us.[7]

And yet both the subtitle and the anonymity of the poem are in themselves an admission. In his 1868 preface the middle-aged Browning rather ruefully conceded that his impersonation turned out to be that of a young poet remarkably like himself at twenty. The poem is in fact essentially lyrical and confessional. If Pauline originates in Eliza Flower, she is certainly a very attenuated, perhaps a merely therapeutic Eliza.[8] One has only to compare this work with "Epipsychidion" to see the difference between an author interested in a woman and an author interested in himself.

The hero of *Pauline* is a rather bewildering montage of real, daydream, and literary Brownings who coalesce after the manner of the *Nude Descending a Staircase.* And as the hero *is* the poem, this surrealist complexity extends to theme and treatment. An aesthetic and spiritual autobiography leads up to a rather pale and regretful victory of intuition and Christian faith over reason and Shelleyan free thought.[9] Here Browning wrote, as Wordsworth says of himself in the preface to *Lyrical Ballads,* with his eye on the object—in this case, his own interior.

Robert begins by imploring Pauline—who certainly has a lovely, abundant, and curtaining head of hair—to shut him in from fear. Had he sat by her always, he would never have "deceived God" and chosen "wild dreams of beauty and of good" and gifts distinct from "theirs."[10] This preference, apparently for atheism, revolution, and poetry over the useful occupations and sober truths of the third-person-plural of society and family, has led him to deep inward conflict and disturbance. The poet would explain or, as Stewart W. Holmes observes,[11] attempt an autopsychoanalysis.

He describes two dreams:

> I was a fiend in darkness chained forever
> Within some ocean-cave; and ages rolled. . . .[12]

Psychoanalytic writers interpret these dreams as symptoms of extreme introversion or preoccupation with self.[13] And indeed it is difficult not to see in the swan and the God the Apollonian "Sun-treader" Shelley, and in the dreams themselves the poet's deep conviction that he has somehow betrayed, defiled, or even destroyed his hero.

What produced in him a terrible sense of betrayal? Having expatiated on Shelley's incomparable greatness and his own unworthy adoration, he will strip "mind bare," and then show how its "first elements" are responsible for his present state:

> I am made up of an intensest life,
> Of a most clear idea of consciousness
> Of self.[14]

To a passionate inwardness was joined a restless and perfervid imagination. This—clearly—is the Robert who from earliest youth responded to the most vivid of the Greek myths, Agamemnon murdered by his wife, Orestes "streaked with his mother's blood"[15]—and that prediction of his future life represented in his favorite engraving of Andromeda. W. S. Swisher emphasizes that Robert identified himself with these legends, that he associated them with his father, with whom he first read them, and that they suggest, at least in the Orestes theme, strong hostility toward his mother.[16] These naïve adventures in the paternal library were followed by a long period of restraint, possibly in the chapel and the school, in which he had first learned to turn his mind against himself.

The effects were "cunning, envy, falsehood, all world's wrong."[17] On that occasion, he had cured himself with verse, singing at first spontaneously, of his fancies and the Greek myths, and then imitatively, of his own thoughts and feelings as more powerfully expressed in "the mighty bards," until, eagerly searching the "White Way" of poetry for a star, he found Shelley:

> A key to a new world, the muttering
> Of angels, something yet unguessed by man.
>
> . . . . .
>
> Much there, I felt my own soul had conceived,
> But there living and burning! . . .
>
> . . . . .

I threw myself
To meet it, I was vowed to liberty,
Men were to be as gods and earth as heaven,
And I—ah, what a life was mine to prove!
My whole soul rose to meet it. Now, Pauline,
I shall go mad, if I recall that time.[18]

This is the most intense passage in the poem. The sense of personal bereavement never finds an adequate consolation.

And yet the poet does not say that he was forced to give up Shelley—he was simply disillusioned. Apparently, Shelley's intellectual atmosphere—that free, heady ozone of revolutionary skepticism with its permanent sunset of utopian vision—simply proved unbreathable. What began in the spirit of *Hellas* ended almost in the spirit of Byron's *Don Juan*:

First went my hopes of perfecting mankind,
Next—faith in them, and then in freedom's self
And virtue's self, then my own motives, ends
And aims and loves, and human love went last.
I felt this no decay, because new powers
Rose as old feelings left—wit, mockery,
Light-heartedness . . .
. . . I laughed and said
"No more of this!"[19]

In short, all worship eventuated in self-worship, and with self-worship came a renewed sense of strength. His "powers were greater" and his soul seemed to be a "temple" itself.[20] But he cannot believe in his poetic powers—for long—any more than he can believe in anything else. He once more falls back on Shelley, whom he cannot quite cast out. And he adds:

I to rise and rival him?
Feed his fame rather from my heart's best blood,
Wither unseen that he may flourish still.[21]

Shelley's ideals he could renounce, but not Shelley as superlative poet and therefore idol.

Still feverishly preoccupied with self, the poet craves pleasure, fame, power, but particularly knowledge. The harpy, knowledge, he perceives, exacts of the pursuer the renunciation of all other pursuit or recompense.

And when I found that I should perish so,
I bade its wild eyes close from me forever.[22]

And now in a passage of baffling and precocious obscurity, he explains the crisis of his history. Apparently Platonic reason confronted him afresh with the possibility of a world beyond the material. But love bound him to sense, even to self, which—when viewed in the light of what a spiritual, unselfish love might be—seemed the more hideous. He would escape into his favorite myths, or overcome self and no longer seek rivalry with poets: he would love England, love Pauline. Swept along in this way by involutions and reversals of emotions bewildering even to himself, he complains somewhat irrelevantly at the deceits of reason and bursts out

Oh sympathies, obscured by sophistries![23]

Does this passage indicate that, like Carlyle under similar circumstances, he had abandoned reason for some form of intuition? Perhaps. Certainly a later passage indicates that he had resolved like Carlyle to "look within no more."[24] This resolve was eventually to become settled habit and inclination.

"Epipsychidion" now follows hard on the heels of confession and self-vivisection. For perhaps the first time, the poet addresses Pauline with feeling, and having at some length expressed an attachment beyond self and Shelley, he turns more frankly and squarely to face his problems. Is there a life after death? he asks. The soul cannot expect to have every question answered, every wish fulfilled. It must lovingly submit to God, to Christ, whom now the poet apostrophizes in phrases curiously uninspired:

Do I not
Pant when I read of thy consummate power . . .?[25]

He contemplates Olivet, Calvary—and once more returns to Pauline. The concluding section begins:

Sun-treader, I believe in God and truth
And love; and as one just escaped from death
Would bind himself in bands of friends to feel
He lives indeed, so, I would lean on thee!
Thou must be ever with me, most in gloom
If such must come, but chiefly when I die,

> For I seem, dying, as one going in the dark
> To fight a giant: but live thou forever,
> And be to all what thou hast been to me![26]

The authentic tone is yet curiously belied by the sense of the passage. The declaration of independence involves further dependence; the escape from death is not an escape; the assertion of principles extremely vague. One notes the suggestion of self-pity, the rather pathetic premonition of "Childe Roland"—"as one going in the dark/To fight a giant." But can the prophet of revolution and atheism be reconciled with Christian Deity? Can Robert have a sense of his mother's approval and a sense of loyalty to his hero at the same time? Perhaps, by that expurgating and rationalizing process so characteristic of him and his characters, Browning is already moving toward the Shelley of his 1852 "Essay," rejecting the shrill defender of "a set of miserable little expedients" and shaping the bold utopian visionary into a safe and reassuring transcendentalist absorbed in "the great Abstract Light" and "the sufficiency of the First Cause." Yet, at the core of every rationalization there is a guilty sense of truth, and that guilty sense was for Browning echoed in the plain meaning of Shelley's poetry, which he continued to read and love. "What I have printed gives *no* knowledge of me," he wrote Elizabeth Barrett in 1845.[27] Her poetry was superior to his because hers, like Shelley's, was subjective and personal, whereas most of his was objective and dramatic. "*My* poetry is far from 'the completest expression of my being'—I hate to refer to it, or I could tell you why, wherefore . . . *prove* how imperfect (for a mild word), how unsatisfactory it must of necessity be."[28] As a subjective poet, Browning was to end in almost complete obscurity, complaining of the limitations of his few critics. As an objective poet—representing with astonishing sympathy the self-dividedness of other speakers—he was to emerge rather quickly into the light.

In the constitutional revolution of the previous year, W. J. Fox had exercised with notable effect his power of making people feel as though they were walking six inches above the pavement: he was now famous as one of the most eloquent and daring speakers for the liberal cause. A few words from such a man might do a great deal for the anonymous work of an unknown poet. Within a week of the time *Pauline* was to appear, Robert sent Fox a presentation copy. "Perhaps by the aid of the subjoined initials and a little reflection," he wrote as one suave gentleman to another, "you may recollect an oddish sort of boy who had the honour of being introduced to you at Hackney some years back." That individual now wished to submit "a free and easy sort of thing which he wrote some months ago 'on one leg.' " Robert also mentioned having heard that Fox contributed to *The Westminster.* He did not mention *The Monthly Repository,* of which Fox was editor. This letter was followed by twelve copies of *Pauline,* and Shelley's *Rosalind and Helen,* "the getting back" of which Robert proposed to make the excuse for an evening call.[29]

Accordingly, a young man appeared soon after at Stamford Grove West. Nearly twenty-one, he was elegantly gloved and caped, dark and rather startlingly handsome, with bright gray eyes and curling brown chin whiskers. His manner was contained and his conversation, dry and satirical. The Flower sisters were at a loss to recognize the impetuous and romantic boy—with his appealing perplexities and eager confidences—of four years before. Sarah soon discovered, apparently with satisfaction, that the new Robert Browning (for all his "great power of conversation," "thorough originality," and "exceptionally poetical"[30] appearance) had an ugly nose. Somewhat later, Eliza says that she had begun admiring him again, but that, apparently by undue self-admiration, "he has twisted the old-young shoot off by the neck."[31] And again she observes: "If he had not got into the habit of talking of head and heart as two separate existences, one would say that he was born without a heart." Perhaps Eliza's patience was a little short. She was then living in a cramped, strained, suffocating little world, the intricacies of which Robert was probably soon to discover with a great deal of secret astonishment.

Domestic life among married "Socinians"—such as those in Fox's set—aroused the moral horror of Carlyle, always eager to cast stones from the windows of his own glass house. He declares them

> a flight of really wretched-looking "friends of the species". . . . frequently, indeed, [they] are obliged to divorce their own wives, or to be divorced; for though this world is always blooming (or is one day to do it) in everlasting "happiness of the greatest number," these people's own *houses* (I always find) are little hells of improvidence, discord, and unreason.[32]

Fox's own house was just such a little hell at this time. Since the Flower sisters had gone to live with him as his wards, he had been seriously ill and, as his wife did nothing, Eliza had nursed him back to the point where he could resume work, had then taken dictation, looked up references, copied out sermons—in short, given him aid, counsel, and encouragement without which he would not, as he wrote his mother, "have been able to hold out at all."[33] Naturally, his wife was indignant, and let her indignation be known. "O you—no not even you," Eliza wrote her friend Harriet Taylor, "can imagine what the wretchedness of this state is—I mean what one *must* bear—and so quietly too! And one's whole existence is condensed into the mere effort of enduring."[34] Sometimes the little hell was complete. "He vexed me too this morning. . . . I feel I am a little insane just now."[35] There was a special reason for Eliza's intimacy with Harriet Taylor. In 1830 Fox had introduced that handsome young lady, the wife of a prominent member of his congregation, to John Stuart Mill, then recovering (on a diet of Wordsworth, music, and debating societies) from a long depression. Mill had been convinced that the habit of analysis had completely undermined his capacity for emotion. A short acquaintance with Mrs. Taylor awakened his emotions with a vengeance. He was soon composing treatises under her inspiration as passionately as ever Petrarch composed sonnets under Laura's, and for the next twenty years he burned platonically with the ecstasies, sorrows, doubts, piques, and nostalgias of youthful—even adolescent—love, until the death of Mr. Taylor permitted a happy marriage.

There was enough talk about this friendship in literary circles to reach the ears of an entirely obscure young poet. Mill was very famous and was now being very absurd. As usual Carlyle could not resist his own satirical talents. He describes Harriet as pale, "passionate and sad-looking," "a living romance heroine"; and after another meeting with her: "she affects, with a kind of sultana noble-mindedness, a certain girlish petulance."[36] At a philosophical radical party, John Roebuck saw Mill appear with Mrs. Taylor hanging on his arm. "The manner of the lady, the evident devotion of the gentleman, soon attracted universal attention, and a suppressed titter went round the room."[37]

Against a world so ready to be amused, Mill and Harriet quite naturally formed a quiet alliance with Fox and Eliza Flower. Quite naturally, also, Fox sent Mill, for review, one of his twelve copies of *Pauline*.

The reviews of that poem were divided. *The Literary Gazette* pronounced it "somewhat mystical, somewhat poetical, somewhat sensual, and not a little unintelligible."[38] *Fraser's Magazine* professed to believe it the work of a madman—probably one, or all, of the Whig ministers. On the other hand, though finding some failures in dignity, language, and metrics, *The Atlas* spoke of beautiful passages, genius, and future success. Alan Cunningham writing in *The Athenaeum* was perhaps even more favorable, and most favorable was of course Fox, writing not in *The Westminster* but in his own *Monthly Repository*. Inevitably, he saw the poem less as a confession by the author than as a confidence to Pauline: "her presence is felt throughout as that of a second conscience, wounded by evil, but never stern."[39] He has no doubts of the poet's future: "we felt certain of Tennyson, before we saw the book, by a few verses which had straggled into a newspaper; we are not less certain of the author of Pauline."

The most critical review was not published. Mill had tried in vain both *The Examiner* and *Tait's Edinburgh*. The rejections were unmerited. Sir William Hamilton's philosophy was not more conscientiously and industriously examined. Mill read the poem four times, made copious notes in the margin, and wrote a critique on the flyleaf.[40] He seems also to have submitted the poem to the judgment of his own "second conscience." Professor Hayek discerns another handwriting, that of Mrs. Taylor, in the marginal comments.[41] The comments in her script are highly yet vaguely complimentary, being chiefly limited to the word *beautiful*. Mill's are of the kind one always wants to write in the margin of a Browning poem: "what power?" "what times?" "who?" "he is always talking of being prepared—what for?" Sometimes he is a little more wicked: "self-flattery," "too much pretension in this motto." Mill's essay on the flyleaf is what one might expect from the devoted admirer of Harriet Taylor and the disciplined pupil of James Mill. Like Fox, he sees the poet in terms of Pauline, but critically so:

> With considerable poetic powers, the writer seems to me possessed with a more intense and morbid self-consciousness than I ever knew in any sane human being. I should think it a sincere confession, though of a most unlovable state, if the "Pauline" were not evidently a mere phantom. All about her is full of inconsistency—he neither loves her nor fancies he loves her, yet insists upon *talking* love to her. If she *existed* and loved him, he treats her most ungenerously and unfeelingly. All his aspirings and yearnings and regrets point to other things, never to her; then he *pays her off* toward the end by a piece of flummery, amounting to the modest request that she will love him and live with him and give herself up to him *without* his *loving her—moyennant quoi* he will think her and call her everything that is handsome, and he promises her that she shall find it mighty pleasant.[42]

On the other hand, he grants that the poet's "psychological history of himself is powerful and truthful," except that the reform is not genuine. "If he once could muster a hearty hatred of his selfishness it would *go*; as it is, he feels only the *lack* of *good*, not the positive evil. He feels not remorse, but only disappointment."

Mill returned the annotated copy to Fox, remarking that "on the whole the observations are not flattering to the author—perhaps too strong in the *expression* to be shown to him."[43] They were shown, nevertheless. What Browning thought of them may be imagined—but need not be imagined, because he could not resist writing some indignant rebuttal into the margins of the same invaluable little book. Two of Mill's "who's" and "what's" are actually answered, and an accusation of vulgarism is buried under a mountain of erudition—and wounded vanity. Mill's criticism cut deep. On a blank page at the front he wrote the bitter, satirical description of his grandiose scheme already quoted[44] and concluded bitterly: "Only this crab remains of the shapely Tree of Life in this Fool's paradise of mine." Browning must have seen with a shock what the poem looked like from Pauline's point of view and what the author looked like from any but his own point of view. And yet—as Masao Miyoshi has shown—his poetic career was hardly altered by Mill.[45]

Browning had an additional reason for disliking his poem: not a single copy was sold. As he produced better and more successful poetry, he seemed willing, and yet not quite willing, to have *Pauline* forgotten. Probably some time after 1838, in making up one of their many tiffs, he gave John Forster the precious copy in which he and Mill had waged their illuminating warfare. Before long he regretted his indiscretion, and he made repeated attempts, during Forster's lifetime and afterward, to recover the gift. But the eager flames of propriety were denied their victim, and the little book found appropriate sanctuary at last in the Forster-Dyce Collection in the Victoria and Albert Museum. By that time *Pauline* itself had been long since rediscovered and its authorship revealed. As early as 1847, Dante Gabriel Rossetti, that discriminating explorer on the seas of neglected poetry, had come upon it in the British Museum and taxed Browning with having written it. In 1863, Moncure Conway, reviewing a three-volume edition of Browning's *Works*, regretted the omission of *Pauline*, a poem "in every way worthy"[46] of the poet. The secret became more and more precariously open until, in 1867, Browning gave R. H. Shepherd permission to publish a few extracts if he would confine himself to the single remark that the work was "purely dramatic and intended to head a series of 'Men and Women' such as I have afterwards introduced to the world under somewhat better auspices."[47] Shepherd did not publish the extracts. At length, to prevent unauthorized publications, Browning "with extreme repugnance" included the piece in his 1868 collected edition, insisting that it consisted in "so many utterances of so many imaginary persons, not mine."[48] Though he declared that he had not altered a syllable, except to correct misprints, he actually made textual changes and thoroughly reformed the punctuation. Finally, in preparing his 1888 edition, he made further revisions, this time avowedly—to mitigate "an eyesore"[49] which he had endured for twenty years.

As though to clarify his rather ambiguous declaration of independence in *Pauline,* Robert emancipated himself in March 1834 almost to the furthest limits of geography. He had recently become friendly with the Russian consul-general in London, the Chevalier de Benkhausen. Having to go on a special mission to St. Petersburg, the consul-general proposed Robert accompany him, nominally as his secretary. Robert was almost twenty-two. He agreed at once.

The long letters which he wrote from abroad to his sister are another casualty to elderly reticence. Even so, it was not a voyage into silence and the void, a voyage into new lands with old thoughts, like Macaulay's visit to India. It stirred many new thoughts and left many articulated traces in his poetry and later correspondence.

The continent was much as Napoleon had left it some twenty years before. The travelers were conveyed by a frail, primitive, piston-palsied little steamer to Ostend, and from there traveled by horse carriage night and day, week in, week out, fifteen hundred miles to St. Petersburg. Fifteen hundred miles of careening wheels and galloping hooves, in the incessant hurry and urgency of official business! The experience must have answered to something very fundamental in Browning's nature. The galloping hooves entered into the very tempo of his meter; the rapidly moving carriage window became, very nearly, his most characteristic viewpoint upon the universe—as native to him as the gunwale of a sailboat to Shelley.

He rumbled swiftly though the country which was later to be the setting of *Colombe's Birthday*—past Castle Ravestein,

> That sleeps out trustfully its extreme age
> On the Meuse' quiet bank,[50]

through Cleves, to Aix, where he saw the oldest existing portrait of Charlemagne, later described in *Sordello*, and where he accumulated impressions which, on a second journey four years after, matured into "How They Brought the Good News." Of the sand-flats of Prussia and of Tilsit, where Napoleon and the Czar met on a raft in midstream, his poems are silent—and indeed, as a sober, conscientious liberal, he was with one exception[51] proof against the enchantments of the Napoleonic legend.

Entering a still ice-bound Russia, he sped day after day through a white, pine-forested solitude so endless and unchanging that he seemed scarcely to move—a real and symbolic journey as fantastic as that of *The Heart of Darkness*. Forty-four years later, when the scenery of the Splügen Pass in Switzerland reminded him of Russia, he wrote a characteristic little moral melodrama, "Ivàn Ivànovitch," in which he gives a glimpse of his long Russian journey:

> In the deep of our land, 'tis said, a village from out the woods
> Emerged on the great main-road 'twixt two great solitudes.
> Through forestry right and left, black verst and verst of pine,
> From village to village runs the road's long wide bare line.
> Clearance and clearance break the else-unconquered growth
> Of pine and all that breeds and broods there, leaving loth
> Man's inch of masterdom,—spot of life, spirt of fire,—
> To star the dark and dread, lest right and rule expire
> Throughout the monstrous wild, a-hungered to resume
> Its ancient sway, suck back the world into its womb:
> Defrauded by man's craft which clove from North to South
> This highway broad and straight e'en from the Neva's mouth
> To Moscow's gates of gold. So, spot of life and spirt
> Of fire aforesaid, burn, each village death-begirt
> By wall and wall of pine—unprobed undreamed abyss.[52]

Finally, at the edge of the white horizon, St. Petersburg appeared, and materialized into a city of glittering baroque palaces, wide avenues and squares, and heroic equestrian statuary. Browning stayed long enough to see the solid ice in the Neva break, and a few days later, to watch the governor, amid the booming of guns, cross the open stream to bear a goblet of clear river water to the Czar.

Exotic, passionate, violent, barbarically colorful and splendid, Russian life was probably much to his literary taste, but it was shut away from him by formidable barriers of distance, language, and culture. The realistic method and the conversational style favor a near view and an easy familiarity. Browning modestly limited himself, for the most part, to western Europe. In 1843, however, he did attempt a play, *Only a Player-girl,* laid in St. Petersburg. He told Elizabeth Barrett that it was "about a fair on the Neva, and booths and droshkies and fish-pies and so forth, with the Palaces in the background."[53] It was never published, and no trace of it has been discovered.

Yet, for a trip that kept him from England less than three months, Browning put a great deal of Russia into his head and kept it there. Half a century later, there was a stir of excitement at a soirée in Venice. Mr. Browning had fallen into a rare talk about Russian music with old Prince Gagarin, a retired Russian diplomat who had been ambassador at Athens, Turin, and Constantinople. At length, moved by thoughts of an experience long past, the poet "sang in a low, sweet voice a number of folk-songs and national airs he had caught by ear during his short stay in Russia," until the prince exclaimed in wonder at a musical memory even better than his own.[54]

Quite naturally, Robert now thought of a diplomatic career and applied for a place on a mission to Persia. The answer, ambiguously worded, seemed to accept him. He was much disappointed to learn, apparently on presenting himself to the "chief," that another man had been appointed. One suspects that in seeking a diplomatic post he had wished merely to make himself more independent and, as he says in *Pauline,* to look further "on real life,"[55] in short, to prepare himself for poetry rather than to make it secondary.

For his poetic powers were developing rapidly at this time. In the icy hurry and distractions of sightseeing in St. Petersburg, he had written "Porphyria's Lover," and on his return (in addition to a sonnet and a song which ultimately found its way into *Pippa Passes*) "Johannes Agricola in Meditation." These two pieces may reflect the sting of Mill's criticism. They are astonishing sequels to *Pauline.* The first, particularly, achieves the drama which *Pauline* merely aims at. Here already is the monologue method, the familiar style, the violent action, the wildly eccentric point of view, and the significant moment of insight—or rather of delusion, for the speaker obviously mistakes Porphyria's weak side, her attachment to him, for her strong side, and, as H. B. Charlton explains,[56] sees her as frivolous and proud whereas she is actually practical, efficient, and all too little discriminating in her friendships. The power of the poem resides in the extraordinary dramatic complication and intensity which it achieves in sixty lines. Here are characters, motives, a highly articulated situation, setting, atmosphere, and an action which, though swift, is elaborately balanced, with neat, ironic reversals—in pantomime—of loosening and unloosening hair and resting of heads on shoulders. The elaborate ghoulish irony of loving embrace and the granting of Porphyria's wish builds up to a smashing "curtain" line. The language is clear and easy, yet less abrupt and colloquial than in the later monologues. In fact, a restraint rare in Browning contributes greatly to the dramatic impact. "Johannes Agricola" presages the philosophical monologues, from "Saul" to "Caliban upon Setebos." It is another excursion into the eccentric consciousness, into the thinking mind laboring under strange delusions. Like "Porphyria," it is admirably concentrated. In sixty jingling, briskly rhyming tetrameters which effectively convey his grinning complacency, Johannes reveals how the Calvinistic doctrines of predestination, election, grace, and damnation make him the demented spiritual prig that he is. As Charlton observes, the poem concludes with a crowning irony: an instant of humility. Though Johannes sees with crystal clarity his own election amid universal damnation, he does not understand it—how could he, a mere man?[57]

These two poems were first published, over the initial Z, in *The Monthly Repository*. With what gusto Fox must have read "Johannes"!

CHAPTER **4**

The Promise of Paracelsus

1834-37

Early in the summer of 1834 a young French nobleman appeared among the Brownings of Camberwell with a letter from one of their relatives in the Rothschild bank at Paris. An ancestor of the young man had served the Bourbons in matters of finance; the impressive and accomplished Count Amédée de Ripert-Monclar himself served them—as he later confessed to the Brownings—more romantically as an undercover agent among émigrés in London. He now discoursed very affably on history, French culture, literature—and perhaps on Robert's future as a poet. He soon proved his friendship. He drew the first existing portrait of Browning, and proposed to him the subject of Paracelsus.[1] To be sure, he retracted the proposal almost in the same breath: the life of Paracelsus contained no fashionable romance.

But this time, apparently, Robert was quite willing to dispense with Paulines. Paracelsus was a favorite study of his father and, represented in the paternal library by the three substantial folios of Frederick Bitiskius' edition, was as familiar a piece of household furniture as the Perseus of Caravaggio's painting. According to Griffin,[2] he had even rather superficially penetrated the Bitiskius edition. Having read the accounts of the Renaissance physicians in the *Biographie universelle* and in Melchior Adam's *Vitae Germanorum Medicorum*, Robert began to write, and by March 1835 had produced a manuscript of 4,152 lines.

Paracelsus is an oblique but sufficiently illuminating self-portrait. Much of what was outward and dramatic in the career of an eccentric Renaissance genius recedes, and much of what was inward and problematic in Robert swells into the foreground. All the great, noisy, obvious events of Paracelsus' career at Basel for example—his burning of the books, his cure of the cleric, his appearance before the magistrate—are seen, like Wordsworth's experience of the French

Revolution in *The Prelude,* in retrospect, across a broad foreground of subjective mood and feeling. The poem is in fact a very elaborate speculation on what might happen to a somewhat hypothetical Robert Browning if he undertook an entirely hypothetical course of action. It is therefore also a passionately lyrical expression of personal ambition, set in a dramatic framework of possible failure. Robert at twenty-three had not disappointed himself seriously enough to doubt that he might succeed. But, consulting his father's books, eating his mother's meals, and gazing at a corner of the sky beyond the paper on his bedroom desk, he could not honestly believe that his achievement so far guaranteed the future. Fox's daughter remembers the young poet at this time "full of ambition, eager for success, eager for fame, and, what's more, determined to conquer fame and to achieve success."[3]

He was almost as eager and determined to exploit dramatically the autobiographical perspective he had used—not with the most lucid results—for *Pauline.* His starting point seems to have been a passage in that poem:

> This restlessness of passion meets in me
> A craving after knowledge. . . .[4]

Apparently, mere knowledge leads to spiritual pride, to the desiccating exclusion of "happy ignorant hopes and fears"—more particularly, perhaps, to the rebellious and critical rationalism which had temporarily made Robert an atheist.

In *Paracelsus* he spells out this nemesis more precisely. The "craving" is now more intense. His new hero affords him an impressive symbol of insatiable thirst for knowledge, of perilous searching into the secrets of life, of Protestant or Shelleyan contempt for established authority. Browning minimizes the comic boastfulness of the historical Paracelsus and reads into him his own uncharitable impatience with the folly of ordinary people. He seems to have aimed at a more realistic Alastor, likewise distinguished by "grey hair" and "faded hands,"[5] equally defective in love and social sympathy, and similarly condemned to waste away—in part, through the intensity of lonely cerebration.

Mrs. Betty Miller has called attention to the strongly autobiographical character of Part I.[6] Like Robert's father, Festus is singularly modest and unassuming; he is a lover of books and has presided over Paracelsus' early education. Like Robert's mother, Michal sings, is fond of gardening, and, significantly, fears that the pursuit of knowledge will bring Paracelsus to ruin. The two live sequestered lives, behind an "old populous green wall"[7] like that of the cottage in Camberwell. Both have for Paracelsus the proud, solicitous affection of doting parents. Like Robert himself, Paracelsus has passed through a period of disturbance and confusion which may adumbrate the crisis in *Pauline.*[8] He is scornful of schools and scholars, and, like Robert decamping from Bedford Square, has broken off an indifferently successful school career to succeed on a plane which defies all competition.

No doubt, had the poem been wholly autobiographical, the hero would have been a Shelleyan atheist and revolutionary. By using the Paracelsus story, Browning could impose a Christian framework on his own intellectual presumption, and so keep within the bounds of Victorian decorum. Even so, he manages to keep remarkably faithful to the spirit of his own adolescence. Paracelsus proposes to serve God and mankind as haughtily, cold-heartedly, and very nearly as irreverently as the poet had served himself in *Pauline.* At one and the same time Paracelsus, like Browning so often, loathes and cherishes:

I seemed to long
At once to trample on, yet save mankind.[9]

His ambition is staggering: he will discover "the secret of the world"—"man's true purpose, path, and fate."[10] Festus asks him whether he is not really more eager for fame than for knowledge. He replies that he trusts in his own "fierce energy" as evidence of God's grace.

Is it for human will
To institute such impulses?—still less,
To disregard such promptings![11]

Thus far, he might seem only a rather overwrought Calvinist. But Browning has him address God in a tone of blasphemous defiance, coupled with overweening ambition:

See if we cannot beat thine angels yet![12]

Browning even takes a hint from the Paracelsan doctrine of the correspondence between microcosm and macrocosm to depict the excess of introversion from which he seems to suffer. Paracelsus plans to discover medical and other truth by looking within:

> There is an inmost centre in us all,
> Where truth abides in fullness. . . .[13]

Why, then, need he leave his cottage? Festus argues the wisdom of staying at home to study in the schools. But Paracelsus' travels are historical and also symbolic: they represent the intellectual search—as do Alastor's—and severance from the Christian love and traditional prudence of Festus and Michal.

In short, Paracelsus departs from "a garden in the environs" of Würzburg as a particularly insatiable Robert might leave Camberwell. Nine years later at the house of a Greek conjurer in Constantinople, worn out and prematurely aged, he has neither the health to enjoy pleasure nor the energy to pursue knowledge. Having heard a song which might have been taken up by the company of failures in "Childe Roland," he encounters the poet Aprile. Paracelsus later exclaims:

> Part? Never!
> Till thou the lover, know; and I, the knower,
> Love—until both are saved.[14]

Knowledge has given him power; love has given Aprile beauty.

What could Paracelsus learn from such a man? Scarcely love, for they were both equally in love with themselves. Perhaps Aprile's weakness is that he had gazed so ardently on all the world's beauties that he had never fastened on one long enough to obtain the knowledge and power to embody it in a work of art. Paracelsus' weakness, on the other hand, is that he had been so ardently obsessed with his own ideas and aspiration for power that he had grown blind to the infinity of God's creation. On the basis of such a distinction, Paracelsus might learn from Aprile the importance of turning lovingly outward on the human and spiritual world.

As the spokesman for Christian love, Festus fittingly expostulates:

> I say, such love is never blind; but rather
> Alive to every the minutest spot
> Which mars its object, and which hate (supposed
> So vigilant and searching) dreams not of.[15]

Festus himself possesses the patience and humility which Aprile and Paracelsus both lack. On the other hand, he lacks the ardor and aspiration which raise them to the possibility of high achievement. Here, again, one thinks of Browning's father, who failed to turn great talents to account.

Paracelsus now resolves to love as well as to know. That resolve makes him a professor: he will share his knowledge with his fellow men—specifically, with the students of Basel. What is the relation of a prophet to his audience? That problem had occupied Browning for some time. It was to occupy him and other Englishmen much longer.

For Browning lived at a time when prophets expected large audiences. In nineteenth-century England, as E. D. H. Johnson[16] has shown, poetry actually attempted to revolutionize, reform, and edify the mass readers of a nation. The history of that adventure, which Browning predicts for Paracelsus, is bitterly ironic. Romantic poets preached revolution and became infamous; they then preached idealized revolution, beauty, patriotism, or religion—and died martyrs or laureates. Victorian poets hesitated between art for art's sake and civic duty, chose duty, trod a cautious *via media* between inculcating conventional virtue and insinuating revolutionary criticism—and received much applause and little serious attention. Late Victorian poets grew desperate, and sought with sensuality, sedition, atheism, blasphemy, and art for art's sake, to shock and outrage where their elders had tried to edify. Browning's own Shelley had preached revolution literally and directly in *Queen Mab* and symbolically and indirectly in subsequent works. Robert himself had preached *Queen Mab* openly in the bosom of his family, and recanted darkly in *Pauline.* He had certainly reflected a great deal about his own reception, and perhaps not a little about Shelley's. In the Basel episode of *Paracelsus,* he presents the possible disintegration of an artist, and in some degree the disintegration of the Victorian artist, in the face of an indifferent audience.

Visiting Paracelsus in Basel, Festus finds him already disillusioned. His students repel him. And here, perhaps, one sees considerably magnified the scorn Browning had felt for the decorum of the lecture hall at London. Unthinking applause offends Paracelsus' pride and encourages him in a reckless cynicism. Niggling criticism, by others, defeats his creative impulse and saps his intellectual energy. He publicly burns all medical books to astonish the crowd and declare his contempt for traditional authority. He uses tricks to gain from his hearers the adulation he had once dreamed of winning honestly. He drinks to comfort himself for disappointed ambition and is bitterly aware that the genius come before his time may at the right moment legitimately win the allegiance of the crowd.

Sometime afterward at Colmar, Festus finds him a refugee from Basel and still further deteriorated. Yielding to his better nature, he had attempted to instruct his students, and been deserted by them to a man. Now, substituting alcohol—and poetry—for youthful inspiration, he once more aspires. But the illusion of love has ended in the reality of hatred. In fact, he allows himself very few illusions except about himself: mind is a disease; men are depraved—he is above them like a god.

Summoned to Salzburg, Festus finds Paracelsus dying. He has come to believe in immortality—apparently because life is so unsatisfactory. He is now humble and full of love. Clairvoyant in the moment of death, he unfolds a vast panoramic vision of the terrestrial creation permeated by divine love and joy. His fine speech owes some of its technique—notably the cosmic loftiness of its point of view—to Shelley, and a good deal of its content (notably the idea of the Great Chain of Being) to Pope's *Essay on Man* and Milton's *Paradise Lost.*[17]

He failed, Paracelsus says, because he gazed on power until he grew blind, because he saw no use in the past, and because he had tried, in a moment, to give men mastery of the elemental world. The passage suggests not only that Browning understood the error of Faust but that he had discovered how ridiculously Faust-like some aspects of his own luxurious day-dreaming had been. Paracelsus describes the faculties of life—power, knowledge, love—vaguely, but with emphasis on the dualism of human strength and weakness. Knowledge is

> not intuition, but the slow
> Uncertain fruit of an enhancing toil,
> Strengthened by love—[18]

Love may well include both the humble, illuminating Christian love of Festus and the joyous, expansive, aesthetic love of Aprile. If divine love and joy sustain the world and are themselves the ultimate reality, then human love and joy are essential helps to insight which will not come from "enhancing toil" alone. Yet where love can mean so many things—humanitarian service, brotherly love, Christian and Platonic love, aesthetic projection—it cannot mean very much. One point of course remains certain: Paracelsus learns that love must be humble and reverent to develop the discipline and charity necessary to a happy, productive life.

Whatever its faults, one has only to compare *Paracelsus* with

"Alastor" to understand what Browning had accomplished. The poem is a remarkable expression of the impulse and the ambition to know and to create works of art. It is also a vivid, lifelike, and even subtle study of genius—and particularly of genius disintegrating for want of an appreciative audience.

In the previous year Sir Henry Taylor's lengthy dramatic poem *Philip van Artevelde* had created a journalistic sensation. To do it justice, the sedate and dignified *Athenaeum* had thrown sedateness and dignity to the wind in fifteen columns. Surely one could look forward to a handsome profit from a really first-rate intellectual tragedy. Robert appealed to Fox for an introduction to the printer Moxon, himself a poet and the publisher of Taylor and Tennyson. Through Fox's friend Cowden Clarke the introduction was managed. Alas! "No sooner was Mr. Clarke's letter perused than the Moxonian visage loured exceedingly thereat—the Moxonian accent grew dolorous thereupon:—'Artevelde' has not paid expenses by about thirty odd pounds. Tennyson's poetry is *'popular at Cambridge,'* and yet of 800 copies which were printed of his last, some 300 only have gone off: Mr. M. hardly knows whether he shall ever venture again, &c. &c., and in short begs to decline even inspecting, &c. &c."[19] The expression on Moxon's face was a portent of the age. Since the financial collapse of 1826, poetry had been a drug on the market; nor were epics and tragedies ever again to be the highly salable commodities they had been in Byron's day. Robert tried Saunders and Otley with no better result. Eventually, Effingham Wilson, a friend of Fox and publisher of radical literature, was persuaded to see radical tendencies in *Paracelsus,* and at the expense of Mr. Browning, Sr., brought it out in 1835.

Robert's poem did not disturb the composure of magisterial journals. *The Quarterly,* the *Edinburgh,* and *Blackwood* received it in stony silence. In seventy-three words, the *Athenaeum*[20] discerned (with difficulty) some talent, but found the work "dreamy and obscure," and concluded with a warning against any attempt to imitate the "mysticism and vagueness" of Shelley. *Paracelsus* seemed fated to make neither noise nor profit until John Forster spoke out in *The Examiner* of September 6. "Since the publication of Philip van Artevelde," he wrote in somewhat feeble superlative, "we have met with no such evidences of poetic genius, and of general intellectual power, as are contained in this volume."[21] Inferring that the author is a young man, he predicts a "brilliant career." Robert Browning "possesses all the elements of a fine poet." Moreover, Forster was not the only critic to applaud.

In November Fox emerged from an intricate warfare against Whigs, Tories, Trinitarians, and Mrs. Fox to publish a lengthy review in *The Monthly Repository.*[22] Fox had heard *Paracelsus* read in manuscript by Robert himself and presumably had discussed it with him, so that in considerable degree his review must reflect the poet's own ideas. It is in effect a vigorous elementary lesson in Browning for critics. Fox begins by roundly declaring that *Paracelsus* is "*a Work.*" It is not—as some bewildered critics have imagined—a mystical fog floating inexplicably out of a metaphysical void, but "the result of thought, skill, and toil." Mr. Browning's "Paracelsus is not a personification indeed, but an individualisation of humanity, in whom he exhibits its alternations of aspiration and attainment." Further, "*Paracelsus* is not a drama; and although generally in form a dialogue, is often in spirit a monologue, the other speakers being introduced as subservient to the delineation, by Paracelsus himself, of the several states of his mental being." Regretting some obscurity in the poet and more density in his critics, Fox concludes by stating very firmly that *Paracelsus* is not only a poem, but a poem with ideas.

Critics believed him—and with few exceptions began to discover merits and beauties. In *The Metropolitan Journal,*[23] the reviewer humbly begged to ask "what *poet of the present day,* Wordsworth himself . . . not excepted," could "express himself more nobly," and John Forster in a second article—this time in the *New Monthly Magazine and Literary Journal*[24]—declared: "Without the slightest hesitation we name Mr. Browning at once with Shelley, Coleridge, Wordsworth."

One might expect that Robert would be content. By no means. He had experienced only one previous failure. The meek forbearance of his father and unremitting attention of his mother failed to prepare him for one eventuality of life. His childhood had echoed and reverberated with applause. Writing of the reception of *Paracelsus* to Elizabeth Barrett in 1845, he remembered chiefly that critics had called it "rubbish."[25] Forster's review was the sort a young poet dreams of reading, but apparently it had caused only a slight admixture of justice in a sea of neglect. Indeed, Browning's acute—and lifelong—susceptibility to critical censure suggests that until he began to publish he had rarely been criticized.

But an important circle of men now recognized the promise of *Paracelsus'* author by offering friendship, new incentive, and new opportunity. Again, Fox proved how essential he was to Browning's career. At about this time, Fox's domestic edifice came down with an appalling clatter of broken glass. Mrs. Fox broke an armed truce and, while her husband was prostrate with illness, informed two members of his congregation of her worst suspicions. In the full thunder and lightning of open scandal in which Eliza Flower, as Fox wrote his mother, was "fiercely and falsely attacked," Fox resigned as minister of South Place. He also proceeded to an open separation from Mrs. Fox. It speaks well of South Place's liberalism that a majority of his congregation actually supported him: forty-six seat holders withdrew, one hundred and twenty remained. Fox's resignation was refused.

Having provided for his wife and his son Franklin, who usually lived with her, Fox migrated with his daughter "Tottie" (later Mrs. F. L. Bridell-Fox) and his deaf son, Florance, to Craven Hill in Bayswater, then a rural village in quiet meadows bordering on Kensington Park. "When the new household was organised," writes Richard Garnett, "Eliza Flower appeared at the head of it."[26] Fox declared that the relationship was platonic and he was generally believed. Nevertheless, he and Eliza found many respectable doors closed to them, and inevitably they were aware, at the edges of their lives, of much attentive horror and of occasional ribald whisperings. "There was a furtive look about the eyes and mouth," wrote D. O. Madden of a thinly veiled fictitious character, "an appearance as if he were playing a part that did not become him. He seemed as if he had done something which made him feel unquietly, like a monk of La Trappe addicted to eating beefsteak in the dark."[27]

Insulated from laughter by green fields, a vine-covered cottage, loyal friends, and an almost perpetual spring of fine weather—which persists remarkably in Eliza's letters and Tottie's reminiscences—the inhabitants of Craven Hill lived a singularly durable and strenuous idyll of labor and love. Eliza sang, composed, wrote letters, copied articles, gave Florry his lessons, played at trapball with him in the back garden, and very naturally worried about him a good deal. "He seems to me," she wrote Fox's sister Sadie, "to need moral training and discipline (though of the kindest kind) more than any being I ever met with."[28] In the afternoons she often sat over sewing or embroideries with her neighbor Mrs. Novello under a great cherry tree on whose trunk Fox had pinned—in fierce philosophical-radical protest against another neighbor who shot blackbirds—a placard reading "Blackbirds May Eat the Cherries Here."

Conquering new worlds as well as old, Fox set forth for London every weekday morning at eight-thirty. "And now I'll tell you what he is doing," Eliza wrote his sister with the unmistakable air of taking up the most important subject in life. "On Tuesday he is preaching a course of lectures on the Reformers, from Abraham, Moses, the old prophets and Greek philosophers—up to Christ and His Apostles, then to Mahomet, Wycliffe, Luther, Knox, and then to those of our own age. I think they are the finest things he ever did, and I wonder how often I've said so before. But in the week the newspaper is the grand object."[29] Fox had sold *The Repository* to R. H. Horne and was now daily writing—it would seem, almost single-handedly—D. W. Harvey's *True Sun.* "The leading articles besides literature and drama, the criticism, with an additional one for the Sunday paper, is his department." The circulation doubled, trebled. Truth seemed to be winning another great battle over error—and perhaps on a more congenial, money-on-the-counter basis. After his first day at *The True Sun,* Fox had come home at what was to be his usual hour of three, exchanged his coat for his dressing gown, and exclaimed, "There, I feel like an honest man who earns his bread by the sweat of his brow."[30] After three, one suspects, the idyll began once more in earnest. Friends arrived; there was more talk, more poetry, more music, and no doubt even finer weather.

No visitor was more assiduous than Robert Browning, at least in Tottie's girlish eyes a very dashing figure.

> One bright morning rises up clear before me, like a sunlit spot through the long misty years. I see myself, a child, sitting drawing at a sunny cottage window in the then rural suburb of Bayswater. . . . Mr. Browning entered the little drawing-room, with a quick light step; and on hearing from me that my father was out, and in fact that nobody was at home except myself, he said: "It's my birthday today; I'll wait till they come in," and sitting down to the piano, he added: "If it wont [sic] disturb you, I'll play till they do." And as he turned to the instrument, the bells of some neighbouring church suddenly burst out with a frantic merry peal. It seemed to my childish fancy, as if in response to the remark that it was his birthday. He was then slim and dark, and very handsome; and—may I hint it—just a trifle of a dandy, addicted to lemon-coloured kid gloves and such things: quite "the glass of fashion and the mould of form."[31]

What did this ardent, bustling, modishly dressed young man think of the new household? Perhaps—availing himself of the remarkably fluid adjustment between head and heart which Eliza Flower had observed—he contrived to think very little about it except in quiet places and in quiet parts of his brain. Probably he was not very much shocked; after all, he had read Shelley; he had written *Pauline,* and was eventually to write "The Statue and the Bust." Doubtless he admired Eliza's courageous action, yet it was not, one suspects, the kind of action with which he would wish to be personally identified. Their relationship had become rather formal, perhaps even rather strained. She thought him egotistic; his letters to her are short and correct; on the other hand those to Fox are long, open, and boisterous, full of syntactical exuberance and literary swagger. In the difficult years ahead, reechoing with accusations of obscurity, the reader who never failed to understand was Fox. "I would, you know I would, always would, choose you out of the whole English world to judge and correct what I write myself."[32]

To be sure, Robert came to Craven Hill only in part to support and enjoy old friends. He was a literary man in search of a literary world. Fox's cottage, somewhat removed by its irregularity from ordinary time and space, was a pleasantly improbable pastoral retreat in which the denizens of diverse literary and intellectual climates came quietly and often intimately together. As a dramatic critic, Fox knew Macready and his friends Dickens, Forster, Talfourd, and Bulwer. As a literary journalist of varied interests, he knew poet-editors like Leigh Hunt and R. H. Horne, popularizers like Cowden Clarke and the Howitts, and wealthy amateurs like John Kenyon. As a radical philosopher and unitarian thinker he knew utilitarians like Mill and Bowring, their transcendental critic Carlyle, and unitarians like the Martineaus. As next-door neighbor to Vincent Novello—who, with his son Alfred, was founding on music a commercial house nearly as solid as that which the Rothschilds had founded on money—he was separated by a low garden wall from a factory devoted to the production of opera singers, literary propaganda, and Shakespeare scholarship. Clara Novello was then on the verge of her career as England's foremost concert soprano; her sister, Mary Cowden Clarke, was compiling a vast Shakespeare concordance; and the jovial, stentorian Charles Cowden Clarke himself was busily explaining English poetry to almost the entire population of Great Britain.

Into this intimate little forest of varied celebrities, Robert did not have to venture quite without a mane and a tail: after all, he had written *Paracelsus.* As the author of that poem, he seems quickly to have made friends with Kenyon, Horne, Talfourd, and Hunt. Far more important, he met, in the rather awful immediacy of Fox's little sitting room, William Charles Macready himself. Robert was twenty-three. The "eminent tragedian," then forty-two, had been reading favorable reviews of *Paracelsus* for more than a month. He intended the meeting with young Mr. Browning to be a success. It was a success. To his diary—the monumental receptacle of so much monumental exasperation with life, the stage, the world, and himself—he purred approvingly:

> Went from chambers to dine with Rev. William Fox, Bayswater. . . . Mr. Robert Browning, the author of *Paracelsus*, came in after dinner; I was very much pleased to meet him. His face is full of intelligence. My time passed most agreeably. . . . I took Mr. Browning on, and requested to be allowed to improve my acquaintance with him. He expressed himself warmly, as gratified by the proposal; wished to send me his book; we exchanged cards and parted.[33]

On that evening of November 27, 1835, Browning began a fateful friendship. Actor, manager, and pre-eminent force in the theater since the death of Edmund Kean in 1833, Macready was as earnestly Victorian as his predecessor had been demonically Romantic. Not that he lacked passion. His Macbeth, particularly in the dagger scene, frequently terrified Lady Macbeth as much as the audience, and his Othello was literally murderous. Desdemona never knew whether she would emerge from the avenging pillow with her life. Yet in Macready conscience was as sharp as passion was violent. He did not, like Kean, strain for points. His Shakespearean roles were carefully meditated attempts to represent the total characters which Shakespeare had conceived—and he examined his artistic conduct on the stage as relentlessly as he examined his moral conduct off it. Of late he had found little reason to be pleased, particularly in the first category:

> *October 21st.*—Went to the theatre, and felt very nervous and unsettled; reasoned with myself, and partially recovered my self-possession; but, in truth, was hurried out in the part of Othello, and was not perfectly possessed of it. The criticism I passed on Malibran's Fidelio will exactly suit my own Othello—it was "elaborate, but not abandoned."[34]

The truth was, first-rate work had become almost impossible. He was thoroughly exasperated with the state not only of the English stage but of his own career. As a fifteen-year-old boy at Rugby, where he was admired by pupils and masters alike, he had felt a strong social prejudice against his family's profession of acting. When forced to adopt it by the sudden bankruptcy of his father and so give up a genteel future in the law, he had resented his own snobbery—and that of society—with a fierce and intrepid egalitarianism. As a Victorian gentleman of sense and rectitude, he obdurately considered the stage a low business pursued by low people. As a born actor with discriminating taste and obsessive ambition, he fervently admired the artistry of a ruffian like Kean and was impelled to labor relentlessly to surpass him, in spite of an awkward carriage, a flat face, and a harsh voice. As a dedicated idealist, he devoted his energies—and later, as manager of Drury Lane, a large part of his fortune—to the impractical task of ridding the theater of its flamboyant sensationalism and making it a dominant cultural force in the nation.

Macready's heaviest cross at this time was the Anti-Christ of the British stage, "Grand-Junction" Bunn, director of the Drury Lane, to whom he was tied by contract and thus "interdicted," as he put it, "from the exercise of his profession."[35] Yet he did not give up his vision of a national theater. Anxiously, tirelessly, he plodded the deserts of contemporary blank-verse tragedy in search of genuine dramatic works which would compel production. In his friend Talfourd's *Ion* he thought he had found one. Might he not get another from this young Mr. Browning?

In the actual reading, *Paracelsus* proved impressive but scarcely stageworthy. "I am obliged to confess that the main design of the poem is not made out with sufficient clearness," he decided on December 8, but the writer himself was clearly "destined for very great things."[36] And great things might well include producible plays. Two weeks later he invited Browning to spend the night of New Year's Eve at his house at Elstree, several miles from London.

Waiting at the "Blue Posts" for the stagecoach, Robert noted a short, stocky young man with a shock of brown hair, a square head, stern features, and broad, high shoulders, impregnably buttoned up in a frockcoat. There was authority in the flourish of the stranger's monocle, irrefutable certainty in the heavy jaws massively shut. Covertly, Robert eyed him. Presently he was aware of being eyed in return. Arriving almost simultaneously at Elstree, the two elegantly dressed young men were introduced. The stranger's name was John Forster. "Did you see a little notice of you I wrote in *The Examiner*?"[37] he asked in a formidable undertone of confidence. Of course Robert had seen it. By that voice, deep and resonant with conviction and lung power, he was to be told again and again that he was a great poet. In the monumental diary Macready recorded with benevolence: "Mr.

Browning was very popular with the whole party; his simple and enthusiastic manner engaged attention and won opinions from all present; he looks and speaks more like a youthful poet than any man I ever saw."[38]

Forster was already developing that vast knowledge of the macrocosm, London, which was to make him the power behind so many literary thrones and the practical agent of so many men of genius. "Whenever anybody is in a scrape," declared Thackeray, "we all fly to him for refuge. He is omniscient and works miracles."[39] He knew everybody important because he made himself indispensable and rose to ever greater heights of servility from Dickens and Tennyson eventually to Palmerston and Gladstone. At this time he descended on a promising young author like a column of army ants on a tropical wilderness in springtime. With massive self-assurance yet often with considerable tact and shrewdness, he explained the young man's talents to the world and to the young man himself, took over his negotiations with publishers, acted as his Mercury to friends and admirers, managed his business affairs, advised him about his private life, and planned his future career. Though as yet Robert's success hardly offered scope for such wide activity, he seems to have been constantly together with Forster—particularly in Macready's dressing room and chambers.

Like so many men who seem to proclaim all they are on the surface, Forster is a puzzling and enigmatic figure. Men so diverse as Dickens and Tennyson, fond of him through many years, saw more beneath that prodigious exterior than a remarkable pair of vocal cords and a servile eagerness. Forster was a shrewd and resourceful man of business, an accomplished amateur actor, a learned and discriminating critic of art and literature, a gifted writer (as his *Life of Dickens* was conclusively to demonstrate), and an affectionate and loyal friend capable not only of boisterous enjoyment but of quiet intimacy and understanding. "He was two distinct men," wrote the Reverend Whitwell Elwin—who broke off a monumental edition of Pope in the fifth volume because he could abide the poet himself no longer—"and the one man quite distinct from the other. To see him in company I should not have recognized him for the friend with whom I was intimate in private. Then he was quiet, natural, unpretending, and most agreeable, and in the warmth and generosity of his friendship he had no superior. Sensitive as he was in some ways, there was no man to whom it was easier to speak with perfect frankness."[40] Splendidly endowed with all the superficial talents to astonish, command, and overawe, Forster could perhaps hardly be expected to resist the temptation of an audience. Percy Fitzgerald saw him as another Dr. Johnson. Actually, he was much more a Boswell in Johnson's clothing. He laid down the law, and talked to win. In the large, reverberating interior of Forster's autocratic personality, there was an un-Johnsonian hollowness which longed to engulf and possess the achievements of other men's talents. To be sure—as Carlyle might have pointed out—there was a principle of generosity in this aggression. Forster valued and admired genius. Therefore he longed to serve it, to embrace it.

Charged with future history as the domicile of Tulkinghorn in *Bleak House,* Forster's impressive chambers at 58 Lincoln's Inn Fields, garrisoned by his cockney servant Henry and subsidiaries, supplied with astonishing stores of wine and brandy, were an even more important part of his strategy against the great city than the authoritative monocle or the coat with the impregnable buttons. In the middle thirties, distant by less than two decades from the Regency, pleasure was still an heroic and dangerous pursuit. "I cannot be one of those," wrote Barry Cornwall firmly, "who will doubtless be found under the table at 4 a.m."[41] Forster's invitations were dreaded more than most. Carlyle dared not trust himself there before the play, and Mrs. Carlyle complained of being "filled half drunk with champagne as usual." What did Browning's mother think of these invitations and their consequences, when Robert, then twenty-four, appeared for a good-night kiss at four or five in the morning?

As passionate and headlong in friendships with men in his twenties as he was cool and cautious in those with women, Robert was not likely to fare smoothly with Forster. In fact, he was nearly as loud, fully as restless and energetic, and, when sorely tried, far more violent and hot-tempered. According to one report, dining with a mutual friend, he became so infuriated with Forster that he "seized a heavy cut-glass decanter with murderous intent, and was only prevented from hurling it across the table by the nimble intervention of his host."[42] This incident may be apocryphal—but Forster possessed the valuable last-minute caution of the blusterer. The two continued to quarrel, pout, and measure injuries.

To know Fox was to know almost everybody under the bucolic influence of domestic life; to know Forster was to know almost everybody else under the more sinister influences of bachelor life. In the festive rooms at 58 Lincoln's Inn Fields, Robert for the first time met Bulwer, a genius in stays; Procter (Barry Cornwall), to whom he later dedicated *Colombe's Birthday;* T. N. Talfourd, to whom he dedicated *Pippa Passes;* the artist Daniel Maclise, for one of whose pictures he wrote ("in those very rooms"[43]) the lines that became "In a Gondola"; and—more interesting to Robert at the moment—the poet Laman Blanchard, for whose *Lyric Offerings* he had as a boy run all the way to Bond Street.[44] That quiet and affectionate convivial of intense and almost feminine sensibility, whose correspondence reads suspiciously like a long invitation to whisky punch, had begun as a gentle worshipper of Byron's violence, had declined into the Victorian responsibilities of laborious editorship and four children, and, after sorrowfully recording the life of the suicide poetess "L.E.L.," was himself to succumb to financial and other anxiety, madness, and eventual suicide. When Robert met him in 1836, he had but lately resigned the editorship of *The True Sun* for that of *The Court Journal.*

A minor figure in two lesser decades of poetry, Blanchard shows little to warrant Browning's lifelong admiration. He seems to have imitated Keats and Shelley as well as Byron, but he is a Keats without passion, a Shelley without ideas. Despair inspired his most intense and effective work; a grandiose ingenuity, his most characteristic. Apparently Browning valued Blanchard for his plumage. "That fine 'sun-bronzed, like Triumph on a pedestal,' that bridge 'dark trees were dying round,' that super-delicious 'song of the wave,' live within me yet, 'being things immortal,' " he wrote Blanchard many years later.[45]

Stimulated and encouraged by so many new acquaintances, Browning was now very eager to prove that *Paracelsus* was only the tip of a marvelous iceberg. Forster was all loyalty. He urged Macready to expect masterpieces from Robert and urged Robert to write the masterpieces Macready expected. Macready was quite willing to expect masterpieces. Indeed the imminent cauldrons of simmering irritation visibly receded from his look and manner at the young man's approach. "Forster and Browning called," he recorded in his diary at about this time,

> and talked over the plot of a tragedy which Browning had begun to think of: the subject, Narses. He said that I had *bit* him by my performance of Othello, and I told him I hoped I should make the blood come. . . . May it be![46]

Narses was rejected. Steeping himself in Shakespeare, Macready, and the theater, Robert pursued his search.

Meanwhile, Macready himself was moving through painful and

intricate darkness toward a literary theater—and Robert Browning. He continued to suffer the martyrdom of long banishments from the stage, a stately martyrdom in frockcoat. At length, walking to the theater one evening, Macready was arrested by the sight of his name on a poster. He turned, and read that he was to appear in the first three acts of *Richard III*, on the same evening with *The Jewess* and the first act of *Chevy Chase*. He and Shakespeare—to be truncated between two melodramas! Macready thought unthinkable thoughts. Then he thought about his duty to his family and submitted. But stalking from the stage on that night of humiliation, he came to the door of the Director's Office. A moment later, "Grand-Junction" Bunn looked up in the dim light from the plotting of future menageries to behold the sinister features and flashing eyes of the murderer of the little princes.

"You damned scoundrel!" thundered Macready, "how dare you use me in this manner!"[47]

Bunn rose. Macready struck him with the back of his hand. There was a scuffle in which the monarch suffered a bitten little finger and the director of theaters a sprained ankle and a closed eye. Gazing down at the yet unsullied page of his diary that night, Macready was already sick with shame and remorse, not so much for Bunn's discomfiture as for his own "intemperate and unfortunate rashness."[48]

But the blow that closed Bunn's eye had opened a way to Macready's objective. Barred from Drury Lane, he speedily obtained an engagement at Covent Garden and was greeted on his first appearance by cheers that continued until he nearly broke down. After a superb performance of *Macbeth*, he stepped forward and, within the limits of the Macreadian style and dignity, laid his tortured conscience before the public. "I was subjected in cold blood," he declared, "from motives which I will not characterize, to a series of studied and annoying and mortifying provocations, personal and professional. . . . I was betrayed, in a moment of unguarded passion, into an intemperate and imprudent act, for which I feel, and shall never cease to feel the deepest and most poignant self-reproach and regret."[49] But a damage suit impended, and the press had given itself up to a robust enjoyment of the scandal. Moving with intense agitation in a dark private world of anxiety and humiliation, Macready began to rehearse Talfourd's *Ion* for its premiere at Covent Garden on May 26, 1836.

The event was a dazzling success—in fact, as Betty Miller has shown,[50] that kind of dazzling success which tempts every man's jealousy. The audience was a national pantheon of living immortals—including even that venerable solitary, William Wordsworth, who sat in a box in the dress circle with Walter Savage Landor. Perhaps the play was too successful, however—even for Macready, whose benefit night it was. Summoned after the final curtain, he made a speech which, according to Mary Mitford, whose *Rienzi* he had refused, gave all credit to himself and none to the author. Talfourd came to his dressing room immediately afterward and asked whether he should go on the stage, as the audience was calling for him. Macready consulted his conscience, and replied with decision, "On no account in the world." That night he explained to his diary, "It would not be right."[51]

Immediately after the performance, a full sixty of the living Pantheon—Wordsworth, Landor, Macready, Douglas, Knowles, Browning, Forster, Miss Mitford, Miss Ellen Tree (the leading lady), and many lesser lights—moved to Talfourd's house in Russell Square, where a "very elegant" supper awaited them. It was then that Macready felt one of his infinitely fleeting moments of "tranquil happiness." Consulting his artistic conscience, he felt that he had never acted better. Consulting his practical conscience, he felt that (in the interests both of his friend Talfourd and of the living drama) he had acted with generosity and restraint, except that he had lost his temper about a stage set before the performance and about an attack in *Blackwood's* after. "Moroseness—unchecked will—when am I to learn and practise a sensible, restrained and philosophic bearing?"[52] Still, within the limits of insatiable conscience, it was a happy night. Wordsworth chatted with him. Forster bustled among the guests—doubtless plotting what the great men should think and say—with a manner that was being increasingly recognized as Macready's stage style. At table, Macready noted with satisfaction, he was seated between Wordsworth and Landor, with Browning opposite. He pointed out to Wordsworth a passage in *Ion* as having been suggested by lines Wordsworth had once quoted to him from a manuscript tragedy of his.

Wordsworth smiled and said, "Yes, I noticed them," and then went on:

> Action is transitory—a step—a blow,
> The motion of a muscle—this way or that—
> 'Tis done; and in the after vacancy
> We wonder at ourselves like men betrayed.

Landor said he had not the constructive faculty for dramatic composition. "He could only set persons talking, all the rest was chance."[53] Nevertheless, he would send his play of *Count Julian*, and he desired to know Macready better.

At this supper Miss Mitford, even then beginning her friendship with Elizabeth Barrett, saw Robert Browning for the first time. Describing the occasion to her father in a letter written the next day, she merely notes the author of *Paracelsus* among "quantities more of poets."[54] But Miss Mitford seldom reacted neutrally to anybody. Writing in 1847 to Charles Boner, she elaborated on her first impression:

> I saw Mr. Browning once and remember thinking how exactly he resembled a girl drest in boy's clothes—and as to his poetry I have just your opinion of it—It is one heap of obscurity confusion and weakness. . . . Do you know him personally? Did you ever see him? I met him once as I told you when he had long ringlets and no neckcloth—and when he seemed to me about the height and size of a boy of twelve years old—Femmelette—is a word made for him. A strange sort of person to carry such a woman as Elizabeth Barrett off her feet.[55]

After the supper, Forster appeared at Macready's elbow. Everybody in the room expected the actor to propose Talfourd's health. Macready contemplated a long vista of toasts converging on a next morning headache—and demurred. Forster became irresistible, and Macready rose. Talfourd responded at once with a eulogy of the actor, Douglas followed with a pledge to Mrs. Talfourd, and the toasting ramified with rapidly increasing warmth until Talfourd, as the Agathon of the feast, proposed Robert Browning, "the youngest poet of England."[56] It was a great moment, even for one who had long since decided "to become the greatest and most glorious man on earth."[57] Robert saw Landor—to whom, he often said later, "he owed more than to any other contemporary"—raise his glass. According to a tradition of Browning biography, Wordsworth leaned across the table.

"I am proud to drink to your health, Mr. Browning."[58]

But, as Betty Miller points out,[59] even this single gesture of warmth and cordiality cannot be attributed to the gray immortal of Rydal Mount. Crabb Robinson records a much more characteristic act: he had accompanied Wordsworth home before the toasting began. What Browning felt, seated across the table from the most famous—and the most formidable—poet of the age is an interesting speculation. He had never particularly liked Wordsworth's poetry, and he was still enough of a Shelleyan to like his politics even less. In fact, he was to publish, nine years later, an indignant poem on the subject.

Toward the end of the evening, when the toasts of friendship produced their apples of discord and poets began to quarrel, Macready, far advanced in the inebriety he had feared, observed to Miss Mitford that the occasion should stimulate her to write a play.

"Will you act it?" she asked quickly—and not without venom.

The unacted *Rienzi* rose up before him like Banquo's ghost, and Macready responded with significant silence. But in shepherding his ladies—his wife, his sister, and Miss Haworth—away from the house, he hastened to overtake Browning.

"Write a play, Browning, and keep me from going to America."[60]

Apparently Robert did not make a decisive reply, for two days later he wrote Macready a very earnest letter: he would allow himself another month to complete a long poem (*Sordello,* which he had actually begun after *Pauline* in 1833) and would then attempt a tragedy on any subject he or Macready thought appropriate. "Should I succeed," he concluded, "my way of life will be very certain, and my name pronounced along with yours."[61] Perhaps he had a subject already in mind, for of late he had not only been reading, but writing, about the Earl of Strafford. Forster had nearly finished a biography of Charles I's great minister, but had been rendered incapable of meeting his deadline by a disturbing event—probably the breaking off of his engagement with the poetess Letitia Landon ("L.E.L."). Robert was readying Forster's manuscript for the press.

On August 3, 1836, Macready heard that Browning had definitely fixed on Strafford as the topic for a tragedy. Macready was delighted. On October 4 Forster told him that Browning had completed *Strafford* in ten days. Macready was astonished but not delighted. "I cannot put faith in its dramatic qualities—the thing seems, not to say incredible, almost impossible." Happily, Forster had exaggerated. But within the month Browning himself announced that the play was all but finished.

At length, withdrawn to the quiet of Elstree, Macready settled down to *Strafford.* "I was greatly pleased with it, read portions of it to Catherine and Letitia"—and the next day was able with entire frankness to reassure a very anxious Browning. But he observes ominously, for the first time in their friendship, "He sat very long."[62] Rereading *Strafford* carefully, he saw that he had fallen into an error he had earlier suspected in Forster. "I had been too much carried away by the truth of character to observe the meanness of plot, and occasional obscurity."[63] He now informed Browning that the decision must wait until after he had brought out Bulwer's *La Vallière.* Meanwhile, he listened to the expostulations of Forster and the explanations of Browning. He read the play to his family, to the green room, to Browning himself—with the most varied and bewildering results. He read it one evening and felt restored to sanity, read it again the next and was assailed by entirely fresh doubts. Bit by bit, and for several hours at a time, he went through the text with Browning, suggesting deletions, additions, and clarifications—and later rejecting most of them when made. Such imposing and conscientious agonies could not but tell on the young author, who, by the end of March 1837, "looked very unwell, jaded and thought-sick."[64] Somewhat anticlimactically, Osbaldiston, the director of Covent Garden, was delighted with *Strafford,* and offered Robert £12 per night for twenty-five nights and £10 per night for ten nights beyond. Momentarily elated, Robert asked permission to dedicate the play to Macready.

Meanwhile *La Vallière*—a pompous and rhetorical ghost—had glimmered weakly, pallidly into oblivion. Macready sat down once more to the nightmare of *Strafford.* He went through it with Forster, pointing out its "feebleness" and "heaviness"—possibly in the hope that the man of infinite practical and worldly resource might somehow bring connection into chaos and excitement into obscurity. Forster tinkered unhappily and, illumined by truth from the higher god, became disillusioned with the lesser. He was gripped by the impulse to assert superiority, to vociferate, refute, humiliate. There was a quarrel.

On April 12 Macready confided to his diary:

> Called at Forster's chambers, whence Browning and he came to mine. There were mutual complaints—much temper—sullenness, I should say, on the part of Forster, who was very much out of humour with Browning, who said and did all that man could do to expiate any offence he might have given. Forster (who has behaved most nobly all through the matter of this play—no expression of praise is too high) showed an absence of sense and generosity in his behaviour which I grieved to see. There was a *scene.* Browning afterwards told me how much injury he did himself in society by this temper, corroborating what Talfourd had just before said of my poor friend Forster's *unpopularity.* I was truly sorry to hear from Browning much that rendered his unpopularity scarcely doubtful. Browning assented to all the proposed alterations, and expressed his wish, that *coûte que coûte,* the hazard should be made, and the play proceeded with.[65]

Two days later, at Forster's chambers, he met to go over further changes with Browning, "who came upstairs and who produced some scraps of paper with hints and unconnected lines—the full amount of his labour upon the alterations agreed on."[66] Macready's dissatisfaction must have been portentous. They went through the play again, and Robert went off like a schoolboy with another assignment for changes. That evening, he was waiting for Macready at his gate. He had done nothing. He wished to withdraw the play. In solemn conference with Forster the next day they debated the question, and resolved to go on at all costs. Macready now lay awake at night brooding about the soporific horrors of the play. He feared that it would be "damned," that it would be hissed.

CHAPTER 5

Macready's Boards
1837

Two months short of his twenty-fifth birthday, Browning plunged as a new playwright into the world of the Victorian theater.

What was that world like? A rapidly growing London proletariat had not only multiplied the number of "illegitimate" houses but trebled the size of the two legitimate, royal patent theaters. By virtue of a monopoly then largely nominal, Drury Lane and Covent Garden were the citadels of serious drama—as well as of artistic acting and cultivated audiences—yet were so vast as to reduce serious drama almost to insignificance. Drury Lane seated 3,600 people and contained a stage ninety feet deep. Its horseshoe-shaped walls towered up, in tier after tier of filigreed boxes, to a gallery from which scarcely audible Hamlets and Lears looked like ants crawling on a pavement.

The best actors struggled valiantly not to be swallowed up in the abyss of astronomical remoteness. They developed a power of attack, an intensity of passion and artistic purpose that often scorched and withered lesser creatures on the stage and radiated far out into the audience. They developed a "nervous athleticism"[1] of articulation which enabled them to stage whisper and breathe love sighs to the rafters. They boomed and bellowed with astonishing melody and range of expression. They stood in monumental attitudes, walked with rhythmic and rhetorical grandeur, gestured in an elaborate pantomime of passionate meaning. They stage-dueled with reckless ferocity and turned the action of a play into breathtaking exhibitions of acrobatic skill and agility. Such a style was for heroes, not for men. "Actors of gigantic or intense personalities could carry it off," says Shaw, "but it made commonplace actors ridiculous."[2] Not only were commonplace actors mere declamation fodder for stage-Napoleons like Kean and Sullivan, but, forced by the repertory system to be ready for a great number of roles on short notice, they reduced the infinite possibilities of dramatic imitation to a few stock roles and a few stock emotions. In this situation, lesser actors turned all plays to stereotype; major actors pumped them up into heroics.

But heroics and stereotype were what audiences liked, even at Drury Lane and Covent Garden. A horde of butchers, bakers, and candlestick-makers had poured into the pit and driven ladies and gentlemen into the remote mountain fastnesses of the gilded boxes. In the safe anonymity of a vast audience, a working man needed not touch his hat to a gentleman or tremble before a constable. On the contrary, he could overthrow a monarch and crown a nobody. Eagerly, clamorously, he reached into the performance of the play, the professional fortunes of the actor, the internal affairs of the theater. With a sarcasm opportunely yelled, an apple-core neatly thrown, he interrupted the meditations of Hamlet or the wooing of Romeo. Even Macready occasionally acted whole plays amid a din which reduced him to a dumb show, and frequently he justified his conduct on or off the stage in speeches—portentously dignified, it is true—to the audience.

The logic of ignorant numbers and colossal size is spectacle. The vast stages of Drury Lane and Covent Garden were honeycombed with formidable engines and undermined with Niebelungen workshops which floated navies and built cities, conjured up Switzerland and Peru, drew down angels and raised up demons. Fêtes, carnivals, fires, earthquakes, pestilences, revolutions, wars by land and sea seldom occurred offstage in the Victorian theater. Joanna Baillie's *De Monfort: A Tragedy* succeeded because it transpired in a splendid seventeenth-century cathedral; Shakespeare's *Tempest* was a favorite because Ariel descended on invisible wires from the ceiling.

The theater—or rather, the drama—could not gain a world of wonders and calamities without losing its own soul; and indeed it had by 1837 very little soul to lose. For the soul of drama is of course action, as a unifying principle which includes diction, emotion, and character. That principle, firmly grasped by the Elizabethans, had fallen into fragments in the heroic play of the seventeenth century. Plot had subsided to an ingenious, hysterical dead level of dilemmas and surprises; character, to an essentially passive, Lockian mechanism driven by impulses of honor and romantic love; the emotions wandered wild in the dialogue, seeking any character or any affecting situation for set rhetorical displays. With some loss of artificial brilliance and some gain in verisimilitude, elements of the heroic play had survived in the domestic and classical tragedy of the eighteenth century. As comedy had declined into farce, in the nineteenth century tragedy declined into melodrama, which in the thirties and forties receded from the aristocratic grandeurs of history to become contemporary, plebeian, prosaic, even literal, feeding on the facts of the police record. Yet it never deepened into realism. The spectator could hate, scheme, and lust with the villain; aspire, adore, be virtuous and brave with the hero; and, after passing through a nightmare of malignant hostility, be luxuriously and virtuously assured in the last moments by a platitude or two, and the union of hero and heroine in life or death, that evil is temporary and good prevails. Indeed, so many Victorians lived in so much fictional melodrama that even the most conscientious and clear-sighted frequently mistook its lurid clichés for the clear white radiance of truth.

In the world of the Victorian stage, the actor-manager possessed the power and the initiative. His sole imperative was to remain solvent, and solvency, at best precarious and temporary, depended on what the audience would pay to see. Acting and ostentation determined the play. The written script was reduced more and more to an expedient impromptu, produced in quantity by a horde of piratical hacks, who for little money pilfered the French and Germans, disemboweled the novelists, and butchered Shakespeare to suit the appetites of the audience and the personality of the actor-manager.

A degree of reform did come from Macready and others like him, desperate at the condition of the theater. Macready played a good deal of Shakespeare—even Shakespeare pure and undefiled. But his "contemporary" repertory, with the possible exception of the Byron plays, looked pretty resolutely backward. In general, even the better Victorian stage drama was as grotesquely eclectic and antiquarian as Victorian architecture. It offered less scope to the talents of the serious playwright than to those of the stage manager, the actor, the painter, the carpenter, the engineer, even the trained lion.

As a medium offering concrete realization of the ideal, with a visible audience and audible applause, the theater has always appealed to the man of letters. Since it failed to produce adequate playwrights of its own, why, in spite of its disadvantages, did it not draw more poets and novelists? Novelists of the period could count on a more reliable audience and a more certain profit, but the expectations of poets were less reassuring. Further, they regarded the drama as poetic, and they rightly suspected that it might be made intellectual and revolutionary. What they were likely to forget, as Romantic artists absorbed in their own unique subjectivity, was that it should be dramatic. Could utopian vision, lyric aspiration, or the poignant intimacies of a bleeding heart be communicated to a large audience?

Of all the nineteenth-century poets who wrote for the theater, Browning seemed the most likely, and was the most determined, to succeed. In the seventeen years between 1836 and 1853 he wrote no less than nine plays. Yet of these, though some were impressive as literature, none really made its way on the stage.[3] From first to last, Browning attempted to depict, as he said in the original preface to *Strafford*, "Action in Character, rather than Character in Action."[4] It was not an emphasis likely to captivate a Gargantuan audience. And yet Browning had observed such an audience night after night in Macready's theater even before he began to write *Strafford.* As his venture grew desperate, he turned from history to romance and violence, but action continued—ever more glaringly—to be an ironic irrelevance to character. Failure utterly exasperated but did not utterly dishearten him. He treated the theater as a gigantic laboratory, and—even when most optimistic—regarded his work "not without apprehension."[5] At once experimenting with character portrayal and compromising with stage requirements in each successive play, he learned to trim his style to a lean efficiency, to depict settings more concretely and human beings more believably. Some lessons he could not learn. Browning was fascinated by motives, but seemed scarcely interested in how motives produced action or how one action must be linked logically and psychologically with another. He could depict character in isolation—even at a moment of crisis—but he could not easily bring one character into dynamic relation with another. In short, he understood the private drama of passions and ideas occurring in the mind, but not the public drama of men acting and conflicting in the great world of politics and business.

At first glance, *Strafford* seems a thoroughly conventional chronicle history revealing, as Charlotte Porter has pointed out, Robert's fondness for *Julius Caesar.*[6] Both plays begin with a crowd, obviously omnipotent yet easily led. Pym and Strafford are paralleled by Brutus and Caesar, though in Browning's play the democratic, whereas in Shakespeare's the autocratic, principle triumphs.

Actually, *Strafford* is neither so Shakespearean nor even so historical as it seems. And it is conventional only in a rather unexpected way. Pym and Strafford suggest not so much a political rivalry as the high-flown estrangements and cross-purposes of conventional romantic love. Pym is overeager to conciliate at first and implacable at the end. Strafford is the haughtily unapproachable romance hero throughout. Again, on closer view, the pair suggest not so much Brutus and Caesar as Paracelsus and Aprile. History—or rather fiction—repeats itself in startling fashion. Strafford pursues power and Pym, liberty, with the same abstract devotion that Paracelsus pursues knowledge and Aprile, love. Lady Carlisle looks even farther backward, combining the functions of a Pauline and a Festus: she serves as an audience of feminine adoration for Strafford, and as a realist who explains to him that he has idealized a weak and unworthy monarch. Not that there is any elaborate drama of disillusionment. Lady Carlisle simply heightens the sense of pathos with which the spectator follows the hero to grandiose failure. In short, Browning's Strafford emerges as another romantic genius: febrile, intense, passionate, unworldly, and already far gone in a quite historical but nevertheless picturesque illness.

The play was written by a singularly cloistered and inexperienced young poet who could imagine mad, isolated monks and mad, isolated lovers—and portray them lyrically and effectively—but who as yet really could not get inside a politician's mind. Browning was too full of himself to get very much inside Macready's mind, either, or to appreciate how improbable it was that dramas modeled on the principles of *Paracelsus* would survive more than a few nights on the London stage. On the other hand, he got inside Forster's *Life* and many of Forster's documents. Harold Orel in 1962 demonstrated that *Strafford* "does not contradict" the known facts of history, and Gordon Pitts in 1970[7] displayed the considerably wide range of Browning's topical allusions to Strafford's epoch. Indeed, after the timelessness and vagueness of setting in *Paracelsus*, one opens the play of *Strafford* to something very different:

ACT I.

SCENE I.—A HOUSE NEAR WHITEHALL.

HAMPDEN, HOLLIS, the younger VANE, RUDYARD, FIENNES, and many of the Presbyterian Party: LOUDON and other Scots Commissioners: some seated, some standing beside a table strewn over with papers, &c.[8]

With such a rush the real world enters Browning's poetry for the first time. The opening scene is at once adequate exposition and a triumph of atmosphere, resounding with the clamor and contention of patriotic debate. On the other hand, the trial scene is nothing but atmosphere. We see Strafford conferring with messengers, discussing his fortunes with Lady Carlisle; but what in any detail he was accused of and what precisely he says in his own defense, we never learn.

Throughout this "historical tragedy" the dialogue, though seldom poetic, is swift, vigorous, vivid, and full of the spontaneity of parenthesis and interjection—so full indeed that we occasionally wonder when someone will finish a sentence. Exclamations, dashes, and ellipses seem to have to have been broadcast over the text like seeds. Wentworth (Strafford) and Lady Carlisle appear at Whitehall:

WENTWORTH.

All the court! Evermore the Court about us!
Savile and Holland, Hamilton and Vane
About us,—then the King will grant me. . . . Lady,
Will the King leave these—leave all these—and say
"Tell me your whole mind, Wentworth!"

CARLISLE.

But you said
You would be calm.

WENTWORTH.

Lucy, and I am calm!
How else shall I do all I come to do,
—Broken, as you may see, body and mind—
How shall I serve the King? time wastes meanwhile,
You have not told me half. . . . His footstep! No.
—But now, before I meet him,—(I am calm)—
Why does the King distrust me?[9]

It is worth emphasizing that elliptical dramatic speech had been written before, and by playwrights better than Browning. In *Hamlet,* a subtlety of intuition and clarity of expression combine in broken soliloquy to reveal the exquisite tensions of a thoroughly modern mind:

Let me not think on 't! Frailty, thy name is woman.
A little month; or ere those shoes were old
With which she follow'd my poor father's body,
Like Niobe, all tears; why she,—
O God! a beast, that wants discourse of reason,
Would have mourn'd . . .
. . . Within a month.[10]

In *Strafford* intuitions do not really coalesce or build upon one another. Nor is the expression lucid except—perhaps—when it matters least:

FIRST SPECTATOR.
More crowd than ever! . . . Not know Hampden, man?
That's he—by Pym—Pym that is speaking now![11]

Yet Browning's play owes to impressionistic passages in Shakespeare and begins to show from the interior viewpoint the momentary impulses and conflicting passions of character. The second scene of Act I seems to open in the middle of a sentence, giving the impression of a camera suddenly turned on the raw continuity of life itself. The second scene in Act II contains a passage in which the characters follow the urgent preoccupations of their own thoughts to the degree that they talk not so much to each other as about each other, expressing essentially private opinion as though in soliloquy.[12]

Attending the rehearsals of *Strafford,* Robert was enraptured at seeing his own conceptions realized on the stage. On the final evening he brought his father into Macready's dressing room to shake hands. Macready was touched, but to the young author he judiciously exuded the gloom he himself felt. Robert thereupon wrote Fox, perhaps too jauntily for conviction, that the outlook was "perfect gallows."[13] Unhappily, the expression was apt. Osbaldiston, the manager of Covent Garden, was on the verge of bankruptcy and would not allow "a rag for the new tragedy."[14] The king was played by Dale, who was stone-deaf; Pym, by Vandenhoff, who proved "positively nauseous with his whining and drawling and slouching";[15] the queen, by Miss Vincent, who usually performed with Burmese bulls; and Helen Faucit, who had less than twenty months' experience on the stage, was Lady Carlisle.

Oddly enough, the play was a success—or nearly a success. The first night was a benefit for Macready, and Covent Garden was jammed to its remotest heavens. Dale and Vandenhoff did their worst, but Miss Faucit put so much tenderness and pathos into Lady Carlisle, and Macready so much majesty and authority into Strafford ("crossing and recrossing the stage like one of Vandyke's courtly personages come to life again"[16]), that the curtain for each act went down on a vigorous round of applause and the final curtain, on cries for Macready, Miss Faucit, Vandenhoff, and "author!" The next morning, May 2, 1837, the *Constitutional* declared the performance a signal triumph, and then rather noncommittally, on the authority of "some very keen critics,"[17] predicted for Browning unsurpassed eminence as a dramatic poet. In *The True Sun* Fox found the play obscure, but of such quality as to promise a genuine revival of the drama. The second night was a little less successful. Muffled in a cloak, Browning sat in the pit, to feel the pulse of the audience. The fourth night seemed encouraging, though Macready was huffed at the *Morning Herald*: "It extolled the play . . . and abused me for 'pantings—a-a-s, etc.' which the writer supposed 'it was too late to cure.' "[18] *Strafford* was promised again for the following Thursday.

Meanwhile, Robert was becoming increasingly incensed with actors, managers, and critics. Actors like Dale and Vandenhoff were a revelation in negative capability. Some of the cast were so ignorant, he told Eliza Flower, that they thought *impeachment* meant *poaching.* (No doubt the play itself did not set them straight.) Forster's review, which appeared in the *Examiner* on May 7, was another shock. Though full of compliments, it pronounced *Strafford* more poetic than dramatic:

> Called on Forster [wrote Macready], who informed me how much he had been hurt by Browning's expressions of discontent at his criticism, which I myself think only too indulgent for such a play as *Strafford.* After all that has been done for Browning with the painful apprehension of failure before us, it is not pleasing to read in his note, "Let . . . write any future tragedies"! Now, really, this is too bad.[19]

At about this point Vandenhoff withdrew from the cast. Macready did not think fit to find a substitute. *Strafford* vanished—not to reappear except on May 30, Fitzball's benefit—and was replaced by Fitzball's own *Walter Tyrrel*, a wild melodrama which enraptured audiences with forest scenes, blue fire, and moonlight effects. Robert's sufferings may be imagined. "Browning . . .," wrote Macready on May 18, "again evinced an irritable impatience about the reproduction of *Strafford.*"[20] No doubt Macready was right about Robert's play, but he was not very perceptive about Robert's feelings. How could a young author feel otherwise than that a great popular success had been arbitrarily snatched from him? The whole episode must have seemed a very subtle and excruciating torture, with Macready as a very high-principled but efficacious hangman. At the moment, Robert resolved never to write another play.

CHAPTER 6

"Sordello"

1837 and 1833-40

As a matter of fact Browning didn't begin another play for nearly a year. He couldn't. *Sordello*—conceived, written, reconceived, rewritten, yet still maddeningly incomplete—hung about him, gloom upon gloom, in a great forest of autobiographical projection. That forest had become an enchanted forest, in which he, as well as Sordello, had met with some very singular adventures. A dream of frustration had resulted in some very practical frustration. Clearly, he must emerge: shuffle off the hypothetical, before he could proceed with the actual, Robert Browning. Indeed, in the process of writing he had begun to rid himself of the habit of excessive introspection.

On April 16, 1835, he had written Fox, "I have another affair on hand, rather of a more popular nature, I conceive, but not so decisive and explicit on a point or two—so I decide on trying the question with this."[1] "This" was *Paracelsus*, which he had composed in the preceding six months. "The other affair" was certainly *Sordello*, which must have been begun soon after *Pauline* had been so acutely neglected by the public and so acutely noticed by John Stuart Mill. It seems in fact to have been intended as a more dramatic and objective *Pauline*, that is, a highly lyrical and subjective poem about Robert Browning under an elaborate and romantically appealing historical disguise.

DeVane believes that Browning discovered Sordello in Daniello Bartoli's *De' Simboli Trasportati al Morale*, of which he had purchased the 1830 edition by Angelo Cerutti, his tutor in Italian. Bartoli directed him to the fifth, sixth, and seventh cantos of the *Purgatorio*. From Dante's tragically retrospective afterworld he turned, DeVane surmises, to that familiar of his father's library, the *Biographie universelle*, where he found a succinct account of the legends surrounding his hero. He read that Sordello was born in Mantua about 1189, that he grew up in the castle of Goito; that he won fame as a troubadour and more as a knight; that he eloped with Cunizza, wife of Count Richard of St. Boniface and sister of Ecelino da Romano; that he deserted her to marry another woman; that he then wisely migrated to southern France and eventually returned to Italy to defend the liberties of Mantua, where the city square is named after him—and that he met a violent end. Quite understandably, Robert felt much in this career, so full of extrovert success and ebullient achievement, uncongenial to his purpose and even to his moral sensibilities. The elopement, the desertion, the wife, the military and political action disappear. Cunizza, renamed Palma after her younger sister, becomes merely the betrothed of St. Boniface. She is called "passion's votaress"[2] but does little to deserve the name, evincing rather, in the later books of the poem, a kind of Lady Carlisle interest in politics. For the hero she is an "out-soul" representing his devotion to beauty. Browning introduces Eglamor as a rival poet to Sordello and Naddo as a kind of critic, who seems not only to reflect Browning's resentment against reviewers in general but to be a satirical sketch of John Forster in particular.[3]

The first version of the poem, as DeVane suggests, was probably the present first two and a half books. These—like *Paracelsus*—combine autobiographically real and hypothetical Robert Brownings: Sordello grows up as a lonely youth at Goito, discovers a world of beauty and reverie in nature, dreams grandiosely of being an emperor in the world of men, attracts Palma's attention by overcoming Eglamor in a tournament of song, adores her at a fairly safe distance, and apparently looks forward to a death by Shelley's disease of over-cerebration.

Browning's adventures with Sordello, no less than Sordello's with Browning, had now begun. One cannot find one's subjects in the mirror without some sacrifice of variety. Robert discovered—probably with surprise—that he had forestalled himself. Paracelsus' youth and aspiration were substantially Sordello's; the contrast between Paracelsus and Aprile was virtually that between Sordello and Eglamor. Clearly, another *Sordello* must be written. This was largely accomplished, says DeVane, in the eleven months after he completed *Paracelsus*, and in the three months before he began work on *Strafford*.[4] In the preface to the play, dated April 23, 1837, Browning says that before launching on *Strafford*, he "had for some time been engaged in a Poem of a very different nature," which had left him with a "jaded mind," and on page vi appears the advertisement: "Nearly ready. Sordello, in Six Books."[5]

For the second Sordello he turned more receptively to the legends surrounding the poet—in short, once more to the *Biographie universelle* and, at its direction, to the Mantuan chroniclers Aliprandi and Platina.[6] The result was a more "popular"[7] poem—probably in the present rhymed couplets rather than blank verse—dealing with a poet-warrior inspired by love for Palma to rise above his morbid self-consciousness and defend his native city against the tyranny of Ecelin. Love and war must certainly have been Browning's themes, for the second revision became abruptly worthless on the appearance in July 1837 of a *Sordello,* also in six books, treating precisely those themes. Forestalled once by himself, he had now been forestalled by a poetess known to posterity by the unlikely name of Mrs. W. Busk.[8] "There were many singular incidents," he wrote Elizabeth Barrett in 1845, "attending my work on that subject."[9]

The singular incidents were discouraging. For a period he considered other possible projects. In August he was asking Fanny Haworth's advice about two subjects for tragedies.[10] On December 23, Harriet Martineau recorded in her diary that he was once more progressing well with the poem. "He must choose between being historian or poet. Cannot split [the] interest."[11] Having read a good deal of history for his plays, as well perhaps as Carlyle's recently published *French Revolution,* which the final *Sordello* resembles very much in its vivid evocation of a past century, Browning apparently elected to emphasize history and fact in the third version. Guided once more by the *Biographie universelle,* he began to read Giambatista Verci's *Storia degli Ecelini,* and was soon deep in thirteenth-century politics. The third or political version of *Sordello,* according to DeVane, first appears in the latter half of Book Two. Before proceeding very far, however, Browning decided to visit Italy, "intending," as he told John Robertson, to finish his poem "among the scenes it describes."[12]

Abroad, he wrote only four lines—and they had little to do with Sordello. Two were addressed to the Queen and two to Fanny Haworth as "Eyebright," in translation of her first name *Euphrasia.* Yet the voyage was thoroughly successful. He discovered Italy, rediscovered humanity—in short, provided himself the materials for his last revision, as well as a fresh mind with which to think about them.

On Friday, April 13, 1838, he sailed from London for Venice. The voyage was seven weeks of desperate seasickness, relieved by a friendship and an adventure. As his vessel passed through the Straits at seven in the morning, the captain himself roused Robert and helped him on deck, in order that he might see Gibraltar. This officer, "a rough north countryman," was so taken with the young poet that he offered him free passage to Constantinople, and "after they had parted, carefully preserved, by way of remembrance, a pair of very old gloves worn by him on deck. Mr. Browning might," continues Mrs. Orr with reverence, "have dispensed with gloves altogether; but it was one of his peculiarities that he could never endure to be out of doors with uncovered hands."[13] Clearly, Robert's zealous regard for gloves —old or new—astonished even his contemporaries. The need to conceal his hands seems to have been one feature of that larger, more intricate need to resort to camouflage in his writing; to conceal the unresolved conflicts in his own personality from the world's eye, and to live almost comfortably and respectably with his mother's religion and Shelley's poetry. Even the most autobiographical passages in darkest *Sordello* suggest that he could not bear to examine his own deepest loyalties too closely or directly.

Robert's adventure on the high seas was in his own most macabre taste. In a letter to Fanny Haworth he gives an admirable account of it, filtered through an appropriate delicacy and another striking facet of his personality. Reverent and somewhat theatrically masculine toward Macready, he was arch, precious, and self-conscious with Fanny, taking out his style and poetic sensibilities for her admiration and thus achieving one of his oblique beginnings in the irrelevant and the minute:

> Do look at a Fuchsia in full bloom and notice the clear little honeydrop depending from every flower . . . I have but just found it out, to my no small satisfaction,—a bee's breakfast. I only answer for the *long* blossomed sort. . . . I have, you are to know, such a love for flowers and leaves—some leaves—that I every now and then,—in an impatience at being unable to possess myself of them thoroughly, to see them quite, satiate myself with their scent,—bite them to bits.

Sordello will be ready in a trice. "Shall I say Eyebright?" he queries. Then:

> The story of the ship must have reached you "with a difference" as Ophelia says,—my sister told it to a Mr Dow, who delivered it, I suppose, to Forster, who furnished Macready with it, who made it over &c &c &c—As short as I can tell, this way it happened: the Captain woke me one bright Sunday morning to say there was a ship floating keel uppermost half a mile off; they lowered a boat, made ropes fast to

> some floating canvass, and towed her towards our vessel. Both met half-way, and the little air that had risen an hour or two before, sank at once. Our men made the wreck fast, and went to breakfast in high glee at the notion of having "new trousers out of the sails," and quite sure she was a French boat, broken from her moorings at Algiers, close by. Ropes were next hove (hang this sea-talk) round her stanchions, and after a quarter of an hour's pushing at the capstan, the vessel righted suddenly, one dead body floating out; five more were in the forecastle, and had probably been there a month—under a blazing African sun . . . don't imagine the wretched state of things. They were, these six, the "watch below"—(I give you the results of the day's observation)—the rest, some eight or ten, had been washed overboard at first. One or two were Algerines, the rest Spaniards. The vessel was a smuggler bound for Gibraltar; there were two stupidly-disproportionate guns, taking up the whole deck, which was convex and—nay, look you, these are the gun-rings, and the black square the place where the bodies lay. Well, the sailors covered up the hatchway, broke up the aft-deck, hauled up tobacco and cigars, good lord such heaps of them, and then bale after bale of prints and chintz, don't you call it, till the Captain was half frightened—he would get at the ship's papers, he said; so these poor fellows were pulled up, piecemeal, and pitched into the sea, the very sailors calling to each other "to cover the faces": no papers of importance were found, however, but fifteen swords, powder and ball enough for a dozen such boats, and bundles of cotton &c that would have taken a day to get out, but the Captain vowed that after five-o'clock she should be cut adrift: accordingly she was cast loose, not a third of her cargo having been touched; and you can hardly conceive the strange sight when the battered hulk turned round, actually, and looked at us, and then reeled off, like a mutilated creature from some scoundrel French surgeon's lecture-table, into the most gorgeous and lavish sunset in the world.[14]

Of his four weeks in Italy, Browning spent two in Venice. That brilliant, somewhat tarnished exhalation rising so melodramatically—and even odoriferously—from the waves, he was soon to render with appropriate bravura in "In a Gondola" and later with more nostalgia and reflection in "A Toccata of Galuppi's." Here indeed was history—as atmosphere, as landscape, as a sumptuous, exotic country of the human heart. And not merely history. In industrial England, poverty had been drab, gigantic, impersonal, economically "logical"; in Venice, it was personal, dramatic, supplicative—it could be seen as a woman, whom one could fall in love with and serve as a knight-errant. Toward the end of the third book of *Sordello,* in one of those maneuvers so characteristic of impressionistic art, Browning comes before the reader as the author in the process of writing his poem:

I muse this on a ruined palace-step
At Venice: why should I break off, nor sit
Longer upon my step, exhaust the fit
England gave birth to? Who's adorable
Enough reclaim a ——— no Sordello's Will
Alack! —be queen to me?[15]

Who would be adorable enough to inspire Sordello to act as the people's champion and—what was much the same thing—inspire the author to write about such action?

Apparently a semi-historical Palma will not suffice. Browning's early devotion to Shelley, his study of Pym and Strafford had prepared him for a less sentimental image. Sitting on his palace-step, Browning eyes the handsome peasant girls nearby. What, he asks, selecting one,

if I make
A queen of her, continue for her sake
Sordello's story?[16]

As he watches another, he is approached by a beggar girl:

You sad dishevelled ghost
That pluck at me and point, are you advised
I breathe?[17]

To be sure, he does not wear his heart—or his social conscience—on his sleeve. He addresses the other girls:

I ask youth and strength
And health for each of you, not more.[18]

In short, he will never again be the naïve Shelleyan idealist whose disillusionment he recorded in *Pauline.* Unsentimental service of the beggar girl will not be easy:

You, no doubt,
Have the true knack of tiring suitors out

With those thin lips on tremble, lashless eyes
Inveterately tear-shot.[19]

Yet, the poet continues in an image quite prophetic of Wimpole Street:

Care-bit erased
Broken-up beauties ever took my taste
Supremely; and I love you more, far more
Than her I looked should foot Life's temple-floor.[20]

In short, Palma must be supplanted by the beggar girl. But, as Mr. Holmes points out, both figures seem to guide Sordello—and Browning—out of a deep little swamp of introversion to an urgent, waiting world. Evidently, Robert could not become less self-absorbed merely by thinking how much the masses of humanity needed him. He had already personified his devotion to beauty in the static but entrancing shape of Palma. He would personify his devotion to humanity in the odder, more alluring shape of a bewitching ragamuffin.[21]

Leaving the palaces and urchins of Venice, Browning passed through Treviso and Bassano to Asolo in the mountains, a gleaming white little city, spacious in time, with vigilant towers and climbing walls, where in four days he absorbed the setting for *Pippa Passes.* And then, apparently with his Verci in hand, he went off in search of Sordello's thirteenth century and the Ecelini, visiting particularly Romano, where the family began, and San Zenone, where, virtually, it ended.

And I think grass grew
Never so pleasant as in Valley Rù
By San Zenon where Alberic in turn
Saw his exasperated captors burn
Seven children and their mother; then, regaled
So far, tied on to a wild horse, was trailed
To death through raunce and bramble-bush.[22]

At San Zenone a cleric told Browning that five years before he had seen Alberic's huge skeleton thrown up from its grave.[23] "Then," Robert wrote Fanny Haworth, describing the rest of the journey without unnecessary ceremony of verbs, "to Vicenza, Padua, and Venice again. Then to Verona, Trent, Inspruck (the Tyrol) Munich, 'Wurzburg in Franconia'! Frankfort and Mayence,—down the Rhine to Cologne, thence to Aix-la-Chapelle, Liège, and Antwerp—then home."[24]

Much restored, Robert took up his London life with zest. He was one of a select group invited to hear the first reading of Bulwer's *Richelieu,* and in later years recalled with satisfaction that he had silently recorded, "A great play."[25] At about the same time he wrote Fanny Haworth of a visit to his "Master," Fox, that "magnificent and poetical nature."[26] There may be an echo of such a visit in the recollections of Tottie Fox, to whom Robert, as a handsome, dramatic young man of inexhaustible parlor accomplishments, was perhaps even more magnificent than her father was to Robert. The poet had a novel mode of illustrating the beauties of Venice. "Taking up a stray bit of notepaper he would hold it over a lighted candle, moving the paper about gently till it was cloudily smoked over, and then utilizing the darker smears for clouds, shadows, water or what not; would etch with a dry pen the forms of light on cloud and palace, on bridge or gondola, on the vague and dreamy surface he had produced."[27]

Apparently not long before Robert's Italian tour, the Brownings had moved from the book-crammed cottage in Camberwell to a larger house in Hatcham. Here there was an upper story of low-ceilinged rooms for books, a large garden opening on the Surrey hills for Mrs. Browning, and a stable in the back for Robert's horse York, the imagined hero of "How They Brought the Good News from Ghent to Aix." Carlyle, then forty-two or -three, first appears in Browning biography as a visitor to Hatcham, riding out from Chelsea for a talk and country air. That prophetic glance, which could drop from the moral summits of the past and future to rest very shrewdly on the piquant trivialities of the present, was mild and benign when directed upon Robert and the Browning household: Mrs. Browning was a gentlewoman, the family were "people of respectable position among the dissenters, but not rich neither," and the little room in which Robert kept his books "was in that sort of trim which showed he was the very apple" of his mother's eye.[28]

Some years later Gavan Duffy asked Carlyle about the still-obscure author of the *Bells and Pomegranates* volumes, in which, despite their small print and inferior paper, the zealous Irishman took a great delight. "Browning had a powerful intellect," replied the sage, "and among the men engaged in England in literature just now was one of the few from whom it was possible to expect something." Duffy suggested that he might be an imitator of Coleridge. "Browning," came the severe reply, "was an original man, and by no means a person who would consciously imitate anyone. . . . It would be seen by and bye that he was the stronger man of the two, and had no need to go marauding in that quarter."[29] This in spite of *Sordello,* which caused Carlyle to beseech the young poet to espouse the light and sanity of prose.

Of all Browning's rivals in those early days Carlyle seems to have had a slightly higher opinion of Tennyson, that "fine, large-featured, dim-eyed, bronze-coloured, shaggy-headed man," who swam "outwardly and inwardly, with great composure in an inarticulate element of tranquil chaos and tobacco smoke."[30] Tennyson was the only poet, apparently, whom Carlyle never advised to give up poetry. On his side, Robert became increasingly enthusiastic about the voluble prophet of silence. "I dined with dear Carlyle and his wife," he wrote Fanny, "(catch me calling people 'dear,' in a hurry, except in letter-beginnings!) yesterday—I don't know any people like them."[31] Macready noted that Browning was a constant attendant at the Lectures on Hero-Worship. Superficially diverse in many ways, Carlyle and Browning resemble each other surprisingly in fundamental outlook and mode of expression. If Meredith was a prose Browning, Browning was not far from being a poetic Carlyle.

Dining one day at Serjeant Talfourd's, Robert was approached by a courteous, elderly gentleman with inquisitorial spectacles. "Was his father's name Robert? had he gone to school at the Rev. Mr. Bell's at Cheshunt, and was he still alive?"[32] Robert answered in the affirmative. Then, said the elderly gentleman, Mr. Browning was certainly his old school chum. The next morning Robert asked his father if he remembered John Kenyon. "Certainly!"—and he sketched a boy's head in which Robert at once recognized the elderly gentleman with inquisitorial spectacles. Mr. Kenyon resumed his friendship with the father, but he formed a closer one with the son. A bachelor of wealth, he made a career of being friends with poets. Wordsworth, Southey, and Landor were all cordially attached to him, and, when in London, Wordsworth sometimes stayed at his house, where perhaps Robert saw most of that taciturn bard. Mr. Kenyon also had the good fortune to be the cousin of another celebrity—Miss Elizabeth Barrett. "I want," Robert wrote Fanny Haworth, looking restlessly beyond *Sordello* to possible dramatic themes, "a subject of the most wild and passionate love, to contrast with the one I mean to have ready in a short time. . . . Give me your notion of a thorough self-devotement, self-forgetting; should it be a woman who loves thus, or a man? What circumstances will best draw out, set forth this feeling?"[33]

Robert did not finish *Sordello* "in a trice," as he had promised Fanny. From his return home in July 1838, he was occupied with it at least until May of the following year, when he told Macready it was done. Browning may have been writing *Pippa, Monsoor* (or the *Druses*), and *King Victor* at the same time, for in the *Sordello* volume they in their turn were announced as nearly finished. In any case he had much to do with *Sordello* itself. Presumably, before departing for Italy, he had constructed an historical frame about the first two books, inserting early in the first an elaborate exposition of party alignments and antecedent events. He had now to write, in whole or in part, four additional books, in which he must represent, together with its consequences, Sordello's espousal of action rather than poetry, and of humanitarian service rather than ambition and power.

Browning was in the habit of exemplifying such alternatives in contrasting characters. The essentially inspired and spontaneous poet had been set off against Eglamor, the merely skilled and mechanical versifier. Now the sensitive introvert hero with a gift for insight should be set off against a robust extrovert with a capacity for action. Reading Verci's *Storia* and more particularly Rolandino's *De Factis in Marchia Tarvisina*,[34] Browning found an admirable man of action in the wily, indefatigable old warrior Taurello Salinguerra, lord of Ferrara, general for the Ecelini, and, after the retirement of Ecelino the Monk, leader of the Ghibellines in northern Italy. Salinguerra offered the solution to another problem: how the author might bring the private events of his own spiritual autobiography, embodied in the character of Sordello, into significant relation with the public events of thirteenth-century history. According to legend, Sordello was of uncertain parentage. Salinguerra had married a daughter of Ecelino and had one son. Any reader of Dickens or spectator of melodrama could see that Sordello must be made the long-lost son of Salinguerra. Learning from Palma Sordello's true identity, his father offers him the Emperor's badge, or leadership of the Ghibellines, at the very moment when Sordello has decided that he must act. But he has also decided, for nineteenth-century reasons, that he must be a Guelf, since the supporters of the Pope seem to represent the people's cause. He therefore tramples the Emperor's badge underfoot, and dies of moral strain. The inward warfare of the soul, which above all merits study,[35] is thus connected by a single climax with the outward warfare between Emperor and Pope, who in their turn symbolize power and humanitarian holiness, the alternatives of Sordello's choice.

Sordello appeared in March 1840—and was greeted by readers with a heavy frown of bewilderment, followed by unmistakable noises of suppressed laughter. The famous words of famous contemporaries are better known than the poem itself. Tennyson declared that he understood only the first and the last lines—avowing that Sordello's story would be, and had been, told—and both were lies. Harriet Martineau recorded that the poem made her physically ill; Douglas Jerrold loved to recount how, picking up the poem after a severe illness, he read a page or two, turned deadly pale, and exclaimed, "My God, I'm an idiot!" Macready tried it both before and after dinner, and, "utterly desperate," pronounced it "*not* readable."[36] Mrs. Carlyle protested she had read it through without discovering whether Sordello was a man, a city, or a book.

The press maintained a bewildered silence, broken by a few outcries of intellectual pain and moral indignation. *The Spectator* did not pretend to understand the poem but it did understand that, in the act of writing, Browning's poetical spirit had been overlaid "by digression, affectation, obscurity, and all the faults that spring . . . from crudity of plan and a self-opinion which will neither cull thoughts nor revise composition."[37] After an interval of three months apparently spent in honest but indignant exploration, the *Athenaeum* reported it had discovered nothing in the cloudy depths of *Sordello* but mannerism, cacophony, and a few commonplaces.[38] *The Examiner*, despite Forster's friendship with Browning, remained portentously silent. *Sordello* had taken seven years to write. It was to take nearly four times as many to expiate.

Browning lived to see *Sordello* forgiven, read, even understood, but seldom appreciated. Many Victorians—notably the reviewers—found something supercilious, unsocial, even hostile, in its obscurity. Others, like Macready, feared for the poet's mind. More recently, Stewart W. Holmes has also feared for the poet's mind: Browning's obscurity is traceable in part to the difficulty all prophetic poets experience in communicating the deeply subjective images of the unconscious, in part to a psychic malady—he was a semantic stutterer.[39] He felt that God required him to speak on high philosophic matters, and yet, because of an irregular early education, he lacked the discipline and training to develop an adequate, consistent vocabulary. Certain confusions in the use of words like "body," "soul," "mind," and "matter" led to blocks which explain his headaches when writing, his irritability—and the obscurity of *Sordello.*

Particularly in his illustrations Mr. Holmes seems convincing, yet one feels that he explains too much with too little. Browning neglected logic not only because he did not know how to use it but because he feared what it might reveal. The outer darkness of *Sordello* corresponds to an inner darkness in Robert Browning—carefully preserved lest he have to face too squarely the divided loyalties and divided inspiration, the conflicting "consciences" and double sense of betrayal so somberly and obliquely described in *Pauline.* If *Sordello* gives cause to fear for the poet's mind, one may observe that there is method in his madness. Surely he could have been so very obscure only on principle. Within the poem he suggests the principle. What is needed is a "brother's speech . . . where an accent's change gives each the other's soul."[40] By one of those paradoxes so characteristic of impressionism, he was sacrificing clarity to gain vividness and immediacy, using the colloquial, dramatic language of a man spontaneously recounting his story to intimates. Hence his maddening tendency to explain thirteenth-century politics as though the reader already understood them perfectly. Hence the bewildering informality in pronoun reference and the blasé, stultifying violations of logical and chronological sequence.

But Browning was attempting not only to be colloquial; he was systematically trying to say everything at once. The possibilities of poetic delineation, says Herman Heuer, lie *"im Bereich des Nacheinander. Browning strebt hinüber zu einer Kunst des Nebeneinander."*[41] Or, as Browning describes his own and Sordello's method:

Accordingly he took
An action with its actors, quite forsook
Himself to live in each, returned anon
With the result—a creature, and, by one
And one, proceeded leisurely to equip
Its limbs in harness of his workmanship.
"Accomplished! Listen, Mantuans!" Fond essay!
Piece after piece that armour broke away,
Because perceptions whole, like that he sought
To clothe, reject so pure a work of thought
As language: thought may take perception's place
But hardly co-exist in any case,

Being its mere presentment—of the whole
By parts, the simultaneous and the sole
By the successive and the many. Lacks
The crowd perception? Painfully it tacks
Thought to thought, which Sordello, needing such,
Has rent perception into: it's to clutch
And reconstruct—his office to diffuse,
Destroy: as hard, then, to obtain a Muse
As to become Apollo.[42]

In brief, he would present an action simultaneously from the point of view of each of the actors,[43] and he would present that point of view not logically but intuitively, not in abstract fragmentation but in whole perceptions—presumably in vivid, graphic renderings of highly subjective images. Hence, in passages of qualification and elaboration, the parentheses, the interjections, the frequent omissions of conjunctions and relatives and the general sacrifice of causality, time, and space to the simultaneity of *and* and what Heuer calls the "*assoziative, additive Satzbild*."[44] Hence in passages of drama and crisis the swift transitions from place to place, from point of view to point of view, from outward to inward and inward to outward; hence the breathless hurry of ellipses, exclamations, rhetorical questions and the intimate, dramatic unifying presence of the author as narrator, stage manager, and cameraman searching out the complex contemporaneities, physical and psychic, of a moment in north Italian thirteenth-century history.

In its entirety *Sordello* is meant to embody a single whole perception. But to glean 5800 lines of poetry from a single perception, to see in a moment a hundred years of history—or many concurrent actions from the separately unique points of view of all the participants—suggests the prerogative of Deity. Both in *Paracelsus* and *Sordello* Browning declares that God is the perfect poet, and the passage on whole perceptions concludes:

as hard, then, to obtain a Muse
As to become Apollo.[45]

But is God too perfect a poet to be imitated? Apparently Browning did not think so in his twenties—or in his fifties when he wrote *The Ring and the Book*.[46] It is not uncommon for Browning to speak moral humility in poems that practice artistic presumption, and at the risk of critical censure that is far more significant to him than the ineffectual balms of critical praise.

In *Sordello* Robert Browning is both himself and his hero, and is felt throughout as an insistent presence, standing, as he himself puts it,

> Motley on back and pointing pole in hand,

or, as his disciple Pound puts it, before his fish-booth crying himself and his wares.[47] The narrative opens in a style somewhere between heraldic announcement and elegant dinner conversation:

> Who will, may hear Sordello's story told:
> His story? Who believes me shall behold
> The man, pursue his fortunes to the end,
> Like me: for as the friendless-people's friend
> Spied from the hill-top once, despite the din
> And dust of multitudes, Pentapolin
> Named o' the Naked Arm, I single out
> Sordello, compassed murkily about
> With ravage of six long sad hundred years.
> Only believe me. Ye believe?
> Appears
> Verona . . .[48]

Rather disappointingly, Verona does not appear at the first effort. Worm-eaten chronicles in hand, the poet stares doubtfully into the cold gloom of the past. After another vain effort he begs—for imaginable reasons—that Shelley be absent and Dante present. Ironies and complications of masked autobiography continue to arise.

The story of Sordello's youth is a lugubrious, intricately psychological little version of Browning's own, over which Naddo-Forster and the poet differ sententiously at long range. Like the hero of *Pauline,* Sordello shows the weakness which Jung adduces for the introvert: excessive ambition and vanity. Again like Robert in the Dulwich woods, he will succeed quite variously. He projects a world of applauding minions into nature, and tiring of that, another into human society, as he gleans it in his isolation.

He is the chieftain Ecelin, then the Emperor Friedrich; then, hearing of Eglamor, a minstrel-emperor—as Browning had wanted to be a super-Shelley. He even wonders whether he is Apollo, mysteriously reincarnated. At length, blundering in the castle on Ecelin's daughter Palma, he falls in love with her. Is she Eliza Flower? Perhaps. The identity is no more certain than in the case of Pauline, for she is not rendered in elaborate detail. Yet Palma importantly provides inspiration for Sordello in the song-contest in which he easily beats Eglamor, the versifier of fashionable conceits. Why does such a triumph resound hollowly? Despite his genius, Sordello—again like the retrospective poet of *Pauline*—values poetry as a means of exhibiting his powers and satisfying his vanity. Experience has taught him that he is in body weaker than most men; in mind, much more imaginative. Obviously, he must realize his boundless ambitions in the realm of mind and poetry. Godlike, he would swallow the whole universe of men into his personality; in imagination he would annex to himself every grace, every virtue, every achievement, every glorious career; so that each listener would find his own highest aspiration reflected in the song.

Unfortunately, he has not taken pains to acquire technical skill. Browning in *Pauline* had imitated "Alastor"'s rhythms, even borrowed some of Shelley's language.[49] Sordello uses Eglamor's very rhymes! He eventually falls into drastic conflict with himself: the man would strive for a mean success with traditional techniques; the poet, for an impossible ideal; neither is effective.

Sordello returns to Goito, the Camberwell-like locale of youthful dreaming. The castle is half in ruins. Once more in the mystic maple-paneled room of inspiration, into which cold streams of air blow up from the dungeon-depths of the unconscious below, he casts his minstrel's crown into a font supported by expiative maidens. The renunciation in *Pauline* seems no less explicit and final.

Yet the moment of despair brings its own illumination. Like Browning, Sordello does not stagnate:

> A presage shuddered through the welkin; harsh
> The earth's remonstrance followed. 'T was the marsh
> Gone of a sudden. Mincio, in its place,
> Laughed, a broad water, in next morning's face,
> And, where the mists broke up immense and white
> I' the steady wind, burned like a spilth of light
> Out of the crashing of a myriad stars.
> And here was nature, bound by the same bars
> Of fate with him![50]

Ambition and vanity had alienated him from the world and blinded him to the intimations of true happiness, which consists in becoming one with the world. Sordello's illusive and elliptical reflections seem to purport that the selfish introvert would become a humanitarian extrovert; the subjective, an objective, poet. After all, Robert was turning from gloomy introspection in front of a mirror to the more amusing—and more objective—study of human behavior in human history. Yet he continued to quarry from autobiographical materials. Sordello is apparently moving toward a change which occurred at a shallower depth in his creator. Browning did *not* become less ambitious, and indeed came to depend more than ever on subjective intuition and subjective "truth." In fact, subjective visions were to enrich objective delineations in the best of his semi-dramatic poems to come.

Standing with Palma later by a campfire, as Robert might have gazed into Fox's hearth, Sordello has a vision of what Rome has been and might be again; but as night falls Sordello's new Rome falls arch by arch. About to bury his vision in mockery, he checks himself:

"Sordello, wake!
God has conceded two sights to a man—
One, of men's whole work, time's completed plan,
The other, of the minute's work, man's first
Step to the plan's completeness. . . .
What is gone
Except Rome's aëry magnificence,
That last step you'd take first?—an evidence
You were God: be man now![51]

This passage, fundamental to the ethics of the poem, sounds like Goethe and Carlyle, and also like Pope.[52] Sordello continues to reflect. Living men build on dead men's achievements; living poets produce a music in which the simpler songs of dead poets can be heard. Great men, having faith and will, are souls who find in multitudes a body with which to realize their vision. Thus Charlemagne had built an empire of physical strength; Hildebrand and his successors, an empire of moral strength. Sordello chooses the latter: the Papal cause is the people's cause. He must persuade Salinguerra to become a Guelf. Plainly, Sordello's view of history resembles Carlyle's: history is the gradual realization of the Divine Idea through the achievements of great men; men and institutions embody ideas; social progress and individual well-being depend on work and humanitarian service.

This is, approximately, the view of history that Browning recommends to himself. The passage suggests that in writing *Sordello* he not only managed to symbolize his own introspective tendencies but to construct a worldview inimical to them. Clearly, great achievement in art must result from the artist's ability to draw upon the great world. And apparently—for Browning—there was no time to lose. Sordello's lifetime of dreaming and posing has undermined his sincerity; despite his fervor, he cannot help thinking self-consciously of the effect he is making when he attempts to persuade Salinguerra. The warrior disposes of him with a witticism. The poem concludes after Sordello's death in a long vista of ironies. Sordello is celebrated in aftertimes for everything he did not do, and what he might have done, is done by Dante, who—though Browning does not mention the fact—was a Ghibelline. The true Sordello is unwittingly perpetrated by the peasants of Asolo in a single imperfect song, which as a youth he had written in a moment of self-forgetful enjoyment of nature.[53]

Sordello is Browning's most grandiose exploit of breaking the beautiful soul on the wheel of commonsense and Christian ethics; his last long adventure on the sofa of self-analysis, carrying therapeutic examination to its logical extreme of privacy and complication. Apparently he had constructed the symbols he needed to find a new and absorbing interest in men and women. He had also discovered much about his art—in seven years' work in his finest verse laboratory. The eloquent indignation and even more eloquent silence of the press hurried him into a future which was already unfolding. In its dramatic, stream-of-consciousness style, its lively portraiture, and its vivid picture of a past age, *Sordello* looks forward to the monologues and beyond.

CHAPTER 7

Mass Attack on the Theater

1837-44

Browning was now in a breathless hurry to succeed before he should fail utterly. In the process of writing *Sordello,* or between versions, he had been turning over a half-dozen subjects in his head and elaborating nearly as many on paper. On August 1, 1837, just after the appearance of Mrs. Busk's *Sordello,* Robert had confided to Fanny Haworth that he was "thinking" a tragedy—an historical one like *Strafford.*[1] This play, which must have been *King Victor and King Charles,* was apparently written between finishing *Sordello* (May 1839), beginning *Pippa,* and "thinking" *The Return of the Druses.* It was well along toward completion by August 21, 1839, for on that evening Browning sounded Macready about it. Unhappily, the master was growing critical; the young disciple, somewhat stridently plaintive and querulous. Perhaps, in spite of the unfinished manuscripts at home, he appeared a little too often at Macready's stage door, dressing room, and lodgings. The eminent tragedian was in a particularly tragic mood, having been suffering from claustrophobia from acting in the Haymarket. "This dog-hole of a theatre," he mutters into the *Diary.* ". . . The audience is so close upon me, and yet I cannot feel their sympathy, if they have any." And he interjects, "Found Browning at my lodgings on my return, and was kept by him long. . . . His object, if he exactly knew it, was to learn from me whether, if he wrote a really good play, it would have a secure chance of acceptance. I told him certainly, and after much vague conversation, he left me to read and rest as I could."[2] The encounter was not auspicious. Two weeks later Browning submitted his play. Macready not only refused it but refused it with emphasis. "Read Browning's play on Victor, King of Sardinia—it turned out to be a *great mistake.* I called Browning into my room and most explicitly told him so, and gave him my reasons for coming to such a conclusion."[3] *King Victor* contains some very good writing, yet for once Macready had no doubts. The word "mistake" seems to indicate a disagreement on principle.

And such there was. Browning's preface once more emphasizes "Action in Character, rather than Character in Action." *King Victor* conforms even less than *Strafford* to the Macready formula. It is tragedy with even less action and spectacle, chronicle history with even less history. In fact, history is something that is pulled out of a drawer—a pile of papers that are laid on a table, gestured at, and barely discussed. Victor's abdication in favor of Charles, Charles's humanitarian reforms, his successful treaties with Austria and Spain, Victor's later machinations and revolt scarcely emerge from the pile of papers. The audience does not see what Charles did. It simply hears how he felt about what he did. Indeed, it might well doubt he did anything at all, for he is a savior of the people who displays all his weakness on stage and accomplishes all his wisdom off stage.

Having laid his tragedy quietly away, Browning continued to explore continents utterly dark and impenetrable to Macready. Even while writing *King Victor*, which was a more radical (and therefore a less successful) *Strafford*, he suddenly struck out on an entirely new path, and discovered not only a new genuinely dramatic form, but almost the whole repertory of modern dramatic techniques. *Pippa Passes* marks a return to all his deeper sources of inspiration—to poetry, art, Italy, and complex autobiography. Mrs. Orr informs us:

> Mr. Browning was walking alone in a wood near Dulwich, when the image flashed upon him of some one walking thus alone through life; one apparently too obscure to leave a trace of his or her passage, yet exercising a lasting though unconscious influence at every step of it; and the image shaped itself into the little silk-winder of Asolo, Felippa, or Pippa.[4]

Pippa, like Browning, is isolated, obscure, neglected—a singer dramatically, pathetically unaware of the magical effects of her songs. She is also variously related to that alter-Browning, Sordello. The closing picture of *Sordello* is that of a boy, "barefoot and rosy," running up a hill by "sparkling Asolo" while singing the poet's surviving youthful song, now become anonymous and popular.[5] Why not expand the picture into a poem—to be sure, a poem in most respects as unlike *Sordello* as possible?[6] As the *trouvère* Sordello had been complicated, self-centered, and ineffectual, the child Pippa—having been appropriately changed into a girl—would very properly be simple, spontaneous, unself-conscious, as a singer of subjective poetry, the direct and efficacious instrument of God's goodness. The play would be concerned with the effect of simple song on complicated people. Asolo would become a world, a stage on which Pippa would walk for a day pouring out in song the spontaneity of her joy and natural goodness, and her song, heard at crucial moments by several sets of people standing amid all the complicated evil and uncertainty of life, would sway them unawares. Here, in infinite possibility, were crisis, action, pathos, sentiment, irony, the nostalgia of the momentary, all wrapped up in an exotic Italian setting and a conception of coincidence and melodrama.

Browning could never resist attempting the impossible. In *Pippa* he failed at it—or succeeded—as brilliantly as anyone could. He begins with a heroine who shares his own tendency to live vicariously in the experiences of other people. Pippa announces that she will share in fancy the pleasures of the happiest four in Asolo—Ottima, Phene, Luigi, and the bishop. She will be loved as they are loved, be happy as they are happy. She is quite aware her chosen four are not altogether exemplary. She knows the town gossip about Ottima, and, after surveying with a somewhat complicated innocence the prospects of married and unmarried love, she reflects, not unlike a cautious bachelor of twenty-seven:

> Lovers grow cold, men learn to hate their wives,
> And only parents' love can last our lives.[7]

Pippa not only thinks but talks rather like Robert Browning. Her taste in figurative language is exotic, not to say baroque. She describes her "martagon" as

> New-blown and ruddy as St. Agnes' nipple,
> Plump as the flesh-bunch on some Turk bird's poll![8]

and dawn, as so many different things at once—a cauldron of boiling light that overflows the world with divine love, a breast that flickers, a chalice to be drunk—that one gives up consistency in despair.

The four episodes that follow are boldly linked by the regenerative influence of Pippa on the one hand and on the other by the world she regenerates. Depicting several classes in several walks of life, Browning presents an entire Italian community in the mid-nineteenth century. Depicting several kinds of love—adulterous, marital, patriotic, religious—transmuted on the very knife-edge of crisis by a girl's articulate love of life and of God, he demonstrates the essentially moral and religious nature of all love and the possibilities of salvation in the moment.

Unlike Pippa, Browning lives in a violently ironical imaginary world. Ottima and her lover Sebald, in Scene I, are already beyond love and happiness, for Sebald has murdered Ottima's husband Luca and is in the first throes of remorse. The episode seems to owe something to the final scene of *Othello,* and a good deal more to Act II, scene ii, of *Macbeth.* Luca is the murdered Duncan. Sebald—diminished to magnify Ottima—is a Macbeth who understands his crime only after he has committed it and who lacks the strength to embrace evil to its final consequences. Ottima glories in her love as remorselessly as Lady Macbeth in her ambition. Apparently she has felt marriage to Luca as a desecration. Now she feels released, cleansed; and as Sebald calls her and himself by all the appropriate harsh names and tries to make her do likewise, she reminds him proudly of the day when they lay in the woods together while a storm (as in *Lear*) raged overhead like an angry vengeance. Now she bids him crown her his "queen . . ./ Magnificent in sin."[9] Roused in spite of himself, he repeats the words but is cut short by Pippa's voice outside, singing what might be taken as a brief summary of Pope's *Essay on Man*:

> God's in his heaven—
> All's right with the world![10]

Appalled that he has intruded crime and the worship of crime on such a world, Sebald turns to Ottima and, in painfully Victorian accents, commands her to put on her clothes and wipe off her paint. Looking out from the deep and rather luxurious isolation of his guilt, he finds her suddenly emptied of all grace and beauty. In one of those impressionistic passages so frequent in Browning's plays, Sebald talks at Ottima—from out of a separate world—as at a lifeless and insensitive object. Then, apparently in a perfect pet of moral indignation against Ottima, Sebald stabs himself. Ottima begs for death, and speaks the last words:

> "Not me—to him, O God, be merciful!"[11]

Are they saved—according to Browning's rules? Very likely they are. In the moment of death, Ottima rediscovers her love and on a level that excludes self and reaches up to God. The mention of God here—and at the crucial moment in the other episodes—is significant.[12] The last words of both Ottima and Sebald suggest that they are penitents of the last hour, like Dante's Sordello and others of the fifth, sixth, and seventh cantos of the *Purgatorio* and therefore saved. How their service and that of less sinful souls rank, in the words of Pippa's first song, "the same with God" is a little harder to see.[13] Guilt is a rather easy liability in Browning's moral books. He draws upon God's benevolence as upon an unlimited credit, producing an unbalanced budget in which a heavy expense of wrongdoing in the present may be defrayed in eternity. The emphasis is not, as in Dante, on the slow payment but on the swift realization and remorse after the expense has been incurred. Yet, despite the sentimentality of its denouement, and the sordidness of its characters, the first episode of *Pippa* is perhaps, as critics have said, the most impressive single scene of poetic drama written in the nineteenth century.

The second and third episodes have distinctly autobiographical ingredients. Jules the young sculptor and lover of Phene, in the second, resembles Browning in many particulars, not only in magnanimity, ambition, and ideas about art, but in his arrogance and angry readiness to duel with those who injure him.

The third episode seems to be an exercise in abnormal psychology—a study of mother-fixation, complete with love for a mother-substitute in native country and hatred for a father-substitute in the Austrian emperor. Psychological insight does not seem to have precluded Browning from identifying strongly with the young patriot. Luigi rejects his mother's and his sweetheart's love and goes forth to assassinate with every blessing which God and the author can bestow. That Pippa's influence was particularly bad here, that God is placed in the position of resorting to crude emergency action to rectify the deeper workings of His system, does not seem to have struck Browning. Probably he was not thinking at all, but simply giving vent, in good evangelical idiom, to his violent hatred of tyrants and his warm sympathy for liberators. In short, he seems to have grasped Luigi's situation quite intuitively, divining from his own intense and disturbed experience of family how mother and father relationships may project themselves—or "metaphor out," in Kenneth Burke's phrase[14]—into the complexities of social life.

Here, too, Pippa's lines about parents' love[15] suggest a degree of autobiography. In this light it is interesting that the mother is essentially conservative, shrewd, and forceful, yet tentative and tactful in dealing with her son; while he is impulsive, passionate, romantically liberal, and decidedly vague about his cause. His mother observes that the Emperor Franz is a kind, gentle, densely stupid old man. Why should he be killed? Luigi tries to explain, but bogs down at the first Austrian treachery—the historical facts aren't worth remembering.

In the final episode, Monsignor the bishop catechizes his wicked Intendant and discovers that Pippa is his own niece and therefore rightful heiress to his fortune. The bishop hesitates, then, hearing Pippa's song, unmasks the Intendant—and presumably sees justice done. Pippa loses stature and symbolic value by being involved in the lives of the people she influences, and coincidence becomes more obtrusive by being enlisted in the service of a happy ending.[16] The episode is chiefly interesting as Browning's first study of an ecclesiastic. The bishop, with his cough, his taste for art, his detective astuteness, his almost comic mixture of religion and worldliness, is the evolutionary prototype of both Blougram and St. Praxed's. In his turn, he seems to derive from Bulwer's Richelieu, who, triumphantly incarnated in Macready, first walked the boards on March 7, 1839.

Pippa's concluding monologue reiterates at once the basic irony and optimism of the play. She wonders whether she might someday affect the lives of the happy four she has dreamed about; and, just before falling asleep, she sings

> All service ranks the same with God—
> With God, whose puppets, best and worst,
> Are we: there is no last nor first.

Three "Talks by the Way," the first two in prose, separate the four episodes in *Pippa.* The first—representing a student conspiracy against Jules—is an admirable imitation of Shakespearean wit and comedy. For a brief run, everybody talks like Mercutio at the top of his bent. The third linking entr'acte, in which several prostitutes discuss their profession, is as realistic a milieu sketch as ever came from the pen of a virtuous and poetic bachelor.

Standing in the chill shadow of *Sordello* and other failures, Robert felt that he could not put his father to the expense of publishing *Pippa.*

It lay in his drawer for about a year, until Moxon, hearing of the situation, offered to publish all new work at low cost in pamphlet form, printed double column on inexpensive paper. Browning eagerly accepted the offer, hoping thus, as he says in a discarded preface,[17] to regain the kind of pit-audience Macready had got him for *Strafford.* In April, 1841, *Pippa* appeared as the first number of the now legendary *Bells and Pomegranates.* Cheapness did not make these pamphlets a success, but early failure ultimately made them rare and expensive.

Appealing at many points to the best and the worst in Victorian taste, *Pippa* was destined ultimately to be the most popular closet drama in nineteenth-century literature. It could not become so at once, for the press received it, with intellect permanently impaired by *Sordello,* either in silence or with admiration deeply troubled by nightmare memories of earlier bewilderment. *The Morning Herald* praised it warmly both for the right and the wrong reasons.[18] *The Athenaeum* prudently took counsel with itself for more than eight months, then lost its temper all over again at the obscurities of *Sordello,* complaining querulously about the poet's persistent determination to think and be original. It professed to find Pippa almost equally baffling, and then belied itself by giving a lucid and admiring account of the poem. The reviewer only wished that so fine a work had been immortalized in a less perishable form.[19] In *The Examiner* John Forster read his old friend a gentle lecture on his career: *Paracelsus* was his promise; *Sordello,* his folly; *Pippa,* his fulfillment. Recently he had nearly ruined himself by writing a bad poem on bad principles. Now he had saved himself by writing a good poem on good principles.

Meanwhile, with hardy enthusiasm, Robert continued to send forth poems and tragedies. He wrote Eliza Flower—who plainly was not always complimentary—"Praise what you can praise, do me all the good you can, you and Mr. Fox (as if you will not!), for I have a head full of projects—mean to song-write, play-write forthwith."[20] And he adds in a postscript: "By the way, you speak of *Pippa*—could we not make some arrangement about it? The lyrics *want* your music—five or six in all—how say you? When these three plays are out I hope to build a huge Ode—but 'all goeth by God's Will.' "

The third play was undoubtedly *Mansoor the Hierophant,* finally called *The Return of the Druses.* Thus far, he had tried to please Macready with his own ideas. In *The Druses* he tried to please Macready with Macready's ideas—love, spectacle, suspense, and action. "A subject of the most wild and passionate love," about which he had inquired of Fanny Haworth in 1837,[21] suggested itself in connection with the Druses of Lebanon. Apparently in the *Biographie universelle,* his main source as well for *King Victor,* Browning came on the story of Hakeem, third Fatemite Caliph of Egypt, who in 1016 announced himself as the tenth incarnation of God and sent out his disciples, Hamza and Darazi, to disseminate the new religion. At home in Cairo, the Caliph soon after disappeared, murder being the most likely noncelestial explanation. In the region of Lebanon, Darazi succeeded in establishing the new faith, the major tenet of which became the mysterious flight of Hakeem to the skies and his eventual return to rule over the entire world.

From these bare details, and perhaps a few vague suggestions from other sources,[22] Browning devised an action which transpires in a long delirium of high-minded moral crisis. He assumes a remnant of the Druse sect driven by the Turks to an island of the Sporades, where for generations they have been oppressed and debased by their "protectors," the Knights of Rhodes. Djabal returns secretly to the island from his wanderings in Europe, falls in love with Anael, a beautiful maiden who has sworn to marry only the savior of her people, and, proclaiming himself the god Hakeem, thus inspires the degraded Druses to attempt rebellion and the much-longed-for return to Lebanon in a Venetian fleet. Löys, prefect-elect of the Knights and devoted to the Druses, learns it is his own religious order that has ruined them.

The situation bristles with the most fascinating psychological questions: How does it feel to impersonate a god, to be espoused to a god, to discover that one's religion is dedicated to ruthless exploitation? These questions are answered—rather on the run. As an idealist with somewhat Shelleyan visions, and a good deal of youthful self-consciousness, Djabal often reminds one of Robert:

> That a strong man should think himself a God!
>
> . . . . .
>
> My mother's arms twine still about my neck. . . .[23]

He feels intensely, and at times is chiefly concerned to express his feelings as beautifully as an elaborated image will allow:

> Avow the truth? I cannot! In what words
> Avow that all she loves in me is false?

—Which yet has served that flower-like love of hers
To climb by, like the clinging gourd, and clasp
With its divinest wealth of leaf and bloom:
Could I take down the prop-work . . .

. . . . .

The old support thus silently withdrawn!
But no; the beauteous fabric crushes too.[24]

A number of psychological monologues are imbedded in the play, dramatic in themselves, though not very dramatic in relation to the action. But in general Browning made a strong effort to produce the Macreadian virtues. What he did produce with certain Browningesque subtleties, originalities, and confusions was ironic-domestic tragedy with strong reminiscences of the heroic play. Anael commits murder to prove herself worthy of Hakeem, only to learn from Djabal himself that he is an imposter. Ever true to the loftiest principles, she promptly exposes him before all the people. The action closes on a fine scene in which, with the Venetian fleet in the harbor and Anael (having expired Desdemona-like with the name of Hakeem on her lips) dead at his feet, Djabal stabs himself in sorrow and remorse, and then leads his people a few steps on the hegira to Lebanon.

One might expect Macready to have been delighted. Actually, sometime in May or June 1840, even before he read it, he advised the original three acts be expanded to five. Browning complied, and felt the result an improvement, but Macready recorded that the play "*does not look well.*"[25] On August 3, he wrote: "Read Browning's play, and with the deepest concern I yield to the belief that he will *never write again*—to any purpose. I fear his intellect is not quite clear. I do not know how to write to Browning."[26] Obviously, Macready was one of those whose intellects had been permanently impaired by *Sordello.* In his letter to Browning, which has not been preserved, he seems to have objected that nobody had ever heard of the Druses, that the initial situation was improbable, and that the role of Djabal was unsympathetic to him—perhaps because Djabal was so extravagantly impious and unsound as to impersonate the Deity. He must have written tactfully, for Robert's reply, though vigorous, was affectionate: "So once again, dear Macready, I have failed to please you! The Druses *return,* in another sense than I had hoped."[27] He urged that audiences need no previous introduction to the oppressed to sympathize with them. As for the part of Djabal, he had written it with

Macready always in mind. Macready had been Macbeth for years. Browning urged him to be somebody new.

Browning was probably as puzzled at Macready's resistance to the play as the actor was puzzled at the author's faith in it. The more Macready resisted, the more Browning argued. What was worse, he argued at the wrong time. "Browning came before I had finished my bath, and really *wearied* me with his obstinate faith in his poem of *Sordello*, and of his eventual celebrity, and also with his self-opinionated persuasions upon his *Return of the Druses*. I fear he is for ever gone."[28] No doubt Browning was at his worst, and Macready was willing to see the worst: "He speaks of Mr. Fox (who would have been *delighted* and proud in the ability to praise him) in a very unkind manner, and imputes motives to him which on the mere surface seem absurd."[29] Nevertheless, he reread what he could of the play—and found it "mystical, strange and heavy."[30] History has confirmed Macready's judgment. Even in the nineteenth century, when taste favored it, no manager was tempted to back it as a commercial venture. In 1881 Henry Irving asked Browning to write him a play in verse. "I have just answered his letter," Browning told Gosse. "I have said that it is very kind of him, very civil and all that, but that if he wants to act a play of mine, there is *The Return of the Druses* ready waiting for him."[31] Irving did not avail himself of the opportunity.

Macready had learned some lessons in Browning's egotism; Browning was now to learn some in Macready's—nor was their friendship to survive so much mutual understanding and misunderstanding. Still persistent, Browning turned to *A Blot in the 'Scutcheon* and within a short time—probably late in 1840—once more wrote Macready:

> "The luck of the third adventure" is proverbial. I have written a spick and span new Tragedy (a sort of compromise between my own notion and yours—as I understand it, at least) and will send it to you if you care to be bothered so far. There is *action* in it, drabbing, stabbing, et autres gentillesses,—who knows but the Gods may make me good even yet? Only, make no scruple of saying flatly that you cannot spare the time, if engagements of which I know nothing, but fancy a great deal, should claim every couple of hours in the course of this week.[32]

To this diffident and almost pathetic letter, Browning received no decisive response for more than a year.

As a matter of fact, poor Macready had at this time far more than his conscience and the English theater on his mind. His friends and authors had been quarreling among themselves. People had been talking, quite unjustifiably, about him and his leading lady, Helen Faucit. His son Henry had been very ill; his daughter Joan had died, for a time he had been unable to act at all. Finally, by way of excruciating irony, Bulwer's *Money* had been phenomenally successful, so that he was compelled, in spite of low spirits, to act the same comedy until he was beside himself with boredom and exasperation. Meanwhile, with all his performing horses and lions, Bunn had gone down to ruin at last, and Drury Lane was available to a new management. Macready saw a last opportunity, perhaps to revive the English drama, at least to be his own master. With a careful and apprehensive look at his pocketbook, he once more, on October 4, 1841, assumed the management of a major theater. In accord with his high purpose, he planned to change his bill frequently and to introduce new plays. Even while anxiously considering his decision as to Drury Lane, he had discussed new plays over dinner with Forster. Forster seems to have rediscovered his faith in Browning at the bottom of a wineglass and, remembering *A Blot in the 'Scutcheon* gathering dust so many months, clamorously urged Macready to read it. With some misgivings about Forster's sobriety and even more about Browning's sanity, Macready read the play and was doubtful. Forster also read the play, and was equally doubtful. They sent the manuscript to Dickens, who himself kept it for a year.

Meanwhile, Macready had gone through one season and most of another—and indeed through much of his capital—acting in many old plays and in two new ones: Marston's *The Patrician's Daughter* and Darley's *Plighted Troth.* The first was at best a moral victory; the second, the kind of failure that does not bear thinking of. Begun in unshakable confidence, it proceeded with a massive gravity broken by catcalls far into the last act, until, to the obvious relief of the audience, Macready lay prostrate on the stage. Limping from his bed to inspect the corpse, the actor Bennett trod heavily on Macready's hand. The dead man sat up with a jerk. "Beast!" he exclaimed in Shakespearean rage. "Beast of hell!"[33] And he died all over again. The audience roared. The play was not repeated.

Macready was in a desperate mood when, in November 1842, out of a not very blue sky, Forster showed him a letter from Dickens:

> Browning's play has thrown me into a perfect passion of sorrow. To say that there is anything in its subject save what is lovely, true, deeply affecting, full of the best emotion, the most earnest feeling, and the

> most true and tender source of interest, is to say that there is no light in the sun, and no heat in blood. It is full of genius, natural and great thoughts, profound and yet simple and beautiful in its vigour. I know nothing that is so affecting, nothing in any book I have ever read, as Mildred's recurrence to that "I was so young—I had no mother." I know no love like it, no passion like it, no moulding of a splendid thing after its conception, like it. And I swear it is a tragedy that *must* be played: and must be played, moreover, by Macready. . . . And if you tell Browning that I have seen it, tell him that I believe from my soul there is no man living (and not many dead) who could produce such a work.[34]

Macready himself had thought as highly of *Plighted Troth.* Still, such praise from Dickens could not be ignored. On December 13, 1842, Browning told his friend Domett that Macready had promised to keep his theater open until he had produced *A Blot.* Robert was not sanguine. "I don't know what will be the end of it," he wrote.[35]

And, in fact, the history of *A Blot* is in itself an oddly perverse, opaque little tragedy which, but for space, one might present after the manner of *The Ring and the Book* in the divergent testimonies of Browning, Macready, Arnould, and others—among whom, as T. R. Lounsbury proves, Browning himself verges with a good conscience and the best of intentions quite consistently toward error.[36] But nobody, either at the time or later, was very detached or very rational. As a preliminary, from motives calculated or mysterious, Forster never showed Browning Dickens' letter. He read it thirty years later, with a shock of pleasure and resentment understandably mixed, in his friend's *Life of Dickens.* From motives less mysterious but more disastrous, Macready did not himself read the play to the cast. On January 29 he called Browning to his private room and told him that his play had been received by the actors with shouts of laughter.

"Who read it?"

"Oh, Mr. Willmott."[37]

Willmott, the prompter, was a grotesque old man with a wooden leg, a red face, and a reputation for vulgar humor that turned everything he touched into buffoonery. Forty years afterward Helen Faucit recalled how, as he read, "the delicate, subtle lines were twisted, perverted, and sometimes even made ridiculous."[38] Browning did not conceal his indignation, and, somewhat conscience-struck, Macready conceded with grandeur that "Willmott was a ridiculous being."[39] He would himself read the play on Monday. But the mischief had been done. Willmott had brought out a weakness which was inherent in the play itself and which the actors were eventually to betray with fatal clarity to the audience.

Macready now told Browning that he would not himself act in the play. A new man, Phelps, would take the leading role. Macready would not read, he would not act. If Browning would only be so good as to see disaster on the horizon. Further cuts and revisions were penciled on the manuscript.[40] But Robert had tried too hard and waited too long to be tactfully receptive to the suggestions of an irascible manager always at war with himself—or to the universal truth that a tragedy without Macready must fail in Macready's theater. One of his Camberwell intimates, Joseph Arnould, explained the situation to Alfred Domett: "Judicious friends, as judicious friends will, had a habit of asking Browning when the play was coming out—you can fancy how sensitively Browning would chafe at this. At length the paramount object with him became to have the play played, no matter how, so that it was at once."[41] Robert accepted Phelps as Tresham—and scandalized Macready further. Everything Robert did now proved that "this young man's head is gone."

On the third day of rehearsal, Phelps became ill, so that, as the eminent tragedian has written with superb humility, "I decided on under-studying his part."[42] The next day Robert observed that Macready was not merely reading but moving across the stage and counting his steps. Actually, he had yielded either to the fascination of a part admirably suited to him or simply to the necessity of making an inescapable venture as successful as possible. Phelps waylaid Browning at the stage door and told him with great emotion that Macready had decided to take over the part of Tresham, thereby greatly improving the chances of the play. But, if Browning were willing to forgo that advantage, Phelps assured him that "he would take ether, sit up all night, and have the words in his memory by next day."[43] Browning replied that he would make known his decision in the green room. There, fixing his hat more firmly on his head, he marched up to "the great bashaw" and interrupted him before his minions in the very act of reading.

"I find that Mr. Phelps, although he has been ill, feels himself quite able to take the part, and I shall be very glad to leave it in his hands."

Macready rose, and said, doubtless with baleful eyes and a diction terrible with baroque incrustations of fury and indignation: "But do you understand that I, *I* am going to act the part?"

"I shall be very glad to entrust it to Mr. Phelps," said Browning firmly.[44]

Macready received the news as Napoleon might have received the intelligence of a fresh treachery of Talleyrand. He crushed up his freshly printed copy of the play and flung it across the room. That night he confided to his diary that Browning had behaved "in the worst taste, manner, and spirit. . . . I could only think Mr. Browning a very disagreeable and offensively mannered person. *Voilà tout!*"[45]

Browning was equally ready to think the worst: "All this," he wrote many years after, "to keep up the belief that Macready, and Macready alone, could produce a veritable 'tragedy,' unproduced before."[46] Perhaps from the best of motives, Macready had suggested that Tresham should not die but enter a monastery. Robert not only declined the change but, to forestall any further cuts in the text, had Moxon rush the play through the press, so that, as No. V of *Bells and Pomegranates,* it was available to Macready as a stage property in the scene just described and to theater-goers on the opening night. Macready did not draw upon his slender resources to make the production brilliant. Existing props and costumes were used; a striking scene from *The Patrician's Daughter* did service a second time. The thirty-year-old poet saw in this economy—perhaps with some justice—a hostile intent. Looking back on the whole episode, Browning wrote William Archer in 1888: "Macready was *'fuori di sè'* from the moment when,—in pure ignorance of what he was driving at,—I acquiesced in his proposal that a serious play of any pretension should appear under his management with any other protagonist than himself. When the more learned subsequently enlightened me a little, I was angry and disinclined to take advice."[47] In short, each was shocked to discover his own coldness in the other. Macready had become impatient of an intimacy which he no longer felt. Browning was indignant at a devious formality which he thought his own warmth and openness did not deserve. The comedy off stage had ended. The tragedy on stage was about to begin.

A Blot in the 'Scutcheon is laid in the eighteenth century, when family pride, which determines the action, seems to have been particularly sensitive and fastidious. As the play opens, Lord Henry Mertoun calls on Earl Tresham and asks for the hand of his sister Mildred. Tresham favors the match. Apprised that a lover has visited his sister's room, Tresham waylays the muffled stranger a night later, discovers him to be Mertoun, and, dueling, inflicts a fatal wound. Overcome with remorse, he then takes poison, receives Mildred's forgiveness as she dies, and dies. Obviously, none of the principals is very rational. Mertoun had not proposed earlier from sheer awe of his idol Tresham. Mildred is paralyzed by remorse when the illicit situation is about to become licit. The play has a certain air of case history about it, and Browning aims a homily at self-righteous moralists: juvenile folly is blown up into tragedy by the violence of a Victorian adult who is too horrified to think. One can see why Dickens was so deeply moved by *A Blot.* It was not only written in his particular key of pathos but spoke to his deepest experience of life and to his most persistent motive for reform.

Desperately anxious to succeed on Macready's stage, Browning appears very nearly to have stopped thinking about character when he wrote *A Blot.* Having filled his head with Shakespeare, he contrived a balcony scene from *Romeo and Juliet,* a scene of awakening vengeance from *Othello.* Guendolen and Austin are Beatrice and Benedick, introduced—apparently as relief from tragic thick-headedness—from *Much Ado.* Mildred is a conscience-ridden Juliet; Tresham, a high-minded (and feeble-minded) Othello. His whole part, in its most effective moments, is an elaboration of the line, "But yet the pity of it, Iago! O Iago, the pity of it, Iago," abounding in pathos admirably suited to the talent of Macready. The attempt to imitate the brilliantly dramatic imagery in the balcony scene of *Romeo and Juliet* is less successful. The sunrise images symbolize the young lovers' hope in contrast to the darkness and secrecy of the past, but they soon fall into paradox and confusion.

The play was in rehearsal for only a week. Still convinced that his talent might somehow accommodate itself to the theater, and probably aware that he had almost turned himself inside out to achieve a success, Robert was, realistically, prepared for the worst. He would not allow his sister or parents to be present at the performance, and he himself came, as anonymously as possible, accompanied solely by Edward Moxon. Helen Faucit surpassed herself. Phelps, a Macready imitator with a good voice and a Macready nose, did well enough to please the critics but not well enough to please Macready or Helen Faucit. Anderson, obsessed by Willmott's comic reading to the cast, played Mertoun in some doubt whether he was tragic or ridiculous; and when, in the very act of ascending to Mildred's chamber, he sang the unfortunate song

> There's a woman like a dew-drop, she's so purer than the purest[48]

the audience tittered audibly. But the sensitive lines and the abundant action and the steadily dripping pathos partly made up for the want of sanity in the characters and suspense or coherence in the action. The audience applauded more and more. At the final curtain, Phelps was called and recalled, and, according to Gosse, a shout went up for author, until Anderson came forward, and with his eye on Browning, said, "I believe that the author is not present, but if he is, I entreat him to come forward."[49] The author chose to be absent, like the actor-manager—perhaps as T. R. Lounsbury surmises, because the shout had not been very loud.[50]

In any case, a dreadful syllogism beginning "Macready acts in all good Macready tragedies" hung like a sword over the play. In a letter to Domett, Edward Arnould gives an account of the second and third performances:

> The second night was evidently presided over by the spirit of the manager. I was one of about sixty or seventy in the pit, and we yet seemed crowded when compared to the desolate emptiness of the boxes. The gallery was again full, and again among all who were there were the same decided impressions of pity and horror produced. The third night I again took my wife to the boxes. It was evident at a glance that it was to be the last. My own delight, and hers too, in the play was increased at this third representation, and would have gone on increasing to a thirtieth; but the miserable, great, chilly house, with its apathy and emptiness, produced on us both the painful sensation which made her exclaim that "she could cry with vexation" at seeing so noble a play so basely marred. Now, there can be no doubt whatever that the absence of Macready's name from the list of performers of the new play was the means of keeping away numbers from the house.[51]

On that very day Drury Lane had announced that *A Blot* was thenceforth to be acted three times a week. But Arnould's impression at the third performance had also been Macready's. The tragedy vanished from the boards of Drury Lane.

The press was less enthusiastic than the audience. That monitor of respectability, *The Athenaeum,* was shocked by a heroine who lacked the obvious credentials of virtue.

> If to pain and perplex were the end and aim of tragedy, Mr. Browning's poetic melodrama called *A Blot in the 'Scutcheon* would be worthy of admiration, for it is a very puzzling and unpleasant piece of business. The plot is plain enough, but the acts and feelings of the characters are inscrutable and abhorrent, and the language is as strange as their

> proceedings. . . . A few of the audience laughed, others were shocked, and many applauded; but it is impossible that such a drama should live even if it were artfully constructed, which this is not.[52]

Browning never forgave this review, and firmly believed it was inspired by Macready.

A Blot in the 'Scutcheon made some stir, and the quarrel with Macready an even greater stir, in the theatrical world. Soon after this time Charles Kean offered Browning a considerable sum—the rather improbable sum of £500, as he later remembered it—for a new play. Browning's reverence for Edmund Kean had not descended to Charles the son. In fact, he had made it a point of faith in Macready to scorn Kean without troubling to see him perform. But all that was over. The prospect of being well paid to prove Macready a bad critic and himself a good dramatist was attractive. He chose a subject and wrote with characteristic rapidity, so that, despite headaches, illness, and much other work, he was able to inform Domett a bare two months later that he must make up his mind to finish a play he had written for Kean. Again rather characteristically, the interval required for finishing was somewhat protracted. But on March 9, 1844, he read the play to Kean and "his charming wife," who was to take the title role.

> . . . all went off *au mieux—but*—he wants to keep it till "Easter next year"—and unpublished all the time!—His engagement at the Haymarket next May, is merely for twelve nights, he says:—he leaves London for Scotland to-morrow, or next day—and will be occupied for ten hours a day till he returns—my play will take him two months at least to study, he being a 'special slow-head, and after the Haymarket engagement nothing is to be done till this time next year.—Of all which notable pieces of information I was apprised for the first time *after* the play was read and approved of . . . for, it certainly never entered into my mind that anybody, even an actor, could need a couple of months to study a part.[53]

Not having published for thirteen months, he decided, in spite of money, to try his readers immediately. His reasons are interesting: "I *must* print, or risk the hold, such as it is, I have at present on *my* public . . . two or three hundred pounds will pay me but indifferently for hasarding the good fortune which appears slowly but not mistakably setting in upon me, just now." He was winning an audience, though still few—and he was in no mood to deal patiently with actors. "The poorest Man of letters (if *really* of letters) I ever knew is of far higher talent than the best actor I ever expect to know . . . can't study a speech in a month. God help them." In April 1844, *Colombe's Birthday* was issued by Moxon as No. VI of *Bells and Pomegranates.* The cost, probably a little more than £16, was once more paid by the poet's father.

In *Colombe* Browning wrote at once a convincing romance and his most accurate prediction thus far of his own courtship. The plot turns on that favorite feudal daydream of the democratic and industrial nineteenth century: the story of the poor man who wins a princess. In fact the play is set in a seventeenth-century Rhenish duchy. But plot and setting seem unimportant. Browning apparently studied the Contest of the Juliers Succession of 1609,[54] only to idealize and simplify it—by turning the political contestants into suitors and the Duke of Cleves into a beautiful and bemused young lady. Despite her obliviousness to anything *but* love and the easiness of her choice of the Advocate Valence—with whom she falls in love at first sight—Colombe seems believable and interesting. One is tempted to forget that her subjects in Cleves are starving and on the brink of revolution. Valence's defection to love is more surprising. Pale and thought-worn, poetically eloquent, and seething with humanitarian idealism, he is obviously a portrait of the author himself. Like Sordello, he sees in a woman a symbol of a people's cause. Of himself and his fellow townsmen, he tells Colombe:

> There is a vision in the heart of each
> Of justice, mercy, wisdom, tenderness
> To wrong and pain, and knowledge of its cure:
> And these embodied in a woman's form
> That best transmits them, pure as first received,
> From God above her, to mankind below.
> Will you derive your rule from such a ground,
> Or rather hold it by the suffrage, say,
> Of this man—this—and this?[55]

One would expect him to arm the citizens, to educate the Duchess in just and democratic rule. Not at all. Browning is concerned to show how lovers communicate their love and the psychological "action in character" which brings them finally together—amid circumstances no more political than those on a particularly idyllic desert island. Especially in the cumulative effects of her flower imagery, in the precision of poetic rhythms,

Presagefully it beats, presagefully,
My heart—[56]

and in her contrasting reactions to the two suitors, one sees in Colombe's portrait how much Browning's style finally gained in subtlety and dramatic clarity as a direct result of playwriting.

Colombe was the last play he wrote for the theater—nor did it reach a theater until 1853, when, with Phelps and Helen Faucit in the leading roles, it was performed seven times at the Haymarket. It then vanished impecuniously, despite the warm approval of the critics.

In 1844, the printed text met with some rather prickly critical reservations, especially from Forster. Having written almost undiluted praise of the play, he turned suddenly on the author and concluded, with his heaviest after-dinner emphasis: "As far as he has gone, we abominate his tastes as much as we respect his genius."[57] The sentence caused a rupture. After waiting a year, Forster called at Hatcham and was "profuse of graciosities." "We will go on again with the friendship," Robert told Elizabeth Barrett, "as the snail repairs his battered shell."[58] He accepted an invitation to see Forster and Dickens in an amateur performance of *Every Man in His Humour.*

CHAPTER 8

Impressionism

During these years, Browning was a great unrecognized master to his intimate friends. They were chiefly members of "The Colloquial," a rather informal "social and literary society"[1] centering about Camberwell, Limehouse, and several families in the shipbuilding business. Their leader was Captain Pritchard, an older man remarkable for benevolence to old maids and secrecy about his domicile. Among the others were the Dowsons, W. C. Young, and two young Camberwell intimates, Joseph Arnould and Alfred Domett, who, with Browning himself, belonged to a soberly aspiring and close-knit "set" within the larger group. Arnould had won the Newdigate prize for poetry at Oxford and then, discovering an appetite for the laborious aridities of the law, had sagely discounted undergraduate fame and settled down to the prose of a professional career, which eventually carried him into a judgeship of the High Court at Bombay. He was an able, warm-hearted man, who paid tribute to poetry in an ardent hero-worship of Browning, appropriately couched, in its more expansive moments, in verse epistles and the portentous idiom of Carlyle.[2]

Domett's career is only a little less remarkable than that which Browning predicted for him in the poem "Waring." There was a quiet air of splendid possibility about this man from the start. Lance's watercolor shows a bold, handsome face under a large amount of romantic hat. The features have a still, inward look and the eyes are veiled under their lids in reverie. Such a man might well see folly in grinding at the law and in pacing up and down

Any longer London town.

His family had not only owned but sailed ships. He had left Cambridge without taking a degree, published a volume of poems, traveled in Italy and Canada, and then—having quietly allowed his friends to grow used to the improbability that he had settled down to the law—suddenly emigrated to New Zealand. Robert was as astonished as everybody else. The abrupt disappearance impelled him to enfold his friend in a cloud of romance and to unfold himself to him in a series of affectionate confidences, sometimes as intimate and mysterious as those in *Pauline*:

> I have a sort of notion you will come back some bright morning a dozen years hence and find me just gone—to Heaven, or Timbuctoo; and I give way a little to this fancy while I write, because it lets me write freely what, I dare say, I said niggardly enough—my real love for you—better love than I had supposed I was fit for; but, you see, when I was not even a boy, I had fancy in plenty and no kind of judgment—so I said, and wrote, and professed away, and was the poorest of creatures; that, I think, is out of me now, but the habit of watching and warding continues, and—here is a case where I do myself wrong. However, I am so sure now of my feelings, when I do feel—trust to them so much, and am deceived about them so little (I mean, that I so rarely believe I like where I loathe, and the reverse, as the people round me do) that I can speak about myself and my sentiments with full confidence.[3]

Browning rose from that first letter, one suspects, with the poem of "Waring" in his mind.

Apparently, these two young men had reason to expect a good deal of each other. Robert constantly urged his friend to produce great poetry. Domett did not immediately do so, nor did he, like Waring, secretly return to London to paint immortal frescoes on the ceiling of a garret. He did not even tread

> the Kremlin's pavement bright
>
> . . . . .
>
> . . . with five other Generals
> That simultaneously take snuff.

On the contrary, he stayed on in New Zealand, lived in a hut, chopped down trees, moved rocks, worried about his potato crop, and eventually broke his leg. Even the distance halfway round the world could not lend much enchantment to these facts. Yet neither Robert nor anybody else lost faith. Previously devoted to literature, the Colloquials now met to discuss the wonderful future of Alfred Domett.

Domett feared that he might be lame.

> I take refuge now [wrote Robert] in what I used to deprecate once, your habit of painting everything *en noir:* as long as you can *swim,* for instance, how should you be "crippled"? All the same, if *black* is the colour about you, and may not be softened away, take ship, in heaven's name, and come here in the cursed six months! There you walk past our pond-rail (picking up one of the fallen horse-chesnuts), and now our gate-latch clicks, and now——[4]

Browning's letters to this lonely, struggling, far-off emigrant, who believed in his friend's poetry as staunchly as he believed in New Zealand, give a vivid glimpse of the man behind the poems and plays of these years—a sensitive, thoughtful, ardent, very ambitious young man, still impatient with his time, his rivals, and much in himself—and very eager to be without delay all that he might be. He is proud to be able to report the doings of Carlyle and Tennyson, yet he praises Carlyle only for his conversation, and Tennyson for but two or three poems. Tennyson's revisions are disasters: there is "some woeful mental infirmity in the man." Again, he praises minor figures like Hood, Blanchard, Hanmer, and Ebenezer Jones; yet, in general "we are dead asleep in literary things, and in great want of a 'rousing word' . . . from New Zealand or any place *out* of the snoring dormitory."[5]

> Contrive, contrive
> To rouse us, Waring! Who's alive?

The quarterlies are full of dry-as-dust philosophy. Macaulay's *Lays* are the quintessence of staleness and commonplace. Bulwer's *Last of the Barons* is "a poor affair"—damned from a single extract.[6] Dickens is "uproarious" and his Pecksniffs "disgusting."[7]

Taken to task by Domett for his own obscurity, Browning humbly resolves to be clear—in not very clear sentences. Since finishing *Colombe,* he feels that he has much more to say and is eager to say it. As for the reviews, he is grateful for praise, almost grateful for abuse. "They take to criticising me a little more, in the Reviews—and God send I be not too proud of their abuse!"[8] He has been deeply moved by a preacher. What moves him, however, is not the message, but the Carlylean phenomena of hero-worship, the psychology of faith and personal power:

> The most notable thing of the year [1843] has been, to me, the visit of Father Mathew to London—this reverting to the simplest form of worship (for the converts are converts to his hand and voice and eye, and nothing beyond), all these men choosing to become *better* because he, who was standing there, better—he *bade* them so become; you should have seen it, as I did. . . . I stood on the scaffold with him, and heard him preach, beside.[9]

Meanwhile, with and without benefit of Carlyle, Arnould describes to Domett endless fresh discoveries of virtue and power in the miraculous Robert. There is no opacity of brothers' speech in his talk:

> in conversation anecdotical, vigorous, showing great thought and reading, but in his language most simple, energetic, and accurate. From the habit of good and extensive society he has improved in this respect wonderfully. We remember him as hardly doing justice to himself in society; now it is quite the reverse—no one could converse with him without being struck by his great conversational power—he relates admirably; in fact, altogether I look upon him as *to be* our foremost literary man.[10]

And again: "His life so pure, so energetic, so simple, so laborious, so loftily enthusiastic. It is impossible to know and not to love him."[11] Indeed, these virtues extend to Robert's sister:

> Sarianna, as my wife now always calls her, we are both very much attached to; she is marvellously clever—such fine clear animal spirits—talks much and well, and yet withal is so simply and deeply good-hearted that it is a real pleasure to be with her.[12]

Domett took such effusions gravely, preserving in a special album every one of Robert's letters, and everything in Arnould's relevant to the poet. Domett was himself beginning, in a homespun, democratic way, to justify Waring. In 1843, twenty-two Europeans were killed during an attempt to arrest a Maori chief involved in a land dispute. Such an event as the "Wairau Massacre" could in those days create a shiver of horror around the world. Domett joined in the agitation against Governor Fitzroy and drafted with great moderation and ability the petition for recall sent to the Home Government. The new governor offered Domett a seat on the Legislative Council. In late middle age, Robert wrote the end of the story to his friend Isa Blagden: "*Waring* came back the other day, after thirty years' absence, the same as ever—nearly: he has been prime minister in

New Zealand for a year and a half, but gets tired, and returns home with a poem."[13] The reunion was achieved on both sides with appropriate cordiality, but the word "nearly" is eloquent. Probably Warings should never return—certainly not in late middle age.

Another relationship of these years was almost the antithesis of the friendship with Domett. Edward Moxon, Browning wrote Locker-Lampson in 1874,

> printed, on nine occasions, nine poems of mine, wholly at my expense; that is, he printed them and, subtracting the very moderate returns, sent me in, only, the bill of the remainder of expense. . . . Moxon was kind and civil, made no profit by me, I am sure, and never tried to help me any, he would have assured you.[14]

These words hardly suggest the *entente cordiale* that existed between the two men. Browning thought Moxon slow, unenterprising, calculating, and parsimonious. What he really could not forgive, of course, was that Moxon had failed to invest in the commodity Browning. But Moxon had invested a good deal in similar fantastic commodities. In his sober, calculating way, he was dedicated to poetry. Rightly somewhat dissatisfied with his efforts to write it, he began in 1832 to publish it. No doubt he meant to make money, but even more he meant to become, in the spacious tradition of Murray and Constable, the friend and patron of poets. Unhappily, a rapidly growing proletariat had done for literature what it had done for the theater. Epics and romances at a guinea a volume had with eye-deceiving swiftness given way to encyclopedias of useful information and pamphlets on religion, sedition, and blasphemy. But Moxon did not give up poetry for encyclopedias. In 1858, having published four generations of great poets, he died a moderately prosperous man.

Short of investing in him, Moxon seems to have felt a sober and cautious interest in Browning. He actually lent his name to *Sordello,* and actually continued to lend his name to Browning afterward. He took the trouble to suggest pamphlet publication for the plays. In 1842, at the point when Robert was most absorbedly determined to succeed as a dramatist, Moxon made a suggestion which showed that he saw, perhaps better than the poet himself, what was to be popular and permanent in his work: Browning should gather some of his shorter pieces into a volume of *Bells and Pomegranates.* The result was *Dramatic Lyrics,* which duly appeared in November 1842.

At first the poems in *Dramatic Lyrics* made almost no stir. Two of them already had been published in a periodical. Yet the appearance of the collection is a notable event both in Browning's career and in literary history. Biographically considered, they present the familiar Browning—of *Paracelsus, Sordello,* and the two plays that had appeared—practicing the unfamiliar virtues of clarity, brevity, and drama. They also present familiar nineteenth-century ideas and literary techniques producing unfamiliar effects in the brief poem. The logic of these effects is found in an elaborate and consistent dramatic impressionism.

Historically impressionism arises out of the romantic and, more particularly, the empirical movement,[15] which, as carried to a rational extreme by Hume, denied reason the power certainly to know the outward world and established the interior stream of sensations and ideas as the sole indubitable reality. Thought, together with the general ideas on which it depends, is traceable to sensations, the mind's ability to recall them and its tendency to associate them according to similarity, succession, and coexistence. The key to impressionism is the disparagement of reason. To depreciate the ordering power of reason is to emphasize that the mind is continually exposed, as it moves through time and space, to an infinite variety and anarchy of sensations and ideas, and their attendant emotions.

Literary impressionism uses techniques calculated to emphasize this variety and anarchy—broadly, techniques which present description, narration, or reflection from the point of view of a limited, individual consciousness. The reader has the feeling, in greater or less degree, of being inside the mind and senses of another person. In shorter works, or in shorter sections of longer works, the point-of-view character in Browning may be markedly eccentric, so that the reader has a sharp sense of a mind different from his own. Moreover, what the mind sees or experiences in a scene or a situation may be graphically recorded, as though by a moving camera. "Soliloquy of the Spanish Cloister" has already worn itself trite. Even so, it is a remarkable achievement of its kind. The speaker follows Brother Lawrence in his gardening, for example, with a careful, lingering, furious identification through hatred—hatred that is ironically like love:

> What? Your myrtle-bush wants trimming?
>   Oh, that rose has prior claims—
> Needs its leaden vase filled brimming?
>   Hell dry you up with its flames![16]

Almost equally important in impressionist theory is the associative mode of progression. What is informally spoken or written, and what is privately thought or felt—insofar as it is coherent and articulate at all—tends to follow an associational order. Brother Lawrence's infuriating solicitude for his plants calls up the solicitous care he bestows on his cup and plate; recollection of the cup-polishing is interrupted by

(He-he! There his lily snaps!).

"Brown Dolores" suggests not only lust, but Brother Lawrence's liberal theology and the pleasant prospect of tripping him on a certain text in Galatians, which bristles for the unwary with twenty-nine distinct damnations, or of tempting him with a "scrofulous French novel" which drips damnation from every page, or even of making a compact (fraudulent, of course) with Satan

till, past retrieve,
Blasted lay that rose-acacia
We're so proud of![17]

Unfortunately, associational order is seldom conducive to either swiftness or clarity, and therefore—having a good deal to say in little space—Browning uses it cautiously in his briefer poems. Insofar as it verbalizes at all, the mind—according to the impressionist—speaks an intimate, colloquial, conversational language, which may vary all the way from the private growls of the "Spanish Cloister" to the comparative order and formality of dramatic language in a play or spoken monologue.

Browning himself calls his poems "dramatic." What, briefly, is the relation of drama to impressionism? Most plays present outward events on a physical stage. An impressionist work—particularly as it emphasizes reverie and recollection—presents inward events on a mental stage. The language may have the racy, colloquial quality of good dialogue, and the action may have conflict, crisis, and reversal—and much graphic concreteness. Thus an inward rationalization may be dramatic, as in "My Last Duchess." But in the long run, inward events are dramatic only insofar as they are vividly and significantly related to an outward situation which is in itself dramatic. Impressionism is undramatic in its tendency to recede into the individual mind.

But the mind can observe as well as meditate. Impressionism can be dramatic in another way. Narrative from the vividly realized point of view of a character makes him a participant. Impressionism may thus brilliantly exploit the drama of recognition and discovery. The limited consciousness acts as a spotlight which may illuminate, sensation by sensation, perception by perception, at once the horrors of the mind within and the horrors of the situation without. Even so, impressionism is here once more beset with limitations that can only be suggested. The point-of-view character cannot be too active, or he will have no time to verbalize and report. He cannot be too violent, or his sensations and emotions may become incommunicable. In short, the reader cannot be too close to the scene of the crime. In Browning's monologues, murderers recollect, but do not commit, their murders.

In the original pamphlet of 1842, *Dramatic Lyrics* has no table of contents. Perhaps to interest and reassure, the poems are arranged—partially at least—according to their subject matter and complication. The "Cavalier Tunes" illustrate two impressionist elements: they combine moving—in this case marching and horseback—points of view with the colloquial gusto of the drinking song:

> Hampden to hell, and his obsequies' knell
> Serve Hazelrig, Fiennes, and young Harry as well!
> England, good cheer! Rupert is near!
> Kentish and loyalists, keep we not here. . . .[18]

In "Porphyria," the madman speaks—convincingly enough—in polished and condensed tetrameters; "Through the Metidja" is hypnotically stark and rapid; "The Pied Piper," definitely post-Debussy. "Waring" admirably suggests the fashionable talk of Victorian men about town; "Rudel," the symbolic elaborateness of medieval troubadours; and "Artemis Prologuizes," the swift simplicity of the Greek tragedians. "One of the very best antique fragments I know," wrote Matthew Arnold[19] of this little poem, which was to have introduced a whole play in the Greek manner.

"In a Gondola" is quite as dramatic as it is impressionistic—a one-act opera produced on a revolving stage with exotic sets—complete with conspiracy, melodrama, and a violent love-death. What is real about this poem is of course the love that overrides all barriers—physical, social, and possibly moral—to find justification in its very intensity and exclusive devotion to the beloved. In a manner highly prophetic of Robert's affair with Elizabeth, the lovers vie with each other in mutual adoration and self-abasement. Love so intense and reckless must, at least in literature, be brief. "In a Gondola" presents the supreme or significant moment, not as in *Sordello* expanded into an eternity of bewildering complication, but contracted to a single ecstatic experience. Such moral impressionism is a boon to the dramatic lyric, for if a lifetime may be explained in a moment, then a lyric may explain a lifetime. Here again movement—this time of a nautical Shelleyan variety—is basic to theme and structure, and indeed to diction and prosody. The first stanza, or song, with its rippling triples and feminine rhymes, gives at once a barcarole effect that determines mood and feeling. The gondola moves with musical ease not through a Shelleyan world of fantastic natural beauty, but through an urban one of sordidness and danger:

> Past we glide, and past, and past!
> What's that poor Agnese doing
> Where they make the shutters fast?
> Grey Zanobi's just a-wooing
> To his couch the purchased bride:
> Past we glide![20]

The refrain suggests Byron's romantic irony in reverse. Realistic perception does not annihilate lyric rapture, but exalts it. The same effect can be observed on a grander scale in *The Ring and the Book.*

A more complex achievement in music, movement, and point of view is "The Pied Piper of Hamelin." The music, urgent as castanets, is elaborately descriptive:

> Rats!
> They fought the dogs and killed the cats,
> And bit the babies in the cradles,
> And ate the cheeses out of the vats,
> And licked the soup from the cooks' own ladles,
> Split open the kegs of salted sprats,
> Made nests inside men's Sunday hats,
> And even spoiled the women's chats,
> By drowning their speaking
> With shrieking and squeaking
> In fifty different sharps and flats.[21]

The dominant rhyme, six times repeated, multiplies the number, sharpens the noise, insists on the ubiquity, and accumulates the nuisance of rats. This passage, and others more extreme and elaborate in the same vein, indicate how important onomatopoeia is to Browning's poetry. The impressionistic emphasis on immediacy, or direct appeal, fosters a tendency to convey meaning by the sound, as well as the symbolism, of language.

Browning suggests point of view with a novelist's skill and resource. The reader shares quickly in the exasperation of the people, the puzzlement of the mayor and his corporation, the ecstasy of the single rat survivor on hearing the Piper's music, the complacent avarice and duplicity of the city officials, and the ecstasy of the single child survivor. Of these, the rat's vision of heaven is a triumph of eccentric point of view.

In "My Last Duchess" we peer, through the somewhat anonymous eyes of the ambassador, at the inhumanly cold and ruthless Duke, and beyond, through the inhumanly cold and ruthless eyes of the Duke, at his victim—the joyous, warm-hearted Duchess:

> Will't please you sit and look at her? I said
> "Frà Pandolf" by design, for never read
> Strangers like you that pictured countenance,
> The depth and passion of its earnest glance,
> But to myself they turned (since none puts by
> The curtain I have drawn for you, but I)
> And seemed as they would ask me, if they durst,
> How such a glance came there.

The portrait and the Count's ambassador are brilliantly brought to life by the effect of one on the other. Here point of view produces drama, irony, complication, and even relativity—at least the Duke seems to feel that his wife was deluded partly by a much mistaken sense of good form:

> such stuff
> Was courtesy, she thought, and cause enough
> For calling up that spot of joy.[22]

Yet the speaker's indignation gives a clue to his sincerity. The denouement contains a suggestion of paradox which Browning must have greatly relished. Confessing murder in a spirit of virtuous indignation, the Duke reveals that his wife was the victim of an impasse: she was unable to grasp his notion of pride, and he was too proud to explain it to her. But why does this polished, fastidious monster draw the curtain for the stranger through whom he is arranging his next marriage? Apparently, to remove any possible doubts regarding his fitness as a husband. Obviously, he had no recourse but to do away with his last duchess.

Drama and impressionism had informed lyric and narrative poetry before Browning so freshly gave inward events the immediacy, vigor, and conflict of outward drama. In *The Canterbury Tales*, the Pardoner's Prologue is in somewhat the satirical manner of Browning's "Sludge." On the other hand, Robert Southwell's "St. Peter's Complaint" is an example of sympathetic projection. The author identifies with the weakness and remorse of the saint. In the eighteenth century, pre-romantic taste for picturesque or ghastly tableaux, together with pre-romantic sympathy with primitives, savages, and other exotics—as well, no doubt, as many other causes—produced monologues in unprecedented numbers. Joseph Warton's "The Dying Indian" represents a Browningesque conjunction of the first person with eccentric character.

The bridge between Browning and the past, however, seems to have been not so much the work of Warton, Gray, and Cowper, as that of Burns and the Scottish pastoral poets. Burns was a poet with a marked dramatic gift, writing a free dialect style in a highly dramatic tradition. James U. Rundle has pointed out how much the "Spanish Cloister" owes to "Holy Willie's Prayer."[23] In its smug and hypnotized Calvinism, "Johannes Agricola" seems equally indebted to the same poem. "The Jolly Beggars" and "Tam O'Shanter" provided precedent for the rough masculine gusto of "Cavalier Tunes," "Fra Lippo Lippi," and other poems—as well as for the weird and jocular rhymes, the combinations of grotesqueness and violence with convincing intimacy and humor, in such a work as "The Pied Piper."

Insofar as it was both dramatic and impressionistic Burns' dialect poetry may well have exerted a strong influence on Browning. What Burns lacked were inwardness, psychological complication, moral and philosophical didacticism, historical dimension. Such qualities Browning seems to have found mainly in nineteenth-century romanticism. He is obviously indebted to Landor's *Imaginary Conversations*—notably for the technique of implying complex scene and action by dramatic speech, and for the precedent of giving a realistic historical setting either to a dramatic episode or to an illustrious personage capable of communicating truth with authority to nineteenth-century readers. Doubtless Browning got some of his historical vividness from Scott, and even more from Carlyle—from the latter, also, some of the impressionistic violence of his style and some of the dramatic didacticism with which he dealt in illustrious personages.

Wordsworth provided a basis in theory and an example of inwardness. Long before Browning, he had depicted "incidents in the development of a soul."[24] From "Tintern Abbey" to *The Prelude,* he analyzed, with an elaborate impressionistic philosophy, moments creatively significant at least to Wordsworth, exhibiting a psychological subtlety comparable to that with which Browning analyzed the lady's sudden decision in "The Glove" or the Duke's failure to act in "The Statue and the Bust." In fact, the romantic interest in reverie, self-analysis, and confession produced what might be called the auto-monologue. "Tintern Abbey" is an auto-monologue with a setting and an auditor. Coleridge's "Dejection: An Ode" is an auto-monologue with a setting and an auditor in a fairly dramatic style.

But the style needed to be more dramatic. With his "selection of language really used by men," his "spontaneous overflow of powerful feelings," and his incidents and situations made interesting "by tracing in them . . . the manner in which we associate ideas in a state of excitement,"[25] Wordsworth had outlined a theory of dramatically impressionistic style. Actually, of course, poets from Chaucer to Pope had been making a sophisticated, satirical use of such a style. More recently, Burns had practiced it—though with less decorum than Wordsworth would have wished—on a dialect level.

Byron practiced it on the level at which Browning wrote—having carried it, in *Don Juan* and other poems, to Mercutian extremities of whimsical association and shocking anticlimax.[26] An original genius fascinated with his own pose of splendid improvisation, a nobleman with a gentlemanly contempt for solemn poetry and careful craftsmanship, a complex sentimentalist half angry he could not take Childe Harold quite seriously and half resolved to grow up to mature commonsense, Byron found in his letter-writing style (as well, apparently, as in Pulci, Freri, Pope, and Dryden) a medium in which he could be at once a titan and a gentleman, a poet and a Regency buck; in which he could talk low scandal and high philosophy, create and annihilate the lyric rapture, deflating poetic first thoughts of romantic spontaneity with prosaic second thoughts of cynical reflection. This style—a kind of *a cappella* choir of all the Byrons—is wonderful enough in limited passages, but in the long run it exalts temperament almost to the exclusion of artistic purpose. Temperament, moralizing and immoralizing, makes *Beppo* all prologue, shriveling the story itself to a mere anecdote.

And yet Browning seems to have read *Beppo* very carefully. Many of his poems evoke the same brilliant Italian setting with the same gusto, the same easy, worldly tone, the same confidential intimacy, the same dramatic, prose-poetry complexity of style. "Up at a Villa—Down in the City" seems to extend the parallel. As Byron declares a preference of Italy to England, mocking and paradoxical to English readers, the preference of Browning's "Italian person of quality" for city over country mildly mocks Victorian romantic readers. Both preferences are expressed in a curious mixture of poetic feeling and prose detail. Byron's seemingly ingenious, actually calculated attack on Englishmen is paralleled in Browning by a subtly limited, eccentric point of view.

Though Byron wrote several monologues, notably "The Prisoner of Chillon" and "The Lament of Tasso," he wrote none in his conversational style. At first, he seems to have associated that style with its traditionally satiric, mock-heroic vein; later he associated it so inextricably with the license and violence of his own moods that he could not possibly tame it to the restraints of a dramatic art. At his best, Browning could. He set the staggering, sprawling beast firmly on its feet, sobered its St. Vitus dance of irony, and taught it to run smoothly in harness. More broadly, he endowed with the psychological inwardness of Wordsworth and the colloquial dramatic articulateness of Byron the lovers, monsters, criminals, and madmen of romantic fashion, and placed them with unparalleled vividness in complex and exciting situations.

Browning continually experimented with point of view. But limited and graphic physical point of view, limited and eccentric psychological point of view, together with the synecdoche which they both involve, appear frequently in romantic and Victorian poetry. Coleridge's "Christabel" is a third-person narrative which at times vividly realizes the psychologically limited, and the physically moving, point of view. "The Ancient Mariner," except for brief passages, graphically presents a surrealistic motion-picture view in a narrative monologue spoken by a demoniac of the Wandering Jew species. Keats' "Eve of St. Agnes" builds up within the omniscient third person interesting contrasts and limitations in point of view, beginning with the cold-numbed animals in the forest and the ancient beadsman in his icy chapel, moving to the warm, brilliant hall full of music and youthful revelers, and coming to rest on Madeline, who, deep in her private solitude of reverie, sees only the dancers' feet as she sits with downcast eyes. Shelley's "The Cloud" is written from the rather surprising point of view of the cloud itself; *Queen Mab*, so familiar to Browning's youth, from the astro-*encyclopédiste* view of a philosophical Fairy Queen of the skies. Most significant of all, perhaps, is "Julian and Maddalo," written in an agony of remorse after Harriet's death: Byron and Shelley visit a Venetian bedlam and encounter Shelley's alter ego, who has been driven mad by the desertion of his beloved and, apparently, by the disappointment of his humanitarian projects. Here guilt and self-pity have devised a situation worthy of Joseph Conrad. Madness speaks not only from the lips of the madman, but from the imagery and the expository frame. In certain passages "Julian and Maddalo" comes close to being the monologue of a madman written by a madman. However little he may have understood Shelley's life and character when he was writing his first monologues, Browning must have seen that there were two Shelleys and a great deal of dramatic potentiality in this poem.

Prose was equally instructive. Doctrinaire and Gothic novels are full of the eccentric, insane, or monstrous point of view more or less clearly defined. In Godwin's *Caleb Williams,* the protagonist speaks out of the nightmare isolation of an innocent man persecuted by society as a criminal. In Bulwer's *Falkland,* the protagonist is a noble savage; in James Hogg's *Private Memoirs and Confessions of a Justified Sinner,* he is an extreme Antinomian who is led by native inclination and pious doctrine into theological argument and personal friendship with the Devil and thence, through weird psychological experiences involving split personality and various *Doppelgänger,* into a high-minded but steadily less satisfactory career of crime and murder.[27] By the thirties literature was moving rapidly in Browning's direction. When he was writing his earliest monologues, another bold technical innovator, Edgar Allan Poe, was in a series of lurid short stories exploiting the same kind of psychological sensationalism by likewise conducting readers inside the minds of madmen and murderers. The narrator in "The Tell-Tale Heart" reminds one of Porphyria's self-satisfied lover; the narrator in "The Cask of Amontillado," of the careful, gloating avenger in "The Laboratory."

It need hardly be said that nineteenth-century drama and melodrama, whether of the closet or the stage, had its own adventures in impressionistic diction, its own physical violence, its own criminals and avengers—often pale, ranting shadows of Iago and Othello. What is interesting for Browning's poetry and particularly for the monologue is a steady romantic tendency toward introspection, reverie, and the single point of view in isolation, noticeable, for example, in such works as *Faust* and *Prometheus Unbound.* Byron might have dispensed with all but a single character. Dr. Frank Sayers and the youthful

Southey actually did—in six monodramas, each spoken by an exotic character about to meet a death more or less suicidal.[28]

Of the writers of verse monologues, the most significant, next to Browning, is of course Tennyson. "Œnone" is an essentially lyrical monologue which owes much to Theocritus and the pastoral tradition. "Ulysses" and "Tithonus" are epic monologues in which, as in "Cleon" and "Rabbi Ben Ezra," the expression of an ideal or a criticism of life is more important than dramatic revelation of character. "St. Simeon Stylites" is less like Browning. The character is well conceived, and he speaks with vividness and passion, but oratorically rather than dramatically, in expository rather than psychological sequence: in short, he explains rather than reveals himself, so that his expiatory column seems distressingly like a very high speaker's platform. Moreover, the auditor, Christ in Heaven, is a Deity apostrophized rather than a presence dramatically felt. On the other hand, "Northern Farmer: Old Style" is very much in Browning's vein. The auditor and the setting are graphically realized; the speech is authentic dialect; the point of view is dramatically and ironically limited. In fact, it is in theme and much else a looser and less elevated "The Bishop Orders His Tomb." But dramatic immediacy, impressionistic complications are the exception in Tennyson; in Browning, they are the rule. No one has really equaled him in writing these singular little closet dramas to which he chiefly owes his fame.

CHAPTER 9

Friends

1842-45

In his early thirties, Browning somewhat fastidiously and coolly enjoyed the friendship of several men of letters. To serve them, he published considerably in periodicals—in fact, more than was suspected until recently.

In 1933 T. Sturge Moore edited *Works and Days*, a selection from the diaries and letters of Michael Field. "Michael Field" was not one poet, but two poetesses. In fact, "Michael" was Katherine Bradley; and "Field," Edith Cooper. These two late Victorian poetesses, the select friends of a few discriminating people, had as young ladies been intimate with the elderly widower, Robert Browning, whom—doubtless for exquisite reasons—they privately called "The Old." In 1895 Michael Field visited Sarianna Browning and Robert's son Pen at Asolo and there, amid conversation heavy with Browningiana, explored alternatively a landscape and a library, sacred to the memory of the great poet. Reading, many years later, the account of this visit in *Works and Days*, Professor Donald Smalley came on the diary note: "Now I am going to read 'the Old's' article on *Tasso and Chatterton* in the *Foreign Quarterly Review* for July 1842."[1] Apparently Professor Smalley was not surprised, and turning to the correct number of the *Review*, read an anonymous article which gave every indication of Browning's hand.

Forster had become editor of *The Foreign Quarterly* in 1842 and was known to have depended heavily on his friends for the first number. Apparently, he had asked Browning, as an Italian scholar, to review R. H. Wilde's work on Tasso. Browning devoted seven paragraphs to Wilde's book, and then some twenty pages to reflections suggested by a quite different book—C. B. Willcox's new edition of Chatterton.[2]

The digression was inevitable. Robert had once dreamed of writing the works of half-a-dozen fictitious authors. Chatterton, when scarcely more than a boy, had actually written the poetical works of a busy, important monk named Rowley, inventing a splendid medieval Bristol for him to live in and a quaint medieval English for him to speak. Unfortunately, Rowley's life and Rowley's Bristol were so thoroughly satisfactory to Chatterton's heady ambitions that he fiercely resented the poverty-stricken errand-boy existence which he led—on the whole, recklessly and amiably enough—in his own shabby eighteenth-century Bristol. In those days a good many people were dreaming, editing, and forging their way back into the Middle Ages. Chatterton managed to impose some of his manuscripts on the credulity of local antiquarians. He attempted a similar deceit on Horace Walpole and failed. Failing once more in London to realize the magnificent success which he was describing in letters to friends and relatives at home, he gave way to despair and committed suicide. Chatterton seems to have resembled Browning a little as Mr. Hyde resembled Dr. Jekyll. He carried through Browning's boyish gusto in secrecy to actual forgery and carried rebelliousness worse than that of the poet in *Pauline* to a defiant self-destruction which that poet hardly dared suggest between long paragraphs of remorse.

Such a Chatterton Browning was far too interested and clever to accept. By ingenious special pleading and by dexterously forcing the facts to argue against themselves, he converted the reckless, amiable self-deceiving young poet into an earnest Victorian, similar of course to Browning, who devoted the whole of his short life to retrieving a single false step.

Having faith in the world and the world's idols, wrote Browning, "genius almost invariably begins to develop itself by imitation."[3] Chatterton differed from other geniuses only in that his imitation was so vivid and real that Bristol antiquarians eagerly accepted it. Their hunger for antiquities betrayed him into forgery, and their indifference to poetry put him in the dilemma of having to give up Rowley if he gave up deceit. And yet what poet does not publish his first work under a borrowed name or no name at all, sensing that the world envies him his gift, for poetry provides "a free way for impulses that can find vent in no other channel"?[4]

In Chatterton's earliest poetry, Browning discerns the beginnings of that kind of moral sense which causes a poet to distrust reason and to fulfill his mission. That moral sense directed Chatterton to leave Bristol behind him and seek an honest career in London. The offer of Rowley manuscripts to Dodsley and Walpole were attempts to wind up the past, for how could he prove his poetic ability without being able to point to Rowley? To be sure, he practiced some deceit in

London, but "it is old as the world itself, the tendency of certain spirits to subdue each man by perceiving what will master him, by straightway supplying it from their own resources, and so obtaining, as tokens of success, his admiration, or fear, or wonder."[5] In his peroration Browning develops Rowley into a symbol of temptation: a life of common drudgery is better than one of deceitful creativity. *"Any thing but Rowley!"*[6] Chatterton's intellect sketched out profitable deceptions; his moral nature destroyed them. His death, like Sordello's, was a moral victory. Clearly, Browning found in Chatterton enough of himself to set the whole exculpatory process in motion once more.

Browning could pity his own weaknesses in Chatterton. In a much more eminent poet, he could see nothing but venality. On April 4, 1843, Wordsworth accepted the poet-laureateship. He deserved the honor and, for the past twenty years a sincere Tory, he could accept it with good conscience. Yet which Wordsworth had won the laureateship—the taciturn, passionate young revolutionary who climbed mountains and wrote unforgettable poetry, or the austere, white-haired old Tory who sat self-importantly at Mr. Kenyon's dinner table and from time to time published quantities of dull verse? Pondering and suffering events, personal and political, a man of great moral and speculative enthusiasm had slowly and cautiously revised a revolutionary creed into Tory Christianity. That circuitous, very English Odyssey was scarcely understood in 1843. Browning gave it the obvious explanation which his old heroes Byron and Shelley had given. His "Lost Leader," written about this time, is certainly aimed at Wordsworth and probably aimed at his acceptance of the laureateship. With considerable savagery of New Testament metaphor that enduring old gentleman is damned in this world, to be rather sentimentally and grandiosely pardoned in the next.

Browning's opinions on Chatterton and Wordsworth afford an unusual insight into the way his mind worked. Where his feelings were at all involved, detachment was out of the question. Few sane and honest men have manipulated the facts so dexterously while apprehending so little of their real meaning. To think was to rationalize an emotion. A very little reflection ought to have shown him that his own surrender from Shelley's ranks was not unlike Wordsworth's political surrender. But his mind was closed: he disliked Wordsworth. In any case, "The Lost Leader" was a mistake. Wordsworth was ceasing to be a political partisan and rapidly becoming a national hero. Browning expiated with a lifetime of embarrassed explanations.

"The Lost Leader" illustrates how much Browning identified himself with contemporary liberalism. Perhaps he did not know politics, but he knew people who did. He knew W. J. Fox and his circle; and on the romantic, poetic edge of that circle, he knew Leigh Hunt, also the friend and neighbor of Browning's scarcely liberal friend Carlyle.

Browning's friendship with Hunt is worth notice not because it was close, but because it linked him with a circle and an era. Hunt was a living repository of Shelleyan tradition, a very vocal relic of the past in which poetry and liberty were one. Like most relics, he was disappointing. Going as a young woman to a small literary tea followed by "a substantial supper at ten," Camilla Toulmin found Hunt playing Sir Oracle with Browning among the listeners. Hunt "harangued rather than conversed." He was "a thickset man of nearly sixty, with fine dark eyes and whitened hair, with his portly person encased in a white waistcoat, which was amply displayed by his habit of throwing back the lappets of his coat and inserting his thumbs in the armholes of his waistcoat. . . . He seemed to me the very type of self-satisfied, arrogant vulgarity, a man without reverence, and, consequently, without the understanding which reverence gives." Browning spoke little, "but I was struck," says Camilla, "with the quiet dignity of his deportment, and his impression of commanding intelligence."[7] Yet if Camilla was harsh with Hunt, Keats had been harsher: "Hunt does one harm by making fine things petty, and beautiful things hateful. Through him I am indifferent to Mozart, I care not for white Busts—and many a glorious thing when associated with him becomes a nothing."[8] Hunt lived by preference in a permanent second-rate Charles Lamb essay, using genuine talents to make himself the hero of innumerable intimate teas followed by substantial suppers at ten.

In fact, he had in youth won permanent fame by being the life of the party on the most solemn occasion of his career. Sent to prison for libeling the Regent, he had with paint, wallpaper, distemper—and the assistance of his wife—converted his cell into a "bower of roses under a Florentine heaven," where, as Byron's "wit in a dungeon," he had practiced his social graces on some of the most distinguished men in the kingdom.[9] Thereafter he had continued to stand by his principles in a very youthful, light-hearted, and even frivolous manner.

Hunt was a romantic who had failed to die young but who had made up for the deficiency by not growing old or at least not obviously old. Caricaturing him as Skimpole in *Bleak House*, Dickens describes "a damaged young man," "a romantic youth who had undergone some unique process of depreciation."[10] The quizzical smile still glimmered on a countenance of cast-iron gravity. The gestures were still exuberant, the puns still rapid and high-spirited, the defense of liberty and nonsense still effortlessly ingenious and eloquent. Many intelligent people adored him and many who did not forgave him. W. J. Linton blamed the negative revolutionism of 1798 for his carelessness about debts and other people's money. Even Carlyle could be sarcastic only about the appalling shambles of his domestic arrangements. By welcoming Mrs. Carlyle's porridge dinners with orations of joy, by stirring up his host to Guy Fawkes exhibitions of logic and denunciation and then rising from the ruins of half-a-dozen flimsy positions to sum up the battle flatteringly to his own disadvantage, Hunt had turned the Scottish Jeremiah into a monument of patience and indulgence—toward himself.

For Browning, Hunt was a man who had once seen Shelley plain, and who had known how to value the privilege. In his fantastic way, Hunt had been loyal to Shelley as he had been loyal to his political principles. Before sailing on his fatal excursion, Shelley had borrowed from Hunt a copy of Keats' last volume of poetry, which, the only one of its kind in Italy, he had faithfully promised to return by his own hand. Hunt made Browning smile by assuring him, with cast-iron gravity unrelieved, that Shelley would one day appear to fulfill his promise. When on the hot, sunny beach at Viareggio the funeral pyre had burned low, Trelawny, the only man present who dared witness the spectacle, had at the risk of a burned hand pulled out Shelley's heart. Hunt begged for and obtained it. Mary Shelley pressed him for it, but Hunt's love for the dead man conspired with his desire to possess keepsakes. He simply could not give his treasure up—and did so only after a severe struggle with himself. In 1856, when the Brownings were showing unmistakable symptoms of immortality, Hunt requested and received locks of hair for his unrivaled collection. "The capillary attractions have been laid up with their illustrious brethren," he wrote with satisfaction.[11]

As most of Robert's intellectual life seems traceable to his father's library, so his social life seems to unfold from the cottage of William Fox and Eliza Flower. There he met another politico-poetic figure, Richard Henry (later Hengist) Horne. Again, Robert was cordial—but reserved. Horne was a middle-aged, athletic man with a bald dome, a dead-white complexion, and flamboyant red whiskers. The red whiskers symbolically announced that Horne had adventures to unfold. He had already lived two consecutive lives. As a young midshipman in the Mexican navy, he had fought in the war of independence against Spain, taking part in the siege of Vera Cruz and the storming of San

Juan Ulloa, and narrowly escaping death before a Spanish firing squad. He had broken two ribs swimming under Niagara on a bet, lost all his money at billiards, been ship-wrecked in the St. Lawrence River, and very nearly gone down in the mid-Atlantic when mutineers set afire the vessel in which he sailed. Restored to his native England, this much-enduring Ulysses turned calmly to literature and produced tragedy and epic as coolly as he had fought the Spanish, publishing, among other works, *Cosmo de' Medici* in 1837, *Gregory VII, A Tragedy,* in 1840, and in 1843 the short epic *Orion,* which, at the quixotic price of a farthing a copy, went through six editions in a year.

Having by 1843 traveled considerably in the realms of gold, as well as elsewhere, Horne astutely decided that the time was ripe for a general estimate of contemporary literature. He chose as his assistant in this delicate and arduous project Miss Elizabeth Barrett, a young lady who was reported to have lain for five years in a darkened bedroom. Mr. Horne had never seen her—hardly anyone had; but, like a surprising number of people, he corresponded with her, and knew her to be well qualified in literature. She was already growing famous as a poetess and was formidably well known as a scholar and bluestocking. Browning also assisted the critical project in the humbler task of selecting mottoes.

Horne called his work *A New Spirit of the Age,* inviting a comparison which neither he nor his collaborator could possibly sustain. The period was hard to judge, one of inflated writing and still more inflated reputation; and Horne was trying to satisfy at once his own better judgment and the most extravagant fashion. *A New Spirit of the Age,* two bulky volumes long, was garrulous, confused, ponderously light-hearted and conscientiously myopic. Dickens, Tennyson, Macaulay, and Carlyle emerge as the important figures, but whole chapters are devoted to men like Talfourd and Ainsworth, who now swell histories of English literature by scarcely a sentence. Browning is courageously declared to be great, yet unceremoniously fitted into a chapter with the now-forgotten J. W. Marston.

Browning himself must have read that chapter with very mixed feelings. Horne begins by referring to "the little known works of Mr. Browning"[12] and then plunges into a five-page discussion of *Paracelsus.* When would critics ever finish with *Paracelsus*? Sandwiching in a few paragraphs on Marston between strong praise of *Paracelsus* and even stronger praise of the Ottima-Sebald scene in *Pippa,* as well as of *King Victor* and *The Return of the Druses,* Horne then actually devotes his remaining twelve pages to *Sordello,* beginning with a very long paragraph about its obscurity and concluding with a fine purple-patch about Browning's future. Horne's treatment of *Sordello* shows both courage and discrimination. He dares to say that it "abounds with beauties" and that it has been treated "with great injustice."[13] Writing of the chapter to Domett, Joseph Arnould was moved to Carlylean splendor: "Horne (Orion Horne) has done him good service. . . . Friend Robert he stirs up to good effect, and makes him roar out very nobly some of the grandest passages in 'Paracelsus.' "[14]

The tragic illness of a friend now led Browning to publish several notable poems in a periodical. Having spent his life writing and editing other people's magazines, Thomas Hood founded in 1844 his own *Hood's Magazine and Comic Miscellany.* The January issue sold well, but difficulties with his partner and his printers proved so exhausting to a delicate constitution that by May both Hood and the magazine were prostrate. F. O. Ward, a contributor, stepped into the breach and got out the June issue with a note explaining that Hood had been stricken with consumption. Immediately, poems, sketches, and articles flooded in from Dickens, Browning, Landor, and many other friends of the gentle and convivial editor. Already in the June issue Browning had contributed both "Claret and Tokay" and "The Laboratory"; in the latter a lady of the Old Regime stops for poison on her way to the King's ball. Like the hero of Wilde's "Pen, Pencil, and Poison" many years later, she plans to murder with taste and ingenuity:

> To carry pure death in an earring, a casket,
> A signet, a fan-mount, a filigree basket.

To the July issue Browning contributed "Garden Fancies," of which the first, "The Flower's Name," seems to celebrate his mother's garden; and the second, "Sibrandus Schafnaburgensis"—at least by token—his father's library. In the August issue appeared "The Boy and the Angel," and in the March issue of 1845, "The Tomb at St. Praxed's,"[15] the product of an Italian journey.

CHAPTER 10

To a Third-Floor Chamber

1844-45

Browning sailed for Naples in August 1844, once more in quest of artistic renewal. The voyage out seems to have restored him considerably, for he wrote "Home-Thoughts, from the Sea" while rounding Cape St. Vincent, and "How They Brought the Good News from Ghent to Aix," while skirting the coast of North Africa.[1] Actually, he was embarked on a double voyage. "I don't think I sent you a copy of my last play—'Colombe,'" he had written Domett in July: "here you shall have it—but I feel myself so much stronger, if flattery not deceive, that I shall stop some things that were meant to follow, and begin again. I really seem to have something fresh to say."[2] The "but" following *Colombe* suggests that plays were the things he meant to stop; and his most characteristic writing at the time suggests that the "something fresh" was to be expressed in dramatic monologues. During the next few years his speakers were for the most part Italians and their intense and eccentric perspectives necessarily directed toward Italian life and history.

To be sure, on his first voyage he had already discovered modern Italy while searching for medieval. The autobiographical excursus in the third book of *Sordello* gives a picture of Italian poverty; and *Pippa,* a picture of Austrian oppression and Italian patriotism. Doubtless Browning found the cause of freedom, like that of poverty, more moving in an Italian than an English setting. There was no doubt who was right and who was wrong. One could put aside all troublesome economic and constitutional questions and burn confidently with poetic indignation. Moreover, recent events had once again put the Italian situation vividly before the minds of all Englishmen and made a popular hero of a refugee named Mazzini. Mazzini was a close friend of the Carlyles.

Of all the lands occupied by Napoleon, Italy had seemed the least infected by revolutionary enthusiasm. It therefore became a chief victim of the Congress of Vienna and of Metternich's genius for turning the clock back. Austria acquired the rich provinces of Lombardy and Venetia and, as the principal military power of the peninsula, guided the restoration. Austrian archdukes were established in Modena and Tuscany, and the old ruling families, nearly everywhere else. All the blessings of legitimacy and foreign domination followed—seven labyrinths of custom walls, seven little chaoses of ignorant and inwardly conflicting bureaucracies, high taxes, dungeons full of distinguished liberals and professors, a languishing commerce, a stagnant intellectual and educational life, a servile press, and a censorship which, in the Austrian provinces, sought to control both the living and the dead, condemning Alfieri and emending Dante. If the Italian eighteenth century seems a long, shabby, petty-court ceremony, the nineteenth century was one long conspiracy—so vast, intricate, elaborately hierarchical, and theatrically futile that it involved almost the whole population in what was itself little more than a dangerous, secret kind of ceremony. Every city and province was thronged with conspirators, secret societies, and secret police, eluding and pursuing each other, plotting and counterplotting, with inexhaustible gusto and ingenuity. Where there were so many revolutionaries, there had to be a little revolution. The spark was a fine, spontaneous, mystical, utterly impractical patriotism, yearning, like unrequited love, for fulfillment in death.

The interval between 1820 and 1844 saw the rise of Mazzini, whose *grande passion* for Italy lasted a lifetime. He gave Italian freedom both a head and a tongue: the one full of German transcendentalism, the other eloquent with a rhetoric equally splendid and vague. Many passages in his writings might serve as footnotes to *Sordello* or *Sartor*. Truth is "hidden in an intention inaccessible to analysis."[3] Progress is but the evolution of divine thought. His slogan was God and the People; his ultimate goal, a universal socialistic republic; his immediate goal, an Italian socialistic republic. Unfortunately, he was nearly all vision and hardly any action. He spiritualized politics and moralized conspiracy, but made neither much more effective than before. His career began characteristically. He was arrested in 1830—ostensibly for recruiting Carbonari, actually for giving every appearance of thinking too much. A half-year in prison produced only further thought; Mazzini decided very wisely that the Carbonari pursued conspiracy too much as *l'art pour l'art*, and he conceived Young Italy, a comparatively straightforward organization which, with a modicum of cloak-and-dagger mystification, was to work for the definite objective of a unified, republican Italy.

Young Italy was founded and grew rapidly. Mazzini directed its affairs from exile—first in Marseilles, then in Switzerland, and by 1837 in England. A slim, extremely handsome man with chiseled features, long curling black hair, a thrilling voice, and brilliant dark eyes through which *la grande passion* burned with a guileless, compelling ardor, he exerted an hypnotic effect on all kinds of people. Italians conspired and died for him. English ladies gave teas and became transcendentalists for him. Even the Carlyles were impressed. Mazzini now attached himself to Mrs. Carlyle's circle of eccentric gentlemen—so firmly that Signora Mazzini, his mother, had to be assured from time to time that his feeling for the Scottish lady was that of a brother for a sister. Meanwhile, he failed pathetically to measure up to the dimensions of a Carlylean hero. Who could have confidence in a man who planned to invade Italy in balloons? Mrs. Carlyle was disillusioned with him as a conspirator. Did he not confide all his secrets to her? A model of Scottish thrift, she was also exasperated with his benevolence. "I never saw a mortal man who so completely made himself into 'minced meat' for the universe!"[4] Moreover, while other Italian patriots died in Italy, he subsisted laboriously on journalism and even declined temporarily into the wine-and-sausage business. Worst of all, he denounced the doctrine of hero worship itself. Though he conceded him all the moral virtues, Carlyle detected a "sick Sentimentalism" in his politics. To the unsympathetic eye of prophecy, the passionate lover of Italy had begun to look like a rather seedy bachelor resigned to a broken heart.

Mazzini's opportunity came just as Robert was preparing to sail for Naples. Revolutionary martyrdom was following its usual course of heroism, treachery, and death when a curious episode, partly Italian and partly English, ensued. Inspired by Mazzini's writings, two young officers—paradoxically the sons of an Austrian admiral—determined to join one of the ephemeral, infinitesimal revolts which were constantly breaking out in Calabria. Mazzini learned of their intentions and tried in vain to dissuade them. With some nineteen others, Attilio and Emilio Bandiera landed on the Calabrian coast, were betrayed by a comrade, fell into the hands of Bourbon troops, and were shot—shouting "Long live Italy!"—by a weeping executionary squad. There, as so often before, the curtain might have gone down, but that Mazzini had noticed that his letters were postmarked twice. Had the British government been opening his mail? With self-addressed letters, with envelopes containing grains of sand or sealed with wax, he performed, in part before witnesses, a series of ingenious experiments which absolutely confirmed his suspicions. He now made a public statement, explaining his experiments, drawing the obvious conclusion, and referring ominously to the death of the Bandiera brothers. Suspicion naturally focused on the Home and Foreign Secretaries—Sir James Graham and the Earl of Aberdeen. Apparently the British government had blood on its hands!

The world was now treated to a display of peculiarly British temperament. The House and the press exploded into one of those hurricanes of rhetorical indignation which are the drama and extravagance of a moderate and sensible nation. Graham was assailed for hours and days by Sheil, Macaulay, Milnes, Duncombe, and many others. His name became a verb for the act of bloody betrayal. Even *The Times* was moved to editorialize, but while roundly condemning the Government, managed to insinuate a snobbish and insular sneer against Mazzini. Carried away by the passion of the moment, Carlyle replied with a masterly letter, in which he turned the sneer with uncharacteristic delicacy and concluded in dignified panegyric of his friend. The situation now proceeded to its final phase: a committee whitewashed the Government in the ritual language of sanity and moderation; while Mazzini, now a famous man and the friend of many distinguished liberal politicians, philosophers, and editors, flooded the press with the ardor and idealism of *la grande passion,* reviewing the ethics of the case with lofty indignation and drawing, in a long and eloquent pamphlet published in 1845, a dark but convincing picture of Italy under Austrian rule. "The best thing that had ever befallen him," observed Carlyle, not without envy, but certainly without any further extravagance of friendship or loyalty, "was the opening of his letters by Sir James Graham. . . . Afterwards he had innumerable dinner invitations, and got subscriptions up and down London for his Italian schools and other undertakings."[5]

Whether Robert knew Mazzini personally at just this time, or how much he knew him through the bold light and dark of the Carlyles' conversation, is not clear. In 1862, he was to accost him rather familiarly at Cheyne Row in the presence of Mrs. Carlyle: "I should know *you* anywhere!"[6] Certainly he already knew him by his writings and reputation, and probably in the flattering light of the Graham affair. How much Italy and freedom, and perhaps even Mazzini, were in his thoughts is suggested by two poems conceived after he landed at Naples and completed the following year: "England in Italy" and

"Italy in England," in 1849 renamed respectively "The Englishman in Italy" and "The Italian in England." The first seems on a casual reading to do nothing more political than to number very precisely the grapes on the vine. All the sights, smells, and activities of a south Italian harvest are described with unexampled sharpness and minuteness of observation:

> . . . girls who keep coming and going
>   With basket on shoulder,
> And eyes shut against the rain's driving;
>   Your girls that are older,—
> For under the hedges of aloe,
>   And where, on its bed
> Of the orchard's black mould, the love-apple
>   Lies pulpy and red,
> All the young ones are kneeling and filling
>   Their laps with the snails
> Tempted out by this first rainy weather,—
>   Your best of regales,
> As to-night will be proved to my sorrow,
>   When, supping in state,
> We shall feast our grape-gleaners (two dozen,
>   Three over one plate)
> With lasagne so tempting to swallow
>   In slippery ropes,
> And gourds fried in great purple slices,
>   That colour of popes.

Altogether, one gets the impression of a numerous, primitive, superstitious population harvesting an abundance only too sorely needed. On closer reading, one sees that the poem is a political pamphlet disguised as an economic treatise. It is cast as a monologue: to comfort a little Italian girl frightened by the sirocco, an English traveler recounts his impressions while exploring the plain of Sorrento. He has ascended the Vico Calvano and, gazing out on the blue infinities of sea and sky, becomes aware in a moment of vision that the watchful, sinuous mountains threaten the soft plains beneath and the pliant, servile curves of their trees and vines.

> 'T is a sensual and timorous beauty,
>   How fair! but a slave.

He looks down at the rocks of the sirens. He, like Ulysses, understands the secret of their song. Alert throughout the poem to the superstitious idolatry of the peasants, the traveler continues with an ominous description of a church festival and an even more ominous reference to a scorpion. He concludes:

> —"Such trifles!" you say?
> Fortù, in my England at home,
>   Men meet gravely to-day
> And debate, if abolishing Corn-laws
>   Be righteous and wise
> —If 't were proper, Scirocco should vanish
>   In black from the skies!

Clearly, the sirocco, like Shelley's West Wind, is as much a political as an atmospheric phenomenon.

Browning might have had the subject of the complementary poem, "The Italian in England," in mind even before he reached Naples. Relaxing for a moment from his writing, an Italian exile recalls in terse, conversational narrative how a brave peasant woman helped him escape his Austrian pursuers near Padua. "The Italian" deals explicitly and more favorably, as "The Englishman" deals implicitly and pessimistically, with Italy's cause: it concedes that Italians may be servile and treacherous, but emphasizes that they can be brave, resourceful, and patriotic. The laborious and single-minded devotion of the exile, who never knew passion except for Italy, inevitably suggests Mazzini; as the situation itself—the flight, concealment, and the betrayal by Charles—suggest the Bandiera incident.[7] Mazzini told Browning afterwards that he had read fellow exiles the poem to show them how an Englishman could sympathize with their plight.

Robert's journey had its microcosm of roadside incident with a grim aftermath. In Naples he fell in with a young Italian named Scotti, who apparently concealed beneath a handsome and romantic exterior a cool and reckoning mind. "As I write," Robert informed his sister, "I hear him disputing our bill in the next room. He does not see why we should pay for six wax candles when we have used only two."[8] The young men traveled to Rome together and there spent their mornings with an old acquaintance of Robert's father, the Countess Carducci, who pronounced Signor Scotti the handsomest man she had ever met. But in the midst of the gaieties and gallantries of a young man's excursion, Signor Scotti had been reckoning up graver matters than those of a night's lodging. Soon after he parted from Browning, he shot himself.

Little is known of this, Browning's first visit to Rome. He seems to have visited the Grotto of Egeria, where that nymph was supposed to have held with King Numa the interviews celebrated by Byron in so many stanzas of melancholy but sensible meditation. He also visited Shelley's tomb in the New Protestant Cemetery—and, apparently in commemoration, wrote the few terse, ironic lines on "Fame" which form the first part of "Earth's Immortalities."

Browning had already recorded in minutely realistic notes his impressions of the plain of Sorrento. Actually, he did not pass over Rome with a few irrelevant lines on the grave of an English poet. Where Byron had rhetoricized *in extenso* about ancient carnage and turmoil, from Romulus to the dying gladiator and the destroying Goth, Browning concentrated with great learning and subtle psychological realism on a single paradoxical case of Renaissance ecclesiasticism, bringing the reader boldly to a prelate's deathbed.

For "The Bishop Orders His Tomb," his point of departure was the ornate, glittering, recently restored interior of S. Prassede's (Saint Praxed's) church, built in 822. The tomb of Cardinal Cetive may have provided the poet with his idea, but, according to DeVane,[9] his extensive knowledge of the d'Este family supplied him with his hero—Cardinal Ippolito the Younger, brother of Ercole II, Duke of Ferrara. Like Tennyson's "St. Simeon" and his own "Soliloquy" this new monologue is a study in the horrors of spiritual pretensions debased. Indeed, it seems to owe something to both poems. Like the Spanish monk, the bishop is obsessed with hatred; and, as St. Simeon bargains with God for a martyr's crown, so the bishop bargains with his sons for a tomb.

And yet it is more. The opening nineteen lines are perhaps the finest exposition Browning ever wrote:

> Vanity, saith the preacher, vanity!
> Draw round my bed: is Anselm keeping back?
> Nephews—sons mine . . . ah God, I know not! Well—
> She, men would have to be your mother once,
> Old Gandolf envied me, so fair she was!
> What's done is done, and she is dead beside,
> Dead long ago, and I am Bishop since,
> And as she died so must we die ourselves,
> And thence ye may perceive the world's a dream.
> Life, how and what is it? As here I lie
> In this state-chamber, dying by degrees,
> Hours and long hours in the dead night, I ask

"Do I live, am I dead?" Peace, peace seems all.
Saint Praxed's ever was the church for peace;
And so, about this tomb of mine. I fought
With tooth and nail to save my niche, ye know:
—Old Gandolf cozened me, despite my care;
Shrewd was that snatch from out the corner South
He graced his carrion with, God curse the same!

The bishop's mind wanders—and the reader sees not merely the whole situation, but nearly an entire life, in all the intricacy of dazzling paradox. His life has seemed so little of a dream to him that his whole vision of eternity is bounded by the encrusted ornamentation of St. Praxed's, seen from the perspective of his burial niche:

One sees the pulpit o' the epistle-side,
And somewhat of the choir, those silent seats,
And up into the aery dome where live
The angels, and a sunbeam's sure to lurk.

The angels of his heaven are painted ones. His religion is revealed in the superbly declining series of bas-reliefs he suggests for his tomb:

The Saviour at his sermon on the mount,
Saint Praxed in a glory, and one Pan
Ready to twitch the Nymph's last garment off.

The bishop threatens feebly to bequeath his villas to the Pope. He is, however, the prisoner of his own sense of property and must leave his own to his sons. But he is not a bleak prisoner. Moving slowly through galleries of an intensely sensual imagination, he turns colors into felt objects, stones into seductions, religion into court-favor in a limitlessly opulent court:

Some lump, ah God, of *lapis lazuli,*
Big as a Jew's head cut off at the nape,
Blue as a vein o'er the Madonna's breast . . .

. . . . .

Nay, boys, ye love me—all of jasper then!
'Tis jasper ye stand pledged to, lest I grieve
My bath must needs be left behind, alas!
One block, pure green as a pistachio-nut,
There's plenty jasper somewhere in the world—

And have I not Saint Praxed's ear to pray
Horses for ye, and brown Greek manuscripts,
And mistresses with great smooth marbly limbs?

He foresees—not without masochistic pleasure in a quick, delirious descent into an aesthete's hell—the tomb his sons will give him:

Gritstone a-crumble! Clammy squares which sweat
As if the corpse they keep were oozing through—

His nearly complete spiritual atrophy, his passionless hypocrisy, his passionate hatred of the dead Gandolf, his eager scheming and utter helplessness—all heighten the element of macabre comedy in the portrait of a sensualist who, at least among other sensualists in British literature, has remarkably few rivals.[10] Also he is a Catholic prelate, whose every word can be held against him. Browning's moral gusto and Victorian prejudice are hard to separate in such stunning lines as

And then how I shall lie through centuries,
And hear the blessed mutter of the mass,
And see God made and eaten all day long,
And feel the steady candle-flame, and taste
Good strong thick stupefying incense-smoke!

Browning regarded the poem as an indictment of the Catholic Church. In submitting it for *Hood's Magazine* in February, 1845, he wrote: "I pick it out as being a pet of mine, and just the thing for the time—what with the Oxford business, and Camden society and other embroilments."[11] It is safe to surmise that many Victorians read the poem in the same spirit. In the light of his opinions, Ruskin's admiration for it indicates moral quite as much as historical zeal: in 125 lines, he declared, Browning had said as much about the Renaissance as he had in thirty pages of *The Stones of Venice.*

It was in Florence that Browning probably conceived, and perhaps wrote, "Pictor Ignotus." The poem indicates a broad familiarity with Florentine painting and is full of the intense, silent, pictorial excitement of the galleries and churches:

All I saw,
Over the canvas could my hand have flung,
Each face obedient to its passion's law,
Each passion clear proclaimed without a tongue;

Whether Hope rose at once in all the blood,
  A-tiptoe for the blessing of embrace,
Or Rapture drooped the eyes, as when her brood
  Pull down the nesting dove's heart to its place.

The theme of the monologue depends on the contrast between the contained religious formalism of the fifteenth century and vivid secular realism of the sixteenth.

I could have painted pictures like that youth's
  Ye praise so. How my soul springs up!

The painter describes what he *might* have painted and then, momentarily overcome with misgiving, breaks off:

O human faces, hath it spilt, my cup?

But he has heard a voice and seen sights. Clearly, he is obsessed by something other than the loving faces he has not portrayed.

. . . Who summoned those cold faces that begun
To press on me and judge me? Though I stooped
  Shrinking, as from the soldiery a nun,
They drew me forth, and spite of me . . . enough!

These are the most passionate and incoherent lines in the poem. He fears the self-revelation of realistic art; fears—like Browning himself—the casual curiosity and coarse judgment of the crowd. Therefore he paints

These endless cloisters and eternal aisles
  With the same series, Virgin, Babe, and Saint,
With the same cold calm beautiful regard,—
  At least no merchant traffics in my heart.

He accepts the fact that he will be forgotten. At the very close he turns directly to the youth:

O youth, men praise so,—holds their praise its worth?
Blown harshly, keeps the trump its golden cry?
  Tastes sweet the water with such specks of earth?

Apparently, the speaker suspects that to have rejected painting in the realistic style of the much-praised youth has been in a deep sense to reject life. Plainly, he wants to see that rejection as a fastidious purity, a preference of a better world to this—as in part it was. That, in a late arrangement of *Men and Women,* "Pictor Ignotus" immediately precedes "Fra Lippo Lippi" is obviously indicative of its meaning and emphasis.

At Leghorn, Robert established another connection with the Romantic past by a visit to Edward Trelawny. The friend of Shelley, the companion of Byron's last years, the ally of the Greek chieftain Odysseus, and the defender of his fabulous cave on the slopes of Parnassus—a mountain only Trelawny should defend—was then fifty-two, a very rich and mellowed combination of freebooter, gentleman, soldier of fortune, and teller of stories. Unfortunately, Robert found Trelawny in a situation little suited to pleasant recollection of Byron and Shelley. A surgeon was probing the veteran's leg for a troublesome bullet lodged there years before. What Browning remembered of the visit was Trelawny's cool courage and stoic indifference to pain.

Altogether, the Italian voyage had been remarkably fruitful, both late and soon. His faith in the monologue had been well justified. Yet the public remained stubbornly indifferent to his work. Were his bitterness and resentment approaching a crisis? "I was scheming," he wrote later, "how to get done with England and go to my heart in Italy."[12] Clearly, he needed very much some special form of encouragement.

Encouragement was soon to be forthcoming. He arrived home from the Continent in the midst of a very considerable sensation about a new edition of Miss Elizabeth Barrett's *Poems.* In the last few years Robert had contemplated Miss Barrett from various angles and perspectives. She had published in *The Athenaeum* of 1842 two series of articles, impressive alike for learning and taste, one on the Greek Christian poets and one on the English. Acknowledging a want of promise in the present generation, she nevertheless saw in Browning and Tennyson two men destined to bring English poetry once more to its former heights. Not to be curious about this learned and prophetic lady would have been inhuman. Two years later, in Horne's *New Spirit of the Age,* Robert had contemplated Miss Barrett briefly through the eyes of that adventurous and much-traveled bachelor. "In consequence of some extremely delicate state of health," wrote Horne, Miss Barrett has lived for five years "almost hermetically sealed" in her apartment. And he allowed himself to fancy, somewhat ponderously:

> When . . . we consider the many strange and ingenious conjectures that are made in after years, concerning authors who appeared but little among their contemporaries, . . . we should not be in the least surprised, could we lift up our ear out of our grave a century hence, to hear some learned Thebans expressing shrewd doubts as to whether such an individual as Miss E. B. Barrett had ever really existed.[13]

Actually, Horne was convinced she existed: if her collaborative work on his book were not quite sufficient evidence, he knew a lady who had seen her many times. That old friend of Miss Barrett's was none other than Miss Mary Russell Mitford, a rosy, blooming maid of fifty or more, who wrote tragedies to pay for her father's dissipations. An accomplished raconteur with a decided eighteenth-century flavor, she had a delightful explanation for Miss Barrett's bad ryhmes, which Horne relished sufficiently to publish many years afterward and which he may well have told Browning at the time.

"Our dear friend," Miss Mitford had told Horne, perhaps on that visit to her country cottage when he had disappointed her so severely by taking three baths in a single day, " . . . has a high opinion of the skill in *reading,* as well as the fine taste of Mr. ———, and she gets him to read her new poems aloud to her, and so tries them upon him (as well as herself), something after the manner of Molière with regard to a far less elegant authority. So Mr. ——— stands upon the hearth-rug, and uplifts the MS., and his voice, while our dear friend lies folded in Indian shawls upon her sofa, with her long black tresses streaming over her bent-down head, all attention. Now, dear Mr. ——— has lost a front tooth—not quite a front one, but a side front one—and this, you see, causes a defective utterance. It does not produce a lisp, or a hissing kind of whistle, as with low people similarly circumstanced, but an amiable indistinctness, a vague softening of syllables into each other,—so that *silance* and *ilance* would really sound very like one another,—and so would *childrin* and *bewilderin—bacchantes* and *grant-es,* don't you see?"[14]

Mr. ——— could of course only have been Mr. Kenyon, and Mr. Kenyon, as Robert himself later confessed,[15] had long been talking to him of Miss Barrett. To be sure, what could so correct an older gentleman communicate to so correct a younger one about an invalid lady? Presumably, they talked about her poetry. Mr. Kenyon had shown Robert the manuscript of "Dead Pan" and carried his enthusiastic praise back to her. He had even attempted to bring the two poets together and had failed only because Miss Barrett had become indisposed at the last moment.

And now Mr. Kenyon was full of Miss Barrett, and so were the journals. *Blackwood's*, for example, bowed in reverence before a "deep-hearted and highly accomplished woman" whose power seemed "to extend over a wider and profounder range of thought and feeling, than was before felt within the intellectual compass of any of the softer sex."[16] Some reviewers, brow-beaten and overawed by Miss Barrett's knowledge of Greek and metaphysics, felt obliged to murmur feebly about her obscurity and mysticism. Mr. Kenyon himself, on grounds of the most cheerful commonsense, had complained of such Browningesque faults. Robert looked around for Miss Barrett's volumes and found that, providentially, Mr. Kenyon had already given them to his sister.

However they may have faded since, these poems seemed gorgeous and new to Browning as to many another discriminating Victorian. In "Lady Geraldine's Courtship," a "Lockesley Hall" with fewer ideas and happier romance, he found that the humble Bertram read to the heroine

> at times a modern volume,—Wordsworth's
> solemn-thoughtful idyll,
> Howitt's ballad-verse, or Tennyson's enchanted reverie,—
> Or from Browning some 'Pomegranate,' which, if cut
> deep down the middle,
> Shows a heart within blood-tinctured, of a veined
> humanity.

Even Tennyson might have read these lines with mild satisfaction. Browning seems to have read them with something more than satisfaction.

One must not go too far. Robert had resolved not to marry. His father could support a poet but not a poet with a family. In fact, proving to Miss Barrett herself, some months later, that he had fallen in love with her and not her poetry, he insisted he had proposed to Mr. Kenyon he write to her for the first time purely out of a sense of obligation. "I did write, on the whole, UNWILLINGLY . . . with consciousness of having to *speak* on a subject which I *felt* thoroughly concerning, and could not be satisfied with an imperfect expression of."[17] He did not in the least "expect" what followed. On the other hand, falling in love as the hero of his own poems with a series of hypothetical duchesses and beggar-girls, he had for several years been industriously predicting his own future—at first, to be sure, rather half-heartedly. But the broken and damaged beauties had been obviously prophetic, and metaphysical conveniences like Pauline and Palma had gradually given way to warm and compelling symbols of substantial possibility like Colombe and the Queen of "Count Gismond." None of the ladies Robert knew answered to this possibility. Certainly not Miss Haworth, the elderly and rather awed recipient of so many chatty and ebullient letters; nor even Eliza Flower, the gifted woman—now obviously dying—who had long ago devoted herself wholly to another man.

But Miss Barrett did. On January 10, 1845, he posted to that lady a letter which seems to have been written from almost any motive but a sense of obligation.

"I love your verses with all my heart, dear Miss Barrett," he began, "—and this is no off-hand complimentary letter that I shall write." He had thought he might find words thoroughly to justify his admiration, "but nothing comes of it all—so into me has it gone, and part of me has it become, this great living poetry of yours."[18] Nevertheless, he has no trouble in articulating virtues: "the fresh strange music, the affluent language, the exquisite pathos and true new brave thought" —all are causes for his emotion. But the final cause becomes clear only after a little more writing: "I do, as I say, love these books with all my heart—and I love you too." He recalls that Mr. Kenyon had nearly gained him access to Miss Barrett's presence. "And now it is years ago—and I feel as at some untoward passage in my travels—as if I had been close, so close, to some world's-wonder in chapel or crypt."[19] The simile might have been startling to a lady who lived in a darkened bedroom and celebrated a perpetual requiem mass in her poetry. In fact, his whole letter might have been startling.

Yet Miss Barrett replied at length with admirable calm. She, too, seemed afraid the correspondence might fall an early victim to the proprieties. She pleaded for a list of the faults in her poems, justified them beforehand, alluded pleasantly to the chilliness of the crypt—and held out hope that he might see her next spring. With an ardor only a little more restricted than his own, she concluded: "I will say that while I live to follow this divine art of poetry . . . in proportion to my love for it and my devotion to it, I must be a devout admirer & student of your works. This is in my heart to say to you—and I say it."[20]

They begin to exchange letters almost weekly.

From a labyrinth nearly as intricate as some in *Sordello,* Robert seems to imply in his second letter that Miss Barrett's poems might sometimes be too detailed and reiterative. On the other hand, "you *do* what I always wanted, hoped to do. . . . I only make men & women speak—give you truth broken into prismatic hues, and fear the pure white light, even if it is in me: but I am going to try."[21] Two days later Miss Barrett hastens to confess—as she never had to Horne—that she is by nature headlong and therefore likely to be guilty of all manner of technical faults. She also insists that Browning is both philosophical and dramatic, "both subjective & objective," in his "habits of mind."[22] Robert refers ironically to his "own gentle audience," and Miss Barrett comforts him by maintaining that his audience is fit though few. And is not poetry its own reward? Her only happiness "lies deep in poetry."[23] She sometimes wonders how people can live without such a purpose. Several weeks have now elapsed since January 10. He thinks she must hate writing letters, as he does—usually. By no means. She does most of her talking by post—"as people shut up in dungeons, take up with scrawling mottos on the walls."[24] She urges Robert to speak out, man to man, without reserve—in his letters. She is curious about the real Robert Browning, the real poetic Robert Browning. They have been exchanging mere pleasantries, it would seem.

Robert replies, in his best monologue manner, with a dazzling display of real and pseudo-Roberts. He had never begun what he hopes he was born to begin and end—"R. B. a poem." He is like one of those Mediterranean lighthouses "wherein the light is ever revolving in a dark gallery, bright and alive, and only after a weary interval leaps out, for a moment, from the one narrow chink, and then goes on with the blind wall between it and you; and, no doubt, *then,* precisely, does the poor drudge that carries the cresset set himself most busily to trim the wick."[25] He writes poetry from a sense of intellectual duty. "I must, if for merely scientific purposes, know all about this 1845, its ways and doings."[26] He markets his poems like cabbage and is amused at his audience not because it is small, but because it laughs in the wrong places. Throughout all this gay cynicism he shows a quite illogical tendency to recur, explicitly or implicitly, to the phrase, "I love you."

"Real warm Spring, dear Miss Barrett," announces Robert one February morning, "and the birds know it; and in Spring I shall see you, surely see you."[27] Unfortunately, Miss Barrett has felt nothing but the east wind. Moreover, she has barely escaped from the winter with her life. Robert is deeply moved. She has touched "a tragic chord" on his "life's harp," to which indeed she has added "octaves on octaves of quite new golden strings."[28] Entirely free as she has never been free, surrounded by loving care from childhood, " 'spoiled' in this world," and touched with sadness only by the slow recognition of his poetry, he finds himself strangely, irresistibly drawn to this woman, so frail, so oppressed, so talented, and so famous. He feels himself rushing headlong upon his fate—and yet, as Dorothy Hewlett observes,[29] he has valued his freedom so highly, has fought so many good battles to preserve it. He is plagued at this time with violent headaches and with a persistent ringing, not at all golden, in his head which he gaily renders to Miss Barrett with a clef and a single note.

Miss Barrett is all sympathy and solicitude. She has been stronger for several winters. Not only does she now expect to live; she is now reconciled to the prospect. She hints at a deep sorrow, an irreparable loss. Since then she has not been able to sleep "except in a red hood of poppies."[30] She is in fact "a recluse, with nerves that have been all broken on the rack, & now hang loosely, . . . quivering at a step and breath."[31] Gently, he asks that, each time she is a little better, she let him know. The implications of this request sink in. Much taken aback, she protests that in principle she is neither pessimistic nor unsocial. She has always insisted on the wisdom of cheerfulness and the duty of social intercourse.

But Robert sets no store by consistency—his, hers, or theirs. She may find her happiness in writing—he dreads and dislikes it; she may approve of a social life—he abhors it; then he tells her he has cured a headache by dancing all night and walking home at dawn. The headaches and ringing in his head persist—so much so that he has had to cancel a whole two weeks of parties and dinners.

She predicts his greatest works are yet to come, and gently dissuades him from writing further for the contemporary stage, which is vulgar. He expounds Aeschylus' *Prometheus* and urges her—apparently in part as an exercise in optimism—to write a *Prometheus* of her own. But the "I love you too" with which he began his letters takes increasingly complete possession of his mind. He cannot think about Greek plays or Danish novels—or any of the topics she throws desperately in his way. Conscientiously, he writes more and more ingeniously and exhaustively about less and less until he succeeds in writing a rather long letter about nothing at all. In his next he runs on for many pages about Dante, Mr. Kenyon, Sorrento, his own recent poems and incessant headaches—and manages to convey quite plainly that he thinks only of her and must see her. This—and a shallow threat that he may leave once more for Italy—brings her to bay. There is some controversy about whether she "trusts" him. She warns him that her poetry is the best of her: "I have lived most & been most happy in it, & so it has all my colours; the rest of me is nothing but a root, fit for the ground & the dark."[32] Not to be outdone, Robert somewhat tactlessly imagines an eager Browning admirer who, after beholding his hero, "noddeth familiarly an adieu, and spinning round on his heel ejaculateth mentally—'Well, I *did* expect to see something different from that little yellow commonplace man.' "[33] They agree on a certain Tuesday, May 20 at two o'clock. The Tuesday draws near; there is a rapidly growing undercurrent of anxiety in their letters—and at the last moment Miss Barrett interjects, "Let it be three instead of two—if the hour be as convenient for yourself."[34]

CHAPTER 11

Chronicle of an Invalid

1806-45

Turning into Devonshire Place from the semi-urban rush and noise of the Marylebone Road, one soon finds oneself in Wimpole Street, by comparison as quiet and hushed as a cathedral aisle, and as likely to have changed. With undeviating rectitude rise up on either side two long impeccable Georgian façades—the quiet opulence of gleaming, neutral-colored plaster below, the blameless respectability of red brick above. Tall iron pickets guard the Avernian descent to basement kitchens below. Freshly painted black doors shut firmly upon the impeccable dignity of spacious front halls. Brass knobs and knockers shine with a virginal, uncontaminated brilliance. Here and there one notes with excitement the cautious deviation of a brown door, the timid effrontery of an ivy runner, even the wild frivolity of a wisteria vine. Behind those almost militant ranks of steadfast doors one imagines whole acres of thick red carpets, whole forests of polished mahogany furniture. "The butlers of Wimpole Street," Virginia Woolf informs us, "move ponderously even today; in the summer of 1842 they were more deliberate still. The laws of livery were even more stringent; the ritual of the green baize apron for cleaning silver; of the striped waistcoat and swallow-tail black coat for opening the hall door, was more closely observed."[1]

To be sure, time, like nature, has left its slight mark on Wimpole Street. No. 50 was destroyed in 1912. Yet one knows the exterior. In fact, standing in Wimpole Street, one can hardly conceive anything else. One also knows that the interior of No. 50 had contained a back drawing room in which Miss Mitford was invited to receive visitors, that over the mantelpiece in the large drawing room hung a "Holy Family," supposed to be by Andrea del Sarto—of which Elizabeth had her suspicions—and that the back area sometimes exploded into the furious barking of a great "Cuban" bloodhound named Cataline.

What one could hardly imagine—without the vast amount of evidence available—is Elizabeth's third-floor bedroom. A tragic life, the Victorian cult of illness, the will of a wealthy and imperious papa, the sympathy of a large family, the exertions of a devoted maid, and the solicitude of a series of grave if somewhat puzzled physicians, had created one of the strangest and most elaborate of invalid existences. A double green door, installed in 1844 at Mr. Barrett's command, shut out the drafts and noise of the house. Dark shades excluded the daylight, and during seven or eight months of the year, paper pasted tightly across the cracks and crevices of the three large windows sealed out the cold and the east wind, a sinister presence which blows malevolently through dozens of Elizabeth's letters. At such times fire burned day and night in the hearth, keeping the mercury at a constant level and depleting an oxygen supply which was meagerly renewed only in spite of human vigilance. Once this warm, dark, airless chamber had been sealed up for the winter, a broom or a duster was of course unthinkable. "At last we come to walk on a substance like white sand," Elizabeth confessed to Miss Mitford, "and if we don't lift our feet gently up and put them gently down, we act Simoom, and stir up the sand into a cloud. . . . The spiders have grown tame—and their webs are a part of our own domestic economy,—Flush eschews walking under the bed."[2]

"Flush's breathing is my loudest sound, and then the watch's tickings, and then my own heart when it beats too turbulently."[3] The inventory is oddly complete: except for occasional visitors, Elizabeth lived alone with silence, her symptoms, her family, and her spaniel Flush. The eccentricities and the adventures of Flush, her own coughs, chest pains, pulse beats, fainting spells and insomnias, as well as her soothing "amreeta draughts" of opium and ether, formed the routine—and an absorbing interest—of her life. On the surface her watch's tickings had little importance. Time seemed to move in circles with the seasons, or not to move at all. And yet she was quite aware of it passing. She detested mirrors. Miss Mitford describes her at thirty as "of a slight, delicate figure, with a shower of dark curls falling on either side of a most expressive face, large tender eyes fringed by dark eyelashes, a smile like a sunbeam, and such a look of youthfulness, that I had some difficulty in persuading a friend . . . that the translatress of the 'Prometheus' of Aeschylus . . . was old enough to be introduced into company."[4] No one would have described her thus at thirty-nine. Gordigiani's well-known portrait, though painted after years of happy married life, curiously suggests a regal captive, a defeated potentate. The head hangs aside in sorrow and acquiescence; the lines about the mouth are bitter and ironical. The large, beautiful eyes look with leaden heaviness.

A door connected Elizabeth's bedroom with her father's. At a late hour every night, the door would open and Mr. Barrett would walk to his daughter's bedside. "Papa," she confided to Miss Mitford, "is my chaplain,—prays with me every night; not out of a book, but simply and warmly at once,—with one of my hands held in his and nobody besides him and me in the room."[5] Her father had not always been so very close to her. Now he was dearer than anyone else, and in a pathetically valedictory manner: "My best hope," she wrote, was "to die beneath his eyes."[6]

May was a period of metamorphic renewal—at least for her bedroom: she moved to her father's room, and her own was unsealed, aired, swept, and cleaned from top to bottom. Then, changing from her one black velvet dress to her one black silk, she returned to find spring in her own four walls. To be sure, she saw very little of the May sky. Ivy grew heavily over her windows, and at her own wish. Her own particular empyrean of roofs and chimney pots did not please her. Perhaps sunlight was too hard a reality to accept. "I had a transparent blind put up in my open window," she wrote in October 1844. "There is a castle in the blind, and a castle gateway, and two walks, and several peasants, and groves of trees which rise in excellent harmony with the fall of my green damask curtains—new, since you saw me last. Papa insults me with the analogy of a back window in a confectioner's shop, but is obviously moved when the sunshine lights up the castle, notwithstanding."[7] In summer the silence was somewhat less deep and intense. Sometimes there was a movement of air, and an Aeolian harp, the gift of her father, emitted its low, mournful music, arousing the suspicion of Flush. Sometimes an ivy branch scratched against a windowpane, and made her think "of forests and groves."[8]

Illness complicates other people's lives; it may simplify that of the invalid herself. Elizabeth had no chores, no duties, no responsibilities. She saw only a few old friends. Illness, sorrow, sensitivity, and solitude had made her extremely shy. The first two times Wordsworth had asked to see her he was refused through her relation, Mr. Kenyon. When her neighbor, Mrs. Jameson, came up the stairs for the first time, Elizabeth's "heart beat itself almost to pieces for fear of seeing her."[9] But shyness and timidity vanished when Elizabeth took up her pen. She became frank, open, curious, loquacious, eager to make confidences and to receive them. Her solitude was mitigated by vast epistolary conversations both with old friends and with a number of literary and artistic gentlemen whom she had never seen. She became sufficiently interested in the adventurous and poetical Horne to be decidedly vexed when she discovered from a picture that he was bald. She inspired so much confidence in the painter B. R. Haydon that after his suicide she found herself—to her own and everybody's astonishment and consternation—entrusted with his unpublished autobiographies.

Elizabeth also used her immense leisure to be a wide reader, a laborious student, and a voluminous, almost feverish versifier. The five years at Wimpole Street had been a period of intense literary activity, sometimes of frequent and exacting deadlines. "For these two, three, four days past . . .," she wrote Miss Mitford, "I really have seemed to myself much like a hare tearing away before the huntsman sweeping over the most fragrant of thyme without the power of pausing to crop the least head of it."[10] And she told her brother George: "I am writing such poems—allegorical—philosophical—poetical—ethical—synthetically arranged! I am in a fit of writing—could write all day & night.—& long to live by myself for three months in a forest of chestnuts & cedars, in an hourly succession of poetical paragraphs & morphine draughts. Not that I do such a thing!"[11]

In romantic fiction, women exist to adore men. Instead of adoring actors, dukes, and dandies, Elizabeth adored poets, artists, and emperors. She even adored great women, though somewhat more critically. "I could kiss the footsteps of a great man—or woman either," she exclaimed, "and feel higher for the stooping."[12] As a child she had walked halfway across London to peer into the windows of Campbell's house, and wondered at the red curtains in his dressing room. As a grown woman, she collected the autographs of poets through Mr. Kenyon, and the mere thought of Shakespeare's *garters* reduced her to awed exclamation. Her bedroom was not only a crypt but a pantheon. Busts of Homer and Chaucer looked down on her from commodes and chests; engravings of Wordsworth, Carlyle, Tennyson, Browning, and Harriet Martineau regarded her from the walls. She had dared meet Wordsworth once, in healthier days, though trembling both in "soul and body."[13] She had courted and interested Carlyle sufficiently to be advised henceforth to write in prose. She read Tennyson with awe as he came out, and speculated curiously and sympathetically about his solitude, health, marriage, and tobacco-smoking. She was breathlessly interested in Harriet

Martineau as an author, woman of intellect, and confirmed invalid successfully cured by mesmerism. In *Paracelsus,* lost between evangelical zeal and romantic aspiration, she had early sensed a kindred spirit, and defended his creator from the robust commonsense of Miss Mitford with an oddly personal resentment.

Hero-worshipers are by temperament immoderate, by vocation uncritical and confused. Mr. Kenyon justly accused Elizabeth of an "immoral sympathy with power."[14] A devoted partisan of the poor and weak, she had moved all England by her "Cry of the Children." Yet autocratic will and authority, from her father's to Napoleon's, drew her strongly. Though she had lived a life of almost quixotic moral idealism, Byron's satanic wickedness aroused only her sympathy and admiration. As a girl, she had dreamed of running away to become his pageboy, and even in her most discreet years, she stridently insisted on the villainy of his wife. In her judgment of most women, to be sure, Elizabeth was not generous. She had early rebeled against her own femininity. "Through the whole course of my childhood," she wrote Miss Mitford, "I had a steady indignation against Nature who made me a woman, and a determinate resolution to dress up in men's clothes as soon as ever I was free of the nursery, and go into the world 'to seek my fortune.' "[15] George Sand was a great heroine because she had overcome her womanhood, though she offered some difficulties to a nice Victorian conscience. However much she might overlook it in Byron, Elizabeth could not condone unchastity in a woman. *Lélia* "made me blush in my solitude to the ends of my fingers."[16] Yet George Sand was "eloquent as a fallen angel." She was "a true woman of genius!—but of a womanhood tired of itself, and scorned by *her,* while she bears it burning above her head."[17]

Worshipping George Sand, Elizabeth seems to have become interested in feet of clay for their own sake. Perhaps the cloisters always cast shadows on the virtue they protect. Elizabeth's mind was sincerely and deeply preoccupied with an imminent death and another world. Nevertheless, she was widely read not only in French memoirs but in the most dubious yellow-cover literature. "Not that I would let it loose in this house for the world"[18]—one can almost see the delicious shudder of apprehension. "I have just done reading," she remarks casually to the startled Miss Mitford, "a romance of Frederic Soulié's which begins with a violation and a murder, and ends consistently with a murder and a violation,—the hero who is the agent of this 'just proportion' being shut up at last and starved in a premature coffin, after having his eyelids neatly sewed up by the fair fingers of his lady-love."[19] She confides a panoramic estimate of this French fictional inferno: "There is Eugene Sue, and Frederic Souliè and De Queilhe . . . why the whole literature looks like a conflagration—and my whole being aches with the sight of it,—and when I turn away *home,* there seems nothing to be seen, it is all so neutral tinted and dull and cold by comparison."[20] In fact, so much vicarious sex and violence seem to have led Elizabeth, English-fashion, to some shrewd commonsense about the hypocrisies of her time. "The squeamishness of this Age, . . . this Ostrich age . . . which exposes its own eggs, and then hides its head in the sand, . . . is really to me quite monstrous. The shrieks on all sides because Mr. such a person tells the astonished public that Mrs. such a person has a nose, could scarcely be louder if he had attacked her character in a public court."[21] And when Miss Mitford discovered that the second illegitimate child of her maid K had been fathered by her manservant Ben, Elizabeth must have startled the good lady by observing: "My dearest friend, one thing I must say—*the want of chastity is the least sin.* The overwhelming sin, in my eyes, lies in the fact of the systematic lying with which she formerly imposed on you."[22] Plainly, this pious and somewhat lugubrious idealist was also a gay and sensible bohemian. How did this extraordinary woman come to find herself, at thirty-nine, in such an extraordinary situation?

As some of Robert's ancestors had been lesser planters in St. Kitt's, so Elizabeth's had been great planters in Jamaica. Since the seventeenth century, Barretts had acquired land; imported slaves and exported cocoa, sugar, and rum; built and helped to build churches; built their fortlike great houses and patiently rebuilt after hurricane, earthquake, and fire; multiplied in spite of malaria, yellow fever, plague, and the great slave rebellion—from the violence of which their own moderate rule had largely exempted them—and humanely provided for their mulatto children while devolving their estates upon their legitimate white heirs. It was thus that in 1798 Edward and Samuel Moulton, their surnames changed by royal decree to Barrett Moulton-Barrett, inherited the extensive North-Side Jamaican estates of their maternal grandfather, Edward Barrett. Both boys had come to England to live. Edward, the elder, went briefly to Harrow, even more briefly to Cambridge, married at nineteen to a beautiful twenty-three-year-old Mary Graham-Clarke, settled down first at his mother's house of Coxhoe Hall, where Elizabeth was born in 1806, and finally on the five-hundred-acre Herefordshire estate of Hope End, where he reared a family of twelve children.

Elizabeth was the eldest and in every respect the most remarkable.

She was beautiful surely to her parents—delicate, slight, elfinlike, and with a fire that makes delicacy doubly charming. In fact, with rather too much fire: "I was always of a determined and if thwarted violent disposition,"[23] she wrote with solemn pedantry at fourteen; and at thirty-nine, with a hint of regret, "Never since I was a child have I upset all the chairs & tables & thrown the books about the room in a fury."[24] No doubt Mr. Barrett gave the fire his most serious attention, and so did Elizabeth herself, at a surprisingly early age. Nevertheless, there were incidents. Once the world was all wrong and Elizabeth withdrew into a hatbox, pulling down the lid to make the exclusion dark and complete. Eventually, the temper disappeared, leaving in its place a boyish tendency to disorder, a tomboyish strenuousness, and a very formidable will. That will won notable victories, even over Mr. Barrett. At eight, through sheer persistence, Elizabeth got herself taken to Paris on what was meant to be an entirely child-free excursion.

Unlike the brothers and sisters springing up so rapidly in her wake, Elizabeth was a prodigy so remarkable that she herself thought it worthwhile, at the age of fourteen, to record her early history. She read romances at four, proceeded rapidly to novels, histories, Pope's *Iliad*, and Shakespeare's plays, made metaphysics her "highest delight"[25] at twelve, and at thirteen, "perused all modern authors who have any claim to superior merit and poetic excellence."[26] Her pen was nearly as swift as her eye. She wrote verses from her infancy, celebrated birthdays and other family events with appropriate odes and verse narratives, began a novel at six, wrote an epic at nine and several tragedies—both in French and English—at ten. At fifteen, she published, at her father's expense, *The Battle of Marathon*, in the manner of Pope's *Iliad*. When she was sixteen, two of her poems appeared in Campbell's *New Monthly Magazine*.

In that happy world of Hope End—increasingly filled with birthday celebrations and cricket games, and apparently sealed off from sorrow by wealth and luxury—Elizabeth's achievements were received with astonished applause and tender appreciation. She was deeply loved and proudly admired by her mother, a gentle, almost too yielding woman; and she was the particular favorite of her Uncle Sam, an M.P. and a cultivated, sensitive man, who on his death left her, alone of his brother's children, a legacy of several thousand pounds. If Mr. Barrett enjoyed cricket more than poetry, he valued virtue and piety above everything else; and Elizabeth was fervently ambitious for all the best things. Her religious experiences, her moral victories over temper and other sins were as precocious as her epics and tragedies. All tasks laid upon her were triumphantly carried out. She never learned to sew, she told Miss Mitford, because sewing was never put to her "in the form of a duty."[27] With such dutifulness Mr. Barrett was well pleased—as with her virtue, ability, and family prestige, his younger children were deeply impressed. In her later letters to her sisters and even to her brother George, Elizabeth writes with confident authority.

To be sure, Mr. Barrett was far from encouraging the habit of authority in children. He was a loving father with a jolly laugh and an infectious gusto and gaiety, but he was also a man of strong convictions, secret counsels, and sudden commands, with a firm sense of his own rights and other people's duties. He had not been born a great slave owner for nothing. Not only authority, but independence of mind, initiative, and even ordinary self-possession failed to flourish in his presence. His daughter Arabel became a devoted social worker, selfless, narrow, and strict. Edward, or "Bro," was, in the mature opinion of his elder sister, too sensitive to be energetic. Stormie was very nervous, stammered, and so shrank "from the shadow of his own personality" that he gave up pursuing his Glasgow degree because, laughed at once for stuttering, he would never utter another word in class.[28]

Charming, brilliant, and determined as she was, Elizabeth was far from immune to either family pressure or the disillusionment consequent on towering ambitions limited by personal capacity. She suffered from one very obvious limitation, and one which her father was not likely to minimize: she was a girl. When a tutor appeared to instruct Bro, she eagerly availed herself of the opportunity, and made more rapid strides than her brother in Greek and Latin. Yet when Bro went away to school, she learned that, in spite of her superior attainments, there was no place for her to go. There was not even a tutor, and she had already tasted disillusionment with her own unaided efforts. Looking back at the ripe age of fourteen on her eleventh year, she writes: "For months during this year I never remember having diverted my attention to any other object than the ambition of gaining fame. Literature was the star which in future prospect illuminated my future days—it was the spur which prompted me . . . the aim . . . the very seal of my being. I was determined . . . to gain the very pinnacle of excellence."[29] In the intoxication of completed composition, she ran downstairs into the library to compare her poem with Pope's Homer, that she might enjoy her own "SUPERIORITY." "I read fifty lines. . . . It was enough . . . I felt the whole extent of my own immense and mortifying inferiority. . . . I wept for an hour and then returned to reason and humility. Since then I have not felt MANY twitches of vanity and my mind has never since been intoxicated by any ridiculous dreams of greatness!!"[30]

But of course disillusionment was very far from producing common-sense. Her posture is well illustrated by a childhood memory. When she was a very little girl, her father used to lift her onto the mantlepiece and adjure her to stand straighter, straighter, until she could feel the wall pushing the back of her head as if to plunge her to the polished hearth below. So the lofty ideals and ambitions of childhood, coupled with the will to be on top, to be a man in a family of men, might well, in an environment where the will by no means made the way, have produced an unusual degree of self-doubt and fear. "I used to be frightened of the dark," she told Miss Mitford, "and could not go to sleep unless the nurse sate there with a candle; and I well remember how I used to think . . . 'I shall not like to be grown up because then I shall have nobody to take care of me,—nobody to *trust to*'. Distinct, very distinct, is my recollection of that feeling."[31]

The feeling persisted. The need of someone to trust to forms the basis of her love for her father, for Browning, even for Miss Mitford. "Do not talk of me in hyperboles, but love me!" she begged that lady.[32] And the essence of her religion was a firm faith that the Divine Will can be completely trusted, though not at all comprehended. But as in later years she doubted that she merited Miss Mitford's love, or Browning's, so in girlhood she had far more fearful doubts that she merited God's. Once, at twelve, she forgot a prayer. "My whole mind was tortured and my prayers that night bespoke the anguish of my heart. It was not the humility of a sinner suing for pardon at the throne of mercy but the violent entreaties extorted by despair from my heart. The next morning I renewed with tenfold ardour my agonising prayers."[33] A flood of sunlight through the mist brought comfort and a sense of forgiveness. Here her history was predicting itself, but in the later, most terrible crisis of her life, there was to be no sunshine of comfort and forgiveness.

During these early years, her inward life was a strange and stormy mixture of pride and guilt, rebellion and submission, pity for herself and contempt for others. She strove both to attain and to mortify her literary ambitions. Sometimes she was lifted up by a thrilling sense of dedication and destiny:

> I always imagine [she wrote in "Glimpses"] that I was sent on the earth for some purpose! To suffer! to die! to defend! To save by my

> death my country or some very dear friends! To suffer in the cause of freedom!! . . . I feel it in my heart core and so strong is this feeling that it amounts almost to presentiment! But this is only sometimes.[34]

There are also moods of extraordinary depression and desolation, when, as she records, "Man has appeared to me black as night and happiness but a name!"[35] Though she grows calmer and more self-possessed without, her inward feelings remain as wild and stormy—and threatening. The back of the wall is still pushing against her head:

> I have acquired a command of myself which has become so habitual that my disposition appears to my friends to have undergone a revolution. . . . Yet were I once to loose the rigid rein I might again be hurled with Phaeton far from everything human . . . everything reasonable! My mind has and ever will be a turmoil of conflicting passions. . . . I have always some end in view which requires exertion, for if that exertion be wanting I should indeed appear to myself a dreary void! . . . I look upon that tranquility which I cannot enjoy with a feeling rather like contempt as precluding in great measure the intellectual faculties of the human mind.[36]

Lofty ideals proudly and uncharitably pursued are of course the common burden of dedicated youth. The weight of that burden in Elizabeth's case was increased by unusual ability, sensitivity, and frustration: she could make peace neither with herself nor with others. When people felt and resented her "uncontroulable contempt for any littleness of mind or meanness of soul,"[37] she had another reason for self-pity. "It is pleasing to all minds," she observes with precocious insight, "to feel that they are judged harshly—it robs Conscience of half her arrows." At a very early age, she was told by a displeased servant that she "was cold and unfeeling and that everyone thought so, whatever they might say. . . . I only smiled—a contemptuous smile I meant it to be—and walked away! And yet I was not angry, only astonished—unspeakably astonished!—that whole day my usual calmness sat on my brow . . . and I gloried in that self-command, but when the shades of night descended, when I was left alone to hold solitary converse with my pillow, feelings so long repressed rushed like a cataract to my heart and tears gushed wildly forth!"[38]

Here, then, were temper chastened by Papa, ambition chastened by Pope, and everything chastened by conscience and religion, with very high ideals, and melancholy and self-pity to fill the gap between ideals and self-estimate. Bro and Sam were away at school. Elizabeth was facing the fact that she was a girl. At fifteen occurred her first grave illness.

> You who keep account
> Of Crisis and transition in this life,
> Set down the first time Nature says plain "no"
> To some "yes" in you, and walks over you
> In gorgeous sweeps of scorn.[39]

Reviewing the case in a letter to Mr. Barrett, Dr. William Coker notes:

> It began with pain in the head, which continued at intervals for seven weeks—The pain then attacked various parts of the body, for a considerable period—and for the last month it has permanently seated itself on the right side. . . . The pain commences here, is carried to the corresponding region of the back, up the side to the point of the right shoulder, and down the arm. The suffering is agony—and the paroxysms continue from a quarter of an hour to an hour and upwards. . . . There are generally three attacks in the day and none during the night—Very considerable debility and consequent nervous irritation, producing smallness and feebleness of the pulse—pain, and weakness in the back, which will not allow her sitting up, without support by pillows, and she is always rendered worse by exercise—The feet are generally cold.[40]

Elizabeth attributed her illness to a spine injury suffered while saddling her pony. The late Dr. D. J. Davis, then Dean Emeritus of the University of Illinois Medical School and long familiar with such cases, finds that "both symptoms and treatment indicate clearly a diagnosis of 'general tuberculosis from girlhood.' "[41] Henrietta and Arabel seem to have undergone similar, though less severe, attacks in the same year (1821). All three cases were arrested, but Elizabeth's malady recurred with shorter and shorter intervals of health until her death. During this early illness, on the advice of her doctors, Elizabeth took opium for the first time. Though she was in danger only a few months, her parents were so deeply concerned that they hardly ever left her "to go anywhere, not even to dine in the neighbourhood."[42]

By the time she had recovered from her illness, Elizabeth was approaching marriageable age. In neighboring country houses, and in those of her relatives to the north, young men were undoubtedly to be met with—in fact, she mentions several in her letters, but with complete indifference. The authoress who at nineteen had completed *An Essay on Mind* was not likely to take much interest in the average young country squire, nor was the average young squire likely to feel anything but fear and awe for the authoress of *An Essay on Mind.* Had Alexander Pope been alive and nearby, he might soon have found himself plunged in eager correspondence with Miss Barrett and in danger of ceasing to be either a papist or a bachelor. But in that part of Herefordshire, there were only two men of any literary or intellectual eminence. One was the venerable Uvedale Price, the friend of Wordsworth and the author of *An Essay on the Picturesque.* The other was Hugh Stuart Boyd, a blind Irish gentleman in his late forties who had memorized an astonishing amount of Greek Christian poetry and who had published quantities of frigid verse and even greater quantities of scarcely less frigid translation. From the septuagenarian Price, Elizabeth enjoyed a sensitive and intelligent guidance and sympathy which she did not find at home. When her father bluntly advised her to burn her long poem, "The Development of Genius," Price gave her tactful and encouraging criticism.

The story of the second friendship is longer and sadder. Great zeal, a fantastic memory, a narrow mind, an obstinate self-righteousness, a passion for esoteric detail and unimportant knowledge had made Mr. Boyd a pedant. His blindness, his ineffectuality, his loneliness, his eagerness for fellowship in study and learning had made him a pathetic and rather lovable pedant. Somewhat absentmindedly he had married a woman indifferent to the Greek Christian poets and was the father of a girl several years older than Elizabeth. Impressed like Price with the *Essay on Mind,* which appeared in 1826, Boyd sent Elizabeth his books and an invitation to call. She was forced to explain that her father considered the visit of a young female to a strange man beyond the limits of propriety. The two now corresponded, for an entire year, on a level of breathless grandiloquence, about Greek, Latin, Italian, and even English literature. She learned with astonishment that Boyd preferred Lucan to Homer and defended herself with indignation against the charge that she thought the Muses had blue hair. At length a pathetic plea from Boyd caused Mr. Barrett to relent. After a terrifying carriage accident on the way to the visit Elizabeth, trembling and speechless, met Boyd in the presence of Bro.

She was soon riding over to Malvern alone, to pay the Boyds frequent and protracted visits. For the next few years she was undoubtedly the most important person in Boyd's life, as he was in hers. He found in her what probably he most desired: an admiring and precocious scholar, an eager and industrious assistant; she saw in him what she longed to worship: a hero of knowledge and literature. Her letters gradually lose their grandiloquence and become eager and affectionate. "My note to him may be *too* expressive of regard!!" she confides to a diary.[43] What she felt seems most like a belated adolescent crush. Only a very innocent and self-righteous idealist could rush so blindly into, and only a belated need for intellectual nourishment could sustain so odd a relationship. Though apparently generous and affectionate toward the visitor, Mrs. Boyd and her daughter were scarcely content with the situation itself, and Mr. Barrett was even less so. His attitude seems to have varied from jealousy to bare indulgence. " 'Well,' he said, with a good-humoured smile,—'so you have *condescended* to come back at last.' And when I told him how happy I had been, the reply was—'I do not doubt *that*. I am only afraid that you will find it impossible to tolerate us, after Mr. Boyd.' "

During the course of this studious and engrossing friendship, tragedy and disaster fell on Elizabeth and her family. In 1828 Mrs. Barrett died. Her husband locked up her rooms and his heart at the same time: her name was never again mentioned in his presence. Elizabeth was taken wholly by surprise in her loss and felt that God had punished her for loving her mother too deeply. Weeks, perhaps months afterward, she wrote Boyd: "I never can forget what I have lost. Her voice is still sounding in my ears—her image is in my heart."[44] Late in 1830, at the age of twenty-four, she had another severe illness. In the spring of 1831, she began to hear rumors that Hope End might be sold, that the family must find humbler quarters, that the servants were leaving because the family was moving to Jamaica. Though terrified at the prospect of living far from England on a slave plantation, she dared not question her father, who remained imperturbable. At length a momentous letter arrived: "just one shadow past on his face while he read it (I marked it at the moment) and then he broke away from the melancholy, and threw himself into the jests and laughter of his innocent boys."[45]

The shadow on Mr. Barrett's face had a long history. His Jamaica estates had for some years been mismanaged. They had also suffered from the loss of a family lawsuit involving the ownership of his slaves and again from damage in the great slave uprising of 1831. To meet losses, Hope End had been mortgaged, and by 1831 the mortgagers were deciding to foreclose. Presently, a "fat gentleman with rings" came up from London, and was "said to have said that '*the place is to be sold.*' "[46] Finally, London and local papers announced that it was in fact to be put up for auction. For some months, parties of curious people in noisy, picnic mood paraded through the house and grounds, striking indignation or panic into the Barretts and frequently driving them into hiding, from which they heard "the trampling and the voices of strangers through the passages everywhere, and in the chambers which had been shut up for years from . . . [their] own steps, sacred to death and love."[47] Mr. Barrett was frequently away on business during this period. When at home, he played cricket with the boys as usual, and over the morning papers, he showed himself a voluble champion of Reform. Nevertheless, he ceased to visit neighbors or even to attend chapel, and, on the one subject on which his children longed for knowledge and certainty, he spoke not a word.

At length an inclusive auction took place: no one bid near the £50,000 the estate was worth. Awaiting a sufficiently wealthy purchaser, the family lived on in a house that no longer seemed their own. Rumors continued to circulate; once Elizabeth heard that Hope End might yet be saved. Meanwhile, her father forebade her longer to wear out her health serving as Boyd's amanuensis, and in May 1832 Boyd moved with his family first to Somersetshire and eventually to Bathampton. Exhausted from nervous strain and beside herself with despair, Elizabeth was once more certain that she had been punished for depending too much on a merely earthly relationship. "For a long time," she wrote Boyd in July, "my powers of feeling pleasure and pain have been clashing against each other—and neither my body nor mind can bear it any longer."[48] She had by then heard a report, which proved to be true, that Hope End had been sold to Thomas Heywood.

Mr. Barrett now briskly emerged from his secrecy. He returned from a few days tour of the southern seacoast towns full of enthusiasm for the climate and, characteristically, with a lease on a furnished house in Sidmouth in his pocket.

On a hot August morning, accompanied by five servants and riding in two carriages, most of the young Barretts rolled for the last time beyond the gates of what Elizabeth later called their "Paradise in Herefordshire."[49] At the time it was an exodus from anxiety. Every mile lifted a burden.

Like most tyrants who build walls and keep secrets, Mr. Barrett was a desperate procrastinator—as reluctant to begin his future as he had been to wind up his past. Planned as an interlude of two months, the sojourn at Sidmouth extended into an almost permanent seaside vacation. The three years she passed there, in her late twenties, were, despite petty irritations, among the happiest and healthiest in Elizabeth's life. She bathed, boated, rode a donkey along the seashore, composed poetry, translated *Prometheus Bound,* and wrote long soothing letters to Mr. Boyd, who—perhaps partly for her sake—was still offended with her father. Boyd not only refused to give up his grievance, but actually complained that he grew tired of listening to such long letters. Much hurt, she wrote a short one. Boyd became more offended still. Elizabeth now wrote an extremely long letter: "The charm of my intercourse with you, was the power of communicating with a person who could feel like me & with me, & of saying within myself—*I cannot tire him. . . .* If you could see into my heart, you could not suspect *me* of thinking ill of *you*!"[50] Boyd immediately moved to Sidmouth.

Elizabeth soon found herself again serving as Boyd's reader and amanuensis, helping him to revise his "Essay on the Greek Article" and prepare a series of translations called *The Fathers Not Papists.* She also found herself the cause and victim of a protracted family quarrel. Annie Boyd had refused to leave Bath at all; Mrs. Boyd had left reluctantly and soon returned. Only an imploring letter, dictated by Boyd and written by Elizabeth, finally brought her once more to Sidmouth. Elizabeth had begun to wish that neither wife nor husband had ever moved from Bathampton.

The family quarrel was bad enough, but what was ultimately worse was the discovery that Boyd conducted his scholarship very like a family quarrel. Anyone who failed to see eternal verity in his wild prejudices and narrow sectarianism must be guilty of gross ignorance or determined knavery. Taking up *The Fathers Not Papists* after the learned author had moved to London, Elizabeth was shocked both by the ferocity of the preface and the crudeness of the translation. In the years that followed, she continued to write soothing letters with unfailing affection but increasing humor. In fact, one is tempted to say that she developed a sense of humor attempting to propitiate Mr. Boyd. More than a decade later, she wrote Browning, "He talks like a man of slow mind, which he is. . . . He is not a man of deep sensibility, and, if he heard of my death, would merely sleep a little sounder the next night."[51] Her *Prometheus Bound . . . and Miscellaneous Poems* (1833) shows that, poetically, she made as little progress in her twenties as she had made much in her teens. One cannot but agree with Gardner Taplin that the friendship with Boyd was a principal cause.

To be sure, she had a reason for seeing through Mr. Boyd. In her seaside travels on a donkey, she had not been accompanied solely by her younger brothers. Her other companion was the Reverend George B. Hunter, minister of the local Independent Chapel. Mr. Hunter was an accomplished scholar and a powerful preacher, with a "talent for anger"[52] and a fund of denunciatory eloquence against wealth and privilege, departments in which he himself had little opportunity to develop a bad conscience. The opportunity of Elizabeth and her father was more ample. Nevertheless, they were deeply impressed by this austere man, and Elizabeth copied memorable passages from his fulminations into a rich morocco notebook. In her own medium she wrote:

How, when I sang of Adam's sin,
I saw you burning, beaming
With eloquent lightnings, fencing in
Earth's crime, for Heaven's redeeming—[53]

When the implacable Mr. Hunter left the local chapel, she journeyed to more distant churches to hear him—once to Exeter where he spoke before a thousand people. Had her old friend Mr. Boyd been less angry and more perceptive, he might have noticed that church politics, churchmen, and particularly Mr. Hunter appeared with suspicious frequency in Elizabeth's letters.

Both his later conduct and his one surviving letter to Elizabeth indicate that Mr. Hunter himself was very much in love. It is true he had grave disadvantages as a suitor. He seldom kept a position long: apparently, wealthy parishioners detected something besides piety in his eloquence against privilege. Graver still—if a letter[54] from Elizabeth to Miss Mitford is accurate—he had besides a little daughter who was very much in evidence, an insane wife who was not at all in evidence.

In short, Elizabeth had once more become interested in a married man and in one who, though intelligent and accomplished, was nearly as ineffectual as his predecessor. History could do little but repeat itself. Elizabeth celebrated Mr. Hunter's virtues in verse, mourned his absence when she moved to London, affectionately and patiently endured his follies when he later followed her—and eventually came to see him quite clearly for what he was. "The power of suffering," she wrote Miss Mitford in 1842, "is not sufficiently balanced by the energy to act,—which produces a despondent character very painful to witness the workings of sometimes, in so dear a friend."[55]

In 1835 the Barretts moved to London, where they lived for two years at 74 Gloucester Place and thereafter at the legendary 50 Wimpole Street. Elizabeth began by thoroughly disliking the metropolis. "London is wrapped up like a mummy, in a yellow mist, so closely that I have had scarcely a glimpse of its countenance since we came," she wrote her old friend Mrs. Martin. "But I dare say I shall soon be able to see in my dungeon, and begin to be amused with the spiders."[56] The dungeon became amusing, but never healthful. Elizabeth gravitated more and more to the sofa and the bed. Finally, a very long cold through the winter of 1837 ended in a persistent cough. In the spring of 1838—soon after moving to Wimpole Street, which she described as "Newgate turned inside out"—Elizabeth burst a blood vessel in her chest. Dr. Chambers was gravely concerned, hoped much from the summer weather, and was gravely disappointed. He spoke unequivocally; her recovery depended on avoiding the London winter—she must go to the south of Europe. Mr. Barrett saw no merit in the idea. His numerous children supported their sister, consulted deviously, and suggested to him Torquay as a compromise. Elizabeth later told Miss Mitford that she went there "against the bias of his desire. I was persuaded—he was entreated. On his side, it was at last a mere yielding up to a majority." In August, accompanied by Bro, George, and Henrietta, Elizabeth set out by ship for Torquay.

Papa's bias hung in thunderclouds over the entire three years at Torquay. At his command, Barretts now began to move constantly between London and the seaside. As a first arrival, Bro soon received the order to leave his sister's side. The news was bitter, for Elizabeth did not expect to live, and Bro was her favorite brother, the being she "loved best in the world beyond comparison and rivalship."[57] One of her aunts interceded with Mr. Barrett. The despot yielded, but again sorely against his bias: "he considered it to be *very wrong in* [*her*] *to exact such a thing.*"[58]

For a few weeks Elizabeth seemed to recover and was able to be taken out in a "chair" nearly every afternoon; but the winter of 1839 found her once more suspended between life and death. Meanwhile, the grief which she had sensed in the air of Torquay had begun to materialize. She had become deeply attached to Dr. De Barry, her idealistic and dedicated physician. On October 2, 1839, he died very suddenly, leaving a wife, a daughter, and an unborn child. The shock left Elizabeth gravely ill for three weeks. On February 17, 1840, her brother Sam, victim of the temptations and the climate of Jamaica, died in lonely grandeur at Cinnamon Hill Great House. Elizabeth was struck down instantaneously "as by a *bodily* blow,"[59] and again gravely ill. And yet she could take comfort in God's will. Tried, Job-like, in the odorous hush of the sickroom, she was to learn more of God's will, and even of her own character.

"You have heard of Arabel's and Brosie's separate romances," she wrote her brother George on June 17.[60] By this time Mr. Barrett must have made known his strong bias against marriage, on pain of excommunication from the paternal income. Elizabeth seems to have regarded Arabel's romance as pathetic and unimportant, but she entered heavily into Bro's, attempting to make over her own small fortune to him, so that he could be independent enough to marry. Mr. Barrett prevented the transaction. There was "a storm of emotion and sympathy on my part,"[61] Elizabeth later wrote Browning, and in the midst of the open rebellion, the blow fell. On July 11, 1840, Bro went sailing with three companions in a small boat. There was a squall, and, as night closed in, rumors spread of a capsized boat in Babbacombe Bay, or even within sight of shore at Torquay. For an "awful agony of three days," Elizabeth and her sisters kept hope alive. The sun shone, the air was still, her sisters "drew the curtains" to show her "how smooth the sea was, and how it could hurt nobody." As hope entirely left her, a catastrophic conviction took its place: "You have done this."[62]

Bro's body was cast ashore weeks later. By then, and for long afterward, Elizabeth lay deathly ill, unable to speak or to weep, or even to "hold on to one thought for more than a moment." She suffered from attacks of delirium and beheld visions of "long dark spectral trains" and of "staring infantine faces" that almost brought her mind to "madness, absolute hopeless madness."[63] She did not pray. She felt "too near to God under the crushing of His hand";[64] or, as she put it to another correspondent, "God's face seemed so close upon me that there was no need of prayer."[65]

Why was God so near and yet so crushing? Though she could not think, Elizabeth at thirty-four was even then choosing between alternatives, for Bro's death represented not only a terrible loss, but a terrible dilemma. Elizabeth had believed all her life, as the cardinal tenet of her religion, that "God's will is always done in mercy."[66] Three days before the tragedy and shortly after a desperate crisis in her own illness, she had written Boyd, "There are so many mercies close around me . . . that God's *Being* seems proved to me, *demonstrated* to me, by His manifold love."[67] Could Bro's death be interpreted as in any sense an act of Divine Mercy? Her extraordinary conscience prevented her from regarding it mainly as the catastrophic end of Bro's life: it was preëminently a transaction between her and the Almighty. Either God was not merciful, or this shattering blow was an act of His mercy, required to instruct and correct her. Characteristically, she clung to her idealism—and chose the second alternative. Was she not responsible, as all her family knew, and she knew best, for Bro's presence in Torquay? Mr. Barrett, she later told Robert, "never reproached me as he might have done as my own soul has not spared—never once said to me then or since, that if it had not been for *me*, the crown of his house would not have fallen. . . . And I could have answered nothing. . . . 'Not with my hand but heart,' I was the cause or occasion. . . . When the time came for him to leave me *I*, weakened by illness, could not master my spirits or drive back my tears."[68]

In short, by keeping Bro in Torquay she had caused his death. But the "weakness" which had thwarted her father's wish was not the sin. Probing to comprehend, she found that she had always been "as willful, as impatient of controul" as she had described herself at fourteen. Had she not only recently supported Bro in his desire to marry, and even attempted to make over her property to him? What God's punishment had revealed to Elizabeth in herself was the crime of willing, of desiring.

After three months of agony, she saw it was God's will she should live. On what terms? She must try, as she later told Browning, to make herself "*pure of wishes*,"[69] she must will no more. No doubt such a response involved an element of moral suicide, a "tendency to lie down to sleep among the snows of a weary journey."[70] But to continue to live and at the same time cease to will proved extremely difficult for one who had surmounted her circumstances by force of that will—however deviously operating—which she wished to annihilate. Soon it became imperative to escape from the nightmare associations of Torquay and return to Wimpole Street. But of course the determination must not be hers. It must be Dr. Scully's. In early spring she speaks of "*honest* Dr. Scully (who would never give an opinion just to please me) saying that I am 'quite right' to mean to go to London. . . . So . . . the only means of regaining whatever portion of earthly happiness is not irremediably lost to me by the Divine decree, I am free to use."[71] Dr. Scully had named June, but in June he "fears the *journey* . . . and has tried hard and vainly to frighten me out of the thoughts of it."[72] As Dr. Scully vacillates, she formulates the principle of discerning Papa's pleasure, but this again proves unsatisfactory. "Papa's *biases* are sacred to me, and . . . I would not stir them with a breath. Yet he says to me 'Decide.'"[73] And Papa was developing quite horrible biases. He threatened to bury the family alive in the Black Mountains, in Michael Church. At least he would move her to Clifton. "That hot, white, dusty, vapory place, & scarcely an 'inland place too'—And then sometimes I grow dizzy & fearful that he looks to Michael Church!—Oh but I WONT fear it. I wont fear anything."[74] Though she called herself "selfish," she was now scheming to bring the more influential members of the family—chiefly her brother George—in line with her wish. Eventually, the tyrant abandoned his whims, and, though frightened of the journey, as was Dr. Scully, allowed his daughter to return home. About the first of September 1841, a patent invalid wagon, suspended on "a thousand springs," came to a stop before No. 1 Beacon Terrace, Torquay; and a bed was drawn out "like a drawer out of a table."[75] On this bed, and in the company of Arabel, Flush, and her maid Crow, Elizabeth traveled by easy stages to London.

The wonder is that this fragile and gravely ailing woman survived at all a loss which she felt so deeply. Thereafter, she feared much, and expected little, from life. And still she was singularly like the Elizabeth of former days. Both guilt and gratitude drew her closer to her father, who, she felt, had been warm and generous in the moment of crisis; yet, though making a strong effort to be loving and submissive, she continued to resent the callous and self-righteous tyranny with which he kept his children in servitude. She liked to think herself dead to desire and will; yet she could admit on occasion that she was very far from being so. In fact, as so often happens in such cases, her fears could be more tyrannous than the most arbitrary will. When Stormie and Henry were "wild with desire to go out" to Alexandria in their father's ship, the *Statira*, they found they could persuade Mr. Barrett, but not Elizabeth. "I bitterly think, even now," she told Miss Mitford after their departure, "that the advantage of being in Aegypt a month, at Gibraltar two days, and at Malta, two days, is disproportionate to the long anxiety of those left at home."[76] And though Bro's death had forced her drastically to reassess her whole former conception of herself, her suffering over it soon became the supreme fact in that elusive principle of "Ba"-ishness which made her unique among mortals, both ordinary and extraordinary. Throughout her life she shows an embarrassing tendency to competition in griefs. She herself realized on occasion that her attitude was morbid, though how much, as Kierkegaard would say, she poetized her sorrows and luxuriated in them, she could hardly suspect. In fact, such phrases as "my heart being broken by that great stone that fell out of Heaven"[77] and "I have wept tears of blood"[78] must have been less offensive to a sentimental age than they are to our own.

Such was the history of the profoundly unhappy woman who, at three o'clock on Tuesday, May 20, 1845, lay with beating heart and fluttering breath, awaiting Robert Browning.

CHAPTER 12

"Not Death, But Love"

1845

Robert Browning's greatest exploit was his own romance. It was thoroughly in the spirit of his poetry: a passionate rather than a rational act; and the daring rescue of a pessimist by an optimist. It was a stratagem against an ogre, the awakening of a sleeping princess in an enchanted palace, surrounded by a thicket, the wooing of a confirmed old maid by a confirmed bachelor, an Orphic descent into a region of shadows and the guiding of an Eurydice upward into the light. Robert himself spoke of his courtship as a warfare against shadows. The shadows existed, of course, mainly in Elizabeth's mind. They were very self-righteous shadows: fears posing as duties and ideals, sorrows luxuriating in their inconsolability—the morbidities of a generous nature. Robert was too idealistic, too much in love, to peer very curiously into these darknesses. He simply urged against them his passionate love, his urgent need, until they fled before an accomplished fact.

Only in fairy tales do sleeping beauties languish in their bowers for twenty years—or even five—without losing some of their freshness. In real life, by a very familiar kind of magic, they are commonly transformed into faded and aging invalids. Why should a promising young poet lay determined siege to such a person? That question haunted Elizabeth throughout the first year of her friendship with Browning, and with particular horror before their first meeting. The ardor of his early letters, the unmistakable tendency toward "I love you," made her dread a disillusionment for him as harrowing as the humiliation for her. Surveying her room, the intimate macrocosm of her work and her ailments, she removed his portrait from its place on the wall below Wordsworth—the *New Spirit of the Age* engraving in which he stares with conventional poetic exaltation into blank white paper—and in a "fit of justice" pulled down Tennyson's as well. At the last minute she wrote, bitterly echoing his own phrase: "Before you come, try to forgive me for my 'infinite kindness' in the manner of consenting to see. . . . Well!—but we are friends till Tuesday—& after perhaps."[1]

She need have had no fears. Yet only after many months and many signs of confirmation did she dare to believe and utter the truth: "Turning the wonder round in all lights, I came to see what you admitted yesterday . . . yes, I saw *that* very early . . . that you had come here with the intention of trying to love whomever you should find."[2] Nor did Robert deny he had felt a "presentiment"[3] he would fall in love. He had fancied her just what he found her. He had known her from the beginning. What he remembered, particularly from that first meeting, was "the dear, dear pale cheek and the thin hand";[4] and what he seems to have felt at the moment, in the warm, hushed darkness of the sick chamber, was the infinite fragility and the shrinking sensitiveness of the small figure, muffled in shawls and rugs, upon the sofa. Even so, he stayed a full hour and a half. "I trust to you," he wrote the same evening, "for a true account of how you are—if tired, if not tired, if I did wrong in anything,—or, if you please, *right* in anything—(only, not one more word about my 'kindness'. . . .) . . . They all say here I speak very loud—(a trick caught from having often to talk with a deaf relative of mine). And did I stay too long?"[5]

After he had left, Elizabeth had a constant sense of his presence in the room, and when her father came in next morning she said, "It is most extraordinary how the idea of Mr. Browning does beset me— . . . it is a persecution."[6] To Miss Mitford, with equally naïve yet significant calculation, she pronounced Robert "younger looking than I had expected—looking younger than he *is*, of course."[7] To Robert himself she replied that she "ought to be better for what was . . . happiness and honour" to her yesterday—and then took him rather stridently to task for placing an embargo on the words "kindness" and "gratitude." They are appropriate to her humble sphere: "We stand on the black and white sides of the shield; and there is no coming to a conclusion."[8] But Robert was past heeding such warnings. He now gave expression to his feelings in a violent love letter.

Elizabeth reacted with vigor and courage. "You have said some intemperate things . . . fancies—which you will not say over again . . . but *forget at once*, . . . And this you will do *for my sake* who am your friend (and you have none truer)—and this I ask, because it is a condition necessary to our future liberty of intercourse." And then she concluded, piteously fearful for the future, "You are not displeased with me? . . . I do not write as I might, of some words of yours—but you know that I am not a stone, even if silent like one. And if in the *un*silence, I have said one word to vex you, pity me for having had to say it—and for the rest, may God bless you far beyond the reach of vexation from my words or my deeds!"[9]

The circumstances were peculiar, yet the facts were clear: He had been rejected as a lover, and he had fallen short as a gentleman, having grossly disregarded the feelings of a lady whom he had every reason to think an incurable invalid. Both pride and conscience were deeply mortified—and he may also have feared that without some sort of disavowal he would not be allowed to visit her in the future. His next letter was one of the strangest and most revealing he ever wrote. In these few pages he managed, somehow, to write all his dramatic monologues at once, multiplying himself protectively into many Robert Brownings and creating a wonderful psychological poetic smokescreen with which to conceal or half-conceal that fiery, impulsive Robert Browning who had got himself so egregiously in the wrong:

> For every poor speck of a Vesuvius or a Stromboli in my microcosm there are huge layers of ice and pits of black cold water—and I make the most of my two or three fire-eyes, because I know by experience, alas, how these tend to extinction—and the ice grows and grows—still this last is true part of me, most characteristic part, *best* part perhaps, and I disown nothing—only,—when you talked of '*knowing* me'! Still, I am utterly unused, of these late years particularly, to dream of communicating anything about *that* to another person (all my writings are purely dramatic as I am always anxious to say) . . . Will you not think me very brutal if I tell you I could almost smile at your misapprehension of what I meant to write?[10]

So much for pride. He now insists on her superiority and confesses the darker Brownings in the intervals of pleading for the better. He does not attitudinize or long for Lethe "à la Byron," but "the heart is desperately wicked"; he is "vain and ambitious some nights"; he has a faculty for self-consciousness "at which John Mill wondered." Nevertheless, he dares call things by their names to himself; and he knows she will forgive him. "Because I am, from my heart, sorry that by a foolish fit of inconsideration I should have given pain for a minute to you, towards whom . . . I would rather soften and 'sleeken every word as to a bird' . . . (and, not such a bird as my black self that go screeching about the world for 'dead horse'—corvus (picus)—mirandola! . . .)." The fundamental Browning, he declares on Mr. Kenyon's authority, is a man of "common sense," and a mild man-about-town.[11] Such she will find him.

Elizabeth apologizes "for having spent so much solemnity on so simple a matter," confesses that she had not suspected the "ice and cold water" part of him—into which she has now taken her first plunge—and assures him she will bear in mind that he is "a dramatic poet."[12]

For a time the correspondence falls back uneasily on literary themes. She is grateful for his help on her translation of *Prometheus*. She finds his "St. Praxed's" the "finest and most powerful" of the poems he had published in *Hood's*; "The Laboratory" is "hideous,"[13] as he had meant to make it. His gratitude is touching, yet almost aggressive: "You do not understand what a new feeling it is for me to have someone who is to like my verses or I shall not ever like them after! So far differently was I circumstanced of old, that I used rather to go about for a subject of offence to people; writing ugly things in order to warn the ungenial and timorous off my grounds at once."[14]

Elizabeth remained cautious. Browning talked a good deal of parties and how much they bored him, of how dull and stupid most people were. How long could a man so exacting, so complexly made up of volcanos and cold water, find much to amuse him in the dismal quiet of a sick chamber? She insisted he choose his visiting days, lest she be brought to the "catastrophe"[15] of asking for a day when he would rather not come. What makes him weary in soul? "Is it . . . that you are tired of a same life and want change?"[16] She could not altogether repress her curiosity: "Upon *second* or *third* thoughts, isn't it true that you are a little suspicious of me, suspicious at least of suspiciousness?"[17] Who gives cause? he demanded. The question of higher and lower was once more aired. He protested that she had benefited his work much more than he hers. She declared: "To judge at all of a work of yours, I must *look up to it*, and *far up*." She saw that he was in love with an image exalted by genius and perhaps by illness. Do not "spoil the real pleasure I have . . . in your poetry," she begged, "by nailing me up into a false position with your gold-headed nails of chivalry, which won't hold to the wall through this summer." To bring herself down to the floor a little faster, she told him she was older than he "*by years*,"[18] though how much older she did not say. Dorothy Hewlett informs us that according to Barrett family tradition, Robert never did know her age while she lived.[19]

On his side, Robert had fallen in love first, and asked himself questions afterward. The questions were nearly all practical. He had at first understood that the lady could not stand on her feet, that her illness consisted in "a spinal injury irremediable in the nature of it."[20] Having learned that it was probably remediable—and sensed that it was in part psychological—he at once set about a cure. Many similar cures have involved an incidental love affair. Gently but persistently, he recommended the fine summer weather; she must take exercise, go into the air. Elizabeth was anything but enthusiastic. Carriage rides were desperate and disagreeable adventures. Every breath of air and drop of moisture was a threat. "You may if you please get well through God's goodness—with persevering patience, surely."[21] What was put to her as a religious duty, she could not shirk. By early August she confessed "living more in the outer life for the last few months than I have done for years before."[22] Robert applauded every achievement. "Never, pray, *pray*, never lose one sunny day or propitious hour . . . . But do not surprise *me*, one of these mornings, by 'walking' up to me when I am introduced . . . or I shall infallibly, in spite of all the after repentance and begging pardon—I shall . . ."[23] Here some words are rubbed out. Robert dared not yet attempt an epistolary embrace.

Meanwhile, the sheer volume of their correspondence was pushing them toward intimacy. Having forbidden expressions of endearment, Elizabeth herself, with a woman's instinctive resourcefulness, was smuggling them into the routine courtesy of her parting sentences. "May God bless you, my dear friend, my ever dear friend!"[24] Robert dared not trust himself beyond a few closing lines, for fear of writing a love letter, yet did not scruple in his turn to exploit the amenities of the final sentence. "God bless you, my best, dearest friend—think what I would speak—"[25]; and she parried, though with deep feeling: "May God bless you, far longer than I can say so."[26] And Robert: "May God bless you, and let you hold me by the hand till the end."[27] These exchanges did not alarm Elizabeth's conscience, and they gave her quiet assurance of being loved. She became motherly about his headaches and forbade him excessive walking and verse writing.

They were now in the classic positions of the hero and heroine in a Victorian romance. Robert wrote dozens of letters with a full heart and a guarded pen. His duty to Elizabeth's pleasure alone imposed the curb. At the same time, her duty impelled her to insult his love periodically by telling him he would soon tire of her. The lighted match could not be flourished indefinitely in close proximity to the fuse. With regard to the sentence "'that I shall be tired of you &c.,'" he wrote on August 27, "though I *could* blot that out of your mind forever by a very few words *now*,—for you *would believe* me at this moment . . . —but I will take no such advantage—I will wait."[28] Elizabeth took offense at the suggestion that she would not believe. "Do not avenge yourself on my unwary sentences by remembering them against me for evil."[29] Robert had received the time-honored provocation of the hero: he responded with an indignant love letter. "I believe in *you* absolutely, utterly. . . . Let me say now—*this only once*—that I loved you from my soul, and gave you my life, so much of it as you would take."[30] These passionate words forced her to a deeper level of her dilemma—from "How could he love?" to "How dare I let him love?" "Could *I* be . . . justified in abetting such a step—" she asked, "the step of wasting, in a sense, your best feelings?"[31] He must force his mind "at once into another channel."[32]

Shrewdly, she had used his own commonsense against him. With equal shrewdness, he used the Victorian ethos against her: will removes all obstacles. She still believed herself incurable. He did not. And now the facts begin to yield to him. Dr. Chambers in September declares her much better and strongly enjoins a winter in a warmer climate, which would probably restore her to health. There is talk of Pisa, of steamers, even of steamer schedules. Arabel and a brother or two would accompany her. Gaily she explains to Robert the difference between her sisters: Henrietta likes polkas; Arabel likes sermons. Arabel is her favorite. The whole family is scheming. Mr. Kenyon has come out strongly for the plan. Of course Robert would be there. He warns her she must not expect Neapolitan scenery in Pisa.

With immense caution and elaborate circumlocution, Robert opens wider the door to the forbidden subject, and now he knows how to urge his cause:

> I am not what your generous self-forgetting appreciation would sometimes make me out—but it is not since yesterday, nor ten nor twenty years before, that I began to look into my own life, and study its end, and requirements, what would turn to its good or its loss—and I *know*, if one may know anything, that to make that life yours and increase it by union with yours, would render me *supremely happy*, as I said, and say, and feel. My whole suit to you is, in that sense, *selfish*—not that I am ignorant that *your* nature would most surely attain happiness in being conscious that it made another happy—but *that best, best end of all*, would, like the rest, come from yourself, be a reflection of your own gift.

To be sure, he continues, "my whole scheme of life (with its wants, material wants at least, closely cut down) was long ago calculated—and it supposed *you*, the finding of such an one as you, utterly impossible."[33] Now all is changed. One hundred pounds a year would suffice them in Pisa. He will do hack work: he will write a play for Kean, a novel for Colburn!

In reply, Elizabeth seizes half-heartedly on one or two inconsistencies to worry the old questions of integrity and worthiness, but at length she confesses that "neither now nor formerly has any man been to my feelings what you are." But God has put a barrier between them—her health. Mr. Kenyon said to her today in smiling kindness, "In ten years you may be strong perhaps." Beyond this, her father "never *does* tolerate in his family . . . the development of one class of feelings"[34]—not that she is dependent financially, for she has an income of her own.

Meanwhile, as talk about Pisa mounts, Papa distinguishes himself by maintaining a "dead silence."[35] All eyes gradually focus on him. Like the rest of the family, he has seen morbidity in Elizabeth's illness. Apparently, when he wanted to, he saw nothing but morbidity. Part of Dr. Chambers' office, he once said, is "to reconcile foolish women to their follies."[36] There is less talk of Pisa, of steamers. Elizabeth sees the stars constellating against her. And then, to the astonishment and horror of the entire family, she faces her father. "I told him that my prospects of health seemed to me to depend on taking this step, but that through my affection for him, I was ready to sacrifice those to his pleasure if he exacted it. . . . He would not answer *that.* I might do my own way, he said—*he* would not speak. . . . For his part, he washed his hands of me altogether."[37] Highly indignant, her brother George urges her to continue her preparations for the voyage. He will appeal the case once more at the last moment.

Here, on the knife-edge between Papa's displeasure and possible death, is a moment for decision. "Well!—and what do you think?" asks Elizabeth. "Might it be desirable for me to give up the whole? Tell me."[38] Robert understands with Mr. Barrett that Elizabeth is a jewel to be guarded carefully, but Mr. Barrett is casting her away. "And you ask whether you ought to obey this no-reason? I will tell you: all passive obedience and implicit submission of will and intellect is by far too easy, if well considered, to be the course prescribed by God to Man in this life of probation."[39] And he concludes: "Now while I *dream,* let me once dream! I would marry you now and thus—I would come when you let me, and go when you bade me—I would be no more than one of your brothers—'*no more*'—that is . . . when your head ached I should be *here.*"[40] Deeply moved, Elizabeth replies that if God "should free me within a moderate time from the trailing chain of this weakness, I will then be to you whatever at that hour you shall choose. . . . Only in the meanwhile you are most absolutely free."[41]

She still talks of steamer schedules, but now she is under the full weight of Papa's displeasure. He has withdrawn his nightly visits; he spends only a few awful minutes with her before dressing for dinner. At the last possible moment, George makes his plea—and fails. Her final comment concedes old servitude almost more than it asserts new emancipation. "The bitterest 'fact' of all is, that I had believed Papa to have loved me more than he obviously does."[42] But she has found an emotional refuge from which she can admit the truth about her father, and she has told Robert she is his for anything but his own harm. After the Pisa episode, he dares to omit the second word from his usual "dearest friend."

Finding Robert more closely committed to her than ever, she makes another supreme effort: why should he not go to Pisa alone, next week? "YOU WILL CONSIDER MY HAPPINESS MOST BY CONSIDERING YOUR OWN."[43] Impatiently Robert brushes aside all lofty motives: "I quite understand the grace of your imaginary self-denial, and fidelity to a given word, and noble constancy; but it all happens to be none of mine, none in the least. I love you because I *love* you."[44] He must himself have been astonished at the effect. Her next letters are full of a new warmth and intimacy. Those words, she declares, mark "the first moment in which I seemed to admit to myself in a flash of lightning the *possibility* of your affection for me being more than dream-work."[45] From childhood she has hungered for "irrational" love because she has felt unworthy of any other. Now she need no longer fear being loved out of pity for her misfortunes or admiration for what Robert calls her "glorious genius."[46] He assures her that if she had told him, "I am not *the* Miss B.—she is upstairs and you shall see her—I only write those letters and am what you see—"[47] he would not love her the less. "It is something to me between dream and miracle . . .," writes Elizabeth in wonder, "as if some dream of earliest brightest dreaming-time had been lying through these dark years to steep in the sunshine."[48]

But Robert had not won his victory by a random shot, nor had he been waging love by letters and visits alone. For months sternly forbidden to use the word, he had, like Elizabeth, fallen back on poetry as a safe subject. But need it be a safe subject? Long before he met Elizabeth he had written poems about her without knowing what he was doing; why not write more now that he knew her and had a very precise idea of what he wanted to do? As early as May 1, she had expressed interest in "The Flight of the Duchess," the first nine sections of which had just appeared in *Hood's Magazine.* On May 3, Robert told her that what she had read was a mere introduction. He had a portfolio which contained much more of "The Duchess." For weeks she continued her inquiries until on June 22 he promised he would finish and transcribe the poem. Thereafter, a few lines at a time as he composed them, he sent her the rest. Then, sternly literary, he asked her to read the poem carefully and write a criticism.[49] By this time, Elizabeth's interest in "The Flight of the Duchess" was by no means exclusively literary.

To be sure, this work may have taken at least vague shape in Robert's mind long before he met Elizabeth. In a sense it originated in the gypsy's song heard in boyhood. Robert told Elizabeth on July 25, 1845, that he had conceived the poem "two years ago, fully," and that originally it was to consist "entirely of the gipsy's description of the life the Lady was to lead with her future gipsy lover."[50] He wrote Furnivall in 1883 that, interrupted after composing the first nine sections, he forgot what he had intended and did not continue until "some time afterwards" when, visiting Sir John Hanmer at Bettisfield Park, he heard a guest say "the deer had already to break the ice in the pond."[51] This detail begins the tenth section. A letter to Domett indicates he was at Bettisfield Park in September 1842. But his statement to Elizabeth implies he had not even conceived the poem until 1843. Probably, then, he made subsequent visits to Bettisfield and may even have completed a final draft of the first nine sections after he began to correspond with her.[52] Or, again, the first nine sections, in approximately their published form, might have been written earlier, and his thoughts about Elizabeth might have occasioned the interruption (mentioned to Furnivall) which brought about the change of emphasis. Certain it is that the first nine sections were published in *Hood's* for April 1845 and that the finished poem emphasized not the gypsy's song and the lady's life with her gypsy lover, but the Duke's domestic situation and the Duchess' escape from it.

In fact, the poem ultimately developed a surprising resemblance to the situation in which Robert was involved. The Duchess is a tiny, intense, vibrant creature like Elizabeth, though without the sadness and morbidity:

> She was the smallest lady alive,
> Made in a piece of nature's madness,
> Too small, almost, for the life and gladness

That over-filled her, as some hive
Out of the bears' reach on the high trees
Is crowded with its safe merry bees:
In truth, she was not hard to please!

The huntsman who tells the story is like Robert a daring prosodist, a fair horseman, a man of passion and gusto, and an adoring inferior. Though not obviously like Mr. Barrett—a still-beloved father—the Duke is, like him and the speaker in "My Last Duchess," a tyrannical egotist who, regarding his wife as property, periodically demands certain clockwork performances from her, and then leaves her to "die away the life between." Again, the Duke is a pedantic, obsessive medievalist who, in opposition to the gypsy, lives a sham and imposes it on others, and is thus tactfully made responsible for the unreality in Elizabeth's own life. He is also a comic villain upon whose absurdities the bluff, hearty narrator proves his own wit and insight—to obtain credence for the romantic miracle shortly to be told. Finally, his dukedom, for all its proud forests and lingering feudalism, is like England a cold northern country where

Beneath they mine, above they smelt,
Copper-ore and iron-ore,
And forge and furnace mould and melt.

Into this sinister, Dickensian domestic comedy—Wimpole Street magnified and medievalized—comes the gypsy, a symbol of nature and reality with suggestions of sunburnt bohemianism. In images and phrases that echo the letters of Robert and Elizabeth again and again, she preaches "How love is the only good in the world," and invites the Duchess to a healthy, joyous life in the open air, presumably in the south. Significantly, reality and happiness are not to be achieved by the mere wish. To be a gypsy, one does not simply climb out the window. An arduous period of probation is necessary before one can join the tribe and find a lover.

Stand up, look below,
It is our life at thy feet we throw
To step with into light and joy; . . .
If any two creatures grew into one,
They would do more than the world has done: . . .
So, to approach at least that end,
And blend,—as much as may be, blend

Thee with us or us with thee,—
As climbing plant or propping tree,
Shall some one deck thee, over and down,
  Up and about, with blossoms and leaves?
Fix his heart's fruit for thy garland-crown,
  Cling with his soul as the gourd-vine cleaves,
Die on thy boughs and disappear
While not a leaf of thine is sere?
Or is the other fate in store,
And art thou fitted to adore,
To give thy wondrous self away,
And take a stronger nature's sway?

In the phrase—"as much as may be, blend"—Professors Snyder and Palmer[53] see an expression of the fear that, because of a supposed injury to her spine, Elizabeth might be incapable of coitus. The Duchess yields to the gypsy's spell and rides off with her, having given a plait of hair to the faithful huntsman, who values it more than a happily married man should. So Robert had long begged, and Elizabeth with infinite maidenly reluctance finally given, a lock of hair. A poem of courtly love, "The Flight of the Duchess" shows a fine aristocratic disdain for the marriage vows. Were the author less obviously loyal and respectable, Elizabeth might well have been alarmed. Actually, she fell more and more in love with this little back-to-nature sermon, and at the same time subjected it to a severe stylistic criticism, proposing no less than seventy-three changes.

Was the sermon any better understood, or followed, than most sermons are? Apparently, Robert was too secretive, and Elizabeth too ladylike, to acknowledge a personal reference in so many words. Yet after receiving a batch of newly written lines, she wrote significantly, "I was sure to be so delighted—and *you knew it.*"[54] On October 13, the very day the poem went to press, she told Robert she would not go to Pisa: "And so, tell me that I am not wrong in taking up my chain again & acquiescing in this hard necessity."[55] The word "chain" establishes a significant parallel to events in the poem: the huntsman had not followed the Duchess because

My father was born here, and I inherit
  His fame, a chain he bound his son with.

On November 6, 1845, all the poems of Robert's portfolio, including "The Flight of the Duchess," were published as *Bells and Pomegran-*

ates, No. VII, Dramatic Romances and Lyrics. On the same day, by a fitting coincidence, Elizabeth sought to recover Robert's first love letter:

E.B.B. to R.B.

Wednesday.
[Post-mark, November 6, 1845.]

I had your note last night, & am waiting for the book to-day,—a true living breathing book, let the writer say of it what he will. Also when it comes it wont certainly come 'sine te.' Which is my comfort.

And now—not to make any more fuss about a matter of simple restitution—may I have my letter back? . . . I mean the letter which if you did not . . . did not punish for its sins long & long ago . . . belongs to me—which if destroyed, I must lose for my sins, . . . but, if undestroyed, which I may have back,—may I not? is it not my own? must I not?—that letter I was made to return & now turn to ask for again in further expiation. Now do I ask humbly 'nough? And send it at once, if undestroyed—do not wait till Saturday. . . .

For the rest . . . yes!—you know I do—God knows I do—Whatever I can feel is for you—& perhaps it is not less, for not being simmered away in too much sunshine as with women accounted happier—*I* am happy besides now—happy enough to die now.

May God bless you, dear—dearest—
Ever I am yours—[56]

In 1845, Robert could scarcely think at all without thinking of Elizabeth. Nearly all the poems of that year in the *Dramatic Romances* relate to her in one way or another. "Saul"—comprising as yet only the first nine sections—reflects her religious earnestness; "Time's Revenges," her replacing Domett in Robert's affections; "The Lost Mistress," the prohibitions she imposed after Robert's violent love letter.[57] But perhaps the most interesting Elizabeth poem, after "The Duchess," is "The Glove." The idea seems first to have caught Robert's eye in "The Glove and the Lions," Hunt's trite and solemn ballad: King Francis I and his court watch the lions fight; a lady throws her glove into the pit; her suitor, De Lorge, recovers the glove and throws it in her face; King Francis applauds, pronounces her vain—and the poem closes. One can understand how, given this ferociously flamboyant situation, Robert would inevitably rush to the lady's defense. But how find a virtuous motive for the throwing of the glove? Obviously, such a gesture invited expulsion from the court—and Browning did know of a lady who had renounced a court on principle. The *Mémoires* of the Marquis de Lassay record the story of the beautiful and virtuous Marianne Pajot, who renounced the Duke of Lorraine for his own good and ultimately yielded to the patient suit of the young Marquis himself, several years her junior.[58] The lady of "The Glove" became Marianne—and of course Elizabeth.

Still, a virtuous lady must be reconciled with a murderous action. Clearly, so singular a case must be given an atmosphere of fact. There must be an eyewitness: Peter Ronsard reports the facts in trimeter couplets so frank and open, so easy and intimate, that unbelief seems a tasteless folly. At the same time he is witty; and the quick double rhymes, falling themselves like witticisms, teach one to expect the unexpected—particularly from a court that plainly esteems fine words, as well as war, a "true pastime." Throughout, the king acts as chorus, a blunt and obvious monarch who understands neither women nor poets. He exclaims at the powerful jaws of the lion, and the glove flutters down. He pronounces the lady vain, and she leaves amid the derision of the court. But Ronsard notices something in her face and, overtaking her, asks her for an explanation. She replies that De Lorge has long besieged her with words, describing the endless dangers he would face for her love. When she sees the lion—a magnificent beast fresh from Browning's boyhood recollections and the old Strand menagerie—she thinks how many humble people have quietly braved death to snare, cage, and transport him to France.

> So, wiser I judged it to make
> One trial what 'death for my sake'
> Really meant, while the power was yet mine,
> Than to wait until time should define
> Such a phrase not so simply as I,
> Who took it to mean just 'to die.'

By this time, throwing a glove beneath the lion's jaws seems scarcely more than the rational precaution any alert Victorian young lady might take against a designing man. As Ronsard turns away, a youth, younger than the lady herself, approaches, and leads her away—to be happy with her ever afterwards. Both the youth and Ronsard are Browning himself. A comic ending further diminishes the seriousness of the lady's impulsive action: De Lorge marries and has to recover *her* glove from the king's chamber.

"Do tell me what you mean precisely by your 'Bells and Pomegranates' title?"[59] asked Elizabeth when No. VII was about to come out.

"The Rabbis," replied Robert somewhat mysteriously, "make Bells and Pomegranates symbolical of Pleasure and Profit, the Gay and the Grave, the Poetry and the Prose, Singing and Sermonizing—such a mixture of effects as in the original hour (that is quarter of an hour) of confidence and creation."[60] She suggested he append some such note to No. VII (Robert did later on to No. VIII). Meanwhile, she exulted over the infinite riches in that slender volume. "Now if people do not cry out about these poems, what are we to think of the world?"[61]

There was very little outcry, and even that echoed the old ritual note of bewilderment. Reviewers read even these brilliant poems through the dark spectacles of the Sordello Legend. *The Eclectic Review* had only recently persuaded itself of Browning's sanity. *The Athenaeum* still maundered about "mist," *The Examiner*, about "transcendental and other fogs."[62] Chorley in *The Athenaeum* thought the versification of these poems almost "Hudibrastic" pushed "to the extremity of all rational allowance"; and yet noted in "How They Brought the Good News" "an animation which Bürger himself hardly exceeds." Everybody complained a little of Browning's virtues. Chorley found "England in Italy" too full of matter; and Forster, who wrote *The Examiner* review, all of Browning's poetry too full of ideas. "Mr. Browning's metaphysics," he said flatly, "have been too abundant for his poetry." And yet, having once more become reconciled to his old friend, Forster conceded that in the present volume, fog and metaphysics were at a minimum. In fact, these poems "look as though already packed up and on their way to posterity; nor are we without a confident expectation that some of them will arrive at that journey's end."

Browning thought Forster "most generous."[63] On the whole, he was. But the difference between a reviewer's generosity and a poet's became evident shortly after, when Landor sent from Italy fourteen blank-verse lines, in which he said of Browning:

> Since Chaucer was alive and hale,
> No man hath walkt along our road with step
> So active, so inquiring eye, or tongue
> So varied in discourse.

"Landor had sent the verses to Forster at the same time as to me," Robert told Elizabeth, "yet they do not appear."[64] They had, as a matter of fact, just appeared in the *Morning Chronicle* of November 22. Meanwhile, intensely proud, Robert's father had caused them to be printed and distributed to his friends. Robert himself had been briefly excited by Landor's praise, but in fact he was listening to only one voice. "I do like these poems better and better," wrote Elizabeth. ". . . You will be tired to hear it said over and over so."[65]

Preoccupation with Elizabeth had carried Browning rather swiftly into his future. He had still other unfinished poetical business that belonged to his past. As early as February 11, when he and Elizabeth were curiously searching each other out, he had referred exuberantly to "this darling 'Luria'—so safe in my head, and a tiny slip of paper I cover with my thumb!"[66] Two weeks later, he explains that Luria is "a Moor, of Othello's country, and devotes himself to something he thinks Florence, and the old fortune follows."[67] In short, he is to be a passionate, "golden-hearted" Othello, done in by three shrewd Florentines. The play emerged rather slowly from Robert's head, which ached a good deal. It was laid aside while he saw *Dramatic Romances* through the press, was resumed by October 27, and by January 22, 1846—except for the fifth act—was sent to Elizabeth.[68] She was highly enthusiastic but could scarcely believe that Luria had been meant to commit suicide in so unheroic a manner. Indeed, the work proved not so firmly under Robert's thumb as he had thought. Struggling with the fifth act, he found he could not make Domizia either fall in love or be quite the panther-beauty he intended. Undoubtedly she suffered from not being like Elizabeth.

Altogether, Elizabeth's fears about the play were only too well justified. Faced with Luria's choice of using a victorious Florentine army to conquer Florence, or of surrendering his command to be executed, Shakespeare's Othello would have enslaved the city first and then committed suicide in remorse at having done so. Unfortunately, Browning had no Iago on hand to bring his Moor to a proper boil. Politically, the play comes down to one of Browning's ironic dilemmas: a society cannot afford to trust its military heroes very far or very long, and yet if the people attempt to defend themselves, they may do the society such spiritual damage that it may never again rise to its former achievements in philosophy and art. The fault is of course not that of the hero or the people, but of "those old fools/ I' the council."[69] The dilemma is further complicated because the hero is "God's model"[70] in the state. Clearly, neither the ideas of Sordello nor the influence of Carlyle had disappeared from Browning's mind.

On February 11, 1846, Robert wrote Elizabeth of still another play which he had completed probably some two years earlier: "For the 'Soul's Tragedy'—*that* will surprise you, I think. There is no trace of you there—you have not put out the black face of *it*—it is all sneering and *disillusion*—and shall not be printed but burned if you say the word—now wait and see and then say! I will bring the first of the two parts next Saturday."[71] These words are eloquent testimony of both how much Robert felt Elizabeth's influence and of how much he felt obliged to be publicly cheerful. *A Soul's Tragedy* languished in dangerous proximity to the flames for almost another month before it reached Elizabeth's hands. She was astonished and delighted: it was certainly superior to the first act of *Luria.* With a cry of triumph she recognized in the hero Chiappino a prophetic sketch of her suitor George Hunter.

In *A Soul's Tragedy,* Browning had written, somewhat involuntarily, his one comedy. Chiappino, a citizen of Faenza, has long boasted he will accomplish that heroic act of Browningesque liberalism: he will assassinate the papal tyrant. His friend Luitolfo does so on impulse and flees the city. Crediting Chiappino with the deed, the people make him their ruler. Ogniben, the Pope's Legate, now appears. He is one of Browning's most engaging cynics, an easy, comfortable man who has seen twenty-three revolts and is perfectly willing to grant two and two make five, so long as his opponent grants four and four make ten. He not only bends Chiappino and the revolution to the orderly purposes of the status quo, but takes over the play, leaving the comic idealist scarcely any room in which to display his folly. *A Soul's Tragedy* suffers from too much Iago, as *Luria* suffers from too little.

On April 13, 1846, *Luria* and *A Soul's Tragedy* were published together as the eighth and last number of *Bells and Pomegranates.* Forster praised the volume in *The Examiner* and J. R. Lowell in *The North American Review.*[72] Otherwise, neither play has received very much attention then or since.

CHAPTER 13

Into the Light

1845-46

In the character of a smartly dressed visitor presenting himself week after week with Victorian punctilio at the correct front door of No. 50 Wimpole Street, Robert had penetrated to the heart of the enchanted castle, found his princess, and won her. Now he was to discover what he had long feared—that in spite of love she was singularly reluctant to escape and preternaturally calm in the presence of the ogre. That threatening presence, always invisible to him, was to grow on Robert through the rest of the adventure with a terrible imminence. Would he lose his Elizabeth after all? Would she break down helplessly before her father's angry ruthlessness? Robert felt his anxiety like a Victorian—and like a human being: he continued to suffer from headaches, dizziness, and nausea.[1]

Her father's confidence lost after the Pisa episode, Elizabeth kept urging caution about the visits. Robert, as a law-abiding Englishman accustomed to the enjoyment of his liberties, was long reluctant to see in Mr. Barrett any impediment that could not be overcome, if not by frank and open dealing, at least by gentlemanly 'legalities.' Why, as precaution, should he not give Elizabeth a signed and sealed paper, with which she could then confront her father? Elizabeth did not think a signed and sealed paper effective magic against the paternal wrath. Blandly unenlightened, Robert proposed an even franker expedient: "The process should be so much simpler! I most earnestly EXPECT of you, my love, that in the event of any such necessity as was then alluded to, you accept at once in my name *any* conditions possible for a human will to submit to."[2]

In reply, Elizabeth assures him at the outset, "I am yours, while I am of any worth to you at all." But no agreement or promise will serve any purpose with her father. "Ah, you do not see, you do not understand. The danger does not come from the side to which a reason may go. . . . I shall be thundered at; I shall not be reasoned with." That her father loves her enough to exempt her from the prohibition imposed on his other children—she no longer hopes. What is that prohibition? Once she said in jest,

> "'If a prince of Eldorado should come, with a pedigree of lineal descent from some signory in the moon in one hand, and a ticket of good-behaviour from the nearest Independent chapel, in the other'—?
> "'Why even *then,*' said my sister Arabel, 'it would not *do.*'"

But there is no immediate danger of discovery. "Let there be ever so many suspectors, there will be no informers," and she concludes, "Why not leave that future to itself? For me, I sit in the track of the avalanche quite calmly . . . so calmly as to surprise myself at intervals—and yet I know the reason of the calmness well."[3] What lay behind this unnatural calm became painfully clear in a subsequent letter: "I have thought sometimes . . . I should choose to die this winter—now—before I had disappointed you in anything."[4]

Robert is horrified at her "frightful wish."[5] She is his reason for being, his highest good, for whom he is profoundly grateful to God. "As I sate by you," he writes somewhat later, "you so full of the truest life, for this world as for the next—and was struck by the possibility, all that might happen were I away, in the case of your continuing to acquiesce—dearest, it *is* horrible—I could not but speak."[6] And yet his remedy is still that he claim a man's right to be the first to inform her father.

Elizabeth continues to expound her father's character and to reveal what passes behind the blameless red-brick front of No. 50. As a religious man who reads his Bible, Mr. Barrett believes that children are by divine arrangement bound to "passive obedience, and particularly in respect to marriage." The other day, downstairs, he was holding forth at length on this doctrine. "One after the other, my brothers all walked out of the room, and there was left for sole auditor, Captain Surtees Cook, who had especial reasons for sitting it out." Very mildly Captain Cook asked "if children were to be considered slaves."[7] Mr. Barrett's reply is not recorded. Some years before, Henrietta was discovered to have a suitor. "At a word she gave up all—at a word. . . . A child never submitted more meekly to a revoked holiday. Yet . . . I hear how her knees were made to ring upon the floor, now! She was carried out of the room in strong hysterics, and I, who rose to follow her, though I was quite well at that time . . . fell flat down upon my face in a fainting-fit."[8] Recently, Henrietta has been "taken by storm,"[9] as she puts it, by that very meek soldier her relative, Captain Cook, who endures the rudeness of her brothers and waits daily in the drawing room four hours at a time, sometimes sobbing uncontrollably. He seems so insignificant that even the head of the house suffers his presence.

By this time Robert has begun to have nightmares in which Mr. Barrett appears as a man with a whip. Elizabeth gently explains her father's many admirable qualities and that she has long striven to keep his love. "I have heard the fountain within the rock, and my heart has struggled in towards him through the stones of the rock . . . thrust off . . . turning in again and clinging." Of late years he has isolated himself more and more. If he were not stronger than most men, he could not endure "the cold dead silence all round." She does not expect mercy. "He would rather see me dead at his foot than yield the point."[10]

Robert is now extremely eager to make decisions and form plans. Elizabeth wants to go on plucking daisy petals in the lion's den. Once more she worries the question of who is to serve whom, who is to sacrifice whose happiness to whom. She confesses she had long regarded Browning the letter-writer and Browning the visitor as two distinct people and could not bring them together. Actually, she was herself guilty in part of keeping them separate, for she frequently commanded the letter-writer: "Do not mention this when you come." She declares that the letter-writer has won her: he is bolder and more convincing. Robert explains that the visitor feared giving way to passion and himself expresses a most vehement disgust at aggressive wooing.

Next summer, says Robert, they must marry and go to Italy. She qualifies: if when fine weather comes she is still well, he must decide—then, not now. Suppose she became ill *after* their marriage. She is thinking of his risk. "As to taking the half of my prison . . . I should recoil from your affection even under a shape so fatal to you . . . dearest!"[11] He replies that to remain in England indefinitely is certain tragedy for both. "You have all my life bound to yours—save me from *my 'seven years'*—and God reward you!"[12]

Through the winter months, Elizabeth resigns herself occasionally and briefly to optimism, and for good reasons. Her health has improved wonderfully. She takes up the looking-glass with a good conscience, stands to tend Robert's flowers, and astonishes the whole family by walking downstairs alone and appearing in the drawing room. These miracles are produced by a deeper and more splendid miracle, of which she cannot resist giving some special confidant a glimpse now and then. "A friend of mine—one of the greatest poets in England too—," she writes Mrs. Martin, "brought me primroses and polyanthuses the other day, as they are grown in Surrey."[13] In this mood she believes, for the moment at least, in her right to love, in the possibility of marriage. If she is exacting in her requirements of marriage, it is for Robert's sake, not for hers. She is horrified at the calculation with which many women are encouraged to marry and at the thoughtlessness with which many others actually do—"from pity, from admiration, from any blind impulse."[14] Robert temporizes somewhat anxiously: marriage as it now exists causes women much suffering, but it is still practicable—the world must go round.

A visit from Mr. Kenyon seems to have brought about a disastrous reversal in Elizabeth's mood. How? As a poet and translator, Elizabeth wrote and published with very considerable talent and boldness. But she sometimes dreaded the world's opinion nearly as much as she scorned its grosser ways and values, and, by a characteristic process of large fears playing upon small symptoms, she had inflated Mr. Kenyon into a formidable symbol of the world's most enlightened judgment of her and therefore of her own severest judgment of herself. He had always been playfully critical of her, and, recently, when she had expressed wonder that he should be deeply moved by "Saul," he had retorted with some heat—and perhaps a twinge of jealousy at her closeness to Robert—that she "never understood anybody to have any sensibility" except herself.[15] Lately, also, she had become more and more aware and fearful of his "scanning spectacles."[16] What did he guess? She knew what he would think. He had "long ceased to wonder at any extreme foolishness produced by—*love.*" He would think her "ungenerous," and Robert "very, very foolish." She concludes, with another brave effort to remain cheerful, "There will be a nine days railing of it and no more!"[17]

But while Mr. Kenyon's spectacles guard the future, there can be no confident looking forward to marriage and happiness. Sanity and cheerfulness fall back into morbidity and despair. She tells Robert that if she had been truly generous, she would not have seen him after their first meeting. "But I had not courage—I shrank from the thought of it—and then . . . besides . . . I could not believe that your mistake was likely to last."[18] When she was in such a mood, Robert had to write carefully. Any awkward phrase might offend her. Even her playful misconstructions—that he had said thinking about her was a "plague"[19]—Robert took pains to explain and expiate. In her despair she brooded afresh on "a letter, written in a crisis long since, in which you showed yourself awfully, as a burning mountain, and talked of 'making the most of your fire-eyes,' and of having at intervals 'deep black pits of cold water'!—and the lava of that letter has kept running down into my thoughts of you too much, until quite of late."[20] Here was an old problem. The fire-eyes and the black pits did certainly correspond to a violence and coldness in Browning, to sudden aversions and a ready contempt—directed toward others, though never toward herself—which had given Elizabeth pause at the beginning of their romance. Moreover, for all their patience, good sense, courage, and splendid passion, his letters remain somewhat opaque, somewhat mysterious. At the end of a thousand pages, one sees her clearly; one does not see Robert so. Perhaps she did not either—and therefore she feared, and resented the more, his repeated "You do not know me."

The discussion now moved away from the problem—however urgent—of ends and ways, downward and inward, to the confidences and confessions beloved of lovers. If they were sometimes mysteries, they were also dreams and destinies long foreknown, to each other. "I seem to have foretold, *foreknown* you in other likings of mine,"[21] wrote Robert. "*I* was thinking the other day," replied Elizabeth, "I had loved you all my life unawares, that is, the idea of you. Women begin . . . by meaning . . . to love such and such an ideal. . . . And here is mine . . . even to the visible outward sign of the black hair and the complexion (why you might ask my sisters!)." She had surprised everybody in the house by consenting to see him. "Then, when you came, you never went away. I mean I had a sense of your presence constantly."[22] She had been frightened of him at first. She felt he had a power over her, that he could read her thoughts as he might read a newspaper.

But once again they found that perfect foreknowledge did not mean perfect agreement. Elizabeth continued to marvel that they had fallen in love through the strange medium of pen and paper. Surely all letters are good. She is particularly enthusiastic about one she has received from Miss Martineau describing a visit to Wordsworth. She sends it on to Robert—and discovers with a shock that he by no means shares her feeling. "Burn anybody's *real* letters . . . they move and live—the thoughts, feelings, and expressions even—in a self-imposed circle limiting the experience of two persons only." But Miss Martineau's is not a real letter. "The carriage-sweep and quarry, together with Jane and our baskets, and a pleasant shadow of Wordsworth's

Sunday hat preceding his own rapid strides in the direction of Miss Fenwick's house—surely, 'men's eyes were made to see, so let them gaze' at all *this*!" But Robert prefers his Wordsworth of *The Lyrical Ballads* to Miss Martineau's prosy wonder. Didn't Shelley say Wordsworth "had no more *imagination* than a pint-pot?"[23] Elizabeth warmly disputes letter-burning. "If the secrets of our daily lives and inner souls may instruct other surviving souls, let them be open to men hereafter."[24] At the same time she admires the cleverness of Robert's letter. He refuses to continue the controversy, and is sorely vexed at her praise. "If I caught myself trying to write finely, graphically, &c. &c., nay if I found myself conscious of having in my own opinion, so written—all would be over! yes, over!"[25] Protesting that she hates literary letters as much as he does, Elizabeth drops the subject with guilty haste—perhaps with a sudden recollection of the thick-growing cypresses, tombs too close for tears, golden nails of chivalry, escutcheons eternally sundered between black and white, and many other labored ingenuities familiar to her pen.

Confidences now proceed to a deeper, more intimate level. Robert confesses, with characteristic reluctance, that, though he loved her almost before he saw her, he loved her much more after he had seen and talked with her many times. "Oh, I know what is old from what is new, . . . but . . . if you let me, love, I will not again, ever again, consider how it came and whence, and when, so curiously, so pryingly." And he repeats, "Ah, dear, dearest Ba, I could, could indeed, could account for all, or enough!"[26] But he would not. Clearly, he has privacies not only from her, but from himself. For all his moral courage and psychological curiosity, he is not eager to explore his own interior volcanos and water pits. Elizabeth suffers from an opposite excess of self-consciousness: she is obsessed with a mountain-top observer. "I have my own thoughts of course, and you have yours, and the worst is that a third person looking down on us from some snow-capped height, and free from personal influences, would have *his* thoughts too, and *he* would think if you had been reasonable as usual you would have gone to Italy. . . . The third person thundered to me in an abstraction for ever so long, and at intervals I hear him still."[27] Robert takes an instant dislike to the third person. He is a busy-body who confuses counsel. Had he thundered at Robert, he would have commanded marriage to some "cook-maid animal" with "You can't kiss Mind!"[28] and then urged the classics of mind against the cook-maid animal. Elizabeth meekly promises to ignore the third person.

Through most of March and early April, the correspondence flowed idyllically in its double stream between New Cross and Wimpole Street, with much joking, teasing, gossip, and a comfortable repetition of old themes and sentiments—until, apparently on a visit of April 6, Robert had the grave misfortune to air his views on dueling. It was now his turn to encounter a critical stranger in the fond lover. It was also his turn to recant and submit. Elizabeth seems to have been too shocked for words on the sixth, but, in her letter of the seventh, she falls on him with heavy sarcasm: "Honourable men are bound to keep their honours clean at the expense of so much gunpowder and so much risk of life. . . . Not only it seems to me horribly wrong . . . but absurdly wrong."[29] So far from hiding Robert after a duel, she would turn him over to the police. Browning replies in the combined manners of Cleon, Karshish, and Bishop Blougram, defending the duel according to the principles not only of Christianity, Stoicism, Asceticism, and Epicureanism, but of ordinary social utility. He is full of surprising points where major principles intersect, of crucial exceptions that prove the rule, of learned and ingenious illustrations. "Say, Christianity forbids this,—and *that* will do—rational Simon renounces on his pillar more than the pleasures of society if so he may save his soul—"[30] and so on for many pages, with even a dexterous stab at Wordsworth in his court dress.

Elizabeth is not dazzled. Far from it. She tries to avoid the issue, to be cheerful and gossipy, but she cannot. "You do *not* well, by any means . . . for my poet of the 'Bells and Pomegranates,' it is very ill, wonderfully ill . . . so ill, that I shut my eyes, and have the heartache (for the headache!)."[31] And the heartache has its own regions and cogent logic. Elizabeth begins to fear that he will tire of her after all. Robert shudders and submits, but still tries to save his dignity: "I wrote *so*, precisely because it was never likely to be my own case."[32] Alas! She opens up a fresh abyss. Her principles will not allow him to submit. He must think for himself, even though his thinking gives her pain. Meanwhile, the logic of pain and heartache remains as cogent and compelling as before: "I think of you, bless you, love you—but it would have been better for you never to have seen my face perhaps."[33] Suddenly the full horror of the situation comes home to Robert. In a letter nearly as long as his original casuistry, he repeats over and over that he could not possibly have cut off loving her; and yet he adds apprehensively, "I *can* fancy your being angry with me, very angry."[34] He begs her to marry him soon, at once—to preserve him from further error. The ensuing letters subside into mutual endearments.

Meanwhile, it is March, April, even May—and observers not at all alpine or imaginary are developing shrewd and alarming suspicions. A lady encamped at No. 16 Wimpole Street sends a rosetree and writes on the card, "When are you going to Italy?"[35] Mr. Kenyon reports quite casually that Mrs. Jameson has inquired how Miss Barrett and Browning are. Elizabeth has a disturbing habit of coloring to the roots of her hair when Mr. Kenyon mentions Robert's name—once so violently that he looked at her with "infinite surprise in a dead pause."[36] And Robert himself confesses that at a dinner of Mr. Kenyon's where George Barrett was present, "I left the talking to go on by itself, with the thought busied elsewhere, till at last my own voice startled me for I heard my tongue utter 'Miss Barrett . . . that is, Mrs. Jameson says . . .' "[37] Browning's visits are much discussed downstairs—and even upstairs—at No. 50 Wimpole Street. Late in May, when she was holding her Sunday levee for all her brothers and sisters together, "Alfred threw himself down on the sofa and declared that he felt inclined to be very ill, . . . for that then perhaps (such things being heard of) some young lady might come to visit *him*, to talk sympathetically on the broad and narrow gauge!"[38] Worst of all, Elizabeth had written somewhat earlier of her father, "it was plain to see yesterday evening when he came into this room for a moment at seven o'clock, before going to his own to dress for dinner . . . plain to see, that he was not altogether pleased at finding you here in the morning."[39]

This portent was gravely discussed by the lovers. Robert bursts out with an immense sentence—tortured with syntax and indignation—which in its later stages concludes, "a mere sympathizing man, of the same literary tastes, who comes good-naturedly, on a proper and unexceptionable introduction, to chat with and amuse a little that invalid daughter, once a month, so far as is known, for an hour perhaps,—that such a father should show himself *'not pleased* plainly,' . . . my Ba, it is SHOCKING!"[40] Elizabeth explains that her father's displeasure was not directed against Robert personally. Robert had "just touched one of his vibratory wires, brushed by and touched it—oh, we understand in this house." And she adds bitterly, "After using one's children as one's chattels for a time, the children drop lower and lower toward the level of the chattels, and the duties of human sympathy to them become difficult in proportion."[41] Robert answers, "If the toad *does* 'take it into his toad's head to spit at you'—you will not 'drop dead,' I warrant. . . . Why prevent the toad's puffing himself out thrice his black bigness if it amuses him among those wet stones. We shall be in the sun."[42] Elizabeth accepts *toad*, and, like the unicorn, it becomes a mythical beast in their correspondence. "I am not afraid of 'toads' now, not being a child any longer." She could not give Robert up if she wanted to. Deliciously, she tells him he is "chained" to her.[43]

Plainly, the moment for decision is not far off. Redoubling his efforts, Robert turns every occasion into a sermon on Italy, on health. He has long since sounded her delicately on her use of opium, and she has responded in a very defensive manner, insisting she takes opium solely on medical advice, to steady her pulse, quiet her nerves, and induce sleep. "I don't take it for 'my spirits' in the usual sense; you must not think such a thing."[44] Robert continues to express a quiet interest, and somewhat later she quotes her medical consultant: slowly and gradually, something will be done. "All the kind explaining about the opium makes me happier," rejoins Robert. " 'Slowly and gradually' what may *not* be done?"[45] Still later, he writes, "I have to thank you with all my heart for the good news of the increasing strength and less need for the opium—how I do thank you, my dearest—and desire to thank God through whose goodness it all is!"[46]

It is now full spring. Elizabeth need no longer limit her excursions to the downstairs of No. 50 Wimpole Street. Robert tells her that he expects everything from her going out of doors, and enticingly describes the view from the upper windows of the house at New Cross—the lambs bleating in the green field behind, the chestnut all leafy and blossoming fruit trees over the garden wall, and, beyond, the hill—which Wordsworth had condescendingly called "a rise"—commanding a vast prospect over the surrounding country. "Do you think that I never saw the chestnut tree before?"[47] demands Elizabeth. Nevertheless, she has bought a bonnet, of which her sisters say that "nothing can be more fashionable";[48] and to prove that the purchase was not a mere gesture, she not only goes driving in it in Regent's Park but actually descends from the carriage and walks along the path. "The sun was shining with that green light through the trees, as if he carried down with him the very essence of the leaves, to the ground. . . . I put both my feet on the grass, . . . which was the strangest feeling! . . . and gathered this laburnum for you." And she repeats with wonder: "The standing under the trees and on the grass, was so delightful. . . . And all those strange people moving about like phantoms of life."[49] Robert protests that he would walk barefoot till he dropped to see the bonnet.

To be sure, the new bonnet brings dangers as well as responsibilities. Elizabeth never knows what bore she may meet at the foot of the stairs or on the doorstep, and once, entrapped in the drawing room, she waits a long time at Henrietta's command for the intrepid Captain Cook to appear in full regimentals from a presentation to the Queen—and is finally rescued by Mrs. Jameson, whom she accompanies up to her stronghold with a sigh of relief. Yet the enchantment of the third-story bedroom with the double green door has definitely been broken. With fear, astonishment, and delight, Elizabeth moves out into the light, noise, and novelty of the everyday world. She drops a letter in the post with her own hand, writes another sitting in the back drawing room (the first in five years written outside her bedroom), walks up the stairs as well as down, and actually goes out for a stroll accompanied only by Flush—a prodigious act of cool independence, except that Flush terrifies her by walking on the other side of the street, in utter indifference to dog-stealers. She drives out with Mr. Kenyon to see the Great Western train come in with a terrifying roar, has tea in Regent's Park with Mrs. Jameson, and on the drive home sees for the first time in many years the gaslight in the shops. A wonderful, miraculous restoration! And yet—"mournful and bitter would be to me this return into life, apart from you. . . . But you are *there,* in the place of memory."[50]

Not that Robert had caused her to forget Bro. On the contrary, in the midst of her happiness, she felt guilty both toward Robert, because she had gained his love, and toward Bro, because she had ceased to suffer from his death. These feelings were of course morbid and obstructive. She had long since accepted Robert's love, but she still refused to accept its consequences and responsibilities. Anxious to be forthright and perhaps to de-etherealize her commitment to marriage and Italy, Robert had been urging her to confide in Mr. Kenyon and to receive Sarianna Browning as a visitor. Elizabeth shrank from doing either. Mr. Kenyon's spectacles had become the very eyes of private and public accusation, and they saw incriminating evidence everywhere. Only the other day he had shaken her with the information that the servants had been turning away visitors by telling them Mr. Browning was with her. To confide in Mr. Kenyon would be to take up an intolerable weight of worldly caution and prudence. To meet Robert's sister would be to confront an even more formidable judge than Mr. Kenyon. "You understand, dearest beloved, all I *could* mean about your sister's coming here. . . . I was afraid of not being liked enough . . . which was one reason, and none the less reasonable because of your being 'infatuated.' "[51] The last word indicates a feeling several times expressed. Poor Elizabeth felt that in choosing her Robert had made a fool of himself. She was ashamed of herself, not only for herself, but for him. Robert now asked that he might tell his parents of their engagement. Elizabeth was opposed to it. If they knew, they would feel obliged to apprize Mr. Barrett. In desperation, she proposes that she go to Italy with her friend Miss Bayley, or that they postpone the whole venture for another year.

Though declaring that he would wait fifty lifetimes for her, Robert shows irritation almost for the first time in their correspondence. He agrees to say nothing to his parents but resents the suggestion they would betray his secret to Mr. Barrett. And, when she begs to be released from a promise just made as to the future, he writes: "Do not for God's sake introduce an element of uncertainty and restlessness and dissatisfaction into the feeling whereon *my* life lies."[52]

Despite the fondest endearments at the end of every letter, a certain amount of friction and heat continues. One seriousness begets another. Sometimes the issue is not even serious. Elizabeth's brothers bring back from the Flower Show the report that "Mr. Browning is to be married immediately to Miss Campbell."[53] The Barretts are both puzzled and amused. Robert is only a little amused. Pursuing the mystery with desperate ingenuity, he discovers that a Mr. Brown, the nephew of Lord Jeffrey, is to marry Miss Campbell immediately. Elizabeth doubts the explanation with perfect good humor, and Miss Campbell joins the unicorn, the toad, and the other mythical beasts that wander through the correspondence.

A much more serious issue is money. Insolvency in Victorian husbands caused far more scandal than sickliness in their wives. In the middle of April, Mr. Kenyon had shown himself in what Elizabeth must have thought his true colors by broaching this ugly truth:

> He began a long wandering sentence, the end of which I could see a mile off, about how he 'ought to know better than I, but wished to enquire of me' . . . 'what Mr. Browning's objects in life were. Because Mrs. Procter had been saying that it was a pity he had not seven or eight hours a day of occupation,' &c. &c. It is a good thing to be angry, as a refuge from being confounded: I really *could* SAY something to *that.* And I did say that you 'did not *require* an occupation as a means of living . . . having simple habits and desires—nor as an end of living, since you found one in the exercise of your genius! and that if Mr. Procter had looked as simply to his art as an end, he would have done better things.'[54]

Mr. Kenyon beat a hasty retreat: Wordsworth had not climbed Parnassus on a steady income either. Robert was forbearing about Mrs. Procter's character, and the subject was dropped. Two months later, Robert once more urges Elizabeth to make her fortune over to her brothers and sisters, and again plunges into impromptu schemes: he will enter the diplomatic service or obtain a pension from Lord Monteagle. Besides, Moxon says that his poems are beginning to sell. Gently, but firmly, Elizabeth informs him that he has little practical sense. She will retain her fortune, at least during her lifetime and his. He must never take time from poetry to earn a living. Once more the subject is dropped, but an atmosphere of frustration and futility lingers. Once more she wonders whether she ought to marry him at all, and he is pained at the appearance of such a very old ghost.

Somewhat half-heartedly, they discuss places to live. Pisa is a possibility and La Cava in Southern Italy is another. Florence has bad water and too many English people. But the discussion of plans fills Elizabeth with a renewed and terrifying sense of immediacy, and she is off into the improbable: "My programme is, to let you try me for one winter, and if you are tired (as I shall know without any confession on your side) why then I shall . . . leave you in La Cava, and go and live in Greece somewhere all alone, taking enough with me for bread and salt. Is it a jest, do you think? Indeed it is not."[55] Robert now rises fully to the occasion. His reply to this demoralizing threat is a model of tact and patience, with the gentlest undercurrent of irony and reproach. "I feel altogether as you feel," he writes, "about the horribleness of married friends." But for him, "there never has been one word, one gesture unprompted by the living, immediate love beneath." And he concludes, "I count confidently on being more and more able to find the true words and ways (which may not be *spoken* words perhaps), the true rites by which you should be worshipped, you dear, dear Ba, my entire blessing now and ever—and *ever*."[56] Elizabeth says no more about Greece, but she continues to make reservations and invent delays. Even Arabel is out of patience with her. Going with her sister to see Mr. Boyd once more after many years, Elizabeth takes fright and tries so desperately to turn back that Arabel bursts out, "Oh Ba, . . . such a coward as *you* are, never will be . . . married, while the world lasts."[57]

Travel fares and the practical aspects of life in Italy bring them back a month later, in the middle of July, to the money question. Accumulated disagreement has brought about a reaction. Both are now ready to be realistic and constructive. Both insist that they attach no importance to money, that they are devoted to the simple life. Robert talks no more about diplomacy and novel writing: his pride will be satisfied if she will "endeavour to live as simply and cheaply as possible. . . . You shall come and live with me, in a sense, rather than I with Miss Campbell!"[58] But Robert's simplicity is complicated by an elaborate modesty. He continues in a more intimate tone:

> Now put the hand on my eyes again—now that I have kissed it. I shall begin by begging a separate room from yours—I could never brush my hair and wash my face, I do think, before my own father—I could not, I am sure, take off my coat before you *now*—why should I ever? 'The kitchen' is an unknown horror to me,—I come to the dining room for whatever repast there may be,—nor willingly stay too long there,—and on the day on which poor Countess Peppa taught me how maccaroni is made,—*then* began a quiet revolution, (indeed a rapid one) against 'tagliolini,' 'fettucce,' 'lasagne,' etc., etc., etc.—typical, typical![59]

Apparently these requirements seem to Elizabeth nothing beyond what John the Baptist, under similar circumstances, might stipulate. She replies that Robert may choose the lodging and order the dinner; she is quite willing to live on locusts and wild honey. On the other hand, she has thought of taking her maid Wilson with her. Her sisters have urged her to do so, and Wilson is eager to travel. To be sure, she is an expensive servant, with a salary of £16 a year. Robert thinks Wilson absolutely indispensable. In fact, recognizing that Elizabeth might again be ill, he will not ask her to give up any of her income. "I have only to be thankful that you are not dependent on my exertions."[60] He is even willing to live on her money at the start. At his request, she writes a paper bequeathing her property after his death to her two sisters equally or, in the event of their deaths, to her surviving brothers. Thanking her for the paper, Robert surmises cheerfully, "There may be even a *claimant*, instead of a recipient, of whatever either of us can bequeath—who knows?"[61] A week later, sturdily facing the more unpleasant aspects of this subject, he asks her for a precise account of her assets and income. She learns from Stormie that she has £8000 in the funds, as well as ship and railroad shares. The total yields annually some £360, which was more than Robert's father earned and a very handsome income for Italy.

Elizabeth was now visited by a macabre consequence of one of her more dashing epistolary friendships. Late in June—on the same morning, she saw his *Napoleon Musing at St. Helena* in Samuel

Rogers' private collection—the painter Haydon committed suicide, bequeathing a trunkful of manuscripts to Elizabeth Barrett, in the hope that she might edit and publish them. Elizabeth at once began to make herself ill. Could she not have saved Haydon's life by sending him money? Should she not edit the manuscripts? Controlling his temper, Robert patiently explained that the whole idea, like its originator, was insane. Edit twenty-six volumes of coarse boasting and reckless scandal-mongering? Moreover, Serjeant Talfourd was of the opinion that the manuscripts belonged to Haydon's creditors. Elizabeth thankfully acquiesced, though with one regretful backward glance: Haydon had told her that the dashing Mrs. Norton had made advances to him. Robert declined to relish the morsel: Mrs. Norton was the "hack-block"[62] of braggarts like Haydon.

Elizabeth quickly recovered from the Haydon episode. Everybody was astonished at her health and strength. And indeed she seemed to have crossed a divide, both physical and psychic. Love had gradually conquered fear, or worn it out. The financial question was settled, and, without being too imminent, Italy had begun to appear real. On July 22, 1846, she wrote: "*I* shall look back on these days gratefully and gladly, because the good in them has overcome the evil, for the first time in days of mine."[63] But while Elizabeth rested content in a rather precarious present, Robert suffered even more severely from headaches and dizziness in contemplating an extremely uncertain and threatening future. He had to accustom his pride and conscience to the prospect of living on his wife's income. He had to keep silent on his intentions both to his intimate friends and to his immediate family, and yet to fear that his open secret might be discovered at any moment by Mr. Barrett. He had to be ready not only to meet Elizabeth's catastrophic backslidings in the present, but at the final crisis to bring her to the pitch of resolve and action. He had to face the fact that, though further incarceration in No. 50 Wimpole Street was unthinkable for her, yet marriage, a long journey, and a new life in a new country involved the gravest risk. Little wonder that his health deteriorated. Elizabeth became increasingly worried about him, consulted Wilson about his pallor, and advised coffee-drinking instead of his noxious habit of taking cold showers.

For a year and a quarter now, first once a week and then twice, Robert had been facing the austere front door of No. 50, been received by a servant or Arabel, braved the hall with its imminent danger of masculine Barretts, and then ascended three flights of stairs to his Elysium on the third floor.[64] His visits had become not only more frequent but much longer. To manage them with a minimum of household noise and incident, to keep his hours and days separate from Mr. Kenyon's or Mrs. Jameson's, to take advantage of a sudden exodus of Barretts on the one hand or warn against a sudden influx of relatives on the other—was a prodigious task of plotting and maneuver, which Elizabeth performed with astonishing vigilance and resource, and with an only gradually weakening discretion. Even so, Robert had adventures. Sometimes he stayed so long he was intercepted by Mr. Kenyon, who then looked "whole catechisms"[65] from behind his spectacles; and once, in the presence of the trembling Wilson, he was followed upstairs by Elizabeth's former suitor, the Reverend Mr. Hunter, whose face was white with jealousy. And Mr. Hunter was no man to be trusted with a secret, even an unsubstantiated one.

What Elizabeth and Robert could not hide from their world was the long history of their discretion. Late in August, Stormie asked Arabel out of the blue whether there was an engagement between Ba and Mr. Browning. "What nonsense, Storm," was the best Arabel could muster. "George was by, looking as grave as if antedating his judgeship."[66] Treppy guessed the secret across the loneliness and infirmities of old age. Mr. Boyd saw it from his dungeon of blindness. If Mr. Kenyon did not know, it was only because he was too cautious to conceive so extravagant a middle-aged folly. In late July he had attempted to bring the whole situation to a sensible solution in a manner that caused the lovers no little embarrassment. Taking Arabel and Henrietta aside one day, he explained that Mrs. Jameson had offered to accompany Ba to Italy. That lady was aware of the difficulties—he had himself made them clear. "Poor Papa was not spared," mourned Elizabeth. Mr. Kenyon urged that Ba be persuaded to accept the offer. Much embarrassed, Henrietta declined to interfere. "Ba must do everything for herself." Mr. Kenyon was puzzled. "But she must not go to Italy by herself. Then, *how*?" "She has determination of character," continued Henrietta, "she will surprise everybody some day."

" '*But* HOW?'—Mr. Kenyon repeated . . . looking uneasy."[67]

Mr. Kenyon's constructive endeavors on that day were far more embarrassing than he dreamed. Hearing that he was in the house, Robert cut his own visit three-quarters of an hour short, then had the further misfortune to meet him on the stairs. Hearty and jovial, Mr. Kenyon proposed an excursion with Landor and himself. Robert discouraged the idea. Conscious of three-quarters of an hour of happiness irretrievably lost and of "a half opened door that discovered sundry presences,"[68] he gossiped vaguely and miserably about literary people for a moment or two, and escaped. In Elizabeth's room, Mr. Kenyon exclaimed at what an amusing anecdote Browning had told him. Later, Robert could remember neither what the anecdote was, nor that he had told it.

Meanwhile, having made her offer, Mrs. Jameson began to make inquiries. Three weeks later, she put Mr. Kenyon's question: what was Elizabeth going to do about Italy? "Just nothing."

> "But what *are* you going to do—" throwing herself back in the chair with a sudden—"but oh, I must not enquire."
>
> I went on to say that "in the first place my going would not take place till quite the end of September if so soon . . . —and that, for the actual present, nothing was either to be done or said."
>
> "Very sudden then, it is to be. In fact, there is only an *elopement* for you—" she observed laughingly.[69]

Elizabeth felt obliged to laugh, but the word "elopement" had shocked her deeply, nor was she ever willing to grant that it applied to the action of a woman faced with her situation.

When the halt and the blind had guessed Elizabeth's secret and the entire household was discussing almost nothing else, how could Papa fail to suspect? Like Paley's Deity, he was nearly always absent; like Hardy's, he was blind. Probably he found it more comfortable not to see too much. Still, Mr. Browning was a regular visitor in the house. His flowers were constantly on Elizabeth's table. Once in April, tacitly acknowledging this phenomenon, Mr. Barrett had himself brought her flowers, which had then withered with ominous swiftness.

Another event threw Robert's visits into the sharpest and most perilous relief. Elizabeth's cousins the Hedleys came from their home in Paris to marry their daughter Arabella to a Mr. Bevan, a giant of a man who terrified Elizabeth with his size and exhausted her with a flood of talk about ecclesiastical architecture. There was to be a splendid church wedding and a marriage breakfast for fifty or sixty people at Fenton's Hotel. Hedleys were now in and out of the house, and everybody was talking matrimony. Mrs. Hedley thought nothing funnier than to turn every occurrence into a joke on the subject. Mr. Barrett brought home a paper for Elizabeth to sign. "Is that your marriage-settlement, my dear?"[70] asked Aunt Hedley. Elizabeth became so nervous she wrote her name wrong, and Papa became cross with her.

At dinner two days later, Aunt Hedley said to Mr. Barrett, "I have not seen Ba all day—and when I went to her room, to my astonishment a gentleman was sitting there." Mr. Barrett looked questioningly at Arabel. "Mr. Browning called here to-day," she said. "And Ba bowed her head," continued Mrs. Hedley, "as if she meant to signify to me that I was not to come in." "Oh," exclaimed Henrietta, "*that* must have been a mistake of yours. Perhaps she meant just the contrary." Mr. Barrett was imperturbable. "You should have gone in," he said, "and seen the *poet*." Unfortunately, Stormie could not let the subject rest. "Oh, Mr. Browning is a *great* friend of Ba's! He comes here twice a week—is it twice a week or once, Arabel?"

Again, when she introduced Mr. Bevan to Elizabeth, Aunt Hedley said, in Mr. Barrett's presence: "'You are to understand this to be a great honour—for she never lets anybody come here except Mr. Kenyon, . . . and a few other gentlemen' . . . (laughing)." Once more Mr. Barrett was imperturbable. "Only *one* other gentleman, indeed. Only Mr. Browning, the poet—the man of the pomegranates."[71]

So much apparent inability to see the fact, Robert could not, under the circumstances, regard as blindness. "I think your Father's words on those two occasions very kind,—very! They confuse,—perhaps humble me . . . that is not the expression, but it may stay. I dare say he is infinitely kind at bottom."[72] Such a view, though it gratified Elizabeth, could not be allowed to stand:

> The difficulty, (almost the despair!) has been with me, to make you understand the two ends of truth . . . both that he is *not* stone . . . and that he *is* immovable *as* stone. Perhaps only a very peculiar nature could have held so long the position he holds in his family. His hand would not lie so heavily, without a pulse in it. Then he is upright—faithful to his conscience. You would respect him, . . . and love him perhaps in the end. For me, he might have been king and father over me *to* the end, if he had thought it worth while to love me openly enough—yet, even *so*, he should not have let you come too near.

After a year of coldness, Mr. Barrett had suddenly relented toward Elizabeth, calling her "my love" and even "my puss." "I quite quailed . . . ," she wrote Robert. "Anything but his *kindness*, I can bear now."[73]

The open secret continued to unfold under Mr. Barrett's nose. While Mrs. Hedley waylaid strange gentlemen and learned little, her husband quietly visited Elizabeth—and learned a good deal. A tender-hearted, matter-of-fact man, he was very fond of his famous niece without in the least troubling himself why she wrote verse or other people read it. Interested in her health rather than her secrets, he had no difficulty in coming directly to the question of Italy. "If you don't go this year, *you will never go,*" he told her. Mysteriously, he urged Pisa and begged that if she went through Paris she would pay him a visit. "When that day arrives," she said, "you may be inclined, perhaps, to cast me off." "Cast you off! Now do explain what you mean." "Ah, no one can tell," replied Elizabeth musingly. "Do you mean," he laughed, "because you will be a rebel and a runaway?"[74] He promised never to cast her off. The next day, while Robert was within, Mrs. Hedley again appeared at Elizabeth's door and was rather "cavalierly" dispensed with. "Pray which of Ba's lovers may *this* be?"[75] she asked Arabel with a half-laugh in the passage way. Mr. Browning's name had to be mentioned. Fortunately, a dinner party that evening swept the matter out of people's minds. Another two days after, while Robert lingered three delicious, dangerous hours in spite of Mrs. Hedley's presence in the house, even Flush became suddenly concerned about the situation, and in spite of Robert's unfailing friendliness and gifts of propitiatory cakes, demonstrated his canine hostility. But once more no harm was done—except to Robert's leg and Elizabeth's feelings. "I did not forgive him till nearly eight o'clock,"[76] reported Elizabeth.

And now the very elements conspired to open Mr. Barrett's mind. On August 1, while Robert was visiting, a violent storm broke out. At first, the situation could not have been altogether unpleasant. Terrified as always on such occasions, Elizabeth clung to Robert's hand and at each flash of lightning or crash of thunder, felt the reassuring pressure of his fingers. But the hour for departure came and passed. The rain rattled and swirled against the windows, and the chimneys howled and creaked. At length, even these terrors faded before the lesser but more practical perils of propriety offended and decorum breached. Elizabeth began to wonder who was listening and thinking downstairs. Then she began to expect Papa's return from the City. Before that awful eventuality, the storm, her bedroom, even Robert himself melted into unreality. "When you sate there yesterday," she confided later, "I was looking at Papa's face as I saw it through the floor." At length, the rain stopped and Robert left. It started again before Elizabeth heard the front door shut, so that, torn between opposite fears, she hoped for a moment that he might return. Eventually, it became quiet outside and then Papa, who had actually been in the house for an hour, appeared in Elizabeth's room like a fresh thunderstorm.

> I was lying on the sofa and had on a white dressing gown, to get rid of the strings . . . so oppressive the air was, for all the purifications of lightning. He looked a little as if the thunder had passed into him, and said, 'Has this been your costume since the morning, pray?'
>
> 'Oh no'—I answered—'Only just now, because of the heat.'
>
> 'Well,' he resumed, with a still graver aspect . . . (so displeased he looked, dearest!) 'it appears, Ba, that *that man* has spent the whole day with you.' To which I replied as quietly as I could, that you had several times meant to go away, but that the rain would not let you,—and there the colloquy ended. Brief enough—but it took my breath away . . . or what was left by the previous fear.

Yet the thunder on Mr. Barrett's brows did not apparently betoken suspicion or intelligence. He was concerned for propriety, and for possible ill-effects from Elizabeth's terror of the storm. " 'And only Mr. Browning in the room'!! . . . He was *peremptory* with Arabel, she told me."[77]

The narrowness of their escape appalled the lovers. "Is not the wonder that this should wait for the eighty-second visit to happen?"[78] exclaimed Robert, displaying the passion—rare and significant in so headlong a man—for commemorative tabulation which had led him to record each meeting as it occurred on the envelopes of her letters. He now urged that they move forward drastically the date of their departure, but Elizabeth must first search his devotion again for cracks and chinks. "Once or twice you have talked as if a change were to take place in your life through marrying—whereas I do beg you to keep in mind that not a pebble in the path changes, nor is pushed aside because of me."[79] And again she threatened him with a flight to Greece. Robert was astonished but patient:

> I want to be a Poet—to read books which make wise in their various ways, to see just so much of nature and the ways of men as seems necessary—and having done this already in some degree, I can easily and cheerfully afford to go without any or all of it for the future, if called upon,—and so live on, and 'use up,' my past acquisitions such as they are. I will go to Pisa and learn,—or stay here and learn in another way—putting, as I always have done, my whole pride, if that is the proper name, in the being able to work with the least possible materials. There is my scheme of life *without* you, *before* you existed for me; prosecuted hitherto with every sort of weakness, but always kept in view

> and believed in. Now then, please to introduce Ba, and say what is the habit she changes?

"What I mean by marrying you—" he concluded, "it is, that I may be with you forever—I cannot have enough of you in any other relation."[80]

A sentiment so heroically conjugal could not be resisted. Elizabeth was now ready to make practical decisions. They reduced visits from twice to once a week. They set their time of departure for late September—a month hence—instead of October or November. They would make Pisa their home, at least for a year. They would go by land across France rather than by sea, since this route was less expensive and less dangerous for Elizabeth. Robert was grave about the responsibility he had assumed: "In the case of your health being irretrievably shaken, . . . the happiest fate I should pray for would be to live and die in some corner where I might never hear a word of the English language."[81] Though he avoided the word, Robert now accustomed her to the idea of elopement. They had no other course, if she was not to be struck down by the sight of her father's anger as by a dagger blow. She began to attend church services with Arabel, apparently to prepare herself for the wedding—she could not see crowds or hear music without bursting into tears. Arabel was impatient. She thought Ba might hear a note or two without falling dead.

Once more Robert urged that they tell Mr. Kenyon and Mrs. Jameson. Toward Mr. Kenyon Elizabeth remained obdurate. Pursuing his inquiries in a fresh quarter, he had recently asked her point blank, "Is there an attachment between your sister Henrietta and Captain Cook?"[82] "Of course Mr. Kenyon *knows*," answered Robert, "and this is the beginning of his considerate, cautious kindness—he has determined to hurry nothing, interfere abruptly in no case, to make you *infer* rather than pretend to instruct you— . . . for 'if the visits of Captain Cook *have* that appearance &c., must not those of R.B., &c., &c.,' "[83] But Elizabeth could not see beyond the glitter of Mr. Kenyon's spectacles. On the other hand, she confirmed Mrs. Jameson's divinations. As that lady was going earlier to Paris, and then on to Italy, they would ask her company from France onward. Robert now told his mother the secret, and she told his father. From him, Robert borrowed £100 to defray the expenses of the voyage. Elizabeth commanded him not to praise her in his foolish way before his parents. Robert was hurt, but reassured her: his parents are utterly generous and loving; they have complete faith in his decisions.

Actually, arrangements proceeded with a minimum of offense on either side. Both lovers were protected by their love from any serious disillusionment. Elizabeth, always a little closer to the facts than Robert, understood that he had certain puzzling faults, some of which she was half-inclined to relate to the old satanic letter of the fire-eyes and water pits. But human limitations continued to be mere incidents in a soaring process of mutual idealization and self-accusal. Elizabeth saw only one grave fault in her paragon: why did he not recognize her own utter and iniquitous inferiority? As a dedicated courtly lover, Robert was equally distressed that she did not perceive *his* inferiority. "There is no love," he insists, "but from beneath, far beneath."[84] Elizabeth had characteristics but no faults—and here his faculty for rationalization was active: her imperiousness is generous pride; her self-righteous humility, "divine diffidence."[85] She tells him he is blind, but for some time she has been willing to accept his blindness: "Love is better than Sight, and Love will do without Sight."[86]

In a less healthy spirit, her sense of guilt was helping to separate her from No. 50 Wimpole Street. "To hear the voice of my father and meet his eye makes me shrink back—to talk to my brothers leaves my nerves all trembling."[87] Psychologically, practically, the time was ripe. At a hint of postponement past September, Robert demands, "Show me one good reason, or show of reason, why we gain anything by deferring our departure till next week instead of tomorrow." And in the same letter: "If . . . you make up your mind to leave England now, you will be prepared to leave by the end of September."[88] Elizabeth agreed to get married at once and leave England as soon as possible thereafter.

At this moment Flush was stolen! On a shopping expedition with Arabel, Elizabeth had stepped into the carriage with Flush at her heels, turned, and—no Flush! Arabel saw her face go white. The rest of that particular letter to Robert alternates lamentations for Flush with railroad itineraries. Flush had fallen among thieves before, and Elizabeth had been warned to expect a ransom price of £10. She dared not haggle—a lady who had done so had been sent her dog's head in a parcel. Elizabeth delegated her brother Henry to pay the "Archfiend Taylor" anything he asked—and learned that her father had forbidden Henry to pay anything at all. The letters carry impassioned debate on the ethics of dealing with dog-stealers. Robert declared he would listen to no nonsense about cutting off heads and paws, but that if Flush were not returned in good health without ransom, he would devote the rest of his life to annihilating the thieves. Elizabeth asked what he would do if Italian *banditti* were to carry her off and send him back her ears. Robert replied that he would pay his last farthing and *then* devote his life to annihilating the thieves. In the realm of practice, Elizabeth and Wilson had driven in terror and desperation to the dens of Whitechapel and been graciously received by Mrs. Taylor in the absence of her husband. Taylor then appeared in Wimpole Street and was angrily shown the door by Alfred Barrett. In this moment of desolation her brother Sette went to Whitechapel and ransomed Flush for six guineas.

Flush had scarcely been washed and fed before a fresh gulf yawned. As early as August 3, Robert had predicted that Mr. Barrett would suddenly carry his family off to the country. On September 10, George was sent forth to find a house in Sussex or Kent. No. 50 Wimpole Street must be cleaned, papered, and painted. Robert did not mince words: "We must be *married directly* and go to Italy—I will go for a licence today and we can be married on Saturday. I will call to-morrow at 3 and arrange everything with you."[89] Elizabeth's comparatively solid world dissolved into shadows in an instant. Despite all her progress, she was only half-emancipated from the sofa point of view. Yet, though she could scarcely believe in the event, she was eager for it: "Will not this dream break on a sudden? Now is the moment for the breaking of it, surely. But come to-morrow, come."[90]

Accordingly, Robert came on Friday for the last time to settle details, and Elizabeth asked him for the last time whether he would repent? His manner was almost too satisfactory: "Yes—my own Ba,—I could wish all the past were to do over again. . . . I look back, and in every point, every word and gesture, every letter, every *silence*—you have been entirely perfect to me—I would not change one word, one look."[91] After he left, Elizabeth prepared Arabel for her absence the next day: she and Wilson would go in a carriage to visit Mr. Boyd; Wilson would return directly; later her sisters should come by to take her for a drive. She also confided her plans more fully to Wilson. "She was very kind, very affectionate, and never shrank for a moment."[92]

Elizabeth did not sleep all night. Saturday morning found her frightened and exhausted. When she walked out with Wilson, she staggered so badly that they had to stop at a chemist's for sal volatile. Elizabeth revived, and they drove to Marylebone Church. Waiting with his cousin George Silverthorne, Robert thought she looked like death when she met them at the door of the church. Later he noted on the envelope of the previous day that the ceremony took place "$\frac{1}{4}$ 11–11 $\frac{1}{4}$ A.M."[93] He also noted that it was the ninety-first meeting between them. Standing beside him in the empty church, Elizabeth thought how many, many women had stood where she did. "Not one of them all perhaps, not one perhaps, since that building was a church, has had reasons strong as mine, for an absolute trust and devotion towards the man she married—not one!"[94] When the brief ceremony was over, she bade her husband good-bye, removed the ring he so lately placed on her finger, and was once more—on that swift day of fantastic dream and irrevocable reality—in the carriage with Wilson on the way to Mr. Boyd's. There she rested on a sofa while her host saw his doctor, was then made to talk and take Cypress wine by the initiated and exultant Boyd and, when her sisters still did not come, was given a dinner of bread and butter so that she would not seem too pale.

> At last they came and with such grave faces! Missing me and Wilson, they had taken fright,—and Arabel had forgotten at first what I told her last night. . . . I kept saying, 'What nonsense, . . . what fancies you do have to be sure,' . . . trembling in my heart with every look they cast at me. And so . . . went on with them in the carriage to Hampstead . . . as far as the heath, . . . —now you shall praise me for courage—or rather you shall love me for the love which was the root of it all. How necessity makes heroes—or heroines at least![95]

Having agreed that scruple forbade Robert's visiting Wimpole Street after their marriage, Elizabeth had now no convincing evidence that she was married or had passed through a long and enthralling romance. It was all dream, delusion, deception. She knew that it had happened only by her fears, her guilt. She saw it in the glitter of Mr. Kenyon's spectacles. The next day began as a jarring irrelevance.

> All my brothers have been here this morning, laughing and talking, and discussing this matter of the leaving town,—and in the room, at the same time, were two or three female friends of ours, from Herefordshire—and I did not *dare* to cry out against the noise, though my head seemed splitting in two (one half for each shoulder), I had such a morbid fear of exciting a suspicion. . . . It was like having a sort of fever.

And yet the fever was swiftly invaded by thrilling reminders of the incredible event: "And all in the midst, the bells began to ring. 'What bells are those?' asked one of the provincials. 'Marylebone Church bells', said Henrietta, standing behind my chair." That afternoon Elizabeth endured the ordeal of Mr. Kenyon's prudent concern for the last time. "*When did you see Browning?*" asked Mr. Kenyon. Elizabeth changed color, and he saw it, yet she answered quickly. "He was here on Friday."[96] The inquisition of this kindly man had become too painful. When he called on a later day, she pleaded a headache; and when Robert wanted to write him a letter confiding their secret before the elopement, she was "terrified" at what could conceivably follow. "Remember that I shall be *killed*—it will be so infinitely worse than you can have an idea."[97]

To be sure, Robert's father had learned of the engagement without feeling obliged to lay the matter before Mr. Barrett; and now hearing of the marriage, he simply looked up from an old book with a start—and was delighted. Mrs. Browning said that if she were well she would write Elizabeth a letter. Elizabeth begged for love and forgiveness. "I feel so as if I had slipped down over the wall into somebody's garden—I feel ashamed."[98]

Few men awake the morning after their marriage day with a sense of freedom and relief, yet such were Robert's feelings. "Dearest, I woke this morning *quite well*—quite free from the sensation in the head. I have not woke *so,* for two years perhaps—what have you been doing to me?"[99]

Necessity, or love, had in fact made a heroine of Elizabeth. She saw at a glance how impossible Robert's ideas about the announcement cards were and took over the task—though on his advice she did omit the West Indies from her territorial title "of Wimpole Street and Jamaica," to appear in the newspaper notice. Stealthily, she and Wilson packed a box and a carpet bag which Wilson—probably, as Dorothy Hewlett suggests,[100] with the connivance of the housekeeper—got out of the house and on their way to New Cross. The new capacity to act gave tongue and scope to Elizabeth's native *hybris.* She wrote Robert on September 14:

> In your ways towards me, you have acted throughout too much 'the woman's part,' as that is considered. You loved me because I was lower than others, that you might be generous and raise me up:—very characteristic for a woman (in her ideal standard) but quite wrong for a man, as again and again I used to signify to you, Robert—but you went on and did it all the same. And now, you still go on—you persist—you will be the woman of the play, to the last; let the prompter prompt ever so against you. You are to do everything I like, instead of my doing what *you* like, . . . and to 'honour & obey' *me,* in spite of what was in the vows last Saturday.[101]

One more heroic task lay before her. What she had long evaded and postponed, she must now with one great effort perform—and no doubt, as a vehement and self-righteous woman, she felt, in spite of her terror, impelled to perform it. Fortunately, she could do so under circumstances congenial to her courage—pen in hand and in the quiet of her bedroom. She must write to Mrs. Jameson, to Miss Mitford, to Mr. Kenyon, to her sisters, to at least one of her brothers, and to her father. Eurydice must give one last look into the long, dark passage behind and, to those who thought it her misfortune or her duty to be dead, explain that she was still alive. The letters to her sisters, and even that to Mrs. Jameson, would be easy enough—spontaneous outpourings of emotions and confidences long held back. That to Mr. Kenyon would be harder because of his spectacles and her long reticence. It would be an appeal to public opinion, but after all to a most kindly and indulgent public opinion.

On the other hand, her brothers presented a delicate problem: she must ask them to exempt her, a mere woman, from the dispensation they lived by. For her intercessor among them and to her father, she chose George, the second eldest and ten years her junior. The choice was a natural but ambitious one. To be sure, George had on at least one occasion looked very grave at the mention of Mr. Browning, yet he had been her strong defender in the Pisa affair. Moreover, as a barrister and a man of business, George enjoyed unusual influence and authority within the family; and as a woman who instinctively allied herself with power, Elizabeth had cultivated him carefully, having corresponded with him regularly ever since Bro's death. In such dreadful crises as the proposed moves to Clifton or the Black Mountains, she had exerted all her energy and skill to win him to her side and use him as an ambassador to Papa. In character, George seems to have been a grave young man full of heavy commonsense and even heavier suspicion of folly in women. On the other hand, he was generous, warm-hearted, and like his other brothers definitely susceptible to Elizabeth's charm. Her letters to him are among her most delightful, as clear and simple in language as those to Robert and Miss Mitford are often florid and labored. In the most loving and inoffensive manner (only faintly tempered with the condescension of an elder sister) she is constantly pricking the bubble of his masculine importance, twitting him with legal terms, teasing him with lawyer's logic, and disarming him with exhibitions of commonsense—particularly about her health, on which he obviously held sensible opinions. She must have realized he was not altogether safe, and yet, if she won him, he would be her most powerful advocate.

The truly heroic letter would of course be that to her father. Here she must plead with the leopard to change his spots. "I will put myself under his feet," she had told Robert beforehand, "to be forgiven a little, . . . enough to be taken up again into his arms." But would he forgive? "He will wish . . . , that I had died years ago! For the storm will come and endure. And at last, perhaps, he will forgive us."[102] But when the moment came for writing, she was too hurried, exhausted, and depressed to predict anything. "I began to write a letter to Papa this morning, and could do nothing but cry, and looked so pale thereupon, that everybody wondered what could be the matter."[103]

Meanwhile, Robert was struggling with travel schedules and his own impatience. *Sordello* was only a little less penetrable to Mrs. Carlyle than the arrival and departure of trains and steamers were to Robert. He saw one railway company where there were two, and confused departures from Le Havre with those from Southampton, discovering fresh complications every day until, somewhat surprised at his incompetence, Elizabeth set him straight.

On Friday evening, September 18, 1846, Elizabeth wrote, "Is this my last letter to you, ever dearest? Oh—if I loved you less . . . a little, little less."[104] On the next afternoon, a rather faded, fragile little lady of forty, her maid, and a middle-aged spaniel left No. 50 Wimpole Street as though for a thirty-minute drive in the autumn sunshine. Somewhat later, George Barrett opened a sealed envelope addressed to him in his sister's handwriting. He read the words, which seem even now to break from the page in the passionate, imploring tones of feminine entreaty:

> My dearest George I throw myself on your affection for me & beseech of God that it may hold under the weight—dearest George, Go to your room & read this letter—and I entreat you by all that we both hold dearest, to hold me still dear after the communication which it remains to me to make to yourself and to leave to you in order to be communicated to others in the way that shall seem best to your judgement. And Oh, love me George, while you are reading it. Love me—that I may find pardon in your heart for me after it is read.
>
> Mr. Browning has been attached to me for nearly two years—At first and for long I could not believe that *he* (who is what you know a little) could care for such as I, except in an illusion & a dream. I put an end (as I thought) briefly to the subject. I felt certain that a few days & a little more light on my ghastly face, would lead him to thank me for my negative.

And she plunges into a fervent yet succinct account of the entire romance, dwelling on her own incredulity and the magnitude of Robert's love. "And this was the attachment, George, I have had to do with, & this the man—Such a man.—Noble he is—his intellect the least of his gifts! His love showed itself to me like a vocation." She touches swiftly on finances, less swiftly on the necessity of acting "in defiance of Papa's will." In accepting Mr. Browning's offer, she has served the best interests of all. "My spirits would have festered on in this enforced prison, & none of you all would have been the happier for what would have [been] bitter to *me*."[105] She firmly believes that she has acted within her rights, even that she has done her duty—and yet, with the desperate iteration of a besetting fear, she begs George again and again to look at all the circumstances, to judge her gently. In short, she knows that she has transgressed against the Commandment of Wimpole Street. She feels guilty. And George finds her guilty, for he did not forgive her for five years.

Apparently George refused either to break the news to Mr. Barrett, or to give him the letter which Elizabeth had enclosed for him. These baleful duties fell upon Henrietta. She found her father on the stairs, with a heavy volume in his hands. When he heard what had happened, he let the volume drop with a slam. In her terror Henrietta lost her footing and fell, thus giving rise to a tradition that in his anger Mr. Barrett had thrown her downstairs. Soon after, Mr. Kenyon called. Having received his letter, he had come to urge that Robert be accepted as a son-in-law. "I have no objection to the young man," Mr. Barrett is reported to have said, "but my daughter should have been thinking of another world."[106] Much or little might be read into this remark, so openminded about the young man, so singleminded about the daughter. On a happier occasion, he had said that Elizabeth was "the purest woman he ever knew"—which meant, she interpreted for Robert, "that I had not troubled him with the iniquity of love affairs."[107] Plainly, she was the keystone of Mr. Barrett's moral and patriarchal arch, a virgin dedicated to a principle that was somehow satisfactory both to him and to God. Acting as a man of principle, he cast Elizabeth from him. Acting as a loyal retainer—and apparently as a zealous prosecuting attorney—George was equally obdurate and accused Arabel and Minnie the housekeeper of connivance in the elopement.

CHAPTER 14

Pisa to Florence

1846-47

Courtships may be idyllic, but honeymoons seldom are. Elizabeth's and Robert's touched the heights and the depths. A marriage founded on the higher love, a husband torn between ecstasy and dread, a middle-aged invalid discovering the world for the second time and sex for the first, a journey which seemed to threaten death in every inn-parlor and railroad waiting room were scarcely conducive to happiness. Some of Elizabeth's friends thought her marriage little more than a sentimental form of suicide. It was, Miss Mitford felt, as if "Dr. Chambers had given her over. . . . I never had an idea of her reaching Pisa alive."[1]

Elizabeth herself seems never to have been greatly worried that she might lose her life, but she was not entirely glad that she had lost her chains. Speeding toward Southampton—her first ride behind one of the iron monsters she had trembled at from the safety of Mr. Kenyon's carriage—she could think of little but the dear dungeon she had now left forever. That night, they had a miserable crossing, and, "exhausted either by the sea or the sorrow," they rested all the next day at Le Havre. At nine in the evening, they set out on another incredible night journey. "A little feverish with the fatigue and the violence "done to herself and beginning to doubt whether she was "in or out of the body" Elizabeth could see "now five horses, now seven . . . all looking wild and loosely harnessed . . . some of them white, some brown, some black, with the manes leaping as they galloped and the white reins dripping down over their heads . . . such a fantastic scene it was in the moonlight." Perhaps she was by then beginning to break out a little from her gloomy thoughts. "Robert," she told Arabel in that first letter, "was dreadfully anxious about me—and after all, he was the worst, I believe, of any of us. . . . You would have been startled if in a dream you had seen me, carried in and out, as Robert in his infinite tenderness, insisted on carrying me, between the lines of strange foreign faces in the travelers' room; back again to the coupé of the diligence, which was placed on the railway."[2]

Once in Paris, Robert lost no time in calling on Mrs. Jameson, who with her niece Gerardine Bate was staying at the Hôtel de la Ville. Mrs. Jameson was not at home. Rising in the crisis to a supreme effort of terseness, Robert scribbled the note: "Come and see your friend and my wife, E.B.B." These nine words illuminated Mrs. Jameson as Elizabeth's many "confidences" and parting letter had never done. Her aunt's astonishment, wrote the earnest Gerardine, was "almost comical"[3] to behold. Still wide-eyed, Mrs. Jameson appeared at the Brownings' suite that evening, and assuaged Elizabeth's conscience by emphatic and reiterated approval of her marriage. Seeing that the bride could scarcely speak from weariness, she urged that they come to her quiet hotel for a week, before continuing southward. Robert eagerly agreed.

But, though very kind-hearted, Mrs. Jameson was herself the victim of an unhappy marriage. To an even more illustrious victim—of all people, Lady Noel Byron, who had the best reasons for being pessimistic about poets—she communicated with many misgivings a rather lugubrious view of the Brownings' honeymoon. Elizabeth, noted Mrs. Jameson, was "nervous, frightened, ashamed, agitated, happy, miserable. I have sympathized, scolded, rallied, cried & helped." (Poor Robert!) The next day, she still thought Elizabeth "in a most feeble state. . . . I really believe I have saved her life by persuading her to rest." And she added—very feebly, as Lady Byron must have thought—"I have not faith in the poetical temperament as a means of permanent happiness."

Robert now suggested that the two parties travel together. Inwardly, Mrs. Jameson hesitated for a moment. The immediate and daily spectacle of conjugal love might give Gerardine ideas. But, as she explained to Lady Byron, the newlyweds "have thrown themselves upon me with such an entire & undoubting confidence, that to have refused help & comfort, or even hesitated, would have been like a brute or a stone."[4]

Resting day after day in the quiet apartment above Mrs. Jameson's, Elizabeth quickly regained her strength and spirits. Robert noted the change, and his dreadful anxiety lifted. He now became irrepressibly gay and talkative, pouring forth, as Elizabeth told Arabel, whole rivers of "wit and wisdom." In her gentle way, Mrs. Jameson rose to the occasion, so that Paris became a long, delightful conversation. Listening happily, Elizabeth regained her legs, walked out to restaurants, and ventured even to the Louvre,where, buttressed by Mrs. Jameson on one side and Robert on the other, she saw "the divine Raphaels . . . unspeakable those are." But her letters had only one divinity. "He will carry me upstairs," she complains to Arabel, "and make me eat too much. . . . We sit through the dusky evenings, watching the stars rise above the high Paris houses, and talking childish things, or making schemes for work or poetry to be achieved when we reach Pisa."[5]

Elizabeth had directed that all letters from home be sent to Orléans. When on September 27, therefore, the entire company set out for that city, Elizabeth began a swift journey back into the dark center of her conscience. Anxiety grew as the minutes passed. She was approaching a moral scaffold, her "death warrant," as she told Robert. At last she found herself in Orléans, in the hotel, in her room. Robert was absent for an awful interval and then returned with "a great packet of letters." She sat holding them in her hands, "not able to open one, and growing paler and colder every moment." Robert wanted to remain with her while she read them, but after some beseeching she got him out the door. She must "meet the agony alone."

The letters from "dearest Papa and dearest George" quite justified her terror. Papa's, particularly, was nothing less than full excommunication, with book, bell, and candle: she was disinherited, cast off forever, and henceforth to be considered as dead. Her sin was quaintly, yet precisely defined—in such a way as to emphasize the difference between Robert and Mr. Barrett himself, and to associate all moral and spiritual values with the latter: Elizabeth had sold her soul "for genius . . . *mere* genius." George's letter seems to have been angrier, less logical, and less theological. He told her she had "sacrificed all delicacy and honour," leaving "the weight of the sorrow and blame to be borne by her family." In fact, she later exploded to her sisters, he had written "precisely as if I had run away without being married at all." Finally, he had said something very disagreeable about Robert. Elizabeth declared that George's letter almost broke her heart. But it had irritated her also—and so carried its own antidote.

Letters from Henrietta and Arabel remained to be read. Had her sisters also cast her off—at Papa's command? With beating heart she opened the first letter. Meanwhile, Robert was still waiting just outside the door. At last he came in, she told her sisters, "and found me just able to cry from the balm of your tender words—I put your two letters into his hands, and *he*, when he had read them, said with tears in his eyes, and kissing them between the words—'I love your sisters with a deep affection—I am inexpressibly grateful to them,—It shall be the object of my life to justify this trust, as they express it here.' He said it with tears in his eyes."

In her letter, Arabel confessed that, on a certain confused and exciting afternoon at Mr. Boyd's, she had guessed Elizabeth was married. "I was afraid of her—," Elizabeth replied, "she looked at me so intently, and was so grave." Little wonder, after Arabel's confession and George's aspersions, that Elizabeth explained very carefully to her sisters, "There was no elopement in the case, but simply a private marriage." The return to Wimpole Street was simply a precautionary measure imposed by Robert "lest I should be unequal to the double exertion of the church and the railway, on the same morning." She then lectured her sisters unmercifully on the virtues and the devotion of her husband. "He rises on me hour by hour. If ever a being of higher order lived among us without a glory round his head, in these later days, he is such a being." And on the very day she wrote, this saint had prostrated himself before *his* saint, telling her "with a deep, serious tenderness . . . 'I kissed your feet, my Ba, before I married you—but now I kiss the ground under your feet, I love you with a so much greater love.' " And this man, so solemnly and loftily devoted, can also be thoughtful in small ways, as well as inexhaustibly gay and amazing. "He encases us from morning till night—thinks of everybody's feelings . . . is witty and wise . . . (and foolish too in the right place) charms cross old women who cry out in the diligence 'mais, madame, mes jambes!' talks Latin to the priests who inquire at three in the morning whether Newman and Pusey are likely 'lapsare in erroribus' (you will make out *that*) and forgets nothing and nobody . . . except himself." He has won Wilson's heart and drawn from Mrs. Jameson a continual stream of gentle superlatives. She concludes her long letter with several pages of endearments for everybody, from Papa to Treppy.

The great packet of mail contained other consolations—a kind note from Miss Mitford, another from Elizabeth's medical advisor, Mr. Jago, who sent her a prescription and ever so many good wishes, and above all a letter from Mr. Kenyon, who showed himself a model of all the virtues she did not think he possessed. "Dear EBB," he wrote, "I sympathize in all you have both been thinking and feeling, and in all you have done. . . . If the thing had been asked of me, I should have advised it." Was there the faintest reproach in the last sentence? Elizabeth did not speculate—at least on paper; she was too grateful for the comfort he gave. "Dearest, kindest Mr. Kenyon, how I love him better than all!" To Robert, his letter "was a great relief, as the verdict of a friend whom he loved and looked up to on many grounds."

The ordeal of the letters, like other ordeals in her life, took their toll on Elizabeth's spirits; and, as many times before, Robert was the best doctor. "He laid me down on the bed and sate by me for hours, pouring out floods of tenderness and goodness, and promising to win back for me, with God's help, the affection of such of you as were angry." He "charms me into thinking of *him* when he sees my thoughts wandering . . . forces me to smile in spite of them all."[6]

Elizabeth did not tell Robert that George had insulted him; she did not tell Mrs. Jameson that she had received any letters whatever from her father and brother. That lady seems to have sensed no disaster. Yet she did happen on that particular day to draw for Lady Byron a contrast between the temperaments of the lovers: in her "there is not a trace of animal spirits, though evidently a sense [of] deep happiness, gratitude & love. As to *him*, his joy & delight, and his poetical fancies & antics, with every now and then the profoundest seriousness & tenderness interrupting the brilliant current of his imagination, make him altogether a most charming companion." In the same letter she observed primly that the "deportment" of the newly married couple "is in the best taste & Gerardine can only gain by all she sees & hears."

From Orléans they traveled by rail to Lyons, and from there—in a dirty, cramped little steamboat, the rain pouring down in torrents—down the Rhône to Avignon. Though to her sisters Elizabeth wrote chiefly of how much she was pampered and cared for, Mrs. Jameson wrote to Lady Byron of how much Mrs. Browning suffered from the rigors of the journey and of how patiently she bore her suffering. "Not only we have had to carry her fainting from the carriage but from her extreme thinness & weakness, every few hours journey has bruised her all over, till movement became almost unbearable. With her present feelings it is not perhaps great praise to say that all this has been endured with *patience*. But the unselfish sweetness of the temper, the unfailing consideration for others, I did not quite expect." Plainly, Mrs. Jameson was thawing toward the poetic temperament. "Whatever may be the issue, what has been done, has been well done & the rest remains with God." To be sure, she herself felt the strain of such travel, as Robert did. "So far on our long anxious journey," she wrote Lady Byron from Avignon, "—ten days since we left Paris, & only *here*!"[7]

After a day in bed at Avignon, Elizabeth once more recovered her strength, and the whole party made an excursion to Vaucluse, the home of Petrarch's Laura, and consequently a holy place. As they were standing at the edge of the river, Elizabeth suddenly began to climb among the slippery rocks, with the spray flying about her on every side. "Ba, are you losing your senses?"[8] exclaimed Robert, scrambling to help her. Looking back on the scene after many years, Gerardine remembered no domestic anxiety or middle-aged caution. "There, at the very source of the 'chiare, fresche e dolci acque,' " she wrote, "Mr. Browning took his wife up in his arms, and, carrying her across through the shallow curling waters, seated her on a rock that rose throne-like in the middle of the stream." Apparently Mrs. Jameson could not do quite such full justice to the spectacle of married love contending with the waves. "A most tumultuous torrent,"[9] she commented somewhat unsympathetically; nevertheless, she sketched Robert and Elizabeth as they sat amidst the spray. "The loves of the poets could not have been put into more delightful reality before the eyes of the dazzled and enthusiastic beholder," wrote Gerardine,[10] not less dazzled and enthusiastic after nearly thirty years of marriage than as an earnest-eyed young girl of seventeen. For Mrs. Jameson's fears about her niece's susceptibility proved only too well founded. The very next spring, in Rome, Gerardine became engaged to, and later married, a painter named Macpherson, who had the romantic qualification of very slender means.

From Vaucluse they traveled to Aix and then to Marseilles, where, on a "burning, glaring afternoon," they embarked for Leghorn. The sea was rough and everybody suffered, but, as they skirted the Riviera, Robert and Elizabeth got up early despite heavy weather and light stomachs and, wrapped in their cloaks, came out on deck. Lofty mountains rose up from the water's edge and shouldered back, high on the horizon, "six or seven deep."[11] Along the Italian coast, they sailed close enough in to see the green blinds to the windows of the houses that nestled under the hills and around the harbors. On October 12, they laid up for twenty-four hours in Genoa. While Mrs. Jameson and Gerardine went off sightseeing, Elizabeth managed to take a short walk with Robert. She wondered at the narrow streets and alleys, the old palaces "looking all strange and noble," the gorgeous interior of a church with its altars of "shining marble encrusted with gold" and its "great columns of twisted porphyry." On the marble pavement kneeled Genovese ladies in veils, nuns in strange medieval dress, and monks in brown serge. "Beautiful Genoa—what a vision it is!"[12]

Another night of storm and seasickness, and they were in Leghorn, from which they traveled by rail to Pisa. While Elizabeth rested at a hotel, Robert looked for a permanent lodging, and after a few days took rooms near the cathedral in the Collegio di Ferdinando, a vast, marble-porticoed building erected by Vasari. "On the front . . . I counted about forty seven doors and windows the other day,"[13] wrote Robert. They had a sitting room and three bedrooms, with hot water "*a discrezione*"—all for only £1.6.9 a week. "Wonderfully cheap!"[14] exclaimed Elizabeth.

Mrs. Jameson lingered some three weeks in Pisa to do what she could do to establish the poetic marriage on sane foundations. Reporting to Lady Byron from the cool elevation of her own experience, she was still delicately balanced between considerations pro and contra. "We have brought our dear Invalid in safety, to what she fondly calls her home." She is "almost helpless," and yet looks "wonderfully well, considering all the fatigue undergone. Under her husband's influence & mine she is leaving off those medicines on which she existed, ether, morphine, &c, &c. I am full of hope for her." Of Browning, Mrs. Jameson wrote with an admiration tempered by one final reservation about the poetic temperament:

> *He* is full of spirit & good humour and his unselfishness & his turn for making the best of everything & his bright intelligence & his rare acquirements of every kind rendered him the very prince of travelling companions. *But* (always *buts*!!) he is in all the common things of this life the most impractical of men, the most uncalculating, rash, in short the worst *manager* I ever met with.[15]

She had reckoned shrewdly with every part of Browning's character but his anxieties about financial independence. Having never earned money, he had a horror of owing it; and now two months married, he had probably discovered several debts he felt he should pay which Elizabeth had left behind her in Wimpole Street—£70 to Arabel and a similar sum to Minnie the housekeeper. "It is not to *my* honour and glory," Elizabeth told Mrs. Martin, "that the 'bills' are made up every week and paid more regularly 'than bard beseems', while dear Mrs. Jameson laughs outright at our miraculous prudence and economy."[16]

Mrs. Jameson left Pisa in early November for Rome, where, assisted by Gerardine, she was to study the paintings and monuments with view to a book. The lovers were now faced with the prospect of living happily ever after. Perhaps no marriage began with its feet quite so far from the ground. Elizabeth lectured her sisters no more extragavantly about Robert's halo than, in his letter to them, he expatiated on the ineffable brightness of her own. "I . . . thought I knew her, while every day and hour reveals more and more to me the divine goodness and infinite tenderness of her heart;—while that wonderful mind of hers, with its inexhaustible affluence and power, continues unceasingly to impress me. . . . Her entire sweetness of temper makes it a delight to breathe the same air with her."[17] Could such ardor and idealism ever survive fulfullment, let alone the wear and tear, of day-to-day married life?

So far from banishing poetry, domesticity became itself poetic. With the professional assistance of Wilson and the devotion and high spirits of Robert himself, facts, as reported for the Wimpole Street perspective of Arabel and Henrietta, seem to fit convincingly into the pattern of the ideal.

> This morning when we were at breakfast, sitting half into the fire and close together, and having our coffee and eggs and toasted rolls, he said suddenly, in the midst of our laughing and talking, "Now! I do wish your sisters could see us through some peep hole of the world!" "Yes," said I, "as long as they did not hear us through the peep hole!"—for indeed the foolishness of this conversation would—on which he laughed and began "abstract ideas," etc. *That* was for you to hear, you understand, to have the reputation of our wisdom.

Their taste in foods and cooking accorded beautifully. "He turns away from beef and mutton, and loathes the idea of a Saturday hash! A little chicken and plenty of cayenne, and above all things pudding, will satisfy us both when most we are satisfied." Robert was of course trying to make her fat.

> At dinner we have Chianti which is an excellent kind of claret; and fancy me (and Wilson) drinking claret out of tumblers! Ask Arabel if she wishes Robert to make me *drunk*. . . . He aspires to make me take more of this claret than he would take himself, pouring it into the glass when I am looking another way, and entreating me by ever so much invocation when I look and refuse! and then I never being famous for resisting his invocations, am at the end of the dinner too giddy to see his face and am laid down at full length on the arm chair and told to go to sleep and profit by the whole.[18]

Elizabeth was also eloquent on the fresh oranges presented by their landlady, and the fish, thrushes, and other delicacies sent in from a nearby *trattoria.* Robert's adoration survived all this eating and drinking. "I begin to wonder . . .," remarked Elizabeth robustly, "whether I may not be some sort of real angel after all." In the evenings they ate grapes and roasted chestnuts, dreamed of the future, and, when they retired, Elizabeth slept soundly on a mattress stuffed with orange-tree shavings.

Robert with his weekly account book in hand proved to be a firmer character than Elizabeth expected. They had scarcely any library, and Elizabeth craved fiction. Robert responded by supplying her with Italian fiction at the moderate library subscription cost of eightpence a month. Unwilling to endure any kind of separation from her, he prepared to share her passion with her. No passion developed on either side. Elizabeth began to expatiate on the "persistent dullness of these modern Italian writers who haven't a soul among them all."[19] On the other hand, "Robert says sometimes, in one of those desperate fits of philanthropy to which he is subject, 'Really Ba, you are too severe!' (yawning) 'really this is not so very heav . . . y.' "[20] Elizabeth began to plead for French novels, and at length, after many jokes "against his little Ba-lamb (one of my names!) 'who in spite of her innocence, couldn't live without wicked books by Eugene Sue,' " Robert took out a more expensive subscription. The new library, Elizabeth wrote with satisfaction, "gives us the privilege besides of having a French newspaper, the 'Siècle,' left with us every morning." Led by Elizabeth, Robert now made a genuine and prolonged descent into prose—and French prose at that. "Robert is a warm admirer of Balzac," Elizabeth wrote Miss Mitford, "and has read most of his books, but certainly—oh certainly—he does not in a general way appreciate our French people quite with our warmth; he takes too high a standard, I tell him, and won't listen to a story for a story's sake." But he did listen—apparently to a great many. He "was properly possessed by the 'Mystères de Paris.' " Yet, wrote Elizabeth, "we have great wars sometimes." As a confirmed lover of the theater, Robert knew the French plays and vaudevilles very well and maintained they were "the happiest growth" of popular French literature. One day they read together *Le Rouge et le Noir.* Robert was much struck and thought it "exactly like Balzac *in the raw,* in the material, and undeveloped conception."[21]

Meanwhile, Elizabeth had begun to argue for a piano—Mrs. Jameson had pronounced Robert's playing "full of science and feeling." But she had unfortunately confessed that she herself could not play. "Though I have talked myself hoarse about my love of music," she reported, Robert "calls it a foolish expense, and won't listen to it."

Robert could be very reasonable, and he could be very unreasonable about the right things—like Elizabeth's neglect of her health—and sometimes about the wrong things—like the occasional intrusions of strangers. Some English ladies threatened to come all the way from Florence to see them. Robert at once began to brood about the horrors and contaminations of casual curiosity. The worst of it was that in April he and Elizabeth would move to Florence. They would then be living in the very jaws of a large and vulgar English colony.

> "Those people will spoil all our happiness, if we once let them in,—you will see—If you speak of your health and save yourself on that plea, they will seize upon *me*—oh, don't I know them?" He walks up and down the room, thoroughly worked up—"But, dearest," say I with my remarkable placidity . . . "*I* am not going to let anybody in! If one of us lets them in, it will be Wilson, most probably—! but we need not suffer it—I desire it quite as little as you"—"There is that coarse, vulgar Mrs. Trollope—I do hope, Ba, if you don't wish to give me the greatest pain, that you won't receive that vulgar, pushing woman who is not fit to speak to you"—"Well . . . now we are at Mrs. Trollope! You will have your headache in a minute—now do sit down, and let us talk of something else."[22]

Was the outside world, then—in this jealously guarded four-room paradise—simply an inconvenience, a threat of contaminating incursion? Elizabeth speaks of a perpetual and absorbing tête-à-tête which in four months of marriage no shadow had crossed. They were discovering with understandable gusto and delight each other's daily selves and daily lives. They had their poetry, their Bible and Shakespeare, their novels and newspapers. Indeed, they found immense resources in doing nothing at all. "What makes Robert perfectly happy," wrote Elizabeth, "is to draw his chair next mine, and let time slip away." And yet both mention, with suspicious iteration, that they see nobody. "We would like to know one or two Italians," confesses Elizabeth, "to have an opportunity of speaking the language." In point of fact, an Italian professor from the university did occasionally visit them and expatiated graciously on the virtues of English classical scholarship.

They also spent a good deal of time looking out of their windows. Near at hand was the convent of Shelley's friend, Emilia Viviani—apostrophized in "Epipsychidion" as "Spouse! Sister! Angel!" and an unfortunate victim of parental tyranny. There was much else to be seen—the Cathedral, the Leaning Tower, and particularly the street itself, which proved quite as fascinating as the square in "Up at a Villa—Down in the City" to the "Italian Person of Quality." Late in November the weather became cold, and then people went up and down "muffled up in vast cloaks, with little earthenware pots full of live embers to warm their fingers besides." In December, the midday sun again grew very hot, and the women appeared with furs and parasols together. At first, both were deeply interested in the funerals, which, says Elizabeth, "throng past our windows"—no doubt because the cathedral was so close. "The monks, sometimes all in black, sometimes all in white (according to the order) chant in a train, carrying torches . . . and on the bier comes the corpse . . . open-faced . . . except just a veil." What Robert thought significant was that the crucifix, as the sign of faith, "should precede the dumb Dead, and 'would rather like it' to be done in his own case!" Soon her old horror sunk into Elizabeth and she could endure the sight no longer. "Ah, don't go to the window!" she would say to Robert. Sometimes he would answer, " 'I can't help it, Ba—it *draws* me.' Such horrible hoarse chanting it is—Like the croaking of Death itself."[23] No less disturbing to her were the cathedral bells, which day and night tolled, caroled, and jangled their Catholic and often gloomy admonitions to the dreaming city—and sometimes searched her out in profoundest sleep with the deep, dull, doomsday voice of the *pasquareccis*, which announced executions.

Art, history, and Italy were beyond their windows, and therefore they did venture outside—not always to their satisfaction. Sometimes they walked to the Campo Santo to see the fourteenth- and fifteenth-century frescoes, which were wonderfully fresh and vivid, and remained so until largely destroyed in the Second World War. On Christmas Eve, wrapped in shawls, furs, and a great cloak, Elizabeth went out with Robert to midnight mass at the cathedral—to the post-facto astonishment and consternation of her sisters. The expedition had no ill effect, but it was a severe disappointment to her. She had expected a thoughtful sermon and a decorous ceremony. What she witnessed seemed to her the superstitions of the temple mixed with the noises of the market place. There was no sermon. Priests chanted hoarsely at the altar. People moved about freely, talking loud enough to be heard three yards off. Two ladies kneeling beside Elizabeth were laughing and chattering "with all their might." The Italians, she informed Arabel, "have the sun and no light."[24] The statement represented a judgment as of that date. Perhaps partly because of or in spite of Robert and his poetry, she had come to Italy expecting to see a renaissance of culture and a reawakening of the people. She found good cooking, cheap lodgings, a soft climate, and a museum of historical splendors. Italy as a sanitarium, as a domestic convenience, as a monument to the great dead, was satisfactory enough; but Italy as a living moral and cultural community had, thus far, little more to offer than hideous funerals, dull fiction, and people who laughed in church. Later, Elizabeth's disillusionment was to be even more drastic.

No doubt, some of these objections applied particularly to Pisa. A great Renaissance city-state which had built navies, recruited and sent forth armies, had shrunk within its buildings to a provincial watering-place in which a small population of doctors, nurses, and lodging-keepers ministered to chronic invalids. Robert speaks without approval of "this strange silent old city." Elizabeth was only a little less frank and more artful. To her friends she confessed that Pisa was dull; to her sisters she emphasized that she and Robert were difficult to please and much preoccupied with each other. Lately a visitor—"an awful interruption"—had revealed "to her astonished ears . . . that Pisa was very 'gay' just now . . . a weekly 'reception' at the Governor's, besides the Baroness." She reported to Robert "where he might go if he pleased, to which he irreverently replied that the Governor and the governed might be hanged first." Here was the idyllic story with a political twist: the inhabitants of paradise scorned a frivolous society enslaved by the Austrians.

Fortunately, Pisa offered more than Italian beauty and an Italian past. It had an English past—both poetic and romantic. Robert and Elizabeth made occasional carriage excursions which she liked better than her Christmas visit to the cathedral. On one fine day, she tells her sisters, "we drove down through the pine forest to the sea side, and met the camels and enjoyed it all exceedingly."[25] Camels were used in the vicinity to carry wood. The pine forest represented in part an excursion into the English past, for there Shelley and Byron had almost daily gone riding and pistol-shooting. At another time the Brownings made a pilgrimage to the historic Lanfranchi palace, which Byron described during a residence of almost a year.

> I have got here into a famous old feudal palazzo, on the Arno, large enough for a garrison, with dungeons below and cells in the walls, and so full of *ghosts*, that the learned Fletcher (my valet) has begged leave to change his room, and then refused to occupy his *new* room, because there were more ghosts there than in the other. . . . There is one place

> where people were evidently *walled up*; for there is but one possible passage, broken through the wall, and then meant to be closed again upon the inmate.[26]

Here he lived his singular afternoon-to-predawn existence, presiding over his large household of truculent retainers, sallying forth with dueling pistols on his daily ride, and dining with the Countess Guiccioli, the Counts Gamba, the Shelleys and Williamses, Taaffe, Medwin, and others—often the light coming in at the windows found him in deep colloquy with a single inebriate survivor. Here again he faced the Pisan mob in the affair of the Italian sergeant-major. Here, in the intervals of a fierce and desolate idleness, he continued *Don Juan*, wrote dashing letters to his friends in England, and ingeniously defended the morality of *Cain* to the pecunious Murray. The substance of this highly un-Victorian history Browning knew, for he had read Moore's *Life.* Yet, like Elizabeth, he came in reverence, seeking the gold in the dross: in the garden they plucked a bayleaf, which, with a lock of Elizabeth's hair, Robert had mounted and inscribed with the note that it was gathered in the first year of their marriage. A rather solemn connubial adventure, imposing itself incongruously on the ghost of a flamboyant profligacy—only twenty-five years stood between.

For one who knew, the streets and environs of quiet old Pisa were poignant with the memory of Shelley's last days. On the Lung' Arno was the Casa Frasi, where he had lived. At the Ponte al Mare was the Torre Guelfa, which he had described in more than one poem. In the neighboring hills were the Baths of San Giuliano, where he had written *Adonais.* To the west were the pine woods which he had haunted—so persistently that, two weeks before his death, certain friends had seen an apparition of him when he was known to be far away. To the west also was the Serchio, where he had sailed—and very beautifully written of his sailing—with Williams; and to the north was the Gulf of Spezia, where the two men had drowned. Influenced by Leigh Hunt, Browning still held a rose-colored view of Shelley's life; but what seems to have interested him chiefly were the poems and the visible scene in which they were laid. Banished daily by Elizabeth from their "perpetual *tête-à-tête,*" he must often have followed in the footsteps of Shelley's meditations.

Yet what Browning really did and thought during these years we must see through Elizabeth's eyes; what remained separate from their common life, we can only glimpse—as she did his microscopic manuscripts from "afar off." The future flames of a London fireplace awaited nearly all of his own intimate letters. Elizabeth herself, writing to Sarianna, enables us to see that he felt his exile from Hatcham as acutely as she felt hers from Wimpole Street. "He is grieved about the illness of his cousin" (James Silverthorne), she writes, and he is always "so anxious" about his mother. "How deeply and tenderly he loves her and all of you."[27]

The daily, hourly history of No. 50 Wimpole Street—an unlimited monarchy still rocking with the tremors of a single terrible revolt—continued to be of overwhelming interest to Elizabeth. No doubt the most industrious historian would have failed to satisfy her thirst for detail, but the number and urgency of her questions suggest that her sisters were not industrious historians. "The new maid, I have taken into my head, is not a pleasant person. Why do you keep her, in that case? . . . Remember to tell me the colour of the drawing room curtains and paper." What she did hear was not agreeable. The retributory anger which had excommunicated Elizabeth herself had sentenced Arabel to a smaller bedroom and an uncomfortable bed. "Do write to me soon, and let me know whether my darling Arabel has her room yet, and whether Papa is kinder to her." In fact, Papa let no one think him downcast. He is "*in high spirits* and *having people to dine with him every day.*"[28]

At first, all the Barrett young men were as virtuously indignant as their father. Apparently they agreed with George, who in his first note condemned all the women in the household for deceit and connivance, and Robert, for unspeakable deceit. But Elizabeth was a beloved sister, and perhaps George had been rereading her last letter. Early in 1847, he sent a second note in which he forgave her but not Robert. Sette also conceded she had been merely "foolish." Robert "was the real criminal." Clearly, he was guilty of a two-headed but rather logical crime: he did not earn money; therefore he had treacherously married it. One Barrett, alone in Jamaica with his brooding memories of Wimpole Street, actually remained obdurate to the second generation. When in 1899 Pen Browning published the *Love Letters* of his parents, Stormie, then an old man, wrote a public letter in which he blamed alike "the careless indifference" of his nephew and the calculating bad faith of his brother-in-law. "Under these circumstances," he summed up, "my father lost his daughter. . . . He never recovered from it. I venture to say few fathers would take the hand of the man who had so acted."[29]

To the accusations of her brothers Elizabeth deigned no reply.

"Money, money, money, nothing but money," she wailed to her sisters, and once more lectured them on the perfections of Robert, who was "infinitely less worldly than any of them."[30] Yet as her brothers continued to love her in spite of her folly, she continued to love them in spite of their mercenary obtuseness. "Does Alfred get on with the railroad?" she asks. "Has Occy made any good drawings lately? Did George go to Cambridge? How is the Law, too, with Jim and Sette? And tell me of Henry. As to dear Stormie, I do trust that he has other plans than for that dreadful Jamaica."

To heal or mitigate this breach, so full of obstinate grievance and obstinate affection, Robert strove optimistically to introduce a note of reason. In a long letter to Elizabeth's sisters—in which, to be sure, he lectured them a good deal on her perfections—he urged that the facts be put clearly before her brothers: she could hardly have survived more than two or three winters in England; a few months in Italy had transformed her. At the same time, apparently, he tried to make Elizabeth see the obduracy of her brothers in a consistent and rational manner.

> We were talking this morning at breakfast [she wrote] of O'Connell and the Irish, and I was describing Stormie's enthusiasm for both. "Indeed," said I, "he is so generous and tenderhearted, that he naturally takes the part of every party or person attacked by others—He defends everyone who is *accused.*" —"Everyone, except *you*" . . . observed Robert gravely. I could not speak a word,—my heart was full.

Robert's good sense on the one side and her brothers' stubbornness on the other did bring Elizabeth to an important and emancipating decision. While still at Pisa, as she recovered from an illness, she resolved never to live in England again. Proximity to her family would only cause bitterness.

The extravagant mutual admiration of the lovers was more even than sisterly flesh and blood could bear. At least one of Elizabeth's strident boasts produced a sharp reaction from Henrietta. Both she and Robert, says Elizabeth, detest Puseyism—

> Robert *so* strongly, that I wish sometimes to "pit" him against Mr. Bevan—only . . . *poor Mr. Bevan*! He understands the scriptures thoroughly and learnedly, and begins by denying that there is any Priesthood but Christ's, or any christianity apart from the doctrine of justification by faith as taught by the first reformers—then wishes for more Martin Luthers, and disdains all saints like San Raniere and San

> Torpé!—thanks God that he is likely to die a dissenter . . . then admits that as a body, the dissenters have quite as many faults as any other class of christian men.

Whatever she thought of such broadminded Roundheadism, Henrietta chose to be much offended by the term "Puseyites." Elizabeth replied with a short, rather peremptory plea for forgiveness and a long, rather impatient justification of the term. After all, "there are high churchmen and high churchmen."

A good deal can happen to three people in four rooms. Late in January, Wilson suddenly revealed that she had been suffering from a pain in the side "just where Arabel used to have hers," and confessed "(making exclamations!) that she had bought and partly taken *eight shillings worth* of English pills for bilious disorders" and that they did not seem strong enough. In the evening Elizabeth sent Robert for calomel and rhubarbs. The pains continued. In desperation Wilson the next morning tried a concoction of herb water and cream of tartar recommended by the people of the house. She begged Elizabeth not to tell Robert, but, growing fearful, Elizabeth did tell. Robert declared that the woman would kill herself at last with medicine: she must go to Dr. Cook. That evening while Elizabeth was putting her feet in hot water by the fire, Wilson "sank down on the sofa, shivering all over," and cried out she would go to Dr. Cook at once. Elizabeth tried to send her in a carriage with the girl of the house. The girl was afraid to go. Drying her feet, Elizabeth put Wilson to bed and ran barefoot to Robert: *he* must get Dr. Cook. The doctor prescribed five leeches. The case was not serious—an inflammation of the stomach originated by seasickness, and perhaps aggravated by spices from the *trattoria.* When all was over, Robert gave Elizabeth "a tremendous scold" for running about barefoot. " 'I wanted to kill him . . . I played with his life' &c &c! Poor me!"[31] One gathers that, where his feelings were deeply involved, Robert did justice to the drama of a situation.

This episode further emancipated Elizabeth. Till now pouring the coffee had been her sole duty, which she had performed every morning with éclat. While Wilson was ill, she told Miss Mitford, "I have . . . learnt how it is possible (in certain conditions of the human frame) to comb out and twist one's own hair, and lace one's very own stays, and cause hooks and eyes to meet behind one's very own back, besides making toast and water for Wilson."[32]

But she was to learn ruder lessons, for, without in the least suspecting her condition, she had now been pregnant for some time.

Six weeks earlier, she had suffered regularly "sudden violent pains which came on in the night, relieved by friction and a few spoonfulls of brandy, and going off as suddenly as they came." These symptoms were not lost upon Wilson, who feared that her mistress's morphine was threatening to precipitate a miscarriage, but she dared not speak frankly. The pains continued. Wilson finally confessed her suspicions. Robert "made a fuss" and implored—no doubt dramatically—that Dr. Cook be called in. Elizabeth was as reluctant as Wilson had been to receive medical attention. Apparently, forty years of maidenhood made confession to a stranger too awful, too intimate—and had she not displayed a laughable ignorance of physiological fact? "I was frightened out of my wits," she wrote, "by the suggestion about the morphine, and out of my *wit* about the entreaty about Dr. Cook." She attempted to quiet her own fears and Robert's by the roundabout expedient of putting the whole case, as a *theoretical* question—to her London physician, Mr. Jago—and realized as soon as the letter was mailed how ridiculous she had been. Robert continued to plead for Dr. Cook and she continued to "put him off with ever so many impertinent speeches, yes, and obstinate ones." In a letter to her sisters she pleads pathetically and with some justification that she was so accustomed to think of her discomforts as symptoms of disease that she could not believe them symptoms of normal functioning.

The pains ceased, and everybody was very uncomfortable. A few days later Elizabeth felt "unwell." In a moment of rational caution she allowed Dr. Cook to be sent for. "He came . . . declares he found the room at seventy, a scandalous fire, a wrong posture, and my pulse very irritable: laid me down on the sofa—commanded cold tea." Though still obstinate and inclined to scoff, Elizabeth did what she was told. On the next day, the pains came on again, and more severely. She felt very superior to them—"I have had worse pain I assure"—and bore up "with so much bodily vigour" that Wilson and Dr. Cook were surprised. But early the next morning—Sunday—Elizabeth suffered a miscarriage, "*of five months date.*" On the whole, Robert seems to have been the chief victim of the experience. When finally admitted to her room that evening, he "threw himself down on the bed in a passion of tears, sobbing like a child."

Elizabeth had begun to feel that he had much better have given her a sound scolding. Dr. Cook told her flatly that if he had been called in six weeks earlier all would have gone well. On the other hand, he felt that the pregnancy would have the best effect on her general health, and in fact, Elizabeth wrote, "I have wondered lately where my chest has gone to." Elderly truculence in gestation now gave way to anger and remorse at her stupidity, and yet, in her letter to Henrietta, a note of confidence and resolution suggests a secret hope for the future.

Still "overcome," Robert lived in the crisis, and thought of heaven as Elizabeth thought of Wimpole Street. "We are rebellious children," he told Elizabeth, "and He leads us where He can best teach us." He could not be persuaded, even by the now infallible Dr. Cook, that there was no danger. Ceasing to eat or sleep, he spent every possible moment by Elizabeth's bedside, rubbing her, talking to her, reading to her—"all with such tenderness, such goodness" that Dr. Cook was astonished and Wilson exclaimed, "I never saw a *man* like Mr. Browning in my life."[33] For the first few nights after the miscarriage, Wilson slept on a sofa in Elizabeth's room, as Arabel had done in Wimpole Street. When, awakening, she caught sight of the shadowy form on the sofa, Elizabeth was forcibly reminded of her old life and of everybody at home from Treppy to "poor dearest papa." The meditations of convalescence brought release, clarification, and notably a humble gratitude for the "noble generous goodness" of Mr. Kenyon, who had not only tirelessly urged her case with dearest Papa, but, unsolicited, had assumed management of her financial affairs after Papa had abandoned them in anger.

Six days after her miscarriage, "all dressed and ringletted," Elizabeth walked from one room to the next. She also rescued her husband from starvation by once more eating her dinners with him. Still unable to believe in her safety, he spoke of taking an apartment that summer in the house with Dr. Cook at Lucca. But that infallible man astonished them both with the verdict that they might actually carry out their earlier plan of meeting Mrs. Jameson in Florence within a fortnight.[34]

Meanwhile, a letter had arrived from Mr. Jago—a wonder of divination after the event. Elizabeth was once more reminded of her folly. "Just at present," she confided to Henrietta, "my mood inclines to be a more obedient wife than I have been." Henrietta addressed an inquiry to Robert: Candidly, is Ba always an obedient wife? "This Ba, who is my wife," wrote Robert, "very *dis*obedient she is—for all my commanding, and imploring to boot, will not make her eat a little more at dinner." Furthermore, he can never cause her to do anything selfish or for her own good. At this point there is a characteristic breakdown of syntax, and when he lapses once more into coherence he is saying "I can find nothing to compare with her entire generosity and elevation of character—and when I solemnly affirm that I have never been able to detect the slightest fault, failing, or shadow of short-coming in her,—recollect that we have lived constantly together for eight months."[35]

On the deeper, more impersonal level of poetry, he was franker. At about this time or a little later, he wrote with intimate knowledge of a marriage in which the wife, after a sharp struggle of words and will, makes unconditional submission to her husband, and calls on him to be masculine and dominant:

1

Let's contend no more, Love,
Strive nor weep—
All be as before, Love,
—Only sleep!

2

What so wild as words are?
—I and thou
In debate, as birds are,
Hawk on bough!

. . . . .

6

Be a God and hold me
With a charm—
Be a man and fold me
With thine arm!

7

Teach me, only teach, Love!
As I ought
I will speak thy speech, Love,
Think thy thought—

8

Meet, if thou require it,
Both demands,

Laying flesh and spirit
In thy hands![36]

And yet he does give the woman the last word, and it is eloquent. Perhaps the husband, if indeed he be Robert, has a fatal and ungodlike capacity for seeing both sides of the argument.

The days before the departure for Florence were full of financial calculation and enlightenment. Poring over his account book, Robert discovered that, for the first six months of married life—including the journey from London and the two weeks in Paris—they had spent only £150. Shortly after, they learned that even so they had spent far too much. An Englishwoman who lived in the house opposite, the wife of a certain Major L———, had been spreading the story that she had very nearly lost her apartment to Mrs. Browning, who had attempted to bribe the landlord with an enormous rent. Robert was of course furious, and with his compliments dispatched an emphatic denial to Mrs. L———. She had gossiped in good faith. Her landlord had started the false rumor—out of a virtuous desire to maintain the prestige of his own house in the face of the exorbitant rent obtained by Mrs. Browning's landlord. A kind Mrs. Turner now showed the Brownings that they also paid extravagant prices for food and had been systematically cheated in weights and measures as well. For their future protection, she instructed the astonished Wilson in the arts of Italian marketing. They would take their education with them to Florence.

On April 17 they set out, rumbling and swaying in the coupé of a diligence over the winding, often mountainous roads. To reduce the buffets, Elizabeth lay much of the time across Robert's lap, but frequently she sat up to view the Tuscan countryside with its "vine-festooned plains," its "sweeps of river,"[37] and its pine-wooded hills crested by castles or towns—a landscape out of a Quattrocento painting or a passage of *Sordello*. Coming up the valley of the Arno, they at length reached Florence, of which Elizabeth seems to have had two glimpses—one as they crossed a bridge, and another as Robert carried her into the Hôtel du Nord. There they stayed for two days: Robert hunted houses and Elizabeth rested, intensely conscious that the monuments, sculptures, and paintings of the city awaited her in a silent, thronged expectancy.

CHAPTER 15

"O Bella Liberta, O Bella!"

1847-49

By 1847 Florence had apparently long since exhausted the possibilities of history. Scarcely had so much ever happened to so few people in so small a space. Rising out of the gloom and anarchy of the twelfth century, she had perfected her crafts and manufactures, gained wealth, invented banking, and become the money-lender of Christendom, financing from her quiet counting houses war and peace, destruction and city-building at the far corners of Europe. She had conquered Tuscany, sent forth fleets to trade or war from Pisa and Leghorn, swayed the destinies of Church and Empire, and finally through far-sighted policy brought comparative peace to the whole peninsula, and even to her own streets and squares. She had nurtured Italy's greatest poet, produced the first modern man, rediscovered ancient literature and learning, realized a more intense and ample kind of human existence, and filling her pantheons and graveyards with generation after generation of famous dead, had carried the fine arts in a long evolution from primitive simplicity and traditionalism through ascending levels and varieties of grace, fantasy, and naturalism up to epic power and again downward into bombast and sentiment. Waging war with the sword, the pen, and the stiletto, turning civil war into a way of life, endlessly fertile in constitutional improvisation, she had run through nearly every possible compromise between aristocratic, commercial, and popular interests, rested briefly and turbulently in ochlocracy, moved through new forms of oligarchy and dictatorship, and at length, after the Napoleonic explosion, subsided into peace and legitimacy.

Under the grand-ducal family of Lorraine, Florence continued to be much that she had been—artistic, refined, adroit, well-dressed, gay, and carnival-loving. She lacked only what had been essential to the old Florence: an openness to great ideas and high aspirations. The depths of Italian misery and the heights of Italian patriotism were alike unknown to her. She was easy, comfortable, even a little stodgy, and quite content with her Austrian rulers. The Grand Duke Leopold I had enacted beneficent laws, moderating taxes to a degree unique in Italy, and as Adolphus Trollope says: "Nature was prolifically generous of corn, wine and oil; and the people, sober and frugal by the inherited habits of successive generations, worked little, dozed, chatted, and sang much."[1]

But Florence did *not* exist for Florentines alone. Here was a splendid climate, a beautiful landscape, an exquisite city of churches, galleries, and palaces full of history and masterpieces, a population of skillful servants, excellent cooks and restaurant-keepers, and gay decorative citizens devoted to pageants and picturesque rivalry—all at very low prices. Little wonder that tourists came in considerable numbers—the great seasonal folk migrations of our day were then unknown—and that foreigners who loved art, or aspired to practice it, men and women with dubious health or dubious reputations, families without marriage certificates or without very much money should come to be permanent residents. Such people, including the English, may have been nearly as bad as Browning thought them. The aristocratic and candid diarist Charles Greville, visiting Florence in 1830, called them "the refuse of Europe."[2] Where money was to be spent, however, the Florentines were not inclined to ask questions, nor was the Grand Duke himself. In fact, making himself at once a good host and a tourist attraction, he invited all the foreign colony to the receptions and balls at the Pitti Palace, where, seated on gilt chairs beneath the great mirrors of the banquet room, the guests made provender with an extraordinary lack of ceremony:

> The English would seize the plates of bonbons and empty the contents into their coat pockets. The ladies would do the same with their pocket handkerchiefs. But the Duke's liege subjects carried on their depredations on a far bolder scale. I have seen large portions of fish, sauce and all, packed up in a newspaper and deposited in a pocket. I have seen fowls and ham share the same fate, without any newspaper at all. I have seen jelly carefully wrapped in an Italian countess's laced *mouchoir*! . . . The Grand Duchess also would occasionally walk through the rooms; but her object, and indeed that of the Duke, seemed to be to attract as little attention as possible.[3]

The reigning Grand Duke, Leopold II, was a timid, sleepy man, whose clothes never fit him, whose manners were as bad as those of many of his guests, and who seemed to suffer from the consciousness that he never had anything to say. When complimented on the prosperity of his people, he invariably replied, *"Sono tranquille."* (They are quiet.) Soon they were not quiet, and the Duke was to prove a more complicated man than people suspected. For the time, however, his ministers ruled well, and the *Grancinco* (great ass) or the *Grandoca* (big goose) was accepted by his subjects with affection and tolerant raillery.

Freshly illuminated as to what money could buy in Italy, Robert soon found—in the Via delle Belle Donne,[4] just off the broad square of Santa Maria Novella—rooms which Elizabeth pronounced "infinitely superior" to those in Pisa. Real cups instead of mugs, a spring sofa and a spring chair, a full compliment of knives, forks, and spoons, of linen, plate, and china, even decanters and champagne glasses: all for four pounds a month, one pound six less than they paid to the "Pisani Traditori." Their whole way of life was on a corresponding scale. A nearby trattoria provided them, by standing order, with port for Elizabeth, ordinary wine (at three- or fourpence a bottle) for Robert, and with ample, excellently cooked meals. Three-o'clock dinner (at two shillings eightpence a day) consisted of "Vermicelli soup—turkey (not a whole turkey, but the third of one at least)—Fish (sturgeon)— . . . stewed beef (done something like fricandeau),—mashed potatoes—cheese cakes." Elizabeth also informed her sisters, with noticeable emphasis, that she had persuaded Robert to get a piano—"a good one, a grand one, a German one, including the hire of music, for about ten shillings a month."[5]

The first Friday after their arrival—April 23—was Shakespeare's birthday. That evening, while Elizabeth lay on the spring sofa, Robert, seated at the piano, was playing "Shakespeare's favourite air[6] (as discovered by poetical antiquaries)" when "a voice said 'upon my word here's domestic harmony!' And lo! Mrs. Jameson stood in the room! Both of us leapt up, one from the piano and one from the sofa, and we had our arms round her in a moment." She also had suddenly realized it was Shakespeare's birthday and hurrying forward from Rome, had arrived a day earlier than expected, to drink a toast, from a bottle of wine bought in Arezzo, with two poets in memory of a third. Soon the four members of the honeymoon party—for Gerardine had of course come with her aunt—were seated at coffee and supper, and there was an immense exchange of "Roman news and Pisan dullness," in which Robert was so wise and witty that Mrs. Jameson exclaimed as usual "Oh, that inexhaustible man!" She reported that because she had fallen in with them so patly in Paris, she had been accused on all sides of having managed the whole affair between Robert and Elizabeth. Rome was full of Italian politics and English politicians. O'Connell had just come—many said, to die. Cobden was there, and had gone with Mrs. Jameson to the Sistine Chapel, where he had tried with touching earnestness to appreciate Michelangelo. Living in "an atmosphere of love and admiration" the new pope, Pius IX, continued to make tentative efforts toward reform in the Papal States. Mrs. Jameson urged, "he is doing *what he can*"; but Robert professed no belief in the permanent miracle of a liberal pope: "A dreadful situation, after all, for a man of understanding and honesty! I pity him from my soul, for he can, at best, only temporise with truth."[7]

In point of fact, Browning had lately been much more hopeful of Pio Nono's career. On March 31, while still at Pisa, he had written Monckton Milnes partly to thank him for a warm letter of congratulation but partly to make, in his style of offhand, insinuating intimacy, an extraordinary request.

> A six months' residence in Pisa is favourable to a great deal of speculation and political study . . . [he began]—what shall I say?—here one sees more clearly than elsewhere that—why, only that England needs must not loiter behind the very Grand Turkian policy, but send a Minister before the year ends to this fine fellow, Pio Nono—as certain, that is, as that his name will be Lord Somebody—against which the time is not yet come to complain. But I should like to have to remember that I asked you, whose sympathy I am sure of, to mention in the proper quarter, should you see occasion, that I would be glad and proud to be the secretary to such an embassy, and to work like a horse in my vocation. You know I have studied Italian literature sedulously . . .[8]

There is no reason to doubt Robert's complete sincerity. But did he not also see an opportunity to make himself a breadwinner? Clearly, he had been thinking about money, for in the same letter he insists—perhaps too much—that he would not accept a pension.

The Brownings had taken a bedroom in the house for their friends and entertained them for a week. Mrs. Jameson was one of those sightseers who travel on their conscience. Every picture, sculpture, and monument in the vicinity became a moral adventure in careful study and just appreciation. She and Gerardine were out early and late, leaving Elizabeth to brood more remorsefully than ever on the expectant wonders outside her door. But Dr. Cook had warned against any early exertion. "Don't be drawn into going out, Ba, I beseech you!" exclaimed Robert, probably in his most demonstrative manner.

The visit did not transpire without some friction, which points up the edge and violence in Robert's nature. Unhappy in her own marriage and a feminist both by default and conviction, Mrs. Jameson had aspired to make her niece, "Geddie," a competent artist and a worthy collaborator. Like any intelligent couple as yet childless, the Brownings had stern and sage opinions on this project. Geddie "was just a pretty, accomplished, gentle little girl, with some want of high motive or apprehended duties—thinking how to please herself, and loving 'Aunt Nina' in a sort of indolent fashion . . . no more fitted to be what Mrs. Jameson desired, a *laborious artist,* than to fly up to Heaven like a lark." Even on the voyage from Paris, Elizabeth had made excuses for Geddie while at the same time thinking Mrs. Jameson too much inclined to adore when she did not reprehend. Robert seems to have taken at once a more critical and a more lighthearted view. He told Mrs. Jameson

> what he took to be the truth in a very blunt fashion, and also what "he should do if he had the misfortune of having a wife like Gerardine" (which was not by any means an agreeable form of sympathy to Mrs. Jameson, though it gave Robert an occasion of showing a wonderful quantity of ferocity and savage determination) that I was half nervous with the discussion.

All that had been before aunt and niece had gone to Rome: there Geddie had brought about a very complex disaster by falling in love: she had contrived to find—all in the same man—"a bad artist! an unrefined gentleman! a Roman catholic! (converted from protestantism!) a poor man!! with a red beard!!!" What could the girl mean? Mrs. Jameson answered her own question with conscientious veracity. "The truth is," she told Elizabeth during the Florence visit, "the dear child who never thought in her whole life before of love and marriage, had it all put into her head at once by the sight of your and Browning's happiness. Oh, I see it, I understand how it was."[9] Elizabeth promised to "speak to Geddie," who denied all but the red beard. Mr. Macpherson was handsome, generous, noble; he might well become a good Protestant and a good artist. Geddie remained obdurate, and on their return to England, Mrs. Jameson was obliged to lay the child's folly before her parents. Despite a moment of shock and alarm, they proved surprisingly tolerant, and after the decorum of two years' wait, Geddie had the inexpressible happiness of becoming Mrs. Macpherson.

After a week that passed with bewildering swiftness, the visitors departed, leaving a vacancy behind. Robert judged the time propitious for a carriage tour of the city. "It was like the trail of a vision in the evening sun," wrote Elizabeth. "I saw the Perseus in a sort of flash." A more elaborate guided tour followed. "I have seen the Venus, I have seen the divine Raphaels," she told Boyd. "I have stood by Michael Angelo's tomb in Santa Croce. I have looked at the wonderful Duomo. . . . The mountainous marble masses overcome as we look up—we feel the weight of them on the soul."[10] Elizabeth's reactions to art seldom got beyond vague superlatives. She was more eager to applaud the genius than to contemplate his works—and perhaps the sight of so much nakedness staring out from walls and ceiling were permanently a trial to the daughter of Edward Barrett. She laughed at Wilson for being "struck back" at the door of the Tribune "by the indecency of the Venus," but she confessed that "the sight of that marble Goddess and Titian's (painted stark, just overhead,) were too much at first."[11] Realizing, no doubt, that she was physically unequal to the arduous foot journeys of the enthusiast, Robert contrived to combine brief sorties into churches and galleries with long drives in an open carriage through the streets and parks of the city. Usually they set out late in the afternoon, "with Elizabeth holding a parasol over her head"; stopped at the Church of the Carmine to see Masaccio's frescoes in the Brancacci Chapel, or at Santa Croce to see those of Giotto; and then took a long drive through the Cascine.[12]

Florence was as gay as Pisa had been lugubrious. Now Elizabeth was disturbed not by funerals and execution bells, but by laughing and singing, which often continued until late at night. Yet she was charmed by these carefree people who were always in the streets celebrating—with or without good cause. Robert and Elizabeth could not resist the chariot races held almost at their doorstep in the Piazza Santa Maria Novella to celebrate the feast day of San Giovanni, the patron saint of Florence. "Up against the houses, up against the great church, up against the convent walls," she wrote to Arabel, "seats were raised one over one, and the people crowded everywhere close as bees, only shining like butterflies, with their pretty dresses and glittering fans. Every seat, every window looked alive. The monks stood at the monastery windows, and we laughed to observe that there was room for just two at each."[13] On another occasion they attended a reception to meet R. B. Hoppner, former British consul at Venice, and his wife told them how she had "seduced" Shelley from vegetarianism with thick slices of roast beef.

An assortment of visitors now began to appear in the Via delle Belle

Donne. The Hanfords, old friends of the Barretts, called on their way through Florence, had dinner and champagne punctiliously served by Robert's order, and witnessed the Brownings' marriage settlement, which neither of the principals read. Another early visitor was the American sculptor Hiram Powers, who dropped in quite informally, drank coffee, talked for more than an hour with Robert, and particularly impressed Elizabeth.

"Like most men of true genius," she wrote, "he is simple as a child, quiet and gentle, calling himself 'a beginner in art' which is the best way of making a great end."[14] As time went on, the English poetess and the American sculptor were increasingly drawn to each other—partly, one suspects, because she liked to admire a genius and he liked to be so admired. Later, also, they discovered they had Swedenborg and spiritualism in common. A true Yankee, he was shrewdly and self-reliantly alert in both worlds, with a decided opinion on every subject, including himself. A self-made man and a self-made artist, he had been a library attendant, a clock mechanic, incidentally an inventor, an artist in a Cincinnati museum, and finally a sculptor, first in Washington and now in Florence. His "Eve" (1839) had made him known, and his "Greek Slave" (1843), celebrated. Apparently, he owed his success to an acquisitive eye for the beauties of ancient statues, a moderate talent for modeling, and a great talent for frank and sincere argument, by which he convinced himself and a good many others that he was a commanding genius. Even so cool an observer as Nathaniel Hawthorne, who knew him in the fifties, could not spend a few hours in his company without coming away half convinced that the man was all he asserted himself to be, and once had to stare very hard at the Venus de Medici to regain faith in it after having heard Powers compare it very unfavorably with his own "Greek Slave," which was apparently in large part but a feeble imitation. What Browning thought of Powers as an artist does not appear, but he thought well enough of him as a man to become a long-standing friend.

As the hot weather of May wore on, Elizabeth began to droop. Robert grappled with the weather on the one hand and Elizabeth's invalidism on the other. Every blind was drawn against the sun; every door and window was opened to the breeze. Yet by early morning the muslin curtains had sighed themselves out with the last breath of air. The indoor temperature rose to seventy-seven or -eight. "After our three o'clock dinner," wrote Elizabeth, "Robert wheels a great chair into his dressing room, which just then has the deepest shadow in it, and makes me sit in the chair, and pours eau de cologne into my hands and on my forehead, and fans me till my eyes shut of themselves. . . . Scarcely a day passes that I have not a regularly sound sleep after dinner." One breathless evening, Robert proposed she come down to the bottom of the house, where there was "quite a bath of cool air." She protested that he would have to carry her upstairs again. "I shall like to carry you—Now come, dear! take courage and come." She did so, and found herself so strong after the descent that they went out into the cool "street of pretty women," then into "what Robert calls 'Trot the jackass Street' " (*Troto del asino*), and so into the piazza. Another evening they walked as far as the Baptistry of Maria Novella, where they sat down and talked of Dante. Presumably on both occasions, Robert carried her up the stairs. This ceremony, so often practiced and so often mentioned, points, one suspects, to an element in his marriage that was important to Browning. Seen through Elizabeth's adoring yet not uncritical eyes, his habits, opinions, and preferences continue to emerge: he had very distinct ideas about ladies' dress; he liked strong, dark colors—"not those fainting-away blues and pinks and lilacs and greens;"[15] he could never imagine marrying a widow; he commemorated the day of his marriage not only on the twelfth of every month but on the Saturday of every week—a practice somewhat bewildering to Elizabeth, who seldom knew the date.

They had now been married ten months.

In July, even Robert could not mitigate the heat, and he worried about Elizabeth. But they still had two weeks' rent paid for. Therefore the contention in generosity was once more set in motion: this time Robert argued for extravagance and Elizabeth for economy. Besides, they hadn't received permission to go where her heart was set on going. They had discussed various cool and luxurious places, but all the while a bold and adventurous idea—abetted by Robert—had been growing in Elizabeth's mind: they would spend the hot season at the monastery of Vallombrosa in the high mountains! Eventually, they received a letter of recommendation to the abbot, urging that for various rare qualities they be allowed to remain in the House of Strangers beyond the usual three days. Robert was confident of his powers of Tuscan eloquence; Elizabeth, doubtful of the abbot's power to endure the presence of a woman very long. Setting out one morning at four to avoid the heat, they traveled to Pelago by carriage, and then—Robert on horseback, and Elizabeth and Wilson on basket sledges, each drawn by two white bullocks—they ascended for four hours—up mountains, through fir forests, past waterfalls—the five miles to Vallombrosa. Exhausted, famished, and happy, they downed a dinner of black bread and beef cooked in oil. "Oh, that bread, with the fetid smell, which stuck in the throat like Macbeth's amen!" For three days they felt welcome. After that, the abbot—a jealously, anxiously holy man with a red face—grew restive. Through a mediating monk Robert conveyed gratitude, hope, persuasion. In vain. "While he is abbot," was the reply, "he *will* be abbot."[16] In spite of her earlier forebodings, Elizabeth was indignant that although, as she read in the "Life of San Gualberto," the monks cleaned out pigsties with their bare hands, they would shrink from touching the little finger of a woman. After the fifth day, they were unceremoniously expelled.

While Elizabeth steamed behind closed shutters and drawn curtains, Robert braved the glaring sun in search of a cooler apartment, and soon found—astonishingly at the same rent—the cool and splendid suite of seven rooms, on the first floor of the Palazzo Guidi, which, after two more changes, was to be their permanent home. Situated between the Via Maggio and the Via Mazzetta on a *piazzetta* at the end of the Via Romana, Casa Guidi is a dark, grim, wedge-shaped building of brown stucco and ponderous rough-hewn stones, having from its thin edge the curious appearance of being all façade and no interior. Actually, the interior was vast enough. Looking out on the *piazzetta* and at one wing of Pitti Palace and of its great square were Robert's bedroom and a bedroom and sitting room for Wilson. On the other side of the central passage were the dining room, the drawing room, and Elizabeth's room, all of magnificent proportions, with high coffered ceilings and eight tall, floor-length windows opening out on a small stone balcony just wide enough for Robert and Elizabeth to walk abreast. Here, on fine summer evenings, they paced up and down, waiting for the moon to rise above the blank gray wall of San Felice Church just opposite and listening to the choir and organ within. As the successors of a Russian prince, they inherited splendid furniture, moving luxuriously among "noble mirrors," "marble consols, carved and gilt," and armchairs of crimson and white satin.[17]

But so much grandeur could be had for so little money only in the off season. Early in October their landlord demanded more rent. They were reluctant to leave, not only because they had grown accustomed to their luxuries, but probably because they already knew that Elizabeth was once more pregnant. The winter in Rome which they had planned was out of the question: Elizabeth ought not to travel.

Robert began to bargain with the landlord, but apparently, like other good-natured but economical persons, he had paid too much too often and broke off at last over a difference of two *scudi*—nine shillings. He was thus condemned to a fresh search. At such times he neither ate nor rested, but ranging the city from one end to the other, came back at intervals, pale and haggard, to describe what he had found. At this season he found nothing. Rooms were too hot or too dingy. There were difficulties about locations, staircases, sofas, even champagne glasses. In desperation he took an apartment in the Via Maggio. They moved in. The rooms were too cold for Elizabeth. Robert was once more walking the streets, and within ten days they were in what he described as "little funny rabbit-hutch rooms; but *so* warm, and cheerful" on the Piazza Pitti just opposite the grand-ducal palace.[18] He now had to pay "heaps of guineas" till their first landlord could relet his rooms. What such a debacle must have meant to a man so orderly and economical in his financial arrangements, one can imagine. "Any other man, a little lower than the angels," wrote Elizabeth, "would have stamped and sworn a little for the mere relief of the thing."[19] Actually, he seems to have felt only remorse. "The taking that cold house was all my fault,"[20] he assured her sisters.

These domestic tribulations would hardly be worth recording at such length did they not illustrate what a revolution had been wrought in the life of a vigorous, buoyant man hitherto dedicated to celibacy, independence, and poetry. At this time, Browning wrote little or nothing new, confining himself to the revision of work already published. Even Elizabeth could not wheedle, scold, or bully him into going out alone at night; nor did Italian music, Alfieri's plays, or private theatricals at the house of Charles Lever tempt this sociable, musical, theater-loving man. The whole tendency of his life is revealed in what he wrote to Elizabeth's sisters. These letters are one long though modest demonstration that in carrying Elizabeth away from all she loved to a new home at the other end of the continent, he had made possible a restoration of her health and happiness. Indeed, the very concentration of his purpose and weight of his responsibility caused him to see a new and rather surprising Elizabeth. A niece of Lord Cork, Mary Boyle, who used to look in on the Brownings at an hour which she considered early but they considered late—as they sat before the fire at their chestnuts and mulled wine—has described once more the Elizabeth that most people saw: "I have never in the course of my life seen a more spiritual face, or one in which the soul looked out more clearly from the windows; . . . and her form was so fragile as to appear an etherial covering."[21] Robert would have emphasized spirituality rather than ethereality. "I wonder," he wrote her sisters, "if she tells you anything about her good looks—her rounded cheeks with not a little colour on them, and her general comparative . . . shall I dare to write it . . . plumpness?" Nobody else ever dared "plumpness," yet Wilson, as well as old friends and relatives visiting Florence, did testify to a radical improvement in her appearance.

Throughout the winter her health continued to improve, but early in March she suffered her second miscarriage. Dr. Harding saw port wine as the cause; Robert himself, excessive letter-writing—so much so that he attempted to enlist her sisters in a program of moderation.

> . . . it is all thro' me [he confessed] you do not receive a great letter from Ba,—whole sheets overflowing, such as I used to see her perpetrating, —while I could not find the heart to stop the quick little fingers, or do more than interpose at intervals with "*now*, Ba"— "What did you promise me?" "There's your face getting red and redder," . . . "Just to the end of this page"—"only a word here,—something I forgot and must say" and so at last the letter was piled up story on story like a Tower of Babel—and then—once the letter safely off at the post—and away, I used to hear "*Perhaps* . . . it was not wise in me to write so much—it may be the cause that I don't feel quite so well!"[22]

She quickly recovered both her health and her fortitude. "Children may be kept for those who have not such a husband as I, perhaps!"[23] she wrote her friend Miss Fanny Dowglass.

At Casa Guidi, and even more in the little rabbit-hutch rooms on the Piazza Pitti, the Brownings' front windows opened on the very stage of Florentine history. What they saw in 1847 and 1848 moved them deeply and changed them a little. The new pope cautiously lifted a finger: attempting to mitigate the rigors of ecclesiastical misgovernment, he had begun his reign by freeing a large number of political prisoners. Apparently, he had meant to stop there. But the whole Italian people had been waiting for a sign, and such books as Gioberti's *Del Primato morale e civile delgi italiani* encouraged them to expect it from the papacy. The result was such a storm of applause and gratitude that, carried away in spite of his sober intentions, Pius made other tentative motions; he considered plans for building railways in his dominions, established a *consulta* which was supposed to have vague legislative functions, and appointed famous secular liberals as ministers of state. Avalanches of patriotism now threatened on other political slopes. Unrest in Sicily was forcing King Frederic of Bourbon into ever wilder paradoxes of extravagant promise and brutal repression. Avalanches of verbal patriotism in the newspapers were also making Leopold of Tuscany extremely anxious. He had no desire to follow in King Frederic's footsteps. Indeed as a pious Catholic and a cautious liberal, he was much inclined to follow in the Pope's. On the other hand, he was Grand Duke of Tuscany because, as a relative of the Austrian emperor, he could count on the authority of Austrian bayonets. After some deliberation, he established a *consulta* on the Roman model and, under heavy pressure from the newspapers, made a gesture of abjuring the Austrian bayonets: the Tuscans might have their own civic guard.

The celebration took place on September 12, 1847, the anniversary of the Brownings' marriage:

> For above three hours the infinite procession filed under our windows—with all their various flags and symbols, into the Piazza Pitti where the Duke and his family stood in tears at the window to receive the thanks of his people. . . . —class after class—troops of peasants and nobles, and of soldiers fraternizing with the people. Then, too, came the foreigners . . .—French, English, Swiss, Greeks. . . . Clouds of flowers and of laurel leaves came fluttering down on the advancing procession; and the clapping of hands, and the frenetic shouting, and the music which came in gushes. . . . I had a throne of cushions piled up on a chair, but was dreadfully tired before it was all over. . . . And then Robert and I waved our handkerchiefs till my wrist ached, I will answer for mine. At night there was an illumination, and we walked just to the Arno to have a sight of it. . . . And even *then,* the people were *embracing* for joy. It was a state of phrensy or rapture, extending to the children of two years old, several of whom I heard lisping "*Vivas,*" with their fat arms clasping their mothers' necks.[24]

However much he had waved his handkerchief, Robert seems, unlike Elizabeth, to have realized that a revolution cannot be all carnival. Watching the civic guard parading as usual one *festa* day in all the splendor of their new helmets and epaulettes, he remarked, "Surely, after all this, they would *use* those muskets?"[25]

Through the next few months the Italian people continued to parade, demonstrate, applaud, publish, and in some instances to fight their way to further concessions. A constitution was granted by the King of Naples in January 1848, by the King of Piedmont on February

8, and by the Grand Duke of Tuscany on February 17. The last event was celebrated by another popular outburst of feeling in which—for the moment at least—the sovereign seemed as happy to surrender power as the people to assume it.

> "Ba, Ba," says Robert at the door, "come this moment out here—I want you to see something."
>
> What in the world is the matter now, thought I—I went to the window—and there, with vehement bursts of acclamation, was the Grand Duke's carriage in the midst of a "milky way" of waxen torchlights. You would have thought that all the stars out of Heaven had fallen into the piazza. Good Grand Duke!

At the end of the day celebrating the new constitution, the Duke had gone privately to the opera and been recognized; shouting replaced singing, and as he left he encountered at the door a great crowd of torchbearers ready to conduct him home. Overcome, the Duke "wept, we hear, like a child."[26]

In Paris, a week later, an event occurred which caused every potentate in Europe to quake in his military jack boots. The constitutional monarchy of Louis Philippe gave way to a republic. Revolution spread swiftly into the German states, and on March 13 there was even an uprising in Vienna.

The proceedings of the new republic in Paris brought out in both Robert and Elizabeth an English distrust of French speculation and experiment. "Republicans as I and my husband are by profession," she wrote Miss Mitford, "we very anxiously, anxiously even to pain, look on the work being attempted and done just now by the theorists in Paris."[27] Their ideas, she told Henrietta, "go up like rockets, and in the midst of our acclamation and admiration, drop down in ashes. Little is consequent and consistent, and still less practically possible." She and Robert were naturally apprehensive about mob rule and legislation for the benefit of a single class; they also condemned the attack on private property. "Whatever . . . touches upon property is a wrong, and whatever tends to the production of social equality is absurd and iniquitous, and oppressive in its ultimate ends. . . . Robert and I agree nearly on all these points, but here and there we have plenty of room for battles."[28]

Sentenced in April 1848 to a fresh search for rooms by the expiration of his lease, Robert seems to have made two notable discoveries. Because of political disturbances and the flight of foreigners from the city, lodgings were at the time both cheap and available. Moreover, unfurnished lodgings rented by the year were always infinitely cheaper than furnished lodgings rented by the month. In climate and in other respects—particularly now that nearly all the English were gone—Florence suited them well. Why not make it their headquarters, renting unfurnished by the year and subletting at a profit when they wished to travel?

At one point in their search, Robert had leaned toward "a ground floor in the Frescobaldi Palace, being bewitched by a garden full of camellias, and a little pond of gold and silver fish; but," continued Elizabeth in her witty, high-flown manner, "while he saw the fish I saw the mosquitos in clouds, such an apocalypse of them as has not yet been visible to me in all Florence, and I dread mosquitos more than Austrians; and he, in his unspeakable goodness, deferred to my fear in a moment and gave up the camellias without one look behind."[29] They now decided—at a rent of twenty-five guineas a year—on their former suite in Casa Guidi, where they could have plenty of room, magnificence, and camellias on the terrace if they wished, with privacy.

The magnificence was important to Robert. "Sometimes, in joke," Elizabeth wrote Henrietta, "I call him an aristocrat—I cry out '*à bas les aristocrats*'—because he really cares a good deal about external things—perhaps it is an artist's sense of grace that he has, only that I choose to make fun of it. For instance about houses, and furniture, and horses and carriages, he is far more particular than I ever was or can be. Then I laugh—and then he says it is for my sake." Whether his taste derived from the artist, the aristocrat, or the Philistine in him, Robert liked hunting furniture as much as he had disliked hunting apartments. For the drawing room he rapidly provided a number of black, antique, Gothic chairs, and to go over the fireplace, a mirror "with the most beautiful carved gilt frame" and two cupids holding lights in the lower part. He also aspired to find Elizabeth a ducal bed, all gilt and carving; but apparently had to be content with a humbler price and white muslin draperies. She coveted sofas; he, chests of drawers. Soon after taking up residence early in May, they found they had eight spring sofas and six chests. Elizabeth protested they had more drawers than they could ever fill, but she was lost in admiration for two chests Robert had bought for her room—one "walnutwood inlaid with ivory," and the other, "ebony and ivory inlaid, with the curiousest gilt handles—Tritons holding masks."[30] He also bought from a convent a great bookcase of carved angels and demons—to hold their books, which were now sent for from England. For an artist's luxury Robert paid only a Puritan's price: the entire six rooms were furnished on the returns from their writings for the last two years. Later, Robert hunted for pictures, and made some notable finds. "The other day," Elizabeth wrote Mrs. Jameson in 1850, "he covered himself with glory by discovering and seizing on (in a corn shop a mile from Florence) five pictures among heaps of trash; and one of the best judges in Florence (Mr. Kirkup) throws out such names for them as Cimabue, Ghirlandaio, Giottino, a crucifixion painted on a banner, Giottesque, if not Giotto."[31]

The Brownings also added to their household a new servant, Alessandro, who acted as cook and manager—partly, perhaps, on the theory that an Italian was needed to bargain with Italians. But Alessandro represented not only an economy: "From beefsteak pies up to fricassees—he is a master, and from bread and butter puddings to boiled apple-dumplings, . . . an artist. He apologized in a set oration the other day for not having sooner provided us with a roast turkey—placing one on the table, as he spoke, to our extreme admiration—just such an one, Wilson thinks, as at this time of the year would cost twenty shillings in London, and the whole price of which was one shilling and ten pence!" Alessandro's excellence was that he was at once an artist and a man of reflection and large experience; his fault was that he knew he was. Any advice or interference from Wilson was most unwelcome. In fact, Wilson had to hear many times a day: "I have been to Paris—I have been to London—I have been to Germany—I must know." And what he knew was even more offensive. "London is by far the most immoral place in the world," he assured her.[32] Poor Wilson usually fled from the scene without the least pretense to a woman's last word. She was engaged to a handsome grenadier in the Duke's Guard and had many problems.

By mid-July Florence was again insufferably hot. Though "dreadfully afraid, as usual" that Elizabeth would "fall to pieces" at the first motion of the carriage, Robert decided they must go to Fano for the benefit "of the sea air and the oysters." He himself had just recovered from influenza, and she was in the earliest stage of a third pregnancy. Traveling often by night to avoid the heat, they set out by diligence on the evening of July 17 for Arezzo, from there crossing the Apennines to Fano. They discovered at once they could not summer there. Except for some beautiful churches and Guercino's "divine" painting "The Guardian Angel," Fano was hot and dull; Ancona, further south, was hot and beautiful—rising up from the brown rocks as though it were a part of them and "elbowing out the purple tides."[33] They continued south as far as Loretto and then, partly retracing their steps, turned north to Ravenna, where Robert had once thought he would like to live. He was disillusioned. Situated on a marshy delta that was building itself out into the sea, Ravenna proved to be a city of glittering mosaics and awful stenches, with one thing of note besides—the tomb of Dante. Returning home, the Brownings crossed the Apennines at Forti.

While at Ancona, Browning wrote "The Guardian-Angel: A Picture at Fano," one of his very few poems of the period. Though not one of the best, it is significant for two strong marks of Elizabeth's influence: Browning speaks in his own voice, and in a deeply religious tone. What he says, however, reveals the obverse of the courageous, resourceful Browning Elizabeth knew daily. In effect, the poet begs for the kind of soothing care and tutelage that the angel gives the kneeling child:

> If this was ever granted, I would rest
>   My head beneath thine, while thy healing hands
> Close-covered both my eyes beside thy breast,
>   Pressing the brain, which too much thought expands,
> Back to its proper size again, and smoothing
>   Distortion down till every nerve had soothing.

How important was this side of Browning? Mrs. Betty Miller thinks it deeply so. And yet a sheltered childhood does not mean a permanent need for shelter. Robert had expected and accepted a good deal from his family but had also long relied on himself in making personal decisions, some of which—his career, his marriage—indicate a vigorously operating self-confidence and basic independence of early ties. On the other hand, Mrs. Miller is probably right in saying that the poem expresses his lassitude and frustration.[34] What is more to the point: a marriage undertaken in the spirit of "Count Gismond" had entailed a very strained, Victorian service at a bedside and over an account book; very little time and strength had been left for poetry. "The Guardian-Angel" seems to represent a moment of awareness and realization—of anxiety before a new and strange home, an invalid wife, and fresh responsibilities of a child possibly impending, as well as of nostalgia for the old home, perhaps the old freedom, and old friends lost in distance and time. Browning twice apostrophizes Alfred Domett and concludes—as though he were writing him a letter—in wonder that they should both be so far away from their childhood home:

> Where are you, dear old friend?
> How rolls the Wairoa at your world's far end?
> This is Ancona, yonder is the sea.

One of the few long Browning letters available from this period presents, in a very different form and context, another view of this complex personality. Writing to R. H. Horne, Browning is for one page intricately and elaborately chatty about every trivial thing under the sun. On page two his purpose becomes clear: Eliza Flower had died in 1846. "I heard [of] it at Pisa, and, three or four months after, wrote a note to Mrs. Adams—a few lines, but they must have shown how I felt, I think. I added . . . that I should be glad to have my letters back—just mentioning . . . [that Eliza had said she kept them] as an excuse for the seeming absurdity of not being sure all such boyish rubbish had not been at once properly disposed of." He continues in tones of increasing horror that he had heard nothing at all, then from Horne himself that there had been "a horrible raking up of the correspondence in general," then that Eliza's sister, "poor Mrs A.," had also died. Would Horne try to get the letters? Robert now speaks of Horne's recent marriage, of an impending revival of *A Blot in the 'Scutcheon* by Phelps, of a new edition of his own poems.[35]

"We have been obliged with quantities of Father Prout," Robert tells Horne dryly in the same letter. "Father Prout" was F. S. Mahony, an ex-candidate for the Jesuit Order, former light of *Fraser's Magazine,* and now Roman correspondent for Dickens' *Daily News.* Having had a faculty for mysteriously appearing in the midst of Robert's bachelor travels on the Continent, he continued to do so in his married travels as well. Robert was continually getting off a steamer or rising from a breakfast table with the exclamation, "Good Heavens, there he is again!—there's Father Prout!" The gentleman was exuberantly fond of Browning. Once, stepping out of his black box—or as Elizabeth says, "spending an hour or two in Florence on his road to Rome"—he "met Robert, and *kissed* him in the street, mouth to mouth."[36] Calling at Casa Guidi on another visit, he found Robert very sick with an ulcerated throat and Elizabeth "quite unhappy . . . over those burning hands and languid eyes." Pointing out that the fever had "got ahead through weakness," Prout mixed a potion of eggs and port wine, and administered it in spite of the moral consternation of Alessandro, who lifted up his eyes and cried, "O inglesi, inglesi!" The Jesuit magic worked: Robert soon threw off the infection. "I shall always be grateful to Father Prout," Elizabeth told Miss Mitford, "always."

The reiterated *always* is significant. For as Elizabeth went on to explain with polite despair, "He has been in Florence ever since, and we have seen him every day; he came to doctor and remained to talk."[37] Indeed he calmly informed them that "Florence agreed with him better than Rome did, that he liked the place, liked the beef, liked the bread and especially liked his Attic evenings with Browning and Ba!" He came morning or evening, expected wine as a matter of course, commandeered one of the Raphael basins for a spitoon, and poured jolly cynicism and tobacco smoke out upon the two poets. Though "sorely tried between his good nature and detestation of the whole proceeding," Robert usually responded to the "sublime confidence" of the man sufficiently to maintain a creditable show of warmth. Elizabeth lay on a sofa, listened, and let herself be called *Ba.* But "when he goes away," she wrote Henrietta, "there's a general burst of indignation and throwing open of doors to get rid of smoke and malice."[38] She was particularly revolted at the spectacle of the black clerical sides heaving with intemperate laughter.

No doubt, to project oneself poetically into Caliban is one thing, and to entertain him every evening in the presence of one's wife would be another. To be sure, Father Prout was not Caliban, nor the Spanish Monk, nor even the Bishop of St. Praxed's. What is interesting about this episode is how little, apparently, Robert was attracted on this occasion to the earthy gusto which he depicts in literature.

Meanwhile, throughout 1848, the Continent responded with the crash of fallen thrones and empires, driving prudent English people out of Florence by the carriage-load and filling Robert and Elizabeth with a heady sense of history audibly transpiring. On March 13 an insurrection broke out in Vienna. On March 18, the provinces of Lombardy and Venetia rose in revolt; and an outraged people, almost without arms, dislodged an army of 20,000 Austrians from Milan. This news reached Florence the next day. On the twenty-first, gathering in front of the municipality, a large crowd of young men demanded arms. The Duke responded with a warm proclamation of Italian patriotism and the dispatch of two columns of troops to the frontier. The proceedings of the patriotic liberal and the zealous Catholic in the grand ducal personality must by this time have caused the cousin of the Austrian Emperor considerable alarm.

Most Italian sovereigns led double lives, though none was quite so placidly sincere in both, perhaps, as the Grand Duke Leopold. Charles Albert of Sardinia alone was powerful and courageous enough to make a clear-cut decision, and even he stood long poised with his army on the banks of the Ticino, balancing the dangers of fighting the Austrians in front of him, or, if he did not, of putting down outraged subjects at his back. The embattled people of Lombardy and Venetia pleaded for his aid; patriotism and ambition echoed that plea. On March 29 he crossed the river and in the ensuing month won several limited victories over the Austrians, notably Pischiera and Goito, in the last of which the raw Tuscan troops sent by Leopold heroically defended the villages of Curtalone and Montenare against the onslaughts of vastly superior Austrian forces. On April 29, however, the Pope struck dismay into the whole Italian cause—and complicated his own double life—by declaring that he could not sanction a war against a Catholic nation. Even so, he still tried valiantly to close the gap between the Pontiff and the patriot by appointing as his chief minister a moderate and statesmanlike liberal, Count Rossi, who might have effected sound and stable reforms had he not been assassinated in November.

Elizabeth's opinions on these events are the chief indication we have of Robert's. She declares several times in her letters that they substantially agree. Having thoroughly enjoyed the Italian revolution as carnival, she has surprisingly little to say of it as revolution. In a letter to Henrietta of June 24th, for example, she dismisses the situation with a sentence: "Austria goes out slowly, but never will recover her position in Italy."[39] Apparently both she and her correspondents were more interested in France. On July 4, she writes Miss Mitford briefly of the Florentine *senati*: "The elections have returned moderate men, and many land-proprietors, and Robert, who went out to see the procession of members, was struck by the grave thoughtful faces and the dignity of expression." But discussion of the French crisis is lengthy. "How did you feel when the cry was raised, 'Vive l'Empereur'? Only Prince Napoleon is a Napoleon cut out in paper after all." She says that Robert was a little more hopeful of the French republic than she. She reiterates that she and Robert are in substantial agreement.

The fullest expression of her own feeling at this time—it can hardly be called thought—is *Casa Guidi Windows*, the first part of which was written before the Italian collapse, and the second part after, in 1851. The poem is a signal instance of the way in which the use of verse pumps Elizabeth up beyond any possibility of coherent and rational discussion. Metaphoric violets, swords, crowns, and croziers accumulate until there is no room for realities. Politics founder in rhapsody and anecdote about dead Florentine poets and artists. Elizabeth is for carnage and for peace, for and against England and France. The pattern of the poem is that of romantic illusion and disillusionment. Part I is naïve and frenetic: geniuses, peoples, individuals, Florence, and liberty are good and wonderful; priests, monks, governments, Austrians, and tyranny are evil. Part II is ironic and gloomy: Pope Pius, admired in Part I as a possible Carlylean hero, is as evil as any pope after all; Florentines are frivolous and fickle beyond any but the stillest small hope of faroff independence. Yet one suspects, making allowance for its childlike vision and its frantic idiom, that this poem sets forth the essential elements of thought and feeling for both Elizabeth and Robert. His "Why I Am a Liberal," for example, is not inconsistent with the sentiments of *Casa Guidi.* Meanwhile, her prose, taking up Italy's story in subsequent letters, once more settles down toward comparative English caution and good sense.

Caught in the dynamics of revolution, Tuscany now moved rapidly toward the left until, in October, the Duke found himself compelled to take as minister Francesco Guerrazzi, one of the most notorious republicans from notoriously republican Leghorn. Guerrazzi suavely urged a constitutional assembly, presumably for the purpose of deposing the Duke. "It is painful," Elizabeth wrote Miss Mitford in all prose sobriety, "to feel ourselves growing gradually cooler and cooler on the subject of Italian patriotism, valour, and good sense; but the process is inevitable. The child's play between the Livornese and our Grand Duke provokes a thousand pleasantries. Every now and then a day is fixed for a revolution in Tuscany, but up to the present time a shower has come and put it off. Two Sundays ago Florence was to have been 'sacked' by Leghorn, when a drizzle came and saved us."[40] Actually, the Duke seemed willing to be deposed. He even said that he would gladly be deposed for his people's good. Privately, however, he must have reflected that in such times a superfluous sovereign is likely to be a dead sovereign. To make matters worse, the Pope, having moved from cautious reform to violent reaction, was even now threatening to excommunicate Leopold if he called a constitutional assembly. Leopold's situation had grown so complex that it was becoming simple; Guerrazzi had frightened the liberal in him; Pius had reversed the Catholic. Still uttering liberal sentiments, Leopold retired to Siena and then to San Stefano.

Now the revolutionary leaders began to complicate themselves or their situation. Mazzini had returned to the Peninsula, breathing republicanism and denouncing the very Sardinian monarchy on which Italian strength depended. On February 8, 1849, Guerrazzi finally deposed Leopold, apparently with reluctance. Power had made Guerrazzi a moderate, even a constitutional monarchist. An intuitive realist, he saw that some compromise with legitimacy was unavoidable. Meanwhile, as the new republic faced a growing anarchy, he ruled with his tongue—a wily, devious, flattering eloquence which filled English observers with gloomy distrust. "Guerrazzi is a traitor, to my mind," wrote Elizabeth; "and though Mazzini is virtuous and heroic, he is indiscreet and mistakes the stuff of which the people is made, if he thinks to find a great nation in the heart of it. The [Italian] soldiers refuse to fraternize with the republicans, and Robert saw a body of them arrested the other day."[41]

The flight of the Pope following his declaration of war on Austria led to the proclamation of a Roman republic on the one hand and a scramble of the Catholic powers to put it down on the other. Pursuing theory to the center of Italy, Mazzini arrived in Rome, became dictator, and, with Garibaldi at the head of the defending forces, presided over a martyrdom of classical Italian republicanism at the hands of the French, who, though republicans themselves, supported the Pope to prevent Austrian control of the entire peninsula. "The poor Pope I deeply pity," wrote Elizabeth; "he is a weak man with the noblest and most disinterested intentions."[42]

To the north, events had also been moving toward a conclusion. Charles Albert of Sardinia was severely defeated at Novara in March 1849 and abdicated in favor of his son Victor Emmanuel. Now helpless and exposed to Austrian invasion, Florence entered on a macabre comedy of counterrevolution. The regular troops refused to obey their officers. Some of the worst elements of the citizenry went about heavily armed. A contingent of ragged Leghornese troops swaggered about in the most elegant parts of the city. Such a powder keg needed only a very small match. "If the Leghornese . . . had not refused to pay at certain Florentine cafés," wrote Elizabeth, "we shouldn't have had revolution the second." At any rate, firing broke out between the civic guard and the Leghornese, and, in a shocking return to Florentine street violence, many of the Leghornese were hunted down and torn to pieces. "Dr. Harding, who was coming to see me, had time to get behind a stable door, just before there was a fall against it and four shot corpses; and Robert barely managed to get home across the bridges." When order was restored, the terrified municipality—

backed or coerced by armed peasants from the neighborhood—imprisoned Guerrazzi, obliterated all emblems and memorials of republicanism, and blandly invited the Grand Duke to return as constitutional monarch. There was now a renewal, apparently quite sincere and spontaneous, of carnival celebrations—processions, illuminations, and *Te Deums.* "The same tune, sung under the windows, did for 'Viva la republica!' and 'Viva Leopoldo!'" wrote the scandalized Elizabeth.[43] In May Austrian troops entered the city, and the Grand Duke returned. Both he and the Austrian commanders promised to respect the *statuto* of constitutional rule—and promptly abolished it. According to Adolphus Trollope, former republicans were punished with severity.[44]

No zealous republican could live through such events without being deeply moved—and greatly disillusioned. "The Austrians are to arrive in Florence to-morrow, and the officers to be quartered on the inhabitants. I am sick at heart, and so is Robert, at the prospect of the country. I, individually, give up the Grand Duke, . . . as Robert did a long time ago. . . . I shed some tears when he went away, and could cry again for rage at his coming back."[45] The Brownings' disillusionment with Italian character, descending from mercantile to deeper moral and political levels, was now complete. "The people wants *stamina,* wants conscience, wants self-reverence," she had written Miss Mitford as early as August 1848.[46] The arrival of the Austrians produced in her a mild reaction of sympathy for the Italians—and something even more characteristic. While Elizabeth was writing a letter, an Italian servant called out, "'Signora—signora—ecco i Tedeschi!' . . . We ran out on the terrace together—and up from the end of the street and close under our windows came the artillery, and baggage-waggons—the soldiers sitting upon the cannons motionless, like dusty statues."[47] In these words one feels a little—and in a longer passage of *Casa Guidi Windows,* much more—that respect for power which bound Elizabeth to her father and was later to affect decidedly her political views. "The word 'Liberty' ceases to make me thrill, as at something great and unmistakable,"[48] she had written Mrs. Martin; and in the long letter to Henrietta which describes the arrival of the Austrians, she says quite simply, "Robert and I agree that it is melancholy work to live on here."[49]

Why, after writing so much good poetry about Italy, past and present, did Browning himself attempt nothing about these events, which, as Elizabeth's letters show, he had taken a great deal of trouble to observe at first hand? He was, to be sure, writing very little poetry at this time. He may have found the liberal catastrophe too dispiriting for a liberal pen. He may even have felt, subconsciously at least, that he could hardly write anything without writing better than Elizabeth had done in *Casa Guidi.*

But, as in *War and Peace,* domestic events now supervened within the Browning family upon political and military; a small future shouldered aside a larger, vanishing present. As early as February 1849, Elizabeth had written Henrietta, "Remember the little petticoats you sent me—four of them. Of the four I have made three. This I did with my very own fingers."[50] Clearly, Elizabeth's third pregnancy was proceeding normally. At length, Robert himself wrote, investing Elizabeth, in reverent gratitude, with some of the divinity with which he later invested Pompilia:

> Dearest Henrietta, dearest Arabel—This is written on the 9th of March [1849] at 4 o'clock in the morning, to tell you that thro' God's infinite goodness our blessed Ba gave birth to a fine, strong boy at a quarter past two: and is doing admirably. She was taken ill at five o'clock yesterday morning, and suffered still increasing pains, with only a few minutes intermission between them, for more than twenty-one hours—during the whole of which time she never once cried out, or shed a tear, acute as the pains were; I sate by her as much as I was allowed, and shall never forget what I saw, tho' I cannot speak about it. Dr. Harding assures me that, without flattery, the little creature is the very model of a beautiful boy; but the only remarkable point in him I can safely testify to, of my own knowledge, is his voice—which made me effectually aware of his existence,—before it had well begun—thro' a thick wall and double door.

At nine o'clock he once more took up the pen: "Ba is going on *perfectly* well—she is as happy as human creature can be." He speaks with unwonted boldness of physiological matters and of "a famous specimen of a wet nurse that is to come"; then proceeds to Elizabeth's "perfect goodness, patience, self-denial and general rationality," citing "that resolution of leaving off the morphine, for instance"; and finally assures his sisters-in-law with all the solemnity of italics: *"rely on one thing, that we will take every precaution with respect to Ba"*—and concludes in a postscript: "Babe has got the nurse he was beginning to call for, and is now feeding like a hungry man."[51]

CHAPTER **16**

Sober Questions

1849-51

The day or two immediately after the birth of his son found Browning poised before many a tall palazzo door to deliver, with his customary punctilio, an appropriate announcement card. Yet his demeanor scarcely did justice to the errand. One maidservant reported to her mistress, "He did not walk, he danced." Still on tiptoe, so to speak, with this dancing joy, he received in quick succession three letters from his sister Sarianna. The first informed him that his mother "was not well"; the second, that she "was very ill"; and the third, that she had passed away. Actually, she had died before the first letter was written. "My husband has been in the deepest anguish," Elizabeth wrote Miss Mitford more than a month later, "and indeed, except for the courageous consideration of his sister, . . . I am frightened to think what the result would have been. . . . I never saw a man so bowed down in an extremity of sorrow. . . . Even now the depression is great, and sometimes when I leave him alone a little and return to the room, I find him in tears."[1]

This period was one of the darkest of Browning's life. Until now he had suffered no deprivation graver than popular indifference to his poetry. Until now he had been sheltered and protected to the point at which he was positively uneasy at his exemption from obvious remunerative toil. His mother had been the beloved symbol and agent of that protection. In late life, he managed to burn great bundles of the notes and letters he had sent her. Even before the letters, he had given up a college education to be near her, sacrificed Shelley's atheism to be in agreement with her. In the midst of his absorbing and romantic courtship, she had been a presence so compelling and intimate that her illnesses had produced sympathetic illnesses in himself. Nor had marriage and wide physical separation greatly diminished that presence in his thoughts. "No day has passed since our marriage," Elizabeth wrote Sarianna, "that he has not fondly talked of her."

Elizabeth's own situation was not enviable. To Miss Mitford she wrote, "It has been very very painful altogether, this drawing together of life and death. Robert was too enraptured at my safety, and with his little son, and the sudden reaction was terrible." But to Sarianna, she touched on a deeper and more personal level of the crisis. "Very bitter has it been to me to have interposed unconsciously as I have done and deprived him of her last words and kisses—very bitter."[2] Inevitably, the baby suffered also. The "poor little babe . . . fell away by a most natural recoil (even *I* felt it to be *most natural*) from all that triumph, but Robert is still very fond of him, and goes to see him bathed every morning, and walks up and down on the terrace with him in his arms."

From the very first Robert "yearned" toward his sister and father. Elizabeth felt that, if she could "give him back" to them at least, the result would be consolatory to all. Unfortunately, they could not leave New Cross, nor could Robert bear to think of looking upon it. To see his mother's roses over the garden wall, and the place where she used to leave her scissors and gloves, he told Elizabeth, would break his heart. June found him still sunk in lethargy and depression. He dropped "heavy tears" over Sarianna's letters, suffered from "loss of appetite, loss of sleep," and looked "quite worn and altered." Elizabeth began to fear that, unless she could get him out of Florence, he might fall ill with a "nervous fever." Finally, pleading that the baby must soon have cooler air, she carried Robert off to scout the vicinity for a summer retreat. Taking a boat, they skirted "the white marble mountains" of Carrara as far as Spezia, which "wheels the blue sea into the arms" of the wooded hills. Dutifully but not cheerfully, they visited Shelley's house at Lerici. His death by drowning linked him with the saddest event in Elizabeth's life; his skepticism, indirectly with the saddest event in Robert's. Anyway, lodgings in the place were much too expensive. They explored the nearby mountain villages without better result and then, at Elizabeth's insistence, went on to Bagni di Lucca, against which Robert particularly "had the strongest prejudice" as a "wasp's nest of scandal and gaming" for the continental English.[3] They found most of the English gone, the prices low, the woods and mountains beautiful, cool, and consolatory. On the spot they rented an apartment in the highest village for four months—and returned at once to get the baby and the servants.

At Florence they stayed only long enough to have the baby baptized Robert Wiedemann Barrett Browning, on June 26 at the French Evangelical Protestant Church. "The service was very simple and evangelical," Robert wrote Sarianna, "just the same as at Mr. Clayton's." Wiedemann, the maiden name of Robert's mother, was Elizabeth's suggestion (though she later dropped one 'n'). Her husband was deeply pleased. "I have been thinking over nothing else, these last three months," he told his sister, "than Mama and all about her, and catching at any little fancy of finding something which it would have pleased her I should do."[4]

Yet he was by no means restored. The roles of the two lovers were now reversed. Robert's eyes were fixed on death; Elizabeth must guide him back into the world. That she attempted to do so with patience, tact, and understanding, many passages in her letters attest. She had also the forbearance to leave him alone, for there were times when he had to search for himself in the shadows not only of the chestnut forest but of a past in which she had no part. "This evening," he wrote Sarianna, "I climbed to the top of a mountain over loose stones in the dry bed of a torrent, and under vines and chestnuts, till I reached an old deserted village, with perhaps a dozen inhabitants—one of whom, an old woman, told me I was 'too curious' by far, and I should lose myself up there." Sarianna must follow his example: "Now you see I do a plain duty in taking exercise and trying to amuse myself and recover my spirits." And then, in a curious attempt to comfort his sister, he reveals how strong his grief still is and how much it is a rejection, perhaps even an accusation, of his present happiness. "Apart from the folly and wickedness of the feeling, I am wholly tired of opening my eyes on the world now—and if I have advantages and comforts of various kinds that you have not, yet—it seems to me, at least—your comforts and memories are infinitely beyond mine, those of the best kind."[5] He concludes with an earnest plea for news of all his relatives and old friends at home. Looking back from a reading of this letter, one sees "The Guardian Angel" as strangely premonitory—an alienation from the present, an awakening to the past, an opening up to such a loss as he was to suffer.

For to envy his sister was in a sense to regret his marriage. Feeling the exclusiveness in his grief, Elizabeth must have used every opportunity of making him sensible of his present "advantages and comforts." She held one trump card: the sonnets she had written three years before on their courtship. Because of something he said then "against putting one's loves into verse," she had never dared show them. Yet she knew what a high value he set on her "poetic genius." One evening at Lucca he "said something else on the other side." The next morning—if a letter he wrote Julia Wedgwood in November 1864 can be credited—she said to him hesitatingly, " 'Do you know I once wrote some poems about *you?'*—and then—'There they are, if you care to see them'—and there [Browning recalled] was the little Book I have here." By 1864 Elizabeth herself had been dead three years. Robert could still see her gesture and hear the tones of her voice as she had handed him the sonnets. He could even see the window at which he had stood, with the tall mimosa tree in front, and the little churchcourt to the right. For the sonnets had their effect: though she expressed herself in the same quaint or inflated metaphors, Elizabeth had experienced love as she had never experienced Nonconformist theology or Italian politics. "Yes," Browning wrote Julia Wedgwood with his usual solemnity in speaking of Elizabeth, "that was a strange, heavy crown, that wreath of Sonnets." "Heavy," perhaps, because they seemed too personal to be made public and yet were too good to be kept private. Of course the argument of merit prevailed. The sequence was included in the 1850 edition of Elizabeth's poems. Robert indulged his rather conspiratorial sense of privacy by taking one telltale sonnet out of its natural order and tucking a new—and irrelevant—secret into the title. "The Portuguese"—purposely ambiguous—refers not to a language but a lady, "that Caterina who left Camoens the riband from her hair."[6]

As Robert's spirits convalesced, in their "eagle's nest" above Bagni di Lucca the summer became a peculiarly satisfying one for Elizabeth. Temporarily, at least, she had regained her health, and she was proving her competence as a woman. Even as she helped her husband return to his middle-aged world of consolations and responsibilities, she could rejoice in watching her baby awaken, with infinite zest and health, to his fresh new world of elemental joys and challenges. "His little happy laugh is always ringing through the rooms," she wrote. Riding in a carriage on Wilson's knee, he "was in fits of ecstacy at the tossing of the horse's head."[7] He has cut a tooth; he recognizes "Papa" and "Mama," and laughs for joy when he meets them out of doors. Elizabeth at first thought him almost the image of his father, but now, heeding the more objective pronouncements of Wilson, she sees that he has the oval face of the Barretts and is particularly like Henrietta—"only the mouth and chin are fac-similes of Robert's."

Still deeply troubled within himself, Robert loved the child with a passionate yet anxious love. One day, rolling over and over in a particularly reckless manner, the little fellow banged his head on the floor. Robert was out from behind his newspaper and down on the carpet "in a moment, to protect the precious head." "Oh, Ba, I really can't trust you!" Elizabeth met the reproof with robust hilarity—as if a baby's head were Venetian glass! Robert also reproached her for talking Italian to the child. "He hates the idea of his not speaking English with his earliest breath."[8] Unfortunately, the nurse talked Italian at the little boy from morning to night. Everybody who wanted to be understood had to do likewise.

The Brownings did not join English society in the villages below, but that society actually came up to them in the person of the Irish comic novelist Charles Lever. "He is the notability *par excellence* of these baths of Lucca," wrote Elizabeth. "He presides over the weekly balls at the casino . . . and is said to be the light of the flambeaux and the spring of the dancers." Though she could never read Lever's novels, Elizabeth was "surprised into being pleased with him." "The animal spirits [are] somewhat predominant over the intellect, yet the intellect by no means in default."[9] In due course, the Brownings returned the call, but Lever never appeared in Casa Guidi. Apparently, he was shocked not by the seriousness but by the liberalism of the Brownings. Lever was a strong Tory.

This summer of reintegration came to a fitting climax in an all-day expedition of the whole household up to the Prato Fiorito, a mountain five miles off. Robert, Alessandro, and three guides were mounted on ponies; Elizabeth, Wilson, and the nurse, on donkeys; and the baby rode by turns with the last two. Their way led up the rocks of exhausted torrent courses and sometimes on precarious heights where "a single slip of the foot would have precipitated one into deep ravines—frightful they were." At the top they looked out "on a great world of innumerable mountains, the faint sea beyond them, and not a sign of cultivation—not a cottage—not a hut. Only there was a shepherd keeping his sheep, and a few goats." They dined among the goats on cold chicken, ham, and tart, while the baby rolled and laughed on a shawl. The way down was even more fearful than the climb. "We *walked* down several of the descents to escape the horrible sensation of being jolted over the heads of our steeds."[10]

In October they returned to Casa Guidi. Elizabeth was determined that the winter should be an industrious one for both herself and Robert. Their honeymoon dreams of writing poetry side by side had somehow not come true. Since their marriage in 1846, Elizabeth had written only the first part of *Casa Guidi Windows.* She was now at work on a revised edition of her poems. In 1849 Robert also had brought out a new two-volume edition of his *Poems*—according to his own statement, with "most careful revision." Here he attempted to present a new, if diminished face to the general view, omitting, besides three of his less attractive lyrics, *Pauline* in deference to his own feelings, and *Sordello* in deference to the public's. Because he thought Moxon too slow, he had made Chapman and Hall his publishers. But there was no new poetry except "The Guardian Angel." "Being too happy," Elizabeth had confessed to Miss Mitford, "doesn't agree with literary activity quite as well as I should have thought." They were becoming less happy. Work imposed itself as a duty not only to art but to peace of mind. "What am I to say about Robert's idleness and mine?" she wrote in exasperation as late as October 1849. "I scold him about it in a most anti-conjugal manner."[11] But Robert heeded the scolding. In the winter of 1849 and 1850, he produced *Christmas-Eve and Easter-Day*, his first important work since marriage.

This double poem is a new battle fought on old issues. In *Pauline* Browning had abjured atheism and embraced a liberal Evangelicalism. In *Christmas-Eve and Easter-Day* he temporarily abjured dramatic anonymity and confessed to a somewhat less liberal Evangelicalism. After all, both mother and wife had been piously evangelical. Mrs. Browning must have looked with anxiety on those influences which, after *Pauline*, had driven Robert out into the world—mistrusting them as diversions from the inward singleness and purity her religion had caused her to want for her son.[12] And, while Robert's degree of worldliness in no way bothered Elizabeth, he may also have sensed in her some concern at the complexity of Roberts.[1] In any case she wished for singleness in his poetry, urging that, for a time at least, he drop the dramatic method altogether and speak out in his own voice—preferably on a religious subject. Poor Robert must have thought with a shudder of *Pauline*. On the other hand, she had done well to discourage him earlier from the theater. Perhaps he could dispense after all with the "broken lights" of dramatic expression and essay "R.B. a poem."[13]

"The Guardian Angel" was an attempt at speaking out. Now his mother's death impelled him strongly in the same direction. Not that he could write anything so personal as an elegy, but death implied religion and in the nineteenth century religion implied the religious question. With that question, Robert's experience had been precocious and extensive. He had been an atheist with Shelley, something of a unitarian with Fox, something of a transcendentalist with Carlyle. DeVane suggests that he may have heard the Reverend Philip Harwood lecture in South Place Chapel on Strauss' *Das Leben Jesu* in

1845 and may later have read George Eliot's 1846 translation of that work. A final impetus may have been a meeting with Arthur Hugh Clough at Florence in 1849, and a reading of that poet's "Epi-Straussium" and "Easter-Day, Naples."[14] In a letter of December 1, 1849, Elizabeth reports that she and Robert had read with admiration Clough's "Bothie of Toper-na-fuosich."[15]

Christmas-Eve and Easter-Day are not entirely direct and open. The speaker in the first poem does not continue into the second, but is succeeded by two voices, one of which maintains that it is difficult to be a Christian, the other, that it is easy. Yet such ventriloquism seems but the obvious projection and modulation of a single voice. The first speaker is essentially a reminiscent Browning; the second and third, an optimistic interlocutor and an austere, bereaved Browning respectively. What perhaps more seriously complicates the effect of plain speaking is the light tone and the epigrammatic rhymes of both poems. Why write about God in the rhymes of *Don Juan*? This question troubled several contemporary reviewers. The answer seems to be that a light, satiric tone could serve as a weapon with which to attack other people's religion and as a cloak of privacy with which to confess his own. It disguises a note of elegy latent in the two poems and enables the speakers gracefully to find fault with every sect. One is a little reminded of Browning's youthful tendency to call other people fools.

Indeed, Browning's tone arises naturally from the sharp, realistic, yet not unsympathetic picture of a dissenting congregation with which the first poem opens. The chapel is not that which the speaker usually attends and indeed it is too humble to be that of Browning's youth in York Street. Nevertheless, some of the preacher's faults are also the Reverend Mr. Clayton's, and the speaker's impatience with them is certainly the youthful Browning's, for the speaker falls asleep and dreams that he paces very contemptuously out of the chapel. Crossing the common, he beholds a lunar rainbow, meets Christ also coming from the humble service, and feels rebuked by Him. The speaker acknowledges:

> Folly and pride o'ercame my heart.[16]

It is difficult not to see in this episode an act of contrition to his mother's memory.

Having assumed the venerable form of the dream-vision *Christmas-Eve* now becomes a justification of English Dissent. Clasping the hem of Christ's garment, the speaker attends first a mass at St. Peter's, and then the lecture of a German professor. The mass is playfully described as magnificent but calculated theater. Catholicism is gross superstition partially redeemed by much true Christian love among the believers. Pio Nono himself is treated harshly.

> And let us hope
> That no worse blessing befall the Pope,
> Turn'd sick at last of to-day's buffoonery,
> Of posturing, and petticoatings,
> Beside his Bourbon bully's gloatings
> In the bloody orgies of drunk poltroonery![17]

Clearly, Robert felt as bitterly as Elizabeth about the Roman debacle. The German professor is absurd, pathetic, somewhat admirable. But Straussian myth is no substitute for Christian miracle. Christian ethics without Christ are no consolation for the grim eventuality which the professor's cough portends. The speaker now awakes, finds himself still in the chapel, joins in the hymn, and in the fervor of song becomes convinced that the simple, unadorned inwardness of the dissenters is the most genuinely Christian sect. It is deliberately a judgment of the heart; for the preacher and congregation described are too ignorant, dogmatic, and exclusive to approximate an ideal. The implication is that all sects are imperfect—but the heart comprehends. Thus Browning identifies himself, on a deep emotional level, with his mother's creed and his wife's. As DeVane points out, *Christmas-Eve* virtually restates, in dramatic and poetic form, a passage in Elizabeth's letter of August 15, 1846.[18]

Christmas-Eve justifies Dissent; *Easter-Day* sets forth, in a kind of dialogue, Browning's own version of Dissent, and demonstrates its superiority both to historical alternatives and to conflicting tendencies in the poet's own experience. The optimistic interlocutory voice urges that any faith, if strong enough, might withstand all trials and bring salvation. The more austere voice of the bereaved Browning replies that faith is necessarily unsteady and needs God's help. Mere nature-worship is not adequate. Nature, for all its beauties, does not reveal God's plan, nor does it clearly intimate the awful facts of the Incarnation and the Atonement. The first voice then urges the safety of choosing asceticism and so deserving heaven. The second voice replies that no one should lose the opportunity to discern in pleasures moderately enjoyed the Divine Love that provides them. To be sure, pleasure is dangerous. The voice then describes, in impressive poetry, his vision of the Last Judgment, which found him still clinging to earthly joys. Christ tells him that he may have his wish: heaven or hell is the kind of interior world the soul chooses to live in after the destruction of the body. Having condemned himself to a simulation of this world, the speaker chooses as a way of life, first, knowledge, which binds perception to the senses; then, art, which permits only a limited version of divine beauty; and last, love, which, Christ tells him, is the true path to heaven and heavenly love. The latent elegy is discernible in this poem. For all its concessions to pleasure, the tone is stern, even ascetic.

Christmas-Eve and Easter-Day added very little either to Browning's reputation or to his pocket book. One is not surprised. For all their brilliance and maturity, they say hardly anything new, and they say it in an old-fashioned, puzzling, and somewhat repellent way. The dialogue of *Easter-Day*, for example, lacks the clarity and the poignant contrasts of Tennyson's "Two Voices." In fact, readers were offended both by the levity of the first poem and the austerity of the second. Even Elizabeth seems to have failed in understanding. "I have complained of the *asceticism* in the second part," she wrote Mrs. Jameson, "but he said it was 'one side of the question.' "[19]

Wordsworth's death on April 23, 1850, left the Laureateship vacant. Elizabeth was proposed as a successor by several English newspapers—particularly by *The Athenaeum*, which urged not only that a poetess was most appropriate under a queen, but that "no living poet of either sex . . . can prefer a higher claim than Mrs. Elizabeth Barrett Browning."[20] Elizabeth was flattered but unhopeful. Judging by need, apparently, rather than by merit or capacity, she thought Leigh Hunt the most deserving choice.

Grief for a parent lost was but the most inevitable of the portentous involvements of Victorian family life. In 1850, after a secret engagement of five years, Henrietta Barrett and Captain Surtees Cook were married. Her father acted up to his principle with gusto. When Captain Cook had the temerity to ask formal permission, Mr. Barrett told him, "If Henrietta marries you, she turns her back on this house forever." With perfect consistency he wrote Henrietta herself that to ask his permission was an "insult," since she meant to marry anyway: her name would never be mentioned in his house again. The reticences of that respectable domicile were now doubled. On this occasion the younger Barretts sided with the married couple, though there seems to have been a feeling, which Elizabeth faintly shared, that Captain Cook really ought to have had a little more money. Even so, Elizabeth had been earnestly recommending marriage to Henrietta. Now her thoughts returned to her father. "I love him very deeply," she wrote Miss Mitford. "When I write to him, I lay myself at his feet."

By 1850 the Brownings had formed a small circle of friends. One hears of Seymour Kirkup, "who disputes with Mr. Bezzi the glory of finding Dante's portrait";[21] of the quiet and cultivated Ogilvys, who inhabited an upper floor of Casa Guidi; of Miss Isa Blagden, who was thought to have been born in India; but particularly of Mr. and Mrs. William Wetmore Story, an American couple, who were to become the closest and most interesting friends the Brownings made in Italy.

Story's career is a Henry James novel that Henry James never wrote. Fortunately, he did write the biography. The theme is a variation on *The Portrait of a Lady*: the discovery of Europe, art, and happiness descends as a catastrophic interruption on a conventional American success. Story had become a distinguished American lawyer almost before he knew what had happened to him. His father was an Associate Justice of the United States Supreme Court, the author of many internationally famous works of jurisprudence, founder and first professor of the Harvard Law School. Following swiftly in the paternal footsteps, William entered Harvard at fifteen, graduated at nineteen, studied law under his father, practiced, married at twenty-three, held important legal offices in New England, and published two lengthy treatises which were used as textbooks in the Harvard Law School. Unfortunately, he had also published two volumes of verse under a pseudonym, and he had begun to model and paint at college. An admonitory letter from Charles Sumner accuses him of being desultory and irresponsible beyond what is expected of the highest type of Boston intellectual. This flaw, perceptible only to the most practiced eye, became disastrous in a strange manner. An act of filial piety proved Story's undoing. When his father died in 1846, a public statue and monument were decreed, and William Story was asked to make them. After a first refusal, he reluctantly agreed on condition that he go abroad for a year to study. He was never the same again. Rome claimed him even more completely than Paris claimed Strether. He returned home, executed the monument, wrote a two-volume biography of his father, turned out another volume on law, and continued to practice law—but at night he dreamed of Rome. After another pilgrimage to that city and another year in Boston, he decided permanently for Italy and sculpture. His destiny was to become famous but not immortal. Like Powers he lacked a sound training in the fundamentals of his craft.

Story must have recommended himself to Browning not only because he was gaily and enthusiastically interested in all the right things, but because he had given up so much to enjoy them. His career was almost a demonstration that Robert need not hanker after a merely worldly or financial success. Essential seriousness with surface vivacity seems to be the impression Story got of Browning. He writes J. R. Lowell in 1849: "The Brownings & we have become great friends. . . . He is of my size but slighter—with straight black hair—small eyes, wide apart, which he twitches constantly together, a smooth face, slightly acquiline nose—and manners nervous & rapid. He has great vivacity, but not the least humor—some sarcasm, considerable critical faculty, and very great frankness—& friendliness of manner & mind."[22] Why does Story deny Robert a sense of humor—because he talked so solemnly about Elizabeth, or because he suffered so much about Italian politics? The Storys had become friendly with the Brownings in 1848 and had then alternated through the next two years between Florence and Rome, so that they had witnessed the last days not only of Florentine but of Roman freedom. These events, so excruciating to the Brownings, had disturbed the Storys very little. While the Florentine Republic was breathing its last, they went to the theater and sought out interesting little *trattorias* afterward. Indeed, one is reminded by contrast what very serious people the Brownings were.

At this time the Brownings also came to know Margaret Fuller. Hers was another Jamesian pilgrimage, with which, in spite of its tragic close, James himself could scarcely sympathize. "The Margaret-ghost, . . ." he wrote long afterward, with much truth, "still unmistakably walks the old passages."[23] Elizabeth Browning might have agreed, but she may also have seen, in Margaret's life, a grotesque similarity to her own. A lonely and precocious childhood, in which Margaret played a Miranda too deeply engrossed in her father Prospero—the learned and puritanical Congressman Fuller—and dreamed wishfully and tearfully of her mother's funeral; a formidable education, in which Prospero supervised voracious reading in many languages; a laborious young womanhood in which she did housework on a farm, educated her younger brothers and sisters, fell passionately in love with older women, and came at length into conflict with her now-retired father because her arduous exile gave no scope to eager ambition—these were stages in an experience which taught Margaret Fuller what it meant to be a woman and which, in general terms, she communicated to the world in her *Woman in the Nineteenth Century.* As spiritual daughter to a somewhat distrustful Ralph Waldo Emerson, she edited and wrote for *The Dial,* reviewed for the New York *Tribune* under Horace Greeley, and, realizing a girlhood dream, set sail in search of Europe at about the age when Elizabeth had set sail. "Such a predetermination to eat this big Universe as her oyster or her egg,"[24] commented Carlyle when he met her in London. In Paris, she met George Sand. Perhaps that encounter added new dimensions to Margaret's view of woman's place. Margaret wrote: "She has bravely acted out her nature, and always with good intentions." And again, "She holds her place in the literary and social world of France like a man."[25] In Rome Margaret's appetite for life and significance was at length almost satisfied and perhaps destroyed. In Mazzini she found her ideal philosopher and statesman; in the last days of the Republic, an heroic role as nurse and conspirator; in the young, handsome, but ignorant Marchese Ossoli, a lover, a father of her child, and—in deference to respectability—a husband.

Fleeing with her family from the ruin of all she had worked for in Rome, Margaret arrived at Florence late in 1849. Elizabeth found the Roman Marquis "amiable and gentlemanly," but no match for his wife intellectually. "She talks, and he listens." Margaret's talk was brilliant, far better than her books, and in spite of her socialism the Brownings fell under her spell. "Over a great gulf of differing opinion," wrote Elizabeth afterward, "we both felt strongly drawn to her. High and pure aspiration she had—yes, and a tender woman's heart—and we honoured the truth and courage in her." Visiting the Brownings on the last evening before the voyage to America, Margaret was full of foreboding. She gave a Bible from her child to Wiedeman with the gloomy inscription, "In memory of Angelo Eugene Ossoli." She and her husband also joked about an old prophecy warning Ossoli to shun the sea on pain of death. The voyage outdid the grimmest ingenuities of clairvoyance. First, Margaret nursed the captain in smallpox and saw him die in horrible suffering. Then she nursed her baby through the same disease and saw him recover. On the eve of entering port, the ship was wrecked by a sudden storm within fifty yards of shore. Many sailors and passengers saved themselves, but Margaret and her family were drowned.

The Brownings were deeply shocked. Elizabeth once more relived her brother's death at sea but also rose above personal loss partly to understand the dead woman's own evident rejection of life: her socialist views "would have drawn the wolves on her," she explained to Miss Mitford. "Was she ever happy in anything?" mused Elizabeth. "She told me that she never was."[26] Perceiving the quick sympathy between his wife and this strange American woman, Robert for once put aside his strict views on female propriety. He wrote John Kenyon at length of "this dreadful loss of dear, brave, noble Margaret Fuller. . . . We loved her, and she loved Ba." Robert could also feel with "poor Ossoli, . . . a quiet, kind, melancholy-looking creature . . . believing in her superiority with a simple and affecting faith." When Emerson, Channing, and Clarke set to work on *The Memoirs of Margaret Fuller Ossoli,* the Brownings wrote out their reminiscences and sent them to the United States. These papers mysteriously disappeared, as did those sent by Mazzini.

Robert had tried to keep news of the Ossoli tragedy from Elizabeth, for on the morning of July 28, 1850, after some two months' pregnancy, she had suffered her fourth miscarriage. "Harding assured me this morning," Browning wrote John Kenyon on the day after, "she had lost over a hundred ounces of blood within the twentyfour hours. . . . I pain you, I am sure, but how otherwise can I put you into my place and make you fancy that, after sitting all night by the little patient white face, that could smile so much more easily than speak, your letter and its proposal for her good reach me?"[27]

The proposal seems to have been an offer of travel expenses to England. Browning refused. In its very opacity, his explanation is illuminating: "All my life I have elected to be poor, and perhaps the reason, or one among other reasons, may be that I have a very particular capacity for being rich, . . . so that there is no poor spiritedness in my choosing to bound my wishes by my means, seeing that fortune could not easily supply me with means which I could not, if I pleased, outgo, at one stride, by my wishes." And so on for another page, with increasing complexity, confusion, and protestation. Clearly, Browning was not content with his motives, and he was afraid other people would be even less content. In this obsessive self-consciousness and fearful concern for what others might think, one sees a reason for Browning's surface conventionality and for his strong sense of privacy. Somewhat in this vein, he tells Kenyon of himself and Elizabeth, "I never see her letters, nor she mine, lest we should lose freedom in writing of each other."[28]

Elizabeth's last miscarriage was by far her worst. For six weeks she could not stand without help. Dr. Harding recommended country air. As soon as she could travel, the entire household went by train to Siena, two miles from which, on a windy hill called Poggio dei Venti, Robert had taken a villa. It had magnificent views from all the windows and was delightfully situated in the midst of its own vineyard and orchard of olive, apple, and peach trees. Here, to her own amazement, Elizabeth once more rapidly regained her strength. In November the family returned to Florence.

During this period, little Wiedeman was of course a great comfort and for the same reason, sometimes a cause for sharp anxiety. "Our poor little darling, . . ." wrote Elizabeth, "was ill four-and-twenty hours from a species of sunstroke, and frightened us with a heavy hot head and glassy staring eyes, lying in a half-stupor. Terrible, the silence that suddenly fell upon the house, without the small pattering feet and the singing voice. But God spared us; he grew quite well directly and sang louder than ever."[29] The child's delicate frame and high-strung temperament were other reasons for worry.[30] Both the Brownings eagerly visited the toy shops, and Robert spent the whole of one Sunday morning, between breakfast and church, in learning to spin a top. "He considered it a religious duty."[31] Wiedeman had become interested in his own religious duties. "Our little Wiedeman, who can't speak a word yet, waxes hotter in his ecclesiastical and musical passion," writes Elizabeth. "Think of that baby . . . screaming in the streets till he is taken into the churches, kneeling on his knees to the first sound of music, and folding his hands and turning his eyes in a sort of ecstatical state. . . . Robert says it is as well to have the eyeteeth and the Puseyistical crisis over together." Elizabeth acknowledged that the child was spoiled—he seems indeed to have been a tyrannical screamer. "If Flush is scolded, Baby cries as a matter of course." He was very small. "Robert is always measuring him on the door, and reporting such wonderful growth (some inch a week, I think), that . . . you will cry out on beholding the child. . . . You'll fancy he must have begun from a mustard seed."[32]

Elizabeth was now at what Robert later called the "very height of her health."[33] Accordingly, having rented, painted, cleaned, and prepared their apartment in Casa Guidi, they set out in May 1851 for Venice on a voyage which was to take them eventually to England. Venice proved to be everything Elizabeth feared it might not be—romantic, gorgeous, quiet, and admirably adapted to a sedentary life. They "swam" everywhere in gondolas but particularly to the Lido, sailed by steamer to see a *festa* at Chioggia, visited the Armenian monastery where Byron had lived and met quite by chance—sitting under a rosetree—the fabulously white-bearded superior who had taught the poet Armenian, went to the opera and a play, and sat every evening beneath the moon in the Piazza of San Marco taking coffee and listening to the music. This bohemian way of life caused Elizabeth to grow fat, Wilson to be sick, and Robert to have insomnia. Neither the food nor the air agreed with him, and he was suffering painful pressure at two other sore points—money and dress. The last installment of ship money was in doubt, and Elizabeth refused to abandon her old-fashioned lace caps or baby clothes for two-year-old Wiedeman. On the lesser issue of dress, Robert won a precarious victory: Elizabeth consented to abandon the caps on important occasions. On the more important issue, he was confronted by a rather complacently impregnable defense. Elizabeth wrote Arabel:

> Robert wants to make the child like *a boy*, he says—(because he is a man)—and I because I am a woman perhaps, like him to be a baby as long as possible. . . . The truth is that the child is not "like a boy," and that if you put him into a coat and waistcoat forthwith, he only would look like a small angel travestied. For he isn't exactly like a girl either—no, not a bit. He's a sort of neutral creature, so far. But it vexes Robert when people ask if he is a boy or a girl—(oh, man's pride!) and he will have it, that the lace caps and ribbons help to throw the point into doubt.[34]

From Venice, they proceeded to Padua, where they made an excursion to Arqua because of Petrarch; then to Brescia and Milan; and, going through the lakes by steamer where possible, to Lugano, Bellinzona, up and down Lago Maggiore, they crossed the St. Gotthard, the sublimity of which caused Elizabeth to shed tears. Robert shed no tears—at least not over scenery. He had been "in a horrible fright all the way"[35] because of shortness of funds. Worst of all, arriving in Lucerne with a bare and awful ten francs, they found the expected ship money amounted only to £50. They decided to cut short their travels and go directly to Paris. Meanwhile, living almost exclusively with his elders, Wiedeman had learned to appreciate churches and scenery with appropriate fervor. At first sight of San Marco in Venice, he kissed Wilson ecstatically. At sight of the Alps, he clasped his hands and cried out "that the mountains were 'due'—meaning a great number." Now beginning to talk, he corrupted "Wiedeman" into "Penini," which, later shortened to "Pen," became the name he was most commonly called.

Having arrived in the French capital, they found cheap lodgings at the Hôtel aux Armes de la Ville de Paris on the Boulevard de la Madeleine. Elizabeth responded at once to "the bright green trees and gardens everywhere in the heart of the town," the beautiful shops, "fascinating hats and caps," even "the disreputable prints," and the brilliant restaurants, where they dined à la carte, mixing up dinner "with heaps of newspapers" full of witty articles about Louis Napoleon. One day she saw "M. le President in a cocked hat and with a train of cavalry, passing like a rocket along the boulevards to an occasional yell from the Red." Paris was "a splendid city—a city in the country, as Venice is a city in the sea." Tennyson called while they were out and left a card inviting them that afternoon to tea at his hotel close by. This old poetical hero had returned on Elizabeth with all his old enchantment, for she had lately read *In Memoriam* and found it so "exquisite," so "earnest and true." Robert also—if one may judge from his wife's phrases—thought that the poem had increased Tennyson's stature, as disclosing a more "earnest personality and direct purpose."[36] In any case, the poet-laureate was not to be denied. "Though half tired to death with the Louvre," Elizabeth "rose up from the sofa in a decided state of resurrection." They were charmed by the Tennysons, as by his sister and her husband. Tennyson was very warm and cordial, apparently from having read Robert's poems aloud the previous evening. He urged that while in England the Brownings make use of his house and two servants at Twickenham, and even wrote a note to that effect. The Brownings accepted the note as "an autograph at once of genius and kindness." Mrs. Tennyson kissed Elizabeth at parting. Elizabeth reported that she had a "soft winning manner, and the gentlest of smiles";[37] while on his side Tennyson observed in his diary that Mrs. Browning was "fragile-looking, with great spirit eyes," and that she met his wife "as if she had been her own sister."[38] One is tempted to lay down the rule that Elizabeth's eyes grew larger in direct ratio as the observer admired her poetry. William Story had thought her eyes quite small.

Both Elizabeth and Robert had long dreaded a visit to England. She feared the implacability of Wimpole Street, and he, the vanished presence at New Cross. Fourteen months had not much changed his dread. Yet he knew he ought to see his father and sister, and after five years' absence Elizabeth could scarcely refuse the entreaties of Arabel, who could not come to Paris. In the event, England was both better and worse than they had feared. It offered the warmth of old love, the shock of old enmity, the petty attrition of old discomforts and old ills, and a few unpleasant surprises. They were to be disillusioned both by what they expected and by what they did not expect. "My first step ashore," wrote Elizabeth, "was into a puddle and a fog, and I began to cough before we reached London."[39] Arriving there on July 22, they went to rooms rented for them by Arabel in Portman Square. Both Elizabeth and Robert felt he should visit his old home quietly by himself first and grow accustomed to the change. What he found does not appear in his correspondence. The fact—which Sarianna must have been desperately eager to conceal—was that his father, so far from adhering to the contemporary decorum of perpetual bereavement, had already yielded to the instincts of an affectionate nature, and was even then writing passionate love letters to a Mrs. Von Müller, an attractive middle-aged lady twice widowed and with three children.[40] So observant and intuitive a person as his son may well have discovered this awful situation. In any case, when the younger Brownings visited at New Cross, Elizabeth received a "most affectionate" welcome and Wiedeman became passionately fond of his grandfather. Meanwhile they had taken up residence in a small, gloomy, expensive apartment in 26 Devonshire Street. Here Sarianna Browning and Arabel Barrett were constant visitors. Henrietta also spent a week nearby, having left her husband and child in Taunton. In August Wilson was given a fortnight's holiday to visit her family in the country. Finding the very foundations of his universe suddenly and treacherously removed, Wiedeman clung to Elizabeth late and soon as his only certainty. She was thus exposed for the first time to the full rigors of motherhood: "*une âme perdue*," she wrote, "with not an instant out of the four-and-twenty hours to call my own." For a time Elizabeth's cough grew so bad that Robert, in his triple character of "husband, lover, nurse,"[41] was half tempted to carry her unceremoniously off to the Continent. Then the cough moderated, and Robert came down with influenza.

The return of the erstwhile captive maiden to the ogre's castle could hardly be altogether satisfactory. Almost every day, as soon as Mr. Barrett had gone off to the City, Arabel sent her maid Bonser to bring Wiedeman, and sometimes Elizabeth, to Wimpole Street. Partly on such occasions, partly in Devonshire Street, Elizabeth met with five of her brothers—Henry, Sette, Occy, George, and Alfred—in various temperatures of cordiality. George Barrett alone became entirely reconciled to both Elizabeth and Robert. On one of her invasions of Wimpole Street, Elizabeth stayed so late in Arabel's room that Mr. Barrett returned home. "I heard Papa come up stairs, go down again, talk and laugh . . . I, in a sort of horror of fright and mixed feelings. . . . I walked home with Bonser while they were at dinner, past the dining-room door. . . . It made me very sad all evening after, and Robert was not pleased, and called it 'imprudent to excess.' "[42]

Meanwhile the great world of London literature flooded in on them. Old friends were warm and attentive, and everybody, one suspects, was curious. Here were the romantic lovers who had created a sensation five seasons ago. The solitary and invisible poetess of No. 50 Wimpole Street was now to be seen in plain view. "I am confounded," wrote Elizabeth, "with the confusion of London—overwhelmed with kindness—suffocated almost. I take half a cup of tea or coffee, morning and evening, and then am sure to be interrupted by somebody."[43] B. W. Procter and John Kenyon were constant visitors. Mrs. Jameson and the R. H. Hornes also came. Elizabeth was particularly impressed when Fanny Kemble appeared, and the Brownings went to see her in *Hamlet.* They dined in large companies with Mr. Kenyon and with the still-overpowering John Forster—the second entertained them at "a magnificent dinner at Thames Ditton in sight of the swans."[44] And Elizabeth announces, perhaps with relief, "Mr. Forster *told* me he liked me, which was satisfactory!"[45] Several observers noted that she was shrouded in hair—as she had formerly been shrouded in mystery. Sara Coleridge thought her hard-featured, but impressive in her eyes and brow. She also adds the significant detail of a "plaintive voice,"[46] which must have contrasted oddly with Robert's bold, loud one.

The American poet Bayard Taylor called at this time on the Brownings in Devonshire Street and has left a graphic record of the visit. He was received by Robert with great cordiality.

> In his lively, cheerful manner, quick voice, and perfect self-possession, he made upon me the impression of an American rather than an Englishman. He was then, I should judge, about thirty-seven years of age, but his dark hair was already streaked with gray about the temples. His complexion was fair, with perhaps the faintest olive tinge, eyes large, clear, and gray, nose strong and well cut, mouth full and rather broad, and chin pointed, though not prominent. His forehead broadened rapidly upwards from the outer angle of the eyes, slightly retreating. The strong individuality which marks his poetry was expressed, not only in his face and head, but in his whole demeanor. He was about the medium height, strong in the shoulders, but slender at the waist, and his movements expressed a combination of vigor and elasticity.

> In the room sat a very large gentleman of between fifty and sixty years of age. He must have weighed two hundred and fifty pounds, at least; his large, rosy face, bald head, and rotund body would have suggested a prosperous brewer, if a livelier intelligence had not twinkled in the bright, genial eyes.

This huge, genial man was of course John Kenyon. Presently he took his leave. The door had scarcely closed when Browning exclaimed, "there goes one of the most splendid men living—a man so noble in his friendships, so lavish in his hospitality, so large-hearted and benevolent, that he deserves to be known all over the world as 'Kenyon the Magnificent!' " Elizabeth now entered the room. Robert "ran" to meet her "with a boyish liveliness." Taylor noted the contrast, physical and intellectual, between husband and wife. They expressed "great satisfaction with their American reputations," and Robert added, "I verily believe that if we were to make out a list of our best and dearest friends, we should find more American than English names." Elizabeth inquired about the arts in the United States. A republic, she thought, could hardly be favorable to them. Somewhat to Taylor's surprise, Browning warmly disagreed. The argument broadened into a general historical discussion, in which the two poets continued to maintain opposite views with great spirit. "I thought both of them seemed to enjoy it," says Taylor.[47]

"What am I to do," Browning wrote Carlyle a few days after arriving in England—"with my five-years' hunger for the sight of you and Mrs. Carlyle?—unless you let me call tomorrow."[48] Elizabeth shared in this eagerness. As yet she knew the great man only through the tremendous style—and the idealism, puritanism, and prophetic vision, so admired by Robert and herself, to which it gave utterance. Yet is not the style the man? Elizabeth had noted Carlyle's even in his personal letters to Robert.[49] In spite of *Sordello*, marriage, five years' absence, and a disciple–master relationship evidenced by "Dear Mr. Carlyle" as opposed to "Dear Browning," Robert was on cordial terms with his older and more celebrated friend. He had very tactfully broken the news of his marriage—after the event—and Carlyle had responded in his most benign manner, gently thundering through smiling rainbows in phrases that suggest the opening of *Paradise Lost*: "You I had known, and judged of; her, too, conclusively enough, if less directly; and certainly if ever there was a union indicated by the finger of Heaven itself, and so sanctified and prescribed by the Eternal laws under which poor transitory Sons of Adam live, it seemed to me, from all I could hear or know of it, to be this!"[50] Elizabeth copied the passage *in extenso* for her sisters' benefit. The Brownings did spend an evening at the Carlyles' and saw them on other occasions in larger company.

The English visit was almost over. Still Mr. Barrett gave no sign. The iron consistence of his "never" was now to become grimly evident at close range. Elizabeth wrote him, and Robert did also. "A manly, true, straightforward letter his was, yet in some parts so touching to me and so generous and conciliatory everywhere, that I could scarcely believe in the probability of its being read in vain." Browning received a most "violent and unsparing" answer, with a packet of all Elizabeth's letters of the last five years unopened. "He said," she told Mrs. Martin, "he regretted to have been forced to keep them until now, through his ignorance of where he should send them. So there's the end."[51]

CHAPTER 17

Paris: Excursions and Alarums

1851-52

In spite of disillusionments, anxiety about Elizabeth's health, and vivid reminders of his mother's loss, Browning had thoroughly enjoyed London. Indeed, home proved as exciting to the middle-aged poet as Italy had to the youthful one. The tenderness of his letters at this time to Talfourd, with whom there had been some misunderstanding, shows how he valued old friendship. "I do believe," Elizabeth wrote Mrs. Jameson, "he would have been capable of never leaving England again, had such an arrangement been practicable." But of course it was not possible. Now October loomed, threatening her with fogs and east winds, worse coughs and chest pains. On September 25, they set out for France with Thomas Carlyle, who delayed a necessary Paris excursion for one day, as he declared handsomely in his diary, to enjoy their company—and experience in travel. To be with Carlyle was to offer one's own failings as a glass in which the great man might see himself magnified. As they got into the train, he noted, Browning talked "very loud and with vivacity," while he was himself "silent rather, tending toward many thoughts." Mysteriously, the prophet's silence seemed both loquacious and eloquent to Elizabeth. "The talk of writing men," she pronounced, "is very seldom as good." She was determined to see no faults in the old egotist: "All the bitterness is love with the point reversed. He seems to me to have a profound sensibility—so profound and turbulent that it unsettles his general sympathies."[1]

How much the point of love was reversed and general sympathies were upset, Elizabeth hardly dreamed. Through the diary of that "profound and turbulent" sensibility one observes a rather absurd Browning and a rather magnificent Carlyle in the act of making a Victorian journey to Paris. What Browning's friendship (or indeed almost any friendship) meant for Carlyle under circumstances of daily association becomes only too clear. At the beginning of his account, the veteran explorer of the transcendental universe vociferates, with immense verbal resource, his utter despair at having to leave at all the sheltered comfort of a Chelsea study. The pandemonium of London Bridge Railway Station finds him in a kind of perspicacious bewilderment at the irrationality of ticket offices. "The air was thick with suppositions, guesses, cautions; each public office . . . proclaimed its own plans. . . . For very multitude of guide-posts, you could not find your way!" He contradicts his own sarcastic anxiety with a sarcasm against his friend: "Browning managed everything for me; indeed there was as yet nothing to manage." Crossing the channel, Carlyle observed "general sordid torpor of sea-sickness, with *its* miserable noises. . . . Browning was sick, lay in one of the bench tents horizontal, his wife, etc., below." Renewed pandemonium that evening at the Dieppe customs: "Now Browning was passing our luggage, brought it all in safe about half-past ten." The next morning: "We strolled back to pay our bill, and get ready for our start to Paris. Browning, as before, did everything; I sat out of doors . . . and smoked." The poet now emerges as a faithful, useful, doglike individual—not to say a Don Quixote who finds significance contending with porters instead of windmills. At the Paris railway station Carlyle once more descends into a crowding, scrambling "tumult, in which the brave Browning fought for us, leaving me to sit beside the women. . . . Cigar ended, I went in again, Browning still fighting (in the invisible distance) about nothing at all." Paris itself proves to be just another imposition on his good nature. He complains about his cold, glaring bedroom at Lord Ashburton's, contemptuously sees through French statesmen at a glance—the more remarkable as he did not understand spoken French—and, having unmasked a series of bores at Lady Sandwich's dinner party, abruptly flees from the "talkee, talkee" to Browning's. "Great welcome there; and tea in quiet; Browning gives me (being cunningly led to it) copious account of the late 'revolutions' at Florence, such a fantastic piece of Drury-lane 'revolution' as I have seldom heard of."[2]

Meanwhile, "the brave Browning" had fought the battle of the lodgings and emerged victorious with a six-room suite on the top floor of 138 Champs-Elysées, at 200 francs (£8) a month. There were abundant sofas, plenty of sun, and a fine view of the avenue. Money was less abundant: they were still living on Elizabeth's inheritance, supplemented by an annual gift of £100 which Mr. Kenyon started to send after the birth of Wiedeman or "Penini." At twenty francs a month, Robert hired a *femme de service* to clean and to prepare meals. Into this compact, economical, well-cared-for little paradise they moved about October 10, 1851.

In the fine October sunshine Elizabeth's cough disappeared and her strength increased. They began, layer by layer, to explore Paris. They were to see even more than they expected. At first they observed boulevard life from their private terrace above the treetops, but sometimes, early in the evening, they walked in the Champs-Elysées and stood on the Pont de la Concorde, looking down the Seine at "the fantastic city drawn out in gaslight."[3] Presently a note came from Lady Elgin, inviting them to her Monday evenings. Lady Elgin maintained one of the "best houses," and she was also noteworthy as wife of the ambassador to Turkey who made a great deal of Greek statuary safe for Englishmen and scholars by having it removed from the Parthenon and sent home. Robert and Elizabeth accepted the invitation, in the hope of meeting French *célébrités* and possibly even some of Balzac's *duchesses.* Over "a cup of infinitesimally weak tea," Elizabeth reported, they talked with many interesting people but no notables.[4] They attended one other evening function, then the weather changed, the cough returned, and Elizabeth was forced to give up all thought of going out at night for several months. Even so, she insisted Robert go out: it was really "good for him, with his temperament."[5]

Accordingly, Robert continued to explore Parisian society, and met a great variety of notabilities. Through Lady Elgin he met Lamartine, who was struck by his "elevation of thought,"[6] and—much more important—through his new friends the Fraser Corkrans he met Joseph Milsand, who in the second of a series of articles on *La Poésie anglaise depuis Byron* published some two months before in the *Revue des Deux Mondes*[7] had accorded Browning the most perceptive and discriminating praise he had received thus far. Originally a Catholic and a student of Italian literature, Milsand had "invented" Protestantism, discovered Ruskin, published *L'Esthétique anglaise,* and then proceeded to a study of the modern English poets. A zeal for ideas, a high Protestant devotion to literary beauty, an absorbing interest in events within the soul had prepared him to admire Browning's early poetry. Browning himself could not but be deeply grateful for an admiration so intelligent and tactful. During the Brownings' sojourn in Paris, Milsand spent every Tuesday evening with them, and thereafter saw them regularly whenever they were in France. Robert was so confident of his friend's taste in English verse that he "invariably sent him his proof-sheets for final revision."[8]

In December, two Victorian puritans had embarked on a supreme Parisian adventure, a series of visits to George Sand. Here Robert's respectability was at secret war with his eagerness to serve Elizabeth. The lady was said to be as unapproachable as she was mysterious. Therefore, at Elizabeth's wish, he had obtained through Carlyle a letter of introduction from Mazzini. George Sand was known to be in Paris, incognito; how to make sure Mazzini's letter together with an appropriate letter of their own should reach her hands? One of her admirers, a M. François, suggested that they be left at the theater where her play, *Le Mariage de Victorine,* was being rehearsed. In the best tradition of stage gallantry, Robert protested that he wouldn't have their letter "mixed up with the love letters of the actresses, or perhaps given to the 'premier comique' to read aloud in the green room, as a relief to the 'Chère adorable,' which had produced so much laughter."[9] Elizabeth dissented with both Robert and M. François, and while she was dissenting George Sand slipped out of Paris. When she returned Robert found in pride a reason for delay: she never saw strangers. "No," said Elizabeth, "you *shan't* be proud, and I *won't* be proud, and we *will* see her. I won't die, if I can help it, without seeing George Sand."[10] Elizabeth wrote a note, which both she and Robert signed. It was delivered by a friend, and the Brownings received an invitation for the coming Sunday. That morning, the air was sharp. Robert developed stubborn scruples about Elizabeth's health. But again he had to yield. She put on her respirator, smothered herself in furs, and set out with a fretful husband in a closed carriage.

That first meeting left Elizabeth deeply impressed and a little disappointed. Cataloguing the lady's features with feminine minuteness, she was surprised that the mistress of so many famous men had a pronounced nose, a slightly receding chin, and a mouth that at best was "not good." On the other hand, her eyes and brow were noble, and her smile was brilliant, though rare. To the adoring young men that surrounded her, she spoke in a low, rapid voice, "without emphasis or variety of modulation." Elizabeth "felt the burning soul through all that quietness." Both she and Robert also felt in all the lady said—"even in her kindness and pity"—"an undercurrent of scorn."[11] For a moment Elizabeth herself was the object of that scorn. "You should have seen the disdain with which she looked at my respirator—I took it out of my muff to show it to her."[12] Though herself in delicate health, George Sand could abide no compromise with physical weakness.

She scarcely moved Robert to chivalric ardor. The ice between them never broke, he declared, but that new frost began to form. Once he met her by chance in the Tuileries, and walked with her the whole length of the gardens. His report was that she was not looking as well as usual, being "too much 'endimanchée' in terrestrial lavenders and supercelestial blues." On her own second visit, Elizabeth saw the "priestess . . . in a circle of eight or nine men, giving no oracles, except with her splendid eyes, sitting at the corner of the fire, and warming her feet quietly, in a general silence of the most profound deference. There was something in the calm disdain of it which pleased me." Robert was not pleased. On the way home, he declared that "if any other mistress of a house had behaved so, he would have walked out of the room."[13] George Sand did not return their visits, though she invited them to the opening of *Les Vacances de Pandolphe.* Did she really like them? Elizabeth wondered. Robert suspected she did not. "He could only imagine," he confided to Mrs. Orr many years later, "that his studied courtesy towards her was felt by her as a rebuke to the latitude which she granted to other men." Eventually Elizabeth became as perceptive as Robert had ever been. The Victorian adjectives of condemnation, couched elegiacally in the past tense, fell from her pen like rain. "She seems to live in the abomination of desolation, as far as regards society—crowds of ill-bred men who adore her *à genoux bas,* betwixt a puff of smoke and an ejection of saliva. . . . I was deeply interested in that poor woman, I felt a profound compassion for her." Elizabeth would still kneel to her, if she would "be herself as God made her."[14]

Events conspired in one way or another, during the winter of 1851 to 1852 in Paris, to confront Browning with most of the problems, past and present, of his life. Robert "has been absorbed," Elizabeth wrote her brother George on December 4–5, "between his father & sister (whom he had to carry about Paris from morning till night when they were here) & the Shelley edition—which is off his hands today."[15] Mr. Browning, Sr., had not come to Paris to see the sights, nor even to announce his marriage to Mrs. Von Müller. Some time before, that lady had made him a confidence; he had interpreted it as a confession that she had married her second husband before she knew certainly her first was dead. Would Mr. Browning therefore sin if he married her? He now became highly indignant with the amiable widow for a transgression she might have committed many years before. Probably this indignation gained strength from a secret sense of having violated both prudence and loyalty in himself thinking of a second marriage. At any rate, the carefree ardor of his love letters became troubled by elaborate theological considerations, which culminated in a blunt accusation: Mrs. Von Müller had been "guilty of crime or gross error." Subsequent letters made abject apology and full retraction, but apparently indignation grew stronger than love as the moment for decision grew inexorably nearer. Once in Paris, Mr. Browning must have found the truth much too shocking a thing to tell Robert, and Mrs. Von Müller's character black enough to bear any amount of guilt. On November 1, 1851, that lady received from the poet a letter in which he stated that "his father had informed him of the manner in which she had annoyed him and of the persecution he had undergone." Shortly after, she received from Mr. Browning, Sr., a letter in which, withdrawing his proposal, he accused her in so many words of marrying her second husband when she knew her first was alive and declared that "his reason for breaking off the match" was "her misconduct from the time she was a girl."[16] In these letters Mrs. Von Müller's son-in-law saw the means of collecting substantial damages for breach of promise and defamation of character.

It was in the midst of this family crisis—in which everyone must have felt the presence of the dead Mrs. Browning—that Robert completed his "Essay" on Shelley. The publisher Moxon had recently bought twenty-five Shelley letters in a sale at Sotheby's and, with a view to publication, asked Browning during his London visit to contribute a preface. That preface was the beginning of a long and disagreeable adventure in disillusionment, of which the least important element was the discovery that only one of the letters was genuine, the rest having been provided by that enterprising impostor de Gibler, who posed as an illegitimate son of Lord Byron while his wife forged plausible and salable documents. The more important discovery—still in store for him—concerned the Sun-Treader himself.

William Rossetti's diary indicates that it was in 1851, when Browning "was editing the forged letters," that he met Shelley's old friend, the publisher Thomas Hookham, and by him was allowed to read a series of letters from Harriet. W. O. Raymond, however, has pointed out evidence of error in Rossetti's recollection of the date.[17] It was either on his visit to London in 1856, or as late as 1858 that Browning was forced by the letters to revise his judgment of Shelley. Until that time, Browning's ideas about Shelley's first marriage seem chiefly to depend on Leigh Hunt's *Byron and His Contemporaries,* in which he found the matter dismissed with such sentences as "the wife whom he took was not of a nature to appreciate his understanding," "they separated by mutual consent, after the birth of two children," and "He was residing at Bath, when news came to him that his wife had destroyed herself. It was a heavy blow." Hunt concludes with a great deal of rhetorical indignation against those "who riot in a debauchery of scandal."[18] So much smoke might have caused Browning to suspect some fire, but as a lifelong disciple he was accustomed to see Shelley as a martyr to calumny. When finally he read Harriet's letters to Hookham, they shook his hero-worship to its foundations. Much later he wrote Edward Dowden:

> Harriet—represented as either uneducated or incapable of becoming so—said that, in compliance with her Husband's desire, she was learning Latin and could already make out the Odes of Horace: she was, for the same reason, practising music, and commissioned Hookham to procure for her pieces—"especially by Mozart": The most striking letter was the last one—written to enquire where Shelley might be—whether, as the writer thought probable, with Hookham,—altogether conceived in such a state of surprise and bewilderment at his disappearance as to completely dispose of the notion, hitherto accepted by Shelley's biographers, that they had parted by common consent.[19]

Browning talked with Hookham at the time he read the letters. As the confidant and perhaps the partisan of Harriet, Hookham must have been frank. As the friend and admirer of Shelley, he may have been sparing. Browning's report of the conversation reflects some palliation: "Hookham said Shelley was suffering from intense bodily pain at the time,—'would roll himself writhing on the ground, pulling the sofa-cushions upon him'—and, to alleviate this, 'he would actually go about with a laudanum-bottle in his hand, supping thence as need might be.' "[20] One contrasts Peacock's unflattering explanation of this illness: "Between his old feelings towards Harriet, *from whom he was not then separated,* and his new passion for Mary, he showed in his looks, in his gestures, in his speech, the state of a mind 'suffering, like a little kingdom, the nature of an insurrection.' His eyes were bloodshot, his hair and dress disordered. He caught up a bottle of laudanum, and said, 'I never part from this.' "[21] Perhaps again the palliative note in Browning's account stems from the struggle in his own mind. In a letter of 1883 to Furnivall, he wrote that Shelley was "at that time of his life half crazy and wholly inexcusable." In a conversation of 1869 with Swinburne, he said "that Shelley during that period of his life was not responsible for his actions; was in fact positively insane, through excess of laudanum."[22] The shock, though nearly calamitous, did not entirely destroy Browning's faith.[23]

In 1851, he wrote in a vein highly favorable to Shelley. Once more, as in *Pauline,* Browning faced the antithesis between an atheist hero and a pious Christian mother, and once more he resolved it by turning the atheist hero into an almost respectable Christian. The "Essay" is an event in the history not so much of Shelley's poetry as of Browning's soul.

He begins with a distinction between the objective and the subjective poet. The first is extrovert, impersonal, realistic and dramatic; the second, introvert, personal, lyrical, and prophetic. The first looks out as from a watch tower on the world around him and fashions poems which appeal to "the common eye and apprehension of his fellowmen" and which as imitations of external reality stand apart from his own life and personality. The second seeks truth "in his own soul as the nearest reflex of [the] Absolute Mind." "Not what man sees but what God sees—the *Ideas* of Plato, seeds of creation lying burningly in the Divine Hand—it is toward these that he struggles."

W. H. Griffin sees in this distinction the influence of Milsand's recent article on Browning in the *Revue des Deux Mondes.*[24] But clearly, from *Pauline* onward, the poet had recognized and cultivated subjective and objective tendencies within himself. He had also, as phrases in the "Essay" suggest, simply taken over current ideas derived ultimately from Schiller, Goethe, and Friedrich Schlegel. Indeed he may at some time have read in *The Monthly Repository,* to which he had several times contributed, an article by his friend Crabb Robinson on "Goethe," which admirably sums up what were thought to be the characteristics of subjective and objective poets.[25] A more particular debt Browning has himself acknowledged. "I have just done," he wrote Carlyle in October 1851, "the little thing I told you of—a mere Preface to some new letters of Shelley. . . . I have put down a few thoughts that presented themselves—one or two, in respect of opinions of your own (I mean, that I was thinking of those opinions while I wrote)."[26] What Browning insists on in the "Essay" is the essentially religious character of the subjective poet. He is sent by providence to provide a heavenly vision when people have exhausted the earthly vision of the objective poets. To be sure, in a universe so thoroughly transcendental as Browning's, all poets must be more or less religious. In any case, that the poet is divinely called, that he appears at the historical or providential moment, that he interprets the divine idea which lies behind appearances are basic ideas of "The Hero as Poet" in *On Heroes, Hero-Worship, and the Heroic in History.* Here Carlyle does not use the terms "subjective" and "objective," but he does draw a contrast between Dante as deep, intense, and other-worldly, and Shakespeare as broad, calm, and worldly. Browning first introduced himself to Carlyle while listening to the lectures on *Hero-Worship*; he would scarcely have missed that on "The Hero as Poet."

If the subjective poet is particularly religious, he must be particularly good: "In our approach to the poetry, we necessarily approach the personality of the poet; in apprehending it we apprehend him, and certainly we cannot love it without loving him." Or—"Greatness in a work suggests an adequate instrumentality; and none of the lower incitements . . . have been found able . . . to task themselves to the end of so exacting a performance as a poet's complete work."

As a great poet, Shelley must have been both good and religious. Yet he did have a bad moral reputation. In what sense, then, was he good or religious? Browning answers neither question directly. The rest of the "Essay" is an allusive, rationalizing dialectic between his theoretical convictions and his practical fears. With reference to goodness, he seems to ask the question nearly as often as he makes the assertion. He passes quickly over Moxon's letters, using them as the text for a rather dubious sermon to future biographers: "A biography composed in harmony with the present general disposition to have faith in him, yet not shrinking from a candid examination, . . . will be found consistent with a belief in the eventual perfection of his character."

Next comes a change of subject and a surprising admission: A poet's work may be obstructed by "a disastrous youth or a premature death." Among the fruits of a disastrous youth, Browning includes "deleterious Queen Mab notes and the like," which had once been his own gospel. Shelley's greatness consisted in his vision of man's future. Unfortunately, his "early fervor and power to *see* was accompanied by as precocious a fertility to *contrive*: he endeavored to realize as he went on idealizing." The result was he found himself committed to a set of "miserable little expedients," and was "dashing at whatever red cloak was held forth to him." In maturer years he left behind "this low practical dexterity" and sought rather to express his utopian vision. That vision was also heavenly, for Shelley was religious in his very atheism: "Every audacious negative cast up by him against the Divine was interpenetrated with a mood of reverence and adoration." Browning seems to understand religion not so much in the traditional sense of reverent submission to an objective Deity as in Carlyle's sense of passionate devotion to transcendental idea and the good of mankind. Thus Shelley's religion becomes utopian humanitarianism, romantic imagination, expansive feeling, even audacious rebellion—but not practical political action.

Browning now once more shifts to the question of goodness and makes an even more surprising admission: "He died before his youth ended." Such a statement invites the retort that Shelley's whole life was one long youthful indiscretion. Having pleaded for great allowances, Browning now asks that "the whole truth be told of his worst mistake. I believe, for my own part, that if anything could now shame or grieve Shelley, it would be an attempt to vindicate him at the expense of another." In further extenuation, he calls attention to Shelley's ailments of soul and body—including "remarkable delusions and hallucinations." Once more he praises Shelley's poetry. It is "a sublime fragmentary essay" toward presenting "the correspondency of the universe with Deity." Each plea for special consideration leads up to the yet stronger claim: "Had Shelley lived, he would certainly have ranged himself with the Christians." The "Essay" leaves one in grave doubt whether Browning should have so ranged himself.

At the end of his manuscript, Browning wrote: "Paris, December 4, 1851." By nightfall on December 4, the cannons of Louis Napoleon could be heard firing on republican barricades in the Faubourg Saint-Antoine. Had Robert been thinking as he wrote how Shelley had championed a revolution and damned a Bonaparte? If so, he must, as Mrs. Miller suggests,[27] have referred with some bitterness and irony, in the last paragraph, to the "signal service" which he had dreamed in boyhood of rendering Shelley's "fame and memory."

No doubt, Browning was hardly in a position to make an heroic gesture—even on paper. The political situation was bewilderingly ambiguous. Freedom seemed at best a parenthesis between two very similar monarchies. The strongest party in the Assembly favored the monarchy of Louis Philippe overthrown three years before. Louis Napoleon, elected president on December 10, 1848, by 5,400 votes, looked forward by family tradition to an empire not yet declared. The Orléanists stood for peace and order; so did Louis Napoleon. True, he had inherited a program of conquest and glory. But Napoleonism had not remained what the great Napoleon's deeds had made it. On St. Helena, Napoleon had edited it toward Promethean Democracy; at Arenenberg, his sister-in-law Queen Hortense had edited it toward humanitarian Christianity; in his comfortable dungeon at Ham, her son Louis Napoleon had edited it toward "Caesarian Democracy," a system of government by which the people directly elected and so pledged themselves to obey one man—presumably a man capable of the strong and imaginative leadership which the Orléanists had failed to provide.[28] But was Louis Napoleon capable of such leadership? And what of the Napoleonic legend with all its implications? Had the people chosen the Napoleon hat or the man under it—or both?

The man was as enigmatic as the thing he represented. He had begun his career with two parodies of the return from Elba ludicrous enough to ruin the chances of an ordinary pretender. The second debacle had landed him in the fortress-prison of Ham. Here he played whist, continued his education, wrote lucid and sensible pamphlets, and finally, with luck and daring, escaped disguised as a woman. Safe in England, he did nothing—in a masterly manner. In other words, he discreetly advertised himself and nobly refused unlikely opportunities. A Bonaparte without dash or brilliance, a sallow man five feet eight inches high—Browning's own height—with a slow tongue, Louis Napoleon brought to the arena of history the tastes of a roué, the phlegm and inscrutability of a gambler, and the tact, patience, intelligence, and humanitarian ideals of a great democratic leader. The impression republican authors give is: he believed that he followed a star and that every man had his price.

Having elected a Bonaparte president, when and how would France become an empire? The Constitution prohibited a second presidential term. In July 1851, Napoleon's adherents in the Assembly introduced an amendment. It drew a comfortable majority but not the three-fourths necessary for constitutional revision. "People say," wrote Elizabeth as early as October 22, "that the troops which pass before our windows every few days through the 'Arc de l'Etoile' to be reviewed, will bring the president back with them as 'emperor' some sunny morning not far off."[29] On the morning of December 2, the anniversary of Austerlitz, Paris awoke to discover with astonishment what it had long expected—troops thronging the public squares and leaflets plastered on every wall. People gathered silently in little groups about the leaflets. There were two proclamations, both from the Prince President. One, addressed to the people, explained the failure of the existing constitution, dissolved the Assembly, and promised a plebiscite on a new constitution, of which the chief feature was to be a strong and responsible executive. The other, addressed to the army, referred to imperial glories, exalted the position of the soldier in the ranks and called on him to save the country by obeying orders. With typical caution, Napoleon did not assume the title of emperor until a year later.

What individuals saw on the day of the coup d'état varied greatly according to the tint of their political spectacles. Neutralists saw crowds of people standing about with their hands in their pockets or their muffs. George Sand saw men whipping down proclamations with their canes or shouting on street corners, *"A bas le despote, à bas les traîtres! Vive la République*!"[30] On the contrary, Elizabeth heard them shouting "Vive Napoleon!"[31] "The president rode under our windows on December 2, through a shout extending from the Carrousel to the Arc de l'Etoile. The troops poured in as we stood and looked. No sight could be grander, and I would not have missed it, not for the Alps, I say."[32] By nightfall on December 4, however, cannon fire was audible even to the most obtuse political ears. Robert "had some writing to do," and, when she had undressed and put on her dressing gown and shawl, Elizabeth sat by the fire with him till nearly one. She was not afraid but "shrank from going quietly to sleep while human beings were dying in heaps perhaps, within earshot."[33] The irreverent and slightly comic phrase hints what indeed is already clear: that, in spite of womanly pity, she was on the side of the cannons. Her extravagant hero-worship, her "immoral sympathy with power"[34]—and with the paternal principle of authority—even her devotion to "the people" in the abstract had made her a fierce supporter of the Prince President. But she pressed the paradoxes of arbitrary power and popular choice rather far. In using military power to quell Leftist resistance, Prince Louis was but invoking a kind of suffrage. For the French army, Elizabeth told Mrs. Martin, was "eminently *civic*."[35] Apparently a soldier obeying orders was not unlike a citizen casting a vote.

A marriage between idealists is not always an ideal marriage. Apparently Elizabeth spared Robert neither her stratagems nor her scorn for opposition. In her letters of this period she seldom speaks with awe of his wisdom and ideas. Testing herself against him in the developing issues of married life, she may have been somewhat surprised at her own strength and success. She may even have come, as Mrs. Miller says, to assume toward him the superior tone habitual to an elder sister from a large family. "Robert & I," she wrote George, "have fought considerably upon all these points—I always think that England influences him just in proportion to his removal from England. Patriotism gets the upper hand of judgement, & he drops into a vortex of national sympathy."[36]

"All these points" in the French political situation Robert seems to have understood vaguely, in any case. Elizabeth's delicate health and nerves inclined him to caution, though spirited differences and picturesque clashes of opinion were quite in keeping with "A Lovers' Quarrel," "By the Fire-Side," and the permanent romance which he saw in his marriage. To her brilliant, fanatically strident offensives for Louis Napoleon, his response was limited war, waged with humor and forbearance. A letter of February 4, 1852, to George Barrett puts his whole situation into a rather large nutshell. The argument reveals a typical tendency to reduce every problem in human affairs to the problem of character. Deeply, Robert's political quarrels with Elizabeth proceeded not so much from a conviction that she was politically wrong, as from a conviction that politics disguises the real facts of human behavior. Louis Napoleon might be judged as one would judge a house-servant. Robert first assures George that he need not worry for their safety: "Our little nest hangs at the far-end of a twig in this wind-shaken tree of Paris, and the chirpings inside are louder to our ears than the bluster without." Then, after a scrupulous and ritual account of that lifelong trust, his wife's health, he adopts a tone of masculine confidence which yet allows charity and respect for Elizabeth:

> Is it not strange that Ba cannot take your view, not to say mine & most people's, of the President's proceedings? I cannot understand it—we differ in our appreciation of facts, too—things that admit of proof. I suppose that the split happens in something like this way. We are both found agreeing on the difficulty of the position with the stupid, selfish & suicidal Assembly—when Louis Napoleon is found to cut the knot instead of untying it—Ba approves—I demur. Still, one must not be pedantic and overexacting, and if the end justifies the beginning, the illegality of the step may be forgotten in the prompt restoration of the law—the man may stop the clock to set it right. But his next procedure is to put all the wheelwork in his pocket, and promise to cry the hour instead . . . Ba says . . . the parishioners, seven million strong, empowered him to get into the steeple & act as he pleased—while I don't allow that they were . . . at liberty to speak their judgment . . . for I or you might join with the rest as to the after-expediency of keeping a bad servant rather than going altogether without one—we might say, 'Now that you have stolen our clock, *do* stay & cry according to your promise—for certainly nobody else will.' And he does *not* keep his promise, as you see by the decrees from first to last; on that point Ba agrees with us again—but she will have it still that 'they chose him'—and you return to my answer above, that denies the facts. And so end our debates, till the arrival of the next newspaper.[37]

Here is neither admiration for Ba's skill nor pain at her shrillness. Evidently it had sometimes been sink or swim at the breakfast table.

The very force and ingenuity of his own argument suggests that Robert had perfected it against his wife.

But there were graver issues in the Brownings' marriage than the life or death of the French Republic. On Louis Napoleon, Elizabeth was perhaps sounder than Robert was. On Penini Browning, she was infinitely less sound. Astonished at having produced a child at all, Elizabeth persisted in regarding Penini as a standing miracle, to be accepted—even applauded—as such. "We don't teach him yet to say grace or even regular prayers. I am so afraid of tying up the pure free spirit in formalisms, before he can understand significances. But he understands perfectly that God is good & makes him good, & gives him gifts—And quite of his own accord, the other day, after breakfast, he said, turning his bright face up to the ceiling & lifting up his right hand,—'The buono—grazie a Dio.' And now he does it constantly." One can imagine why he did it constantly. With some misgivings, she was also pleased that he preferred to speak Italian rather than English, and his mispronunciations in both languages were wonders not to be tampered with. Pen was not only encouraged to be odd, but had oddness thrust upon him. "Now," she told Henrietta, "we have bought him a white felt hat, white satin ribbons and feathers—really the prettiest hat I ever saw, and he looks lovely in it—with a trimming of blue satin ribbon inside at each cheek. . . . People stare at him, Wilson says, and turn round to stare again."[38] People also frequently asked Wilson whether the child was a boy or a girl. In an interesting speech given on the centenary of Elizabeth's death, Mr. E. R. Moulton-Barrett observes that it was the loving father in Edward Barrett that made him unwilling to let his children grow up, learn a profession, or marry.[39] Elizabeth seemed reluctant that Pen should grow beyond babyhood or indeed be an ordinary mortal in this prosaic world. "The 'elf'," she informed Mrs. Jameson, "is flourishing in all good fairyhood, with a scarlet rose leaf on each cheek."[40]

Against this extravagant folly, Robert had as yet made little headway. He was totally unable to emancipate Pen from feathers and ribbons, though, as a son who adored his father, the boy sometimes echoed masculine feeling—as when, "looking into the mirror with profound dissatisfaction," he said, " 'I not a bit like a boy, wiz mine turls.' "[41] Robert insisted that he be taught English, yet, in the summer of 1851, Miss Mitford had been astonished to hear "the English father, English mother, and English nurse talk Italian" to the two-year-old; nor did he speak English readily for another year. Robert was only gradually successful in imposing a modicum of discipline. Once during the Paris winter when the child misbehaved his father reprimanded him, telling him that he was "molto cattivo." "Upon which," wrote Elizabeth, Pen's "lip began to quiver directly . . . and I interfered and insisted on it that he meant to be 'very good' on the contrary. 'Go and kiss Papa,' said I—and off he ran and kissed his coat; as high up as he could reach. The child is too susceptible—the least word overcomes him. . . . I really don't know a fault in his temper and disposition."[42] Thus instructed, Pen soon learned that the kiss was a deadly weapon against authority, moral or pedagogical.

But why did Robert find it so difficult to assert himself? Later he was to introduce some commonsense into the rearing of his son. No doubt the habit of deferring to a mother had led to the habit of deferring to a wife—significantly, both suffered delicate health. No doubt, also, love and reverence for his mother in life was connected with adoration and service of the lady in his poetry. Passages in the *Love Letters* suggest that he found in Elizabeth something both of the mother and the lady. There were two opposing images in Browning's life, each with its load of significance, love, and guilt. Freedom and revolution assumed for him the masculine image of his hero Shelley, whom he betrayed in youth and remembered with remorse and nostalgia in his middle years. Dependence, conformity, and reverence assumed the feminine image first of his mother, whom he had preferred to Shelley as a spiritual guide, and then of Elizabeth. The feminine image was probably charged with even deeper remorse and obligation than was the masculine: he had ultimately forsaken his mother for a wife; and he had risked Elizabeth's health in marrying her; and more gravely risked it, in making her five times pregnant. He revered her for her purity, her poetry, and her infallibility. In spite of her panics and fanaticisms, her follies and morbidities, she remained for him "perfect" and "divine." Browning was too skillful a rationalizer not to adjust both images to his convenience—as he adjusted Shelley to religion. But such maneuvers are not achieved without inward expense. Browning was becoming more respectable, more conservative, less political, and more transcendental—with a bad conscience.

An episode of just this period illustrates how little inclined Robert was to defy Elizabeth. In May 1852, James Silverthorne died. He had been Robert's favorite cousin and best man at his wedding. Robert was meticulous in matters of ceremony, and as the darling of the family, he must have known how important his presence at the funeral would be. Sarianna had particularly asked him to come. Suddenly terrified, Elizabeth pleaded not to be left alone. Many other relatives would come: surely his presence was unnecessary. Sarianna wrote again, and this time, deeply shaken, Elizabeth said he had better go. But when he was on the point of leaving, she looked so pale and wretched that he stayed after all. To Arabel, Elizabeth explained everything in terms of Robert's sensitivity and Sarianna's obtuseness. Though always "good and true, affectionate and generous," Sarianna was "not made of the same stuff as Robert," and had no "notion of what he would suffer in going."[43] For Browning, this episode may have been a turning point. Never again was he to be overawed by one of his wife's panics.

Does Browning's poetry illuminate these events? Having been very lazy in Florence the previous year, he made a New Year's resolution that in 1852 he would write a new poem every day. For three days he actually kept his promise. On January 1, he wrote "Love Among the Ruins"; on January 2, "Women and Roses"; and on January 3 "Childe Roland."[44] "*Women and Roses* is the record of a vivid dream, occasioned by some magnificent roses . . . sent Mrs. Browning":[45] the poet longs, in succession and each time in vain, for a passionate experience with famous ladies long dead, living ladies, and ladies yet to be born. What deters one from speculating on this picture of somewhat portentous frustration is that the poem seems an exercise in carrying out a resolution rather than something deeply meant. "Love Among the Ruins"—with its skillfully alternated pictures of ancient splendor and idyllic love; its echoing rhymes, meditative, nostalgic, strident, or ironic; its intricate, fluid, yet perspicacious syntax—is obviously a more difficult task achieved with greater inspiration. It depicts an authentically, almost archeologically described civilization—in Jerusalem, Babylon, or Nineveh—[46] well lost and ruined for love:

> In one year they sent a million fighters forth
>   South and North,
> And they built their gods a brazen pillar high
>   As the sky,
> Yet reserved a thousand chariots in full force—
>   Gold, of course.[47]

In short, politics and history, glory and conquest, building and destroying, Louis Napoleon perhaps as well as Ozymandias, are rejected as brutal—and Elizabeth is best. One thinks of Browning's letter to George, in which the harmony of the chirping nest is contrasted with the blustering imperial winds outside.

Robert Langbaum seems quite right in saying that "Childe Roland" is essentially "about the sheer questing—the experience not the situation."[48] Indeed the want of any intelligible situation may be an expression of Browning's deep, residual skepticism. In giving Roland no explicit motive or objective, he seems to say that the quest—and therefore life itself—is meaningless and irrational, or at least in a deep sense dark and mysterious. This interpretation is the more likely in that Roland's quest is commensurate with his life: he had spent "a lifetime" in preparation. To introduce modern skeptical doubt upon the medieval idealism of the quest may incidentally involve a comment on poems like Tennyson's "Sir Galahad."[49] In the blank face which it presents to the reader—as well as in its ambiguities, its nightmarish swelling of light and sound at the close, and its total lack of any ultimate rationale—the poem resembles a dream. "Childe Roland came upon me like a kind of dream," says Browning. "I had to write it."[50] The sources used also suggest that he was expressing images and emotions that lay deep in his mind.

So far as they are known, the sources of this poem, at least in their effect on Browning, are singularly uniform in their implications. DeVane suggests that forgotten memories of a chapter in Lairesse on deformed and horrible landscape may account for many details.[51] The most obvious source—and that from which the poem derives its title and essential idea—is the snatch sung by Edgar in the storm scene of *Lear*:

Child Rowland to the dark tower came:
His word was still 'Fie, foh, and fum,
  I smell the blood of a British man.'

These words are uttered, without reason or relevance, by a man feigning madness to a man actually approaching madness. The world of the storm is chaotic and irrational, hostile to man and his characteristic values. In the song itself—if indeed it is a consecutive unity—the 'Fie, foh, fum' is pretty clearly the "word" of the giant who inhabits the dark tower. Harold Golder points out that it is echoed in Browning's "A Lovers' Quarrel," where Tom Thumb is confused with Jack the Giant-Killer.

I would laugh like the valiant Thumb
  Facing the castle glum
And the giant's fee-faw-fum![52]

Like Roland, Jack does indeed travel over a wasteland to a castle where he finds a host of lost adventurers kept prisoner by a giant. The childhood tale has other echoes in Browning's poetry. Golder reminds us that the lost adventurers parallel the lost poets to whom April beckons and the sages who stand about the deathbed of Paracelsus.[53] One might add a further parallel from *Pauline*:

> For I seem dying as one going in the dark
> To fight a giant.[54]

Or again, the hero of *Strafford*:

> Seldom with you, my king! I—soon to rush
> Alone—upon a Giant—in the dark![55]

In short, allusions to the old tale appear in scenes which involve disillusionment, failure, and death. Recently Thomas P. Harrison has pointed out an elaborate parallel in language and plot between "Childe Roland" and "Peter Bell."[56] Still, one may doubt that Browning intended deliberately or chiefly a comment on Wordsworth or Wordsworth's poems. Rather, "Peter Bell" may explain a certain Gothic-novel ingenuity in the landscape of "Childe Roland," and it suggests that Browning may have thought of his hero as, like Peter, a guilty man. The world through which Roland passes is not only sterile, deathly and grotesque, but purgatorial, malignantly hostile, and even punitive. Seeking courage in old memories, he thinks of two comrades, noble once but—as he immediately remembers with horror—each corrupted to crime: Cuthbert, condemned for "one night's disgrace," and Giles "spat upon and curst" for treason. Pretty clearly, Cuthbert had committed adultery. One need not suspect Browning. Rather—if the nature of the crime is important rather than the corruption of fair promise—both Giles and Cuthbert have sinned against their loyalties. Roland dismisses them with

> Better this present than a past like that.[57]

When a great black bird sails past, brushing Roland's cap with a wing, the knight looks up and sees, instead of the plain, a line of hills that in their suggestions of dilemma and deadlock seem to look inward on the mind:

those two hills on the right,
Crouched like two bulls locked horn in horn in fight.[58]

When he catches sight of the Tower, his reaction to the surprise is angry self-reproach at a failure in military alertness:

Dotard, a-dozing at the very nonce,
After a life spent training for the sight![59]

Immediately after, he speaks of

The round squat turret, blind as the fool's heart.[60]

Roland had just called himself a fool. Is the Tower, then, in some sense his own heart?

Now comes one of Browning's infinite moments, a moment of intense illumination, fraught with suggestions of failure, entrapment and death—and once more in terms of the childhood tale:

The dying sunset kindled through a cleft:
The hills, like giants at a hunting, lay,
Chin upon hand, to see the game at bay,—
"Now stab and end the creature—to the heft!"[61]

The noise in the air becomes bell-like and then articulate, with suggestions of fame, the sweep of history, and, perhaps, the misery and guilt of which history is made up:

Not hear? When noise was everywhere? it tolled
Increasing like a bell. Names in my ears,
Of all the lost adventurers my peers—. . .
Lost, lost! one moment knelled the woe of years.[62]

The crisis of recognition finds him steadfast as ever:

Dauntless the slug-horn to my lips I set.[63]

Admirable as the knight's courage is, one thinks inevitably of Browning's conventional optimism—a public response hardly adequate to the inward exigencies of the adventure.

And what were the inward exigencies of the adventure? In general the ambiguous direction of the cripple, the inevitable entrapment, the deadlock looming in the hills, and the reiterated mention of despair, folly and blindness suggest the kind of confusion, dilemma, self-deception, and frustration one sees in the "Essay on Shelley." "A Lovers' Quarrel" may, at the risk of anticlimax, give further insight into the context of Roland's experience. The poem contrasts a period of winter harmony by the fireside with a period of springtime enmity under the blue sky. For the wrongs of the world, "endurance is easy there," but "the one thing rare" has gone wrong. The causes for the quarrel are not specified, but the points at issue between Robert and Elizabeth turn up like obsessions in everything the speaker talks about—for example, Louis Napoleon, whose marriage dates the poem:

> What's in the "Times"?—a scold
> At the Emperor deep and cold;
>   He has taken a bride
>   To his gruesome side,
> That's as fair as himself is bold:
>   There they sit ermine-stoled,
> And she powders her hair with gold.[64]

Another moot subject—Elizabeth's interest in the occult—appears as a recollected pastime:

> Try, will our table turn?
> Lay your hands there light, and yearn
>   Till the yearning slips
>   Thro' the finger-tips
> In a fire which a few discern,
>   And a very few feel burn,
> And the rest, they may live and learn![65]

Though his tone is uniformly light, the speaker grows serious when he pleads the importance of harmony to himself:

> Love, if you knew the light
> That your soul casts in my sight,
>   How I look to you
>   For the pure and true,
> And the beauteous and the right,—
>   Bear with a moment's spite
> When a mere mote threats the white![66]

The mote is not important, but the issues between Robert and Elizabeth are. It is perhaps even more important that a poem dealing with those issues—written around January 1853, in a period of complete harmony—produced an echo of the obsessions with disharmony and dark frustration in "Roland."

A winter in Paris implied another summer in London. Indeed, Robert had to be in London. On July 1, 1852, his father appeared before Lord Campbell at the Court of Queen's Bench as defendant in a suit of breach of promise and defamation of character. The trial, reported at length in *The Times* next morning, could hardly put a revered father in a more ridiculous light or cause a loving son with an acute sense of privacy greater suffering. The plaintiff's attorney, Sir A. Cockburn, began in a tone of heavy jocularity. This suit had less romance than most of its type because of the advanced age of the principals—Mrs. Von Müller was about forty-five; Mr. Browning was seventy. The court listened to some fifty letters, in which the defendant began by addressing the lady as "My dear Mrs. Von Müller" but quickly warmed—and here Sir A. Cockburn again became heavily facetious—to "My dearest, dearest, dearest, dearest, dearest, dearest, much-loved Minny." The barrister then took up Mr. Browning's theological scruples, "the influence of his son," his breaking off the match, and his point-blank accusation that Mrs. Von Müller had married her second husband when she knew her first was alive. That statement, said Sir A. Cockburn, was "a deliberate lie," and an act of "the most cruel cold-blooded cowardice."

For the defense, Mr. Willis could do little but plead with jocular frankness that "his client was a poor old dotard in love." Lord Campbell then summed up, calling attention to the attainments and the hitherto exemplary life of the defendant. "If the old gentleman, thinking better of the matter," had told Mrs. Von Müller plainly that a second marriage would be imprudent at his time of life, he would not have been found greatly blamable. As it was, he had acted "in a most cowardly manner." A clerk in the Bank of England testified that Mr. Browning's salary was "about £320 a year."[67] A verdict was then given for £800 damages.

The Brownings arrived in London about five days after the trial, moving into comfortable lodgings taken for them by Arabel in Welbeck Street. In the gloomiest of reunions with his sister and father, Robert learned that they wished to exile themselves beyond the arm of English law courts to avoid paying the onerous damages to

Mrs. Von Müller. The case could be appealed, they realized. But that would be to invite further publicity. At length Robert accompanied Mr. Browning and Sarianna to Paris, where he settled them in an apartment not far from the consolations of the Louvre, the Bois de Boulogne, and the bookstalls along the Seine embankments. By July 20 he had "safely deposited the poor victim," as Elizabeth a few days later wrote Henrietta, "and left him tolerably composed and comfortable." Robert himself returned in a state of nervous exhaustion. "The vexation of it all is immense."[68]

Meanwhile, a variety of Barretts paid calls at Welbeck Street, and Elizabeth herself ventured high into the parental dungeon with Pen for secretive feasts in Arabel's room. Yet she longed for a *rapprochement* with the terrible presence who made her shudder in her concealment each time she overstayed her visit at Wimpole Street. Finally in fact she wrote her father a letter to announce that she was in London and to beg, once again, for the immense favor of an interview. Mr. Barrett—miraculously—condescended to reply, in a letter so brutally crushing that Elizabeth, through her tears and her rising bitterness and anger, looked through clouds of sentimentality to the truth. "It was, I confess to you, with a revulsion of feeling that I read that letter," she told Henrietta, ". . . written after six years, with the plain intention of giving me as much pain as possible. It was an unnatural letter, and the evidence of hardness of heart . . . is unmistakable." Indeed she was instructed by her own years of marriage and motherhood. "I have a child myself. I know something of the parental feeling. There can be no such feeling. . . . There never can have been any such . . . where that letter was produced. Certainly the effect of it is anything but to lead me to *repentance.* Am I to repent that I did not sacrifice my life, and its affections to the writer of that letter?"[69]

Less repentant and more confirmed than ever in the loving wisdom of her choices, she was able to enjoy their own friends with something like gusto. They chatted and dined with the Ruskins, with W. J. Fox, with the American poet James Russell Lowell and his wife, and with a very robust Charles Kingsley, whose "wild and theoretical" ideas about Christian Socialism impressed Elizabeth rather less than his "almost tender" masculine solicitude.[70]

"Oh, such a fuss the Brownings made over Mazzini this day!" exclaimed Mrs. Carlyle after taking the revolutionist to call upon them on July 27. Plainly Robert's fuss had been the more obnoxious, for he impressed Mazzini's earnest-minded Scottish chaperone as being very little other than a "fluff of feathers."[71] Yet their real friends were more than appreciative, were affectionately, ardently interested in all three of the Brownings, with the result that October arrived all too quickly.

Now there were protracted leave-takings, and then the bustle of the Folkestone boat, and presently new reunions in the tensely expectant atmosphere of the French capital. From the vantage point of the Fraser Corkrans' high balcony on October 16, Robert, Elizabeth, and Pen were treated to the spectacle of Napoleon's entrance into Paris astride a charger "at least ten paces" from his nearest escort.[72] So much heroism and so many troops filled the youngest Browning with ecstasy and Elizabeth's fervid letters with exclamation points. Robert must have kept several of his opinions to himself.

A week later they left by train for Chalon, whence they boarded a steamboat on the rainswept Saône. Ahead lay the dim outline of mountains.

the Book, the Ring, & the Poet

By courtesy of the Radio Times Hulton Picture Library. From J. C. Armytage's engraving of a sketch by Beard.

Camberwell friends. Robert Browning in 1835, from an engraving. Left: Alfred Domett, future Prime Minister of New Zealand, sketch of 1836. Right: Joseph Arnould, a painting by Middleton in 1838.

From a watercolor sketch by Lance.

Robert Browning, Senior, and Sarianna Browning.
Below: Joseph Milsand, the poet's friend.

From the Browning photograph album, Balliol College.

By courtesy of the Fitzwilliam Museum, Cambridge.

Robert Browning, 1855. From a portrait in colored chalks, pencil and watercolor by D. G. Rossetti.

From a photograph in *Works and Days*, eds. T. and D. C. Sturge Moore (London, 1933), John Murray.

By courtesy of the Radio Times Hulton Picture Library.

Above: "Michael Field" (Katherine Bradley and her niece Edith Cooper), who knew of Browning's early anonymous essay on Chatterton. Below: No. 50 Wimpole Street, the Barrett residence, and Elizabeth's maiden sister, Arabel Barrett. Opposite page: Elizabeth Barrett Browning and Robert Browning, from Field Talfourd's two crayon drawings in Rome, 1859.

From the Browning photograph album, Balliol College

By courtesy of the National Portrait Gallery.

By courtesy of the National Portrait Gallery.

Robert Browning, 1860. From an oil painting by Michele Gordigiani.

By courtesy of the British Museum.

One of Pen's first portraits, in pencil, of his father. The parental inscription is: "Jan. 23, 1853. 'I done this for Dear Papa.'" Below: Pen at eleven, with his mother in Rome, 1860.

From the Browning photograph album, Balliol College.

By courtesy of the Mansell Collection.

At left: Casa Guidi in Florence, the fifteenth-century building in which the Brownings rented an apartment. Below: Asolo, near Venice; and the Casa Guidi salon from George Mignaty's painting in 1861.

By courtesy of Sotheby & Co.

By courtesy of the Armstrong Browning Library, Baylor College

Elizabeth Barrett Browning, 1861, from Pen's enlargement of the "last portrait of E.B.B. taken in Roma." Below: her tomb in the Protestant cemetery at Florence.

CEMETERY, FLORENCE, designed by Count Henry Cottrell and Sir Frederick Leighton.
By courtesy of the Radio Times Hulton Picture Library.

From a photograph by Julia Margaret Cameron.

Robert Browning, 1870, near the time of *The Ring and the Book*.

By kind permission of the Marquess of Northampton

Louisa Lady Ashburton and her daughter in 1862, from Sir Edwin Landseer's oil painting. Below left: Edith Story. To the right: Mrs. Sutherland Orr (Alexandra Leighton).

From the Browning photograph album. Balliol College.

From the Browning photograph album, Balliol College.

From a photograph by Evelyn Barclay.
By courtesy of the British Museum.

By courtesy of the Armstrong Browning Library, Baylor University.

Left: Robert Browning and Pen at the steps of the Palazzo Rezzonico on the Grand Canal in Venice, 1889. Right: Robert Wiedemann Barrett Browning (Pen) in middle age. Below: the Palazzo Rezzonico.

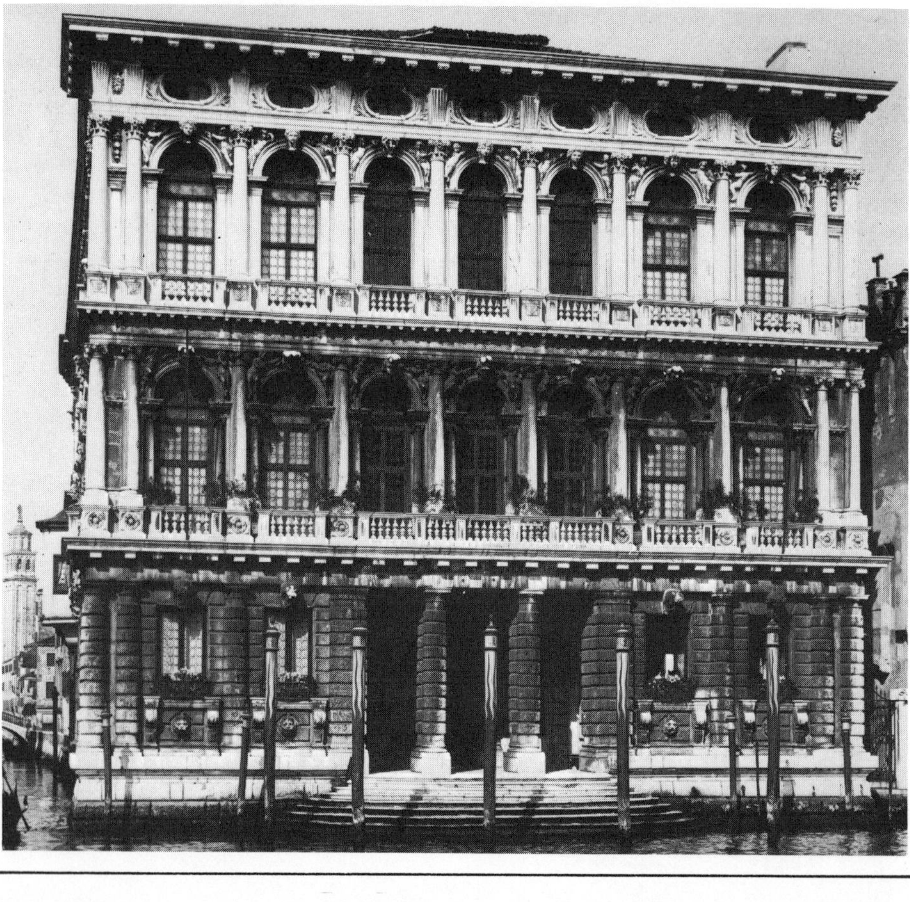

Photograph Osvaldo Bohm, Venice.

By courtesy of the Ashmolean Museum, Oxford.

"Mr. Robert Browning, Taking Tea with the Browning Society." From a cartoon by Max Beerbohm. Emily Hickey with prominent teeth and F. J. Furnivall bearded at the left, the poet seated, and Arthur Symons apparently at the far right. Below: No. 19 Warwick Crescent, London. Browning's house center, to the left of the gap.

From a painting by Margaret E. Wilson. By courtesy of A. N. Kincaid.

By courtesy of the Mansell Collection.

A characteristic portrait of Robert Browning in 1881, from a photograph issued to members of the London Browning Society. Below: The vicinity of Browning's grave, from a photograph taken at the Poet's Corner in the south transept, Westminster Abbey.

By courtesy of the Radio Times Hulton Picture Library.

CHAPTER 18

"Two Souls, and Not a Third"

1852-55

Seduced by the eloquence of Bradshaw, the Brownings crossed the Alps through the high Mont Cenis pass. Early November in that region proved surprisingly cold. Elizabeth began to cough and droop and to Robert's alarm grew weaker and weaker—until they reached the warm sunshine of Genoa. There she soon found herself able "to stand on Andrea Doria's terrace, and look out on that beautiful bay with its sweep of marble palaces." From Genoa onward the journey was a happy regression into the enchantments of the familiar and the congenial. "Everywhere in Italy we have found summer, summer. . . . Such mornings, such evenings!" With mounting exaltation she rediscovered the lovely Italian language, Florence, the Arno, Casa Guidi itself—"our house, our tables, our chairs, our carpets, everything looking rather better for our having been away. . . . Wiedeman's nurse rushing in, kissing my lips away almost, and seizing on the child. 'Dio mio, come bellino!' the tears pouring down her cheeks." Elizabeth felt a delicious "sense of repose," of security. "I could turn myself on my pillow and sleep on here to the end of my life."

Robert did not at first share this feeling. A city which offered the advantages of a bedroom did not please him. "Fresh from the palpitating life of the Parisian boulevards," as Elizabeth put it, he frankly found Florence "dead, and dull, and flat."[1] But he soon saw virtues in his necessity. Exile from Paris had restored him to Elizabeth's world. Among the portraits, inlaid chests, and spring sofas of Casa Guidi, he sat evening after evening and contemplated his wife opposite,

> Reading by fire-light, that great brow
>
> And the spirit-small hand propping it,
>
> Mutely, my heart knows how.[2]

That vision could not fail of its old effect. The winter and spring of 1853 was a period of renewed intimacy, of deeper understanding, of more concerted purpose and effort. They had rediscovered the solitary happiness of their Pisan honeymoon without its idleness. Perhaps they had attained the ideal Pisa at last, for they were actually writing poetry side by side. Elizabeth had at length begun *Aurora Leigh.* Robert was working with redoubled energy at the poems which were to make up *Men and Women.* The quiet study, the orderly desk, the blank white sheet of paper were sights that seldom filled Browning with enthusiasm, but now he had reason to face them with fortitude, even with cheerfulness. "I am in stress and strain with a great day's work before me," he wrote Forster; and to Chapman he predicted "I shall give you something saleable, one of these days—see if I don't."[3]

"Robert and I have had a very happy winter in Florence," Elizabeth wrote in March. "We have been quiet and occupied; reading books, doing work, playing with Wiedeman; and with nothing from without to vex us much."[4] Aided by their new servant Vincenzio—whose only fault was that he looked so very much like a groom—they had developed exemplary habits. Robert got up every morning at seven. "He is longer dressing than I am." Meanwhile Wilson dressed first Pen and then Elizabeth. They breakfasted regularly at nine—"which is a great reformation since we were in England, and gives us whole ribbands of long bright morning time."[5] After dinner, also served with promptness and dispatch, Elizabeth retired to her sofa and Robert went for his walk. In the "dying stillness" of those streets and squares, and particularly in the quiet gloom of the churches and chapels, where, brilliant and vibrant, crowds of painted faces looked out, each "obedient to its passion's law,"[6] he found an older, intenser life, a city congenial to his pen, though its ghost was not congenial to his temperament. When he returned, Pen gave his almost daily theatrical performance with the tambourine. "Such steps, such attitudes—," writes Elizabeth, "and everything in time to the music! He tells Robert to play first slow and then fast, and he begins in the most languishing manner! His one fault is considerable vanity."[7] Next came tea, and at length, having bestowed his last kiss and shouted his last "Dood night," the drowsing tambourine dancer was carried off by Wilson. Robert and Elizabeth now settled down before a roaring fire to their books, of which Elizabeth's letters say a good deal. One hears of Moore in "diary and letters," which Robert found tainted with "flunkeyism"; of Swedenborg, whom Elizabeth began to think greater than Plato; of Lamartine, Dumas *fils,* even of Proudhon. "Robert has been reading a tale of [Dumas *fils*] called 'Diane de Lys,' and throws it down with—'You must read that, Ba—it is clever, only outrageous as to the morals.'"[8]

In the midst of his fresh excitement about the new poems, Robert was partly encouraged, partly daunted by a voice out of the past. A letter came from the actress Helen Faucit, now Mrs. Martin, proposing to revive *Colombe's Birthday* at the Haymarket. Robert braced himself for a show of indifference. "I told Miss Faucit to do just what she liked, and dare say she will do neither more nor less, one whit, on that account."[9] Elizabeth also emphasized that Robert "has prepared nothing at all, suggested nothing, modified nothing. He referred them to his new edition; and that was the whole." At the same time, she was herself deceived by Robert's pose. "I am beginning to be anxious," she confided to Mrs. Jameson, "about 'Colombe's Birthday.' I care much more about it than Robert does."[10]

The play was performed seven times at the Haymarket in April 1853, and then Mrs. Martin took it to the provinces. On May 2 Elizabeth wrote her brother George, "I insisted on going down . . . yesterday morning early to get the letters & afterwards examine the newspapers at Vieussieux's before anybody else arrived—So frightened I was." Browning played his role elaborately to the end: "Robert was calling on me to admire this bright light across the mountains—that black shadow on an old wall—but I couldn't look at anything for my part—My heart beat so I could hear it with my ears. Well! on the whole, I am satisfied."[11] So was Robert—or at least he took elaborate care not to seem disappointed. The closest he came to complaint is in a letter to Reuben Browning: "You were the first to give me news of its success—for such, on the whole, it may be called. I have heard nothing more since the beginning of June, when Miss Faucit was playing it at Manchester, with much the same result: everybody praised her highly, which really delights me; the other actors seem poor creatures, and I won't admit that the play, with its Hero left out, is a play at all."[12]

As Robert had responded to Elizabeth's instinct for solitude, so apparently as far as she was able she responded to his for company. The first eight or nine months of 1853 were perhaps the one prolonged convivial period in her life. She could not keep pace with him in Paris, but by a quiet Florentine fireside, she could enjoy "a few intelligent and interesting persons."[13] "We found most of our old friends here," Robert told Kenyon, "Kirkup wonderfully well, and Powers moving into a larger house, which he has earned, like the brave fellow he is . . ., finishing a fine simple and heroic 'Washington,' and a charming *conceit* of a thing 'California.' "[14] They met also two newcomers to

Florence. One was Robert Lytton, secretary of the British legation and son of Browning's old friend Sir Edward Bulwer-Lytton. The child of a worldly, highly successful father and a handsome, insanely egotistic mother, this young man had grown up with a morbid sense of guilt, an insatiable craving for affection, and a secret tendency to write poetry. His father had commanded him to desist; the son had tried to obey, but somehow the poetry had grown both in quantity and quality until he eventually became, as Owen Meredith, a poet of moderate reputation—as, by a process equally slow and apparently inevitable, he became, as Earl of Lytton, an ambassador to France and a Viceroy of India. The second newcomer was the elder brother of the laureate, Frederick Tennyson, a huge, shy, ruminative, heavy-smoking, inarticulate man, who sometimes stayed late to loosen his tongue—and left Elizabeth exhausted for the next day. A recluse who at Cambridge discomfited the dons with stentorian defiance, and endeared himself to the undergraduates by a hearty eccentricity, he steadily refused to take up a lucrative profession, and having inherited a small property, swiftly retired to Italy, married a handsome girl from Siena, begot four children, wrote vague and melodious verse "with too much personification,"[15] and indulged his taste for music. Elizabeth reported that he had once hired an orchestra to come to his villa and play for him while he sat alone in his armchair. In him the Tennyson morbidity had taken a religious turn. Enjoying music, begetting children, and writing poetry, he looked forward with conviction to an imminent end of the world. Robert and Elizabeth "quite loved" Tennyson while he thought them "the very best people in the world," and Browning in particular, "a wonderful man with inexhaustible memory, animal spirits, and bonhomie."[16]

There was method in Elizabeth's sociability. Everybody in this little group, except Robert, was deeply interested in spiritualism. Through the course of years, Robert was to be critical, interested for Elizabeth's sake, amused, less amused, and finally exasperated or worse. More than Pen's lace and ribbons, spiritualism was to be damaging to the Brownings' marriage.

What was the background of this strange movement that swept over America and Europe and turned so many heads, both wise and foolish? Fundamentally, spiritualism was superstition brought up to date—something as old as the witch doctor made to seem as modern as Victorianism, science, and the idea of progress. In the mid-eighteenth century, Emanuel Swedenborg, a writer on chemistry, physics, and biology, undertook a scientific study of spirits. Having received many communications from them and also developed the power of "traveling clairvoyance"—so that he once predicted a fire at a considerable distance—he came to the following conclusions: This world is "a laboratory of souls, a forcing ground, where the material refines out the spiritual."[17] Selfishness is the root of all evil. Atonement and original sin are delusions. The spirit world is much like ours, with houses, temples, libraries, and scientific institutions; but essentially it consists of graduated spheres of luminosity and happiness each inhabited by those spirits best adapted to it by their previous spiritual development. There is always hope because there is always evolution. A spirit may evolve through successive hells up to happiness. Some decades after the work of Swedenborg, Anton Mesmer, the discoverer of hypnotism, became convinced that there was a mutual influence between celestial and terrestrial bodies. The means of this influence was an impalpable fluid, which was subject to mechanical laws. Mesmer called the human faculty on which this fluid acts "animal magnetism."

A basis for scientific knowledge had thus been laid down; an age of wonders shortly ensued. Apparently Swedenborg continued his researches after death, for in the nineteenth century his spirit communicated at length with Andrew Jackson Davis, leader of the American movement, and became responsible, among other things, for a five-volume work. As time went on, many ordinary, unsuspecting people discovered to their astonishment that they were "mediums" by which spirits and spirit powers might invade the material world. Slade became famous for slate-writing, Daguid for spirit-painting, Home for levitation, Eglinton and Florence Cook for "daylight and outdoor materializations."[18] The eminent physicist, Sir William Crookes, reported he saw Home float out of an upper-story bedroom window, pass over a street seventy feet below, and reenter the house by a sitting-room window on the same story. At another time he saw Florence Cook materialize with wonderful solidity the ghost of Katie King, daughter of Henry Morgan the pirate. Stepping up to the ghost with scientific calm, Sir William felt her pulse and found it to be seventy-five. His reports met with a cold reception from the Royal Society and the British Association. Nevertheless, not only Crookes, but scientists as distinguished as Lord Rayleigh and A. R. Wallace became converts. In the fifties Louis Napoleon, the King of Holland, and the Czar of Russia were all said to consult the spirits as they did their ministers before undertaking important political action. What was impressive was the suddenly and immensely increased volume of messages from the other world. Somewhat as though he were addressing the House of Commons on improvements of the Atlantic cable, Mr. Lytton told Elizabeth he hoped he might "live to see the great day which is opening on the world."[19] In short, history was at a turning point: man would now turn from the conquest of matter to the conquest of spirit.

But spirits as yet seldom reentered the world in all the vividness and completeness of terrestrial life. Usually they could do no more than twitch curtains, float furniture, or rap out messages in alphabetical code. Thus religion became a parlor game and miracles occurred in drawing rooms. They were nonetheless productive of faith. Skeptics have said, cried Elizabeth, " 'Let me see a table move, and I will believe anything.' Now the table moves, all Europe witnessing."[20] Spiritualism enabled the casual to amuse themselves—or the exotically romantic to indulge their nostalgia—and at the same time to feel mystical, scientific, and modern. It enabled those who mourned a beloved relation to dwell morbidly on their bereavement under the illusion they were communicating across the grave.

Jeannette Marks calls attention to a passage in a letter which Elizabeth wrote a few months before her death, to Harriet Beecher Stowe: "My husband calls me 'peculiar' in some things—peculiarly *lache,* perhaps. I can't articulate some names, or speak of certain afflictions—no, not to *him,*—not after all these years! It's a sort of *dumbness* of the soul. Blessed are those who can speak, I say. But don't you see from this how I must want 'spiritualism' above most persons?"[21] Elizabeth had long been familiar with mesmerism and spiritualism, as well as with the ideas of Swedenborg. She had read how mesmerism had "cured" her friend Harriet Martineau of both cancer and the opium habit. Might not spiritualism give her solace from unmentionable sorrows and so keep her mind in the daylight? Actually, like her opium, her novel reading, her political obsessions, her fervid invalid's idealisms, it seems to have reinforced the intense, dark inwardness of her nature. Ultimately, Browning feared it, as he feared her opium habit.

During their Paris sojourn in the fall of 1852, she had first become definitely interested in spiritualism. Henrietta Corkran witnessed as a child a moderate passage of arms between husband and wife at the apartment of her parents in the Boulevard des Italiens. Though it goes somewhat beyond the issue of spiritualism, one cannot forbear to present the scene in all the concreteness of Henrietta's remorselessly sharp, clear recollection. The Corkrans lived up five flights of stairs, so that when she arrived, Mrs. Browning "panted a great deal and was very pale." Henrietta remembers her as "being all eyes and hair, not unlike a spaniel." She also recalls Pen's girlish ringlets and "white drawers edged with embroidery." Mr. Browning was disappointingly unpoetic. His dress was fastidious and conventional, his thick hair well brushed, his manner unsoulfully cheerful, his voice suprisingly loud. Henrietta was shocked to see him "eat with avidity so much bread and butter and big slices of plum-cake." At an early point Mrs. Browning called Henrietta to her, and said in a feeble voice, " 'You and Pennini must be friends, dear. He is my Florentine boy,' stroking his head lovingly. 'Has he not got beautiful hair? so golden.' Then she kissed me and placed my hand in Pen's." During most of the visit, she "kept her right arm around her son's neck, running her long, thin fingers through his golden curls." Mrs. Corkran spoke favorably of spiritualism. " 'What!' boomed out Mr. Browning in astonishment. 'A clever woman like you to be taken in by such humbugs and charlatans!' Then Mrs. Browning in her thin, little voice, said something about her interest in the subject, and then everybody spoke at once. Flush barked and Pen yawned."[22] Though rather carefully contrived, the scene is illuminating. One sees Elizabeth's folly in rearing Pen, and her gently voiced, unyielding resistance on the subject of spiritualism. One sees Robert crashing about with somewhat naïve joviality—a sacrificial bull in the China shop of his own adoration.

After she returned to Florence in November, Elizabeth became increasingly preoccupied with spiritualism—probably because she was then exhuming her memories of Bro, who was the actual hero of *Aurora Leigh*. Rather anxiously, Robert brought reason to bear. In her usual manner, she seemed open to argument, expressed doubts, admitted trickery. Yet her opinions lived a charmed life. To a salient objection, which Robert was fond of urging, she replied: "Why are our communications chiefly trivial? Why, but because we ourselves are trivial, and don't bring serious souls and concentrated attentions and holy aspirations to the spirits who are waiting for these things."[23] And sometimes she answered reason—not Robert's, of course—with rage. Michael Faraday's letter to *The Athenaeum* explaining table movements as unconscious muscular action by the participants drew from her paragraphs and even pages of sarcastic indignation.

On the other hand, favorable facts were received with a passionate eagerness that sometimes bewildered Robert. The spirit had predicted that Lytton's father would meet with a serious accident. "The other day, in comes Robert from the reading room. 'Bulwer-Lytton has had an accident with his arm and can't attend the House of Commons—a serious accident.' I seized upon Robert:

" 'What do you say? an accident?'

" 'Why Ba,' said Robert, 'it's not young Lytton, it's his father.' " Gradually he was made to understand that Sir Edward's misfortune involved a triumph of "science."[24]

When he realized Elizabeth was in earnest, Robert considered the subject more carefully. He read Swedenborg with her, joined her in examining current miracles, and went so far as to say—in a statement to be sure more impressive for skepticism than for faith—that we have "as much evidence of these spirits as of the existence of the town of Washington."[25] He even took his own and other people's arguments seriously enough to waver a little, as well he might, being almost the only infidel he knew in Florence. "We were a company of believers, except Robert, who believes every other day, with intervals of profound scepticism," Elizabeth wrote George. "He will make no profession of faith till he has the testimony of his own senses, he declares."[26]

Indeed the most important difference between them was that he did draw inferences from the evidences of his senses. Both believed in a world of spirits, even in a Swedenborgian world of spirits, for the resemblance of Browning's heaven to Swedenborg's is obvious. Both also believed that mediums practiced trickery, except that Robert felt trickery explained nearly everything and Elizabeth felt it explained very little except the venality of mediums. Browning's "Mr. Sludge, 'The Medium'" contains Elizabeth's ideas, and refutes many of them. In short, she and Robert differed on certain points—and so came eventually to what Mrs. Orr calls the only serious difference of their married life.

The Brownings had long planned a visit to Rome. But money was short. Casting an anxious and practiced eye along debit and credit, Robert decided Rome must wait. Neither he nor Elizabeth had reason to be sorry. In spite of spiritualism, the warm spring sunshine ushered in an even happier period of successful work, gay parties, and romantic excursions. "To-morrow Robert and I have a scheme in our heads, of going to Pistoia and Prato by the railroad, and of dining at a caffé somewhere 'like two lovers,' Robert says. In order to which we leave our respectability and Penini behind us." They drove in the Cascine and along the surrounding heights—once in an open carriage to Fiesole, from which they saw "a vision of sunset over the mountains" and "the wonderful valley where Florence lies enchanted."[27] They witnessed probably with much amusement the rather portentous conversion to spiritualism of the former American representative at Turin, W. B. Kinney, who invested his faith in the new doctrine by taking a poll of the spirits of the great American dead. "Within these few days, & since I last saw you Mrs. Browning," he declared, "I have received accounts from America of the most extraordinary character—The first men of the country, jurists, statesmen, economists—my own personal friends—have come out frankly before the public—committed themselves entirely with the public & risked their political deaths in doing so—testifying to their own spiritual experiences & to their having received communications specifically from the spirits of Calhoun, Webster, & Clay. Now, I ask you—Am I to sit in this chair & say . . . these men are insane?"[28] The evidence was even more businesslike. The spirit of Calhoun had not only given his endorsement *viva voce,* but backed it with an absolutely authentic material signature—executed under a table.

By July both the heat and the fleas became insufferable. Elizabeth took to shaking out her petticoats and rushing about "in a frenetic state, like Io from another sort of fly. Then Mr. Tennyson would calmly observe in the course of conversation—'Don't you find the fleas worse than usual this year, Mrs. Browning?' 'Yes indeed, Mr. Tennyson.' " Hearing accidently of a house to let in Bagni di Lucca, the Brownings engaged it. Two days before their departure, Robert Lytton invited them to a splendid tea on the terrace of his villa, "perched high up at Bellosguardo, close to Galileo's." The occasion was memorable to Elizabeth for historical association, natural beauty, and a spirit of camaraderie which she had rarely known. There was a magnificent double view—"on one side, Florence seething away in the purple of the hills—on the opposite, wood & mountain pressing, gaining on one another, into the far horizon-line still bloodied from the sunset." Besides the Brownings, the guests were Tennyson, Powers, and Senator Villari. As the only lady, Elizabeth had a couch drawn out on the terrace especially for herself. They "consumed floods of strawberries & cream," condemned Faraday as "insolent & arrogant" for attributing table movements to mere muscle, swore to miracles, and told ghost stories. "The old ghost-stories, George," she assured her brother in describing the event, "are effete, stale—they are nothing to the everyday events of the present generation that eats strawberries & cream in talking of them."[29] Little wonder that in such a company Robert's "coat of respectable scepticism" seemed—perhaps even to himself—"out of elbows and ragged about the skirts."[30] Finally, "the stars pressed out over us to meet the fireflies underneath." "I dont know," wrote Elizabeth, "when I have enjoyed anything more."[31]

The shadow of their first visit to Bagni di Lucca did not fall upon the second. Their house, the Casa Dolomei, was situated on the main street of the Villa, though surrounded by a large garden which offered, through a row of plane trees, a fine view of the hills. The cicadas sang all day long in the trees, and the cool shadows from the steep hills on either side crept refreshingly back and forth across the bottom of the gorge. The house was large. As symbols of the awful moral alternatives of work and play, there was a sitting room for Robert to work in and a spare bedroom to house a guest. Elizabeth's letters breathed good resolutions: she and Robert will work *"à faire frémir."*[32]

But very soon after their arrival, the door opened and good intentions seemed likely to fly out the window. "Think of our surprise," Elizabeth wrote Isa Blagden, "when Mr. and Mrs. Story ran into the room for our first visitors here."[33] The Storys were on the top of the hill at Bagni Caldi. "She and I go backward and forward on donkeyback to tea-drinking and gossiping at one another's houses, and our husbands hold the reins." Story notes in his journal: "The whole day in the same woods with the Brownings. We went at ten o'clock, carrying our provisions. Browning and I walked to the spot, and there, spreading shawls under the great chestnuts, we read and talked the live-long day, the Lima, at our feet, babbling on, clear and brown, over the stones, and the distant rock-ribbed peaks taking the changes of the hours." One evening Browning told the company at length the story of Mrs. Procter's step-father Basil Montagu, "which was in other words," explains Henry James with gusto, "the story of the *cause célèbre,* late in the eighteenth century, of Lord Sandwich and Miss Ray, Montagu's romantic progenitors, and of Hackman, the infatuated cleric who murdered, in a passion of jealousy, the nobleman's mistress."[34] What a theme for Browning, whose own moral elevation sometimes provided him with a fascinating bird's eye view into the most iniquitous depths! One thinks also of Elizabeth's own "infatuated cleric," Mr. George Hunter.

Well pleased to be once more part of a gay, intimate little circle, the Brownings actually looked to Florence for further recruits, putting the spare bedroom into requisition. Robert addressed one of his elaborate little invitations, stately in compliment and intricate in grammar, to Mrs. Kinney—"a vivacious, demonstrative, rather pretty woman, with what Alexander Smith w^{d} call a cataract of auburn ringlets"—and with what, apparently, Elizabeth Browning felt was a cataract of

American affability.[35] The Kinneys could not come nor could George or any other Barrett. Eventually, Robert Lytton occupied the guest room for a fortnight. Once more the summer was climaxed by a grand excursion to Prato Fiorito, "six miles there and six miles back, perpendicularly up and down"—a journey so arduous that, when near home, Elizabeth began a conversation with Lytton thus: "I am dying. How are you?"[36]

In fact, this romantic, philosophical picnic led to a romantic, philosophical poem. "After climbing an hour," Story wrote in his journal, "we arrived at a little old church, nearby which the view was magnificent."[37] The little church and many details of Story's description connect time and place with "By the Fire-Side." Plainly, in spite of the exigencies of donkey-back, a perpendicular landscape, and a large company, Browning's eye had been tirelessly and minutely observant. The poem is transparently autobiographical. It involves a lady as "divine" as Elizabeth and a speaker as romantically adoring as Robert, and opens on a fireside occasion in old age when the two look back on the Prato excursion as one which provided a supreme moment of mystical union in a long and happy married life. The adjective "perfect," the phrases "great brow" and "spirit-small hand" clearly exalt Elizabeth above any human folly of spoiling Pen or dallying with spirits. She is the embodiment of soul, aspiration, even divinity.

> Oh I must feel your brain prompt mine,
>   Your heart anticipate my heart,
> You must be just before, in fine,
>   See and make me see, for your part,
> New depths of the divine![38]

One day in Florence Lytton had asked whether Pen, now four, could read. The truth was gently confessed. Pen determined to learn directly, and do "mine lessons evelly day." He was warned not to say it unless he meant it. He persisted. The next day Robert asked,

"Well—are you going to learn to read? God loves truth."

"And I!" returned Pen with dignity.

Each morning he peremptorily announced "mine lesson," was heard for five minutes, and departed in triumph—until one day he was inattentive. There was no difficulty, says Elizabeth. She simply refused to hear the lesson. Pen took a moral view of this refusal but departed. Returning a little later, he asked,

"You dood now, Mama?"

Elizabeth said she was if he was, and the lesson was heard "to perfection."[39] So ends Elizabeth's story to Henrietta, but by late summer the lessons had grown longer and the lapses more serious. Pen had discovered what wonderful fun it was to go with his new hero, the servant Ferdinando, to net fish or coax Flush to bathe in the river. Once, making out words on Elizabeth's lap within tantalizing sight and sound of the mountains and the river, he shut his eyes, kicked his legs indolently, and said, "I not lite mine lesson a bit."[40]

For this act of rebellion Robert shut him in a room by himself. If Elizabeth made no protest, what she thought may be judged from advice she gives Henrietta about her son Altham: "Don't teaze him about his lessons for Heaven's sake. Teach him only if he likes it."[41]

Authorities agree that Browning wrote "In a Balcony" during the three months at Bagni di Lucca. Probably, then, Helen Faucit Martin's revival of *Colombe* had inspired a dramatic work curiously like it. *Colombe* looks forward to his romance with Elizabeth; "In a Balcony" looks back on that romance. The prime minister Norbert wants to tell the faded, lonely Queen of his love for Constance. Constance demurs and persuades him to tell the Queen that he has served her because he loves her, but that since he cannot aspire so high he will ask to be rewarded instead by the hand of her beautiful cousin. The decision itself has very little to do with the realities of Browning's romance. Indeed E. E. Stoll points out that it involves a subterfuge at once transparent and extremely dangerous.[42] But improbability, he declares, citing the great Corneille for authority, is "the inescapable price of a supreme situation." Like *Othello* and *Oedipus Tyrannus*, "In a Balcony" quickly establishes a tragic situation by invoking a convention, in this case the convention that everybody is motivated by romantic love. If that assumption is accepted, the denouement becomes inevitable.

What is remarkable about the play is how closely the invoked convention, and the characters it involves, are related to Browning's experience. For his romance with Elizabeth did in fact make love very nearly the dominant motive of his life, and it also provided him with the psychology of the three characters in his play. Norbert is clearly Robert, suprisingly blunt and headlong for a statesman, and yet—for so blunt and headlong a man—surprisingly tractable to a woman's guidance. Though less clearly, Constance seems to derive from one side of Elizabeth. She is cautious and devious in protecting those she loves. She is somewhat afraid of life and prefers a secret dream-romance to forthright marriage. She shrinks from impoverishing the worldly fortunes of her lover by marrying him—and here we see a prominent theme of *Sonnets from the Portuguese.* She fears that after marriage his love of power will return upon him as a reproach to herself. In short, we see the limitations imposed on Elizabeth by age and chronic illness. But Constance is young and beautiful. Browning tries to overcome the improbability by making her a poor cousin to the Queen, a humble stranger to the brilliant court in which she lives.

There remains the Queen herself. She is certainly not Mr. Barrett, except as a shadowing doom upon the lovers. Rather she represents other aspects of Elizabeth during her romance. She has the very disabilities which might justify the timidity of Constance: she is old, emaciated, ill; she lives in a narrow world of fiction and convention, seeing pictures instead of living realities and receiving homage instead of love. Unlike Elizabeth, however, she has not grown fond of her chains. Robert's love had filled Elizabeth with all the terrors of Constance. Norbert's proposal fills the Queen with the ardor of a young girl. In the first ironic turning point in the play she says to Constance:

> You have the fair face: for the soul, see mine!

In short, the slow, painful ascent of Eurydice toward the light, the very gradual awakening of Elizabeth, becomes sudden and dramatic in the Queen.

The action is essentially, says Mr. Stoll, "a superbly ironical *contretemps.*"[43] Each crisis floods the situation with fresh ironies; each character—as in the principal monologues of *The Ring and the Book*—unfolds his soul in turn. The Queen shows how daringly she can love; Constance, how nobly she can sacrifice; Norbert, how purely he can prefer love to any useful compromise. Then the Queen suffers her bitterest disillusionment. In a moment not very complimentary to either, the two women stand glaring at each other. The Queen leaves to summon the guard.

For once in a Browning play, the characters do not analyze their emotions in the presence of a tragic situation; they grapple purposefully with the situation itself. With brief lapses, the language is clear, rapid, vivid, and elevated—at once poetic and dramatic, foreshadowing ironies to come and reflecting those that have been realized.

In early October, with snow on the heights and chill in the valleys, first the Storys and then the Brownings reluctantly left Bagni di Lucca for Florence. Both families were to spend the winter in Rome. While the Storys visited old friends, the Brownings packed and cleaned house. In the evenings they dallied with the spirits. Robert was at this time in a state of good-humored boredom with supernatural visitors. He "just laughs & jokes," wrote Elizabeth "—we had to turn him away after five minutes—there was only Mr. Story, . . . his wife & I assisting . . . & I am almost immediately stupified with the mesmeric effects. Mr. Story would mesmerize me with looking at me almost, if I did not get out of the way."[44]

Once more preceded several days earlier by the Storys, the Brownings set out on November 14, 1853, on "a most exquisite journey of eight days," stopping to see Perugia, compact and populous on its hilltop, Assisi with its "great monastery and triple church," and the falls at Terni, "that passion of the waters which makes the human heart seem so still." They entered Rome in the highest spirits, Robert and Pen singing, and arrived at lodgings taken for them by the Storys in 43 Via Bocca di Leone to find "lighted fires and lamps as if coming home" and a glimpse of the smiling faces of their friends.[45]

The next morning, tribulation was followed by disaster. First, "in a state of bilious irritability . . . from exposure to the sun or some such cause, and in a fit of suicidal impatience," Robert shaved away "his whole beard, whiskers and all." Elizabeth wept when she saw him. "For no human being was ever so disfigured by so simple an act. Of course I said, when I had recovered breath and voice, that everything was at an end between him and me if he didn't let it grow again directly."[46] Robert consulted his glass and consented. This crisis over, the Brownings were about to sit down to breakfast when Edith, the Storys' little daughter, pale and silent, was brought in by a manservant, who delivered the message, "The boy was in convulsions; there was danger." Leaving Edith with Wilson, the Brownings hurried to the Storys' apartment. All that day they watched by little Joe's bedside. He "never rallied, never opened his eyes in consciousness."[47] In the evening they saw him die in convulsions.

Meanwhile, Edith had come down with the same disease—"gastric fever, with a tendency to the brain"—and could not be moved. As the Brownings had no room for her, she was taken in by William Page, their latest American friend, who lived on the floor below. In no time Page's youngest daughter and the Storys' nurse developed the same symptoms. Soon they were horribly ill, all but given up by the physicians. "After the first absorbing flow of sympathy," Elizabeth wrote, "I fell into a selfish human panic about my child."[48] She was desperate to take him out of Rome. Robert told her flatly that she had lost her head, while the physicians earnestly assured her there was no danger of contagion whatever. Slowly, painfully, Edith Story, Emma Page, and the nurse recovered.

Meanwhile, the Brownings mourned the death of little Joe Story. They witnessed its impact on Pen's Christian innocence. Looking at Elizabeth with earnest blue eyes, he asked, " 'Did papa *see* the angels when they took away Joe?' And when I answered 'No' (for I never try to deceive him with picturesque fictions . . .)—'Then did Joe *go up* by himself?' In a moment there was a burst of cries and sobs." The Brownings' first drive out was to the Protestant cemetery, where Joe was laid "close to Shelley's heart." Nearly swooning with thoughts of shrouds and coffins, Elizabeth looked with wonder at the "poor stricken mother," who "sate so calmly" in the carriage beside her. "Our first step into Rome," she wrote Mrs. Jameson, "was a fall, not into a catacomb but a fresh grave."[49] Such ingenious phrases indicated self-consciousness, perhaps, but no want of feeling. On the contrary, for Elizabeth Rome became the city, not of eternal mortality, but of one mortality. Joe and his stricken parents stood between her and the 175,000 people living decadently, miserably, historically on the massive, mouldering ruins of a much vaster city.

At first, Robert's feelings were quite as gloomy. "We shall be obliged," he wrote Sarianna with an almost audible sigh, "to see some of the Christmas sights, I suppose,—midnight mass, etc. All the city will be illuminated with gas for the first time,—I don't care a straw about such things."[50] They did go Christmas morning to St. Peter's, where they saw the Pope and many cardinals; and later for Pen's sake several times to the carnival, where he accumulated bonbons "and blew out the Duke of Prato's moccoli as fast as they were lighted, with a vehemence of impudence most amusing to the spectators."[51] Of the sights of Rome the Brownings saw only the most obvious: the Forum, the Colosseum, St. Peter's, the Sistine Chapel, and parts of the Vatican museum.

What they did come to know was the foreign colony in the midst of which they lived—round about the piazzas di Espagna and del Popolo. Very early Thackeray and his daughters called. Robert thought the novelist "genial";[52] Elizabeth, "an amusing man-mountain enough," though she was repelled by his bohemianism. "He 'can't write in the morning without his good dinner and two parties over-night.' From such a soil spring the Vanity Fairs!"[53] The Thackeray girls were open and friendly: with his accustomed courtliness Robert responded by taking them walking. Through an introduction from Thackeray's mother, Mrs. Carmichael-Smythe, they met the then notorious Mrs. Brotherton, wife of a landscape painter. She had recently been involved with Saville Morton, of whom with round eyes Thackeray had written his mother a year earlier: "He is shocking about women. Directly I hear of his being fond of one, I feel sorry for her. He lusts after her and leaves her."[54] Recently a jealous husband had disposed of Morton with a butcher knife. Mrs. Carmichael-Smythe had feared the news might "kill" Mrs. Brotherton. Browning triumphantly reported her "quite happy and content with her great bearded husband . . . and so much the wiser she."[55] Elizabeth found Mrs. Brotherton interesting for other reasons. Watching Thackeray and his daughters experiment with automatic writing, Mrs. Brotherton decided, though skeptical, to make the attempt herself. She was greatly surprised when the pen began to move as though by itself—and even more surprised when it wrote not only English but Greek, of which she knew not a syllable. "The character is beautifully written," notes Elizabeth somewhat tensely, "and the separate words are generally correct—such words as 'Christ,' 'God,' 'tears,' 'blood,' 'tempest,' 'sea,' 'thunder,' 'calm,' 'morning,' 'sun,' 'joy.' No grammatical sort of construction hitherto, but a significant sort of grouping of the separate words, as if the meaning were struggling out into coherence. My idea is that she is being exercised in the language . . . in order to fuller expression hereafter."[56] But fuller expression never came. Mrs. Brotherton gave up automatic writing. She found that it gave her severe headaches.

Surrounded by studios in the Via Bocca di Leone, the Brownings could not ignore contemporary art. They admired the statues of the now-forgotten American Crawford, were shocked by the tinted Venus ("more like a grisette than a goddess") of the usually austere and classical Gibson, were personally attracted to a pupil of Gibson's, the youthful Miss Harriet Hosmer, who worked early and late at her statues and breakfasted and dined "at *cafés* precisely as a young man would."[57] Their favorite, however, was the painter who lived a floor below them, William Page, "the American Titian," with whom, in the same breath, Americans did not like to hear Titian compared. He attracted Elizabeth by his spiritualism, and Robert by his goodness of heart. Having noted their admiration for his brilliantly colored portrait of Miss Cushman, the American actress, he did one of Robert and presented it to Elizabeth. Robert pronounced it "the finest of even *his* works";[58] and Elizabeth, "a wonderful picture, the colouring so absolutely *Venetian* that artists can't . . . keep their temper when they look at it." Unfortunately, Page had a technical "secret": he obtained some of his effects by undertoning. Browning's portrait eventually turned black. He also sat to the English painter, Fisher, who had done Landor and Kenyon. "The expression is an exceptional expression, but highly characteristic; it is one of Fisher's best works," pronounced Elizabeth with conviction.[59]

"What happened to me, think you, some six weeks ago?" Browning wrote Forster. "I was talking on the Pincian to an acquaintance, when a stranger touched my arm and said in French, 'Is that *you*, Robert?' It was my old friend Monclar, who, after an absence of seventeen years, had recognized *my voice* (my back being turned)."[60] Reflecting on the loudness of Robert's voice, Forster may not have thought the incident so remarkable. To Count Ripert-Monclar, Browning had dedicated *Paracelsus*. Among other old friends the Brownings called of course on Mrs. Jameson's niece Gerardine, who, married to her red-bearded Macpherson, had borne two children and lost one. "Your lovely, languid, refined unreliable Gerardine has disappeared," Elizabeth wrote "Mona Nina." "In her place is a blooming matron, cleaving to her husband and her household."[61] Mrs. Jameson's husband died about this time, and left her in straitened circumstances. Mrs. Procter took up a private subscription, to which the Brownings contributed. The result was so satisfactory that Mrs. Jameson was able to travel and appreciate art in comfort for the rest of her life.

The Brownings became close friends of the Kemble sisters. Adelaide Kemble had given up an operatic career to marry E. J. Sartoris; and Fanny had given up an uncongenial American husband, Pierce Butler, to return to the stage. Elizabeth pronounced them "noble and upright women." Mrs. Sartoris was "the more tender and tolerant"; Mrs. Kemble, the more brilliant and formidable—indeed she thought Elizabeth "credulous and full of dreams." Even so—"what a voice, what eyes, what eyelids full of utterance!" exclaimed Elizabeth.[62] The sisters, at once artistic and beautiful, drew out Robert's best powers of conversation. Inevitably, they were intrigued with him. One afternoon he marched into the lofty Roman drawing room of the Sartorises, with its "great windows at the farther end," to find himself in a group of ladies "exclaiming, half laughing, half protesting." The hostess, "dressed in some flowing pearly satin tea-gown," sat with an open book in her hand. The "burst of voices" suddenly hushed, and Robert realized that the book was a volume of his poetry. Calling him to her side and showing him the text, Mrs. Sartoris demanded that he "define his meaning."[63] A jarring note from an otherwise delightful lady. He changed the subject.

Robert was also drawn by the people he met at the Sartorises. "The best society at Rome," wrote Elizabeth; "exquisite music, of course." They even met John Gibson Lockhart. "If anybody," wrote Elizabeth, "wants a snow-man to match Southey's snow-woman (see 'Thalaba'), here's Mr. Lockhart, who, in complexion, hair, conversation, and manners, might have been made out of one of your English '*drifts*'." In fact, the "Scotch Reviewer" who had "killed John Keats" was so frosty with premature age, brought on by what his doctors called "excessive abstinence," that his traveling companion, a duke, worried and wondered whether he would get back to Abbotsford alive. "Robert was present when the question was mooted on the Duke's last evening. *Should* he send the body to England or bury it? Would it be delicate to ask Lockhart which he preferred?"[64] Frostily indifferent to the awful questions which surrounded him, Lockhart faced the problem of dining out in Rome, and uttered frosty commonsense about the troubles of his friends. " 'Well'—said he to me—with his lean frozen voice—'I am sorry to hear that Mr. Thackeray is ill.' I said what I have been saying to you—'Dining out at Rome' he exclaimed—if a staccato effort of the voice may be called an exclamation—'Why who *can* dine out at Rome? *I* have never dined out at all since I came—I have seen nothing I could eat—And for the wine—nobody touches it unless in search of poison—No—I will tell you what hurts Thackeray—Those girls hurt him—Those girls annoy him & teaze him. If he wants to be well, he should get a governess, or an aunt, & dispose of the girls.' "[65] What caused Elizabeth to warm toward this man of snow was that he took to Robert at once. Browning was "not at all like a damned literary man."[66]

With the Sartorises, Fanny Kemble, Lockhart, Thackeray, and others, the Brownings went on a number of picnics into the Campagna. Of one such occasion at which she was not present Elizabeth wrote: "Everybody was brilliant, and Lockhart genial, which was more remarkable—they made a fire out of doors, and boiled a kettle and had tea—to say nothing of Champagne and lunch for those who preferred it. Three carriages-full of people!"[67] Elizabeth went on five such picnics; Robert, on no less than fourteen. The proportion pretty well expresses the degree to which she could follow him into society. Now, for the first time in their married life, he did what she had long begged him to do: he went out without her in the evenings. Similarly deserted by their father, the Thackeray girls often came over, chaperoned by the family cook, through the dark streets and up and down stone staircases, to spend the evening with Elizabeth in her quiet room.

As the year before in Florence in the happy solitude *à deux* Browning had written "By the Fire-Side," celebrating a moment when two souls become one forever, so now, in a period of somewhat separated ways, he wrote "Two in the Campagna," describing a moment when such a union just fails. Is "Two in the Campagna" as autobiographical as "By the Fire-Side"? Betty Miller thinks that it is, and since the setting is plainly that of the "Roman picnics," she joins her allusions to the poem with an anecdote about one of these occasions: The company had finished their champagne and mayonnaise. They decided to walk to a distant spot. Feeling unequal to the exertion, Elizabeth excused herself. Robert at once insisted on remaining with her—whereupon Fanny Kemble roundly declared that "he was the only man she had ever known who behaved like a Christian to his wife."[68] Husband and wife are left alone on the "champaign with its endless fleece/Of feathery grasses everywhere." For Robert's thoughts, Mrs. Miller quotes "Two in the Campagna":

> I would that you were all to me,
> You that are just so much, no more.
> Not yours nor mine, nor slave nor free!
> Where does the fault lie? What the core
> O' the wound, since wound must be?
>
> I would I could adopt your will,
> See with your eyes, and set my heart
> Beating by yours, and drink my fill
> At your soul's springs,—your part my part
> In life, for good and ill.[69]

Failure here is closely paralleled by success in "By the Fire-Side," but the lovers in the earlier poem are clearly Robert and Elizabeth; those in the later need not be. The most that one can conclude safely from "Two" is that Robert was in the mood to deal analytically or tragically with romantic love.

Yet spiritualism seems once more to have become an explosive issue. Lady Ritchie recalls that about this time "Mr. Browning was always irritated beyond patience by the subject. I can remember her voice, a sort of faint minor chord, as she, lisping the 'r' a little, uttered her remonstrating 'Robert!' and his loud, dominant baritone sweeping away every possible plea."[70] Evidently Robert had passed beyond good-natured skepticism—perhaps because Elizabeth's faith had deepened. In January 1854, she went with Penini and Wilson to see Isa Blagden, then also in Rome; and watched attempts at automatic writing by Isa's maid and a Miss Hayes, George Sand's young translator, who "dresses like a man down to the waist."[71] Suddenly Wilson, till then a laugher, asked for the pencil. Thereafter, a flood of communications came from her mother, recently dead, with allusions to family affairs, advice, and expressions of affection so deep and tender that Wilson broke down in tears—"You laugh, George," accused Elizabeth, abruptly turning on her correspondent—but continued her story. On a later day, Elizabeth sat down alone with Wilson and asked "if any spirit present would write its name. . . . The pencil turned itself round in her hand & began immediately to *write backwards & upside down at once, presenting the letters to* ME. . . . I could read, though she couldn't—'*Mary*' was written distinctly—I said 'It is a christian name only—Will you write the other name?'—'*Barrett*' was written after—I commanded myself & asked again 'There are two bearing that name in relation to me—Will you write what relation?'—O George—'*Mama*' was written under my eyes."[72]

The next day, Wilson's pencil wrote again with inverted, backward letters. "Then came a beloved name," Elizabeth wrote George. Such eager wishful believing, such willingness to play hocus-pocus with the deep privacies of her life must have pained and humiliated Browning, and when epitomized in the plaintive resistance of the faint-voiced, protesting "Robert," must have irritated him also.

One must not exaggerate. Robert could on occasion still keep his temper about the spirits, and he and Elizabeth could easily drop back into close harmony. One evening just at this time, for example, they stopped in at a party of the Pages' after having already been at the Sartorises'. Elizabeth "stayed by the fire with Mr. Page & talked spiritualism" while Robert, clearly in fine humor, stood "in the doorway of the quadrille-room, admiring the pretty women, & protesting that his own venerable age would prevent his dancing again." Presently he came over to the spiritualists to remonstrate with his wife, in the manner of an exhausted husband, on the lateness of the hour. In fact, he was delighted that she had been capable of two parties in a single evening. "Robert is charmed, you know, when he can accuse me of 'dissipation' before a witness—'He was dreadfully tired—but as for me I never was tired'—& so on."[73]

So many social engagements had left neither of the Brownings much time for writing. They did manage, however, to fulfill two requests for contributions. Arabel Barrett asked them each to write a poem to be printed and sold, with the holographs, for the benefit of the Ragged Schools. Though doubting the financial success of such a venture, they wrote the poems, and paid for paper and printing at Chapman and Hall's. Elizabeth contributed a frank "Plea for the Ragged Schools of London"; and Robert, "The Twins," a little poem with the motto " 'Give' and 'It-shall-be-given-unto-you,' " versed and rhymed in the rather Browningesque spirit of the original, based on a passage from Martin Luther's *Table-Talk. Two Poems,* an octavo pamphlet of sixteen pages, did not sell—and eventually became an expensive collectors' item. Bryan Procter also asked them to contribute to an annual, *The Keepsake,* to help Marguerite A. Power, the editor. Elizabeth sent "My Kate" and "Amy's Cruelty"; Robert, "Ben Karshook's Wisdom."

The death of little Joe Story had continued to cast its shadow on their stay in Rome, and now once more—whether Robert had eyes to see it or not—Elizabeth put herself in a bad light. Edith Story had never recovered her health. "Roman fever followed the gastric," and through the winter recurrences persisted.[74] Browning did what he could, mediating "between the parents and the great Roman doctor of that time, Pantaleoni, at a moment when some of the results of the physician's judgments . . . had caused them to doubt."[75] In April, resolved to try a change of situation, the Storys set out for Naples but had only reached Velletri, their first stopping place, when the child was stricken with "congestion on the brain and heart" and lay "in a state of almost insensibility." Story wrote Robert "a despairing letter saying all hope was over" and pleading that he "*must* go and be with them at the end." Elizabeth did not see the necessity and, in the few minutes in which Robert made hurried preparations, expressed her fear so plainly that, as the carriage drove away, Pen burst into "the most piteous screams and sobs." Robert made the journey in a few hours, "found things had taken a favourable turn," "sate up a night, and left them much lighter of heart next morning."[76] To allay his wife's fears, Robert hurried back to Rome and arrived, laughing, at four in the afternoon with the good news. Elizabeth had spent a sleepless night and was not in a laughing mood. She wrote Arabel that Story should have faced the situation "in all manliness and fortitude." After all, he had with him his wife, two servants, three physicians, and "full pecuniary resources."[77]

By May 1854 the Brownings were ready to leave Rome. They had found it expensive, subversive, ill-starred, and disillusioning. They had been "reduced to live upon woodcocks, snipes, hares and turkeys, because of beef and mutton being so high."[78] Penini had finally suffered a slight attack of "Roman fever," and lost his "ripe cheeks." Robert had got very little work done. "I have let myself be too much entangled," he confessed to Forster, "with people's calls, cardleavings, and kindnesses of all sorts, having not been without social engagements for each evening for many a week now." Finally, spiritualism or the misfortunes of the Story family had for the Brownings cast a shadow not only on the old city itself, but perhaps allowed a shadow to lengthen out beyond an obscure corner of their own married life. "The place is ill-starred, under a curse seemingly," Browning wrote Forster, "and I would not live there for the Vatican with the Pope out of it."[79] And to Mrs. Jameson, still more ominously, Elizabeth wrote, "I lost several letters in Rome, besides a good deal of illusion."[80] The Brownings arrived in Florence about the first of June.

They had meant only to pause there before going northward. Actually, they paused for a year. They were so short of money even Elizabeth was worried. There had been no ship money for that year, and Kenyon had forgotten to send his customary six months' gift of £50. Elizabeth told Arabel they had only £100 for the next six-and-a-half months. "Will you be so good," Browning wrote Chapman in July, "as to give us the half year's account, which will be more interesting than usual, just now?"[81] Hearing nothing for a month, he sent off a more peremptory note. The account came in August, with very little money. Even Bagni di Lucca was out of the question. In September the *David Lyon* finally came in, bringing them an unprecedented £175 and making all things possible.

Meanwhile, Florentine solitude, industry, and bliss had once more succeeded metropolitan, gaiety, idleness, and disillusionment. Life became, in part even for Pen, a quiet, absorbing routine. They rose early, breakfasted; Elizabeth heard Pen read for an hour; then Robert taught him music for another hour. The music lessons show Robert to have been precise and methodical, not only in teaching Pen but in drawing a useful line between maternal and paternal authority.

> Penini has remarkable quickness; and we might, by a little *pushing*, make him do anything: but we won't push, be certain! Robert says if he pushed him in music for instance, he would make an "infant wonder" of

> him in two years. We want instead an intellectual man, of healthy development. . . .
>
> Robert teaches him beautifully. I confess I thought the system rather dry for so young a child—all those scales! But Robert insisting that I should interfere as little with his music as he did in my departments, I was silent, and now I confess him to have been right and justified in his resolution of well-grounding his pupil. I hear Penini answering questions I should be a little puzzled at myself. He is very *vif* and ardent about his music,—anxious to get on—and of course the advantage is great of having such a teacher as Robert, who is learned in music and teaches nothing superficially. The child sits by the fire with a music-book and reads the notes aloud, quite fast. It's funny to hear him "e, *tot*chet, sharp," &c.

Both parents wrote through the long mornings, and after dinner Elizabeth "criticised" Robert's manuscripts, which now she saw for the first time. "Robert's poems are magnificent," she told Henrietta, "and will raise him higher than he stands."[82] A cautious prediction for "magnificent" poems, but for Robert's own sake, predictions of future popularity had to be cautious. Elizabeth's true opinion appears in her steady refusal to speak of her poetry as comparable to his.

Their old intimates reappeared. En route to Rome Mrs. Sartoris spent most of her time in Florence with the Brownings. They drove out to Tennyson's handsome Villa Torrigiani, where with Lytton, Seymour Kirkup, T. A. Trollope and his mother, and—at various times—Landor, Charlotte Cushman, Kate Field, Harriet Hosmer, and the Hawthornes, they listened to music, usually played by an orchestra more numerous than the auditors. As famous people, the Brownings continued to be visited by many strangers. We hear of Lord Fordwich, Lord Cowper's son; Mr. Harrison, a cousin of Wordsworth's; and over a longer period, Brinsley Norton, son of the brilliant and notorious woman who became the model for Meredith's heroine in *Diana of the Crossways*. Like Frederick Tennyson, Norton seems to have simplified his life by retiring to Italy, and simplified marriage by espousing a peasant girl from Capri; he was now employing his leisure in self-admiration. The Brownings welcomed the peasant girl, but eventually tired of the self-admiration.

Elizabeth continued to talk spiritualism but with deference to Robert's impatience. One of her confidants was the American art critic, James Jackson Jarves, who was apparently a better judge of a painting than a religion. Jarves described the London exploits of the American medium Home, and showed Elizabeth specimens of spirit handwriting. When Browning entered the room, the conversation changed to another subject. But easily the most fantastic of Elizabeth's spiritualist friends was Seymour Kirkup, a deaf, white-bearded, skinny-handed, glittering-eyed old necromancer of a man who inhabited several dusty, book-and-manuscript-crammed Faust chambers hanging over the Arno. He had known Blake and Haydon in earlier days and was famous in Florence for having discovered in the Bargello Giotto's portrait of Dante. A long-time friend of the Brownings, Robert valued him for his library and his knowledge of the occult sciences.

One day he called to announce a dramatic conversion. All his life he had been the next thing to an atheist, denying a spiritual world and a future state for the soul. "Always I have said that unless a special revelation should come to myself, I would not believe." The revelation had come—in the very simple form of three raps so loud and sudden that they made the deaf old man leap. Though interested, Elizabeth was dubious. "To my mind, the man was somewhat hasty, after having heard in vain the mystical knockings at all the doors and windows of the universe his whole life long to come round suddenly through a rap on a door by means of a clairvoyante."[83]

A story of Robert's throws further light on the aged philosopher's spiritual adventures. Robert had called at the Faust's chambers to borrow a book.

"Come in," cried the old man, miraculously answering his first ring. "Come and see. Mariana is in a trance."

Browning entered. In the small clear space of a room heaped crazily with "all kinds of curious objects of 'vertu,' stood a handsome peasant girl," rigid, with eyes fixed.

"You see, Browning," said Kirkup, regarding her with his wild look of permanent surprise, "she is quite insensible, and has no will of her own. Mariana, hold up your arm."

Slowly, the girl raised her arm.

"She cannot take it down till I tell her." Kirkup was immensely excited.

"Very curious. Meanwhile, I have come to ask you to lend me a book."

"Wait a bit." The old man shuffled out the door.

At once the girl relaxed, winked, and bringing down her arm, leaned it on Browning's shoulder. When Kirkup returned, she once more became rigid.

"Wonderful," said Browning, and left the room with his book.[84]

The name "Mariana" is interesting. Other friends mention having seen in Kirkup's chambers another peasant girl, also handsome, named Regina Ronti, who received frequent communications from the spirit of Dante. In 1856, at the age of nineteen, and a year or two before she died, Regina bore the old man a child, Imogene, who eventually also mocked him with trances and manifestations. Long after the Brownings left Italy, at eighty-seven, Kirkup was to marry still another Italian girl of twenty-two. "There is a real *poem* being lived," Elizabeth wrote Mrs. Jameson in 1857, "between Mr. Kirkup and the 'spirits,' so called. If I were to *write* it in a poem, I should beat 'Aurora' over and over. And such a tragic face the old man has, with his bleak white beard. Even Robert is touched."[85]

In March 1854, England and France became allies for the first time in two centuries to save the Ottoman Empire from Russia. The Ottoman Empire was soon saved—and the Russians were kept out of the Mediterranean. But would they stay out? To elicit a promise of good behavior—just as though that were worth anything—an allied army, no longer necessary on the Bosporus, was sent into the Crimea, like a needle into a haystack. Seldom have so much folly and incompetence accumulated in high places, so much bravery and endurance remained below. Napoleon asked council on the conduct of the war from the ghost of his imperial uncle. Generals went into battle without plans, intelligence, almost without maps. Meanwhile, beset with filth, disease, and a scarcity and confusion of supply that was enriching jobbers at home, parade-ground armies were actually displaying the fantastic courage they were supposed to possess. The greatest victory in the war, one need hardly repeat, was that won by a woman over supply, sanitation and the treatment of the sick. Little wonder that a young artillery officer on the Russian side, Leo Tolstoi, decided that wars were won not by generals, but by privates.

The Crimean adventure produced, along with some nonsense, a delightful vein of rationality in Elizabeth. To be sure, she found it hard to be enthusiastic about the Turks. Nevertheless, she informed Henrietta that the war was a necessity. Somehow, "the liberty and civilization of all Europe, and the good of the world for centuries" were at stake.[86] In fact, she accepted the war because Napoleon was in it, as Robert accepted it because England was in it. They were appalled by the loss of life and outraged by the follies of English generals and ministers. "Robert has been frantic about the Crimea," Elizabeth wrote Sarianna in June 1855, "and 'being disgraced in the face of

Europe,' &c, &c. When he is mild he wishes the ministry to be torn to pieces in the streets, limb from limb." She could afford to be amused. French troops had taken Sevastopol after the British had failed. Uninhibited by excessive patriotism, she saw through English excuses to faults in the English system. The purchase of a commission does not change a gentlemanly civilian into a trained officer. "Soldiers should have military education as well as red coats."[87] Once in motion, she showed how very far she could go. The English habit of "incessant self-glorification" explains English illiteracy, the ugliness of London, and English corruption in general. "I begin to think," she informed the sober Mrs. Martin with great cheerfulness, "that nothing will do for England but a good revolution, and a 'besom of destruction' used dauntlessly."[88] Such announcements—and he probably heard them—must have made Robert's blood run in reverse, as her brilliant diatribe against Florence Nightingale must have bewildered the mildly emancipated Mrs. Jameson: the angel of Sevastopol had actually damaged the feminist movement. She had succeeded too well in woman's traditional sphere. "Every man is on his knees before ladies carrying lint, calling them 'angelic she's,' whereas, if they stir an inch as thinkers or artists from the beaten line, . . . the very same men would curse the impudence of the very same women and stop there."[89] In any case, the alliance between England and France served to smooth over one area of disagreement between herself and Robert. He now began to see some good in the French Empire and considerable genius in Napoleon.

The Brownings were further united by the worst chest attack Elizabeth had suffered in Italy, caused by the "exceptionally severe weather" of January 1855.[90] "Poor darling Robert!" she exclaimed to Henrietta. "His nights have been diversified by keeping up the fire, boiling the coffee, and listening to the horrible cough which made sleep out of the question for either of us."[91] Each was anxious about the other, and both were full of tenderness. By February 24 she had recovered, and was soon plying herself with cod liver oil so as to appear before her English friends in the summer "with due decency of corporeal coverture."[92]

Putting away the medicine bottles, the Brownings once more took up their pens. By April Robert was dictating four hours a day to a friend. By June, two weeks before their departure, he had ready the eight thousand lines he had set himself, but Elizabeth was short of her equal quota by almost a thousand.[93] And now she must see to shoes and stockings for all, and particularly to the tucks and frills of Peni's trousers; she must answer half-forgotten letters, repay visits of long ago. In the midst of this rather frantic moral, literary, and actual house-cleaning—and a few days before their departure—it was rumored that cholera had broken out in a street behind Casa Guidi, that fourteen people had died, and that their bodies had been carried out under the Brownings' windows. Once more Elizabeth "lost her head." Robert must take Pen and her away within twenty-four hours, to wait for their ship at Leghorn. Robert begged her to wait another day. They did so—and physicians assured everyone that "there was no epidemic, nor would be an epidemic." In fact, there was no cholera. Because of the "excessive abundance and cheapness of fruit and vegetables," people had been ill through "imprudences of diet."[94] A day or two later, about the middle of June, they embarked at Leghorn for Corsica and Marseilles.

CHAPTER 19
Publications
1855-58

The voyage was singularly eventful. Robert and Elizabeth had scarcely settled in their hotel at Marseilles when they discovered Alfred Barrett in the room next door. He greeted them with strange warmth, treated them to champagne, and showered Pen with presents. Though he gave no explanation, Elizabeth understood both his change of heart and his presence in Marseilles. Arabel and Henrietta had informed her that he was soon to marry his pretty young cousin Lizzy Barrett, recently a ward in Mr. Barrett's house. Elizabeth disapproved of the marriage, ironically—though perhaps reasonably—on financial grounds. Alfred was heavily in debt. The paternal predestination duly fulfilled itself: later in the summer and nine days before the ceremony, Alfred wrote his father, received no reply, married Lizzie, and was disinherited.

After a few days' rest in Marseilles, the Brownings proceeded to Paris, taking up lodgings in a suite of rooms below those of Sarianna and Mr. Browning. Elizabeth now had to face further matrimony, for her Wilson had long planned to marry Pen's hero, Ferdinando Romagnoli. Though she did not approve of marriages between Catholics and Protestants, Elizabeth thought Ferdinando an unusually reliable and tender-hearted man. But Ferdinando was reluctant to allow his children to be reared as Protestants, and the priests of Paris were even more reluctant. The Brownings had to stay another ten days to settle the matter. Elizabeth was "horribly vexed" at both the delay and the expense. At length, strangely tractable, Wilson herself yielded the point, and was married on July 10, 1855. Now, though Robert told her "you can't separate a man and his wife," Elizabeth was upset that Wilson would no longer sleep beside Pen, who might need instant attention at any moment.[1] The final blow came in September, when Wilson had to confess she was expecting a baby in October.

Elizabeth could take a tolerant view of premarital pregnancy in Miss Mitford's maid, but in her own Wilson! "Oh so shocked and pained I have been through Wilson," she wrote Henrietta. "But, after the first, I turn and try to think chiefly of her many excellent qualities and of what she has done for me in affectionate service."[2]

Their seventeen days in Paris were busy enough without the tribulation of Wilson's marriage. They not only saw such old friends as Milsand, the Corkrans, Thackeray and his daughters, but at Madame Mohl's ran into a whole galaxy of French genius, including Cousin, Mérimée, and the actress Adelaide Ristori, whom, when he saw her later in the *Médée*, Robert thought "very fine," though hardly equal to Rachel. They also visited Rosa Bonheur, "the greatest woman-painter, it is considered, who ever lived."[3] On July 11, the day after Wilson's marriage, they left Paris and arrived next morning in London, where they occupied an apartment at 13 Dorset Street.

Elizabeth returned to London as to a chronic disease, savoring its disadvantages like inveterate symptoms. The cold numbed her fingers so that she couldn't write; the heavy, rainy air oppressed her heart. It took the curl out of Pen's ringlets and frequently drew from Ferdinando the philosophical remark, as he looked out on the wet street, "*Povera gente che deve vivere in questo posto*"—a refrain which Pen took up with a great air of Florentine superiority. Arabel brought the child regularly to 50 Wimpole Street, and Elizabeth herself soon came "sliding" and "creeping" after—ostensibly to see Minnie the housekeeper. One day, when Pen was playing with George in the hall and was "in fits of laughter," Mr. Barrett "came out of the dining-room and stood looking for two or three minutes. Then he called George and went back. 'Whose child is that, George?' 'Ba's child,' said George. 'And what is he doing here, pray?' Then, without waiting for an answer he changed the subject. To hear of it thrilled me to the roots of my heart."[4] Yet, when the opportunity offered to face her past in a straightforward way, she drew back in horror. Mrs. Martin had invited her for a visit to her old neighborhood of Herefordshire. "If I went there, the thought of *one face* which never ceases to be present with me (and which I parted from for ever in my poor blind unconsciousness with a pettish word) would rise up, put down all the rest, and prevent my having one moment of ordinary calm intercourse with you."[5]

This summer she saw very little of one sister and nothing at all of the other, in spite of the busy scheming of the three sisters, who alternately exulted and cried their eyes out as one house of cards rose and collapsed after another. One morning when—as she wrote Henrietta—Elizabeth was on the crest of a particularly hopeful new idea, "in comes Arabel to say that papa had proposed to them all '*to take a house at Ramsgate, and after a time, if any of them should like to go to Paris where there is much to see! (fancy Papa!) why they might go.*' "[6] Robert declared he would move to Ramsgate in a fortnight. Returned from a scouting expedition, Occy reported that Ramsgate was brimful of Londoners. His father shifted to Eastbourne. Now Arabel swore she would not leave London. Mr. Barrett commanded. All the Barretts migrated, though Arabel, to Elizabeth's intense admiration, boldly returned for a few days' visit. Mr. Barrett stayed in town to supervise the refurbishing of 50 Wimpole Street. The Brownings stayed in town also. Mr. Kenyon had once more forgotten to send their £50. Inveigled by promises of taking care of a little dog, Penini alone went uneasily to Eastbourne, remained even more uneasily for a time, and was sent home after he had awakened Arabel one night by screaming in his sleep, "Oh untle Otty, untle Otty, I must do to Mama!"[7]

As September emptied London, the stream of visitors all but ceased. Earlier in the season one hears many old names—Carlyle, Fox, Mrs. Sartoris and Mrs. Kemble, the Procters—and some names newer to the Brownings—P. J. Bailey, the author of *Festus*, and A. W. Kinglake, the author of *Eöthen*. Robert sat for a portrait to Rossetti. They had lunch with Ruskin on Denmark Hill and saw his Turners. No allusion appears in the published correspondence of either Robert or Elizabeth to the awful absence of Mrs. Ruskin. In the previous summer, however, young Lytton had written them from his new post in Paris: "Mrs. Ruskin is seeking a divorce from her husband. . . . It seems that on the very day of their marriage, Mr. R. . . . informed his bride that he had no intention whatever of having children; and from that day to this, it is avouched, they have been living together as brother and sister."[8] The visit of Frederick Locker-Lampson to 13 Dorset Street is interesting for a sharp first impression of Elizabeth. He sees her resolutely in animal metaphors. "Her physique was peculiar: curls like the pendant ears of a water-spaniel, and poor little hands—so thin that when she welcomed you she gave you something like the foot of a young bird." Having been clever and nasty, he dissolves into sentiment about "her incomparable sweetness, I might almost say affectionateness."[9] What is worth notice is that the woman whom Robert saw—from the "great brow" to "the spirit-small hand"—as the physical index of soul could strike some one else as so decidedly peculiar.

A unique visit—indeed, the one blessed event of this miserable summer—was a two-day descent, September 26 and 27, of the divine Alfred, in a cloud of port fumes and tobacco smoke. The Laureate, wrote Elizabeth, coming down from the Isle of Wight for three or four days, "spent two of them with us, dined with us, smoked with us, opened his heart to us (and the second bottle of port), and ended by reading 'Maud' through from end to end, and going away at half-past two in the morning. If I had had a heart to spare, certainly he would have won mine." Clearly, here was one late night that brought no animus down on the head of the offender. And Tennyson, now in the fullness of his fame, evidently felt he could be openly and articulately himself. "He is captivating with his frankness, confidingness and unexampled *naïveté*! Think of his stopping in 'Maud' every now and then—'There's a wonderful touch! That's very tender. How beautiful that is!' Yes, and it *was* wonderful, tender, beautiful, and he read exquisitely in a voice like an organ, rather music than speech." Sarianna Browning alone noticed that as they listened to Tennyson, D. G. Rossetti, present on both evenings, secretly made the now famous pen-and-ink sketch. Browning was impressed with *Maud*, agreeing with Elizabeth that its general reception was unjust and that in some respects it represented an "advance" on previous achievement.[10] Even so, with two volumes of poetry just completed, he was willing to be heard from, and responded to *Maud* by reading "Fra Lippo Lippi" in a manner as dramatic as Tennyson's had been musical.

Arabel Barrett, also present, much preferred Robert to Tennyson: Robert did not smoke. Elizabeth thought that perhaps he ought to smoke. "It would do him good occasionally."[11]

Elizabeth had resolved to meet "the American 'medium' Hume," who was "turning the world upside down in London with this spiritual influx."[12] Daniel Dunglas Home, or Hume, had been born in Scotland, migrated at an early age to the United States, and by his early twenties become the most famous of all mediums. He specialized in spirit sounds and music and in the materialization of spirit hands, but before the eyes of apparently sober and rational people had on one occasion easily lifted a grand piano with one hand and on another occasion floated out high above a city street. "He's the most interesting person to me in England out of Somersetshire, and 50 Wimpole Street," Elizabeth wrote Henrietta.[13] Robert could hardly refuse to gratify so ardent an interest.

Home was staying in Ealing at the house of a wealthy solicitor named Rymer, who had lost a twelve-year-old son, Wat, three years before. Having received an invitation through Anna Jameson, a friend of Mrs. Rymer's, the Brownings drove out to Ealing on the night of July 23. In preparation for poets, Home and Miss Rymer, also a medium, had woven a wreath of clematis and placed it in the room. At about nine the company were seated round the table as Home directed. Elizabeth had warned them of Robert's skepticism. Perhaps for that reason, Mr. Rymer, clearly a sensitive and even refined person, asked that there be no questions during the seance. Soon the table vibrated and tilted in various ways; there were noises, then raps, which the Rymers recognized as "the utterance" of their usual visitor, Wat.[14] The raps ceased, and Home explained that Wat desired five of the company to leave the room. They did so. The table vibrated again. Mr. and Mrs. Rymer felt the touch of Wat's hand. Elizabeth's dress was softly uplifted twice. The lamp was then extinguished, so that only a faint, clouded moonlight was visible at the windows. A hand, "clothed in white loose folds, like muslin," appeared from the edge of the table opposite the Brownings.[15] Both saw the hand as coming from under the table. At an earlier seance, with more creative vision, Lytton had seen it rising "out of the *wood of the table.*" Presently a larger hand appeared, pushed the wreath off the table, picked it up from the floor, carried it toward Elizabeth—now seated next to Home at his desire—and placed it on her head. The hand bearing the wreath was, as she saw it, "of the largest human size, as white as snow, and very beautiful."[16] At her request, it now carried the wreath under the table and gave it to Robert. He was touched several times on the knees and hands—"a kind of soft & fleshy pat," he told Mrs. Kinney, "but not so that I could myself touch the object. I desired leave to hold the spirit-hand in mine, and was promised that favour—a promise not kept." After an indifferent performance by the spirits on an accordion held under the table first by Home and then by Browning, the medium explained that the hand which had placed the wreath on Elizabeth's head was that of a particular relation of hers. To confirm this fact, the spirits rapped out several names by a prearranged code. "Misses all," reported Browning with satisfaction.

Home now "went into a trance, & began to address Mr. Rymer, in the character of his dead child—in a sort of whisper, at first, to represent a child's voice, but with Mr. Home's own inflexions, peculiarities, and characteristic expressions—beginning 'Dear Papa, —is not God *good,* isn't he *lovely*?' . . . By degrees, Mr. Home's natural tones were resumed." The Rymers were deeply moved—and the Brownings much repelled. Home asked all but the Rymers to leave. When they returned, they found the table lifted about a foot from the floor. There were further appearances of hands, at which Wilkie Rymer was several times admonished by Home "not to look so closely"—and the seance came to an end.

Browning thought "the whole performance most clumsy, and unworthy anybody really setting up for a 'medium.'" He was particularly disgusted by Home himself. "Mr. H. says he is 'twenty,' but properly adds, that he looks much older—he declares he has 'no strength at all' (why? even if it was so!) and affects the manners . . . of a very little child indeed—speaking of Mr. & Mrs. Rymer as his 'Papa & Mama' [partly erased] & kissing the family abundantly."[17] Betty Miller sees "an element of self-recognition in Browning's recoil from Home."[18] Perhaps. But surely Home was objectionable enough in himself. And there were other reasons for Browning's sudden hatred. Home had implicated Elizabeth in "a vulgar fraud," and—for all Browning's contempt of his skill—he had shown what an adroit medium could do with people. On August 30, Browning wrote to a Miss de Gaudrion in the third person an oddly ceremonious little letter, in which he explains that "the best and rarest of natures" may begin by a "proper mistrust" of extravagant spiritual pretensions, may be led on by the affections to an "abnegation of the regular tests of truth, rationality," and thus "end in a voluntary prostration of the whole intelligence" before what is assumed to transcend all intelligence.[19] Among "the best and rarest of natures" Browning evidently counted Mr. Rymer. Did he not see in his wife a possible Rymer? Describing the incident of the wreath, Home himself notes, "Mrs. Browning was much moved."

Two days later, Browning tried to make another appointment with Home at the Rymers, proposing to bring not his wife, but the actress Helen Faucit Martin. Home pleaded illness, but soon after called with Mrs. Rymer and her son on the Brownings. Home describes the encounter at length. As they were shown into the drawing room, Browning shook hands with Mrs. Rymer, passed Home by, and shook hands with the son. As he repassed, Home held out his hand, but "with a tragic air, he threw his hand on his left shoulder, and stalked away." Meanwhile, Mrs. Browning stood, "pale and agitated," in the center of the room. Home approached, and she placed both hands in his. "Oh, dear Mr. Home, do not, do not blame me. I am so sorry, but I am not to blame." There was a moment of confusion, then all were seated, and "in an excited manner" Browning began, "Mrs. Rymer, I beg to inform you that I was exceedingly dissatisfied with everything I saw at your house the other night, and I should like to know why you refused to receive me again with my friend." "Mr. Browning," interjected Home, "that was the time and place for you to have made objections regarding the manifestations, and not now. I gave you every possible opportunity, and you availed yourself of it, and expressed yourself satisfied." "I am not addressing myself to you, sir." "No, but it is of me you are speaking, and it would only be fair and gentleman-like to allow me to reply." Mrs. Rymer said Mr. Home was quite right. Home reports that "Browning's face was pallid with rage, and his movements, as he swayed backwards and forwards in his chair, were like those of a maniac." As the company left, Elizabeth once more shook hands with Home, crying, "Dear Mr. Home, I am not to blame. Oh dear! Oh dear!"[20] This account, one suspects, is not too greatly exaggerated by malice. With something of a spoiled child's pride in his anger, the poet confesses as much in his letter to Miss de Gaudrion: "Mr. Browning had some difficulty in keeping from an offensive expression of his feelings at the ———'s; he has since seen Mr. Hume and relieved himself."

Meanwhile Elizabeth had hung Home's wreath on her dressing table certainly not as a peacemaking gesture. As the wreath withered, Robert's anger grew, until finally he grasped it with fierce scorn and flung it into the street. Elizabeth warned her sister not to mention spiritualism in her letters.

By the middle of October the proof for *Men and Women* had been read. The Brownings retired to Paris and awaited publication. They did not wait in comfort. Commissioned to find them lodgings, the Corkrans had fallen irresponsibly in love with a pair of yellow satin sofas, and leased an apartment which had no other advantage—no sunlight, no carpets, no space, no dressing room for Robert, no bedroom for Pen. "We fell upon evil days and yellow satin sofas in the Rue de Grenelle—due east in aspect, and with draughts flying about like frantic birds." Elizabeth promptly came down with a cold and a cough. She and Robert did "nothing but smoulder over the fire and read George Sand's memoirs," which everyone but Elizabeth found dull because they weren't wicked.[21] Now and then visitors came into the yellow satin desolation—Mrs. Jameson, Madame Mohl, Mrs. Sartoris, D. G. Rossetti, J. J. Jarves, Sir Edward Lytton and his son: Jarves to announce that he was now awakened at night by the spirits; Sir Edward, to report his own turbulent encounter with Home. Elizabeth thought the elder Lytton over-authoritative, over-worldly, and overdressed.

Meanwhile Robert had been industriously thawing out the icy aristocratic avarice of the *Baronne,* their landlady. At length she melted—and released them from their agreement for a mere two-months' rent. Robert now found roomy, comfortable lodgings in the Rue de Colisée, just off the Champs Elysées. To celebrate so notable a victory, he performed on an heroic scale his rite of masculine protectiveness: "That darling Robert carried me into the carriage, swathed past possible breathing, over face and respirator in woollen shawls. No, he wouldn't set me down even to walk up the fiacre steps, but shoved me in upside down, in a struggling bundle—I struggling for breath—he accounting to the concierge for 'his murdered man' (rather woman) in a way which threw me into fits of laughter afterwards to remember! 'Elle se porte très bien! elle se porte extrêmement bien. Ce n'est rien que les poumons.' Nothing but lungs. No air in them, which was the worst!"

All this while the Brownings were living in the shadow of the publication of *Men and Women.* Elizabeth wrote John Ruskin that she was ready "to die at the stake" for her faith in the book. To be sure, so desperate a faith implied some doubt—at least of the event itself. "You please me—oh, so much—by the words about my husband," she continued. "When you wrote to praise my poems, of course I had to bear it—I couldn't turn round and say, 'Well, and why don't you praise him, who is worth twenty of me?' "[22] Two years before, in the secret flush and ardor of composition, Robert had promised Chapman "something saleable,"[23] and even earlier he had told Milsand, "I am writing a sort of first step toward popularity (for me! 'Lyrics') with more music and painting than before, so as to get people to hear and see."[24] But now the excitement of writing was over. The poems were moving rapidly toward the cold light of the public eye. The omens continued good. The "trade" had subscribed generously, so that the expenses of publication were covered within three days. The *Revue des Deux Mondes* had made translations of nearly half the poems, and Milsand himself had quietly told Elizabeth that the book was "superhuman."[25]

Men and Women was published by Chapman and Hall on November 17, 1855. Browning had reason for his early confidence, for he had produced his finest collection of poems thus far. Not only had he shown people how to "hear and see," rendering the musician's ear and the painter's eye as never before in literature, but he had brought the monologue to a new level of development.

Browning's personal development had been moving to a different level. Five or six years of traveling about in Italy, London, Paris, with a delicate wife and without much money, apparently freed and clarified his mind—to an extent. He had brought off the precarious adventure of Elizabeth Barrett Browning's well-being. He was now in his early forties. The cosmopolitan facets of the recent years inevitably added perspective to his earlier, narrower way of seeing things. He was more detached than ever from the puritan ideals and commonsense notions, as well as from the somewhat austere and unpoetic amenities, of nineteenth-century middle-class England. The discipline of going into society had drawn him out of his private speculations, whether autobiographical or of the limited monster-psychology portrayal in his poetry.

As Paul Turner has shown in a thoroughly illuminating Oxford edition of these poems in 1972, modern critics have disagreed sharply in their commentary on *Men and Women.*[26] The best monologues seem to mean five things at once; they admit of directly conflicting interpretations: Bishop Blougram may be seen as hero or anti-hero, admirable or scandalous, honest or false, even honest and false, admirable and scandalous. Certainly, the diabolic monster and the aesthete monster, the Spanish monk and the Duke of "My Last Duchess," have no counterparts in the new collection. Browning's most significant and characteristic speakers now are men of genius or at least of high professional talent—painters, poets, and philosophers. As such, they are men of ideas, and appear as the spokesmen or critics of professions, creeds, philosophies, and even civilizations. Yet often—apparently through the action of historical forces—they are in conflict with themselves, so that they sin against the ideals of their professions or find themselves strangely attracted to alien beliefs and ideas.[27] Their conflicts are not necessarily Browning's own, nor are their pronouncements about art, history, sexual love, economics, or even food. However, a particular application to the Victorian age is visible in several of the poems, and their speakers are such as might speak for Browning with point on contemporary issues.

By the fifties the present had become as exciting as melodrama. The integrity of British intellectual life seemed threatened by the sinister advance of Roman Catholicism from one side and of scientific rationalism from the other. In 1850 the Roman Catholic hierarchy had been established by papal bull, and Father Wiseman had been made a cardinal. Throughout the fifties England continued to terrify and debauch herself with Strauss's *Das Leben Jesu* and, having brought forth a series of geological and biological heresies, was even now rising in fearful pregnancy with Darwin's *Origin of Species.*

"Fra Lippo Lippi" is perhaps a case for caution. Sexual frustration and fulfillment are presented at first in a comic light. A monk is caught by the watch in the very act of leaving the house of a prostitute. The shocking fact is rather safely removed into history, and even more safely conventionalized by a medieval tradition about monks gratefully believed by Victorian Protestants:

Ouf! I leaned out of window for fresh air.
There came a hurry of feet and little feet,
A sweep of lute-strings, laughs, and whifts of song,—
Flower o' the broom,
Take away love, and our earth is a tomb!
Flower o' the quince,
I let Lisa go, and what good's in life since?
Flower o' the thyme—and so on. Round they went.
Scarce had they turned the corner when a titter,
Like the skipping of rabbits by moonlight,—three slim shapes—
And a face that looked up . . . zooks, sir, flesh and blood,
That's all I'm made of![28]

Held now by the yawning night watch, Lippo bribes and flatters with fine crashing effrontery and a lack of success before telling his life-story—which is also a vigorous attack on society. Under pressure of poverty, he is brought as a child to the Carmelites and vowed to monasticism. This event is viewed broadly in both its economic and Christian implications:

I did renounce the world, its pride and greed,
Palace, farm, villa, shop and banking-house,
Trash, such as these poor devils of Medici
Have given their hearts to. [29]

As a young monk, Lippo is also alert to the hypocrisy of his Prior, who wants painters to preach an austerity which he does not practice. The criticism of Christianity is summed up in the double gesture of the young man who finds his father's murderer at the foot of the church altar:

Shaking a fist at him with one fierce arm,
Signing himself with the other because of Christ
(Whose sad face on the cross sees only this
After the passion of a thousand years). [30]

In short, traditional Christianity is too lofty an ideal for human nature—and consequently for Lippo himself. This image, which pictorializes the very basis of Lippo's apology, ironically dominates the poem on its negative side.

The fuller extent of the attack suggests that Browning had his own contemporaries in mind. The church has saved Lippo from starvation; by way of payment it has forced him to deny his own nature. He has been unable to take a wife or—until lately—to paint the kind of pictures which satisfy his own affirmative and realistic genius. At the sacrifice of all he is, he has had after his fashion to serve an ideal in which nobody believes, least of all such pillars of society as the Prior and the Medici. The implications of this indictment are fairly drastic: neither property nor established authority is exempt. Browning's intentions are perhaps clearer in that his main source, Giorgio Vasari, says nothing of the Prior's niece, economic pressure, or Lippo's licentiousness—except that he eloped with an intended nun and lived with her thereafter as though she were his wife. Thus, one is tempted to see in Lippo the Victorian writer and in the Prior and the Medici the wealthy, respectable, indifferent audience who demand of literature lip service to their own hypocrisy.

With the hypocrisy of pretending to live by too lofty a code, Lippo contrasts the sincerity of responding joyously to the world and one's own biology. To deny one's impulses, to do what most people expect is to tell a lie. "As it is, / You tell too many lies and hurt yourself." To recognize "The value and significance of flesh," to see, if possible to paint "The shapes of things, their colours, lights and shades, /Changes, surprises," and count it a crime to let a nuance slip—is honesty and art both. Reaction to the philistine produces the bohemian—even a rather Pateresque bohemian, for, with more gusto and religiosity, Lippo wants like Pater to burn always with a hard, gemlike flame, to gather all he is into "one desperate effort to see and touch."[31] If Browning sympathizes with Lippo's sensualism, he is under some suspicion of sympathizing with his attack on Christianity also. Yet in the end—not entirely for the benefit of the night watch—Lippo displays a bad conscience about his amorous adventures, and declares he will do penance by painting a religious picture on his own account. The ideas of the poem are thus undercut by irony: one is left mainly with the personality of Lippo himself. Still, Browning seems to prefer a bohemian to a philistine, and to weight fornication against some forms of respectability.

"Bishop Blougram's Apology" carries a similar drama of character and ideas to the point of straining the monologue convention. Piqued by the unexpressed contempt of an obscure journalist, a Roman Catholic bishop invites the young man to dinner and at great length argues the soundness of his own faith and the desirability of his own worldly position. Why does Browning make so much of Gigadibs? The basic idea of the poem might be the paradoxical confrontation of faith and skepticism in such a Catholic as Newman. This confrontation is realized in Blougram himself but seems to gain immensely in emphasis and dramatic quality through the setting off of an idealistic agnostic against a shrewd and worldly believer. Superficially attractive, Gigadibs proves to be a broad, uncomfortable mirror for those who live in a gray, unexciting world of pretentious uncertainties, who confuse their ideals with their ambitions and their ambitions with their capacities. Through the interminable condescension of the cabin metaphor, one sees that the bishop is a practical man and—perhaps with striking freshness—that religion is a practical matter. "Life is for action," says Newman. "If we insist on proofs for everything, we shall never come to action: to act you must assume, and that assumption is faith."[32] Blougram seems to stretch and degrade this pragmatism to take care of his luxuries and his self-importance. And thus, standing disconsolate between a fool and a worldling, who at least broadly represent two dangerous intellectual forces of the midcentury, skepticism and Roman Catholicism, the reader is left to draw his own conclusions. Of course, like nearly all of Browning's Catholic prelates, the bishop is a sound Protestant beneath his miter. In fact, he would throw away his tall hat in a moment for the lofty enthusiastic role of a Luther:

> Why, to be Luther—that's a life to lead,
> Incomparably better than my own.
> He comes, reclaims God's earth for God, he says,
> Sets up God's rule again by simple means,
> Re-opens a shut book, and all is done.
> He flared out in the flaring of mankind. [33]

This outburst makes the bishop's Catholicism very nearly the pious fraud Gigadibs had thought it. Browning later denied he had intended any satire through Blougram. He had simply used Cardinal Wiseman as his model! The facility of the bishop's style and imagery seems to indicate the poet's hostility[34]—though the bishop's superiority to his critic would suggest Browning's sympathy for a man contending inwardly as well as openly with religious doubt.

A very interesting case is "An Epistle Containing the Strange Medical Experience of Karshish, the Arab Physician." As critics have done, one may take the poem as the psychological study of a first-century physician confronted by a miraculous cure and a religious faith that answers his deepest instincts. How intricately Browning has developed the ironies of the situation, Wilfred L. Guerin has shown.[35] The poem presents, with compelling vividness, a scientist almost tempted to give up his allegiance to natural causes by encountering at close quarters a miracle, a superhuman personality, and a novel religious doctrine. The effect is to give freshness and immediacy to an incident of the New Testament. Would it not therefore be meant to fortify that document against the attacks of contemporary scientists and higher critics?

Since Strauss's analysis of the gospels depends in the first instance on the rejection of miracle as historical fact, Browning would present a miracle with all the realism of living witness. Since the higher critics argued from biblical documents, he would eschew the monologue and in the epistle provide a document of his own.

The language had to be authentic and convincing. What more so than the style—associated by all readers with the era in which Karshish lived—of the New Testament epistles in the King James version? Necessarily modernizing, Browning gets his atmosphere partly by imitating the elaborate opening in the first chapter of Romans, but even here one must admire the syntactical virtuosity with which he adapts an elaborate convention to the needs of condensed exposition. Apologetically, yet eagerly, Karshish introduces Lazarus, and gives a scientist's description of the miracle—it is the result of epilepsy, of trance. Astonishing facts are mentioned in parentheses and subordinate grammatical elements:

> And first—the man's own firm conviction rests
> That he was dead (in fact they buried him)
> —That he was dead and then restored to life
> By a Nazarene physician of his tribe. [36]

The next astonishing fact is that Lazarus clearly believes he has been in heaven. The psychological effects are described with more than medical zeal.

Browning has not presented evidence but manufactured it. Yet what is the calculated effect on the reader? In the first place, it compels him to consider a Christian miracle with scientific and supernatural explanations placed side by side, but in such a way as to emphasize the enormous inward advantages—in terms of the pragmatism E. D. H. Johnson[37] has pointed out in Browning's thought—of the second explanation. Again, this alternative is reinforced by the whole impact of the speaker's personality. Both Aristotelian and Longinian principles are involved. That Karshish is not only a very probable scientist, but with equal probability a very warm, human, and sincere person; that with convincing psychology and emotion the impulse to believe declares itself against his strong resolution; that he speaks intimately and appealingly to a trusted friend in a private letter; that his language is authentic, passionate, spontaneous, and wonderfully graphic—all contribute powerfully to make the miraculous convincing. Sincerity is persuasive. Seeing is believing.

"Cleon" is less compelling than "Karshish." The speaker is less interesting and attractive; the perspective on Christianity, less immediate and clear. A Greek poet-sculptor-musician-philosopher writes to thank the tyrant Protos for lavish gifts, and then confesses at the end of an abstract discussion to a sense of futility and to the need for a deeper permanence and a higher solicitude. "Karshish" seems to dramatize curiosity and inquiry; "Cleon," pride and possessions. In one, human nature measures scientific materialism against Christianity; in the other, against late Hellenism. Do Greek thought and religion have a nineteenth-century reference? Certainly, and late Hellenism is strongly sympathetic to Victorian *Weltschmerz.* A. W. Crawford maintains convincingly that the ideas and spiritual outlook of Cleon were suggested by *Empedocles on Etna* (1852), which Browning admired and urged Arnold to republish.[38] What is striking, however, is that Cleon lacks the inwardness of Arnold's Empedocles. Both men regard the higher human faculties as ill-adapted to a purely naturalistic universe—here both authors express an argument of late nineteenth-century pessimism—but whereas Empedocles longed for true virtue, happiness, and the consolation of Deity, Cleon seems to want chiefly perpetual youth and pleasure. The reiterated mention of the beautiful woman slave gives one a dubious view of Cleon's heaven. Browning needed a sharp contrast between paganism and Christianity; but very often his own Christianity, with its insistence on personal immortality and the incarnation almost to the exclusion of original sin and the atonement, seems curiously to lack deep feeling. Nevertheless, "Cleon," like "Karshish," belongs to the great discussion in which Victorians attempted to evaluate the elements in their cultural inheritance.

Do other monologues have a notable contemporary reference? "Andrea del Sarto," despite its complementary relationship to "Lippo," is less Victorian. "Mr. Sludge, 'The Medium' " and "Caliban upon Setebos," though written somewhat later than *Men and Women*, both belong to Elizabeth's lifetime; both deal with general ideas and seem to comment on contemporary issues. "A Death in the Desert," possibly written after Elizabeth's death, does employ the strategy of "Karshish" in a rather stark manner, but it is a mediocre achievement.

Why did Browning largely abandon the discussion of contemporary ideas hereafter? Grief seems to have caused a temporary contraction of interest, and meanwhile he had become absorbed in the great project of *The Ring and the Book*. He became less willing to explore the ambiguity of his own attitudes, overpreoccupied with Pen and with Elizabeth's memory. And yet an interest in human motivation would inform all of his significant work.

If only reviewers had not tried to think, if they had given themselves up to frank, unreflective enjoyment, they would have been thoroughly pleased with *Men and Women*. Actually, they did find much to admire. What was exasperating was that they could not fit Browning's work into any satisfactory notion of what poetry ought to be or what an author ought to do. There is evidence they feared he might be doing something quite rational. In this respect, the obscure clarity of *Men and Women* was even more disturbing than the patent obscurity of *Sordello*. Naturally they explained their bewilderment at the expense of Browning's verse and his personal character.

Setting the tone with an article published on the same day as the work itself, *The Athenaeum* once more grieved "over energy wasted and power misspent—over fancies chaste and noble, . . . overhung by the 'seven veils' of obscurity." Particularly regrettable was Browning's "audacity in Hudibrastic versification." Colloquial phrases and fantastic rhymes were perfectly splendid in humorous verse like "Up at a Villa," but serious poetry should take itself seriously. Wit in a love poem was a painful blemish. Indeed, Browning even seemed uncertain of what poetry should be written about. Why should he go to so much trouble "to rhyme the pleadings of a casuist, or the arguments of a critic, or the ponderous discoursings of some obsolete schoolman?"[39] Otherwise, the critic had almost nothing but praise. He admired the love poems. He much preferred "In a Balcony" to Hugo's *Marie Tudor*.

Fraser's Magazine took a much harsher view of similar faults.

Browning was not only a genius unfaithful to his trust, but unfaithful because of "laziness and vanity," because of the "selfish temper and carelessness for the gratification of others which lie at the root of [his] faults." "If a poet will but be slovenly, [silly people] will applaud his graceful audacity, and if obscure, will worship his profundity." "Childe Roland" seems "very much like making a fool of the public." Yet even as he strikes about in anger, this critic sends off sparks of truth. "Old Pictures in Florence," for example, reminds him disagreeably of "Whistlecraft or Beppo."[40]

Again, why does Browning refuse to give his poems any kind of unity and order? "He scorns the old style of beginning at the beginning," fumes *The London Quarterly Review*; [41]and *The Christian Examiner and Religious Miscellany* discovers with astonished indignation that he "gambols" and "raves"; he "shows no purpose, or tendency, or effect, in any high, moral direction."[42] More moderately and intelligently, *The Spectator* enters "a passing protest against his fashion of presenting incidents so allusively as to baffle ordinary penetration."[43] In an unsigned notice in *The Westminster Review,* George Eliot complains that Browning's poems are deeply subjective and private: "This [whimsical] mannerism is even irritating sometimes, and should at least be kept under restraint in *printed* poems, where the writer is not merely indulging his own vein, but is avowedly appealing to the mind of the reader."[44] Both the future novelist—who had just translated Feuerbach and whose *Adam Bede* was then three years ahead—and the critic in *The Spectator* conclude with high praise.

Offensive both for praise and blame is a review in *The Rambler,* later attributed to Cardinal Wiseman but actually by Richard Simpson.[45] He notes "a keen enjoyment of dirt as such, a poking of the nose into dunghills and the refuse of hospitals . . . accompanied by the peculiar grunt which expresses not only the pleasure experienced but also the nature of the experience." Browning is not simply a porcine poet. He gathers virtues and talents as the review proceeds until Simpson declares at last: "If Mr. Browning is a man of will and action, and not a mere dreamer and talker, we should never feel surprise at his conversion."[46]

To read for *Men and Women* something very like the reviews of *Sordello* was a nightmare beyond Robert's darkest fears. He had invested prime years of his life in this effort. He was now nearly forty-four, and must succeed soon or never. His immediate reaction was fury, expressed in the manner of "Sludge" or the "Spanish Cloister."

On December 17 he advised Chapman: "Don't take to heart the zoological utterances I have stopped my ears against at Galignani's of late. 'Whoo-oo-oo-oo' mouths the big monkey—'Whee-ee-ee-ee' squeaks the little monkey and such a dig with the end of my umbrella as I should give the brutes if I couldn't keep my temper, and consider how they miss their nut[s] and gingerbread!"[47] He was somewhat consoled later by praise from *The British Quarterly* and by rumors of "fabulous" sales in America, where the "miraculous Mr. Fields" had brought out the poems.[48]

Early in 1856 Browning wrote Chapman, "I had a capital letter from Forster the other day, one from Carlyle, three from Ruskin."[49] Those from Ruskin were friendly but too disputatious to be quite satisfactory to a middle-aged poet drowning in the waters of oblivion.[50] Though desperately appealed to for advice and encouragement, Carlyle also failed to understand the seriousness of the case—or was constitutionally incapable of unstinted praise. Depicting himself as a rough old veteran with a heart of gold, he scolded his friend gently for obscurity, grudgingly allowed him verse rather than prose as "a dialect"—since it now came "more naturally"—and closed with the fervent hope that his old friend, as well as other people, would someday come to understand his "private notion" of what poetry is. Along with such unpalatable paragraphs, however, Carlyle did manage to say very nearly what Browning wanted to hear: "There is an excellent opulence of intellect in these two rhymed volumes: intellect in the big ingot shape and down to the smallest current coin;—I shall look far, I believe, to find such a pair of *eyes* as I see busy there inspecting human life this long while. The keenest just insight into men and things;—and all that goes along with really good *insight*: a fresh valiant manful character, equipped with rugged humour, with just love, just contempt." Indeed, with only a little quibbling, Carlyle dotted his i's and crossed his t's: "Nay, in a private way, I admit to myself that here apparently is *the finest* poetic genius, finest possibility of such, we have got vouchsafed us in this generation."[51]

For the time being, Robert attempted no fresh poetry. Urged by Elizabeth, he undertook the purgatorial labor of clarifying *Sordello*, and went with his father to draw at the Louvre. "After thirteen days' application," boasted Elizabeth, he has "produced some quite startling copies of heads." As he put increasing time and energy into this hobby, however, she saw its significance and grew alarmed. Every Wednesday he went to read poetry—the first time, Keats—to Lady Elgin, who was now paralyzed. He also dined out. At Mrs. Sartoris', he saw Dickens and—for the first time in many years—Macready. On another occasion he dined "with Mignet, Cavour, George Sand, and an empty chair in which Lamartine was expected to sit. George Sand had an ivy wreath round her head, and looked like herself."[52]

Elizabeth met Robert's misfortune with truly heroic self-sacrifice. Once more she attempted to free him from the restraint imposed by her ill health; he must make the long-dreamed-of journey to the Holy Land, leaving her and Pen at Casa Guidi. He refused point blank. Mere pleasure would never keep him from her for a week. He in his turn dealt gently with her fanaticisms. Observing Napoleon's concern for the poor, his astute handling of socialism, and what seemed his enlightenment about literature, Robert conceded that here was an example of "genius using his opportunities."[53] He was good humored about spiritualism and actually calm about Home. "Think of my horror at Robert's having heard to-day that Hume the medium is in Paris. . . . I looked so scared that Robert promised me that he would be 'meek as maid' for my sake, and that if he met the man in the street he would pass without pretending to see." When Sir Edward Bulwer-Lytton proposed the Brownings accompany him to a seance, Robert astonished Elizabeth by readily assenting. When Story wrote them at staggering length about mediums walking in the air over his head, they "read the letter together on the sofa, like the lion and the lamb—but Hume personally is still a bone in the lion's throat." To ease the lion's pain, the lamb kindly reduced the size of the bone. Home was "certainly a young man of very unreliable nature, as weak as a reed, and more vulgar—but a most wonderful medium in spite of all."[54] Her tone toward the man continued critical. Spiritualism had once more become a discussable, even a jokable subject. When they were visited by "a raw intensely American American, who came into the room without gloves and sate down and did the conversation in the manner of the 'highest black circles,' " they deliberately drew him on "the spirit-subject." After describing the mania in Florence, he turned to Elizabeth with a particularly prepossessing air and remarked, "But I observe that believers in these things are usually of *one-horse power*." Robert was vastly amused. Elizabeth contented herself with telling Henrietta that the American was "rather of one-asspower himself."[55]

By early May 1856, news came that Mr. Kenyon, now seventy-three, was dangerously and incurably ill. Robert offered to go at once to be with his friend. Receiving a "kind negative," he immediately renewed the offer. "It would be a consolation to us if Robert might go," Elizabeth wrote Mrs. Jameson. In a whisper she explained their concern: "It is easier for a rich man to enter, after all, into the kingdom of heaven than into the full advantages of real human tenderness."[56] To Henrietta she wrote, "a *very delicate position*."[57] Mr. Kenyon's brother arrived in London, and the patient improved sufficiently to be moved to the Isle of Wight. He insisted that the Brownings occupy his London house when they came to England in June. They had planned to spend the summer there to see *Aurora Leigh* through the press. Elizabeth had worked hard on it all winter and was now on the last book but one. ("Robert speaks well of the poetry—encourages me much."[58])

Toward the end of June they moved into Mr. Kenyon's home at 39 Devonshire Place. Surrounded by the splendid reminders of a princely hospitality, they settled down, with the assistance of two of Mr. Kenyon's servants and two of their own, to protect the bric-à-brac from Pen and their own elbows. The intermittent chill and perpetual drafts of a great London mansion drove Elizabeth to the softest sofa in the warmest corner, where, enswathed in shawls, she worked hard on *Aurora Leigh*. Even so, she found time to make surreptitious visits to Wimpole Street nearby. She and Robert received their usual succession of literary visitors. Charles Eliot Norton called one evening to find them with the younger generation of the Pre-Raphaelites recently arrived from Oxford—William Morris, who had discovered *Men and Women* with so much gusto, and Burne-Jones, who was being put at his ease by the kindly interest of the hostess. The Brownings dined at the Procters, and went to a breakfast at the Monckton Milnes', where Elizabeth sat next to Nathaniel Hawthorne, since 1853 American consul at Liverpool. That shy but critical author recorded in his notebook that Mrs. Browning was "of that quickly appreciative and responsive order of women" with whom he talked more easily than with men. Altogether, he liked her "a great deal better than her poetry," which seemed much too shrill and strident for "such a quiet little person." After breakfast, in the library, Browning introduced himself to Hawthorne. "A younger man than I expected to see," the latter wrote in his notebook, "handsome, with dark hair, a very little frosted. He is very simple and agreeable in manner, gently impulsive, talking as if his heart were uppermost."[59]

By July, Elizabeth's industry had involved them both. On a page of the manuscript of *Aurora Leigh* appear the reverent words: "Read this Book, this divine Book, Wednesday night, July 9, 1856—R.B., 39 Devonshire Place." By August 3, Elizabeth had all eleven thousand lines ready for the printer. They had also to prepare a second copy of the manuscript with the greatest speed, for C. S. Francis had offered her £100 to publish the book in the United States at the same time that Chapman and Hall did so in England.

Toward the end of August Mr. Barrett discovered the Brownings were living almost under his nose. The very same day he gave orders that his family should go for the rest of the summer to Ventnor on the southern coast of the Isle of Wight. Elizabeth's despair was so evident that even Pen grasped the hostile nature of the paternal dispensation and offered advice. "Mama, if you've been very, very naughty—if you've *broken china*! . . . I advise you to go into the room and say, *'Papa, I'll be dood.'*"[60] Instead of being good, the Brownings promptly uprooted themselves. Gathering up manuscripts, proofs, and pencils, they boldly accompanied the younger Barretts down to Ventnor. George and Occy were particularly warm to Robert. Arabel was in low spirits. With very little future to look forward to and very little past to take satisfaction in, she suddenly saw how abject a prisoner habit, duty, and financial dependence had made her. Her situation went to her sister's heart and provoked a retrospective crisis in conscience that is curiously revealing: "The fact is, she wants companionship and never have I been so near to repent my marriage as in seeing how dull she is, poor thing, all alone."[61]

In sending his family to the Isle of Wight, Mr. Barrett had after all done the Brownings no disservice. After two weeks at Ventnor, they spent another two weeks with Mr. Kenyon at West Cowes, in the northern part of the island. Scarcely a pleasant visit. Pen had to be kept quiet and proofs efficiently read in the midst of a tense, hushed, strained household. "Our stay is uncertain," Elizabeth wrote Mrs. Martin. "We may go at a moment's notice, or remain if he wishes it." Mr. Kenyon was very ill indeed. "The face lights up with the warm, generous heart; then the fire drops, and you see the embers. The breath is very difficult—it is hard to live. He leans on the table, saying softly and pathetically 'My God! my God!'"[62] Elizabeth pleased him by showing him the handsome dedication of *Aurora Leigh* to himself.

Meanwhile, Henrietta was writing the most irresistibly tender letters imploring them to visit her in Taunton. But her "cottage" already contained five Cooks and four servants. "You had better plant us," Elizabeth wrote, "in some out-house, farm-house, something of that kind. . . . Remember, Henrietta, there are four of us! Robert, Peni, Wilson, and me!"[63] The cottage proved larger than Elizabeth had expected and Henrietta, happier than she might have hoped. She and Pen were particularly interested in Henrietta's little girl—Pen, because he had fallen in love; she, because she approved of little girls. "One boy is enough for honour and glory," she had written Henrietta some months earlier. "Boys in the long run are more troublesome."[64] After a crowded fortnight, in which intensive proofreading alternated with an even more intensive exchange of family histories, the Brownings returned by rail to London. The journey was as strenuous as everything had been that summer in England—coffee and sandwiches on the train, Peni asleep with his head on the knee of his adored father. Someone in the carriage said, "I think papa spoils you." On which he opened his eyes and gravely explained: "No, it isn't papa: it's mama."

They arrived at Devonshire Place about eleven—Elizabeth so tired that she scorned the fire and spread tablecloth, and breaking "through a panegyric of Ferdinando's upon a certain ham ('eccelentissimo')," rushed up to bed at once. The next morning, October 1, London was wrapt in fog. "Dear, it was so sad to come away," she wrote Henrietta, "that, almost, one lost the sense of the blessing of having gone."[65]

Three more weeks of proofreading faced the Brownings before they could leave for the Continent. Worse, Elizabeth had to read through Miss Mitford's letters "to let Mr. Harness have what is not unfit for publication." An odor of mortality combined with the fog and the east wind to make this final period miserable in every respect. She worked hard all day and coughed hard most of the night. Robert became grave and urgent. Arabel had written that Mr. Barrett was ailing at Ventnor. Elizabeth found time to worry about him as well as Mr. Kenyon. "I have been very anxious—," she wrote Henrietta, "and shall be sadder than usual in leaving England this year. May God help us all."[66] She was never to return.

They left London on October 22, and after stopping a day or two in Paris and a few days in Marseilles, reached Florence early in November, finding their apartment in excellent condition and feeling as though they had "dropped suddenly down a well out of the world."[67] At the moment, drawing rooms were reverberating with new gossip about new miracles. Home had recently spent some time in Florence, leaving astonishment, hostility, and spiritualism behind him.

Home was soon forgotten—at least by the Brownings. *Aurora Leigh* was published on November 15, 1856—and rapidly became a great popular success. Certainly it offered something to everybody. Nothing if not serious and didactic, Elizabeth began with a load of themes: the sufferings of the poor vs. the frivolities of the rich, English coldness vs. Italian warmth, the aesthetic idealism of the artist vs. the moral idealism of the philanthropist, the right of women to have careers, and the hollowness of all achievement without love—which put to requisition poetry and the novel, from *Paracelsus* and "The Palace of Pleasure" to *Oliver Twist* and *Jane Eyre.* The narrative first person is based on a thinly disguised inward autobiography, which in the First Book is a pious and conventional *Prelude,* and thereafter a record of travel and literary composition, told in an inflated, overelaborate variant of her letter-writing style, with suggestions of Tennysonian music, Byronic satire, and Browningesque stream-of-consciousness. The result is frequently vivid and frequently mawkish. At any rate the "Pythian shriek" is seldom heard. Mounted on this rather elaborate autobiographical structure is an entire novel of intrigue, of which both plot and characters—complete with the burning down of a family mansion, abduction to a brothel, rape, an aristocratic villainess and a maiden of indestructible innocence—are all drawn from the teeming recollections of twenty years' compulsive novel-reading.[68] The heroine is Elizabeth plus half-a-dozen novel heroines, frozen by romantic idealism and the conventions of romance into an iceberg of haughty snobbery. The hero is the St. John Rivers of *Jane Eyre,* plus suggestions of "Bro" Barrett—who eventually suffers the blindness, inward illumination, and happiness of Rochester. The upshot is of course hardly convincing. An inevitable marriage becomes after eleven thousand lines incredible and unthinkable. Even so, one can understand why the poem was popular. In an atmosphere of high romance and lofty idealism, it presents a series of situations familiar and beloved to Victorian sentimentality. Besides, it was written by a lady with a romantic past and a blameless reputation. In fact, abduction, rape, brothel and all, the poem is a long confession of innocence.

Elizabeth expected to be abused for her ideas. Instead, she was criticized for poor taste and a want of humor. Most reviewers thought the poem rather hackneyed and overblown, but the poetess somehow greater than ever. Everybody else gave himself up to unbridled enthusiasm. "Half drunk" with this good "hearty draught of poetry," Landor thundered about "the wild imagination of Shakespeare";[69] and Ruskin, who had written Browning a letter of conscientious objections about *Men and Women,* pronounced *Aurora Leigh* the greatest poem in the English language. A great flood of epistolary praise rolled in upon the Brownings; edition after edition rolled from the press. Elizabeth was highly pleased and a little amused. "The extravagances written to me about that book would make you laugh," she wrote Mrs. Martin.[70] Occupied with sales and epistolary applause, she scarcely realized how unfavorable the reviews had been, though she was hurt by the defection of Mr. Chorley in *The Athenaeum* and indignant at the frequent accusations of heavy indebtedness to novelists. She was certain that she had borrowed nothing from anybody.

Robert gave himself up without a twinge of envy to the sensation created by his wife's "divine book." "That golden-hearted Robert," she told Sarianna, "is in ecstacies about it—far more than if it all related to a book of his own."[71] Yet *Aurora Leigh* seems not to have been an altogether healthy experience for him. With an eagerness and relish born of hunger, he "managed" her success in detail. Writing Chapman on December 2 when excitement was at its height, he warns that in a new edition none of the "'modern' passages" could be "detached without capital injury to the rest of the poem," but chiefly urges that people not be kept waiting a moment for "*Us*—I am the church-organ-bellows' blower that talked about *our* playing, but you know what I do in the looking after commas and dots to i's." This sharp irony about his own significance is directly followed by a paragraph which reveals a bitterness toward reviewers hardly to be explained except in terms, also, of his own experience at their hands.

> I saw the *Athenaeum, Globe,* and *Daily News,* that's all, hearing of eulogy from the *Lit. Gaz.* and blackguardism from the 'Press'; all like those night-men who are always emptying their cart at my door, and welcome when I remember that after all they don't touch our bread with their beastly hands, as they used to do. Don't you mind them, and leave me to rub their noses in their own filth some fine day.[72]

In the midst of their resounding triumph the expected happened. Mr. Kenyon died on December 3, 1856. His brother had died shortly before, making him sole heir, so that Mr. Kenyon had two large fortunes to dispose of. His will read like a roll-call of English arts and letters: there was a large number of bequests, and that to the Brownings was the largest of all—£11,000; £6,500 to Robert ("marking delicately," said Elizabeth, "a sense of trust for which I am especially grateful") and £4,500 to herself. Their grief was deep, but articulate. Mr. Kenyon had been a father to her, nor did England seem possible at all "without that bright face and sympathetic hand, that princely nature." The Brownings were distressed at the many letters of congratulation they received on their good fortune. "People are so obtuse in this world—as Robert says, so *'dense'*."[73] They were not troubled with Mr. Barrett's congratulations. Arabel reported he was "much vexed."[74]

Receiving their inheritance about a year later, Robert invested most of the money in the Tuscan funds. From this source they then received £550 a year, £175 came as before from English government bonds, and royalties continued to trickle in. They did not alter their way of life and so gradually began to feel rich. Robert no longer felt financially dependent on his wife. He now indulged in a luxury of which he had been passionately fond: he began to ride once more.

The winter was a hiatus, almost an irrelevancy, in the Brownings' lives. Elizabeth had written herself out; Robert was too depressed to write. For the first time in his career he had acquiesced so far to public opinion as to turn his writing room into a studio: "He has taken a passion for drawing," Elizabeth told Henrietta, "and through the facilities of Florence, devotes himself to it too much, perhaps, neglecting his own art."[75] He frequently went out in the evenings, and carried his correctness one step further by listening patiently every Sunday to the interminable Scottish sermons of a Mr. Hanna. Before breakfast on week days, he drilled Pen on French verbs and improved his writing of English. Pen, now nearly eight, continued to resist. On the other hand, carnival was a rapturous success. Having teased his parents into giving him a domino, he went rushing about the streets in a blue satin mask talking Italian to strangers and leaving the anxious Wilson far behind. His enthusiasm may somewhat have infected Robert and Elizabeth, for, having himself accepted several invitations through the winter, Robert ended by hiring a box at the opera for the masked ball, going himself in "a beautiful black silk domino," and actually persuading Elizabeth to go. Everybody was there, "even the Grand Duke, poor creature, wretched man, though he couldn't bear it for long, to mix with them as if he were innocent!"[76] Elizabeth went home at two, Robert at four.

Yet one doubts that he was at his best. Certainly the visit of his old friend Fanny Haworth had not been successful. To be sure, the weather was very cold. "'Is this Italy?' says poor Fanny Haworth's wondering face."[77] She confided her vague love affairs to Elizabeth and half converted Robert to homeopathy, which soothed his irascibility against Home. Yet after Fanny had left, Elizabeth felt it necessary to write her: "Be gentle in your thoughts of poor Robert who means more affectionately than appears sometimes."[78]

Particularly since *Aurora Leigh,* Elizabeth had, as Mrs. Miller observes,[79] definitely become the most eminent figure of her little Anglo-Florentine society of minor writers, youthful diplomats, and exiles from higher prices. She was the one person whom all pilgrims to Florence must see. Thus Harriet Beecher Stowe paid homage, and the two sly lionesses roared softly together. Elizabeth even took herself seriously enough to write, in imitation of George Sand, a letter to Napoleon III pleading that Victor Hugo be forgiven and allowed to return to France. But she didn't send the letter.

On April 17, 1857, shortly before his seventy-second birthday, Edward Barrett died—and left with unimaginable feelings the inhabitants of No. 50 Wimpole Street. In the previous summer both Mrs. Martin and their aunt Mrs. Hedley had begged him to "forgive" his three married children. To Mrs. Martin he wrote "that he 'had forgiven' them, and that he even prayed for the 'well being and well doing' of the three families."[80] Yet only in his prayers did he acknowledge their existence. After her second visit to London, Elizabeth believed she had resigned hope of her father's slightest relenting. "I knew then," she later wrote Henrietta, "that this which we have suffered was before us to suffer. Yet when it came, it seemed insufferable as if unforeseen."[81] She had found words to express her grief for Kenyon. Her grief for her father found her wordless, motionless, comfortless. Something had ended, and something had begun—something over which she had little control. Weeks after the event, she wrote Henrietta, "I take up books—but my heart goes walking up and down constantly through that house of Wimpole street, till it is tired, tired."[82] The bitter memory sank inward, joining that of the other Edward Barrett—Bro—and drawing the mind, as time went on, back into a darkness from which Browning had rescued it.

Meanwhile, he was attempting to do so again. For a time he wrote her letters for her—even those to her sisters. His report to Mrs. Martin was gentle:

> Ba was sadly affected at first; miserable to see and hear. After a few days tears came to her relief. She is now very weak and prostrated, but improving in strength of body and mind: I have no fear for the result. I suppose you know, at least, the very little that we know; and how unaware poor Mr. Barrett was of his imminent death: 'he bade them,' says Arabel, 'make him comfortable for the night, but a moment before the last.' . . . So it is all over now, all hope of better things, or a kind answer to entreaties such as I have seen Ba write in the bitterness of her heart. There must have been something in the organisation, or educa-

> tion, at least, that would account for and extenuate all this; but it has caused grief enough, I know; and now here is a new grief not likely to subside very soon. Not that Ba is other than reasonable and just to herself in the matter. . . .[83]

After a month he thought Elizabeth less "reasonable." On May 22, he wrote Hatty Hosmer, "She has seen nobody but Isa Blagden since then, nor once left the house. (But she shall, if I carry her, and before the week is out.)"[84]

And in some degree, she did recover—by clutching at straws and violent remedies. She seized on the phrases with which her father had put off Mrs. Martin. "Those were the words. Let us hold them fast, beloved Henrietta. He prayed for us." She also hoped for a reconciliation beyond and across the grave. "In that world, spirits learn and grow faster. It has been a great help to me that of later years I have apprehended more of the ways of life in that world."[85] Significantly, she wrote Fanny Haworth a year later, regarding spiritualism, "My interest grows deeper and deeper."[86] So much deeper, in fact, that many of her letters on the subject to George Barrett during this period seem to have been destroyed at Browning's request.[87] Such excesses were the symptoms of "a weight of gray and black thoughts" which were never to be thrown off.[88]

Mr. Barrett had wanted his family to go on living together—perhaps even at Wimpole Street. Such an arrangement even a lifetime of habit could not make possible. Inevitably, each Barrett wanted above all to be independent, to do precisely what he wished. This inevitability Elizabeth could not understand. Even in the midst of her grief she found herself worrying about Wimpole Street. "When can another letter come from Storm? Is not Arabel uncomfortable about Bonser? It seems to me that there must be a great deal of discomfort and dreariness, *over and above* what is necessary . . .; and I am moved in the spirit always to get up and meddle, and put everybody in the place I want them to stand in—which is foolish, and very provoking, I dare say."[89] Still, what was more logical than that Arabel should live in Florence? Elizabeth "pushed and pulled" until she made Arabel cry—and then gave up.

Circumstances did not help Elizabeth to recover from her father's death. On July 30, she and Robert once more took a house at Alla Villa in Bagni di Lucca. She had been reluctant to come at all, because Robert, still seeking people as an escape from poetry, would rather be anywhere than in a mountain solitude, and particularly one which must have reminded him of half the poems in the collection that had proved such a failure. But neither did the place provide Elizabeth with the rest and peace of mind she needed. In fact, their stay could hardly be worse for both. Robert had scarcely had time to get bored or she to bury herself in the great pile of German and French novels she had brought from Florence when Robert Lytton (accompanied by Isa Blagden and Annette Bracken) took lodging at a hotel only a few steps away, and promptly came down with gastric fever. As promptly—having perhaps fallen half in love with him—Isa resolved to nurse Lytton back to health. Browning was the not-very-good-humored victim of that resolve. "Through sentimentality and economy combined," he wrote his sister, "Isa would have no nurse (an imbecile arrangement), and all has been done by her, with me to help: I have sate up four nights out of the last five, and sometimes been there nearly all day beside."[90] The illness and the vigil continued for three weeks. Heroically emulated by Pen, Robert solaced and revived himself by taking icy baths in the Lima at half-past six in the morning. He also received a solacing letter from Chapman, who suggested that if he could but write badly enough, he might make a fortune by publishing in the twopenny papers. By the end of August, Lytton was convalescent, and began to think not of Isa, but of apple puddings.

During this or another blessed interval, Robert and Elizabeth made an excursion to Gallicano with some new American friends, the David Eckleys. While there, Robert and Eckley set out in the middle of the night to climb the great mountain peak nearby and then meet Elizabeth and Mrs. Eckley in the gorge for dinner. "Think of this happening. In passing a narrow ledge of gravel, the earth gave way and the horse fell under him, . . . (Robert catching at the rock and so saving himself) the horse falling some sixty feet." Even the horse was uninjured, but the saddle was broken and the ascent seems to have been abandoned. "My imagination reels," Elizabeth wrote Henrietta.[91]

Two days after Lytton's recovery, Peni fell ill of the same disease—less severely, though as Elizabeth could not forget "little Joseph Story died of it before our eyes in Rome." "Two nights he was very ill, and one morning he looked dreadfully—as white as this paper. Oh my Peni, what I suffered in looking at him."[92] Apparently Robert suffered looking at her. "Robert blamed me," she told Arabel, "for looking like a terrified ghost."[93] Meanwhile, Wilson had to go away because of a second pregnancy, and Annunziata, who was replacing her, also came down with gastritis. By then nursing in earnest, Elizabeth took comfort in "the child's sweetness and goodness, too, his patience and gentleness." He said to Elizabeth: "You pet, don't be unhappy for me. Think it's a poor little boy in the street, and be just only a little sorry, and not unhappy at all."[94] Perhaps there was a little of the actor in this saintly patient. Certainly there was in the boisterous convalescent of a few days later. *"Per Bacco,"* he exclaimed to a little girl that came to visit him, *"ho una fama terribile, e non voglio aver più pazienza con questo Dottore."*[95]

The masculine gusto of the last remark was one of many signs that Pen was becoming unmistakably a boy. Earlier in the summer he had inadvertently demonstrated the impracticability of lace clothing. "The first time he rode a donkey . . . through wild places in a wild manner, he came back with his embroidery all in rags—such of it as was visible at all: and when Wilson and I exclaimed, he said consolingly—'Oh, but I have it still! I have taken great care of it!!' And straightway pulled the fragments out of his pocket. He had rescued the torn pieces from the rocks and briars as he went on."[96] Elizabeth bowed slightly to the inevitable—and ordered a pair of "white jean trowsers" only for riding. "They are so ugly, Henrietta," she protested, and added firmly, "Pen wears black silk, or black velvet blouses, and a black hat and feather: but he has never put off his embroidery for the collar and the trowsers."[97]

When they returned to Florence, Pen was enchanted with Wilson's baby—"as if he were the papa and mama both in one. . . . He holds my hand fast—I really think he loves me." "Well," said Robert, improving the occasion like a good father, "if you are kind to him, he will love you." But a world of parental didacticism was still lost on Pen. Elizabeth admitted that he continued to be inattentive at lessons, "kissing" instead of "pleasing" her. He still hadn't "an idea" of arithmetic.[98] On the other hand, "he reads German, French, and, of course, Italian, and plays on the piano remarkably well, for which Robert deserves the chief credit."[99] Pen was now able to do simple pieces and duets with Robert. "You can't think how the child's face lights up while he plays," wrote Elizabeth.[100] Meanwhile, Robert was wisely putting instruction on a more formal basis. Pen already had a teacher for music and was soon to have one for Latin.

That winter in Florence was something less than blissful. Robert was still too restless to stay at home. Elizabeth was too weak to go out. He still sought distraction from thoughts of failure. She struggled in vain against a melancholy produced partly by her father's death, partly by increasing ill health, spending her time "brooding, brooding, brooding, and reading German, German, German." She told herself that cheerfulness was a Christian duty, that gloom was "proof of a low spiritual state. . . . But I have a horrible vibrating body—If I am uneasy in mind for half an hour, I am unwell; and then, being unwell makes me uneasy again."[101] She thought without enthusiasm of wintering next year in Egypt, where Robert wanted to take her for her health. And yet her letters flow with a humor that seems if anything brighter and more effortless than before. "Tell me," she asked Henrietta, "do you and Arabel give in, or rather give out to the hoop-decrees? I have a regular hoop-petticoat, and sweep out into an excess of majestic circumference, much to Robert's satisfaction, and Mrs. Jameson's displeasure."[102]

Robert spent three or four evenings a week at Isa Blagden's villa on Bellosguardo, and went out every day for a drawing lesson. "He has made a great purchase of a skeleton," Elizabeth wrote Fanny Haworth, "and has discoursed upon it till he made me dizzy and sick, . . . enlarging on the beautiful gutta percha finishing of the joints, and the facility with which the head comes off and on—and how, two months ago, this was a Florentine of thirty-six, straying, at evenings perhaps, by Casa Guidi. . . . If I tolerate Robert's bones in the house, he should my spirits."[103] Now deep in homeopathy, Robert had acquired a homeopathic medicine chest and given up wine. "The irritability of his nervous system is calmed down to a degree which I never should have expected from any physical remedy," Elizabeth told Arabel; "and his appetite is ameliorated in a regular way, and his very countenance shows the improvement."[104] Elizabeth toyed with the idea of giving up morphine and embracing homeopathy.

She still clung to spiritualism, but combined it with a reassuring hostility to Home, who had become engaged to a young Russian lady of quality. "Would you not rather be thrown to the lions," she asked Fanny Haworth, "than be his bride? . . . between epilepsy and an influx of bad spirits."[105] Elizabeth was shocked at Orsini's attempt on Napoleon's life and fulminated against everybody in France, England, and Italy who condoned or supported it. "I do fear that Mazzini is at the root of the evil; that man of unscrupulous theory."[106] Now forty-six, Robert does not seem to have defended either assassination or the hero of "The Italian in England."

One evening in that melancholy winter of homeopathy and skeletons with gutta percha joints, Nathaniel Hawthorne came to see them and found the poet in somewhat the position of Arnold's merman reversed. His Notebook tells the story: The street was dark and narrow, "but on entering the palace, we found a spacious staircase and ample accomodations of vestibule and hall, the latter opening on a balcony, where we could hear the chanting of priests in a church close by." Robert and Pen came out into the anteroom to greet the Hawthornes, and perhaps in answer to a question about the nearness of the music—which must have been a prominent ingredient of the atmosphere of Casa Guidi—Browning explained that "this was the first church where an oratorio had ever been performed." Hawthorne felt about Pen as Wordsworth had felt about Hartley Coleridge. He was "so slender, fragile, and spirit-like. . . . His face is very pretty, and most intelligent, and exceedingly like his mother's. He is nine years old, and seems at once less childlike and less manly than would befit that age." Would he ever grow up? Was it desirable he should? Hawthorne decided that he should be fed a great deal. Mrs. Browning was more elfin than he had remembered from a breakfast at the Milnes' where "she did not impress me so singularly, for the morning light is more prosaic than the dim illumination of their great tapestried drawing-room." Hawthorne found himself concerned for the husband. "I do not see how Mr. Browning can suppose that he has an earthly wife any more than an earthly child; both are of the elfin race, and will flit away from him someday when he least thinks of it." Browning looked substantial enough.

There were other guests, chiefly American: the Eckleys and William Cullen Bryant and his daughter. "Mr. Browning was very efficient in keeping up conversation with everybody, and seemed to be in all parts of the room and in every group at the same moment; a most vivid and quick-thoughted person, logical and common-sensible, as, I suppose, poets generally are in their daily talk." Even so, the conversation was not remarkable, dealing mostly with "the now wearisome" topic of spiritualism.[107]

The Eckleys had by now become intimate friends of the Brownings. They seemed an average American combination of naïveté, enthusiasm, and wealth. Sophie Eckley wrote poetry, communed genteelly with the spirits, and burned with a quiet, delicate idealism. She came almost every day to see Elizabeth, having in fact "taken it into that enthusiastic head of hers to fall into a sort of love" with her.[108] Partly from devotion to his wife, partly from natural impulse, Mr. Eckley longed to put his head under the Brownings' feet. Hearing that their new friends would summer in England, the Eckleys hoped to go with them. But the Brownings must spend all their time with their families. Seeing her friends off for France with a flood of tears and a shower of presents—a ring, a brooch, a traveler's bag, Damascus slippers, and a rosary from the Holy Sepulcher—Sophie and her husband set out once more for Bagni di Lucca.

The Brownings traveled by steamer from Leghorn to Marseilles and from Marseilles by express train to Paris, stopping overnight luxuriously at Lyons and Dijon. There, "in a passion of friendship," Robert "went out twice to stand before Maison Milsand (one of the shows of the town), and muse and bless the threshold."[109] Actually, Milsand was in the house at the moment, having come from Paris because of the grave illness of his mother. Within a few years the Brownings had experienced a revolution in travel. The horse carriages which had exhausted Elizabeth almost to the point of death had given way to swift, smooth trains which she found a positive "luxury." With hardly any companions in the carriages and novels provided by Isa Blagden, she was half sorry to arrive in Paris, and Robert, rising to the occasion by adapting his own poetry, wished they might travel on forever so.

Arriving in Paris on July 6, 1858, they stayed in the Rue St. Honoré at the Hôtel Hyacinthe, where Elizabeth lay on a sofa amid the ticking of many clocks. Their stay was pleasant and uneventful. Old Mr. Browning had forgotten Mrs. Von Müller and the law courts among the bookstalls of the Seine, and looked ten years younger. Robert himself vindicated homeopathy by demonstrating a fine appetite and "boasting of his influx of energies." They visited the paralyzed Lady Elgin, and, as they left, she signed to Robert, "as well as she could, that he should kiss her forehead before he went away. She was always so fond of Robert, as women are apt to be."[110] After a fortnight, the Brownings departed with Sarianna and Mr. Browning in search of a house along the Norman coast.

The rocky picturesqueness of Etretat attracted them, but prices were high and bathing was public. "The bay is so restricted that whoever takes a step is 'commanded' by all the windows of the primitive hotel and the few villas, and as people have nothing whatever to do but to look at you, you may imagine the perfection of the analysis."[111] Eventually they settled at Le Havre in a large, airy house close to the sea. Robert found a "hole" through which Elizabeth could crawl as a short-cut to the beach. Arabel, George, Henry Barrett, and his bride came to stay with them. Robert thought one was too much jostled on the street, and their house "in a hideous angle," so that the sea, though close, was invisible.[112] There were too many Brownings for Elizabeth to pursue her absorbing tête-à-tête with Arabel, and too many Barretts for Robert to be anything but very dull and idle. "I go mechanically out & in," he told Isa Blagden, "and get a day through—whereof not ten minutes have been my own—so much for your 'quantities of writing' (in expectation)—I began pretty zealously—but it's of no use now: nor will the world very greatly care."[113] On the other hand, he saw that Elizabeth was growing stronger. Each seems to have concealed his boredom from the other. Then Milsand came for ten "precious" days. After some two months, they left Le Havre with a sigh of relief. Elizabeth carried Arabel back to Paris with her for a few weeks of uninterrupted tête-à-tête and of "dissipation" among the shops.

Setting out on October 13 for Florence by way of Mont Cenis and Genoa, they had a journey as arduous as the last had been easy and pleasant. Elizabeth was exhausted by troubles with the diligences at St. Jean-de-Maurienne, ill with cold in the pass, and everybody was seasick between Genoa and Leghorn. The one, somewhat lugubrious interlude was a night at Chambéry, where, always devout and informed, they visited the shrine of Rousseau at Les Charmettes. "Robert played the 'Dream' on the old harpsichord, the keys of which rattled in a ghastly way, as if it were the bones of him who once so 'dreamed.'"[114]

CHAPTER 20

"The Cycle Is Complete"

1858-61

Arriving in late October, they found Florence bathed in sunshine. A few days after, snow fell. Should they seek a milder winter in Rome? While they debated, Elizabeth noted with some wonder that Mrs. Eckley "kept her family for weeks" in a Florentine hotel, waiting to see what they would do.[1] When they announced their intention, the Eckleys proved also to be going to Rome and to have an extra carriage for the Brownings and their servants. The Brownings accepted—and Elizabeth was rewarded with the present of an expensive pair of fur muffs. The journey—by way of Arezzo, Perugia, Spoleto, and Terni—was pleasant, luxurious, beautiful, and adventurous. Their horses were spirited, and once drew the carriage very nearly over a precipice, and another time, very nearly into a ditch. Then Mr. Eckley lent them his courier, who assisted the coachman on the box. "Such generosity and delicacy, combined with so much passionate sentiment!" exclaimed Elizabeth of both Eckleys. Later on, "there was a fight between our oxen-drivers, one of them attempting to stab the other with a knife, and Robert rushing in between till Peni and I were nearly frantic with fright."[2] They came safely into Rome on November 24, and rented their former apartment at 43 Bocca di Leone.

Elizabeth remained shut up in the house, keeping one eye on Roman fever and the other on the health of her son, who had just resolved to read at a gulp the whole of Dumas, with his father's favorite *Madame Bovary* for dessert. With gulps equally gigantic, Robert was swallowing Rome as his oyster. "I get up every morning in the dark at 1/4 6," he wrote Isa Blagden, "& go out with Eckley for a good hour before breakfast—we go all about Rome, up & down, in & out, the worst & best of it, so that I see it thoroughly on the outside & like it *so* much—so much more than last time: this practice, moreover, improves my health remarkably."[3] So remarkably that, according to

Elizabeth, "the loaf perishes by Gargantuan slices" at breakfast, and "a lark or two is no longer enough for dinner." He had also "plunged into gaieties of all sorts," going out not only every evening for a fortnight, but sometimes to several parties in the same evening. "So plenty of distraction," wrote Elizabeth, "and no Men and Women." She could not otherwise disapprove: "dissipations decidedly agree with Robert."[4] And indeed he was fully himself in all but his poetic faculty.

The city was rapidly filling up with nobility. In February 1859, the Prince of Wales arrived. Lady William Russell, mother of the English representative Odo Russell, informed the Brownings that the young man, then only seventeen, was not to go to balls, but to do his lessons and converse with men of distinction. Sure enough, his governor Colonel Bruce called at 43 Bocca di Leone and explained that *"it would be gratifying to the Queen that the Prince should make Mr. Browning's acquaintance."*[5] Robert left cards at Colonel Bruce's in return. There was an interval of five or six weeks and then a "command" to dine with the prince on Friday. Elizabeth reminded Robert of his republican principles and his impulsive ineptitude in paying compliments. "He said the other day to Mrs. Story: 'I had a delightful evening yesterday at your house. *I never spoke to you once.*'"[6] The experience was less trying than he expected. The prince, "a fair, gentle youth, with a frank open countenance," listened intelligently, asked a few questions—and Robert "found himself talking quite naturally of the wrongs of Italy."

That subject was once more in everybody's thoughts. Since the disaster at Novara, that statesman of genius, Count Camillo Benso Cavour, had been building up the power and prestige of Piedmont. He improved agriculture and industry, strengthened the army, sent 15,000 troops to aid France and England in the Crimea—where they won a victory at Tchernaya—and was invited at the end of the war to the Congress of Paris. There, after isolating Austria, he attempted to interest his allies in Italian freedom. He would have preferred England's aid, because she would have asked for no territory in return, but England—to Elizabeth's great indignation—wanted to keep the peace. The promise of Nice and Savoy, however, did secure the support of France. Accordingly, on January 10, 1859, the King of Piedmont declared from the throne that he could not remain deaf to the cry of pain that reached him from all Italy. Everybody saw that war was inevitable. Elizabeth watched events like a bird fascinated by a snake. "My interest in Italian politics has set me eating my heart lately; and verily the diet has been bitter."[7] One of her few visitors and a new hero was the Marquis D'Azeglio, the Piedmontese ambassador to Rome: "a noble chivalrous head, and that largeness of political *morale* which I find nowhere among statesmen, except in the head of the French government."[8] However noble and chivalrous his head, D'Azeglio had been displaced as prime minister of Piedmont by Cavour.

With a genius for doing the wrong thing at the wrong time, Austria on April 23 sent Piedmont an ultimatum to disarm. She refused, and Austria declared war. France then declared war on Austria. "Louis Napoleon has acted—I was going to say—sublimely—and why should I not?"[9] By land and sea, French troops poured into Piedmont and Italy. "I pass through cold stages of anxiety and white heats of rage," Elizabeth told Isa. "Robert accuses me of being 'glad' that the new 'Times' correspondent has been suddenly seized with Roman fever. It is I who have the true fever—in my brain and heart."[10] Arabel wrote in alarm about their money in the Tuscan funds. Neither Elizabeth nor even Robert was alarmed. "We are not likely to suffer when the crisis is over."[11]

Meanwhile, Robert sat for a portrait to Leighton; both sat for drawings to Field Talfourd. Elizabeth's had been commissioned by her friend Ellen Heaton, a fact which Mrs. Eckley regarded as a "slight" to herself. Elizabeth was used to such rivalries between her intimate friends, yet was becoming oppressed by the voracious, bribing friendship of Mrs. Eckley. "My fault with her," she explained to Arabel, "is that I have to keep my hands and pockets open to be filled with gifts. Really it is quite painful." She had constantly to be alert to ward off generosity. "'Do you like those mosaic buttons for jackets?' 'No,' I say, 'not at all.'"[12] Yet Elizabeth still thought her "a pure, sweet, & noble nature." Another pure, sweet, and noble nature had recently proved disappointing. Julia Ward Howe, reformer, idealist, and author of "The Battle Hymn of the Republic," had in 1854 sent the Brownings a volume of verse called *Passion Flowers.* It had been intercepted by a friend, so that their acknowledgment was long delayed. Mrs. Howe's next volume, *Words for the Hour* (1858), contained two poems attacking them. The second, "One Word More With E.B.B.," attributed Elizabeth's achievements to her use of drugs:

I shrink before the nameless draught
That helps to such unearthly things,
And if a drug could lift so high,
I would not trust its treacherous wings.[13]

Elizabeth told Mrs. Eckley that she felt only pity, but Robert once more felt the need to relieve his feelings. Mrs. Howe's sister was the wife of his friend the American sculptor Crawford, who lived in Rome. On January 7, 1859, he wrote Isa: "I called a few days ago on Mrs Crawford—in order to show how much I despised her sister Mrs Howe. . . . I find out people soon enough & know just what they will do one day to us, if they have the chance. Mrs C. looked black & disconsolate enough, poor thing."[14] Late in May, the Brownings returned to Florence with the Eckleys. The country was "like a solitude between Rome and Sienna." They drove fast.

As they came into Florence they found the French encamped in the meadows of the Cascine. Pen waved his hat out the window and shouted "Viva!" The city itself "was winged with tricolor flags from every window, and there was quite a murmur of festivity and triumph in the streets. . . . The feeling toward the Emperor is beautiful to see. It is an enthusiasm of gratitude."[15] When they were settled in Casa Guidi, Pen hung a great Italian tricolor at one end of the terrace and a great French tricolor at the other, keeping between them a small movable flag, which he intended to take out in the carriage sometimes. "If I were a great boy and hadn't a wife," he declared, adding the second condition in imitation of Ferdinando, "certainly I would go and fight for dear Italy."[16] Robert was quick to bring such motive power to bear on Pen's education. Himself contributing ten scudi a month to the cause, he gave Pen half a pound a day for the same purpose if he did well in his lessons. Pen composed poetry, even an opera, and continued to find his lessons a bore.[17]

The Grand Duke had once more fled from the Pitti in April. The cabinet, the communes, and a representative assembly had all declared for annexation to an Italian kingdom under Victor Emmanuel. From the front came news of a great victory over the Austrians at Magenta on June 4, and a still greater one at Solferino on June 24.

At this point Elizabeth could neither eat nor sleep, nor indeed do anything but think, read, talk, and argue about the war. She lived only in the wrongs of Italy, the exploits of the emperor, and the crimes of his enemies. Did Robert see no cause for alarm in the "insistent voice and fixed eye," observed by their old friend Story, nor in the whole manner and speech of one who entertained her convictions "as a malady and a doom?"[18] Perhaps he was helpless. Perhaps he thought her by now strong enough to bear the excitement. Certainly he was himself deeply involved in that excitement; and, though a good deal less trustful than she of Napoleon, he was only a little less bitter against the Derby government in England. Elizabeth knew she suffered both physically and spiritually from her obsession; though how passionately and crudely she had projected on the complex realities of politics the pattern of romance—of a beautiful woman weeping in chains, of an ogre applying the whip, and a knight riding up in shining armor and ideals to the rescue—she could not of course suspect. Her personal life was not without distress ironically similar. "Imagine my horror, when after a cheerful meeting with Wilson the night of our arrival, she came to me afterward in my room, and I found her to be *quite mad.*" From reading the Bible, Wilson had learned that the world was soon coming to an end, that she was "too near in blood" to live with Ferdinando any more, and that her two sons, Orestes and Pilades, were the "first fruit of the first resurrection."[19] Elizabeth listened to her former servant's words uttered with a fixed, mad expression and in a voice of intense conviction. Wilson now kept a boarding house in the city. Apparently no one suspected. Robert advised Elizabeth to warn Ferdinando.

Meanwhile, political realities were about to declare themselves. The Allies had lost 17,000 men at Solferino, and Napoleon III had not his uncle's stomach for corpses. Prussia had massed 400,000 soldiers on the Rhine, and England was full of grave concern for the peace of Europe and the useful well-being of her old ally Austria. At the same time Napoleon had accomplished more than he intended. What he really wanted was military glory at low cost and three prosperous Italian kingdoms under the protection of France, rather than a dozen poverty-stricken vassals under the tyranny of Austria. In the genius of Cavour he now recognized a force that bade fair to create a strong nation on his southern border. On July 8 he met with the Emperor Franz Josef at Villafranca and concluded an armistice. Austria ceded Lombardy to France, and France handed it over to Piedmont. Eventually France would receive Nice and Savoy in return.

Under this vision of truth Elizabeth collapsed. Of the physical symptoms, she wrote more than a month afterward: "Violent palpitations and cough; in fact, the worst attack on the chest I ever had in Italy. For two days and two nights it was more like *angina pectoris*, as I have heard it described; but this went off, and the complaint ran into its ancient pattern, thank God." Of what she suffered inwardly—what frantic, futile marches of the mind up and down the paths of its beloved illusion, what pathetic glimmers of the unattainable on the precipices of sleep—one has glimpses: "I dreamed lately that I followed a mystic woman down a long suite of palatial rooms. She was in white, with a white mask, on her head the likeness of a crown. I knew she was Italy, but I couldn't see through the mask. All through my illness political dreams have repeated themselves, in inscrutable articles of peace and eternal provisional governments. Walking on the mountains of the moon, hand in hand with a Dream more beautiful than them all, then falling suddenly on the hard earth-ground on one's head, no wonder that one should suffer. Oh, Isa, the tears are even now in my eyes to think of it!"

One grievance and one illusion she could not give up. "*I* never will forgive England the most damnable part she has taken on Italian affairs, never."[20] There spoke her father's daughter. For one moment indeed she did doubt that the French emperor was unselfishly devoted to Italian liberty; and as for one day his busts had disappeared from the public places of Florence, she insisted the reluctant Peni take off his Napoleon medal. But then she saw her hero "did at Villafranca what he could not help but do. Since then, . . . he is walking under the earth instead of on the earth, but *straight* and to unchanged ends."[21]

For three weeks Robert tended her night and day with unremitting care and tenderness. But still she "could do nothing but weep and talk in impotent rages."[22] At length, Robert, the doctor, and Elizabeth herself saw that she must be removed not only from the stifling summer heat, but from the scene of excitement and the friends with whom she talked politics. Robert proposed the high, windy hills outside Siena. "Her strength," he wrote Mrs. Eckley, "was absolutely *gone*—she was carried down-stairs, carried into the railway-carriage, carried up to bed in the Hôtel—and she left Florence in so pitiable a state that Grisanowski set off by the next train and spent two days at the Hôtel with us to be of any use he might."[23] For their abode, Dr. Grisanowski himself selected "a wild, rough old villa" with plenty of room, wind, and quiet.[24]

Meanwhile, besides nursing Elizabeth, managing the household and teaching Pen all his lessons, Robert was actually taking care of Walter Savage Landor. The year before at Bath, the eighty-three-year-old poet had, as usual, with the fresh, passionate impatience of a child been fretting and fuming away at the minor tribulations of an easy life. Suddenly, as though waking from a dream, he realized that he was being robbed of paintings and money by a clergyman's wife and a young girl of whom he had become fond. At once he began to erupt satirical verses against the clergyman's wife. A pamphlet of these appeared in print. He was saved from a libel suit by a retraction urged on him by Forster. Unfortunately, the old man was not clear in the head. Try as he would, he could not keep some of the libels out of *Dry Sticks*, a volume of verse he was seeing through the press. The volume appeared. He was sued and found guilty. Flying before the consequences, he came to rest at last—after an absence of thirty-three years—in the bosom of his family at Fiesole. The family quarrel was resumed as though never interrupted. Playing the gentleman of inflexible patience, the poet listened imperturbably to his wife's endless invectives at dinner, but he suspected her of having the ornamental lions at the villa gate repainted, and his favorite terrace torn up, just to annoy him. When he accused her of these crimes, she turned him out of the house with an order never to come back. Shabby and ill, with only a few pauls in his pocket, the old man set out in the burning sun for Casa Guidi. Browning happened to meet him in the street, heard his story, and took him home. After some illuminating interviews with Mrs. Landor, Robert arranged through Forster a guardianship, supported by modest funds from Landor's brothers in England. When after Elizabeth's collapse Robert took her to Siena, Landor came also to be a guest of the Storys, who occupied a villa nearby. "It was the case of old Lear over again," said Story. Landor had of course been playing the role with immense gusto and self-pity.

"We look at scarlet sunsets, over purple hills, and have the wind nearly all day," wrote Elizabeth.[25] Except for Landor and the Storys, their solitude was absolute. Somewhat to her own surprise, she began to recover. She ate solid foods, moved from the bed to the sofa, swayed and staggered a few steps on Robert's arm, walked, and at last took carriage rides through the countryside. Meanwhile, Landor was setting her a prodigious example. Moved after three weeks at the Storys' to a little cottage about a stone's throw from the Brownings' Villa Alberti, he was clearing his head and restoring his body by eating enormous omelettes, walking in the garden, and tranquilly savoring his anger. "The poor old lion," observed Elizabeth indulgently, "is very quiet on the whole, roaring softly, to beguile the time, in Latin alcaics against his wife and Louis Napoleon."[26] Having no gratitude and affection invested in Landor, she could see him clearly—as Robert could not. "Robert always said that he owed more as a writer to Landor than to any contemporary." Naturally, she pitied the nurse more than the invalid. "Dear darling Robert amuses me by talking of his 'gentleness and sweetness.' A most courteous and refined gentleman he is, of course, and very affectionate to Robert (as he ought to be), but of self-restraint he has not a grain, and of suspiciousness many grains. . . . What do you say to dashing down a plate on the floor when you don't like what's on it?"[27]

Robert kept an eye on his two invalids, on the war, on the effect of the war on them. Rising every morning before six, he walked the two miles to Siena, read the news on the city-hall door, and brought it first to the Storys and then—perhaps after some editing—farther down the road to the Villa Alberti. Under his loving surveillance, Elizabeth was becoming a more rational, less neurotic Italian patriot. Odo Russell stopped off at Villa Alberti, and managed, with the tact of a Whig aristocrat, to give the news to Elizabeth's satisfaction. Apparently his one mistake was to view England's faults with patience.

But what of Landor's mistakes? He was growing day by day more formidably himself. Further negotiations with Mrs. Landor—conducted in part by Seymour Kirkup—had brought about the arrival of a rough linen bag, from which had emerged "a blue coat with brass buttons, a beflowered waist coat, and a frilled shirt, which," wrote Edith Story, "he put on in my honour, saying that he and Count d'Orsay had had them made exactly alike to wear at Lady Blessington's marriage."[28] Landor's conversation was also a Regency piece. "Every evening," wrote Story, "we sit on our lawn under the ilexes and cypresses and take our tea and talk until the moon has made the circuit of the quarter of the sky."[29] Elizabeth, carried by Robert, frequently made her appearance. Landor talked mostly of thirty or forty years ago. "Mrs. Browning was often convulsed with laughter at his scorching invective and his extraordinary quick ejaculations, perpetual God-bless-my-souls, &c! . . .His stories were admirably told, full of point and often of pathos. His mention of Rose Aylmer—and he often mentioned her—always brought tears to his eyes, if not to ours; for there with her he had evidently buried his heart."[30] But sometimes his "scorching invective" would be directed against Napoleon III. Edith Story remembered how "Mrs. Browning, with her face hidden under her large hat and curls, would be stirred past endurance by these assaults on her hero who was her 'Emperor evermore,' and would raise her treble voice even to a shrill pitch in protest, until Mr. Browning would come into the fray as mediator."[31] Indeed Elizabeth's old vehemence was just below the surface. When H. F. Chorley dedicated to her his novel *Roccabella,* in which the chief villain is an Italian patriot, she thanked him with somewhat forced courtesy in the intervals of sharp criticism and bitter irony. At one point she wrote, "I dissent from you, dissent from you, dissent from you."[32]

In October the Brownings returned to Florence. Robert was "picturesque" in "a moustache and beard" together; and Elizabeth, so "right in looks and ways" that the doctor opened his eyes. Still, he forbade another winter in Florence. The Brownings decided to leave for Rome as soon as Landor had been settled. For a time he refused to be settled; he wanted to live in a hut in Viareggio. At length he returned, grumbling about the ugliness of Florence. A caretaker was found in Wilson—not so very mad after all—and a lodging, not far from Casa Guidi, in a little house under the city wall just back of the Carmine. "Rooms small," pronounced Elizabeth, "but with a look out into a little garden; quiet and cheerful."[33] Landor had quarreled with Forster, because Forster would not permit further lampooning of the clergyman's wife. He was attracted to Wilson by the sweetness of her voice, but she also objected to having a platter of mutton thrown out the window. "There is," Browning wrote Forster with plaintive surprise, "some inexplicable fault in his temper, whether natural or acquired, which seems to render him very difficult to manage."[34] He was not told until almost the last moment about the Brownings' winter in Rome.

Because of Landor, the Brownings did not leave Florence until November 28; but the weather was warm, and finding that Elizabeth bore up well, Robert thoroughly enjoyed the journey, beguiling two days with the two volumes of Hugo's *La Légende des siècles.* "He gives you *panforte* for the sacramental wafer," complained Browning; and the preface, blown up with a portentous and self-conscious modesty, was "one big bubble of mere breath." All three Brownings were much interested in the performance of Pen's new pony on the journey, who ended each day, Robert noted professionally, "fresh as at starting and without having turned a hair."[35] Pen had been given the pony in Siena, after elaborate negotiation with each parent separately and then together. One suspects, however, that Robert had won a victory: he was devoted to riding—and no doubt to what riding might do for his son. He was fiercely proud of Pen's skill in riding and swimming. "My boy swims capitally," he had boasted more than once to Chapman the previous summer.[36]

The Storys met them just outside Rome and accompanied them to their hotel. Later they found them lodgings in 28 Via del Tritone. "Four front rooms in the sun," Elizabeth wrote Isa, "besides 'verge enough' for the domesticity behind; two salons very nicely furnished and a dining-room—secondo piano—fifty scudi."[37] The French garrison were thought to be leaving at any moment: Rome was apprehensive, restive, full of rumors, empty of people—and consequently cheap.

Nursing Elizabeth in Rome and Landor in Florence, Robert began a very unpromising winter. Soon after their arrival, they drove in a closed carriage to Castellani the jeweler's shop to see some swords presented by Romans to Napoleon III and Victor Emmanuel. Received with flattering attention, they viewed the exhibit, dispensed autographs, and returned with much glory—and a cold for Elizabeth. "All my bad symptoms came back," she told Fanny Haworth. "Suffocations, singular heart action, cough tearing one to atoms."[38] Listening to the cough, Robert had little patience for the letters he received in abundance from and about Landor. The old man was now quarreling with his staircase, on which he daily threatened to break his neck. He had offered his landlord twenty percent down to improve it. "I would prefer even a mason's ladder," he wrote Browning.[39] Meanwhile, frightened at living in the same house with a tiger, Wilson had taken once more to looking at pictures of the Last Judgment in the churches and was thinking about the end of the world. "A grasshopper's is the stouter soul of the two," Browning wrote Isa in utter disillusionment.[40]

Robert had particular reason to be impatient with grasshopper souls. Four days after he and Elizabeth arrived in Rome, they had met through the Storys Theodore Parker, Unitarian minister of Boston and one of the most remarkable Americans alive. Parker read books, accumulated facts, made friends, influenced people, understood business, commerce, and industry as easily and naturally as he breathed. Quite as naturally, he subordinated these magnificent practical gifts and acquisitions to conscience and aspirations. His object had been to make a somewhat secularized and modernized Kingdom of Heaven prevail in the United States—there was scarcely a major abuse against which he had not launched a massive, superbly eloquent one-man propaganda campaign—while, behind the scenes, in the intimacy of his innumerable friendships, he had scolded senators and investigated the consciences of governors. Ostensibly, Parker had come to Italy to be cured of tuberculosis. Actually, he had come to die of overwork. No invalid was ever so strenuous.

"What a masterly statement! What a wonderful man!" exclaimed Elizabeth after hearing Parker expound and analyze a pamphlet.[41] Browning saw a great deal of Parker that winter. In many ways, the two men were much alike. Both were dynamos of energy, geysers of aspiration. Parker was a Unitarian. Browning had long been friendly to Unitarians. Both detested theology and scorned Calvinism. Both believed that man had an intuition of perfect, impersonal deity, though whereas Browning held that man needed deity also to be human and incarnate, Parker maintained that he anthropomorphized deity through a want of intelligence or culture—and the more so the lower in the evolutionary scale he stood, for Parker had just been reading Darwin's *Origin of Species*, published in November 1859.

Since *Men and Women* in 1855, Browning had apparently not written a single poem. He seemed to have accepted defeat. Here before him, in temperament and ideas much like himself, was a man to whom defeat was unthinkable. Indeed Parker may have provided not only an example but a subject. Just before his death, he began "A Bumblebee's Thoughts on the Plan and Purpose of the Universe," apparently aimed at the homocentrism of such theologians as Paley.

In an admirable article, C. R. Tracy[42] suggests "A Bumblebee's Thoughts" as the immediate source of "Caliban upon Setebos; or, Natural Theology in the Island." Of course, "Caliban" might have been composed any time between late 1859—when Darwin inspired Parker—and 1864—when Browning published his poem among *Dramatis Personae.* The ape-man or missing link was if anything even more notorious in the early sixties, when Huxley had defended his ancestors against the Bishop of Oxford and published *Man's Place in Nature.* But, in the early sixties, Browning wrote poetry with less irony and color. And indeed "Caliban," as theology from an animal or evolutionary perspective, is obviously very much like "The Bumblebee." It is certainly a satire of the narrow, vindictive anthropomorphism of the Calvinists:

> 'Thinketh, such shows nor right nor wrong in Him,
> Nor kind, nor cruel: He is strong and Lord.
> 'Am strong myself compared to yonder crabs
> That march now from the mountain to the sea;
> 'Let twenty pass, and stone the twenty-first,
> Loving not, hating not, just choosing so. . . .'[43]

How far is "Caliban" a satire of characteristically Darwinian ideas —of the survival of the fittest and the elaborately interdependent economy of dog-eat-dog? Such satire is faintly suggested by the sinister, savage beauty of the island and by the passage describing animals hunting, which concludes:

> He made all these and more,
> Made all we see, and us, in spite: how else?[44]

Having read *In Memoriam* carefully, Browning must have had some inkling of "nature red in tooth and claw." On the whole, however, he seems to have understood Darwin only later, if at all. Evidence of Darwin's view—the luxuriant, ticklish multitudinous life that climbs through the mire, the snapshot impressions of exotic animals hunting exotic prey—is but the psychological data by which Browning lovingly depicted a subhuman monster and his world from the inside. Indeed "Caliban" could scarcely be, like "The Bumblebee," a satire of anthropomorphism *per se*, for Browning held that, on its highest level, anthropomorphism is natural and proper for man. Man must not only revere God as an abstract principle; he must love Him as a person. Christianity is unique in permitting man, at least ultimately, this double faith. Basically, "Caliban" is another optimistic study of evil. Thoughts that grovel in the slime may yet reach to the stars. If Caliban's soul lies in the grip of the biblical and Miltonic Belial, it may yet win release from horrendous shackles.[45] The Quiet clearly involves recognition of God as a moral principle; and even Setebos, though now anthropomorphic in the bad sense, may grow into goodness, "as grubs grow butterflies" (l. 248). In this sense, Caliban's case is better than Cleon's: he can see the possibility of Christianity.

On March 12, 1860, Elizabeth's *Poems before Congress* were published in a slender octavo volume by Chapman and Hall. Composed partly in the ecstasy before Villafranca, partly in the revulsion that followed, they are a poignant record of art and reason struggling with folly, rage, and bitterness. All contain admirable passages. "An August Voice," in which Napoleon ironically offers the Florentines their Grand Duke back, is full of vigorous satire. What is impressive throughout—but particularly in the preface—is the insistence that nations must rise above their jealous and parochial selfishness to a genuine internationalism. Elizabeth fails to see that politics must be political, but at least she approaches a rational, coherent view of her position. On the other hand, she is still too intemperate to practice what she preaches. No partisanship is so violent as her own. She flaunts her adoration of the emperor and cannot conceal her animosity against England. There is much eager talk of blood, wounds, and death; an underlying suggestion, perhaps, that beautiful Italian women would like to repay French and Italian heroism with their favors. To make the unity of the book doubtful, there is a final poem—"A Curse for a Nation"—in which, in a kind of rhetorical hysteria, an angel curses the southern American states for practicing slavery. Almost equally mysterious was the book's title, for the congress of leading powers, planned for early 1860, never took place.

"I expect to be torn to pieces by English critics," wrote Elizabeth. She was. In fact, English commonsense about the war was itself somewhat neurotic. Lord Houghton explained the matter in Paris with beautiful simplicity. *"We want, first, that the Austrians should beat you French thoroughly; next, we want that the Italians should be free, and then we want them to be very grateful to us for doing nothing towards it."*[46] Upon most Englishmen, turning calmly from their newspapers to their poetry, Elizabeth's little volume burst like a shriek from Bedlam. That this shriek proceeded from the romantic and admirable Mrs. Browning only made matters worse. In the tone of letters to *The Times* protesting cruelty to an animal, reviewers read her lectures on manners, patriotism, and the proper sphere of woman. Nearly all agreed that her poetry was as bad as her politics. Still smarting under her sarcasms against his *Roccabella,* Chorley of *The Athenaeum* found intemperance and bad writing everywhere but particularly in the last poem, in which he supposed the curse to be directed against England rather than the southern states. Hurt by so potently unjust a review from a friend, Elizabeth wrote *The Athenaeum* explaining the direction of the curse. *The Athenaeum* did not print her letter but simply reported the situation in a paragraph, suggesting that its mistake had been rather natural. Robert was of course furious with Chorley. As usual, his anger bestialized its object. "Chorley's cat-scratch was offensive from the creature's spitting at the same time," he told Isa.[47] Elizabeth later wrote Chorley a frank, warm letter of reconciliation, received an answer in the same spirit, and then read him a last gentle lecture on Italy and Villafranca, of which one sentence is poignant: "A calm scholastic Italian friend of ours said to my husband at the peace, '*It's sad to think how the madhouses will fill after this.*' "[48]

Meanwhile, Italy was fitting together like the pieces of a more-than-half-solved puzzle, divulging both good and evil. In July 1859, Garibaldi and his volunteers had conquered Sicily. In the same month Napoleon III presented his bill—a formal request, on the condition of a favorable plebiscite, for Nice and Savoy. Elizabeth was pained. Besides, she had to hear Robert say, "It was a great action; but he has taken eighteenpence for it, which is a pity."[49] Momentarily, she descended from knight-errantry to politics for an exoneration: since Italy was to become a powerful nation, Napoleon owed it to his country to extend her territories to the natural barrier of the Alps.

One sees how deeply Robert was involved in public events from the fact that his ardor for Italy overcame his repugnance to write. "Robert and I began to write on the Italian question," Elizabeth apprised

Sarianna, "and our plan was (Robert's own suggestion!) to publish jointly. When I showed him my ode on Napoleon he observed that I was gentle to England in comparison to what he had been, but after Villafranca (the Palmerston Ministry having come in) he destroyed his poem and left me alone."[50] In short, his poem was harshly critical of English Tory policy. That same winter in Rome he roughly sketched out a monologue highly critical of his wife's hero. Eventually it became *Prince Hohenstiel-Schwangau.* On January 1, 1872, he wrote Edith Story, "I really . . . conceived the poem, twelve years ago in the Via del Tritone—in a little handbreadth of prose."[51] Certainly, from Villafranca to 1871, when he wrote the poem, Napoleon did nothing to impress Browning. He was not a man of steady vision: even at the moment a French garrison was blocking the Italian unity which he had himself set in motion. In him Browning saw the opportunist, the adventurer, and the voluptuary. Probably he knew too little of internal French politics to recognize the champion of progress and the "Saint-Simon on horseback."

Elizabeth's health did not improve with the political situation. On March 17, 1860, Mrs. Jameson died, leaving "a blot more on the world" for her.[52] Robert also was deeply grieved—at the same time angry with Gerardine Macpherson for sending the news directly to Elizabeth, along with some photographs. With a still greater shock Elizabeth finally allowed herself to discover the wickedness of Mrs. Eckley. Her fault was a vanity "monstrous enough to present a large foundation for an extraordinary falseness of character."[53] Mrs. Eckley had maintained her close intimacy with Elizabeth partly by practicing deceptions as a medium. Robert had long suspected her and repeatedly warned Elizabeth in the spirit of his letter to Miss de Gaudrion.

Here was a medium caught red-handed. A tempting subject, yet of course he could not ridicule a lady. Fortunately, his old enemy Home was once more astonishing Europe with his exploits. Elizabeth reports that Robert "has been writing a good deal this winter—working at a long poem which I have not seen a line of, and producing short lyrics which I *have* seen, and may declare worthy of him."[54] The long poem was almost without doubt the extremely disagreeable "Mr. Sludge, 'The Medium'." Not only is the speaker repulsive, but his auditor and victim, Hiram Horsefall, seems as absurd and unsympathetic as his name suggests. Here the first-person voice has a curious action. Particularly at the outset, one feels in the flattering, propitiating self-abasement of Sludge not so much the scornful triumph of Horsefall as the fierce enjoyment of Browning himself. One feels the angry pursuit of sordid motives, the gusto in cringing villainy detected. One savors the accumulation of repugnant animal imagery as Sludge describes himself through the eyes of disillusioned clients. As the monologue proceeds, however, the first person recovers its self-justifying sympathy-magnetizing functions. A natural medium, Sludge had even as a boy been tempted into deceit by the eager credulity of those he attracted. A world of determined dupes had made him a sharper—and here again, as in "Bishop Blougram," one feels a hostile attitude toward the reader. Nor is Sludge totally perverted or deluded. His trade has taught him, though in somewhat debased form, the importance of the unseen, of religion, in human life. He goes on to express a good many of Browning's own ideas. He is an aspect of the poet's optimism. Like Caliban, from his habitat he can still see up to the stars. Significantly, Sludge reverses the logic of the letter to Miss de Gaudrion. Instead of the medium debasing the auditor, the auditor debases the medium. Probably this reversal is in large part due to the rationale of the first person. Still, one thinks of a later remark of Robert's to Isa: refusing to open her eyes, Elizabeth deserved to be hoodwinked by Mrs. Eckley.[55]

In his spare time, Robert rode a great deal with Pen, talked politics with Odo Russell, had mysterious contacts with Sicilian patriots, and in the evenings sometimes investigated Bohemia with two young painters. One of these, Val Prinsep, has described two expeditions. On the first, they witnessed a poetical contest: "Gigi (the host) had furnished a first-rate dinner, and his usual tap of excellent wine. . . . The *Osteria* had filled; the combatants were placed opposite each other on either side of a small table. . . . For a moment the two poets eyed each other like two cocks seeking an opportunity to engage. Then through the crowd a stalwart carpenter, a constant attendant of Gigi's, elbowed his way. He leaned over the table with a hand on each shoulder, and in a neatly turned couplet he then addressed the rival bards. 'You two,' he said, 'for the honour of Rome, must do your best, for there is now listening to you a great Poet from England.' "[56] On a second expedition to the same restaurant when Story was along, they hired a little band of musicians, which was rendering the Hymn to Garibaldi with traitorous fervor when the police arrived. The police accepted a drink and ignored the treason. Browning's party—and the four musicians—set off in two carriages to see the Colosseum by moonlight. The story of that festive night's progress was one which Browning loved to tell.

June 1860 found them back in Florence for a month before leaving for the Villa Alberti outside Siena. Landor looked more Jovian than ever. "He has the most beautiful sea-foam of a beard you ever saw," exclaimed Elizabeth, "all in a curl and white bubblement of beauty."[57] When Kirkup tried to convert him to spiritualism, Landor responded with such unquenchable Olympian laughter that even Kirkup heard. Yet his laughter expressed no happiness. He took satisfaction in finding nothing satisfactory in his life—except when Robert kept him soothed "by quoting his own works to him."[58] Elizabeth felt that his genius and his gratitude to Robert gave him a claim on her sympathy, but "he is so selfish, so self-adoring, and so little earnest."[59] Robert was at the moment philosophical about the old man. "Whatever he may profess," he told Forster, "the thing he really loves is a pretty girl to talk nonsense with."[60] The pretty girl of the moment was the American Kate Field, who simply adored old literary lions. Another visitor brought Robert good news. In Florence to moderate the expenditures of the novelist Charles Lever, Edward Chapman's son reported that *Men and Women* was selling better and that a new edition would soon be wanted. Elizabeth was momentarily entranced by the romantic, popular heroism of Garibaldi. "We are all talking and dreaming Garibaldi just now in great anxiety," Elizabeth told Sarianna. "Scarcely since the world was a world has there been such a feat of arms. All modern heroes grow pale before him."[61]

Once more in Siena, the Brownings looked forward to a restful summer among old friends. The Storys were down the road in a villa; Isa Blagden was in a rough cabin fifteen minutes' walk away, and Landor was with Wilson close by in a cottage. They were scarcely settled when Elizabeth learned that Henrietta was painfully ill of an internal growth. Elizabeth must have feared cancer and thought how much Kenyon had suffered as he sat in the garden at Ventnor whispering softly, "My God, my God!" "The thought of that pain is the worst thought I have to bear—" she wrote George. "If anything here ever approaches with me to a pleasurable feeling . . . if I look at the blue hills, or hear Penini's musical chatter, or get news even of our triumphant Italy,—instantly comes the idea . . . 'My precious Henrietta is in great pain at this moment perhaps.' "[62] At first she wanted to go at once to England, but "everyone here and there was against it." One bitter thought led to another. "My 'destiny' has always been to be entirely useless to the people I should like to help (except to my little Pen sometimes in pushing him through his lessons, and even so the help seems doubtful, scholastically speaking, to Robert!)."[63] And was she not a heavy drag upon Robert's freedom of movement?

Living wretchedly in the shadow of Henrietta's illness, the Brownings returned to Florence on October 11 and began to prepare for another winter in Rome. Through October Henrietta seemed to suffer less. Elizabeth revived and began to worry about the Mazzinians plotting at Garibaldi's elbow. Toward the middle of November she was nearly prostrated by very foreboding news from George. Robert understood what George was keeping back, and, deciding he must get Elizabeth to the warmer climate before the final shock came, he persuaded her to leave for Rome the next day. He knew also, as he wrote George, that the "necessity for exertion would do good." The journey was made in an agony of suspense; the letters awaiting them at Rome reported no change. Then came days of silence. Robert telegraphed Florence and Taunton. From Florence came five notes of George's "kept back through the infamous negligence of the officials." Not until December 3 did they learn that Henrietta had died on November 23, the day Robert had telegraphed. But Robert felt no indignation whatever at the slow arrival of the final news. It had been part of his plan to give Elizabeth as much time as possible to prepare herself. "She has borne it, on the whole," he wrote George, "as well as I should have thought possible."[64]

To Isa he wrote, "There is little more to suffer—it is better than the suspense of the last ten days. You know Ba's ways—know she hides herself in such a trouble as this: she has seen nobody yet."[65] Or, as he had explained to George, "The wounds in that heart never heal altogether, tho' they may film over."[66] The truth was that the lives of all the Barretts, as well as the features of Italy and France, were woven into the fibers of that heart. Moreover, the heart was proudly, morbidly self-conscious in its suffering. In her letter of condolence to Surtees, she said, as though contesting property in Henrietta and her death: "And though I do confess, Surtees, that your loss is the greater (seeing that she was closer to you & loved you above all) yet mine goes back further into the past and devastates my memories of life & youth."[67] In her fears, her suffering, her capacity to die by inches, one sees the same tenacious sense of unique claim as in the drastic, pseudo-religious tyranny of her father.

From then onward—though she tried to be good, to "eat a little, listen to talking, attend to Pen, & so on"[68]—she was pointed toward death. "I struggle hard to live on," she told Fanny Haworth.[69] Her letters to old friends conclude with valedictory expressions of love: "Yes, I love you, dearest Isa, and shall for ever."[70] She wrote Mrs. Martin: "I believe that love in its most human relations is an eternal thing." She continued to seek comfort in spiritualism: "Also there are other beliefs with me with regard to the spiritual world and the measuring of death, which ought, if I had ordinary logic, to rescue me from what people in general suffer in circumstances like these. Only I am weak and foolish; and when the tender past came back to me day by day, I have dropped down before it as one inconsolable."[71] To protect her at least in some degree from the assaults of the past, and with her consent, Robert had since early autumn been censoring all letters from England. That from Surtees was totally censored. But, whether she read the letters or not, the dead past drew her thoughts backward and downward into the darkness. "Ba is very low & weak," Robert wrote Isa on December 27, "she will get over this grief in some respects but it wears her still—such a wretched Christmas Day did we have."[72]

Across her dark thoughts, Elizabeth watched Robert and Pen admiringly, lovingly. Pen was now instructed in Latin by a kindly abbé, but coached in music and arithmetic by Robert, in German by Elizabeth. He had gone to a children's party at the French ambassador's. He had encountered the French troops, marched in rank with them, discussed Chopin and Stephen Heller with the musical officers, and in his character of small boy been brought safely home. In spite of the Pope, Garibaldi, the Emperor, and the King of Italy, Rome was once more gay: there were parties and Robert went to them "free from responsibility of crinoline—while I go early to bed, too happy to have him a little amused."[73] Next morning Elizabeth and Pen heard his adventures. There was "a great ball at Mrs. Hooker's—magnificent. . . . All the princes in Rome (and even cardinals) present. . . . The princess Ruspoli (a Buonaparte) appeared in the tricolor. She is most beautiful, Robert says."[74]

Robert became positively stout, and Elizabeth tilted with Sarianna over his current degree of beauty. Receiving a photograph of him—plump, gray-bearded, bushy-headed, solemn-eyed—Sarianna complained with a sister's boldness that the cut of his hair made him look like an *épicier*. Considerably offended in her trusteeship, his wife entered at length on the niceties of beard and side-whiskers, concluding almost defiantly: "He is not thin or worn, as I am—no indeed—and the women adore him everywhere far too much for decency. In my own opinion he is infinitely handsomer and more attractive than when I saw him first."[75] She had told George with amusement that when Robert wrote his old friend Arnould a letter of condolence on the death of his wife, Sir Joseph had replied that "he had taken another wife 'young & pretty'!"[76] Elizabeth was quite willing to foresee Robert might do the same. Regarding a new will—not undertaken in anticipation of death—she wrote her brother George: "Agreed that Robert will probably survive me,—agreed even, on my side, that he may remarry . . . being a man . . . nay, 'being subject to like passions' as other men, he *may* commit some faint show of bigamy—who knows?"[77] Indeed, both her letter and Robert's—enclosed in the same envelope and each meant for George's eyes alone—express the deepest mutual trust and understanding.

Coming a few months before her death, Elizabeth's letter to Sarianna is curiously significant: in momentous form defending Robert's haircut, she goes on to defend her whole responsibility for him—as man and poet—to the woman who was to be his companion for the rest of his life. This winter Robert had taken up modeling under Story's direction—and written no poetry whatever. Elizabeth confesses that she has "struggled a little with him on this point." She has told him that "Tennyson is a regular worker, shuts himself up daily for so many hours." But now she accepts the fact that Robert must wait "for an inclination," must work "by fits and starts." The problem is to fill up the intervals. Mere reading "hurts him. As long as I have known him he has not been able to read long at a time." Only "an active occupation . . . saves him . . . from the process which I call beating his dear head against the wall till it is bruised, simply because he sees a fly there, magnified by his own two eyes almost indefinitely into some Saurian monster. He has an enormous superfluity of vital energy, and if it isn't employed, it strikes its fangs into him. . . . Nobody understands exactly why—except me who am in the inside of him and hear him breathe. For the peculiarity of our relation is, that even when he's displeased with me, he thinks aloud with me and can't stop himself. . . . Whatever takes him out of a certain circle (where habits of introvision and analysis of fly-legs are morbidly exercised), is life and joy to him." Last summer that life and joy was riding; now it is modeling. "The more tired he has been, and the more his back ached, poor fellow, the more he has exulted and been happy—'*no, nothing ever made him so happy before.*' "[78]

What Saurian monster—in his circular casuistries of self-accusation—had Robert been thinking aloud about? Some incurable obscurity, no doubt, some fatal want of gift which stood between him and a wide audience. The real Saurian monster, as Elizabeth well knew, was the British public, whose treatment of him had been "an infamy."[79] She had been thinking carefully about this matter for some time. "As a sort of lion," she had written the year before in a shrewd little estimate of her husband's whole position, "Robert has his range in society, and, for the rest, you should see Chapman's returns; while in America he's a power, a writer, a poet. He is read—he lives in the hearts of the people. 'Browning readings here' in Boston; 'Browning evenings' there."[80] In the letter to Sarianna, she once more recurs to his American popularity. Clearly it promised that England would one day be worthy of him.

In spite of her weakness and grief, Elizabeth continued to follow political events with the painful suspense of an overexcited child watching a melodrama too late at night. She almost never went out and saw few visitors, yet she did see the famous English liberal Sir John Bowring, who admired Napoleon and wished Italy well, and the great Italian doctor Diomede Pantaleoni, who, as a secret agent for Cavour, had been treating with some of the more liberal Cardinals. If the Cardinals could persuade the Pope to give up his temporal power, Napoleon might feel sufficiently armed against Catholic opinion in France to permit a united Italy. But the French emperor continued to struggle against the future he had fathered. Meanwhile, England, now under a liberal government, stood forth as the champion of Italy. When Cavour sent an army across the papal borders, England kept the continental powers from intervening; and when, having defeated the papal army commanded by the French general Lamoricière, the Piedmontese joined Garibaldi in the siege of Gaeta, England insisted that the emperor withdraw the fleet which had prevented the capture of the fortress. On November 7, 1860, Garibaldi and King Victor Emmanuel entered Naples together. On February 18, 1861, the first Italian parliament met in Turin. Viewing these events, Elizabeth neither abjured her emperor nor forgave England. She rejoiced in victory but not so much as she grieved when, returning to Florence on June 5 after an arduous journey, she heard next day of the sudden death of Cavour. None of her heroes had survived the vicissitudes of history quite so well as Cavour, "that great soul, which meditated and made Italy." Now Napoleon must save Italy. "There is a hope that certain solutions had been prepared between him and the Emperor, and that events will slide into their grooves."[81]

Robert had not seen his father and sister since Le Havre three years before. He had long counted on spending the summer with them in France. As warmly as she could, Elizabeth wrote Sarianna of living quietly outside Paris in the forest of Fontainebleau or perhaps meeting on the coast. Actually, hiding away with her grief and her newspapers, she gave herself up more and more to her own gigantic, highly colored vision of public events or—though reluctantly—to her tender, shattering memories of a past heavily laden with pain and guilt. Meanwhile, the upper world of hard sunlight and living faces became more and more intolerable. "I should like to go into a cave for the year," she told Mrs. Martin.[82] "I think with positive terror sometimes," she confessed to Fanny Haworth, "less of the journey than of having to speak and look at people."[83] By May, even before they left Rome, Robert pronounced that France was out of the question. So long a journey was much beyond her strength. She protested the decision so vehemently that Robert was vexed. "He fancied I had set my selfwill on tossing myself up as a half-penny, and coming down on the wrong side."[84] He said there was risk; she insisted she would gladly take the risk for his sake. He said that he would not—and made her admit she was relieved.

Florence was hot, deserted—and decked with crepe-hung flags and banners to commemorate at once the death of Cavour and the virtual recognition of Italy by the powers. Though still mourning Cavour, Elizabeth felt stronger. "My cough has got well at once," she told Robert, "as is always the way in such weather." But now the heat itself became oppressive. "Let us *go* at once," he urged.[85] Happening into Count Alberti on the street, he learned that the villa outside Siena would once more be available. But he was unsure what view to take of his wife's health. She would not go out, and when he urged her to walk with him on the terrace as they used to do—"just once"—she came to the window, took two steps, and had to go back.[86] Since Napoleon's peace at Villafranca he had watched closely the effect on her of one blow after another through the two years. At the moment, she seemed calm, even cheerful. The few friends who saw her thought she was much improved. She "is regaining strength now," he wrote Story on June 13—and added, being somewhat relaxed, that Landor was "very well and rationally disposed," though—by a whim—completely shorn of his ambrosial locks and whiskers.[87]

A week later, returning Thursday from the newsroom, he found Isa Blagden with Elizabeth. As so often when oppressed by the heat, Elizabeth was sitting between the windows where the air was stirring. They had tea, and then she complained that she had a sore throat. Alarmed at once, Isa explained to Robert that she had vigorously protested the sitting between windows. A cold developed, and with the cold a cough which prevented sleep. Toward evening on Saturday she felt worse and by one at night was suffering from an accumulation of phlegm which she could not cough up. Robert left Annunziata in charge, and "knocked up (with difficulty) Dr. Wilson, a physician of great repute here, and specially conversant in maladies of the chest." He applied "a sinapism to breast and back, and hot water with mustard to the feet." By five, she was easier. Later Dr. Wilson "examined carefully and reported, with a very serious face, that one lung was condensed (the right) and that he suspected an abscess in it." Robert told part of this to Elizabeth. Having lived for so many years a life of feverish vitality in the presence of great physical weakness, she seems to have felt strangely secure in her frail mortality. "It is the old story," she insisted, "—they don't know my case—I have been tapped and sounded so, and condemned so, repeatedly. . . . This is only one of my old attacks."[88]

Performing with deep concern his ritual of masculine protectiveness, Robert carried her each morning into the great gloomy drawing room and laid her in her chair where, clad only in her nightgown, she read the newspapers a little, dozed, and sometimes seemed unaware of Robert's movements. She took only liquid nourishment—strong brodo or ass's milk. In a voice "all but extinct" she still protested that "it will be nothing." On Friday they discussed somewhat more drastic plans for the future. Casa Guidi had suddenly grown distasteful to both—"noisy, hot, close." Robert proposed the Villa Niccolini. She urged him to inquire. He declared he would take it at once. "Oh, that's not it," she cried, and began to talk about a change of air. Both noticed that she was light-headed, yet Robert was not alarmed. She had eaten so very little and the doctor had increased her dose of morphine. Later on, the window "seemed to be hung in the Hungarian colours." Isa came in the evening, and as she took her glass, Elizabeth smiled at her, "I not only have asses' milk but asses' thoughts—I am so troubled with silly politics and nonsense." Isa told her something from the day's news, but Robert intervened at once: "No talking, come, go, Isa."[89] Isa went, convinced she was better. Pen came in to say good night. Apparently he had caught something of the gravity of the situation, for he asked her three times, with great earnestness, "Are you really better?" Each time she replied, "*Much* better." "Perhaps a little better," said the doctor.[90]

That night as usual Robert sat by her. She dozed, and when he spoke, knew him, smiled, said she was better, and begged him to come to bed. Later he noticed her feet were cold, and presently she exclaimed, "What a fine steamer—how comfortable." Robert called Annunziata, bade her get hot water, and sent the porter for the doctor.

Smiling, she sat up murmuring, "Well, you do make an exaggerated case of it!" She was eager to obey, and, when Robert offered her a fowl jelly she had refused with repugnance earlier, she ate it to the last as he fed her. "My Robert—my heavens, my beloved!" she exclaimed, kissing him. "Our lives are held by God!" She put her arms round him. " 'God bless you' repeatedly—kissing me with such vehemence that when I laid her down she continued to kiss the air with her lips, and several times raised her own hand and kissed them [*sic*]." He once more asked how she felt. "*Beautiful!*" She began to sleep again. Sensing that she must be raised, Robert took her in his arms. He felt the struggle to cough begin, then fail. Her head fell forward on him. He thought she had fainted. Then there was the least knitting of the brows. "*Quest' anima benedetta é passata!*" cried Annunziata.[91] Robert saw her at that moment transfigured. "She looked," he told Story, "like a young girl." The outlines of her face were "rounded and filled up, all traces of disease effaced," and on her lips there was a smile "so living" that for hours he could not persuade himself she was really dead.[92]

The Storys came in from Leghorn as soon as they heard the news. Story was much taken by surprise, "for though she had always been so frail that one only wondered what kept soul and body together at all, we had become as accustomed to thinking of her as different from all others in the matter of health that we began to think that she might even outlast us."[93] At Casa Guidi they found Browning in the drawing room, and in better control of his grief than he would soon be. "The cycle is complete," he said, looking round the room; "here we came fifteen years ago; here Pen was born; here Ba wrote her poems for Italy. . . . Every day she used to walk with me or drive with me, and once even walked to Bellosguardo and back; that was when she was strongest. Little by little, as I now see, that distance was lessened, the active out-doors life restricted, until walking had finally ceased. . . . Looking back at these past years I see that we have been all the time walking over a torrent on a straw."[94]

The next day, June 30, he wrote a long letter to Sarianna. "My life is fixed and sure now," he told her. "I shall live out the remainder in her direct influence, endeavoring to complete mine, miserably imperfect now, but so as to take the good she was meant to give me. I go away from Italy at once. . . . I have our child about whom I shall exclusively employ myself, doing her part by him. . . . Pen has been perfect to me: he sate all yesterday with his arms round me; said things like her to me. . . . She will be buried tomorrow. Several times in writing this I have for a moment referred in my mind to her—'I will ask Ba about that.' "[95]

To his dismay, Story found he had arrived too late to take charge of the "arrangements." To him the funeral seemed unimpressive. There were fewer people than he expected, and "the services were blundered through by a fat English parson in a brutally careless way."[96] Browning remembered only "a flash of faces,"[97] but the fact was that the shops were closed in their street, that by a special privilege the coffin was carried through a part of the city, and that a considerable crowd followed. Elizabeth was buried in the old Protestant cemetery, now an oval, iron-fenced, tree-shaded island in a broad street of steadily increasing traffic. There the almost indestructible Landor was soon to follow, the loud irrational laughter still at last.

CHAPTER 21

Booths at the Fair

1861-62

"The staying at Casa Guidi was not the worst of it," Browning wrote Story on August 30 from St. Enogat on the Brittany coast. "I kept in my place there like a worm-eaten piece of old furniture, looking solid enough; but when I was *moved,* I began to go to pieces."[1] After the funeral he spent his nights at Isa's villa on Bellosguardo, where Pen had been staying since his mother's death. There indeed the gentle, black-eyed nurse and comforter of so many Anglo-Florentines had for a time listened to the outcries of a truly frantic grief. Afterward, Browning seems to have been somewhat ashamed, for on July 18 he wrote Macready, "Do not imagine that I am prostrated by this calamity," and repeated himself in almost the same words to Leighton the next day.[2]

Before the furniture of Casa Guidi was packed and stored, Robert had a very exact painting made of the drawing room. The past would not, could not, be forgotten. On the other hand, the future must be as unlike it as possible. No more housekeeping for him, he told Fanny Haworth, even with his own family. He and Pen would live very simply, and with a minimum of possessions, so that they could move at any time. He was not sanguine about himself. "I shall grow, still, I hope—but my root is taken, [nothing?] remains."[3]

Indeed he was eager to begin a future which seemed more promising than his own. "I shall give myself wholly up," he wrote George Barrett, "to the care & education of our child; I know all Ba's mind as to how that should be, and shall try and carry out her desires."[4] As time went on, however, what he chiefly carried out in educating Pen were his own revolutionary corrections of his wife's ideas. One innovation was not postponed, and concerning it he put the facts bluntly enough. "Pen, the golden curls and fantastic dress," he told Sarianna six days after Elizabeth's death, "is gone just as Ba is gone:

he has short hair, worn boy-wise, long trousers, is a common boy all at once: otherwise I could not have lived without a maid."[5] Again, he had determined to live in England. Therefore he could scarcely recognize the strong loyalty of his wife and son to Italy. The issue was underlined by a visit from Ubaldino Peruzzi, Minister of Public Works under Cavour. He said "he and all the Italians were hoping I should not leave Florence—and that Pen would be brought up as a Tuscan—every career would be open to him, even if he went away for a year or two."[6] Browning's underlying attitude on this point, as expressed to Forster, has an irritable, self-justifying violence about it: "Of course Pen is and will be English as I am English and his Mother was pure English to the hatred of all un-English cowardice, vituperation, and lies."[7] When Mrs. Story suggested a compromise arrangement for Pen, Browning wrote her husband in words that clearly reveal how repugnant some of Elizabeth's ideas had been to him: "I mean to get a very good English Tutor, capable of preparing Pen for the University without, if possible, necessitating the passage thro' a Public School: and if I delay this, as my original notion was, I may lose the critical time when the English stamp (in all that it is good for) is taken or missed. . . . Such a school as dear Edie described would have been desirable had Peni been brought up in England from the first—but I distrust all hybrid & ambiguous natures & nationalities and want to make something decided of the poor little fellow."[8] The tutor was his only concession to the past—one which would exclude Pen from any experience with competitive or gregarious education till he should reach the university.

On the other hand, in justice to Pen, Robert had to put a stop to Elizabeth's follies. In justice to himself, he no doubt did well to reestablish his own career in London. His fault was a violent abruptness which sprang from grief and from old quarrels with Elizabeth and with his own boyhood. He failed to see that in seeking to restore his own identity, he was in danger of obliterating his son's. At one blow, this happy, precocious, much-indulged, much-made-over boy was parted from his mother, his friends, his native language, and his beloved native city—to become anonymous in a country where his earliest memories had been of miserable separation from the adoring Wilson. And now indeed he gave up—perhaps forever—that beloved second mother and his hero Ferdinando—a leave-taking in which, reports Betty Miller, the sobs of nurse and child were terminated by the crash of crockery on the pavement below.[9] Landor had been kept too long waiting for his dinner. Robert's letters say nothing of Pen's sufferings. And yet, at University College, he had himself ignominiously succumbed under much less provocation to the agony of homesickness. Perhaps, in rearing Pen, he was unconsciously setting himself against much in his own childhood.

On August 1, Robert, Pen, Isa Blagden and—to Robert's great credit—Pen's pony left Florence for Paris. Isa had come along so that they would not be alone on the sad journey. At Paris she parted from them, leaving for England, while they, with Robert's father and sister went on to St. Enogat. "Out by the sea—wholly alone" except for Pen, Robert tried to "walk it" out of his head. Pen "amuses himself with my father," he told Isa, "whose kindness & simplicity make him a wonderful child's friend certainly,—they sketch together, go home & paint &c and Pen's loud merry laugh is never out of my ears. He requires not even supervision now in the business of the toilette; is regular, orderly & reliable. He bathes every day—to-day will be the twenty fifth time—with a good swimming master, and really swims very well: he is delighted with it, stays in a long twenty minutes or half hour, then rides for two hours: I walk myself to death by his side. . . ."[10] Lessons were wisely postponed. In October the whole party returned to Paris, and then Robert, Pen, and the pony started for England.

As befitted the entry on a new life, the journey to Boulogne was full of echoes and portents. Misinformed at the central office regarding the right train for horses, Robert—and the pony—were not allowed to board. He demanded that the pony travel by express, the next train. After two hours' debate, urbanely polite on both sides, Robert won his point and the pony traveled safely on the express. Looking around at Amiens station, Robert saw Tennyson step onto the train. "He was changed, had a great beard, but I could not be deceived." At Boulogne Robert avoided an encounter, but as the Folkestone boat was about to leave, he said to Pen, " 'I'll show you Tennyson,'—& presently he came forward with his wife & two beautiful children."[11] They learned in London that the later train, appropriate for horses, had been wrecked at Amiens.

In London Robert took lodgings at No. 1 Chichester Road, but after nine months—despite his resolutions against housekeeping and worldly responsibilities—he moved into a rather considerable establishment. A tall, narrow segment in a wall of white stucco, No. 19 Warwick Crescent looked out over a narrow front garden and the Grand Junction Canal, which at that point widened into a lugubrious little lake with an island, thinly wooded, in the center. The view, on sunny days, suggested Venice. The canal provided boating for Pen. The house was close to Arabel Barrett's in Delamere Terrace. Browning lived there for the next twenty-five years. Some time after he had moved in, an astonished dock official announced the arrival of enormous packing cases from Florence. They were opened in Warwick Crescent, and Robert once more contemplated the massive, elaborately inlaid, ebony furniture of Casa Guidi. Wondering whether he liked the pieces "best here, or there, or at the bottom of the sea," he arranged them in the small English rooms.[12]

His early days in London were passed in solitary walks through a desolate neighborhood, in sad visits to old friends and in zealous pursuit of his dedication to Pen and Elizabeth's memory. We hear of Pen "at his music lesson two yards off" or hard at his German close by.[13] We also hear of the chance visit of a red-haired Italian boy whom Pen used to play with in Florence. "I was amazed at hearing a chatter of Tuscan and seeing emerge his unmistakable locks!" Robert told Isa.[14] So long as he was in London, Alessandro was urged to come to Warwick Crescent as often as he could. In January 1862, Robert had engaged a tutor to his mind—"rather than to Pen's, perhaps—but he is sound to the core in grammatical niceties." Isa accused Robert of being a "monomaniac" about Pen's education.[15] He assured her Pen was doing so well that he had ceased to be a worry. Robert guided Elizabeth's *Last Poems* through the press, dedicating them "To Grateful Florence" in response to an inscription which was being set up on Casa Guidi. Occasionally he saw Forster and Dickens, and once or twice Rossetti, who, one evening not long before, had returned from "a working-men's class" to find his wife dying in proximity to an empty laudanum bottle.[16] Robert saw Arabel Barrett daily, but even more he depended on Isa Blagden, who was spending a number of months in England—mostly in Stone House at Broadstairs, but at first just opposite No. 1 Chichester Road, "in a house," Robert told Story, "no farther from this than your ball-room from the green drawing-room."[17] With her he enjoyed a tranquil, therapeutic friendship, though not without moments of longing or even, perhaps, of caution. Contemplating the possibility of an Isa permanently in England, he wrote, "Why should Italy be barred to you? It should be open to *me,* I know, if the least duty to go there presented itself: even if my own health imperatively required my return I would go . . . *you* probably ought. . . . for me,—I should lose something by every inch that you were removed from me; you know that."[18] Contemplating the loneliness of his own life with Isa away in Kent, he wrote: "How much I miss you every day when I go on my dreary walk as Mr. Gillespie [Pen's tutor] makes his appearance you can hardly guess. . . . I do trust you will return to us."[19] Browning was not a man in love; he was a very lonely man grown accustomed to the unobtrusive sympathy of a black-eyed lady. He wanted, as he told her somewhat tactlessly, to lose himself in the superficial details of life: "I can never,—shall never try to go an inch below the surface—but what need is there of that with you?"[20] Eventually, he proposed, they should spend the last years of their lives near each other in Italy, like the two serpents Cadmus and Harmonia of whom Callicles sings in Arnold's *Empedocles on Etna.* "Last of all will come the pythons incubating their addled eggs in Italy,—eh?—."[21] Meantime, they agreed to write each other every month—she on the twelfth and he on the nineteenth. "I shall not again tell you," he wrote, "that your letter arrived & made me happy: understand without more telling, as I think you do, that I look for it thro' the long month as I never looked for anything else in the letter way."[22]

What cheered him up very considerably was an offer, in March 1862, to succeed Thackeray as editor of *The Cornhill.* "My first answer," he told Story, "was prompt enough—that my life was done for & settled, that I could not change & would not." But "the conveyer of the message" urged him to consider in so flattering a way that he delayed his reply for a week. He did consider—and found that he was very well pleased both with the offer and with himself. Here at his disposal was the power to realize an old ambition—to occupy a substantial position and earn a substantial salary—and indeed, whether Browning knew it or not, Thackeray had received £2000 a year. The letter to Story shows Browning gay for the first time since his wife's death: "O Story, O Emelyn (dare I say, for the solemnity's sake?) and O Edie—the Editorship has, under the circumstances &c &c been offered to—*me*!" He resolved to be very shrewd, to draw up "a full statement" of what he expected to do, to accept not a farthing less than Thackeray had got.[23] Then he refused the offer. To Isa he maintained that he had "never thought for a moment of accepting it."[24] Still, the offer was a fact.

The incident, insignificant in itself, seems to mark a turning point. From about this time onward, he writes Isa more often of social events—of a dinner at Lady William Russell's where he heard the French news, of a very grand dinner where he "saw a great deal" of the "neck & shoulders" of the beautiful Mrs. Petre, whom he nevertheless thought silly and expressionless.[25] Certainly, his taste in beauty remained exotic. He writes—appropriately to Isa—of some Parsee girls "prettier to my corrupt & rotten cheese loving taste than any of the English fineness & loveliness (aquiline nose between two pudding cheeks with lightish hair & eyes, & 'fine' complexion—give me these coal black little bitter-almonds!)."[26] Soon the parties become very grand indeed and pile up sometimes two or three high of an evening. Isa hears of Lady Westmorland's, Lady Salisbury's, Lady Palmerston's, of Robert's taking Pen—at fourteen—to balls, and even to the Derby—"privately, by going to a friend's house close by the course," as in the anxiety of imperiled correctness Robert assures Isa twice in the same letter.[27]

His attitude toward the past and Florence also became more healthy. At first, that city forced on him only gloomy, repugnant, or nagging thoughts, happiness lost, death, the defects of Italian character, cemeteries, gravestones, and the business details of burial and commemoration. From there came the steady stream of Landor's letters—sometimes four in a week—full of complaints, vituperation, self-pity, and absurd requests. What wonder Robert's letters mentioned Florence with sighs and groans. When Isa returned there in July 1862, however, he found suddenly that he was interested in precisely what villa she had taken, in what his old friends were doing, in the beautiful old city itself. Frederick Leighton submitted a design for the monument for Elizabeth's grave, and Robert considered with patient care Isa's criticisms, Cottrell's preference for the Italian artist Mathas, and Kirkup's warning that columns over an open area were dangerous. He sympathized with Leighton's embarrassment, and defended his ideas—which he liked—with the utmost good humor. "You say," he wrote Isa, "'Rafael would have consulted Michel Angelo'—now, I don't say L. is Rafael—but does anybody call the other Michel Angelo? I really want to know."[28] In October 1864, Leighton wrote from Florence that nothing could be "more *impudently* bad than the execution of his designs," which had been placed under the supervision of Count Cottrell. Robert was forbearing: "Cottrell has done his best, I daresay."[29] He then wrote an encouraging letter to Leighton.

In certain areas his sensibility remained thoroughly Victorian and morbid. When Elizabeth's grave had to be disturbed in preparation for Leighton's monument, the thought turned his spine—and his syntax—to water. He appealed to Isa, "Will you, whenever those dreadful preliminaries, the provisional removement &c—when they are proceeded with,—will you do,—all you can,—*suggest* every regard to decency and proper feeling to the persons concerned? I have a horror of that man of the graveyard."[30] When he learned one George Stampe was writing a biography of Elizabeth and had already obtained her letters to Hugh Stuart Boyd, he exploded: "Think of this beast working away at this, not deeming my feelings, or those of her family, worthy of notice—and meaning to print letters written years & years ago, on the most intimate & personal subjects. . . . What I suffer in feeling the hands of these blackguards . . . what I undergo with their paws in my very bowels, you can guess & God knows!"[31]

As he worked through his mourning, however, his attitude toward both past and future became steadily more sensible. "The presence of Her," he wrote Isa in November 1862, after a year in England, "is now habitual to me,—I can have no doubt that it is my greatest comfort to be always remembering her,—the old books & furniture, her chair which is by mine,—all that is comfort to me."[32] He planned to have cut in marble and placed where he could always see it an exact copy of the Casa Guidi inscription. A year later he wrote: "Yes—the years go—we are in the *third*: at first, when you were here, the business was of the hardest, for nothing seemed *doing*, nothing *growing*,—only the emptiness and weariness of it all: now, there seems really use in the process, & fruit."[33] And the year after that, in December 1864: "Well, for myself, I am certainly not unhappy, any more than I ever was: I am . . . '*resigned*'—but I look on everything in this world with altered eyes, and can no more take interest in anything I see there but the proof of certain great principles, strewn in the booths at a fair: I could no more take root in life again, than learn some new dancing step. On the other hand, I feel such comfort and delight in doing the best I can with my own object of life,—poetry,—which, I think, I never *could* have seen the good of before,—that it shows me I have taken the root I *did* take, *well*."[34]

Actually, as Henry James has shown, Browning was intensely interested both in the booths at the fair and in the great principles they proved. Now after many years, he was steadily experiencing the discussion which makes contemporary intellectual history, not from the remote quiet of a provincial city but in one of the great capitals where the discussion takes place. The Catholic menace had faded. People were bewildered, terrified, enraged by the new theory in biology. They were alarmed and dismayed by a whole series of new books that put religious beliefs and traditional dogma into question: Darwin's *Origin of Species* was published in 1859; the multiauthored, skeptical *Essays and Reviews* in 1860, Colenso's Critical Examination of the Pentateuch in 1862, Renan's *Vie de Jésus* in 1863, and Strauss's *New Life of Jesus* in 1864. Browning arrived in England too late to witness the sensation created by *The Origin*, though he had heard the book explained to him in Italy—one suspects, without comprehending it better than most people did. He had read enough of some of the other books to be angry at them, for the old, odd legend of "Gold Hair" turns out to concern them very closely.

> The candid incline to surmise of late
>   That the Christian faith proves false, I find;
> For our Essays-and-Reviews' debate
>   Begins to tell on the public mind,
> And Colenso's words have weight.[35]

No book on Jesus was likely to please a man of Browning's unique convictions—even with their deep element of uncertainty—and least of all a book dealing with Jesus as merely human. Browning read Renan's *Vie de Jésus* in November 1863 and promptly poured out to Isa his contempt and indignation. "Take away every claim to man's respect from Christ," he snorts, "and then give him a wreath of gum-roses and calico-lilies."[36] The rather ghastly wreath pretty clearly refers to the atmosphere of pastoral operetta, after the fashion of Rousseau's *Le Devin du Village*, that pervades the whole account of Jesus' youth. The wreath seems justified. On the other hand, "take away every claim to man's respect from Christ" seems mild in the light of Renan's tendency to portray Jesus as a communist and a revolutionary who, having a taste for bohemianism and low life, consorts with beggars, publicans, and prostitutes. Browning seems to have read Strauss's *Das Leben Jesu,* at least in part, sometime before writing *Christmas-Eve and Easter-Day,* which treats the higher critics not without respect. Though there is no reason for thinking that he had ever read *The New Life of Jesus,* he had come to know George Eliot, the translator of the earlier book. That he admired her novels, we know from several passages of praise in his letters. Indeed, when she pointed out the want of a motive in "Gold Hair," he promptly added stanzas 21, 22, and 23. Could his admiration for the artist and subtle investigator of Christian souls lead him to hear with patience the many-sided rationalist, Hegelian, Comteist, and Millite?

Already in August 1862 he speaks of writing a poem of 120 lines—probably "Gold Hair" or "James Lee's Wife." In October, he says that he is going to print another volume like *Men and Women* and make a "regular poem" out of the murder-trial of Count Guido Franceschini.[37] He could scarcely have faced so soon the painful, failure-haunted prospect of publishing another volume without some encouragement. Actually, he had received quite a little encouragement. The offer of the *Cornhill* editorship, which seems to have roused him from his grief, was only the first and most persuasive sign. Now Chapman wanted to bring out a new three-volume edition of his works, and his friends Forster and Barry Cornwall had in the press a volume of *Selections*.

CHAPTER 22

A Sunning Hawk

1862 and 1860-65

The *Selections* appeared on December 22, 1862. A "pretty little book enough," as Browning told George Barrett, it sold improbably well and won compliments from old friends.[1] Rossetti felt that it would send "pangs of selfishness" through his compeers: "'Had I,' each will say, 'but had the doing of it.'"[2] Critics now vied with one another to acknowledge the appalling fact that Browning was still rather unacknowledged and to explain why this was so. "A Poet Without a Public," *Chambers's Journal* lamented in February 1863, eyeing the *Selections* and wondering why "the poetic idol of men who give laws to cliques and coteries" had absented himself in Italy for so long.[3] The critical chorus modulated to an even more auspicious key as Chapman's edition began to appear. *The Reader*, in May, hailed the first installment of the *Poetical Works* in tones of Genesis. "Let there be an immediate demand for this volume," it commanded, "in preparation for its successors."[4]

Clearly, a change was in the air. Readers, even reviewers were waiting for more of Browning—who, for his part, had attempted to make the rough places plain in *Sordello* to the extent of clarifying its syntax, altering its punctuation, and adding 181 new lines to the old, bewildering text. And now Browning was forced to wait, not idly or unhappily, for more of himself. Chapman wanted to postpone publication of the new poems, *Dramatis Personae*, in order "to take advantage of the sort of success (for me) that the edition is getting," Robert told Mrs. Story with barely concealed delight.[5]

Meanwhile, he added two more poems to his steadily thickening manuscript, "Apparent Failure" and the Yeatsian "Epilogue," in which Renan is made to sing plaintively of "gyre on gyre" and the decline of Christianity. He also set up a tiny Story-like studio at Warwick Crescent, "letting the memories curl round me while I preposterously meddle and make," and sculpted a bust of Keats. He discussed religion and the Civil War on city walks with Moncure Conway—the radical divine who had sailed the Atlantic to propagandize Lincoln's cause and who would soon fittingly inherit Fox's ultraliberal pastorate at South Place.[6] Above all, unremitting attention was to be paid to Pen's progress—"morally & intellectually as physically"—and for an urgent reason. "I had the satisfaction of getting Pen entered on the books of Balliol 'for residence in 1867,'" Browning told Isa in March 1863. "Balliol is immeasurably the best College for Pen—if he will but resolve to rise to their high standard of scholarship, as I hope & trust he will."[7]

Quite definitely, the future was already casting ominous shadows on a fourteen-year-old's lessons. Robert Scott and Benjamin Jowett had helped to enter Pen's name at Oxford. Together they symbolized —and by themselves nearly embodied—what Browning or any other properly ambitious mid-Victorian parent would mean by Balliol's "high standard of scholarship." Scott, then Master of the College, was famous for having collaborated with Liddell on a widely used Greek lexicon. Jowett was even more famous. He reminded Stephen Coleridge, it is true, of a parrot: a "little round man of undistinguished features, a small high voice, a receding chin, and a round nose."[8] Yet his achievements were scarcely those of a parrot. A prodigy at eleven, Jowett had spent much of a lonely childhood in the gloom of a school library at St. Paul's. At eighteen he was the best Latin scholar his headmaster had ever seen. From St. Paul's, he had moved to Balliol's splendidly stored bookstacks, in and out of which he was to troop with pudgy and heavily-laden arms for the rest of his life, accumulating spectacular honors and loyalties, and a reputation for instilling a "doctrine of work" and sheer horror of failure in a long line of Balliol undergraduates who duly became (in numbers quite out of proportion to those other colleges could muster) distinguished viceroys, high commissioners, ecclesiastics, philosophers, historians, generals, lawyers, and poets. Indeed, the scholar who was quickly turning Balliol into a "famous nursery of Public men"[9] had recently helped to turn England inside out. Jowett's commentary of 1855 on Thessalonians, Galatians, and Romans very carefully and blasphemously accuses St. Paul of ignorance and bad Greek. It created a small panic. Five years later he helped to create a more lasting and devastating panic. His essay "On the Interpretation of Scripture" is the lengthiest of those separate pleas for accuracy and common sense in theology by the "seven against God" who contributed to *Essays and*

Reviews. Of course, nearly any parent could forgive Jowett for heresy in the light of his indubitable talent for rearing diplomats.

But could Pen reasonably be expected to matriculate in Jowett's and Scott's college? Browning was deeply determined that he should, "ambitious," as he confessed to Emelyn Story, "and nervously anxious as I am."[10] Nervous anxiety had its causes. Certainly Pen was dutiful, willing, affectionate, alert, and even truthful and manly for his age. Two more summers in Brittany had brought out the very best of his traits. In 1862 and 1863, Robert with his father and Sarianna and Pen had taken rooms in the Mayor's simple peasant cottage in the Rue des Tulipes at Ste. Marie, then a lonely and "stark-naked" little hamlet of a dozen houses huddled near the brink of sloping gray rocks overlooking the sea.[11] Near the end of the first summer, the Mayor's wife had suffered an attack of pleurisy, had lingered in a state of delirium and pain while her four small children were "dragged upstairs to 'bid goodbye,'" and—in a scene that must have been of Dickensian proportions—had finally died, "in the room next to mine & Pen's."[12] Pen was urged to sleep with their friends Mrs. Bracken and Willy the next night lest only a thin partition separate him from a corpse. "*I* go away?" Pen flung back. "As if I shall not be more comfortable knowing she is out of her pain to-night than I was last night when she was in such pain." Browning was justly proud of Elizabeth's "brick-coloured and broad-shouldered" son.[13] A year later, Pen actually helped to stave off a death when an unconscious bather was pulled from the sea. "He ran into a house, got brandy & vinegar, and on being directed by somebody to do some stupidity or other, bade him 'Allez au diable!'—So, you see," Isa was told, "he *promises.*"[14] But if Pen could remember the Humane Society's rules, could he also remember Greek participles? With Willy Bracken, nearly his own age, he quickly learned to box, skate, and fence; and at length—after the Siena pony was inevitably given away—demonstrated that he could manage a plunging stag-hunter for eight hours and twenty-five miles at a stretch. Could he manage equations as well? Pen took in lessons slowly. Browning tried not to grasp at straws, yet his letters to intimate friends in Italy at this time are filled with straws. They hear that Pen is the equal of any Eton boy "I suspect," and that "I have clever masters, & Pen really loves them all," and again that "he certainly satisfies me on the whole—without more *love* for lessons than (at bottom of my heart) I should like."[15]

Yet obviously, a student of Jowett's would have to love lessons with an unquenchable and nearly omnivorous passion. With a little more attention to Pen's own mild and quietly budding passion—"he is increasingly . . . observant," Story read in one letter, "then his drawing is very good"—Robert might have packed off the boy with his crayons and sketchbook to a Roman studio, possible success, and almost certainly greater happiness. But when Story intimated either that some such plan or at least that an Italian sojourn might be desirable, Robert merely thumped his fist. "You should not talk so . . . no Rome, no *you*—except in remembrance & hope."[16] The trouble was that his determination on his own plan overruled the evidence. Pen, no less than Sir Austin Feverel's well-beloved son, was the victim of a Victorian father with a "System."

The past impinged in another way at about this time. When news came from Rome of a new "manifestation" of Mrs. Eckley, who was now loudly accusing her husband of unfaithfulness, contempt for Elizabeth's female betrayer was hurled anew to Isa and the Storys—and celebrated anew in a curious little ritual at Warwick Crescent. "I solaced myself the other day," Browning wrote to Story of Mrs. Eckley in the pleased tones of a discoverer of voodoo, "by placing two portraits of her, one on each side of a delicious drawing of a 'model' in the costume of Truth, just given to me by Leighton." And why had Browning preserved two portraits of a "dunghill of a soul"? For very much the same reason that such a soul speaks twice in *The Ring and the Book,* one suspects. In few men at any epoch can the fascinations of love and hatred have been so intertwined, at times so nearly identical. "I should like above most things," he gloats, "to have a good talk with her: no hurting *me,* alas!"[17] One more fully understands in this context some words he sent Isa at almost the same time: "As for Pen, I love him dearly, but if I hated him, it would be pretty much the same thing."[18]

On February 12, 1864, Browning drew up his will in the portentous presence of Palgrave and Tennyson, who signed as witnesses. The inevitabilities of the future had to be attended to. Sarianna would have £200 a year when he died, plus a sum sufficient "to maintain and educate my son" until he attained legal maturity, at which point Pen would inherit nearly everything else.[19]

Three months later, the present impinged. *Dramatis Personae* was belatedly published in a plum-colored octavo volume by Chapman and Hall on May 28. Critics in London recognized their duty. Here were eighteen new poems that looked a good deal like those in *Men and Women*—but obviously could not be treated so condescendingly. With a distrustful parting glance at a Muse who "lays on us the burden of the incomprehensible in a most wickedly provoking way," *The*

Athenaeum bravely hitched up its skirts, descended Olympus, and discovered "a great dramatic poet." A pity that he had not lived and died an Elizabethan. "Caliban" would have "delighted Shakespeare himself, who would have been the first to have acknowledged that it faithfully represented the inner man of his own creation."[20] Not to be caught out of step, *The Spectator* noted a few days later that the new Caliban "soars far above Shakespeare's conception of the monster," and even found some pleasant things to say about "Sludgehood."[21] A "superabundant power," E. P. Hood wrote in the July *Eclectic and Congregational Review*, flattering his readers with an almost inevitable qualification: perhaps there was a pathos here "too deep for any but eclectic hearts [and] sufferers." Yet "we suppose we are not alone in making the confession that, of the living masters of English poetry, Robert Browning gives us the greatest measure of delight."[22]

In some eyes, then, the Laureate appeared to be eclipsed. In most other eyes, Browning's poems still had egregious faults, were no better than Tennyson's, if indeed they were as good: in short, were harsh, difficult, intellectual, queer, powerful, and rather brilliant. But they were patently better than ever. Only *The Edinburgh Review* dissented rashly from the consensus. Its incapacity to believe that any of Browning would survive "except as a curiosity and a puzzle"[23] provoked a savage letter by Gerald Massey, the *Athenaeum* reviewer, in *The Reader*, and an even more withering frontal attack on *The Edinburgh* (four columns long and bristling with ironies) in *The Saturday Review* of January 7, 1865.

Before the dust from this had settled, Walter Bagehot explained in *The National Review* how it was that Browning could be ugly, distasteful, and significant all at once. If Wordsworth's poems are "pure," Tennyson's must be "ornate," and Browning's "grotesque"—at their worst and best: "Hardly any one could have amassed so many ideas at once nasty and suitable as there are in 'Caliban'." Bagehot's neat categorizations and gentle dogmatisms, his pellucid style and incisive wit—"Poetry should be memorable and emphatic, intense, and *soon over*," he wrote—and even the narrowed aesthetic viewpoint and glaring misogyny in this review-essay would pique readers for decades to come.[24] The possibilities in literary naturalism—or in a new "grotesque realism" of a kind then only budding in France and hardly out of the ground in England—Bagehot only dimly saw. Even so, Browning had attracted an English critic fit to be mentioned in the same breath with "J. Milsand, of Dijon"—to whom he had dedicated his new and slightly emasculated *Sordello*.

No doubt the earlier *Selections* had opened many critical eyes. With the new praise of Browning, reviewers were partly making amends to a perverse Anglo-Italian who had proved to be a brave widower and an almost lucid Englishman. "Prospice," for instance, was to be quoted often in future reviews. Its brevity and clarity were obvious. So too was the evidence that Browning was speaking in his own person, embracing with one arm his heathen Saxon peers, "the heroes of old"—and reaching out the other to the dead Mrs. Elizabeth Browning in her well-lit Christian heaven:

> And the elements' rage, the fiend-voices that rave,
>   Shall dwindle, shall blend,
> Shall change, shall become first a peace, then a joy,
>   Then a light, then thy breast,
> O thou soul of my soul! I shall clasp thee again,
>   And with God be the rest!

With a certain robust bravery, Robert anticipates the "best" battle he will have to fight. Death, "the Arch Fear," stands between himself and the reunion with Elizabeth:

> I would hate that death bandaged my eyes, and forbore,
>   And let me creep past.[25]

.Here indeed was an expression of Britannic courage, appropriately couched in terms of a defiant attitude toward fog, snow-flakes, and nightfall, that would be matched only by Matthew Arnold's quite equally melodramatic and heroic "Rugby Chapel" a few years later. The imagery and the sentiments in both poems are characteristically Victorian.

No less popular then or since, "Rabbi Ben Ezra" is perhaps more typical of Browning. Here again one listens through a series of ringing injunctions and affirmations, the more vibrant in this case for their deliberate cacophony, to the hale voice of a Dissenting Victorian of fifty. In contrast with Blougram or even Caliban, the Rabbi seems a disembodied spirit. He exists in the crabbedness of his syntax:

> Irks care the crop-full bird? Frets doubt the maw-crammed beast?[26]

One feels that the atheism, pessimism, and rampant hedonism of FitzGerald's Omar Khayyám are being countered, if not directly answered, by the religious feeling, optimism, and somewhat abstemious habits of Ben Ezra's Robert Browning; and also that Browning fully intended his poem as a reply to the Persian-Victorian one. The elaborated metaphor of the biblical potter's wheel seems to link the two poems circumstantially. Moreover, as David Fleisher has closely pointed out, Ben Ezra is less indulgent toward Youth's joy in the flesh than a casual reading of stanzas 9–12 would suggest.[27] The Rabbi is hardly assailing puritanical asceticism when he shouts:

> Would we some prize might hold
> To match those manifold
> Possessions of the brute,—gain most, as we did best!
>
> Let us not always say
> "Spite of this flesh to-day
> I strove, made head, gained ground upon the whole!"
> As the bird wings and sings,
> Let us cry "All good things
> Are ours, nor soul helps flesh more, now, than flesh
>   helps soul!"[28]

He is really assailing the flesh—and Youth. In Youth "pleasant" lures of the flesh impede and tend to defeat the soul's would-be flights of grandeur. In Age, soul and flesh are no longer at loggerheads since flesh now projects "soul on its lone way" in a perfectly harmonious if somewhat subservient manner. More percipient and brave, Age outclasses Youth and is not simply the latter half of life but the "best" of being. Youth sees poorly. It needs to be remade. Age sees "the whole design" and the "perfect" plan of life—and so can well afford to be stridently cheerful. Little wonder that Browning could hardly wait for Pen to grow up and declared that he was taller than Willy Bracken when he was not.

There is an implied equation in this poem between the flesh (before it is transformed into soul's valued help-mate) and the "possessions of the brute" that is at least faintly ominous. Perhaps a very hearty welcome extended to joys that are "three-parts pain!" is also a bit ominous. Still, if DeVane is right about the date,[29] "Rabbi Ben Ezra" was completed in the bleak year of 1862 when a deeply bereaved poet needed to affirm everything he could. A year after Elizabeth's death, it took some courage to affirm anything, let alone old age with its personally haunting prospect of uncongenial solitude and artistic decline.

Less consequential, less sinewy, more ironic, and more nearly lyrical are "Confessions," in which a dying libertine reconstructs with the help of his ether bottle and to the mute astonishment of his confessor the scene of a delicious *amour*, and "Apparent Failure," in which three male suicides in the Paris morgue are eulogized with scandalous wit. One "blue" occupant of an abominable slab, we hear, must have been driven to his demise by lust for women. In half a dozen poems in *Dramatis Personae*, love appears to be unfulfilled, regrettably lost, distorted, or bitterly tragic. One has the impression that Robert's own loss strongly influenced these melancholy lyrics.

Altogether *Dramatis Personae* is not so near to being another volume of *Men and Women* as Browning had intimated. Edward Dowden was disappointed to discover in it "less opulence of colour; less of the manifold 'joys of living'"—and very little attention to pictorial art.[30] Opulence has turned into abstract argument in many cases, and the joys of living also tend to be more abstract now and dependent upon a tough-skinned stoicism. The spiritual victories of a musician, a preacher, and a monster seem painfully won in solitudes that make one realize, by contrast, how greatly earlier dramatic auditors contribute to the well-being and self-fulfillment of earlier monologuists. Andrea del Sarto can take a perverse comfort in a wife's fickle charms so long as she is present; Abt Vogler, on the other hand, ascends alone through a "palace of music" to a most indefinite and insubstantial heaven and descends as promptly to the C Major of a life in which the chief ingredients seem to be orchestrions and sleep. An impression of ecstasy is nearly defeated by the starkness of abstractions. So many bare soliloquies from the pen of an inveterate diner-out and lover of gossip and Americans seem strange. Browning did not turn his dinner parties into literature, as Henry James did. Indeed, James himself was to note with increasing amazement that the dividing line between his older friend's brooding creative life and his invariably gay social one was very thick. Elizabeth's death seems to have scored and accentuated it.

In the late spring of 1864, Robert embarked on a curious friendship with a self-confirmed spinster who took immense pains to remind him of Elizabeth. Frances Julia Wedgwood—called "Snow" by numerous kinsmen, including Charles Darwin—at thirty-one had a slight figure, a disproportionately large brow, a primly tight hair-do, and an ailment. She was congenitally hard of hearing. Mrs. Miller thinks that her eyebrows and her nose resembled those of the author of *The*

Origin of Species,[31] who was in fact both her cousin and uncle-by-marriage. In other respects there were echoes of Elizabeth Barrett. Here, again, was a pious, intellectual, superstitious, rather *au courant* authoress given to forming friendships with elderly gentlemen of impeccable repute and spiritual inclination. James Martineau, Frederick Denison Maurice, and Thomas Erskine of Linlathen were all very fond of her. Julia Wedgwood was a good deal more than fond of a brother called "Bro"—who was dying. As before in history, an enthusiastic reading of Mr. Browning's poems and a morbid obsession *vis-à-vis* a "Bro" were to precede intimacies between a sheltered old maid and Robert.

Still, her published writings make luminously clear how few traits of that earlier and unique mortal Julia really shared. Of Elizabeth's gaiety, taste, curiosity, finesse, love of art she had little or none. "I never saw anything prettier than Snow dancing in a pink silk frock" could only have been said of Miss Wedgwood when she was two. Girlish charm had yielded to womanly piety before a succession of eminent spiritual teachers—whose doubtless very instructive lectures Snow had audited from time to time at Queen's and Bedford Colleges in London. Piety in turn soon came to be tinted with self-righteousness, which at length would express itself in anti-vivisectionist tracts and in a rather shrill ethical history of civilization entitled *The Moral Ideal*.[32] In 1888—quite surreptitiously—Julia Wedgwood dedicated this volume with the aid of a noncommittal formula to Robert Browning. "In the perspective of an individual memory," she solemnly added at the time, "years dwindle to a point, and moments expand to an age."[33]

What moments in the blameless life of a nearly deaf Victorian spinster might seem, in retrospect, so immensely expansive? One wonders. In 1864, of course, all the world might know of her brisk philosophical dialogue—published in *Macmillan's Magazine* for July 1861—in which she firmly drew "Boundaries" between religious faith and the domain of her cousin's new theory of natural selection. But who would suspect her of two novels, as well? Surely few beyond her family circle knew that she had published *Framleigh Hall* anonymously and *An Old Debt* under the modest pseudonym of "Florence Dawson" within a few months of each other at the age of twenty-five. Were these merely the last, dreamy stirrings of her girlhood? Both novels rather wearily "exalt sacrifice as a good in itself," as a reviewer of one of them was cruel enough to say out loud.[34] But the heroine of

Framleigh Hall is nonetheless a woman tormentedly in love, suggesting a dilemma in which a perfectly real Victorian heroine of fastidious principles and excessive piety might find herself:

> The thought that the most intense, spontaneous feeling of her soul was one with which she must struggle as a deadly sin, overwhelmed her with a sense of injustice. At what point was it in her power—when could she have stopped and said, 'Here esteem ends, here passion begins—I will go no farther.' She could remember no such point. She knew her love was hopeless . . . and yet so much dearer was it to her than any other joy that she wished to sink into nothing rather than survive it.[35]

"You were an old friend to me long before I saw you," Robert Browning read without surprise on May 14, 1864, "so that it does not seem unnatural to me to express the deep sympathy which I long have had for such a loss as yours, and which is now brought out afresh . . . as the dark shadows close around us."[36] Indeed he knew of Miss Wedgwood's flattering devotion to his poems. The poignancy of a lady in nearly inconsolable distress over a brother was doubly familiar. Nor was he a stranger to this lady's home, for off and on in more agreeable circumstances he had been wined and dined at her parents'—the Hensleigh Wedgwoods—all that past winter. Like many another affluent social impresario of London, Mrs. Wedgwood thrilled to the causes of Mazzini. A "very charming and accomplished Lady," Robert had noted to Isa of Julia's mother, "the daughter of Sir James Mackintosh."[37] On Hensleigh Wedgwood's possible charm and antecedents, Browning's letters maintain a forbidding silence. Yet this man was a grandson of the celebrated potter—that perfect exemplar of all self-made men in Samuel Smiles' *Self-Help*—who in his own right had resigned on principle from a Lambeth magistracy and then written philological tracts and an etymological dictionary. There is little to wonder at in the grandson—a gentle, shy, retiring scholar whose philology was less rewarding to a loquacious widower than chatter about Italy's wrongs. Certainly this house was not guarded by an ogre, but neither did anyone think of carrying off the distressed maiden within.

Instead everyone waited for mortality to take its slow, lamentable course. More than once, as May turned into June, Browning must have found himself noisily hurled toward the hushed parlors of No. 1 Cumberland Place in the airless intimacy of the new underground railway. Then, on June 25, he received a lengthy letter that began with an echo from the past—"Dear and kindest friend"—and ended with a portent for the immediate future, "When I can see any one, it will be you." In between these limits Miss Julia Wedgwood announced very plainly that "Bro" was dead, and less plainly that she would never marry, that she was entirely capable of safeguarding her feelings, and that she longed to tell Robert Browning something more but obviously would not—perhaps could not—do so. She was in a "delirium of sorrow," as she explained several months later.[38] Grief for the loss of beloved "Bro," sudden doubt about the benevolent governance of this world and a tendency to fall in love with Mr. Browning seemed all to be mixed in one gloomy, yearning emotion.

Robert managed to reply on the very same day. That a lady in extreme distress had chosen to call him "a cordial in this swoon of life"[39] could not be thought alarming—what, after all, had he cried out to Isa in the throes of a wilder distress? "Three years ago, in this very week," he fittingly reminded Miss Wedgwood, "I lost my own soul's companion." Yet women console and men are meant to be consoled. A reversal of these roles now tested his syntax—and his theology—to a degree. "If I have any instinct or insight—if I can retain and rightly reason upon the rare flashes of momentary conviction that come and go in the habitual dusk and doubt of one's life," his next sentence began and wavered on after a parenthesis, "—if the result of all this can no more be disputed as *something*—or even, as *much*—than pretended to be *everything*, then," it paused in a luminous cloudbreak, "I dare believe that you and that I shall recover what we have lost . . . ," only to conclude in a slightly darkening rush, "and my belief is a very composite and unconventional one, and I myself am most surprised at detecting its strength in the unforeseen accidents of life which throw one upon one's resources and show them for what they exactly are." Grief would be consoled as much by sympathy's effort as anything. Of "your feeling and mine," Browning thought he also "must write a little—the impulse being to write much, because very many earnest thoughts are excited by your letter—and . . . all of the multitude would confuse us in speaking and hearing." ("I have a fine ear for any strain in intercourse," Miss Wedgwood had warned.[40]) What then did he have in mind to say? "I shall tell you then," Robert wrote a little desperately, "that I do understand you, and know that you understand me."[41]

Darwin's cousin was pleased by this elaborate and highly successful effort to say nothing and promptly showed his letter to her mother. Proprieties first at Cumberland Place. The worldliest of the Wedgwoods was "startled"—seemingly less by Browning's style than by her eldest daughter's behavior—but "satisfied."[42] With this *imprimatur* from the social primate of a proper Victorian household, a precious friendship might be expected to run a smooth course.

For nearly a year it did. Through the summer Robert continued to call and to write, Miss Wedgwood continued to write back and to receive him—with an ear not a bit the worse, one suspects, for his clear, loud voice. "Bro" was resuscitated less often in her letters, layers of self-protecting cloud lifted steadily from his. There is a familiar debate as to who is feminine and who is not. "I am 'feminine,' if you are not," Robert tells her, and pleads twice for her photograph. Miss Wedgwood implies that he is a "Setebos" and prays "that you may continue to me what you are."[43] No photograph is sent. Robert grows candid, even deeply searching about himself. "I live more and more—what am I to write?—for God not man—I don't care what men think now, knowing they will never think my thoughts; yet I need increasingly to tell *the truth*—for whom? Is it that *I* shall be the better, the larger for it, have the fairer start in next life. . . ? Is it pure selfishness . . . ?"[44] And yet he is obviously very much taken up by this life. He tells Miss Wedgwood exactly how he would rewrite "Enoch Arden." He slays a reviewer or two for her. He dislikes Jenny Lind.

For Miss Wedgwood, the "next life" cannot conceivably begin soon enough. She is solemn, priggish even in moments of comparative levity. His heartiness baffles her. "Oh how long life is!" she cries from the gloomy spiritual stronghold of her Woburn aunt's, where one dare not open a newspaper on Sunday, and every day is "chiefly spent in prayers and meals" with two sanctimonious cats.[45] Her drab religiosity is gently rebuked by Robert, who owns to a "Devil's Gospel" and slyly praises the "practical atheism" of children. Her persistently annoying themes—that he is hideously "old," that death will snatch him soon, that his bereavement is unbearable—are likewise deftly parried. Is he so old? "I know that I possess at this minute every advantage that I had thirty five years ago, even to the health and power of physical enjoyment," he triumphantly boasts.[46] No doubt Miss Wedgwood's manner and outlook are antiquated enough to make him feel proportionately seventeen again. And yet clearly—while he is not in love—what invigorates him is the natural role of Orpheus that he plays with another helpless Eurydice confined in the thick darkness of morbid fears and besetting scruples. Once more Robert points upward to the light, to the restorative world beyond the worn edge of a prayer-book, to the colors and sounds this time beyond dismal Woburn and sedate Cumberland Place. He is wittily persuasive. And still of Eurydice hears him, she does not turn in the dark.

Early in August Robert—quite in need, after several weeks' Orphic effort, of new sounds and colors himself—took Pen to Paris where they spent an uneventful week, and then all four Brownings ventured south to Arcachon, beyond Bordeaux, for its "beautiful pine-forest" by the sea. Numerous Frenchmen had recently fancied Arcachon. On arrival, Robert found that the pine-forest had been "turned into a toy-town," with boulevards through the sand-hills, shooting galleries, a gambling casino. A weary two-day search in the environs sent them on to St. Jean-de-Luz and thence to the "awful Biarritz." Nowhere along the coast could they discover a house to let. Finally, giving up the prospect of swimming, they rented a house near Bayonne in the Basque village of Cambo, "with plenty of oak & chestnut woods, and everywhere the greenest of meadows" among mountains that resembled the Tuscan ranges for consolation. Consolingly, too, "charming girl-faces abound,"[47] Robert wrote Mrs. Story. However, he promptly found himself bored, sleepy, and "bilious." Ought he to have taken along something more to read than Euripides, George Sand's plays, Rabbi Benjamin of Tudela—and "Virgil—for the boy's plague"—he wondered?

He found a diversion. "I went this morning to see the mountain-pass called 'Le pas de Roland'," Browning wrote Miss Wedgwood on August 20, "—the tradition being that he opened a way through a rock that effectually blocks it up, by one kick of his boot, and so let Charlemagne's army pass." Sarianna drew a sketch showing a massive, jagged, nearly diamond-shaped opening in a layer of cliff through which a hillside distantly rises. But Robert's letter to Miss Wedgwood reveals decidedly more than his sister's sketch. Details in the scene are selected and heightened so as to become suspiciously symbolic: the effect at once reminds one of "Childe Roland" and suggests that Robert may have been looking at the Pass of Roland very deliberately for symbols. He notes the green river, the sharp mountain walls—"but I think I liked best of all a great white-breasted hawk I saw sunning himself on a ledge, with his wings ready."[48] One is tempted to say that Browning sees himself at this time as a sunning but ready hawk; and again, that the "white" soul of his heroine as well as the "hawk"-like visage and rapacity of his villain in the great poem he is about to write are quite opportunely caught up in the image of "a great white-breasted hawk." At all events, the "paladin's achievement" of Roland's prodigious and rock-shattering foot now seems to become a personal symbol for poetic achievement against great odds. ("Boadicea," he tells Tennyson two months later, for its metrical innovations brings to mind Roland who "hollowed a rock that had hitherto blocked the road . . . so have you made our language undergo [for] you."[49]) Browning planned to hollow a very large rock himself. The spectacle of Roland's legendary "one kick" inspired him, he told William Rossetti in March 1868, to lay out "the full plan of his twelve cantos" then and there in Roland's mountain-gorge.[50] Probably—as Paul Cundiff very persuasively suggests[51]—Browning had considered the organization of *The Ring and the Book* much earlier. Yet Roland's feat seems to have unloosened some obstacles in his mind, for late in September Isa Blagden suddenly hears that besides having had "a great read at Euripides" he has been attending to his new poem and has the "whole" of it in his head—"the Roman murder story you know."[52]

By then, the faces of Basque peasant girls had yielded inexorably to holiday uproar, sky-high prices, and the warm sea at Biarritz. The "standing attraction at one of the bathing-places," Robert reported as a concession to Julia Wedgwood's permanent mood, "is the increasing probability of somebody's being drowned in a certain ugly current which sucks you unawares under [a] rock: I saw one man who, two days ago, all but gave us the due entertainment."[53] The sea-loving Brownings survived the current—and by October 11 Robert and Pen were safely back in London. News of Landor's death in Florence on September 17 at the age of eighty-nine—"without pain, and, at the last, very patient"—had come as no shock in the meantime.[54] Some words of that magnificently harassed, acidly enduring, self-exiled egotist were virtually his own epitaph: "the elephant is devoured by ants in his inaccessible solitudes." "Bless us," Robert exclaimed, "if he had let the world tame him and strap a tower on his broad back, what havoc he would have made in the enemy's ranks!—as it was, they let off squibs at him and he got into a rage and ran off."[55] Browning himself was inclined to get into rages but of course enjoyed them too well to run off. Only Landor's two sons had followed the untamed elephant to his grave.

Autumn proved to be the most productive season yet spent at Warwick Crescent. In one sense, Browning was only following the oracle of Chelsea's advice. "Well," it had spoken in 1856, after a quantity of grudging and grumbling over *Men and Women*, "the sum of my ideas is: If you took up some one *great* subject, and tasked all your powers upon it for a long while, vowing to Heaven that you *would* be plain to mean capacities, then—!—."[56] No one's punctuation was ever more eloquent than Carlyle's. Four years after this oddly prophetic letter, Browning had unearthed a subject with no inkling it would prove to be his "*great*" one, had indeed mulled over it, put it aside, tried to get rid of it, perhaps even temporarily forgotten about it. Yet even the circumstances of his discovery were not to be forgotten.

On a day in June Browning had ventured into the furnace of a Florentine noon and at length into the Piazza San Lorenzo. As usual, the square was packed with make-shift wooden stalls peddling a vast assemblage of sun-baked and dilapidated junk, "odds and ends of ravage, picture frames,"

> Bronze angel-heads once knobs attached to chests,
>
> . . . . .
>
> Modern chalk drawings, studies from the nude. . . .[57]

Robert's upbringing stood him in good stead. Robert Browning, Sr., had an experienced kleptomaniac's eye for junk as well as a bibliomaniac's for bargains. Hard by the Ricardi Palace, the younger Robert now found what he had always been looking for—a vellum-bound collection of legal briefs, pamphlets, and manuscript letters pertaining to a forgotten and perfectly grisly *cause célèbre* involving a child bride, a disguised and probably adulterous priest, barter-in-the-flesh, vengeance and duplicity, triple murder, four hangings, and the beheading of a destitute and crazed nobleman straight out of "My Last Duchess."

Not waiting to read the Old Yellow Book's title-page, Browning fished for a coin. "Stall!" he shouted; and "a *lira* made it mine." One *lira*—as he repeats—a mere "eightpence English" for such a prize![58] Why, it would have darkened his father's face if that gentle old man had been capable of envy! In the broiling sun, Robert moved near a fountain and opened the old mottled covers. *Posizione Di Tutta La Causa Criminale,* he read in very beautiful hand-lettering, *Contro Guido Franceschini. . . .* "A Setting-forth of the entire Criminal Cause against Guido Franceschini, Nobleman of Arezzo, and his Bravoes, who were put to death in Rome, February 22, 1698. The first by beheading, the other four by the Gallows. Roman Murder-case. In which it is disputed whether and when a Husband may kill his Adulterous Wife without incurring the ordinary penalty." Not so absorbed that he failed to notice the bare ankles of girls who were filling copper pots at the fountain, Robert was still very absorbed. Finally, he remembered his invalid wife.

> . . . And on I read
> Presently, though my path grew perilous
>
> . . . . .
>
> Through fire-irons, tribes of tongs, shovels in sheaves,
> Skeleton bedsteads, wardrobe-drawers agape,
> Rows of tall slim brass lamps with dangling gear,—
>
> . . . . .
>
> Still read I on, from written title-page
> To written index, on, through street and street,
> At the Strozzi, at the Pillar, at the Bridge. . . .

By the time he reached "Casa Guidi by Felice Church,"[59] his eyes had run through with clairvoyance more than a score of documents relating to two cases of the utmost complexity and written for the most part in a particularly stilted, clipped, and barbarous form of seventeenth-century legal Latin.

> Under the doorway where the black begins
> With the first stone-slab of the staircase cold,
> I had mastered the contents, knew the whole truth.[60]

The account of this hazardous journey among Florentine bedsprings was composed four years after the event. Yet that he had "mastered the contents" of the Book within a few days of his lucky purchase is fairly certain. Reading the Old Yellow Book in C. W. Hodell's or J. M. Gest's translation, one discovers a sufficiently absorbing chronicle of human misery, filtering through a long-winded, case-citing, slow-motion duel between teams of competent professional advocates.

"My plan was at once settled," Browning told Rudolf Lehmann many years afterward. "I went for a walk, gathered twelve pebbles from the road, and put them at equal distances on the parapet that bordered it. Those represented the twelve chapters into which the poem is divided; and I adhered to that arrangement to the last."[61] Certain it is that in 1860 and 1861 Robert was of two minds about using the Yellow Book himself. On the one hand, he took it to Rome to see if there was "a tradition extant of such facts" and also pressed inquiries at Arezzo, where he found a few meager records of the Franceschini family in the town's annals.[62] On the other hand he tried—perhaps not very hard—to give it away. In Rome he offered the Book as the basis for an historical narrative to W. C. Cartwright, who for unrecorded reasons declined it. As the basis for a novel, he handed it to the very unlikely and surprised Miss Ogle, authoress of "that very pretty book" *A Lost Love,* who could make "nothing out of it." Mrs. Orr was practically certain that he sent it on approval "for poetic use" to a leading contemporary—who seems to have been none other than Tennyson. And, finally, an entry in William Allingham's diary reveals that Browning said at luncheon, on May 26, 1868, he had "offered [the Book] to [Anthony] Trollope to turn into a novel, but T. couldn't manage it; then R. B. thought, 'why not take it myself?' "[63]

Why not, indeed? Certainly no poetic structure he had devised so far seemed adequate to its complexities. Like Henry James later, he perceived a novel in the contrasting depositions and pleas of a murder case whose antecedent events were extraordinarily complex. The trial documents called for techniques in handling multiple viewpoints with an illusion of simultaneity that would tax the novelistic art of a Richardson. Even as late as 1868, Browning was dubious as to whether he could get people "to read through in proper order" virtually the same story told ten or eleven times. Again, he seems to have wondered whether it was worth telling at all. "He has told the story over and over again to various friends," Allingham drearily noted.[64] Robert of course had tested it on his wife. Elizabeth was perfectly repelled by its unexampled sordidness and had quite refused "to inspect the papers."[65] Perhaps while she lived—more surely for some months after her death—a definite decision to celebrate Count Guido's murderous exploits in verse would have been tantamount to infidelity. At some point in Robert's intermittent deliberations, the Book's victimized heroine acquired a new significance. Francesca Pompilia ceased to be an ignorant, angular, dark-haired, luckless, plucky, and brazen fourteen-year-old wedded child of questionable Roman parentage and took on the qualities of a saint on earth and in heaven. She became Elizabeth Barrett. She also became the effective center of an intricate architectonic framework, a focal and pivotal figure in an enormously spreading canvas, the dominant persona among so many dramatis personae, ultimately the justification of *The Ring and the Book* and of Robert Browning's personal vision of human history and human truth.

According to Professor Cundiff, "two years of both spasmodic and intensive preparation" for writing the poem lay behind him.[66]

Through Isa Blagden's help he had received from Mrs. Baker, a mutual friend in Rome, a manuscript account of Guido's trial and execution—"particularly useful to me," he told Isa, though not "correct in several respects."[67] He began writing optimistically: "[I] shall write the Twelve books of it in six months," Miss Wedgwood heard from Biarritz early in October, "and then take breath again."[68] To Isa he predicted the "Italian murder thing" would be "ready by the summer." Browning devoted at least three morning hours to it daily into the following spring. The phenomenal resurgence of his creative activity owed little to the recent approval of critics (for whom Robert's letters continue to exhibit scorn) and much to the exhilarating documents he had at hand. The Old Yellow Book seemed incontestably to prove the rightness of his view of life. The "Book" affected him quite physically—releasing his talents, filling him with industry, and lightening his mood:

> I turn its medicinable leaves [until]
>
> . . . . .
>
> A spirit laughs and leaps through every limb,
> And lights my eye, and lifts me by the hair,
> Letting me have my will again . . . .

"I am about a long poem to be something remarkable," he reminds Isa in March 1865, "work at it hard."[69] Indeed his diligence would have astonished Elizabeth herself no less than it would have pleased her: "for I used to idle enough in Italy—but here I stick to my business honestly."[70] When Edith Story visited England in July and invited Robert and Pen to Walton-on-Thames, Browning found that only a short Saturday visit would do. "I have no time," he pleaded, "—can never call, much less leave town for a day, but I neither am forgetful nor ungrateful, I hope: It is now the end of the season . . . and *my* working season," he emphasized significantly, "for I have written *8400* lines of my new poem since the autumn,—there's for you!" Even the Saturday had to be canceled. Edith told him he was "perverse." Robert admitted he was. "Then, Regattas," he apologized as lightly as he could, "—what has a grey owl like me to do with Regattas & the lovers of the same? No, no! the dark for me!"[71] So much darkness had seen him through hardly more than a third of the 21,116 lines he would write for his now phenomenally expanding murder story.

Not that he had spent three seasons altogether in the dark. Pen's "dreadfully incipient mustachios" were a new reminder of the frightful prospect of Balliol's examination for matriculation. Just before Christmas Browning's wish "to have talked over all these troubles of mine with Jowett" had been forestalled. The maker of diplomats was ill. But early in June 1865, a highly successful interview was arranged at Oxford. "I thought I was getting too old to make new friends," Jowett jubilantly reported to an old friend. "I believe that I have made one—Mr. Browning, the poet, who has been staying with me during the last few days. It is impossible to speak without enthusiasm of his open, generous nature and his great ability and knowledge. I had no idea that there was a perfectly sensible poet in the world, entirely free from vanity, jealousy, or any other littleness." Robert of course was on his best behavior. "Of personal objects he seems to have none," Jowett further noted, "except the education of his son, in which I hope in some degree to help him."[72] No doubt this very comforting hope was made known to Robert.

Robert was impressed with Balliol and told Isa later, "I was much struck by the kind ways, and interest in me shown by the Oxford undergraduates." The Oxford undergraduates were even buying and reading his poems. "Chapman says, 'The orders come from Oxford and Cambridge', and all my new cultivators are young men," he informed Isa in the same letter. As a matter of fact, *Dramatis Personae* already had gone into a second edition, and Moxon even now was printing in his *Miniature Poets* series a new "Selection" to complement Forster and Barry Cornwall's. Macmillan was "anxious to print a *third* Selection, for his Golden Treasury," Isa also learned, ". . . but *three* seem too absurd."[73]

Nor were Browning's social engagements very drastically curtailed during this first siege on *The Ring and the Book.* One hears of concerts, of a dinner spent elbow to elbow with Millais, of an Easter trip to Paris partly for the sake of Joseph Milsand's wedding. One even finds, on a night in May shortly after his fifty-third birthday, a very jovial and grizzled Robert "jammed between two ladies" on the crowded landing of a fashionable staircase and laughing out loud in this cozy human sandwich.[74] Less uproarious had been a letter from Julia Wedgwood on March 1 requesting him not to call upon her again. "I have reason to know that my pleasure in your company has had an interpretation put upon it that I ought not to allow," she had explained a little obscurely. "You will feel at once that it is a mistake which must be set right by deeds, not words."[75] Browning seems to have felt "at once" mainly puzzlement. In fact was Eurydice a trifle weary of Orpheus? Did she perceive that Orpheus had grown slightly weary of her? Or, perchance, was there truly mischief afoot? Unfounded rumors that linked him in impending remarriage to a whole host of breathlessly eligible ladies had been circulating in London parlors and drawing rooms all winter long. Robert was inclined to hear rumor's vicious tongue operating in the present case. He was annoyed—but sturdily tactful. "I thought from the beginning it was too good to last," he admitted to Miss Wedgwood, "and felt as one does in a garden one has entered by an open door,—people fancy you mean to steal flowers." He would "withdraw" his visits but not one whit of his "appreciation." If their friendship was incomplete, he then explained very gracefully, it was only so through his wife's absence: "she never had any woman-friend so entirely fit for her as you would have been—I have told you so sometimes." He could pay no higher compliment. Yet one detects a note of relief in the cheerful buoyancy of this letter from a very hard-working, very much sought-after poet. "Therefore, no goodbye! But, out of sight or in it, there will never come a change to my impression of you: and it is with no particular emphasis that I bid God bless you, my dearest friend."[76]

Perhaps Browning felt that a cessation of his visits would be only temporary. With more time at his disposal and in an absence of rumors, might he not find Miss Wedgwood willing enough to see mutually pleasurable attentions renewed? What he failed to understand was that in these last few months of grueling labor and intermittent gayety, his attentions had been less than adequate. Miss Wedgwood's pride was injured mortally. She sensed that his feelings were incommensurate with her own. Later she would offer a somewhat different explanation for her abrupt action—one nearer to the truth—and would write him exactly what she felt about *The Ring and the Book*. But she did not speak to him again.

CHAPTER 23

The Muse in Her Strength

1865-69

"Nothing is changed," Robert assured Isa from Ste. Marie near the Vendée on August 19, 1865. "Pornic itself, two miles off, is full of company, but our little village is its dirty, unimproved self—a trifle wilder than before." He and his family were once again in the Mayor's house. Mrs. Bracken with her "mild mournful voice" and the inevitable Willy were nearby. The weather matched Mrs. Bracken's voice: "rain every day," Robert noted nostalgically, "a contrast to the wonderful Biarritz & Cambo blaze of last year." Still the place suited him. He went for a daily swim in a creek. Umbrella in hand, he watched Pen and Willy race beneath granite cliffs in the chilly sea, "which after a time turns Pen's face into blue-black and makes his teeth chatter unmistakably." Healthy-faced, Pen raced headlong on dry land with his father through five books of the Aeneid and a quantity of translation into Greek—"which I correct." With Pen now sixteen, definite signs of progress were reassuring: "Oh, I am sure he'll *do*!"[1]

Robert relaxed almost thoroughly, found himself disinclined to "explore" out of doors even in a sunny September, each day taking the very same walk. Yet the Mayor's menage was unfailingly interesting. Out of "pure preference for piggishness," Isa was told, "he sleeps in one room with his son and three daughters" and "the somewhat less ugly than usual maid servant, . . . four beds in a row—and the notion that such an arrangement is queer will not enter a head in the village for the next fifty years." Manners so primitive had to appeal to a poet attempting to depict every level of a seventeenth-century society with minute fidelity. But Robert enjoyed the playful shock to Isa's sensibilities: "Fancy," he wrote a month later, "(. . .shall I be cruel enough to bid you? . . . yes, I will—) fancy the buxom servant girl, aged some 20, washing clothes before my window (on the pianterreno]), dressed in blue gown & nothing else, I can see, just covering the naked legs below the knees—and so kilted, turning her back to me and burying herself with linen she has to stoop for on the ground!"[2] One is left to wonder if Browning noted the effect of a buxom servant girl on Pen's sensibilities.

Having watched his son plunge seventy-three times and having himself plunged sixty into bone-chilling water in two months, he escorted his father and sister back to Paris, and a week later crossed the channel with Pen. They arrived home in time to read "the usual amount of insincerity" in the morning papers over Palmerston's death. Would the reckless old prime minister be remembered for longer than a week? "Yet I have an ambition that way for Pen, you know," Robert confided to Isa on October 19.[3] What encouraged him to believe that his son was cut out for a political career at all, even with Jowett's pedagogical wizardry? Determination in swimming? Manliness? Dutiful attention to Aeneas? As usual, Browning's oceanic self-assurance and optimism were at marvelous high-tidal crests after "the longest possible holiday." The sea-air made him feel "sixteen."

This autumn and winter he saw something of George Eliot, something of the hemisphere-trotting Storys, and a good deal of Tennyson—who, in a positive fit of sociability, "lit up the blackness" of London three or four times in a phosphorescent week in December.[4] Normally Robert ventured into the blackness only to find that anecdotal soirées and sumptuous dinners left very little impression.

But spring was full of the most alarming events and portents. On his regular visit to the French capital for a fortnight at Easter, Robert found that his elderly father was gravely depleted and unwell. "I went no where,—did not make a single call in Paris lest I might be induced to spend an evening away."[5] Back in London he heard from John Forster, in a perfect "paroxysm of grief," a detailed account of Mrs. Carlyle's sudden death while out riding with her dog in a carriage.[6] Carlyle, absent in Edinburgh, where he was being fêted as the new Rector of the University, had not yet been informed. What effect the shocking news would have on that emotionally unstable, deeply devoted, and profoundly dependent old philosopher, Robert could hardly imagine. Actually Carlyle faced his loss with remarkable philosophy. Some months later, Thomas Woolner found "the dear old fellow in good spirits" at the house of a very lovely widow who "rejoiced in having the mighty man to pet and honour and make cozily comfortable."[7] It is true, Louisa, Lady Ashburton, seldom failed to comfort the mighty.

In May 1866, Robert was looking forward to taking Pen to visit Jowett at Balliol—"and don't my heart just beat!" And yet, for all his concern with the present, he had been living again for months in his own past and in the Italian past. He had lovingly edited a selection of "Ba's poems" for Chapman ("how I have done it, I can hardly say") and made immense progress with his murder story. "Browning must think himself the greatest man living," the Laureate had snorted to Allingham. "His new poem has 15,000 lines—there's copiousness!" "16,000 lines, or over,—done in less than two years, Isa!" the greatest man himself exclaimed in weary triumph on May 19, "I having . . . [given] the precious *earlier* hours of the morning to it, moreover, which take the strength out of one."[8] His problem as he saw it was to transmute history into poetry, to cause once-living Italians to speak for themselves again within his own gigantic, revitalizing, blank-verse framework. If *The Ring and the Book* was composed consecutively, as he later claimed, he had just finished resurrecting Giacinto de Arcangeli and Giovanni-Battista Bottini. His weary letter to Isa is filled with exasperation for Italians, both dead and living.

Sarianna's terrible telegram arrived in June. Robert Browning, Sr., was dying. Leaving Pen in care of Occy and Arabel, Browning hurried with unimaginable thoughts to Paris, arriving in the Faubourg St. Germain on the thirteenth at eight o'clock in the morning to be met on the staircase by his haggard sister: his father was in convulsions. That momentary crisis past, Robert promptly packed Sarianna, who had kept vigil two nights, off to bed, greeted Milsand, took his own station at the octogenarian's bedside, and listened to medical reports. There was a tumor, an internal hemorrhage. Yet even as he watched, the stricken patient calmly opened his eyes, and, recognizing his son, said "with just the usual air, that he was perfectly well," as Robert informed Pen in a note scribbled at 2:30 that afternoon. There could be no doubt about the melancholy outcome. "I shall stay to the end. . . . Let me have the comfort of knowing, dearest, that you do your work well,—and act like a man in my absence." Pen was also adjured "to take exercise, to row as usual, and to walk more than usual." Meanwhile the old man lingered on. Toward midnight, he asked to shake hands with Milsand, and then said very mildly to his son and daughter, "If we do not meet again, I hope we shall meet in Heaven." Once more Robert ordered Sarianna to bed.

"Shall I fan you?" Robert gently asked.

"If you please, dear," responded the dying man. "I'm only afraid of tiring you."

Sensing something amiss, Sarianna again bounced up in her nightdress, but Robert resolutely coaxed her to her room so that she should not "witness the last struggle." That struggle ended—"to my infinite joy, for the suffering was terrible to see," as he wrote a little dramatically for Pen's benefit—at 8:25 the next morning, twenty-four hours after he had reached his father's bedside.[9]

Robert was profoundly touched, but scarcely devastated, by the loss of a parent who had lived the life of an inveterate child. Fortified by his daughter's daily ration of a few coppers, this wiry little widower with blue-gray eyes and a sheep's nose had spent his last, happy years sauntering and sketching along the Seine with his pads and pencils, and returning home at nightfall with Hogarthian caricatures of faces, worm-eaten eighteenth-century volumes, a clear conscience, and quite horrible anecdotes. At his son's bidding, he had compiled an immense dossier on a pope—"a regular book of researches, and a narrative of his own, exhausting the subject"—and proudly collected a whole shelf of periodical reviews of Robert's poems.[10] But the biographical novel about the illustrious Romans that he had always intended to write had never been written. Erratically erudite and almost infinitely gentle and ineffectual, he was at least "worthy of being Ba's father," Robert solemnly told Isa. "*He* said . . . while gazing at her portrait, that only that picture had put into his head that there might be such a thing as the worship of the images of saints." The old gentleman's legacies were chiefly two: a vast library of literary curiosities and Sarianna herself. "My sister will come & live with me henceforth. You see what she loses," Browning observed with a strong sense of familial guilt, "all her life . . . spent in caring for my mother, and, seventeen years after that, my father: you may be sure she does not rave and rend her hair."[11]

Indeed, Sarianna never had been one to rave and rend her hair. She was far too practical. So devoted a family caretaker could hardly have found time to indulge in those luxurious demonstrations of feeling with which her brother had once rocked the walls and shattered the quiet air of Hanover Cottage. Wisely, Browning left her in charge of their father's effects.

He returned to London in the grim mood suitable for a housecleaning of his own. The morning after his arrival he wrote an exasperated letter to Chapman. Real and imaginary sins of the publisher had been accumulating. Careless in sending accounts and remittances, he had grossly offended Miss Blagden—whose unprofitable and tepid romances he published with an eye to keeping Browning on his list—and lately even William Story. Somehow *Dramatis Personae* had proved a comparative failure even after glowing reviews. "I am profoundly discontented with him," Browning announced to Isa, apparently with no great concern for the tepid romances, "and shall dissolve our connection,—on my own account, not yours only."[12]

Chapman at once took alarm. New documents and new promises were speedily forthcoming. A brittle *rapprochement* was effected that lasted for little more than a year. Beginning in 1868, George Murray Smith—publisher of a dazzling constellation of Victorians including Darwin, Ruskin, Trollope, Matthew Arnold, and Charlotte Brontë—brought out Browning's poems. The truth was that Chapman had demonstrated his belief in the poet's unpopularity once too often, whereas Smith had shown every little sign of confidence and friendship over the past two decades. Certainly a *magnum opus,* now nearing completion, could not be allowed to fall into the clutches of "a scatter brain creature" who "forgets, makes excuses, and worse."[13]

In July, with Brackens at heel, Robert took his son and sister to Dinard, thence to St. Malô, and then farther south in Brittany to the sea-surrounded fishing village of Le Croisic, where he discovered "the most delicious & peculiar old house I ever occupied." Several of its cavernous rooms looked across a loop of sea to the distant moat, towers, and walls of fortified Guérande. Nearby were flat, rectangular salines tended by gaudy paludiers from Batz who still dressed as their forefathers had in white tunics, white breeches and stockings, and immense black flap-hats fringed in red. Sensuality on the sandy peninsula vied with an easy austerity. The Croisickese—Robert delightedly noted for Seymour Kirkup's scandal-loving eyes—were "still Pagan a couple of hundred years ago, despite the priests' teaching and preaching, and the women used to dance round a phallic stone still upright there with obscene circumstances enough,—till the general civilization got too strong."[14] For Isa, he noted "two pretty sisters" who waited on table at Les Guérandaises Inn, and confined himself to the picturesque.[15]

How did Pen, now bewhiskered and seventeen, react to sensual enchantments? Either this summer or next his activities seem to have extended beyond swimming, shooting, and going with Willy to the local races. Frances Winwar reports that Pen fathered two daughters by different "peasant girls of Brittany" before he turned nineteen.[16] Browning himself, regularly digesting *The Times, The Athenaeum,* and the *Illustrated News,* and sightseeing with two middle-aged ladies, wondered wistfully if Pen would very much longer continue to kiss him "morning and night, as he now does." He decided that Pen was still "growing,—a boy: he seems to me able to do many things for which at present he has little or no inclination,—and that inclination may arrive at any moment." Did he understand which inclinations might momentarily arrive? Again his view of Pen seems rose-tinted with prospects of Balliol and also reminiscent of earlier self-congratulations. "The bases of a strong and good character . . . are more than indicated," Isa is told. "He is good, kind, cautious, self-respecting, and true: I ought to be satisfied."[17]

Satisfaction, at any rate, continued well into the new year. Work on *The Ring and the Book* alternated with ever more urgent tutorials at Warwick Crescent. "I have my poem to mend and end in the gaps between Greek and Latin." A talkative monologuist in a manuscript could be made to wait a little, but hardly a candidate for Jowett. Late in January 1867 that deeply obliging Olympian suddenly spoke about another matter. Matthew Arnold intended to vacate the Oxford poetry professorship in June. Would Browning be willing to become a candidate for the chair? With nightmarish anguish and vividness, Robert saw himself writing lectures. Then—almost immediately—Jowett retracted the offer since the Oxford Council declined to propose the requisite Master of Arts degree. Had the professorship definitely been offered, Browning wrote Isa, "I should have accepted it—simply on account of the wish I have to stand well with,—and, above all, near to—the University where Pen will spend the next three or four years. . . . Had they wished me to blacken their boots instead of polish their heads, I should not have demurred, you understand, in the prospect of possible advantage to Pen."[18]

Jowett, also wishing to be helpful, invited the boy to Oxford for a week in March. The result, a monumental prescription for nine months' reading in Homer, Thucydides, and Livy, duly reached Warwick Crescent along with a firm suggestion that Pen's hurdle be postponed. Browning nervously wrote to delay the matriculation, and heard soon afterward from Jowett's lips that Oxford intended to heap astonishing and glorious honors on his very own head. First, he would receive the Master of Arts degree by diploma at Convocation—"before the assembled universe," as he reported gleefully to Isa in June. Not since Dr. Johnson had any literary Englishman been similarly honored. "Of course, it is purely for Pen's sake—though I am not insensible to the strange liking for me that young & old Oxford seems to have—WHY?" There was even better in store. "For they are going, once the degree given, to elect me Honorary Fellow of Balliol!!!"[19] To the accompaniment of renewed applause from the assembled universe, the honorary fellowship was bestowed in October 1867—by which time his son's matriculation had been again ominously postponed. Could such very delicious academic honors turn to ashes in the mouth?

For her part, Sarianna contributed sanity and stability to his household this year as she did for the next two decades. Slim and briskly energetic, with thick blue-black hair now turning gray, she kept a matter-of-fact eye on jam-pots, linen, and servants, dusted tapestries, entertained visitors, spoke crisply and sensibly, and left Robert to the heady ardors of poetry and his season of dinners. She preferred to retire early with a good book. Moncure Conway found her to be a "bright and cheery lady"[20] and Henriette Corkran always envied her implacable spirit and resourcefulness as a *raconteuse.* Having determined to begin an anecdote, Sarianna completed it, pausing on one occasion only for a moment or two when a friend burst into the room to announce a mortal calamity. "She generally stood up when she related anything, and as she was very short she would stand all the time on tiptoes. Though not handsome, she had an extremely pleasant, shrewd face, sparkling brown eyes, and a nice figure."[21] Robert had little reason to regret his sibling inheritance or the influx of possessions Sarianna had brought with her. Surrounded now by shelves of his father's books—many of them comprising his own first literary inspirations and redolent of the emotional securities of his boyhood—and with a devoted and uncritical sister as household companion and châtelaine, he actually managed to grow fatter. When John Stuart Blackie paid a call on May 14, he was surprised to discover the widower of six years "an active, soldier-like, direct, rather stout little man—a fine contrast to the meditative ponderosity of Tennyson."[22] Robert demonstrated how unlike Tennyson he could be by chasing around the room a tame owl, which glowered back at Elizabeth's correspondent of old with its black, beady eyes.

Three days after this visit, he felt quite direct and soldierly enough for a moderate passage of arms with the inscrutable Miss Wedgwood. Her mother had written from out of the blue to ask him to dine. "I shrink—altogether for my own sake," Robert informed Julia with elaborate caution, "—from beginning again, without apparent reason, what may be stopped once more as abruptly and as painfully without reason one whit more apparent."[23] Julia quickly replied that she had not wished to see him anyway and twitted him over "the long delay of the appearance of your Italian,"[24] which, as Browning had told her, now consisted of eighteen thousand lines and might be ready for her approval in the autumn.

Certainly his progress with the poem had fallen off just of late. Intimate dinners with "very interesting" people such as Gladstone and Lord Russell and rather less intimate ones with "perhaps three hundred" others had kept him out at all hours. Even the past had proved distracting in the shape of Wilson—once more adrift after having wavered between the seducements of starting a cigar shop or a pastry-cook's, and dismally failing as a lodgekeeper in Scarborough. With her equally incapable husband she wished to return to Florence—"where," Robert pronounced, "she will infallibly go mad."[25] Not without feelings of guilt for his neglect of the unlucky pair, he had tried to forestall madness, first by interceding with Wilson's sister in East Retford and then by offering employment to both Wilson and Ferdinando at Warwick Crescent. No doubt for Pen's sake he was relieved when they shook their heads. Isa was told that he feared for his household economy.

In Croisic this summer distractions seemed faint and far off. Again the roomy old Maison du Bochet was available, and again "great rushing waves,"[26] salt air, and Breton enchantments of the past and present wonderfully cast their spell. Robert observed that he could paddle in cold sea-water for three quarters of an hour without tiring. One hears little of his murder poem but something of another one. In a village guide-book called *Notes sur le Croisic,* by Caillo *jeune,* he discovered the story of a common sailor, who in 1692 had saved D'Amfreville's fleet from the English and the Dutch by piloting twenty large frigates at night through a slim channel into St. Malô Harbor. As his reward Hervé Riel had demanded and received an absolute discharge from the French Navy. Perhaps for this reason French authorities had forgotten to honor his memory. Browning, who usually read French without a fault, later claimed to have mistaken the phrase *congé absolu* to mean a single day's shore leave.[27] Thus "Hervé Riel"—the touching and even rather stirring ballad that he now wrote and dated from "Croisic, Sept. 30, 1867"—romanticizes and sentimentalizes history, for the poetic Riel with his "frank blue Breton eyes" and manly directness asks his officers for nothing more than twenty-four hours in which to visit a handsome wife:

> "Since on board the duty's done,
> And from Malo Roads to Croisic Point, what is it
> but a run?—

Since 'tis ask and have, I may—
  Since the others go ashore—
Come! A good whole holiday!
  Leave to go and see my wife, whom I call the Belle
      Aurore!"
  That he asked and that he got,—nothing more.[28]

Browning's own feeling is evident in the sailor's ardent yearning for the Belle Aurore. One also sees impressively how many of his doctrines he could squeeze into a ballad that is simple and colorful enough to appeal to a child: the helplessness of institutions, the necessity of self-reliance, the redemptive value of decisive action, the supremacy of love, even the "infinite moment" that transcends time and makes human history significant.

Has Riel cheated himself? Probably Robert could not imagine a greater reward for a hero. Moreover—though ballad heroes are notoriously simpleminded—the apparent simplemindedness of Riel's choice seems less impressive than his uxoriousness and his navigational skill. The peaceful seafaring citizens of Le Croisic agreed: some years after the poem was published an heroic bronze effigy of the Breton at his helm was erected on a high pedestal near the entrance to their own harbor. Material for a longer and funnier poem was also discovered in Caillo's guidebook—but Browning postponed his mock celebration of two Croisickese poets until 1877.

London was an awful reminder that he had postponed his murder poem too often. Precious morning hours seemed too few. In the middle of October Robert resolved to get up at five without the comfort of a fire, and kept to his stoic schedule but for a half-dozen "exceptional times"[29]—when he rose at six—until well into the following spring. Still the date for the poem's completion steadily advanced. In July, he had predicted that it would be printed in October. In October, Edward Dowden read: "I am finishing the exceedingly lengthy business, . . . hope to be rid of it in a few months." In November he wavered to Isa: "It will be out about May next—I *trust*." Yet on no account would he be rushed. "It won't appear a day before it is ready if I wait another two or three years. . . . I have all my time to myself: not only do more but with infinitely greater freshness."[30]

Freshness owed something to the fact that home tutorials had come to a merciful end, for by the autumn of 1867 his son was imbibing the inspirational air of Oxford with a favorite tutor and was thoroughly enjoying—at least—his own boat. Not for nothing did Pen obey the parental injunction to pull on an oar whenever he could. "I heartily like him," Jowett comfortably reported on December 22. "He is repairing his deficiencies in Greek Grammar & will I think be quite ready for Examination at the beginning of the Easter Term." Admittedly, Olympian eyes detected two new deficiencies: Pen seemed to have a bad memory and was also "unused to writing in English."[31] Robinson Ellis, the distinguished Catullus scholar of Trinity, was prescribed for Greek; nothing was prescribed for bad English or a bad memory. Pen met the champion of Catullus three times a week, continued with his regular tutors, attended Jowett's Greek lectures, rowed his boat, sat for his matriculation on April 2, 1868—and failed. "The boy himself stoutly maintains he was 'not very nervous,'—which of course is an illusion," declared Robert directly afterward. "But don't contradict him, as it may do harm instead of good. He intends to rest here a fortnight, return and study hard . . . [and] try again."[32] Failure only indicated to parental eyes the need for redoubled application, leaving unaltered the view Robert had expressed some years before in a lighter mood: "I cannot venture to disturb the regular roll of the disciplinary wheel that is to grind a Balliol student out of the little long-curled, velvet-clad fellow."[33] For a few months more the mechanical wheel would continue to grind. Pen's tutors, at any rate, were not to be blamed. "Anything like teachable youth, *he* will teach," the father wrote of Mr. Gillespie, with whom Pen worked that summer until he joined Jowett's instructive reading party at St. Andrews for five infinitely hopeful weeks.[34]

Yet it was an agonizing time even for an optimist. In June—by now the month of all his worst disasters—Robert discovered that Arabel Barrett was almost at death's door and that her doctor did not sufficiently recognize the gravity of her condition. "I made him call in a second wise man," he wrote Isa, "who saw with the eyes of the first." Scornfully noting a superabundance of female attendants at her house on June 10, Browning went to hear Rubinstein play at a party, returned home late, and was wakened at dawn with an urgent message. He dressed hurriedly, rushed along empty streets, and again at Arabel's bedside awaited the delayed arrival of trained medical eyes—which soon gave him an opportunity to indulge his rich hatred of them. The doctor "repeated that there was no immediate danger. . . . So he went, and, five minutes after, I raised her in my arms where she died presently."[35]

Now a nerve-wracking week passed before George—"the useful brother"—could be reached in Ireland. Occy Barrett in the meantime was a study in futility, and Browning himself felt equally futile, deeply depressed, and—as he admitted—"full as a sponge of vinegar & gall." He remembered a morbid note that he had written in a copy of Elizabeth's *Poems before Congress* on July 21, 1863. On that day Arabel had told him of a singular dream in which with startling vividness she had seen "Her." " 'When shall I be with you?' " she had inquired of Elizabeth's hovering apparition. " 'Dearest, in five years,' " had been the ghostly reply. Arabel knew "her question referred to her own death." The prophecy had been uncannily fulfilled, Robert now observed. "Only a coincidence," he told Isa on June 19, "but noticeable."[36] The larger, more noticeable fact was that he had lost in a brief span of seven years his wife, his father, and the one sister of Elizabeth Barrett's whom he had truly loved. His emotional ties with the living were steadily narrowing. His sister's well-being could practically be taken for granted now that that eminently sane and happily unmarried middle-aged lady dwelt with him under his roof. His hopes and worries were inevitably to concentrate even more intensely on Pen.

Of course, there was also poetry to live for. J. T. Nettleship was publishing a whole book about his poems. Murray Smith had recently brought out in six handsome volumes *The Poetical Works of Robert Browning, M. A., Honorary Fellow of Balliol College, Oxford.* "A pretty piece of respect, after all," Browning wrote about this conspicuous display of his academic honors, "and I like it better than tokens from nobody." As a matter of fact, the instructive edition had reached his critics' hands at an opportune time—for the Italian murder poem was "as good as done."[37] With eyes nevertheless focused on the stark realities of timetables, Robert took Sarianna in August on a sightseeing tour of Brittany. To Isa Blagden, he reports with the factuality of a stationmaster a list of places visited. But finally—in Audierne, out near the westernmost tip of continental Europe, where brother and sister were to rest for six weeks and also correct proofs—Robert found a setting worthy of a few adjectives: "a delightful quite unspoiled little fishing town, with the open ocean in front, and beautiful woods, hills & dales, meadows and lanes . . . so [we] have no cares, for the moment."[38]

Indeed his cares were confined to the British Isles—as he rediscovered when he returned to them. A letter postmarked from Scotland arrived at Warwick Crescent on almost the same day that Robert did. In the clear air of St. Andrews, a veil seemed to have fallen from distinguished and conscientious professorial eyes. "We were very glad to have him with us, . . ." Jowett politely wrote of Pen on October 8. "I wish I could say that he was quite certain of getting through [his Balliol matriculation]. But I see that to accomplish that is a more difficult matter than I supposed. Shall I tell you . . . the exact truth?" The exact truth appeared to be that while the young man could do some "really difficult things" with Thucydides and Homer, he could not do the very simplest ones. "I have scolded him a little but only to impress on his memory," Jowett added, "that λύπη does not mean a wolf."[39]

What could be done for a boy who had no heart to remember the meaning of λύπη? Whose weakness of memory perhaps was a sign that he remembered all too vividly the limitless indulgence of his mother, the truancy and gayety of Ferdinando, the lusty, wild, whitecapped, zigzagging freedom of Tuscan mountain torrents? "My son is well," Browning informed Miss Wedgwood on November 5, "—just going not to Balliol, alack, as I hoped would be,—*why* after all?—but to the more congenial Ch[rist] Church: he will never be an adept at grammatical niceties."[40] Perhaps Balliol stressed grammar altogether too much. Surely diplomats need not be nurtured on Greek? Robert struggled to conceal the fury and bitterness of his disappointment, and also to avert his eyes from the harshest of the facts. Jowett was remorselessly cooperative. "If he is not unwilling," he wrote on November 13, "I think that he had better stay here for a time & get some help in his work."[41] In consequence, Pen fumbled on obediently with his books, sat for an easy trial of his Latin and Greek, and early in the new year was matriculated at the most populous of Oxford's colleges—one having "a large number of undergraduates," gravely warns a contemporary academic handbook, "who do not, and perhaps do not intend to, take their degree or even pass any examination."[42] But even with its vast floating population of dandies, its gentlemanly cricketers and its somewhat lax standards, it was still Oxford.

Robert was pleased and relieved both for Pen's sake and for his own. "They have given him good rooms," he glowed to Isa in January, "and he is enjoying himself extremely. I chose my own rooms at Balliol—side by side with Jowett's—it will be pleasant, won't it?"[43] No less pleased to be sure was Pen, who would soon have several handsomely engraved Christ Church cups to show as tangible proof of his skill at rowing and at billiards.

Browning was perplexed and worried as late as May 1868 by the problem of presenting his Italian murder poem. What method would be most advantageous? He needed to turn the limited stamina and patience of readers to best account. He had planned to let the resourceful Smith bring it out in two attractive volumes—but the poem had grown to a positively enormous size. Perhaps in the manner of nineteenth-century novels it should appear serially in a magazine—"but no," Robert contradicted himself at one of Allingham's convivial little luncheons, "I don't like the notion of being sandwiched between Politics and Deer-Stalking." It had not been designed to be swallowed on the run in railway depots. "I think of bringing it out in four monthly volumes," Allingham heard over the tea-cups, "giving people time to read and digest it, . . . but not to forget what has gone before."[44]

Smith—who seems to have proposed the plan of monthly installments—came to a "definite arrangement" with Browning about format and publishing dates on July 11, 1868. He also liked the poem well enough to offer £1,250 for the English publication rights for five years. Fields, the American publisher, was having prophetic doubts. When he insisted on only two volumes and £50 as payment, Browning promptly exploded, but when he explained that "four bites at such a masterful cherry" would "puzzle the American appetite" and slyly raised his offer to £200, he had his way. Unhappily, Browning puzzled the American appetite even in two bites. Fields lost several thousand dollars, to the bitter chagrin of a businesslike wife who could see nothing but "twaddle" in the murder poem.[45]

Smith, at any rate, with his quiet encouragement, his exceptional munificence, and his everlasting patience clearly was proving to be the ideal publisher. The only remaining problem appeared to be that of a title. "I have been thinking over the 'name' . . . ," Browning wrote Smith uneasily on July 30, "—but do not, nor apparently shall, come to anything better than 'The Franceschini;' *that* includes everybody in the piece. . . . I think 'the Book & the Ring' is too pretty-fairy-story like."[46] Actually, the more Thackerayan title would soon impress him with its advantages—for "the book" and "the ring" would allude to his poem's central source, to its circular pattern of monologues, to its villain's "round" of diabolic journeyings, and even to Elizabeth—its muse. Not long after this letter, Browning perhaps noticed that *The Ring and the Book* suggested his own initials—and therefore, of course, what he had told Elizabeth he had always wanted to write, "R. B. a poem."[47]

To his most trusted critic and closest friend Joseph Milsand he showed in advance of publication only Books I and II. But Julia Wedgwood was to read it all. "Now, I shall have your sympathy," he wrote her this momentous autumn. ". . . I shall be as sure of your honesty," he took care to add, "but I may beg—not so much for your courage, as your confidence in my own somewhat stiffish texture of mind, and my ability to bear banging, if you see cause to bestow it."[48] Conceivably he might be in for a little critical banging from Miss Wedgwood. Why was he anxious to have her read *The Ring and the Book*? Indications of her incurable morbidity and philistinism, her solemn rigidity and utter lack of interest in common humanity could not have escaped his notice. But almost equally evident is Browning's tendency—dating from their intimate exchanges of sympathy after "Bro" Wedgwood's death—to regard her among living mortals as the person most nearly like Elizabeth. For Julia's intelligence, virginal purity, ethical elevation, renunciation of the world, and moral earnestness were in themselves closely akin to those of the one saintly soul for whom his long poem had been written.

"Ah, dear friend," Miss Wedgwood responded from Dundee, whence she had gone to superintend Thomas Erskine's imminent departure for a better world, "how vain is the attempt to criticise when I hear your voice in my ear again!" Still she promised to look for him "only" in his work—and a few days later had read his first two volumes. "You give a stereoscopic view," she pronounced on November 15, ". . . and the solidity is quite satisfactory." Less satisfactory was nearly everything else. Above all, why did a sense of evil so seethingly predominate in *The Ring and the Book*'s portrayals? "But surely, surely we have more of this than that small white figure can bear,"[49] Julia complained on Pompilia's behalf; she hungered for a better demonstration of the supreme lesson of love's power that Mr. Browning must have learned from an incomparable marriage.

Robert was grateful for her comments and also—at first—nettled. "I value your criticism," he replied almost by return mail, "over and above its being an utterance of yours, beyond what words are likely to make you believe." Yet she must understand that he had overstressed neither good nor evil in the poem and had only attempted to explain certain *facts* recorded in his source. "I was struck," he replied firmly, "with the enormous wickedness and weakness of the main composition of the piece, and with the incidental evolution of good thereby—good to the priest, to the poor girl, to the old Pope . . . and, I would fain hope, to who reads and applies my reasoning to his own experience." That "curious depth below depth of depravity" which he had found "in this chance lump . . . might well have warned another from spreading it out,—but I thought that, since I could do it, and even liked to do it, my affair it was."[50] Nor could he promise her anything more salubrious in the two volumes to follow.

"I thought I shared your interest in morbid anatomy," Miss Wedgwood responded with noticeably increasing dismay on December 3. "You say," she quoted him, " 'this is God's world, as he made it for reasons of his own.' I demur. Guido seems to me not at all to belong to the world, as God made it." She found his Italian villain utterly unrelieved, contemptible, unredeemable, unfathomably depressing. "Shame and pain and humiliation need the irradiation of hope to be endurable," Julia poignantly cried; ". . . you have no right to associate them in our minds with hopeless, sordid wickedness."[51] Browning tactfully delayed seven weeks before returning with more elation to battle. Already he had read aloud some earlier parts of the poem to Tennyson—who doubted in private that it could be popular but found it "full of strange vigour and remarkable in many ways."[52]

Not even a bindery fire delayed George Murray Smith's preordained plan. Four dark-green monthly installments of *The Ring and the Book* duly appeared in London under the Smith and Elder imprint on November 21 and December 26, 1868, and on January 30, and February 27, 1869. Browning's most daring poetic experiment was at last before the world.

Grief had been the incentive to an effort of imagination that transformed seedlings of Old Yellow Book "facts" into a Gothic forest of interpreted experience. Indeed *The Ring and the Book* integrates all of Browning's important experience—it is a final reconciliation of his religion, his England, his Italy, his poetic career, and his love for his wife.

What had he actually seen in the Old Yellow Book?

He claimed—in his poem, in letters, in conversation for twenty years afterward—that he had not changed its story by an iota: he invented nothing. If he created some thirty-three characters out of a "mass of almost equally balanced evidence,"[53] every detail of his poem that describes any one of them—whose very names he has extracted from the Old Yellow Book—is "*true.*"[54] His constant affirmation and reaffirmation of fidelity to the trial records is enough in itself to send one to the Yellow Book. Actually he took over an astonishing wealth of circumstantial data; he rejected or overlooked the more vital and less tangible matters of history—the real Count Guido's imbecility, the real Pope Innocent's political motives, the real lawyers' professional acumen—and fashioned a Caponsacchi and a Pompilia out of the heroic prototypes in his personal romance. As in "The Glove," he defends again the weaker, optimistic, more paradoxical side of a case. Carlyle expressed much of the commonsense side when he said "the girl and the handsome young priest were lovers."[55] Beatrice Corrigan's[56] patient research in *Curious Annals,* of 1956, seems to confirm commonsense and Carlyle.

As Elizabeth was once, Pompilia is imprisoned in a castle guarded by a watchful monster. As Browning once, Caponsacchi is confronted by a strict social code and even stricter scruples, which he defies to save a mortally threatened lady by flying south with her in a jolting carriage through Italian scenery. The priest's experience of feminine weakness on a journey is Robert's of Elizabeth, but the chasteness of the rescue suggests Robert's offer at one point during their courtship to "live as a brother" with his lady, if only he might be allowed to rescue her. Caponsacchi's love can burn all the more intensely in that it never will attain, and yet rise in conformity with Browning's doctrine of failure into a pure ozone where soul disinterestedly worships soul. The attributes of Caponsacchi's own soul are those of Browning's—enthusiasm, impulsiveness, chivalry, courage, and a rich capacity and an instant readiness to hate as well as love. If the pre-Pompilian priest, holding duchesses' hands and sipping mild refreshments in well-decorated chambers, is a fair prediction of what the poet is to become, the later priest is a picture of what he always was. For Caponsacchi—too—fervently trusts in action and just as fervently distrusts intellect. When he deliberates he is wrong (as when he delays in coming for Pompilia because he is lost in thought with Aquinas)—but when he answers his instinct without a thought for consequences, he is right. He exists rather as Browning did in order to feel intensely, and to expose the futility of most traditions and the corruption of most institutions—the Catholic Church in particular. Even his poignancy derives from an acutely felt bereavement:

> . . . My part
> Is done; i' the doing it, I pass away
> Out of the world. I want no more with earth.[57]

Pompilia, in her turn, expresses the grandest illusion of Browning's life—his belief in the childlike innocence and divine goodness of Elizabeth. She is the priest's and the poet's *donna angelicata.* Her dark beauty, charity, articulateness, and perfect naïveté clearly derive from the middle-aged child Browning first saw at her father's house and last saw in the "young girl"[58] who expired in his arms. As DeVane has shown, the poem contains no fewer than thirty allusions to the twin and cognate myths enacted at Wimpole Street.[59] Moreover its two great, central crises involve both a Perseus who carries off an Andromeda and a St. George who balks a dragon to save a virgin. As Caponsacchi snatches up a soul of purity from the beastly Guido, so at the last moment Pope Innocent slays Evil's sophistries to preserve Truth. The first crisis celebrates the decisive outward action of Browning's life, the second, most of its inward and mental action.

Though he read the Old Yellow Book autobiographically, Browning also read it eight times over. At the outset, his poem boldly highlights its chief source:

> Do you see this square old yellow Book, I toss
> I' the air, and catch again, and twirl about
> By the crumpled vellum covers . . . ?[60]

Giddily, the precious Book spins. Robert Browning dandles it, twirls it, thrusts it figuratively into the reader's hands, and whisks it away in a wink. His jubilation is understandable enough. The Victorian age was turning into a helter-skelter race for "documents" and becoming Comtian with a vengeance. Wilkie Collins' poised notebook as he peered through narrow spectacles and an omnibus window into London's tenements was a small sign of the times; Dickens' busy inquiries into prison records and opium dens, a greater. In a continuing landslide caused by the tremors of scientific rationalism and the higher criticism, what could remain in place for long but primary documents and provable facts? "Why, I almost have you at an unfair disadvantage," Browning tells Miss Wedgwood, "in the fact that the whole story is *true*!"[61]

But it is important that trial records are—by their very nature—impressionistic documents. Realities partly filter through limited, subjective viewpoints in the depositions of witnesses and the pleas of lawyers, and they partly consist of these same viewpoints. The viewpoints conflict and develop in the bud drama, irony, complication, and distortion. The materials of the Yellow Book suggested not only an enormous experiment in literary impressionism, but how such an experiment might be organized. Here was an action large, violent, and paradoxical enough to lend intense interest to the mental operations of nine people who would not reenact it, but think and talk about it.

Suspense in *The Ring and the Book* would be psychological and intellectual. Between Books I and XII—a capacious outer frame in which the poet's voice broadly interprets—ten versions of the past action gradually reconstruct its truth in entirety. The truth is difficult because it involves not only whether Francesca Pompilia was innocent, but what kind of person each character concerned with her was, and even the whole inward experience of each. Thus the poem's movement is partly from outward inward—from peripheral and superficial viewpoints of spectators to profounder and more central viewpoints of the three surviving participants and of the Pope, whose sincere and sympathetic projection enables him to see and to judge actors and action alike. It is at the center of the action treated in turn by each speaker that inward life is the most rich and various, in the consciousnesses of Caponsacchi, of Pompilia, and even of Guido, whose second monologue is the reversal that shows real inwardness in his case. A gradation from worldly to spiritual motives is implicit. Caponsacchi and Pompilia suddenly rise above the sordid level of bourgeois litigation and civic murder to reveal themselves in all their splendor. The larger movement is also circular and dialectic. Each speaker regards the past action from a different point at the edge of a round compass of possibilities. From a plea in favor of Guido, to an antithetic one for Pompilia, to a monologue of more impartial synthesis, the poem edges ahead in three cycles of intricate grandeur—each a mirror of the murder trial—to an ultimate resolution in the Pope's synthesizing judgment and in Guido's unwitting vindication of it in his last self-exposure.

"Do you see this Ring?"[62] As in a sculpture half-emerging from the rough marble Rodin indicates his material as well as his finished work, so Browning in his story's frame indicates the matter out of which he fashioned his poem—the valuable Castellani ring that Miss Blagden had given his wife, the Yellow Book, Italy, Elizabeth herself, and his own experience. The ring is weighted with all the symbolic freight that it can bear. Is it overweighted? Quite probably Paul Cundiff[63] is right when he says that Browning understood Castellani's craft well enough. The process of mixing alloy with pure gold to shape the ring parallels that by which Browning mixed imagination with pure fact for his poem. If a quick spurt of jeweler's acid at last removed alloy from the ring's face, so the poet's imagination in effect vanished from the surface of his work—to be enveloped and subsumed by the psyches of his historic monologuists, whose speeches owe to it for their artistic design, interrelations, and ultimate meaning. "Do you see this square old yellow Book . . . ?"[64] Everything we do see relates to the Book. Further, Browning minutely describes the process of his reconstruction. "This is the bookful," he confidently says at line 364—and a little later, "You know the tale already. . . ." We are told what he thinks of each actor—who was noble or ignoble, courageous or cowardly, wise or foolish, good or evil—and even what each reconstituted monologuist looked like and sounded like when he spoke. Yet we are still called upon to judge nine speakers for ourselves when we have heard them, and in our turn to experience the difficulty of positive judgment.

> See it for yourselves,
> This man's act, changeable because alive!
> Action now shrouds, now shows the informing thought;
> Man, like a glass ball with a spark a-top,
> Out of the magic fire that lurks inside,
> Shows one tint at a time to take the eye:
> Which, let a finger touch the silent sleep,
> Shifted a hair's-breadth shoots you dark for bright,
> Suffuses bright with dark, and baffles so
> Your sentence absolute for shine or shade.
> Once set such orbs,—white styled, black stigmatized,—
> A-rolling, see them once on the other side
> Your good men and your bad men every one,
> From Guido Franceschini to Guy Faux,
> Oft would you rub your eyes and change your names.[65]

We rub our eyes in bewilderment when called upon to judge human actions absolutely—even after being told where to look for guilt and for innocence. Acts are inevitably deceptive—"changeable"—and not to be judged until we have recovered all of the viewpoints and motives of the actors and those who were acted upon. And this means participating in the relevant psychological experience—the complexity of which *The Ring and the Book* is intended to illustrate.

At the same time—and paradoxically—ten dramatic monologues are ten consciousnesses within the consciousness of Browning himself. Multiple points of view here do not suggest skepticism or relativism in the poet's ultimate attitude to history but re-present his experience in approaching it. Guessing at the way Caponsacchi and Guido may have spoken "from the facts undoubtedly in the mind of each," as he told Furnivall, "I raised the whole structure of the speeches."[66] But he "guessed" and raised the structure to confirm his own visionary apprehension of the truth, described in Book I, and to persuade the reader of its rightness. Fundamentally, Browning has very little in common with Ranke and his contemporary school of historiographers who believed in the value of massive primary documentation as a basis for historical judgment, and much in common with Carlyle who believed that historical facts and "viewpoints" are useless until a great man arrives with transcendental insight to interpret them. As Professors Altick and Loucks point out,[67] Carlyle's own essay "On History" (1830) nearly predicts the method of *The Ring and the Book.* Honest and perceptive though their recollections may happen to be, even the makers and eyewitnesses of events—here, Pompilia or Caponsacchi—understand fewer of "the real cardinal points" about what has happened than do history's seers—here, the Pope, Fra Celestino, and Browning himself.

Why then are the voices in "Half-Rome," "The Other Half-Rome," and "Tertium Quid" permitted to speak in the poem at all, let alone at such length? Representing the "noise of Rumour's thousand tongues" in Carlyle's essay,[68] they initiate recorded history by offering along with gross illusions and petty prejudices ascertainable facts. In Books II–IV, they give detailed and surprisingly complete accounts of Pompilia's story, and vividly reconstruct for the poem that seventeenth-century religious and social *mise-en-scène* that elicited the wonder of Henry James. Their "wonderful dreadful beautiful particulars"[69] steadily accumulate. Many of the particulars carry special conviction—as when Half-Rome describes the multiple murder wounds, or the behavior of Pompilia's judges, or the taunts of his Aretine countrymen who believed Guido to be cuckolded. Half-Rome's "feel after the vanished truth," The Other Half-Rome's "opposite feel," and Tertium Quid's elegantly "reasoned statement of the case"[70] ascribe false motives to the principal characters, and yet furnish the stage upon which those principals are to be revealed so completely.

"Devils are made to serve," Browning remarked to Emerson while gazing at a gargoyle in the South Kensington Museum.[71] If Pompilia's saintliness is one outstanding effect of *The Ring and the Book,* Guido's diabolism is certainly the other. Auras grow round both characters as the poem proceeds, the final irony lying in our suspicion that the poet is almost equally attached to both. At least if he adores Pompilia, he is delighted with Guido—a villain who feelingly observes all of Browning's rules for heroic villainy. Guido *acts*: he plots, schemes, traps, tortures, hates furiously, smashes, tears off in wild pursuit of Pompilia twice with blood-lust in his eyes, and finally stabs three people to death. Then he further obliges at his trial by proving to be the ideal casuist in "Count Guido Franceschini" and, still later—when he progressively strips off layers of psychic camouflage before our very eyes—the ideal self-revealer in "Guido." Indulgence for him is suggested not only in Browning's letters to Miss Wedgwood, but in the simple fact that Guido is given 500 more lines than Pompilia and Caponsacchi combined. He is so much in motion—his character always is—that one is not too surprised by his apparent recognition of a saint in his final line:

> Pompilia, will you let them murder me?

As with Ottima and Sebald in *Pippa Passes,* and again with Dante's Sordello and certain others in the *Purgatorio,* he is probably to be regarded as a penitent of the last hour. Far beneath him in the Pope's and Browning's estimation are his brothers Paolo and Girolamo, who neither act much nor expose themselves much.

Where does Guido come from? Very little from the Old Yellow Book. Iago, Milton's Satan, Richardson's Lovelace, Dickens' Sikes, and perhaps a half-dozen tormented Gothic monsters in Mrs. Radcliffe, Maturin, and Bulwer-Lytton seem to blend in him; Swinburne—writing in *The Fortnightly Review* for May 1,1869—detected a mild resemblance between Count Guido and Shelley's Count Cenci. Considerably stronger resemblances are ascertainable in the vigorous, antisocial intelligences of "My Last Duchess," "The Laboratory," "Soliloquy of the Spanish Cloister," and of Maffeo in *Pippa Passes.* As a matter of fact, Guido had been in preparation all along, and had even been showing terrible glints of himself from time to time in every real D. D. Home or Mrs. Eckley clever and evil enough to trick and humiliate a personal saint.

Certainly his climactic monologue has intensity, grotesque beauty, psychological and pathological interest, and—though its 2,425 lines do not seem too many—immensity. If Browning's earlier dramatic lyrics are quick visits to haunted houses of ego, "Guido" is a nightmarish plunge into an immense labyrinthine Inferno of the mind, Dantesque in ingenuity as well as vividness, where at each turn of the descending passage grotesque effigies of fear and death flare up. In his first monologue, hatred darts—"that mongrel-brat, my wife."[72] Now its ferocity is fully exposed. Cardinal and Abate who kneel in Guido's cell only infuriate him with the mumbled prayer and the upraised cross, since he is at once the post-Darwinian Victorian who believes in nothing but the sensuous, graphic reality of death and the hardened, seventeenth-century Roman murderer who would tear himself to pieces to escape it:

> Leave my teeth free if I must show my shag!
> Repent? What good shall follow? If I pass
> Twelve hours repenting, will that fact hook fast
> The thirteenth at the horrid dozen's end?
> If I fall forthwith at your feet, gnash, tear,
> Foam, rave, to give your story the due grace,
> Will that assist the engine half-way back
> Into its hiding-house?[73]

This monologue is realistic in being an examination of the diseased psyche of a splenetic and shabby provincial intellectual who has turned killer—the sort of examination John Jasper's mind might have received at the end of *Edwin Drood* had Dickens lived—and symbolic and mythic, as well, in being an anatomy of evil's titanic power and resourcefulness in the world since Adam's fall. "We differ apparently in our conception of what gross wickedness can be effected by cultivated minds," Browning informed Miss Wedgwood, "—I believe the gross*est*—all the more, by way of reaction from the enforced habit of self denial which is the condition of men's receiving culture."[74]

Only apparently—not in essence—does an archfiend have the final word in a series of ten extended self-revelations. Everything that Guido says confirms not only the exalted wisdom of the Pope but the pure folly of the Roman lawyers in the two preceding monologues. "Archangelis" and "Bottinius" are admittedly violent caricatures—the one moderately hilarious, the other thoroughly emetic in the vein of "Mr. Sludge"—that reduce the institution of law to absurdity and lawyers to hypocrites or impercipient buffoons. "As for the lawyers, why . . . just so, I have known them," Browning blandly insisted. And he had known Italians: D. G. Rossetti wrote to say how Arcangeli recalled the domestic pleasures of a childhood "passed wholly among Italians, though in England."[75] Actually, Arcangeli's monologue seems to lampoon many domestic Victorian virtues along with the law. It is also a masterpiece of impressionism. By presenting the coarse and trivial *bon vivant* at work on his case for the defense, Browning gives himself unlimited access to associational progressions. Every distraction that can beset a mind as it approaches, and haltingly accomplishes, a task beyond its grasp is recorded by a mini-camera and soundtrack positioned inside blubbery Arcangeli's mouse brain—which at last produces a mountainous brief for Guido that is nine-tenths rhetoric and one-tenth sheer viciousness. Bottini's brief for Pompilia certainly mixes rhetoric with viciousness in approximately equal parts. There is doubled ironic energy in the fact that the lawyer who speaks in her behalf cannot recognize, much less trust in human goodness.

Pope Innocent XII, on the other hand, repeats Browning's own performance by conjuring up the presences of the actors, and a few other presences besides, to evaluate persons and events with dispassionate wisdom. Like Browning, Innocent makes up his mind instantaneously. He sees into and assorts moral complexities in the flick of an eyelash. His judgments are Last Day Judgments—apocalyptic in their strength and confidence of expression, lack of equivocation, extremity and decisiveness. Only the Comparini seem to be left in the middle ground between absolute guilt and absolute innocence: everyone else is either everlastingly damned or saved. Browning's view of things admits of no purgatory, or at the most, of a purgatory thinly inhabited. As the other speakers do, Innocent invents images that illuminate something about the person who speaks them as well as about the persons they describe. The Pope's animal images and colors are uniquely and starkly emphatic and final in their suggestiveness. Black, blue, and yellow are all linked with hideous evil. Twice Guido is the "wolf"—a metaphor he himself obligingly embraces later on; Paolo is "a fox"; the accomplices, "swine." White is for Pompilia, red for the valiant Caponsacchi. At the same time, Innocent's soliloquy is among the chillier features of a poem in which the speakers seem even farther apart in time and space than do the characters of *Paradise Lost,* whom we see interacting. Half-Rome and The Other Half-Rome, Caponsacchi and Pompilia, Guido and the Pope do not communicate —nor collide—with each other. Tertium Quid's listeners seem bored and aloof. Bottini and Arcangeli never meet. They are all brought together in the mind of Browning—and therefore by transference in the mind of his dramatic representative, the old Pope, who manages to talk in effect, with nine or ten shadows.

The Pope's Catholicism is anachronistic, even fraudulent, since he begins his discourse with the gruesome account of Pope Formosus patently to refute the doctrine of papal infallibility:

> Being about to judge, as now, I seek
> How judged once, well, or ill, some other Pope.
>
> . . . . .
>
> Which of the judgments was infallible?

He then comfortably and amply expounds Victorian Nonconformist theology. As E. D. H. Johnson has shown, Innocent is something of a William Jamesian pluralist.[76] He is very nearly a Kierkegaardian existentialist. His doubts about the ultimate basis and value of Christianity finally lead him to contend with the summoned shade of Euripides, who in lines 1669–1789 points out that souls cannot be judged, that his own pagan teaching is at least as good as Christ's, and that the modern Church, infested with corruption, is beyond redemption.

"How should I answer this Euripides?"[77]

Matthew Arnold's glorious pagan is never really answered, and Browning's yearning in "A Death in the Desert," in "Cleon," and in "Karshish" for an earlier, less ambivalent, more dramatically uplifting "day-spring" of Christianity is once again apparent. Equally apparent is a somewhat unsurprising garden of flowering theses, most of which had taken root in Browning's thought as early as *Christmas-Eve and Easter-Day* in 1850—that life is merely probation, that probation involves a sore trial of human endurance, that intentions and efforts are more important than accomplishments, that disbelief actively sustains belief, that imperfection leads to aspiration, and that God perfectly manifests Himself through self-sacrificing love. A. K. Cook's note on life as probation fittingly alludes to Leslie Stephen's remark that Browning "repeats the most familiar of all arguments . . . as if they had never occurred to any one before, instead of being the staple of whole libraries of theology."[78] Pope Innocent's arguments show him more impressive for his sincerity and decisiveness than his wisdom. But ultimately, of course, his decisiveness is his wisdom—for it symbolizes the bold, brave readiness to believe that will save humanity in an age of overwhelming doubt soon to be ushered in by Voltaire. Belief is equivalent to action, and *action* saves. Appropriately enough, his harshest general censure is reserved for mere talk:

None of this vile way by the barren words
Which, more than any deed, characterize
Man as made subject to a curse: no speech—
That still bursts o'er some lie which lurks inside,
As the split skin across the coppery snake,
And most denotes man![79]

Lest we miss this and certain other dignified, didactic pronouncements by the Pope, they are reiterated in Book XII by Browning disguised as Fra Celestino, and then by Browning without a disguise.

It is perhaps when *The Ring and the Book* is read after the Italian monologues of his middle years—"The Bishop Orders His Tomb," "Andrea del Sarto," or "Fra Lippo Lippi"—that one sees in it the seeds of Browning's decline: his didacticism or, more, his increasing lack of faith in himself and loss of force in his visions and beliefs, his consequent need to trumpet them too loudly. Self-justification is never more apparent than in his final, condescending address in Book XII,

> So, British Public, who may like me yet,
> (Marry and amen!) learn one lesson hence
> Of many which whatever lives should teach:
> This lesson, that our human speech is naught,
> Our human testimony false, our fame
> And human estimation words and wind.[80]

—an address that reveals the Shelleyan seer more than a little embittered. Didacticism and self-justification are weeds that Browning henceforth is to let grow.

Yet *The Ring and the Book* remains a magnificent—and very readable—colossus. More impressive than the dogmatic pronouncements by Celestino or Innocent, or Browning's Carlylean view of historic truth, or the manner in which Caponsacchi and even a grudging Guido cooperate to glorify Pompilia—are the poet's splendid intuitions into the operations of minds, his unprecedented and largely successful exploit in dramatic structure, his circumstantial and thoroughly convincing Italian backgrounds, and his simultaneous management of techniques in imagery and symbol and allusion as well as in syntax and word choice and sound to convey character traits indelibly and intimately. In several respects the poem is remarkably in advance of its time. Its style looks forward and undoubtedly contributes to impressionistic modes of the twentieth century. To convey mannerisms of the speaking voice, the poetry steadily deprecates itself by prose expressions, by abrupt transitions, by sudden touches of humor or violence, by offhand allusions, by seemingly unstudied interjections, and even by unmelodious strings of compound epithets. There is the fat Pauperum Procurator, thinking of his slim legal rival Bottini:

> Don't I know his trick!
> How he draws up, ducks under, twists aside!

> He's a lean-gutted hectic rascal, fine
> As pale-haired red-eyed ferret which pretends
> 'Tis ermine, pure soft snow from tail to snout.
> He eludes law by piteous looks aloft,
> Lets Latin glance off as he makes appeal
> To saint that's somewhere in the ceiling-top:
> Do you suppose that I don't see the beast?
> Plague of the ermine-vermin![81]

When the style rises to lyricism—as in the invocation to Elizabeth in Book I—it verges on the embarrassing:

> O lyric Love, half-angel and half-bird
> And all a wonder and a wild desire,—
> Boldest of hearts that ever braved the sun. . . .[82]

But it could not be more adept than in the two colloquial gossip monologues of Books II and III—the one crass, masculine, vindictive, and vulgar,

> Serves the priests right! The organ-loft was crammed,
> Women were fainting, no few fights ensued,
> In short, it was a show [of corpses] repaid your pains
> For, though their room was scant undoubtedly,
> Yet they did manage matters, to be just,
> A little at this Lorenzo. Body o' me!
> I saw a body exposed once . . . never mind!
> Enough that here the bodies had their due.
> No stinginess in wax, a row all round,
> And one big taper at each head and foot . . .;[83]

the other sentimental, self-pitying, intuitive, and effeminate:

> Another day that finds her living yet,
> Little Pompilia, with the patient brow
> And lamentable smile on those poor lips,
> And, under the white hospital-array,
> A flower-like body, to frighten at a bruise
> You'd think, yet now, stabbed through and through again,
> Alive i' the ruins. 'Tis a miracle.[84]

The novel that Henry James with so much gusto and approval

detected in the poem's "inordinate muchness" was not fully possible until 1922, since its techniques in imagery at least are too demanding for pre-Ulyssean prose. On the other hand, *The Ring and the Book* owes to novels from *Clarissa* and *Humphrey Clinker* to Dickens and Collins for its skill and resourcefulness in telling a story with conviction—and much excitement—from limited points of view. The last poem of epic length in English of indisputably high stature, it advances beyond the epic in its mature psychological content, paralleling the contemporary fiction of Meredith and of George Eliot and, in this respect, the later fiction of Mann and of Proust, of Joyce, of Virginia Woolf—and, indeed, of Henry James. We "can only take it as tremendously interesting, interesting not only in itself but with the great added interest, the dignity and authority and beauty, of Browning's general perception of it," wrote the author of *The Ambassadors*, in 1912, adding typically—and perhaps as truly—"We can't not accept this."[85] In his boldest handwriting, Browning some fifty years earlier had indicated his own opinion of *The Ring and the Book* in Pindar's Greek on the stained flyleaf of the Old Yellow Book:

For me the Muse in her might hath in store her strongest shaft.[86]

An immense landslide even in the literary world presupposes many big and little rocks on a brink. Nudged into position by the sympathetic legend of his bereavement and by their familiarity with his works, by their suspicion that greatness somehow had become attached to his name, by their love of culture heroes, and by their sense of something extraordinary in a poem four volumes long, the British weeklies and monthlies of Browning's day were poised to topple. At times, in 1869, their roar was something much more than rational—mindless, violent, and deafening. "The fascination of the work is still so strong upon us," thundered Robert Buchanan in *The Athenaeum* of March 20, 1869, "...that we feel it difficult to write calmly and without exaggeration; yet we must record at once our conviction, not merely that 'The Ring and the Book' is beyond all parallel the supremest poetical achievement of our time, but that it is the most precious and profound spiritual treasure that England has produced since the days of Shakespeare."[87] ("I had long regarded [Browning] with idolatry," Buchanan partly explained later.[88]) Pompilia "will rank among the highest of the great women of art," boomed *The London Quarterly* in July.[89] Not in "the whole range of English literature" could there be found "a creation worthy of being compared with her," *Chambers's*

Journal loudly echoed at the end of the same month.[90] "There is no writer who is so thoroughly acquainted with all the sorrows," resounded *The Edinburgh* in its turn.[91] "He presents a boundless chaos of accidental knowledge," plunged with an unsteady roar *The North British Review*—after some hesitation—down the same slope of acclaim.[92]

What was most impressive about the landslide was the sheer bulk of periodicals and columns of print involved in it and perhaps also the force of a few crashing boulders that seemed to sweep everything before them. After *The Saturday Review* of December 26, 1868, had paused to fret over the poem's resemblance to an actual legal trial, there came J. A. Symonds' compelling notice in *Macmillan's Magazine* of January. "We are content to peruse," he wrote in part, "the modern law-case; why should we not bring the same freshness of interest to bear upon this tragedy, not stripped, as happens in newspapers, of its poetry, but invested with all the splendours of a powerful imagination . . .?"[93]

But nowhere was that powerful imagination better defended than by John Morley in *The Fortnightly*—in a thirteen-page notice that quite coincidentally demolished Julia Wedgwood, and that was followed, perhaps less coincidentally, by her humble admission to Browning four days later, "I find the British Public is beginning to like you."[94] "After we have listened to all the whimsical dogmatising about beauty," Morley proclaimed on March 1,

> to all the odious cant about morbid anatomy, to all the well-deserved reproach for unforgivable perversities of phrase and outrages on rhythm, there is left to us the consciousness that a striking human transaction has been seized by a vigorous and profound imagination, that its many diverse threads have been wrought into a single rich and many-coloured web of art, in which we may see traced for us the labyrinths of passion and indifference, stupidity and craft, prejudice and chance, along which truth and justice have to find a devious and doubtful way.[95]

Of course few notices lacked some reservation, and several huge rocks stubbornly refused to budge. Confronted with Browning's virulent anti-Catholicism, *The Dublin Review* was immobilized by horror. "Caponsacchi is a failure," it murmured in July. "If the author meant to make a hero of him, he ought to have been less like a young English parson."[96] *The Westminster Review* and *The British Quarterly* rolled a few feet with the avalanche in January, but came to a halt with the bitterest disappointment in March and April. To give "eight versions of the same story," said the *Quarterly*, obviously too weary to count straight, "yet nowhere to tell the story in its true and direct form, is of course original, but it is certainly inartistic. It is the newspaper in blank verse."[97]

Yet misgivings were couched in respectful accents. Not even the theme of adultery or the occasional bawdiness of Browning's language shocked very many Victorian sensibilities. Obviously the poet himself was pure, and just as obviously the idealization of his hero, heroine, and villain indicated that he could plainly distinguish good from evil, that he believed the old verities were still in place, and that he earnestly wished to edify.[98] His methods and design were curious, debatable, alarmingly bold—"Everybody has heard by this time what the plan is of this wonderful story," explained *The Cornhill* in February, "and knows how original and how daring was the attempt"[99]—so that the poem seemed morally impeccable and artistically modern.

Royalty soon heard that he had done something or other that was important, moral, and modern. On March 4, along with Lyell the geologist, Grote the historian, and his old friend the sage of Chelsea, Browning was presented to Queen Victoria in the dreary long drawing room of the deanery at Westminster. Carlyle, who very naturally did most of the talking, noted how the plump little queen "came softly forward" and "gently acknowledged with a nod the silent deep bow of us male monsters." To Browning, Carlyle heard Her Majesty say, "'Are you writing anything?' (he has just been publishing the absurdest of things!); to Grote I did not hear what she said: but it was touch-and-go with everybody; Majesty visibly *without* interest or nearly so of her *own*. This done, Coffee (very black and muddy) was handed round." Then Carlyle, shepherded forward for a *tête-à-tête* with the Queen of England, promptly sat down in her presence. "Nothing of the least significance was said, nor *needed*; however my bit of dialogue went very well," he gloated in his report.[100] Victoria, nevertheless, committed her own opinion of the various "celebrities" she had met that day to her private journal. Mr. Carlyle impressed her as a "strange-looking eccentric old Scotchman, who holds forth, in a drawling melancholy voice . . . upon Scotland and upon the utter degeneration of everything," but Mr. Browning was "a very agreeable man. It was, at first, very shy work speaking to them," she quietly admitted.[101]

"Yes, the British Public like, and more than like me, this week, they let their admiration ray out on me," Browning wrote Miss Wedgwood on March 8, "and at sundry congregations . . . I have seen, felt and, thru' white gloves, handled a true affectionateness not unmingled with awe—which all comes of the Queen's having desired to see me, and three other extraordinary persons, last Thursday."[102] But in April he told Sir Frederick Pollock that he thought he had secured the popular ear at last.

CHAPTER 24

"Some Faint Show of Bigamy" 1869-72

Not that the grand tumult of praise deeply moved a poet who could never forget *Sordello, Men and Women,* and the inconstancy, intellectual dishonesty, shallowness, and moral depravity of critics and reviewers in the mass. "So & so means to review [me]," Robert had told the Storys in a typical outburst when his fame was clearly on the rise in the 1860s, "and somebody or [other] always was looking out for such an occasion, and what's his name always said he admired me, only he didn't say it, though he said something else every week of his life in some Journal. The breath of man!"[1]

In the Spring of 1869, he had had enough of fashionable rave notices and spotless white gloves. Tigers who roared today would remember their claws tomorrow, and his popularity "this week"—as Robert suggests in the letter to Miss Wedgwood about the royal interview—could evaporate at any time. Actually, the Italian murder poem had secured him a lofty niche beside Tennyson, if not an astral one just beneath Chaucer or Milton.

In an irritable mood, Robert escaped to Paris, only to discover in April and May the depth and circumference of his own cynicism. He was worried about Pen's incentive and ill at ease with himself. Conversation with Joseph Milsand may have had its usual soothing effect. But Isa Blagden hears his scorn for an honorary dinner for Dickens, again for James Anthony Froude's "making such a Froude of himself" over the lord rectorship of St. Andrews—an honor that Browning had firmly declined; more scorn for Gustave Doré's pictures, which the painter had invited him to see; and more yet for an Academy fête back in London "where *perhaps* I was to have been called on to return thanks for—literature!" Impatient with the famous, Browning developed curious sympathies for the infamous. Girding himself in his crustiest armor, he called upon Mrs. Eckley, and came away with a milder opinion of the American demon who had duped Elizabeth and with a fresher memory of his wife's old capacity to be duped: "I say, in the bitterness of the truth, that Ba deserved it for shutting her eyes and stopping her ears as she determinedly did."[2]

His vexed mood was little appeased when he returned to Warwick Crescent in the middle of May. The next few months were to lead him down a treacherous slope from impatience and anger, through despair and bewilderment and physical illness, to an unguarded act he would come bitterly to regret. An insinuating attack in *Temple Bar* on his claim to be a poet certainly cut—but at the moment not deeply. "[Alfred] Austin's opinion," Browning acidly jotted in his copy of the magazine.[3] But Dean Liddell must have communicated news of an impending disaster for Pen at Christ Church—and this would strike beneath superficial grievances. One suspects, further, that it was during this spring that Robert learned of his son's sexual waywardness at Le Croisic. "An extraordinary press of matters,—if I dare not call them 'business',—matters for consideration, fell on me at the end of June,"[4] he mysteriously told Thomas Kelsall. To Isa he wrote from the Highlands in August that circumstances out of his control had forced him to forswear Brittany. "Whether travel in Scotland *please* me or no," he emphasized with sudden distaste for his favorite French province, "it does me more good in one week than Brittany in eight."[5]

By July 17, his eyes ached. Ten days later he was apologizing to old friends, the Lehmanns, for reneging on a dinner invitation. "I was unwell, having been so for some time—and felt the grasshopper a burden all day long in the house from which I never stirred." He was deeply in earnest about "being frightened a little by all this bad luck."[6] A few days later when he set out with Pen, Sarianna, and the Storys for a sightseeing trip through Scotland, Robert ran into a perfect stranger who "confessed (afterwards) he thought me dying."

Obsessed by his new worries over Pen, tallowy hued, and "thoroughly worn out & unwell," he accompanied his party to North Berwick, and then left with Sarianna for three days in Edinburgh. Later he followed the Storys to Abbotsford. Eventually, tiring of fashionable hotels, the three Brownings departed in search of quiet lodgings in village inns at Garve and Achanalt. This move proved to be a mistake. In a "hideous confusion of three weeks' constant inconstancy," Robert tottered "from bad place to worse."[7] There were picnics in damp heather during which he recited "loudly" from *Rob Roy* and also from the peroration of *The Ring and the Book.*[8] Fortunately he was not far from Louisa, Lady Ashburton's many-chimneyed and many-windowed Gothic-revival lodge at Loch Luichart. Robert had politely declined an invitation to visit her shortly before he left London. But now at last, one of the century's most talented comforters appeared in a shimmering cloud of pitying smiles and heartwarming entreaties, and "by main force" compelled them all to enter her resplendent estate.[9] For Robert, the visit was to have unforgettable consequences.

Not a few of Lady Ashburton's friends regarded her loyally as a colossal force of nature, or even as an immortal. "It seemed to my bewildered senses," wrote Hatty Hosmer after her first astonished meeting with Louisa in Rome, "that the Ludovisi Goddess in person, weary, perhaps, of the long imprisonment of Art, had assumed the stature and the state of mortals and stood before me." Admittedly—some months before this encounter—a resemblance between Lady Ashburton and Juno had been pointed out to Hatty by Mrs. Jameson on a casual stroll through the Ludovisi Gallery.[10] Moreover, time is kind to one's earliest recollection of a munificent patroness. But Henry James himself viewed Louisa as something larger than life—as a whole novel in the bud—and even the lynx-eyed Lady Paget beheld her as a threatening storm. That few people saw her steadily attests not only to the beauty of "square-cut and grandiose"[11] features, but to certain rather puzzling contradictions.

Browning's hostess had been trained almost from the cradle to entertain, to employ, to enthrall, and—if necessary—to marry great men. In this vocation she distinguished herself. Her mother, heiress to the immense Ross-shire estates of the Earl of Seaforth and social chieftainess of the Highland Mackenzies, was an admired friend of Sir Walter Scott and the probable original of Ellen in *The Lady of the Lake.* Her father was the Right Honourable James Alexander Stewart Mackenzie, a nephew to the Earl of Galloway. When Louisa was four, Stewart Mackenzie was returned as M.P. for Ross and Cromarty. When she was ten he was appointed Governor of Ceylon. When she was thirteen he was elevated to the Lord High Commissionership of the Ionian Islands. Shortly thereafter he died. Pretty "Loo" Mackenzie's upbringing was hardly disturbed by this anticlimactic event. Her mother continued to supervise her education in brief, culturally instructive trips to museums and art galleries on the continent. A whole succession of governesses and private tutors dutifully attended the child's needs at the family home of Brahan Castle. "Loo's" three brothers gravitated to the army and her two sisters to matrimony. One of her governesses was none other than Anna Jameson. Possibly on his honeymoon Browning heard something of the charming Mackenzie girl from that kindly, garrulous companion on the flight from Paris to Pisa.

Assuredly, when he first met the Mackenzie girl in 1862, less than a year after his bereavement when he was still dining out night after night therapeutically "in a cold-blooded way,"[12] she had begun to fill the splendid social role that destiny had prepared. By then John Ruskin had supplied a finishing touch to her training. He had taught her to draw. And by then Louisa was very happily married to a timid, distinguished widower, twenty-eight years older than herself, who was able to supply the few tangible and intangible necessities that she had lost with the death of her father.

Indeed William Baring, Baron Ashburton, had an unusual talent for happy marriages. For thirty-four years his first wife, the former Lady Harriet Mary Montagu, had kept him in a bright, absolutely necessary whirl of dinners, attracting no less famous and diverting figures than Carlyle and Thackeray while her husband pursued with muted diligence his dignified interests in national finance and state-sponsored education and served for one year as Ambassador to the United States. In due course, *Henry Esmond* was dedicated to him. Then, in 1857, the first Lady Ashburton died at Paris. Baron Ashburton, inordinately shy and instinctively conservative, soon recovered his equilibrium by wedding one of the most high-spirited young ladies in English society.

Certainly this quiet man possessed everything that "Loo" Mackenzie's heart legitimately required: fatherly kindness and tolerance, an international reputation, enormous estates to complement her own, available funds, and very celebrated and brilliant male friends, who quickly became her own. At Loch Luichart Bishop Wilberforce and Thomas Carlyle debated the value of conscience in the new Lady Ashburton's presence. ("With *his* good conscience," Carlyle pronounced of St. Paul, "he was one of the most meeserable of men."[13]) Alfred and Emily Tennyson soon succumbed to Louisa's remarkable talent as a hostess. D. G. Rossetti, Thomas Woolner, and Monckton Milnes swelled her dinner parties. Jane Welsh Carlyle confided in her—and the sage of Chelsea, who seems to have fallen in love with the first Lady Ashburton, with astonishing consistency fell in love with the second. After the birth of her daughter and her elderly husband's death, Louisa's undoubted charms and eccentricities became increasingly apparent to others.

Even in the mild glow of Henry James's recollections there is a hint of something awry, for, when James thought of her, "a liberal oddity, a genial incoherence" appeared "to declare itself as the leading note."[14] Another friend had a chance to listen to this leading note attentively in England and during Lady Ashburton's frequent whirlwind visits to Rome. "She was most attractive and very remarkable," Lady Paget recalls. "Generous, violent, rash and impulsive, ever swayed by the impression of the moment, she was necessarily under the thumb of somebody. Bevies of impecunious artists hovered about her like locusts, trades-people made fortunes out of her. . . . [She] threw large sums away for any object that caught her fancy. Though she not infrequently offended, she always fully and graciously retracted," and yet with "all her *engouement* for people and her enthusiasm for artists, a certain grim matter-of-factness ran through her, which told its story." In short, Louisa was "all contradictions," only a few of which appear to have been cultivated. She believed in mediums and wickedly ridiculed mediums; admired Gladstone and gayly applauded Carlyle when he did "nothing but abuse" Gladstone.[15] However, there were deeper inconsistencies that friends and foes alike were rather hard put to it to explain. At her various stately homes, Lady Ashburton entertained guests with unimaginable kindness while ruling over them in unmitigated tyranny. She exploded in wrath and outright violence, wilted in meekness, commanded, threatened, retracted, wept, and showered expensive gifts. Many veteran acquaintances learned as Henry James did to treat her "with a kind of traditional charmed, amused patience."[16]

But there could be no ambiguity whatever about her wealth or her taste. The Raphael, the Titian, the Rubens, and the Reynolds at Melchet Court were real enough, as were the stunning rooms hung with yellow and offset by black doors at her Kent house, where "semi-ruined" cartoons by Paul Veronese lined the staircases. Woolner and Rossetti were exceedingly well paid to sculpt and to sketch for her. Landseer did her portrait. Platoons of gardeners labored in miniature groves of tamarisk and ilex at the "enchanting little paradise"[17] of Seaton. In her impulsiveness, in her flaring generosity and usual neglect of the clock and the calendar, in her disregard of the ordinary feelings of others and in her very spontaneous efforts to console the world's sufferers, in her predilection for older, distinguished men indulgent of her foibles, as well as in her need to dominate occasions while being "necessarily" under someone's thumb, one detects more than a hint of the eternal adolescent in "Loo." Nor was emotional immaturity altogether a handicap. If at the age of forty-two she was somewhat spoiled, Louisa was still an entrancing mystery to all but a few who knew her.

"All goes well," Robert pronounced at last. [18] "The place is most beautiful," reported Sarianna, who rarely saw any earthly need for a superlative. "Lake and mountains, moorland and waterfall, everything is here; with abundance of books, newspapers, magazines and periodicals."[19] Pen donned his hunting costume, went out stalking in the birches around trout-filled Loch Luichart and promptly shot a royal stag—"the head of which," Browning boasted a day after Sarianna's letter, "will glorify his rooms at Ch[rist] Ch[urch]." As for himself, he was now becoming positively "russet" in the cold, invigorating air. Having been "bothered in the last three weeks beyond most folks' bearing,"[20] Robert could feel that the worst was over. As August turned into September he became unwontedly buoyant, optimistic, somewhat giddy in the well-provisioned realm of a handsome lady who maintained an exceptional complement of domestic servants. There were fresh grouse to whet the appetite, peat-water baths to console the limbs. On September 5 he composed a round robin.

> Dear Hosmer; or still dearer, Hatty—
> Mixture of *miele* and of *latte,*
> So good and sweet and—somewhat fatty—

he rhymed merrily for his old friend, whose Roman atelier already had been depleted of many a sculpted gewgaw and marble pile by Lady Ashburton's purchases.

> Why linger still in Rome's old glory
> When Scotland lies in cool before ye?
> Make haste and come!—quoth Mr. Story. . . .
>
> . . . . .
>
> Say not (in Scotch) "in troth it canna be"—
> But, honey, milk and, indeed, manna be!
> Forgive a stranger!—Sarianna B.
>
> Don't set an old acquaintance frowning,
> But come and quickly! quoth R. Browning,
> For since prodigious fault is found with you,
> I—that is, Robin—must be round with you.
>
> P.S.
> Do wash your hands, or leave the dirt on,

But leave the tools as Gammer Gurton
Her needle lost,—Lady Ashburton
Thus ends this letter—ease my sick heart,
And come to my divine Loch Luichart!

In Rome, Hatty dropped her chisel long enough to send Browning eleven innocent quatrains in return.

Tell him who stole my early love
  And while these tears abound
Rob' erst by name, to cherish me
  As he goes Robin' Round. . . .[21]

Meanwhile honey, milk, and manna were having some effect on the entire party. Everyone at the Gothic lodge except Pen and the servants had signed the robin. Spirits continued to mount in a general euphoria. The distinguished, widowed poet and the brilliant, widowed hostess discovered in each other much to esteem. And then—before many more days had passed—Browning found an opportunity to converse in private with a reigning divinity and to ask her in his most direct manner whether she would marry him.[22]

Lady Ashburton could also be direct—and the form of the proposal was mortally offensive to her. Indeed one wonders if in every layer of his consciousness Browning was as bewildered, then and thereafter, as he seems to have been by "the capital point of her quarrel with me . . .—having said that my heart was buried in Florence, and the attractiveness of a marriage with her lay in its advantage to Pen: two simple facts,—as I told her."[23] How far Robert got in expressing more palatable considerations can only be conjectured. But it was one of her own friends who likened Lady Ashburton to bolts of lightning. The wrath of offended goddesses is terrible and immediate, and the two humiliating qualifications to his proposal apparently resulted in more than one memorable scene. The degree of Robert's lasting fury at Louisa's response and the intensity of his reaction to subsequent gossip suggest emergency reserves kept—and used—to flood out doubts that his direct approach had been the most propitious and to swamp out other doubts more deeply disturbing.

As early as November 1863, Browning had written to decline an invitation from his new friends the Ashburtons—hoping that his "piece of self-sacrifice"[24] would be forgiven. Four months later, Baron Ashburton was dead, but Louisa shortly thereafter returned to London's drawing rooms "looking lovely in a spruce little mourning bonnet" as Jane Carlyle noted.[25] Browning did not see much of the spruce bonnet. His name seems to have been linked at this time in successive hypothetical marriages to various muses—Miss Gabriel the composer, Miss Bonham Carter the sculptress, and Miss Ingelow the poetess—but not to Baron Ashburton's widow despite a considerable number of acquaintances they had in common. There is no reason to believe that the "old friend" he came to see at Loch Luichart in August 1869 was in any sense an intimate one or that he really understood her.

Nor in all probability had he traveled to Scotland with marriage in mind. "It is funny people think I am likely to do nothing naughty in the world," Browning had told Isa in 1867, "neither rob nor kill, seduce nor ravish—only honestly *marry*—which I should consider the two last,—and perhaps the two first,—naughtinesses united, together with the grace of perjury."[26] With unremitting energy he had deflated rumors about his impending union with this lady or that. "When I feel my will going . . . ," he wrote the Storys, "I'll tell *you*, first people of all, so, till then, you know what to say."[27] Clearly for him another marriage would be a bigamous one—tantamount to perjury, or a certain sign that he had losts his wits. Was he not "married" in the deepest and most lasting sense to a soul whose connection with him strongly transcended the grave?

Considerations such as these were hardly of a kind to evaporate in the morning mist at Loch Luichart, or even in the rarer light of Louisa's Scottish beauty. They could not, would not be forgotten later on. Though he "had never left her in ignorance about, for a moment" the two "simple facts"[28] of his incomparable devotion to Elizabeth and their son, still a lingering sense that he had indeed perjured himself in Scotland remained his guilt-ridden incubus—diminishing with the years, but driving him at times into frenzies of remorse, into a fury with gossipers and a much deeper fury with himself. At the time of his proposal, Robert's "worry"[29] over Pen was acute. If his son left Oxford in disgrace Pen's future would be closed. Certainly his own marriage to a prominent statesman's socially well-connected widow could not help but unlock a dozen doors to the inner sanctums of politics, diplomacy, the law, commerce, even the military. Louisa had the power to lay the future at Pen's feet. A marriage of convenience would be honorable, so long as the premises were forthrightly declared.

Lesser insults on occasion had driven Lady Ashburton to tantrums. Yet it is clear that something more than her pride was shaken in

Browning's stolid presence, and that for months and even years she "tried on' conciliation"—as he once put it. Not even the mild, well-intentioned efforts of the three Storys mollified the dreadful hostility and bitterness of a rejected Robert. "I see every now and then that contemptible Lady Ashburton," he told William Story in June 1874, "and mind her no more than any other black beetle—so long as it don't crawl up my sleeve."[30] As late as "Parleying with Daniel Bartoli," Louisa is the nightmarish Present that intercepts the Past, a wickedly "bold she-shape,"

> A terror with those black-balled worlds of eyes,
> That black hair bristling solid-built from nape
> To crown it coils about . . . ,
>
> . . . . .
>
> As some war-engine from whose top was sent tall
> One shattering volley out of eye's black ball,
> And prone lay faith's defender!

One is not surprised to find in the poem a suggestion that Robert Browning's bitterness is that of a man who had fallen in love with black hair, black eyes, and limbs of "war-tower tallness"[31] quite against his will.

As the Loch Luichart party broke up, he was in any case a man profoundly stunned and angered. Moving unsteadily southward with the Storys, he seems to have become the object of their earnest alarm. In the company of other guests at Lord Carlisle's Naworth Castle—on the spectacular brink of a deep glen near the Cumberland border—he soon read aloud in what Sidney Colvin remembers as a strident tone of voice from "Pompilia." Story watched and took out his pencil. In his two sketches the poet bends forward from the waist, hand on hip, nose buried in *The Ring and the Book.* In the middle of the recital Robert burst into tears; within a few moments he had "nearly all his audience in tears with him." During this brief stopover Story was loud, robust, affable, and heroic. He kept the sufferer of Loch Luichart engaged hour by hour in a lusty marathon of anecdote, reminiscence, and repartee—so that apparently no one else suspected anything amiss. Colvin found the poet's conversation inconsequential, but amiably noted his "cordial greetings" and "confidential and affectionate gestures."[32]

At Warwick Crescent the familiar testimonials to his wedded life awaited him: busts and portraits, the haunted ebony furniture, the faded tapestries of Casa Guidi. His first night at home was interminable. "Having somehow got out of my good old habit of soundly and expeditiously sleeping," as he wrote Edith Story in response to two anxious letters that had awaited his arrival, "I continued to weary myself in bed—but in the end the sleep came, and I woke aware of the accustomed curtains and furniture, and none the worse for a little tossing and tumbling."[33] Perhaps he could learn to sleep again. But he could not work and he could not remain static in London. Within a few days, he had embarked on a prolonged, restless round of autumn and winter visits to the great fortified posts of barbarians situated outside the city. "Some dozen" country houses in succession opened their doors to him. From the Marquess of Lothian's fortress of Blickling Hall at Norfolk, on November 16, he risked his first allusion to Loch Luichart. "The fact is, the holidays are over"—Robert rather obliquely wrote the Storys, now in Rome—"with (for me) an end of boys'-play, which,—it is said,—men ought to know when to leave off: and 'left off' it all is, I very sincerely assure you."[34] His decisive tone suggests that he had replied to the first of Lady Ashburton's "cajoleries and pathetic appeals" which were to run for "two years together."[35] Pathetic appeals were considerably more dangerous than maddened explosions of vanity for sooner or later they would enlist mutual friends in her cause. The consequences of the proposal were not to be purely inward and psychological.

Edith, Emelyn, and William Story, to their credit, managed to preserve cautious neutrality in the years ahead. Hatty Hosmer on the other hand succumbed to gossip and practical loyalties. "I should like to know," Browning fumed to Edith on April 4, 1872, "what business Hatty had with my behavior to L^{y} A. in L^{y} A's house . . .; does Hatty instantly practise impertinence on any friend of hers who intends to make an ambitious or mercenary marriage? As for her devotion to Lady A: begetting this chivalrous ardour in her,—Lady A. has got plenty of friends quite as intimate, who never fancied for a moment that they were called on to fight her battles." The crucial test for his own friends was whether they credited gossip and blamed his behavior with Lady Ashburton. "So, now, I have done with Hatty, for once & always." Still the behavior of Hatty and others in his circle came as no surprise to Robert: "I retained exactly as much as I was disposed to value of the esteem and attention of every one of our common friends and acquaintance," he staunchly informed Story in late life.[36]

The behavior of Lady Ashburton's circle seems to have been reasonably discreet. Louisa, too, must have made some attempt to disguise the situation—though at least on one occasion by rather flamboyant methods. Finding herself at Belton House with Browning amid a swirl of excitable young ladies in the spring of 1872, she managed to give out the impression that he was courting her.

With paranoid intensity, Browning had begun to interpret the world in the ghastly illumination of a single event. On January 19, 1870, he had told Isa that he could barely "avoid despising" himself in the light of Rossetti's new memoir of Shelley for having terribly misjudged the Sun-treader's marital scandal. Then in turn, Miss Mitford's collected correspondence only pointed up "the usual woman's characteristic" of reacting to "all according to the personal liking or disliking of the moment." And if Miss Mitford was practically a gloss on Louisa, Tennyson's new Idyll in *The Holy Grail and Other Poems* "about a knight being untrue to his friend and yielding to the temptation of that friend's mistress" might have been another gloss on himself—except that, in Robert's eyes, Tennyson had skirted the burning issue. "I should judge the conflict in the knight's soul the proper subject to describe," Browning harshly complained to Isa. "Tennyson thinks he should describe the castle, and the effect of the moon on its towers, and anything *but* the soul."[37] What was the conflict in the perjured soul of a tormented knight but his own subject?

Under Oxford towers in June of this year, Pen shriveled to the size of an abbreviated entry in a college register. He had failed "Smalls," and was "obliged to take his name off the books" at Christ Church. At last his father declined to try for "yet another respite." In suppressed fury he turned to George Barrett. Beneath his superficial, self-justifying reasonableness in three urgent appeals to his brother-in-law there is a bitterly mocking petulance clearly directed at Elizabeth. George, too, was her living representative. "All my plans are destroyed by this double evil—the utmost self-indulgence joined to the greatest contempt of work and its fruits." Somehow his twenty-one-year-old son had run through £160 in barely five weeks of term—but not money alone has been squandered wildly. "I can hardly make a greater [sacrifice] than I have done—of the last nine years of my life, which have been as thoroughly wasted as if they were passed in playing at chuck-farthing. All I can do,—except to give money,—is *done* & done in vain. What do you think of the army? Or will it all end in my pensioning off the poor fellow to go & rot in the country?" His only qualification for diplomacy was his talent for expensive living.

Pen preferred the career of a cavalry officer to rotting in the country, but then, the young man's "exquisite stupidity" must be "unconquerable," Robert cries out on July 1. "I will not hear of a life,—first of all, hateful to his Mother: next, as hateful to me,—finally, involving all the worst temptations to every sort of weakness. It is all miserable to contemplate. The poor boy is simply WEAK." He was perfectly immune to parental influence: "I am merely the manger at which he feeds, and nothing is more certain than that I could do him no greater good than by dying to-night and leaving him just enough to keep from starving." Having neatly eliminated himself and reduced Pen to animal imagery, Browning could now write as though his son were a minor character in *The Ring and the Book.* "There is something infinitely pitiable in this butterfly-nature . . .," he concludes for George's benefit, "a restive horse may be broken of his vice and made win a race against his will,—but how can you make a butterfly cross the room to his life, much less yours?" Several days later, apparently with no very hopeful sign from George, he proposed that the butterfly might be turned into a barrister. At Lord Houghton's the young man had distinguished himself for "coolness and readiness"[38] in a game of charades.

Pen's ignominious calamity perhaps had a soothing effect as well. Robert could take consolation in the thought that a marriage proposal for his son's "advantage" had been warranted by hard, demonstrated facts; loyalty to Elizabeth—plainly—had not been compromised for any other advantage. Still, not even the exigencies of his son's case obliterated from an overactive conscience the fact that concert had been sought with another woman. Browning's lasting paranoia during these years owed much to his sense that Elizabeth's soul was estranged from his own, and his urge to restore the lost sense of union with her becomes in the 1870s very nearly the motivating principle of his life.

Not that the modern world utterly failed to arouse his curiosity. Europe was teetering in 1870 on the brink of chaos—and public chaos was more than compatible with Robert's state of mind. Chancellor von Bismarck had discovered a perfect scarlet cloak with which to taunt a Gallic bull. The Spanish throne had fallen vacant after the deposition of Queen Isabella; if France now permitted Prince Leopold of Prussia to reign in Madrid she would be outflanked by her enemies; but if she declared war on her tormentors she might—as Bismarck devoutly wished—drive the squabbling Teutonic states into a potent political union. At last, editing an account of the Kaiser's mild rebuff of the French ambassador at Ems to read as if the Second Empire had been slapped soundly in the face, Bismarck managed to enrage the legislative body at Paris. Louis Napoleon was suddenly astride a whirlwind; in July war credits were enthusiastically voted in the French capital, and a few days later—to Bismarck's intense delight—the Second Empire declared war on Prussia.

Modern nitroglycerin and antique horse-flesh featured in a rather brief holocaust. Against von Moltke's three disciplined armies, wheeling into the east with alarming rapidity, the Empire would have to rely upon ill-coordinated ranks in shakos and flaming red trousers, upon the accuracy of her *chassepots,* the terror of her *mitrailleuses,* the daring of her mounted cavalry—and, not the least, upon the uplifting presence of her emperor. On July 28 Louis Napoleon with his powdered postilions arrived by train at Metz to lead his undersupplied countrymen into battle. The rouged cheeks and neatly waxed moustache of Elizabeth's hero of Paris, now sixty-two, did not conceal the puffiness and pallor of a man suffering from an intern's list of mortal ills—gout, flatulence, hemorrhoids, stones, cystitis, and worse. In considerable pain, Napoleon mounted a waiting saddle in Lorraine amidst a wide sea of cheering and weeping troops; unfortunately neither he nor his generals could think of anything better to do than occupy Saarbrücken and then quickly vacate it. A few days later the French fled in wild disorder from the Spicheren heights, and then at Froeschwiller, lost 20,000 soldiers in less than twelve hours.[39] Imperial victory was no longer expected on the battlefield—if Napoleon had ever contemplated it.

Not so much the coming magnitude as the sheer inevitability of the emperor's defeat had been forecast in England. Browning fairly glowed at the prospect. In "the interest of humanity," he wrote Isa with high-minded ardor in July, Louis Napoleon "wants a sound beating this time & probably may get it." The ghosts of old personal battles stirred. "Oh, oh, Ba," Isa read with mild surprise, "put not your trust in princes neither in the sons of men,—Emperors, Popes, Garibaldis, or Mazzinis,—the *plating* wears through, and out comes the copperhead of human nature & weakness and falseness too!" Several days after the bloody reversal at Froeschwiller, he lightly announced that he and Sarianna as a "necessary change"[40] were setting out on a holiday visit to embattled France! One wonders if his sister believed the horrendous reports she read in the daily press.

The two Brownings reached Joseph Milsand in perfect safety at St.

Aubin-sur-Mer, in Calvados, on August 12. The weather at least was remarkably fine. From a sunny cottage at the edge of "miles and miles" of vacant beach, Robert contemplated a forlorn village whose able-bodied men were conspicuously absent and congratulated himself on having escaped the boredom of English country-house life. "The sadness of the war & its consequences go far to paralyse all our pleasure," he wrote on August 19; but apparently the war had become an important part of his pleasure. The downfall of the gouty architect of Caesarian democracy elicited little sympathy but an increasing amount of morbid interest. "Surely," Browning writes Isa on August 22, "all this 'brag,' and immorality too,—wanted the treatment it is getting only too energetically. The effect will be, that we shall all be forced into the Prussian system, of turning a nation into a camp; nothing but soldiering to concern us for the next generation."[41]

In fact, the Prussian treatment was every bit as energetic as he supposed. Outflanked by von Moltke's heavy guns and infantry early in September, Louis Napoleon exposed his erect silhouette to enemy shellfire at Sedan on the Meuse and then, unluckily not hit, surrendered his ornamental sword and 80,000 troops to the King of Prussia. Within forty-eight hours, the Second Empire collapsed and the Third Republic was shouted from Parisian housetops. Empress Eugénie fled to the channel with her quick-witted American dentist. German armies now easily encircled General Bazaine's famished and typhus-ridden troops in their stronghold at Metz, and soon afterward, encountering little resistance along the way, invested the French capital in a stranglehold. With Napoleon III in captivity and northern France practically at their mercy, Bismarck and his field marshal could not understand why they had not won the war.

Meanwhile, news of "misfortune huddling upon misfortune to poor France" had not very appreciably disturbed Browning's bathing. Washing the cobwebs from his brain, he had enjoyed his "three dozenth good swim" and was still reluctant to leave Normandy. By this time Milsand's house at Dijon was overrun by Prussians, the house near Paris "emptied of its furniture, & waiting the bombs"—and the Brownings' escape-route by train and ship to England was imperiled.[42] Joseph Milsand's frantic alarm for his two placid friends seems to have been the real reason for their belated, hurried departure from the coast.[43] Possibly it was he who guided Robert and Sarianna first to the port of Le Havre, which was all but closed, and then on to Honfleur—where, in the loud, tangily redolent, and homely company of a boatload of cattle bound for Southampton, they took leave of besieged France at midnight.

This autumn, Louisa's suitor contrived to spend a majority of weekends at Warwick Crescent. Robert turned down many an invitation, and perhaps with a twinge of guilt in the winter—while surrounded Parisians barbecued rats and cats and awaited the arrival of von Moltke's slow-moving but infallible siege guns—sold "Hervé Riel" for £105 to *The Cornhill Magazine* for the benefit of the French Relief Fund.

So far, his recent sufferings had not resulted in poetry. Browning had written nothing but a round robin and an indifferent sonnet since the publication of *The Ring and the Book.* In January 1871, the dismal vacillations of General Trochu inspired some topical doggerel for Lady Charlemont:

> Ay, Trochu, in Paris which Prussians environ,
> Has mettle,—but hardly the metal to win:
> In vain you protest that "the man is cast-iron"—
> These five months have taught me he's simply block-tin![44]

But in May, Browning began to compose and before the month was over brought to completion a more revealing work. In this case yet another accomplished lady—the youthful Katrine Cecilia, Countess Cowper—had "imposed" upon him the task of translating the *Alcestis* and perhaps even writing a poem about it. Having considered such a project for over a year in the somewhat fractured light of Loch Luichart and his other memories, he produced in a flurry of penstrokes a "May-month's amusement."[45] *Balaustion's Adventure, Including a Transcript from Euripides* contains a fair quantity of clear, pedestrian verse that illuminates Browning at the expense of Euripides. Douglas Bush[46] has pointed out that Balaustion talks like a radiant mixture of bluestocking and Girl Guide—that is, like a particularly youthful Elizabeth. All the same, she combines the gaiety and girlish grace of a lyric Pippa with the readiness to act and the wit of a tragic Pompilia, except that she is not tragic. Threatened by pirates, she inspires her oarsmen to pull harder by singing them a song from Aeschylus, and then, debarred from safety by Syracusans, she promptly recites her way into their hearts by remembering Euripides. It is at least as appropriate that Balaustion should prefer Euripides, as that her name should signify wild pomegranate flower. Symbolically her prologue reconstructs the key events in Elizabeth Barrett's life—at least as Browning wished to understand them on the eve of the tenth anniversary of her death.

Threatened by the encroaching will of an overbearing parent, she too had saved herself by turning to Aeschylus and then Euripides. Frail and beautiful as Balaustion, Elizabeth also had won over the hearts of the populace by offering them exquisite poetry. A few obdurate hearts had not been moved. The brisk little "critic and whippersnapper"[47] who rages over Balaustion's interpolations is obviously Alfred Austin—Browning's most hostile critic—and also as the archetypal myope who cannot see beyond conventions, all of Elizabeth's hostile critics together. Attracted by her voice, somebody had been moved to an extraordinary extent:

> But one—one man—one youth,—three days, each day,—
> (If, ere I lifted up my voice to speak,
> I gave a downward glance by accident)
> Was found at foot o' the temple. When we sailed,
> There, in the ship too, was he found as well,
> Having a hunger to see Athens too.
> We reached Peiraieus; when I landed—lo,
> He was beside me. Anthesterion-month
> Is just commencing: when its moon rounds full,
> We are to marry. O Euripides![48]

What is emphasized at the deepest level of this account is the indeflectable adoration and the resourceful subservience of Robert during his visits at Wimpole Street and directly afterward. Poetry is power, transforms indifference into sympathy and may transform it into personal and perfect love. A parental pirate who threatened a poetess does not loom on the blue horizon again.

But in the hushed temple where her suitor listens in rapture, Balaustion is not content to recite the *Alcestis* word for word; nor—to the understandable horror of modern classical scholars—is Browning disposed to remember the satyr-play as Euripides left it. Indeed he seems to forget that it is a satyr-play and that Admetos is a king and Heracles something of a merry drunkard. By virtually suppressing the original chorus, turning Heracles into a supernatural Caponsacchi, Alcestis into the doomed and self-conscious Elizabeth who speaks in "Any Wife to Any Husband," and Admetos into Browning, Robert offers an abject apology to his dead wife for his behavior with a living goddess, as well as a stern investigation of his new relationship with his conscience.

The prologue themes of salvation and of love are strongly reinforced in the balaustionized "Transcript." To propitiate a god, Alcestis has volunteered to die in her husband's stead. Poignant emphasis is placed upon her heroism, upon her concern for her children's future, and in particular upon her fervent wish that Admetos should never remarry. Who in an evil hour might tempt him? Gifted with unusual insight, the Queen seems to have in mind the fully revealed and utterly vile Lady Ashburton of that bitter September,

> For hostile the new-comer, the step-dame
> To the old brood—a very viper she
> For gentleness![49]

—as, cowardly and selfish and deceived by mere appearances, the King seems to envision only the glittering and highborn seductress of August. "All this shall be—shall be," he sobs not insincerely.

> Fear not! And, since I had thee living, dead
> Alone wilt thou be called my wife: no fear
> That some Thessalian ever styles herself
> Bride, hails this man for husband in thy place!
> No woman, be she of such lofty line
> Or such surpassing beauty otherwise![50]

Biographically viewed, the crucial difference between the play and the transcript lies in what has happened to Admetos, for he is no longer a dignified and hospitable Euripidean prince but a rather complacent and self-enamored Meredithian egoist, whose childish indifference toward feminine heroism must be purged in a bitter ordeal of death and bereavement, temptation and sudden recognition. No doubt such an alteration appealed to Victorians, who sentimentally worshipped and unsentimentally neglected their wives. "The very best translation I ever read," muttered Carlyle.[51] For Admetos, widowerhood is a bleak purgatory of short duration in which he is able to see with perfect clarity why his wife needed to die and also able to ride up a steadily moving moral escalator to a point at which he is worthy of her soul's companionship. Though his suffering is acute its outcome never seems in doubt. Heracles—who conspires with the hero's conscience to purify and test it—cheerfully wrestles with death and brings back from the grave a veiled and speechless feminine form which the King is reluctant even to touch, let alone embrace. Whom does Admetos-Robert believe the god has tucked under his arm? Certainly not Lady Ashburton. In shape, the veiled lady resembles his lost Alcestis-Elizabeth, and the very finality of his rejection of her as a possible bride is reminiscent of Browning's attitude toward that pseudo-Elizabeth of Cumberland Place, Miss Wedgwood. Assured with her unveiling that she is his very own wife, Admetos receives her as a lost part of himself.

In an illuminating study,[52] Joseph H. Friend has shown that *Balaustion's Adventure* revises the easy, optimistic thesis of "Prospice." Though both poems look forward in sturdy confidence and optimism to an ultimate reunion with Elizabeth, the earlier presupposes that a quick, climactic battle in which to pay "glad life's arrears" will suffice to prepare Robert's soul, and the later that he must first pass through a deep vale of mortification. Apparently fifteen years of marriage had too much indulged that soul; ten years of bereavement have shown the extent of the indulgence and also done something to repair it, or at least convinced him that it could be repaired. Balaustion's revised and condensed scenario in her epilogue suggests the poet's lasting difficulty in defining his relationship with a woman at a far remove in heaven. But the poem concludes in the most halcyon manner with a languid and flattering description of one of Leighton's paintings—"Heracles Wrestling with Death for the Body of Alcestis."

Perhaps Pen was the immediate beneficiary of this investigation of a bad conscience. Less than two months after the exorcisms of *Balaustion,* Browning could see that the young man's "considerable" abilities after all might spell "success . . . though not in the way which lay most naturally before him." Certainly on better terms, father and son journeyed north together in late July to Ernest Benzon's newly acquired estate above Loch Tummel, where Pen proceeded to depopulate the Scottish air and scrub. "Shot, by himself, to-day 14½ brace of grouse, 4 hares & a plover," his father noted with mingled pride and alarm on August 19.[53] Jowett and Swinburne were staying nearby at Tummel Bridge. On one occasion the Brownings demolished with them a salmon; on another, Robert walked over to discuss a "fanciful rendering"[54] of the *Alcestis* with the sun-tanned Master of Balliol. "I don't know whether I am 'vivacious' as ever," he admitted to Isa Blagden with something of the insight of an Admetos, "but I am susceptible enough of pain,—perhaps, pain which I make for myself by unnecessary anticipation,—still, pain no less."

Father and son had the use of an isolated hunting lodge, "three rugged miles from the house." As Pen set off early to his shooting, Robert was "blessedly alone" with a piano, a few books, and some blank sheets of paper.[55] Not all of the paper in front of him was blank. Contemplating the yellowed sheet and faded Italian ink used a dozen years before to outline a poem about Louis Napoleon, he set himself the orderly task of writing a full-blown monologue in the name of a modern emperor who had ruled for twenty years, compromised democracy, led an army to disaster, and at length escaped to Chislehurst to write his memoirs. *Prince Hohenstiel-Schwangau, Saviour of Society* was duly perpetrated "at the rate of so many lines a day, neither more nor less"[56]—if one of Jowett's Tummel guests is to be credited—and the mechanical results do little to discredit this mechanical procedure.

At first imagining himself seated at a table opposite a bud-mouthed "arbitress"[57] in a neat little room off Leicester Square, the fictitious prince soon annihilates the table, room, and the young prostitute herself with heavy cigar smoke and yet heavier rhetoric. In clattering polysyllables he portrays himself as the evenly spinning cogwheel of a complex leviathan state, threatened from within and without by heroes of every description who would destroy it. His solitary claim to greatness must be that of the self-effacing but resolute bureaucrat: he did preserve order and prevent bloodshed for two difficult decades. What other nineteenth-century bureaucrat with so little understanding of industrial economics and the rivalry of states, one wonders, could have done so well?

No doubt, *Hohenstiel-Schwangau* fails in superficial aspects because Browning himself knew and cared so little about economics and government. What he cared chiefly about were the casuistical operations of his own mind; highly congenial was the problem of what a fallen prince would say to justify a grave moral failure—when under no external pressure. His interest became less topical and satirical than exploratory and psychological. "Well, dear," Browning told Isa a few months after baffled reviewers had begun to interpret the Prince, "I am glad you like what the Editor of the Edinburgh . . . calls my 'eulogium on the Second Empire': which it is not, any more than what another wiseacre affirms to be a 'scandalous attack on the old constant friend of England'—it is just what I imagine the man might, if he pleased, say for himself."[58] Such a man would say something in the pragmatic vein to defend his long regime, as the Prince vaguely does. What Browning alone could "imagine" him to say, in the very process, is that he is not one man so much as he is five or six: a Chislehurst exile, a cautious Prince, a fervent Idealist, a disillusioned Sage, a Dreamer, and an old insomniac in the Residenz. Each of these assumed voices "throws doubt upon all others," as Professor Roma A. King observes,[59] so that only the rather shadowy image of a rhetorical robot remains. Nonetheless—one might add—of a robot reminiscent of just that peculiar fractionated Robert Browning who appears and reappears in *Balaustion's Adventure*, suppressing himself in the prologue, debasing himself in the "Transcript," and idealizing himself in the epilogue. In *Hohenstiel-Schwangau* he seems to become yet another guilty prince of shifting and canceling identities. Louis Napoleon's monologue in fact gives vent to the very Browningesque idea that a truly guilty mind cannot construct a perfectly consistent case for itself.

The proximity of Loch Luichart to the hunting lodge where the poem was all but written by October 1 had been creating vivid images in Browning's mind—and in his son's as well. Having shot enough fowl and rabbit for one season, Pen wanted to go on to Lady Ashburton's for deerstalking. "I shall not accompany him," Browning had declared flatly on August 19; but even then he may have predicted that he would change his mind. Some words from Isa Blagden inspired, at that time, an estimate of Elizabeth's immense superiority in comparison to himself. "But, NO, dearest Isa," he emphasized with urgency in August, "—the simple truth is that *she* was the poet, and I the clever person by comparison: remember her limited experience of all kinds, and what she made of it—remember, on the other hand, how my uninterrupted health & strength, & practice with the world have helped me." And then very optimistically: "I shall wash my hands clean in a minute, before I see her, as I trust to do."[60]

A cleansing interview with a woman who had nearly destroyed his soul may have seemed an ugly necessity, an act of contrition to be endured—and perhaps enjoyed a little, when one recalls Robert's keen fascination with soul-destroyers. In any case, Lady Ashburton could not have failed to detect an unregenerate hardness in his mood when he reached her Lodge with Pen on October 2. "Knowing she had only succeeded," as Browning later told Edith Story with the indignation of an outmaneuvered colonel, "after nine or ten months' teazing with her invitations, to get me to promise to visit her for one day, and so get handsomely done with it all,—[she] wanted to have the air of shutting the door in my face with a final bang."[61]

Not long afterward in London he began to turn this resonant bang of a heavy door into the alexandrine couplets of *Fifine at the Fair*.

As the heavily corrected and interlined manuscript at Balliol would indicate, *Fifine at the Fair* was composed with unusual care and deliberation, between December 1871 and May 11, 1872.[62] Victorians misunderstood a work that purported to amass 2,355 lines of rational argument in favor of adultery. Mrs. Orr was shocked by a "piece of perplexing cynicism" and a "leaven of bitterness" in the mind that produced it.[63] Clearly, *Fifine* reflects bitterness in the mind of a former proponent of Shelleyan free love and latterly reconstructed husband and loyal widower. Yet its peculiar energy, its air of conviction, even its moments of genuine gayety suggest that it did much to restore Browning to himself. More realistically concerned with the whole panoply of his frustrations than either *Balaustion* or *Hohenstiel-Schwangau,* more autobiographical and probably more therapeutic, *Fifine* is also as fine a work as he wrote in his later years.

Unquestionably it is demanding. Rather than its thematic ideas or its casuistry, Browning may have been thinking of the sheer tortuosities of its argument and of its involuted style when he told Alfred Domett that he had "just finished a poem, 'the most metaphysical and boldest he had written since *Sordello,* and was very doubtful as to its reception.' "[64] Even the most sophisticated readers were amazed. Accustomed to such complacent and extroverted seducers as the Don Juan of Molière or Byron, who expected a legendary conqueror of the boudoir to talk like Sordello?—or to rationalize at length on the spiritual merits of a girl with velvet brows and a Greek-nymph nose?

Moreover, Browning's modernized Don Juan—the speaker and anti-hero of *Fifine*—is quite unconcerned with the art of seduction, much concerned with the most ethereal of Elvires. Can his wife, in any sense, be said to exist? One cannot believe in her material presence as one believes in Gigadibs's or even Horsefall's. *Fifine* is a dramatic soliloquy in the tradition of "The Pope," with its array of hypothetical auditors, or, more particularly, of *Prince Hohenstiel-Schwangau.* For if at first Elvire seems almost as real as a bud-mouthed arbitress of Leicester Square, she soon fades into an equally pale translucence whose throbbing heartbeat and tearfully imploring replies are only imagined by an aloof, solitary, obsessed, and truly immortal Don Juan. He now perceives among the performing gypsy troupe at the annual fair of St. Gilles in Pornic one more fribble to add to his immeasurable list—the "fizgig"[65] Fifine. Somewhat like Tennyson's Tithonus, who longs for death and is condemned to pace in the haunted wilderness of life, Browning's Don Juan longs for constancy and the lost prize of an adoring wife, and is condemned to move forever within the boundaries of a footnote in *Queen Mab. Fifine* transpires in circles: from a fair of noise, sensuality, and sputtering lights to a twilit beach of intellectual calm, and then—by implication—to frenetic embraces in a garish gypsy caravan; from loving thoughts about Elvire to adulterous ones about Fifine, and then again back to notions of permanence and constancy. "Love ends where love began," declares Juan, a somber planet now at its apogee, as he stands in cool darkness on the very steps of the villa at Ste. Marie where he imagines himself to be living in faithfulness with Elvire. At farthest remove from the sensual Fair, his mind loses its grip on its imaginings:

> How pallidly you pause o' the threshold! . . .
>
> . . . . .
>
> Suppose you are a ghost! A memory, a hope,
> A fear, a conscience! Quick! Give back the hand I grope
> I' the dusk for!
>
> . . . . .
>
> Be but flesh and blood, and smile to boot!
> Enter for good and all! then fate bolt fast the door,
> Shut you and me inside, never to wander more![66]

Obviously the door never shuts and the bolt never drops for the wanderer is condemned to further wanderings. An "impertinent on tiptoe" has slipped into his hand on the beach an invitation to a tryst, in return for a goldpiece dropped in her tambourine.

> Oh, threaten no farewell! five minutes shall suffice
> To clear the matter up. I go, and in a trice
> Return; five minutes past, expect me! If in vain—
> Why, slip from flesh and blood, and play the ghost again![67]

Elvire will meekly revert to her "ghost." His own restless peregrinations and even the substance of his hallucinatory interview with his wife are to be repeated with minor variations, it would seem, until the end of time. In short, Don Juan's ordeal dramatizes the logical and moral inconsistency of the romantic axiom that free love implies freedom of the spirit, since he revolves into eternity in sexual chains.

In the prologue "Amphibian" and the epilogue, "The Householder," Browning dissociates himself from the voluptuary and imagines himself in direct communication at first with the heavenly sphere in which Elizabeth resides, and later with Elizabeth herself. "Amphibian" recalls Donne in its delicacy, intellectual complication, and metaphysics. Floating on his back far out in a placid bay and gazing near the sun, the poet encounters a creature that might symbolize a soul:

> . . . the membraned wings
> So wonderful, so wide,
> So sun-suffused, were things
> Like soul, and nought beside.
>
> A handbreadth over head!
> All of the sea my own,
> It owned the sky instead;
> Both of us were alone.[68]

Because the sea which bears him up is like heavenly air which supports a metaphysical butterfly, he can imagine that the sea is the "passion and thought"[69] of his own poetry. The sun-suffused soul is Elizabeth's. In his poems, indeed, he comes as close as he can to living in his wife's element and to communicating with her.

However, in "The Householder" he is no longer floating placidly at Pornic but brooding blasphemously in London, where not even verse seems to narrow the metaphysical divide:

> Savage I was sitting in my house, late, lone:
> Dreary, weary with the long day's work:
> Head of me, heart of me, stupid as a stone:
> Tongue-tied now, now blaspheming like a Turk.[70]

Astonishingly, "half a pang and all a rapture," Elizabeth is with him.

> 'What, and is it really you again?' quoth I:
> 'I again, what else did you expect?' quoth She.[71]

Lady Ashburton's suitor is no more prepared for such a visitation than the twentieth century is for the return of Saint Joan. He cries with terrible alarm,

> hie away from this old house—
> Every crumbling brick embrowned with sin and shame!
> Quick, in its corners ere certain shapes arouse![72]

Elizabeth is frankly amused by the familiar self-dramatizing violence of his words and reminds him of the proprieties. Robert now responds very movingly:

> 'Ah, but if you knew how time has dragged, days, nights!
> All the neighbour-talk with man and maid—such men!
> All the fuss and trouble of street-sounds, window-sights:
> All the worry of flapping door and echoing roof; and then,
> All the fancies . . . Who were they had leave, dared try
> Darker arts that almost struck despair in me?
> If you knew but how I dwelt down here!' quoth I:
> 'And was I so better off up there?' quoth She.[73]

He yearns to die and be reunited. In the last line she corrects his myopic misconception: "'—Love is all and Death is nought!' quoth She." Like a loved familiar voice banishing a nightmare, Elizabeth is saying no separation exists. The interchange points up a belated recognition of selfishness in his obsession with recent sufferings. Have the sufferings been so intense? In between the prologue and epilogue—that is, in Don Juan's cathartic monologue itself—Browning reaches a new understanding of them that in itself must have diminished their intensity.

Barbara Melchiori must be correct when she identifies sexual frustration as one of them.[74] Don Juan alludes to sex with the air of a ragamuffin gazing at bonbons through the window of an expensive shop. One is reminded a little of an attentive young poet observing exotic gypsies in Dulwich from a safe distance. The allurements of Mimi, Toinette, and Fifine are linked with images of deception and even perversion: a six-legged sheep, an oddly human ape, girls dressed up as boys. Wandering out beyond the wooden platform upon which they are all to perform, Juan catches sight of a red pennon fluttering in a brisk Breton breeze over their tent.

> Frenetic to be free! And, do you know, there beats
> Something within my breast, as sensitive?—repeats
> The fever of the flag?[75]

His heart in immediate response makes the same "Passionate stretch, fires up for lawlessness" and would impel him to throw off his nagging social responsibilities and run with the gypsies. But in *Fifine* the symbolism of "The Flight of the Duchess" is reversed. Gypsy lawlessness and sensuality are the norms of society, after all, whereas domestic fidelity and contentedness are as uncommon as a spectral wife. The voluptuary realizes as much when he compares Elvire to a painting by Raphael and Fifine to so many leaves in "Doré's last picture-book."[76]

Still, like the genteel monologuist of Rossetti's "Jenny," Juan is attracted to a prostitute who inspires him to philosophize—on and on—about a whole universe in which she is the bewitching center. Juan explains his astonishing loquacity variously. Probably his aim is to discover the key that will unlock the heavy shackles of his own licentiousness, reveal to him the basis of his compulsive behavior with ten thousand Fifines. Unlike a contented swimmer who perceives in an insect's "sun-suffused" wings a glorious symbolic unity of sense and soul, Juan can see only as irreconcilable alternatives Fifine and Elvire, the impulse to be free and the impulse to be loyal, the whirligig of sensuality and the serene prize of spirituality. Deep in aesthetic theory, he reveals himself as a modern empiricist for whom "soul" is nothing but a relativistic concept depending upon the intuition of the artist:

> Art is my evidence
> That something was, is, might be; but no more thing itself,
> Than flame is fuel.[77]

Soul as flame is probably intended as a parody of Walter Pater's metaphor for experience, already public in his review-article on William Morris in 1868 and soon to reappear famously in the *Studies in the History of the Renaissance.* Indeed, as Charlotte Watkins ably demonstrates, Browning's voluptuary seems to be "a type of Pater's characterization of the intellect of contemporary man."[78] Juan unwittingly paraphrases the philosopher of the Aesthetes on Winckelmann and Morris and denies most of the allegorical meanings of Browning's prologue. For Juan, as a matter of fact, too, has taken a plunge off the rocks at Pornic—but in a sea reminiscent of the dark and nearly meaningless one in Swinburne's "Hymn to Proserpine." The experience has taught him that metaphysical truth is illusory, that air is only air, that water is "watery,"

> that I am I, who have the power to swim,
> The skill to understand the law whereby each limb
> May bear to keep immersed.[79]

Sensations and outward appearances then must provide every certainty for his aesthetic judgment, his epistemology, even his morality. Inevitably the certainties by which he would live are few. Art becomes primarily a matter of taste in response to style; truth responds to fashions, and morality, to anyone's point of view. Little wonder that he finds it difficult to believe in the genuineness of "A memory, a hope, . . . a conscience" or that his creator should condemn him to appalling frustrations.

Certainly, Robert is in part Juan. Implicit in point-of-view monologues such as "The Bishop Orders His Tomb" or "Fra Lippo Lippi" is just that relativistic morality that is here condemned. Juan's yearning for personal liberty, his sensuous intensity and impressionism, and scorn for institutions: all partake of a side of Browning's personality richly expressed from *Dramatic Lyrics* to *The Ring and the Book.* Ironically, too, the very pronouncements of Pre-Raphaelite poets and Aesthete philosophers here satirized owe some of their inspiration to Browning's earlier example. Yet Juan radically extends and systematizes what is sensuous and relativistic in Browning, utterly excludes what is transcendental or metaphysical.

In so doing, he stands for modern intellectual forces that seemed to the poet to deny verities tested and matured through a lifetime. Fifine, in turn, is not only Lady Ashburton as seductress but modernity in its distracting and enslaving glitter and falsity. "In moments of spiritual depression," as W. O. Raymond observes,

> the world must have presented itself to [Browning] in the guise of a beguiling but treacherous gipsy, 'an enemy sly and serpentine,' dazzling his eyes with tinselled show, and seeking to wean him from the cherished past.[80]

Robert was undoubtedly setting himself against much in art and thought that might have inspired him in the present. As a rule, his poems from this point on draw rather less upon fresh observation than cherished memory.

Fifine at the Fair was published by Smith and Elder on or about June 4, 1872. No one was more astounded by its repudiation of a good deal of modernity than Dante Gabriel Rossetti. But then, everywhere Rossetti looked in his presentation copy he saw to his unspeakable horror only Rossetti—his own "Jenny" and "The Blessed Damozel" duplicated in their situations and lampooned for their psychology, his own guilt-ridden feelings for a dead wife flouted in "The Householder," himself cast as a sneaky, sense-crazed, prostitute-chasing

Don Juan. Already reeling from Robert Buchanan's venemous attack on him in "The Fleshly School of Poetry—Mr. D. G. Rossetti," and imbibing doses of chloral and whiskey, Rossetti at last impressed his amazed brother as being "not entirely sane." What had he ever done to his famous mentor other than rename *Balaustion's Adventure*—in the intimacy of familial banter—"Exhaustion's Imposture!"?[81] He began to conceive of Browning as a prime agent in Buchanan's conspiracy against his rather vulnerable sanity. For his own part, Browning had given aid and comfort to the enemy by imparting to Buchanan an estimate of Rossetti's "*scented*" poetry, and furthermore, as DeVane suggests,[82] certainly had had "Jenny" in mind when he wrote *Fifine*—but he could not understand Rossetti's continuing hostility and probably knew little of a state of mind that would soon lead to an attempted suicide. At last he told Holman Hunt he could neither bear nor pardon the younger poet's "insolence."[83]

Fifine's reviewers were baffled and outraged in 1872 for rather different reasons. "For the ordinary reader," *The Westminster Review* declared in October,

> it might just as well have been written in Sanscrit. There are such breaks, digressions, involutions, crabbed constructions, metaphysical hair-splitting, that reading becomes a positive fatigue.[84]

The Literary World coyly detected "affectation," while *The Guardian* and *The Galaxy* rang somber admonitory changes on the grand old theme of obscurity.[85] After a deep, brief plunge into the menacing submarine world of its argumentative intricacies, Sidney Colvin came up bubbling with mingled admiration and bewilderment in the July *Fortnightly Review* to report that he had seen in *Fifine* Browning's "most perplexing and intellectually involved and complicated self"[86]—but few others possessed nerve or fortitude for the descent. In rather sullen reply to everybody—but particularly to his reviewers—Browning contented himself by jotting in Greek on the manuscript of the poem two quotations, the first from Aeschylus' *Choephoroe,*

> And reading this doubtful word he has dark night before his eyes, and he is nothing clearer by day

—to which he added in plain English, "if any of my critics had Greek enough in him to make the application!" The second quotation was from Aristophanes' *Thesmophoriazusae,*

> To what words are you turned, for a barbarian nature would not receive them. For bearing new words to the Scaeans you would spend them in vain.[87]

Undoubtedly it was galling first to dread being told that one had written another impenetrable *Sordello,* and then to be told it.

Late in February 1872, after three eventful decades of farming and politics in New Zealand, Alfred Domett, or "Waring," had returned to London at the age of sixty and, almost before shaking the travel dust from his shoes, appeared at No. 19 Warwick Crescent. As if by way of a portent for the immediate future, the poet was not then at home.

> But Miss Browning was [as he writes in a factual and punctilious diary for February 29]. So I sent up a card & presently heard an emphatic "Mr. Domett"—and met Miss B. coming down. Warm welcome followed in Miss Sarianna's old frank and slightly energetic style. She really did not look so very much altered considering that 30 years precisely had passed since last we met. . . . I don't know exactly why, but I had not calculated on finding Browning or his family so soon or easily.[88]

Domett's diary does not record quite so warm a welcome from Robert. Perhaps he had not calculated on being found so soon or easily.

In May he celebrated his own sixtieth birthday—enhancing it by dedicating a new volume of his *Selections* in the same month to Tennyson: "In Poetry—Illustrious and Consummate; in Friendship—Noble and Sincere."[89] He walked and talked, dined and reminisced with Waring, and yet was frequently out of the house when Waring called. Early in September Domett learned with surprise from a servant that his devoted old Camberwell friend and his friend's sister had left for Normandy without a word.

CHAPTER 25

Murder, Natural Death, and the Greeks

1872-80

If Browning escaped Alfred Domett with a little relief, he alighted with bitter dissatisfaction near another old friend. In fact Robert and Sarianna had reached the seacoast at St. Aubin, where Joseph Milsand was staying, in August 1872. The poet soon discovered that Anne Thackeray was living in a château at Lion-sur-Mer, five miles along the French coast. This past winter Browning had deliberately snubbed Anne, apparently going so far at a soirée as to dig her with his elbow for spreading rumors about his "second marriage."[1] Sensing now Robert's constraint at the mention of her name, Milsand marched to Lion and laid the groundwork for prompt reconciliation.

The next day, if Miss Thackeray's memory is correct, Browning sailed purposefully into her courtyard in full regalia. As if to signify a truce, he wore a white suit and held a large white sun umbrella overhead. Anne saw Robert at the window and rushed downstairs in tears. "Don't ask," the dazzling apparition spoke—somewhat hastily. "The facts are not worth inquiring into; people make mischief without even meaning it. It is all over now. . . ."[2] Then he dried Anne's tears and otherwise consoled the latest victim of his own indiscretion.

At any rate, the meeting was not auspicious. Confessing that his brains were "squeezed as dry as a sponge," Browning cast about for new relief from desiccating memories—and perhaps from bleaker self-scrutiny. He was uneasy now in the presence of old friends, and furious with a renewed sense of the malevolence of critics. So furious, indeed, that one feels he may on occasion have seen justice in what they wrote of *Hohenstiel-Schwangau* or *Fifine.* Pen's dilemma looked extremely baffling—the more so because it was intensified emotionally for Browning with seizures of regret over the recent past, and with the old, vexed, guilt-haunted problem of fidelity to Elizabeth's memory. He was lonely and uncertain of many of his old cherished notions.

Moreover, even with intellectual resourcefulness, it is difficult to satiate natural sexual hunger with wooden puritan resolve. The underlying fury and bitterness in Browning's mind would erupt with significant effect in the years ahead: no amount of self-analysis or evasive action would entirely put dark problems to rest. Meanwhile, he sought relief by plunging into brains more troubled than his own. In fact, he discovered his own fondness for a tempered naturalism in the rather nauseating case history of one Antoine Mellerio.

In the gentlest manner near the sea, Milsand told Browning how this rich landowner of nearby Tailleville had attempted suicide in the Seine, burned his hands to ashen stumps on a grate, and vaulted to his death from a high stone tower. Even now the Normandy newspapers were full of a noisy trial at Caen instigated by relatives who wanted to impugn the sanity of Mellerio's will. Could one entirely explain his mutilated limbs and broken corpse?

After Milsand recounted a few more particulars, Browning decided that "religious considerations as well as passionate woman-love" must be to blame. "I concluded that there was no intention of committing suicide; and I said . . . I would myself treat the subject *just so.*"[3] At Tailleville he listened to gossip and inspected the fateful tower. With rather blinding clarity one morning he also caught sight of Mellerio's surviving mistress, Mme. de Beaupré, as she darted from her garden gate:

> . . . although
> I noticed that her nose was aquiline,
> The whole effect amounts with me to—blank!
> I never saw what I could less describe.
> The eyes, for instance, unforgettable
> Which ought to be, are out of mind as sight.[4]

Later on the beach below his cottage, he recited with some appropriateness to a reformed Miss Thackeray a free version of the whole grisly story. Anne offered a title: "White Cotton Night-cap Country," after the immaculate headdress worn by the women of Calvados. Robert was exultant. "I bring back with me, for winter-work in London, a capital brand-new subject for my next poem," he reported to Isa Blagden.[5]

At Fontainebleau before the end of September, brother and sister hired a *bonne* and "tried housekeeping and 'the family' " for a month in private lodgings, while paint dried and air cleared in their redecorated rooms in England. They walked in fine autumn forests, saw Mrs. Orr in Paris, wined and dined Miss Egerton Smith. Alarming news arrived from Pen, who had nearly broken his neck in Scotland in a flying plunge over the low railing of a bridge and through a tree. "Shooting, riding, & dancing the Highland Reel," the uninjured acrobat seemed less wild and more filial than his playmate of old, Willy Bracken, who lately had defied fate and "planted" his mother by marrying in the wrong direction. "The sooner *he* breaks his neck, the better," the poet told Isa.[6]

Despite a lingering cold that he caught on the Folkestone steamer, Browning began *Red Cotton Night-cap Country* at home on December 1 and finished the more than four thousand lines by January 23, 1873—whereupon what took seven weeks to compose took fourteen to publish. Murray Smith expressed grave concern about a possible action for libel. Browning, who had foreseen no such dilemma in using the names of living French persons, at once wrote a formally worded "Advertisement," which failed to please Smith's solicitors. The poet grew aggressive. Could a foreigner press libel in an English court of law? *"Is there one such case in the Books?"* Browning demanded of his publisher with rising anxiety and on his own right solicited the advice of the Attorney-General and later, from the American minister, procured a magnificently irrelevant promise to be given "a Bill of Indemnity against any results in America." To Domett's amusement, he fulminated on the density of the legal intellect and declared poets "clearest-headed after all." Then, vexed to compromise with the problematic facts of history, he fictionalized the French proper names in Smith and Elder's proof sheets.[7] *Red Cotton Night-cap Country or Turf and Towers* appeared in London—safe from the law—in a dark green post-octavo volume in the first week of May 1873.

As a narrative told in his own voice to a nameless, manipulated Miss Thackeray, the poem seems oddly lucid. A portrayal of character in action overshadows one of action in character. Léonce Miranda (or Antoine Mellerio) remains the center of an immense anecdote until he is seen—or rather overheard—high on his tower and about to leap into the arms of ineffectual angels.

The angels seem important. Conceived of as animated balloons or autogyros, they suggest gullibility and innocence rather than calculation or inner conflict. Failing to reason out his faith, Miranda has taken it on blind trust. Even so, his instant resolve in youth to adore a stunning married lady might have preserved him twenty years later:

Whatever be my lady's present, past,
Or future, this is certain of my soul,
I love her! in despite of all I know,
Defiance of the much I have to fear,
I venture happiness on what I hope,
And love her from this day for evermore!
No prejudice to old profound respect
For certain Powers![8]

The intensity of his romantic ardor and the caution of his romantic defiance are reminiscent of Browning's—if little else is reminiscent. Ecclesiastical and implacable powers accept Miranda's money but not his adultery when he tries to renounce the world, but not Clara de Millefleurs, to save his soul. He ends by appealing to the Holy Virgin of La Ravissante for a miracle of levitation that will redeem his and Clara's names and purify every soul in Europe. The narrator does not think him mad or unwise to try to fly over the tree tops, at last, but victimized.

As a victim of the Church, he is simply a victim of Browning's anti-Catholic prejudice. Yet he seems victimized mainly by time. Vignettes of a captive Louis XVI and an "incident of 'Ninety-two" paraphrase Carlyle and link the Carlylean view of modern history as a series of revolutionary changes to Miranda. Contemporary man dives into the Seine, roasts his limbs, and plunges from towers because his ethos is violent. Clothes, much as in *Sartor*, reflect the modern epoch and the modern psyche. The innocence and inner quietude of a white cotton night-cap are clearly less appropriate for Miranda than the blood and turmoil emblemized in the red night-cap Carlyle already had depicted in *The French Revolution*. Robert Browning means to approximate the novelistic realism of that gusty and forward-looking work. Natural and architectural motifs—"turf" for the life of the senses and "towers" for religious aspirations—further suggest Carlyle,[9] and also recall in their interplay the incessant maneuvering between sense and soul in *Fifine*. But whereas Don Juan thinks, Miranda *acts*, and thereby resolves an environmental dilemma in the annihilation of self.

Peering intently into Browning's gloom on May 5, 1873, *The Daily News* failed to detect the shadow of Joseph Milsand—celebrated in a short, morally uplifting passage as that "man of men"—but it could hardly overlook Miss Thackeray, to whom the poem is dedicated. Its reviewer treated with irony Anne's connection with a "quaint Carlylean sort of meditation over Night-caps," and then wagged a portentous finger:

> We may fairly question whether psychological puzzles are fit subjects of poetry, or whether explorations in the mournful phantom-haunted borderland between Illusion and Guilt are the best exercises of the poet's genius.[10]

Miss Thackeray had written him, "somewhat mysteriously," Browning told his publisher on May 9, "so as to give me the impression that she has taken some of the . . . *Daily News'* article as offensive to *her.*" With "disinterested zeal," he recommended to Murray Smith a so far unpublished but approving review by Mrs. Orr. Then he took pains to assure Anne that she was an innocent bystander on a long road of inglorious martyrdom. "Remember," Browning wrote her, "that everybody this thirty years has given me his kick and gone his way."[11]

Other journals grumbled over a heroine who confused love with adultery and over a hero who confused holiness with self-mutilation and free falls. Readers seemed ill-prepared for the horrors of naturalism in colloquial blank verse. R. H. Hutton, the editor of *The Spectator,* denied in Domett's presence there was a line of poetry in the whole work. ("Certainly wrong there," Domett recorded in his diary. "I mentioned the allusion to Napoleon. He admitted this was."[12]) Even Carlyle doubted in private that anyone out of bedlam could have chosen its theme.

Browning next embarked on a theoretical defense of his excursion among naturalistic horrors, and published it two years later on April 15, 1875. In 5,700 lines—composed with apparent gusto—he undertook a good deal besides and too much altogether. Nearly the formless compendium that its title implies, *Aristophanes' Apology, including a Transcript from Euripides, being the Last Adventure of Balaustion* suggests a masque staged by two muttering Greek professors in the airless corridors of a large library. Married and mature, Balaustion seems a curious hybrid cross between Elizabeth Barrett and Robert Browning, Sr.

Only a year ago, as Balaustion reminds her stenographic husband, Aristophanes had burst drunkenly into their apartment at Athens:

> And no ignoble presence! On the bulge
> Of the clear baldness,—all his head one brow,—
> True, the veins swelled, blue network, and there surged
> A red from cheek to temple,—
>
> . . . . .
>
> While the pursed mouth's pout
> Aggressive, while the beak supreme above,

While the head, face, nay, pillared throat thrown back
Beard whitening under like a vinous foam,
These made a glory, of such insolence—
I thought,—such domineering deity
Hephaistos might have carved to cut the brine
For his gay brother's prow, imbrue that path
Which, purpling, recognized the conqueror.
Impudent and majestic: drunk . . .[13]

Euripides had just died that day, and the tipsy rival demanded instant debate on the tragedian's merits. Balaustion, always ready to talk, took up the cudgels with ingenuous boldness and surprising erudition. But Aristophanes, undismayed by her insults, spelled out a crucial disagreement.

Both playwrights, as he points out, have soared to fame as realists. But whereas he himself has taken care to label real toads in real gardens for the enlightenment of mankind, the writer of tragedies portrayed wretched beggars and glittering heroes indiscriminately in the most tawdry of plays. "He wants," cries Aristophanes with disgust written large on a glowing face,

not falsehood,—truth alone he seeks,
Truth, for all beauty! Beauty, in all truth—
That's certain somehow! Must the eagle lilt
Lark-like, needs fir-tree blossom rose-like? No!
Strength and utility charm more than grace,
And what's most ugly proves most beautiful.

In a perfectly well-defined genre, Euripides descended to cramped phrasing, uncouth songs, vile situations, and "earth's dung."[14] And why? Primarily because he could believe character to be instructive and beautiful.

Obviously, Robert had descended at his peril for very much the same reason. If critics had been able to condemn *Red Cotton Night-cap Country* with Aristophanean eloquence, presumably they would have. Had he not deliberately eschewed lyricism to find beauty in atrocities, constancy in adulterers, and truth in an apparent suicide? Browning's conviction is clear enough from the *Apology* that in every abyss of human degradation a revitalizing, soul-saving principle is to be discovered. On the other hand, as Donald Smalley[15] points out, he could hardly approve such literal cataloguing of the moral depths as French exponents of naturalism were beginning to undertake in 1875.

More than her own arguments, Balaustion's wide-eyed candor and enthusiasm condemn the fallacies of her opponent. Apparently Aristophanes has thought a little too much. Thinking in comedy after comedy, he has forgotten that the poet's role is not to titillate the intellect, but to lead his audience through vibrant re-creations of experience to simple, liberating insights. And to *move* the world the poet must aspire to stellar attainment. Directly after Balaustion's recital of Euripides' *Heracles*—a stupendous interlude in the debate during which the writer of comedies can sit down and mop his brow—Aristophanes recalls Thamuris, a singer so stellar in aspiration that he was doomed to challenge the gods in song, and perish. Browning's lyrical tribute to Thamuris, with its syncopated rhythms and astonishing imagery, suggests that the doom hardly mattered. A cheerful and defiant Greek electrifies the morning as he marches to his fatal song-contest. Aspiration and intensity of feeling, enshrined forever in art, triumph over mortality:

> Thamuris, marching, laughed "Each flake of foam
> (As sparklingly the ripple raced him by)
> "Mocks slower clouds adrift in the blue dome!"
>
> For Autumn was the season; red the sky
> Held morn's conclusive signet of the sun
> To break the mists up, bid them blaze and die.
>
> . . . . .
>
> Say not the birds flew! They forebore their right—
> Swam, revelling onward in the roll of things.
> Say not the beasts' mirth bounded! that was flight—
>
> How could the creatures leap, no lift of wings?
> Such earth's community of purpose, such
> The ease of earth's fulfilled imaginings.[16]

"Browning was especially fond of reading aloud this splendid song in later years," writes DeVane. Nevertheless the song of Thamuris did little to offset the stupefying effect of intricate, arid, allusive, and seemingly endless argumentation. Reviewers politely admired the learning and preferred the earlier Balaustion.

Fiercely undeterred, Browning flaunted before their eyes only seven months later a more radical illustration of naturalistic principles.

Again, the sordidness of the subject seems a general measure of the bleakest feelings he has about himself. At first intended for the boards—until he heard that Tennyson was writing *Queen Mary* and decided not to compete—*The Inn Album* resembles a Webster tragedy superimposed upon a Balzac boarding house. At least two of its four characters owe to the rather theatrical trial of the Tichborne Claimant, several of whose jampacked sessions Robert, possibly seeing a little of himself in a famous and articulate impostor, went out of his way to attend. (Carlyle predicted a connection when he declared that Browning would take up the Tichborne *cause célèbre* next and call his poem "*Gammon and Spinach*, perhaps.") Though an earlier scandal about Lord de Ros became the "nucleus of the story," homely British curtains are drawn back to reveal dancing skeletons in respectable Victorian closets—as in the exposure of Roger Tichborne's career. Tawdry sensationalism and contemporary allusions give the poem a journalistic aspect that must have surprised editors of *The New York Times*, which published *The Inn Album* from advanced proof sheets, in its Sunday issues of November 14, 21, and 28, 1875, and paid one hundred guineas for the privilege.[17]

The inn parlor is a kind of dumb courtroom, and the guest album in the parlor, a register of inane public comment.

"Hail, calm acclivity, salubrious spot!"

reads the scrawl of a departed guest; another on the same page prompts the Elder Man to exclaim,

That bard's a Browning: he neglects the form:
But ah, the sense, ye gods, the weighty sense!

Eager to recover solvency, the Elder Man is in a vindictive mood. Having lost £10,000 in a single night of cards, he reveals to his young adversary that his luck began to turn after he seduced a magnificent woman, his bewitching "life's prize," and then lost her to an impoverished curate. Though £10,000 the richer, the Younger Man is no happier since he believes the lady of his dreams has rejected him for a "fifty-years-old reprobate." At this point, the stern law of dramatic propriety brings to the inn the enchantress who eluded both gamblers. The Elder Man counsels the younger to court the peerless beauty, after he has threatened to disclose her secret to the curate unless she gains him £10,000 by compliance to the youth. Recaptivated by her grace and truth, the Younger Man proposes eternal devotion rather than a sordid bed. The lady responds to the suitor by accepting his devotion and to the threat of the Elder Man by taking poison. When the roué returns and reveals his venal maneuver, the true lover tenses himself on his toes and becomes airborne.

One is left in mild uncertainty as to whether the Elder Man is summarily stabbed or summarily choked:

> A tiger's flash—yell, spring, and scream—halloo!
> Death's out and on him, has and holds him—ugh!

The poison is working its effect on the lady. She has just time to write a few explanatory words in the inn album:

> *"I die now through the villain who lies dead,*
> *Righteously slain. He would have outraged me,*
> *So, my defender slew him."*[18]

Apparently the young man is to escape the gallows. A "curtain" drops on a modest pile of two corpses, at any rate, just as an innocent cousin enters the room.

Reviewers rubbed their eyes at the rough, impressionistic texture of *The Inn Album*'s style and the melodramatic morbidity of its vision. In the American *Nation* of January 20, 1876, Henry James could hardly "say very coherently" what he had just read. "It is not narrative, for there is not a line of comprehensible, consecutive statement in the two hundred and eleven pages. . . . It is not lyrical, for there is not a phrase which . . . chants itself, images itself, or lingers in the memory." J. A. Symonds in *The Academy* charged Browning with deliberate grotesquerie and loss of poetic integrity. And A. C. Bradley—who obviously had read until he thought he understood—offered in *Macmillan's Magazine* an epic catalogue of complaints ranging from coldness of portraiture to eccentric syntax and vulgar, unnecessary allusions to "Dizzy" and "the Laureate."[19] *The Inn Album* dropped into a deep well of neglect in which it remained until Professor Hitner discovered it in 1969.

Browning, according to Domett, "laughed at some abuse in the *Guardian* on the style, confessed to a slip in grammar noticed by the *Saturday Review*. . . ."[20] He named two hissing and snapping pet geese "Edinburgh" and "Quarterly"—and so far in public had managed to keep his temper. Yet ever since their contentment at the sun-drenched summit of *The Ring and the Book*, critics were retracing their steps back down the historical slope of his reputation. The general descent was only slightly exaggerated in the critical mountaineering of Alfred Austin, whose little iron crampons Browning had watched with narrowed eyes.

Not that it was easy to keep pettiness and absurdity in focus. A self-confessed Byronite, a very dapper, fastidious, five-feet-tall and cocksure egotist, Austin had been saved in youth from pious instructors by his own cynicism, and later from the dullness of the law by the timely death of a rich uncle. He had published ballads and satires and then, having drifted into literary journalism, thrilled readers of *The Temple Bar* by demonstrating that Tennyson was a third-rate poet. Anyone might have predicted whose turn had to follow. Decades before Wilde, Austin proved in the magazine's issue of June 1869 that Browning's poetry consisted entirely of prose, concluding:

> Small London coteries, and large London salons may stick their trumpery tinsel wreath upon [Mr. Browning's head], but these will last no longer than the locks they encircle. They may confer notoriety, but fame is not in their gift.[21]

That supper parties had conferred Apollo's bays was an insult that might have outraged an even-tempered poet. "I . . . only get an ignoble touch of satisfaction when I think that . . . it 'riles' such a filthy little snob as Mr. Alfred Austin to read in the Morning Post how many dinners I eat in good company," Browning wrote in his best manner to Isa Blagden, whom Austin had closely befriended. And a year later: "I stimulate myself by the reflection that it stings such vermin . . . to the quick that I 'haunt gilded saloons.' "

Robert was before long to lose this loyal confidant of a third of his lifetime. Miss Blagden died in her villa at Florence on January 20, 1873, watched over at the last by a Mme. Linda White Mazini.

When this vigilant friend requested a subscription to a memorial volume of Isabella Blagden's verse to be edited and prefaced by Austin, Robert's contempt almost obliterated his grief: "When the book is perpetrated," he replied, "—I *may* buy it, and, by help of penknife and ink-blotting, purify and render it fit to be read."[22] Allusions to his tormentor mounted. "He has been flea-biting me," Browning wrote with passion, "for many years past in whatever rag of a newspaper he could hop into." Who but "the small satirist"[23] could be responsible for niggling anonymous reviews replete with misquotations and stark misrepresentations?

In the spring of 1876, Browning decided to teach most of his tormentors a lesson at last. "Of Pacchiarotto, and How He Worked in Distemper" was composed in two weeks. A title pun in "*distemper*" introduces a poisonous portrait in jolting Hudibrastics. Alfred Austin, the angry satirist and bad rhymester, appears in fifteenth-century Siena as Giacomo Pacchiarotto, the angry reformer and bad painter. Pacchiarotto has Austin's sublime egotism, if less than his wit and more than his nerve. When a famine breaks out, he denounces the Sienese bailiffs to their faces, puts himself forward as their chief, then flies in panic before their wrath to shudder two days in a pestilential tomb and repent his indiscretion. Reeking, vermin-ridden, and chastised by an abbot, he returns to his miserable brush and frescoes. Lest anyone miss a contemporary target, Browning announces with glee that Xanthippe, his housemaid, has a brimming basin to empty on the heads of dwarfs that dance under his window:

> Banjo-Byron that twangs the strum-strum there—
> He'll think, as the pickle he curses,
> I've discharged on his pate his own verses!

Having fixed Austin in South London music-hall style, Browning turns with a long memory to Austin's tribe:

> Come, critics—not shake hands, excuse me!
> But—say have you grudged to amuse me
> This once in the forty-and-over
> Long years since you trampled my clover. . . ?
>
> . . . . .
>
> Was it 'grammar' wherein you would 'coach' me—
> You,—pacing in even that paddock
> Of language allotted you *ad hoc*,
> With a clog at your fetlocks,—you—scorners
> Of me free of all its four corners?
> Was it 'clearness of words which convey thought?'
> Ay, if words ever needed enswathe aught
> But ignorance, impudence, envy
> And malice. . . .
> You'd know, as you hissed, spat and sputtered,
> Clear cackle is easily uttered![24]

Pacchiarotto and How He Worked in Distemper: with Other Poems, a slate-colored collection of nineteen old and new lyrics, appeared on July 18, 1876. Bitterness and hostility glared from many a page in the first assemblage of shorter poems Browning had offered since *Dramatis Personae* twelve years before. "At the 'Mermaid'" rebuked critics on the elementary distinction between a poet's dramatic and personal utterances. In "House" and again in "Shop" they heard themselves lectured on the right of authorial privacy, in the "Epilogue," vilified for their inveterate obtuseness toward Shakespeare, Milton, Pope, Byron, and Robert Browning. With such a fusillade aimed at their heads, reactions even to most of the neutral lyrics were disgruntled.

Somehow a few of the new poems escaped censure. "Numpholeptos" was praised warmly by James Thomson in *The Secularist* and in *The Academy* hailed with an appreciative murmur by Edward Dowden, who cleverly saw in it a "pathetic personal significance" having to do with the late Mrs. Browning.[25] It only remained for Betty Miller[26] to point out that the poem is a thinly draped allegory of Browning's fleeting rebellion against his loyalty to Elizabeth's memory.

Understandably perhaps, critics found less to say about "St. Martin's Summer." Presenting the dilemma of living lovers haunted and thwarted by vivid memories of dead ones, it seems to keep Robert's problem with Lady Ashburton at a comfortable distance by simplifying issues and romanticizing personalities.[27] The speaker enjoys his second lady almost as much as the panic caused by the ghost of his first.

"Pacchiarotto" itself elicited crocodilian tears of regret, glancing critical thunderbolts, dignified admonitions. How had a flea managed to drive an eminent poet nearly out of his mind? A whole month before the poem's appearance, Austin in fact had published an elaborate disclaimer in *The Examiner* to deny that he had ever dreamed of attacking Robert Browning anonymously in *The Standard.* And now—a month after "Pacchiarotto's" appearance—*The Examiner* dug up and printed some doggerel quatrains, oddly reminiscent of the satirical Austin, but plainly addressed to Master Critic and signed "R——— B———," that had the effect of throwing a poet's gratuitous vulgarity into the limelight:

> You say my large poems are only a spate
> Of dirty brown water, a hullabaloo!
>
> . . . . .

But I am a favourite of the Numphs,
  And if you knew your place, you'd drop
Upon your knees, you niggery sumphs,
  In the back slum of the editor's shop.[28]

A week later, having donned the most immaculate of judicial robes, *The Examiner* loftily defended an injured critic and remorselessly denounced the author of *Pacchiarotto*.[29]

"It was not worth while, perhaps," Browning wrote George Barrett on August 12th, "to amuse myself for once (first time and last time) with my critics—I really had a fit of good humour—and nothing worse."[30] The fit indicates a growing perversity not wholly attributable to old age, a new failure in self-control and more deeply in self-assurance, all to be manifested again in October 1877 when Browning published his "transcription" of *The Agamemnon of Aeschylus* partly to prove Euripidean superiority, but perhaps primarily, as DeVane has suggested,[31] to refute Matthew Arnold's conviction that "the Greeks are the highest models of expression." "I will not deny that I prefer your manner in *Artemis Prologizes*," Arnold wrote Browning with immense tact, "but I can truly say . . . that, given a certain problem which you had fixed for yourself . . . , I am filled with admiration of the vigour and ability."[32] A translation of Aeschylus so literal and graceless as to bury him would have irritated Elizabeth Barrett, and indeed it irritated Carlyle, who had suggested it: "O dear!" that witness of the world's monumental nonsense told William Allingham, "[Browning's] a very foolish fellow. He picks you out the English for the Greek word by word, and . . . then again he snips up the sense and jingles it into rhyme! I could have told him he would do no good whatever under such conditions."[33]

Nevertheless, in the summer of 1876, when critics were still squealing from pulled tails, Robert could feel that he had settled an old score. An illuminating report of a luncheon at Warwick Crescent that summer suggests how pleased he was to have settled it. Upon arrival at Browning's door, Edmund Gosse was hustled aside by a "quite grieving" Locker-Lampson "to mourn over the attack on Austin" in hushed accents. "Browning," Gosse noticed after he had escaped to his host, "was in fine cue, full of spirits and geniality, with more literary and less mere fashionable tone than usual. He has rather suddenly become snow-white in beard and hair, having been merely grizzled, and presents a finer appearance, I suppose, than ever before." The young disciple smiled and nodded his way through luncheon a little uneasily. Yet his host was very affectionate and solicitous—"in the uncomfortably self-conscious way he always is, half confidential, half distant and all inscrutable."

The party over, Gosse followed the magisterial presence upstairs to a book-lined study, where, after his host's patronizing comment on Davenant's "Madagascar," the talk took a more reminiscent turn. Dilating on his earlier lack of readers, Browning explained that any new book of his own could be expected to sell "about 1,500 or 2,000 copies . . . quite irrespective of the opinions of the press." Then with a casual air he plucked a volume from the shelf.

"What have we here? Ah! this is the entirely-unintelligible *Sordello. . . .*"

Which remark "made me laugh nervously," as Gosse remembered, "it was said so drily."[34]

But the past few seasons had been furnishing Robert with a more salubrious reason for geniality and affection. Pen Browning had now set out in a direction that fate—if not his father—had been quietly and steadily preparing him for all along. Shopping among the arts for a vocation, even before his debacle at Christ Church, he had burst into six hundred verses about an experience at Le Croisic. Later he had carried paintbrushes along with birdshot into Scotland and kept up with the piano at home. Displaying for his father and aunt every promise of a consummate dilettantism, he suddenly impressed John Millais while daubing water colors by the painter's side at Birnam. When Millais recommended formal training Browning in a London studio consulted Felix Moscheles, who knew just the right master. Accordingly, Pen crossed the Channel and took rooms over a butcher's shop near the atelier of Jean-Arnould Heyermans, at Antwerp, while hope surged in a paternal heart.

"His master," Browning wrote Story in June 1874, "evidently *is* the master, and, from Pen's letters, which are unremitting, I can see that he is happier than he ever was in his life."[35] Happiness soon manifested itself in paintings from Belgium: an old man gazing at a skull, a dead hare on a damask cloth, a cobbler at work. Engravings in aquatint and stipple, studies in pencil and chalk, prints in line and mezzotint all marvelously testified to industry. Millais declared that "under *nobody* in England could Pen have made such progress," Browning reported to George Barrett. In the summer of 1875, while Robert and Sarianna were visiting him at Dinant, Pen was persuaded "after much entreaty"[36] to daub a parental portrait. Completed in four days and promptly photographed for Millais's approval, the oil shows a recognizable profile of a straight-nosed and curly-headed gentleman, with glimpses of a checkered cravat under a spray of white beard.

"He is a man now, not a mere mouse," Browning pronounced with categorical finality to Henriette Corkran.[37] Artistic friends at Warwick Crescent began to understand a new role. Millais considered a picture brought home at Christmas showing a priest reading a book and declared "the drawing perfect." When Rudolf Lehmann went a step further and offered 150 guineas for it, the son demurred. "Pen, don't be a fool," Browning coaxed after a few days' beaming impartiality about the money, "take it as offered." Pen did. "I doubt if anything ever made me more happy," Browning stretched and purred for Lehmann afterward. Alfred Domett, who had not risen to a prime ministership for nothing, sniffed in the air "a little *practical flattery*."[38]

Obsessive as his rage and despair over Pen had been, Browning's immense pride and relief in discovering that he was more than a mouse are understandable. But he failed to grasp that the self-approval his son lacked could only come through unaided effort and also that Belgium and France were the arena of an entirely new life. Rejected several years before by Fannie Coddington, a neurotic and wealthy American who would later change her mind about him, Pen struck up at Dinant an intense liaison with another girl and refused to return to Heyermans' studio. Robert's anger when he heard marriage was contemplated certainly owed as much to his fear that the young painter might not return to England at all as to horror over an indifferent Continental pedigree. For a time communication between father and son all but ceased. Through zealous intermediary efforts—to judge from Joseph Milsand's doleful letters to Sarianna—matrimony was narrowly averted. Pen became an exuberant and florid bohemian, acquired a ten-foot python named Jean-Baptiste and then a whole menagerie, lost his hair, put on weight, wrote home more often, and continued to paint and to sculpt. He was the "one novelty at Dinant," as Thomas Westwood observed, "quite a droll little figure in knickerbockers, with short, fat legs, and a ruddy countenance, . . . painting Dinant immutabilities. . . . He was very popular at the hotel, and seemed thoroughly good-natured, and quite at home."[39]

Still, despite parental eagerness, the artist really succeeded—for a while. British critics rejoiced in his debut because they could not conceivably forget whose surname he bore. At the age of twenty-nine, with the exhibition of his large painting, *A Worker in Brass, Antwerp,* at the Royal Academy, Pen was skyrocketed into the firmament of contemporary art. W. M. Rossetti detected in it "conspicuous promise" and *The Athenaeum*, an astonishing talent, but *The Times* perhaps came nearer the truth: "Vigorous, well-drawn, well-coloured, and well-composed," it judged, "and only sinning in size."[40] Unfortunately Pen did not take the hint. Size had recently been in fashion. But whereas Delacroix or Géricault had filled walls of great rooms with single paintings because the walls needed to be filled, Pen filled large walls with single efforts, one suspects, because he could never overcome his lingering sense of inferiority: magnitude was almost the only answer to extravagant expectations. *The Times* pronounced again: "As for Mr. Browning's pig, . . . we do not remember a painter who has ventured on so literal and so nearly life-sized a presentation of a porker as we have here."[41]

Loyally and lovingly, Browning hung as many of Pen's efforts in his own room as would "go there." And now—with a passion for detail that a museum director might have envied and something of the ebullience and energy of a public relations executive—he became in his mid-sixties his son's popularizer and curator in England. "To listen to him talking," Wilfred Meynell recalled years later, "one would sometimes suppose that he 'cared for nothing else' but painting." Alma-Tadema and G. F. Watts, Millais, Hunt, and William Rossetti were called upon for professional hints. Browning sent suggestions for new works, summaries of exhibits, and long letters of encouragement to Dinant and Antwerp and later to Paris, where for a brief interval Pen undertook a "dose of modeling" with Rodin. Meanwhile the humble and the great were summoned or cajoled to advanced "views" he arranged at Warwick Crescent, or in rooms loaned by Murray Smith at No. 17, Queen's Gate Gardens, South Kensington. "I barely mention . . . that a picture by my son is just arrived," Browning delicately notifies Tennyson. "If, by any happy chance, you should extend once again your walk so far as this place,—at any time of the day,—it will be a gratification indeed." Not that the visits of the great invariably gratified. Allingham reports that Carlyle was received at the poet's home with unusual emphasis and led upstairs. "How good and dear of you to come! dear Mr. Carlyle!" Browning expanded. "How dear!" Placed in an armchair squarely facing *A Worker in Brass, Antwerp*, Carlyle inquired into the etymology of the word *Antwerp*, said nothing at all about the picture, presently rose, descended on the poet's arm to the front door, and took his leave.[42]

But ordeals were borne with aplomb. "His devotion to his son, his triumphant joy," Lehmann remembers, were "most touching to behold." For hours on end Robert played the *cicerone* in chilly and carpetless rooms, greeting every visitor with a complimentary wink, a smile, or a few meaningless words. Late one evening he grasped the hand of his own deceptively well-dressed cook. "I'm only Martha, sir!" she protested. "And why not, Martha," he replied with the staunchest cordiality, "I am very glad to see you!" Nothing muted his verve. Laura Troubridge, then a young girl in the company of her trusted "Signor," encountered the poet at the Grosvenor Gallery in front of an undraped Venus.

"Well," Browning inquired, lowering his eyes from the picture, "what do you think of this?"

"It is rather funny," replied the schoolgirl shyly.

"Well, let us make a funny rhyme about it, shall we?"

"You begin," commanded Laura, and Browning recited:

> He gazed and gazed and gazed and gazed,
> Amazed, amazed, amazed, amazed.[43]

Yet a grand haughtiness toward fame had little application when he considered his son's career. Frederick Leighton was assiduously courted, apparently the more so after his elevation to the Presidency of the Royal Academy. At about that time Robert began to take long, almost daily promenades in sunshine and in drizzle with his old friend, whose shoulder was so high it touched the top of the poet's head. Both father and friend were put to the test, when the Royal Academy was asked to consider *Dryope Fascinated by Apollo, in the Form of a Serpent*—a life-size bronze costing a thousand pounds to make, and for which a model had stood countless hours with Pen's python draped about her neck. Leighton pleaded in vain; the conservative academicians rejected it as coarse. With mounting anguish, Browning went to the Grosvenor Gallery, and there wept openly in the presence of a surprised official who explained a rule against accepting "works rejected by the Academy."[44] Later he succeeded with Sir Coutts Lindsay, the founder of the Grosvenor, who was happily spared the sight of a distinguished white-maned poet dissolving in tears. The *Dryope* and several of his son's paintings attracted praise and won coveted prizes both at home and abroad. Pen's reputation plummeted to ignominy in the art world only at the sale of the Browning Collections in 1913, when *Dolce Far Niente* and *A Stall in the Fish Garden, Antwerp* (together 143 square feet of canvas) fetched sixteen shillings at auction; twenty-eight square feet of *Landscape*, seven shillings; and a sea piece, just five.

A penchant for depicting nudes with realistic fidelity caused fewer embarrassments than might have been expected. Pen's *After the Bath* survived an International Exhibition at Paris without incident. But his Joan of Arc without clothes, let alone armor, provoked a scandal in the eighties. "I am ashamed at the objection taken by some of the critics to the Eve-like simplicity of Pen's peasant-girl," Robert protested to the sympathetic Furnivall.

> If they knew anything of Joan's habits even when advanced in her saintly career, they would remember she was no prude by any means. Her favoured young cavalier, the Duc d'Alençon, mentions that he had frequently seen her undress, and that "aliquando videbat ejus mammas quae pulchrae erant"—in his very words.[45]

Summers were set aside for strenuous recuperation. In 1876, Browning, his sister, and Miss Egerton Smith had spent August and September near Lamlash on the Isle of Arran off the Scottish mainland. The good influences of a charming spot and an old friend had justified a "trial of novelty." For years Anne Egerton Smith, as a companion at concerts and an occasional guest on holiday, had been a cultivated reminder of Robert's youth. She had been an intimate of the Reverend W. J. Fox and of the Flower family. Elizabeth had made her aquaintance in Florence; later Miss Smith had settled in Notting Hill, from which she sometimes called for the poet in her brougham. As part proprietor of the Liverpool *Mercury*, she was a woman of independent means, and as a tall, quiet, shyly affectionate maiden conversant with theological principles and sharing an ardent enthusisasm for music, she combined several qualities of the poet's mother. Robert and Sarianna seem to have accepted her instinctively as a member of the family.

Early in August 1877 they departed with Miss Smith for Paris and thence for Collonges in the Haute Savoie, where second- and third-floor rooms were engaged in a substantial balconied chalet known locally as "La Saisiaz" or "The Rock-cleft." At first Browning plunged into one of his darkest moods. What he saw did little to draw him out of it. The spectacle of an "ignoble" peasantry absorbed in a daily routine of money-grubbing struck him more forcefully than French and Swiss mountain scenery. What had promised to be splendid woods materialized as "poor forest—thicket, say rather." He could scarcely bring himself to look at Homer or Grillparzer. The heat of the valley was oppressive, the great bulk and peak of the Salève, requiring a hard hour and a half to ascend, rather too close behind the house, intercepted the fresh air and beat back the sunlight.

Yet the scenery and silence soon took effect. In the middle of August, he sits on his balcony "aerially like Euripides," watching a steady progression of clouds and "Geneva lying under us, with the lake and the whole plain bounded by the Jura and our own Salève." He bathes twice a day in a stream-fed pond, "a marvel of delicate delight framed in with trees,"[46] hikes alone and with his ladies, accompanies them one day on an excursion to Voltaire's Ferney, on another to a peak in full view of glistening Mont Blanc. English journals arrived in the post to help his little party through the summer evenings—including a whole issue of the *Nineteenth Century*[47] filled with theological debate. On the evening of September 13, they made plans for a companionable and leisurely ascent of the Salève. A French friend, Gustave Dourlans, volunteered to join them. Miss Smith was enthusiastic and in "exceptionally good health and spirits," though Sarianna elected to stay behind.

A fine day dawned. Browning rose early, went for a morning swim, and returned more or less invigorated to the breakfast table only to hear that Miss Smith was still in her room. "Quite right," he announced, "she reserves her strength for our expedition." Then he went upstairs and, strolling round the second-floor balcony, came to their friend's bedroom windows. Mildly uneasy at no sight of her, he peered closely through a window and discerned the tall figure in an alarming position—kneeling forward with her head upon the floor. Robert called Sarianna, and as soon as he could join her in the room, raised Miss Smith's body, finding it "quite warm." Servants were sent in three directions for a doctor—but "no sort of assistance would have been to any avail," as Browning wrote the next day. "She must have died *standing,* and fallen as we found her."[48]

The immediacy of the event shocked him even more deeply than his grief. Browning "came to my rooms in Gloucester Place," Robert Buchanan remembers of this autumn, "and we had scarcely shaken hands before he began volubly. . . .This particular occurrence, he suggested, was so extraordinary, so unanticipated—he had been familiar with Death before, but it had always approached with some kind of *warning.*" Though in London he seemed to Buchanan "completely agitated and unstrung,"[49] in the Alps Browning had the presence of mind to telegraph Miss Smith's sister in Paris and to arrange the funeral at Collonges.

But a day or two after an abrupt little burial, he set out for reasons more therapeutic than sentimental to climb the Salève alone. Solitude was a necessity and so, perhaps, was ascent. There was relief in the uphill scramble, ledge by ledge, among mountain ash and cyclamen. The depression of a month back, now terribly vitalized by the sudden death, demanded that he examine—no matter with how much churning and confusion—one very stark, horrendous, indubitable reality.

La Saisiaz, dedicated to Miss Smith and completed in London on November 9, 1877, explores the circumstances and several of the reasons for a nightmarish crisis. Most nightmares dwindle in retrospect. A prefatory lyric skims gayly over mortality, and his personal monologue opens on a note of triumph. Apparently one cannot scale the Salève at sixty-five without feeling a little like Christopher Smart:

> Dared and done: at last I stand upon the summit, Dear and True!
> Singly dared and done; the climbing both of us were bound to do.
> Petty feat and yet prodigious: every side my glance was bent
> O'er the grandeur and the beauty lavished through the whole ascent.[50]

New vistas and new perspectives in the symbolic climb have suggested life's journey; and the vast spatial gulf between the summit and Collonges is but the cleft that divides the living from the dead—or Robert Browning aloft from Miss Smith in a grave.

Her shy, delicate, misunderstood personality exists in a fragile recollection. But where else?

> 'Does the soul survive the body? Is there God's self, no or yes?'[51]

Answers to eschatological questions must be personal and finite, for one cannot respond to universal conundrums in a manner that yields ultimate or divine truth in its full splendor and complexity. Like Bishop Blougram, Browning will plumb selfhood for imperfect answers to unfathomable mysteries, and then only with the arm of rational analysis. Indeed, as Blougram has chosen to ignore in himself

> certain hell-deep instincts, man's weak tongue
> Is never bold to utter,[52]

the poet of *La Saisiaz* seems deliberately to ignore disorderly and frightening contradictions of self that might underlie an almost traumatic reaction to natural death:

> Life is stocked with germs of torpid life; but may never I
> wake
> Those of mine whose resurrection could not be without
> earthquake!
> Rest all such, unraised forever![53]

The "germs" perhaps constitute much of the explanation for his crisis, and yet a cautious rationality unearths a few certainties.

Clearly, survival in memory alone would mock the suffering and striving of an individual's life. Positivism gives cold comfort in its insistence that "after the last spark proves extinct" others may attain the perfection one has endeavored to reach. Yet the imperative need to believe in an ampler, later existence does not make immortality a fact. The need may even mitigate against the possibility of the fact and signify moral cowardice. Browning's "Why should I want courage here?" leads to a parallel that perhaps took courage to state:

> Is it fact to which I cleave,
> Is it fancy I but cherish, when I take upon my lips
> Phrase the solemn Tuscan fashioned, and declare the soul's
> eclipse
> Not the soul's extinction? take his 'I believe and I declare—
> Certain am I—from this life I pass into a better, there
> Where that lady lives of whom enamoured was my soul'—
> where this
> Other lady, my companion dear and true, she also is?[54]

Miss Smith's heaven is also Elizabeth's—and Dante's—if it exists.

But does it? Confronting the problem rationally, one must begin with the corollary presuppositions of being: immediate knowledge of the self ("the thing itself which questions") and the not-self, and the independence of the two entities. All the multitudinous phenomena of life are "surmise" except what the self has endured. And what have sixty-five years taught?

> This—there is no reconciling wisdom with a world
> distraught,
> Goodness with triumphant evil, power with failure in the
> aim, . . .
>
> . . . . .

If you bar me from assuming earth to be a pupil's place . . .

. . . . .

I must say—or choke in silence—Howsoever came my
fate,
Sorrow did and joy did nowise,—life well weighed,—
preponderate.[55]

The vital proviso that world is a "pupil's place" is familiar. As Professor Priestley has indicated,[56] it reflects an assumption at least as old as Browning's *Paracelsus* that, whatever the distance between them, the mundane and the eternal are sufficently related.

And yet if assumption has become conviction, the poet insists that the most he can forge is a personal conviction, a credo:

O world spread out beneath me! only for myself I
speak,
Nowise dare to play the spokesman for my brothers strong
and weak,

. . . . .

I shall 'vindicate no way of God's to man'. . . .[57]

Rationality ends—persuasively enough—at a mystical border. But there is a defensive and troubled note in the insistence that Browning cannot speak for anyone but Browning—itself remarkable in the testament of a poet who has achieved fame by entering so many "strong and weak" minds to write their monologues.The wounded, self-limiting posture seems to indicate a temporary loss of nerve, rather than the beginning of a philosophic retreat to the worst of his intuitions about himself and the world. Self-inspection, at any rate, hardly sinks beneath academic postulates and gestures of disapproval in what follows. A mocking debate between Fancy and Reason sounds suspiciously like nervous chatter among tombstones in the dusk. At length Browning seems almost restored as he contemplates the hollowness of fame and descends in a significant, luminous sunset—or, rather, remembers it from London's "mid-November":

I have lived all o'er again
That last pregnant hour: I saved it, just as I could save
a root
Disinterred for re-interment when the time best helps to
shoot.

What did he perceive at the twilit hour? Walking back to the chalet, he "found the chain, I seemed to forge there,"[58] of reconciliation to Miss Smith's death and certainly knew he would need time to set its linked argument in order. He also seems to have glimpsed his own very vivid, unanswerable horror at the notion that death may be the grand finality. That Buchanan thought the horror resembled "terror"[59] is perhaps no more surprising than the passing of Browning's anxiety as he wrote *La Saisiaz.* His delightful and gay *Two Poets of Croisic*—which resurrects two Bretons from the darkest penumbra of French literature to prove that worldly fame is a humbug—was begun on November 10, 1877, a day after he had finished complaining of life's preponderating pain.

Other friendships helped to fill the vacancy left by the loss of a kindly lady. Indeed, pessimism and loneliness were kept under control through Browning's increasing sociability—and flirtation. He would write the attendant lyric for "Plot-Culture" and possibly one or more of the "Bad Dreams" for Mrs. Clara Sophia Bloomfield-Moore, the eccentric Philadelphian widow and philanthropist who bought several of Pen's paintings. On occasion in the 1870s and more often in the 1880s, Robert seems to have indulged in inconsequential romantic kissing. Without troubling his conscience, he took increasing advantage of the prerogative of an elderly, respectable, and rather jovial widower—embracing his ladies when he welcomed them and again when they parted.[60]

Frederick Leighton's sister, Mrs. Sutherland Orr, had alighted in Kensington Park Gardens after a life on the fringes of aristocratic grandeur. Born in St. Petersburg and christened Alexandra after her godmother, the Empress, she had met the Brownings twenty years before in Paris, then married into the army, and after a tragic year in India returned widowed to Bath. At fifty, she had lost her demure fragile beauty and become an odd little creature given to superstitious fears and impenetrable silences. Julian Hawthorne noticed that as her face twitched her weak eyes rushed "away to right and left." Robert recited to Mrs. Orr faithfully on Tuesday and Saturday afternoons and was repaid with the most attentive, enterprising devotion. From writing appraisals of his poetry and theology in the seventies, she graduated in the eighties to producing a handbook to Browning's works. After his death she was to publish an authorized *Life and Letters* that dismayed Pen, who "hates Mrs. Orr's *Life* as we do," the Michael Fields noted in 1895, "—the puling invalidism attributed to a man who never stayed in bed."[61]

Much less complicated were the demands and rewards of Mrs.

Charles Skirrow, the wife of a Master in Chancery who endured large dinners. When the rank of other distinguished guests kept Browning from her at table, she would shoot him "affectionate glances" and "little swift noddings, or gentle grimaces, by which he might understand he still occupied the first place in her mind," as W. B. Maxwell recalls. The poet would nod his handsome head. Sometimes Mrs. Skirrow's incessant gifts bedeviled. "What on earth (or under it) *can* you mean by 'fearing your owl is a vexation to me?' " Browning writes bravely about a brass inkstand with beady little eyes. ". . . As long as I live, it shall be near me."[62]

Not every woman thrilled to harmless intimacies, or was overly impressed by Robert's brushed silver locks, immaculately barbered beard, and Piccadilly and Pall Mall attire. "He talks everybody down with his dreadful voice," Mary Gladstone complained after a hectic evening at Cambridge, "and always places his person in such disagreeable proximity with yours and puffs and blows and spits in your face. I tried to think of Abt Vogler but it was no use—he couldn't ever have written it." Lady Knightley of Fawsley, too, lost an idol when she first encountered "a loud-voiced, sturdy little man, who says nothing in the least obscure or difficult to understand."[63] In fact, Browning had begun to prefer ladies who provided amenities without demanding intellectual gymnastics in return.

Mrs. Thomas FitzGerald, who tended rhododendron bushes named "Lord Tennyson" and "Robert Browning" at her immense manor of Shalstone, was a wealthy philanthropist who had known grief. When Robert met her in 1872 she was a mildly bookish and resigned widow of sixty-two. Four of her eight children were then dead and another was losing his mind. Profiting from her epistolary friendship with Pen, and quite unembarrassed by offerings of figs and cuttings from creepers, he called regularly upon his "Learned Lady" at 22 Portland Place when she was in town—or wrote to her on Saturdays when she was not.

On August 9, 1878, Robert informed Mrs. FitzGerald that "the only part of the world" that might stimulate him a little would be Italy. Not even his study of Spanish and reading of Calderón of late have forestalled lassitude.

Having last seen "the Italian side" in the year of Elizabeth's death, Browning approached the country this year as cautiously and gradually as he could. Stopping at the Splügen Pass, he and Sarianna daily and strenuously savored hours of Alpine paths and roadways and felt "renewed like the eagles."[64] Here Browning wrote at least two—

perhaps as many as five—of the half-dozen short poetic narratives that were to appear as *Dramatic Idyls* on April 28, 1879. Indeed he worked so hard that Sarianna became alarmed for his health.

In "Ivàn Ivànovitch" a Russian mother throws her children to hungry wolves that leap behind her troika and then pleads for death, and in "Ned Bratts" an old rogue with great spontaneity confesses his wickedness at the Bedford Assize. Both protagonists plead for punishment with a contrition and intensity that recall the mood of a young poet who has just abandoned Shelley. Two or three other idyls suggest the speaker of *Pauline* more distantly—as if through a reversed telescope. Remorse that persists through a lifetime in "Martin Relph" and in "Halbert and Hob" seems counterbalanced by Pan's thoughtful gift of early death to the runner in "Pheidippides." At least "He died—the bliss!" implies that one escapes imprisonment in guilt through sacrificial acts in grand, impersonal causes. Apparently to be Pheidippides, the chosen sprinter of Greece,

> Who could race like a God, bear the face of a God, whom
> a God loved so well,[65]

is to be a type of the selfless revolutionary, or the purest martyr, perhaps the Shelley of Shelley's poems.

"Clive"—written later in five days for *Dramatic Idyls, Second Series*—regards youthful and impulsive behavior with a determination to make amends in candor and humility. Yet a paradox is involved. If the young Clive's defiance in a duel was truly accompanied by fear, so the suicide of the ruined, drug-haunted conqueror of India was perhaps motivated by courage. Browning ransacked memory to write this idyl, recalling a story Mrs. Jameson had told him thirty years earlier. Yet the style of his modern jingoist narrator almost predicts Kipling's:

> Fear I naturally look for—unless, of all men alive,
> I am forced to make exception when I come to Robert
> Clive.[66]

Altogether one sees why reviewers applauded the *Dramatic Idyls*—the second series a little less exuberantly than the first. Their pungency and narrative clarity complemented Browning's rather clear, "helpful utterance" of *La Saisiaz.* Only a few of these versified stories, however, seem much more consequential than "Tray"[67]—a rather trivial assault on vivisectionism, materialism, and Harrisonian positivism.

In September 1878, weather at the snow-covered slopes of the Splügen Pass turned bitterly cold. With an enthusiastic sister who had never seen Italy before, Robert descended into sunlight and warmth, proceeding "in pursuance of an old desire" to Asolo. More than a few reminders of a bachelor's excursion of forty years ago remained. "It was *too* strange when we reached the ruined tower on the hill-top yesterday," he writes Mrs. FitzGerald on September 28. "I said [to Sarianna] 'Let me try if the echo still exists which I discovered here' . . . —thereupon it answered me plainly as ever, after all the silence."[68] Some things were new—or unremembered. The screaming of vendors in the open-air market left him feeling quite confused.

For their stay in Venice, an English traveler had recommended the Albergo dell' Universo, a small, decrepit family hotel on the shady side of the Grand Canal managed, as Mrs. Orr records, "by a lady of good birth and fallen fortunes," whose Austrian husband and two grown daughters "did not lighten her task." Browning consulted a Russian lady at the hotel on the names for "Ivàn Ivànovitch," greeted the Willy Brackens on their way to Florence, and with less anxiety than on a previous occasion encountered the benefactor of the Grosvenor Gallery. "We take gondola" with Sir Coutts and Lady Lindsay, "stroll on the Square, and return—all by the brilliant moon." The poet and his sister spent seven of the next eleven autumns in Venice,[69] usually pausing *en route* for a few weeks at some quiet elevated spot for meditative walks. In 1879, 1880, and 1881, they returned to the Albergo dell' Universo, after which the pleasant, decaying hotel suffered eclipse and reemerged as an art gallery. Once over the Alps, Browning took care to avoid the principal localities associated with his marriage.

On June 14, 1879, he had an opportunity to defend Elizabeth's rights in public at the trial of Shepherd *v.* Francis in London. Richard Herne Shepherd, a freelance journalist, had been characterized by *The Athenaeum* as a "literary vampire"[70] and worse, after his republication of Miss Barrett's earlier poems, now unprotected by copyright. He was successfully attempting to recover damages.

Advised in advance that his own essay on Shelley might figure in the proceedings, Browning cannot have been eager to appear as a witness.

"I need not ask who you are," Mr. Serjeant Parry, for the defense, began soon after court had come to order. "I would as soon ask William Shakespeare."

"I have been before the public for some years," Browning admitted, and then alluded to Shepherd's callous disregard for the feelings of a dead poetess, and also to his own "Hervé Riel," part of which Shepherd had published without authority.

Mr. Waite, for the plaintiff, inquired whether the witness had not outraged Shelley's living son by writing a preface to letters supposed to be by Shelley?

"I wrote the preface to Shelley's work in 1867," Robert testified, evidently rattled. "I did not get his son's permission to do so."

"So you too are 'outraging the feelings of the living.' "

"No," replied Browning, "the whole passage had been anticipated."

"You knew that Shelley had suppressed 'Queen Mab'?"

"Yes."

"And that these letters were forgeries?"

"Yes," Browning assented, "forgeries. . . . I have the preface here and I shall be very happy to read the whole of it."

"I think not," interposed the judge, to the accompaniment of laughter from the benches.

"Shelley was a great poet and a great dramatist," Serjeant Parry remarked soothingly a minute or two later.

"A great dramatist," Browning concluded with apparent relief, "—almost as great as Shakespeare."[71]

Trivial in itself, his brief, rather embarrassing participation in a process for slander seems to have reinforced Browning's determined air of neutrality and detachment in public. To some extent, he took increasing refuge in an unassuming, philistine blandness. Eveline Forbes remembers how dreary his dinner anecdotes seemed to her as a girl of seventeen at a Balliol College weekend in 1879. Yet late one night apart from the other guests, Browning took her arm, and walking slowly round the quadrangle in flickering shadows, gave her the striking impression that she was listening to the "real man":

> He spoke of the German poets [she wrote later], of Goethe chiefly, and told me of his theory . . . that it was Judas Iscariot's intense faith in Christ which led to his betrayal of Him. . . . As he spoke, from the shadows of the old college buildings a picture slowly formed, then leapt into the light—the picture of a young disciple, ardent, adoring, seated at Jesus' feet. . . . a sombre light in the dark eyes, the thin hand outstretched to meet his Master, as He offered the sop which should be given to 'that one of you who shall betray me.'[72]

The annual summer voyages renewed the oldest ties. In 1880

Browning and his sister found themselves "literally in the arms of Milsand & Dourlans" at Paris, the Storys were in Venice, and the cook employed by one of the many lionizing Americans was—of all persons—"my old Ferdinando of Florence."[73]

In London, Browning attended the funeral of George Eliot in December and caught a bad cold in an appropriate downpour as he stood next to Herbert Spencer at Highgate Cemetery. He was much more deeply affected when Carlyle died on February 5, 1881. "His opinions about men and things one inch out of his own little circle never moved me with the force of a feather," Browning wrote Mme. Belloc in a letter that oddly suggests affection and indebtedness while denying both. "But we must not ourselves prove ingrates. . . . He wrote *Sartor*—and such letters to me in those old days!"[74]

CHAPTER 26

Lion and Sage

1881-85

Potentially, there had always been enough ghastliness, love, and religion in the works of Robert Browning for an extravagant world-wide success. The Italian murder poem in four volumes apparently turned him into a monumental curiosity in England. And, so far, he had pleased some readers and baffled many others with literary impressionism for almost fifty years. Early in the 1880s, Browning really became a public institution. "There is not a creed which is not shaken, not an accredited dogma which is not shown to be questionable," Matthew Arnold proclaimed in 1880 with his normal percipience, surveying the recent toll of scientific advancement and historical and textual investigation, "not a received tradition which does not threaten to dissolve."[1] In fact, people would now turn to *Sordello, Men and Women,* and the rest of Browning as a complex substitute for shaken creeds and questionable dogmas. His legendary difficulty and optimism implied that he had challenged, and quite probably defeated, every one of the pernicious scientific and philosophic specters of the epoch. Obviously however, fate required that he should first be discovered by an energetic and resourceful new herald and champion.

Frederick James Furnivall—the man who formally institutionalized him—was in himself a whole cluster of institutions. A vegetarian socialist and a Shavian before Shaw, he lectured on grammar to laborers, denounced the House of Lords, harangued in the streets, organized shilling dances at the Working Men's College, sculled on Sundays, and in his spare time laid the groundwork for modern literary scholarship. Planning in its initial stages with Hensleigh Wedgwood the *Oxford English Dictionary,* Furnivall had discovered that willing, unpaid, and capable people could be organized for research. Rapidly he conjured up new societies: the Early English Text Society in 1864, the Chaucer and the Ballad Societies in 1868. Capping these valuable labors, he persuaded Browning to accept the nominal presidency of the New Shakspere Society in 1879—just as the poet was honored by Cambridge with an LL.D. degree.

No sooner had "Robert Browning, M.A., LL.D." been hoisted above the names of sixty-six distinguished vice presidents than the hurricane commenced. Furnivall and Swinburne took this moment to insult each other's Shakespearean expertise in print, and moved swiftly on to less distinguished insult: Furnivall wrote of "Pigsbrook and Co.," Swinburne retaliated with "Mr. Flunkivall Brothelsbank." Later, Swinburne bludgeoned the name Furnivall into "Brothelsdyke." For almost two years the controversy swelled and reverberated, and the New Shakspere Society trembled from stem to stern.

Robert did his best to remain impartial. "I know nothing whatever of any function belonging to the figurehead of the ship except to face the salt-water," he explained to one more seasick passenger.[2] Almost undrenched and unperturbed, he rode out his presidency. Furnivall was a man to his taste. His father, a physician at Egham, had been bold enough to call Mary Shelley a dictatorial "toad"[3] to Shelley's face, and the son demonstrated exactly the same candor with all but the few people close to his heart. Robert grew extremely fond of this cheerful, gymnastic, selfless scholar who spoke of Wyclif and Chaucer as if they were personal friends—and treated Browning himself as one of their peers.

On Sunday, July 3, 1881, the founder of societies accompanied Miss Emily Hickey, his protegée, on a meteoric walk across Regent's Park to No. 19, Warwick Crescent. "What do you think of a Browning Society?" he suddenly demanded. "Would you help in one?"

Miss Hickey was breathless, enthusiastic. But what ought they to do if Robert Browning did not approve?

"Go on all the same and not mind him," Furnivall told her.[4]

Defiance proved unnecessary. Browning listened to the queer proposal in jovial silence, laughed aloud, and then recited a transparent anecdote about a gentleman who had "the greatest respect" for Monckton Milnes but no inclination to pay good money for his poems. Browning was now earning about £100 a year from poetry, whereas Tennyson's verse earned some £5000 annually.[5]

This interview mercifully past, Dr. Furnivall sent a notice to the *Academy,* and then wrote a prospectus that declared Browning "*the* most thought-full" poet alive and the obscurity of his style something of a blessing. "At any rate," Furnivall relented a little,

> the Browning student will seek the shortcoming in himself rather than in his master. He will wish . . . to learn more of the meaning of the poet's utterances; and then, having gladly learnt, 'gladly wol he teche,' and bring others under the same influence that has benefited himself. To this end *The Browning Society* has been founded.[6]

"Il me semble que ce genre de chose frise le ridicule," Browning was heard to murmur.[7]

But a month later he was indignantly refuting a pessimistic rumor: "I suppose that it has been by spontaneous generation," he lectures Mrs. FitzGerald from St. Pierre-de-Chartreuse, "that I have on the table here the proofs of a 'Bibliography of R.B.' . . . mentioning every variation in any edition of every line and word that has been altered at any time." At once he corrected proofs. Earmarked to appear with a reprint of the essay on Shelley as an early release of the Society, the Bibliography would go far to atone for rankling neglect.

While Browning in Venice sent back annotations and contended with gondoliers, in England a curious small army assembled. Domett, Leighton, and Milsand swiftly became ornamental captains. On October 28, as a hush fell over three hundred people at University College on Gower Street, Dr. Furnivall rose from the chair. "Some low-minded folk have attributed unworthy motives to me," he announced very grandly. "'Tis their nature to. I pass them by."

He then annihilated "a ducal correspondent" who had supposed it was "300 years too early for a Browning Society," and introduced the Reverend Joshua Kirkman—who classified Browning's works, commented on his style, and claimed for him "the distinction of being pre-eminently the greatest Christian poet we have ever had." Kirkman also observed that the poet was still hale:

> We can hardly help feeling that if Browning would *take our advice*, we should "make him all he ought to be." But at least we will study, while he laughs kindly on us.[8]

A press cannonade resounded. *The Nation* fired at the "mysteries" of the Browningites, *The Cambridge Review* at their "congregational spirit," and *The Echo* at their dense honorifics. Shot and shell as usual galvanized Dr. Furnivall to a barrage of confident and rather hyperbolic letters: "As to the interpretations of difficult poems," he serenely defied *The Echo* from Primrose Hill, "our Society will soon be able to make all clear."[9]

"What has touched me," Browning pronounced on his return from Venice a safe fortnight after the launching solemnities, "is the sudden assemblage of men and women to whose names, for the most part, I am a stranger." Dr. Furnivall is "most warm-hearted, whatever may be the mistakes about me of which his head is guilty." And when Edmund Yates, editor of the London *World,* begged permission to print a scathing notice:

> As Wilkes was no Wilkeite, I am quite other than a Browningite [Robert explained]. . . . The exaggerations probably come of the fifty-years'-long charge of unintelligibility against my books; such reactions are possible, though I never looked for the beginning of one so soon. That there is a grotesque side to the thing is certain.[10]

Unwilling either to endorse or disavow the Society, Browning avoided monthly meetings and declined to correct Papers, but he entertained disciples and talked with loyal dons and undergraduates at Oxford and Cambridge. Cautious and amazed at first, he nevertheless gave his keenest admirers many covert signs of his approval. He evidenced a sudden interest in literary clubs, which led him to a meeting of the Wordsworth Society, where he conducted proceedings for half an hour, in the presidential absence of Lord Coleridge. A torrent of inquiries was answered: "Once for all," Browning tells Furnivall in 1882, "I never read a line, original or translated, by Kant, Schelling, or Hegel in my whole life."[11]

Furnivall's demand that Murray Smith issue a one-shilling text, and again that Browning prefix lucid "arguments" to his poems, though irritating and impossible, paled to insignificance as the fire aimed at Furnivall began to fall close to the poet. "Pray don't imagine I can't understand the mock compliments to myself . . . in the censure of those who make so thoroughly-appreciated a person 'ridiculous,'" Browning declares after perusing several journals. "The *ridiculus mus* is the inveterate nibbler at, and spoiler of the fruits of a man's whole life's labour." Yet apparently "gibing and gibbering" enemies were beginning to writhe a little.[12]

At any rate, Furnivall's banners advanced like Charlemagne's. Though attracting a skeptic or two (Bernard Shaw, who was learning to speak wittily in public, and Thomas Wise, who was learning to forge expertly in private), the London Browning Society could almost agree that its poet was an unparalleled "thinker and philosopher."[13] The notorious darkness of his style as well as the ambiguity of his dramatic portraits encouraged not only endless debate, but a zealous endeavor to discover and explicate the heart of his "message." With pleasing difficulty, people found in his work almost everything they urgently needed to find. Ranging from headquarters, Browningites spoke and recited everywhere. Some of the Browning clubs blossomed with splendor and promise, only to droop and die soon afterward, but others sipped tea and heard papers with a positive rage for elucidation.

A "Browning craze" addled the United States. Ladies wearing brown, in a room decorated with brown curtains, served brown bread on brown china from a brown tablecloth—to the uncontrollable delight of the press. Already a Midwestern railway company had transferred *Pauline, Paracelsus,* and *Sordello* to its timetables.[14] A Sordello Club sprouted in St. Louis. Chicago booksellers, besieged by a dozen conventicles, could not keep the required texts in stock.

Robert of course had lived long enough to be utterly fascinated. The societies made him "startlingly" aware of the inexhaustible potentials of criticism:

> I write, airily, "Quoth Tom to Jack, one New Year's Day," and one "Student" wants to know who Jack was,—another sees no difficulty there, but much in Tom's entity,—while a third, getting easily over both stumbling blocks, says, "But—*which* New Year's Day?"[15]

He could now refer bothersome "students" to the *Browning Society's Papers,* later to Mrs. Orr's *Handbook.* He told gift-giving Americans he had to conclude he was better understood in Chicago than anywhere else.

Journalists steadily rifled his poems and distorted his features. "The Girton girls have proved faithless," *The Academy* wept invisible tears with Dr. Furnivall after a moral lapse at Cambridge. "They have formally dissolved their Browning Society, and . . . voted that the balance of funds in hand should be spent on chocolates."

> Oh, the dull meetings! someone yawns an *aye.*
> One gapes again a *yea.*
> We girls determined not to yawn, but buy
> Chocolate Menier . . .,

funeralized *The Journal of Education,* as the story ricocheted. The chocolates "would be much better for them than my sour stuff," Browning commented benignly.[16] Occasionally he even added to the store of hilarious reports, as when he regaled the company at Leslie Stephen's with an account of himself chased round and round the Albert Memorial by a bevy of foreign sightseers.

Indeed, there were private compensations for whatever public embarrassment Furnivall's legions cost him. Robert was never on better terms with himself. His jollity and exhilaration steadily impressed the people who paid homage at his door or caught sight of him about town. Privately, he viewed the debate over his work as a public debate over himself. As such, the debate obscured much of his past life and simplified his entire life, as he looked retrospectively over the years. The problem of his betrayal of Elizabeth's faith and trust, his possible obtuseness and wrong-headedness with Pen, his earlier defection from radical ideals, and many other issues and episodes of the past were conveniently blurred or blotted out in the starkly colorful challenge between Browningites and anti-Browningites—between those who simply affirmed and those who simply denied the value of everything he had ever done. Less troubled by guilt and perplexity, self-doubt and philosophic doubt, Browning took a magnified view of those who had tried to oppugn him in the past, and an almost comfortable view of his defenders and conventicles of the present. "If you 'wince' at every little instance of spite at 'Browning's' very existence," he told Mrs. FitzGerald, who had loyally joined the Browning Society, "it is well you did not know that personage nearly half a century ago. . . . I begin to greatly appreciate the services of the Society which 'furifies' these survivors of the *un*fittest. What sort of notice would you expect Mr. Furnivall to take of a scur[r]ilous article in the Saturday Review—written, very probably, by one of the young men who lose no opportunity of spitting at me[?] . . . . When I set up a review and puff myself therein, I presume Mr. Furnivall & his friends will think—and justly—that *their* 'occupation is gone.' "[17]

Glorification—solemn or comic—did not tempt him to remember anything more vividly and intensely than his virulent critics. Decades of uncompromising hostility provided him with a comparatively happy and manageable obsession, to the apparent exclusion of far blacker considerations. He kept an unchanged perspective, even as he wore out the adjectives of gratitude. In June 1882, while he sat in the Sheldonian Theatre, attired in a flame-colored gown and awaiting an honorary D.C.L. from Oxford, an immense cartoon of himself descended from a thronged upper gallery. Lowered jerkily on a string, a red cotton night cap collapsed on the head of a Professor of Divinity. As if aware of a sublime error, it hopped away, paused, and alighted at last on Robert's white curls.

Authorities threatened terrible reprisal until Browning worked wonders: "Am I, or am I not, a member of your University?" he demanded of the vice chancellor.

"Certainly you are one," came the deferential reply.

"Then let that poor boy off!"—whereupon an irreverent student was entirely pardoned.[18]

His respect for youth was reciprocated. In 1884 he made a point of attending an optional reception at the end of a ferociously ceremonial week at the University of Edinburgh. "Browning!" the Scottish undergraduates rose and shouted after a tedious round of tercentenary encomiums. Now they stomped in chorus. They scrambled on to benches, they waved their sticks: "Browning! Browning! Browning!"

The old poet rose: "Some people are good enough to say that my writings are sometimes unintelligible," he had to remind the new generation, "but I hope to make myself intelligible now, when I say how affected and impressed I am by this noble, this magnificent welcome . . .!"[19]

So much for unrestrained adulation.

"Suppose in the midst of this green quiet there were concealed a corpse," Browning had asked himself in a meadow at St. Pierre, back in the summer of 1881. To report a hypothetical corpse to the gendarmes would mean hypothetical incarceration, he had just about decided, when a corpse *was* discovered in the meadow! How could he account for his bizarre prevision?

"By a law of the association of ideas," he concluded a whole year later, "*contraries* come into the mind as often as *similarities*—and the peace and solitude readily called up the notion of what would most jar with them." He had never acknowledged an indebtedness to a law of Wordsworth's and Hartley's more explicitly—or succinctly.[20]

By whatever law of poetic productivity, in the summer of 1882 at St. Pierre, Robert began one of his periods of rapid composition, writing several poems for *Jocoseria,* an inconsequential collection published on March 9, 1883. In "Donald," a stag in the woodlands of Ross-shire twice saves a young hunter who seems too cruel and boastful to be Pen. "Ixion" is less horrible and more interesting. Shelleyan fury at the notion of perpetual punishment is mitigated by the presence of a "Potency" who implicitly forgives Ixion, rotating unhappily in Hades, for making love to a goddess. "Pambo" also implies forgiveness—toward literary critics—if it doesn't quite imply reform:

> Darkling, I keep my sunrise-aim,
>
> . . . . .
>
> And *look to my ways,* yet, much the same,
> *Offend with my tongue*—like Pambo![21]

Jocoseria was twice reprinted in a short period. Robert told the Reverend J. D. Williams: "It all comes of the Browning Societies."[22] Leaving his admirers somewhat at a loss to know what to do with themselves, Robert took Sarianna the following summer to "a paradise of coolness and quiet" at Gressoney St. Jean in the Italian Alps.

For years, Browning had entertained his friends by instantly finding comic rhymes. For Tennyson, he had accepted the splendid challenge of Thomas and Jane Carlyle's Scottish birthplaces—

She, a pearl where eye detect no speck can,
He, ordained to close with and cross-buttock
Cant, the giant—these, O Ecclefechan,
These your glories be, O Craigenputtock![23]

Again, he would rise to the challenge of a fashionable marriage—

Venus, sea froth's child,
Playing old gooseberry,
Marries Lord Rosebery
To Miss de Rothschild![24]

In September 1883, at Gressoney, he wrote the Prologue to *Ferishtah's Fancies* in his most outrageous and anti-lyrical party manner—

Pray, Reader, have you eaten ortolans
  Ever in Italy?
Recall how cooks there cook them: for my plan's
  To—Lyre with Spit ally.

. . . . .

So with your meal, my poem: masticate
  Sense, sight and song there!
Digest these, and I praise your peptics' state,
  Nothing found wrong there.[25]

One is reminded of the tone of *Pacchiarotto*. The Prologue, an Epilogue, and the twelve "Fancies" of Ferishtah were published after a shrewd tactical delay by Smith and Elder on November 21, 1884. Browning told Mrs. FitzGerald how eager he was to see the volume published. The "Prologue" seems at once temperamental and satirical. It even seems directed against the facile philosophic poems of Persian Ferishtah that follow—as if the ironist in Robert Browning were laughing at the buttery lion of the Browning Societies. Ferishtah abominates materialism, asserts that faith transcends logic, and accuses the age of intellectual presumption in tones suggestive of the Reverend Thomas Jones of Swansea. That Browning admired the Welsh Nonconformist preacher is clear, for he wrote a brief, pleasantly reminiscent preface to Jones's posthumous *The Divine Order and Other Sermons and Addresses* in 1884. Jones's recurring theme, "Foolish intellect! Foolish intellect! Thou art not supreme in this universe!"—is of course rational enough, and the interpretation of it in *Ferishtah* is perhaps neither anti-intellectual nor Panglossian.[26] On the other hand, Ferishtah is little more than a loquacious puppet; he seems disinterested in the implications of his outlook and quite addicted to the booming of platitudes:

> But love is victory, the prize itself:
> Love—trust to! Be rewarded for the trust
> In trust's mere act. In love success is sure,
> Attainment—no delusion, whatso'er
> The prize be: apprehended as a prize,
> A prize it is.[27]

Why did Browning write so badly in 1883? The vigor and precision of the lyrics he wrote later for *Asolando* show that he could still write well. Apparently, at the moment, he doubted whether he had any right to wear the costume of a Victorian sage. One returns to his recognition of something "grotesque" in the Browning Society. At all events, in *Ferishtah* he gave his admirers exactly what they wanted. Behind "a thin disguise of a few Persian names and allusions" one sees a very luxuriant white beard. Yet behind the "Epilogue," written at Mrs. Bronson's balustraded palace on the Grand Canal, one sees a great deal more—Italy, Elizabeth, the ironic psychology of his monologues, his own integrity:

> Only, at heart's utmost joy and triumph, terror
> Sudden turns the blood to ice: a chill wind disencharms
> All the late enchantment! What if all be error—
> If the halo irised round my head were, Love, thine arms?[28]

Through London seasons, Robert kissed Mrs. Orr, Mrs. Bloomfield-Moore, and the Michael Fields "when they came and when they went away,"[29] watched his plays stalk the boards like melodramatic ghosts under the auspices of the Browning Society, and did not dwell very much on his joys and triumphs. Nor did he dwell at all upon gloom, despite the darkness of the text he copied at the Lehmanns' to prove that he could see with one eye shut just as well as ever:

Shall we all die?
We shall die all:
Die all shall we,
Die all we shall.
Robert Browning, Jan. 1, '86.[30]

CHAPTER 27

"The Summit Attained"

1886-89

With immense concentration, Browning set himself the goal of crossing new boundaries of the impossible at seventy-three. He took "no interest in what was said," Churton Collins noted with mild surprise in March 1886. "Conversation there is none," echoed Helen Faucit Martin after a seemingly endless luncheon at Llangollen with the usually receptive Robert.[1] He was writing an autobiography—not of events, of course, nor in any form which would enable contemporaries to identify the new work as self-explanation. But he was writing in his own voice, and his subject was, to a degree, a vague medley of those ideas he had lived with preeminently—many of them since boyhood. *Parleyings With Certain People of Importance in Their Day*, the result, was published in reddish-brown boards in London on January 28, 1887. The poem was dedicated to the memory of Milsand, who had died in September at Villers-la-Faye.

Reviewers were dumbfounded by a gigantic, intricate mixture of reminiscence, anecdote, vindication, and mayhem. Even Mrs. Orr felt that Browning's "powers of exposition"[2] were strained in seven confabulations with ghosts. Indeed confusion is apparent. Ignoring Mandeville's wicked irony in the *Bees*, Browning asks that hearty pessimist, who saw evil as the essential basis of society, to cure Carlyle of pessimism:

> Grant
> His bilious mood one potion, ministrant
> Of homely wisdom, healthy wit![3]

He then lectures the dead Carlyle on heavenly love, illusory evil, and the necessity of ignorance.

"Daniel Bartoli" dismisses the wrong Bartoli to deal a blow to chroniclers of saints' legends, then chronicles a miracle of the kind to which Browning gave credence, extracting virtue from the context of evil. But "Christopher Smart" accepts a legend of divine insanity complete with its lore of Smart's scratching "Song to David" in the wainscot of a madhouse cell. Bubb Dodington and Disraeli are treated almost as coeval, wily despots of the supernatural. In "Francis Furini," chronology and coherence dance a jig that rattled even DeVane. Robert urges the seventeenth-century Tuscan to refute Darwinian evolutionists, and then commands Furini, who on his deathbed repented his own frank nudes, to paint Pen Browning's *Joan of Arc and the Kingfisher.* Pen's picture is described in lines that had already explained the purity of Pen's interest in nudes to viewers at the Grosvenor Gallery:

> *Now as she fain would bathe, one even-tide*
> *God's maid, this Joan, from the pool's edge she spied*
> *The fair blue bird.*[4]

And yet, throughout the landscapes of "Gerard de Lairesse" and the musicology of "Charles Avison," as elsewhere in the work, Browning did pay tribute to the influence of a few spirits who had accompanied him in the corridors of impressionism most of his life and, with convulsions of reticence as well as of style, revealed glimpses of his own intellectual and psychological history as he saw it.

The *Parleyings* were a vast elegant bone for the Browning societies to chew, and a hostage to the future in a continuing skirmish with biographers yet unborn. Having disclosed what he thought legitimate, Robert set himself much more systematically to prevent illegitimate intrusion. Froude's intimate disclosures of Carlyle—and everybody else's of Shelley—had doubled his lifelong horror at the public appetite to get inside the artist's private life. Thomas Wise found him stooped over an old leather trunk near a Dantean grate. "Whilst we remained talking the work of destruction continued," the young forger noticed with the roundest eyes. Bundles of letters, manuscripts in a boyish hand, the salable relics of a lengthy career whizzed to the flames! By the time Browning put aside "*two* copies of the original edition of *Pauline,*" Wise lost his voice. Nor were immolations concealed from Symonds, Palgrave, or even Tennyson, to whom Robert wrote instructively about three mornings spent in "long deferred duty" at the fireplace.[5]

However, he was too pleased with the tangible present to worry much about the vague future. At seventy-five he was stout and hale, infinitely fêted, respected by young poets who dared not step too near him at parties, and loved by sedate matrons who recovered their bloom in his presence. Browning's habits had become regular as clockwork. William Grove, the valet who photographed him in sober meditative poses, would find his employer already up at seven "munching an apple, or reading out loud from a book in Greek." Disdaining tea but gobbling the apple—or a few pears, plums, a wedge of pineapple, strawberries in season—while Grove drew the bath, Robert would then climb in and "splash violently, singing at the top of his voice."[6] Tuneful ablutions culminated in a waterfall that pummeled on his head from an overhead tank, to the peril of nearby bookshelves. Dressing with dispatch, Browning would bang the piano a little, open the morning mail, and then at his desk accept or decline dinner invitations and even write poetry—with some reluctance, according to Pen, who remembered in 1912 that his father "would rather do almost anything else."[7] In the afternoons there were galleries to see, Felix Moscheles' cluttered studio to visit, walks and rides with ladies in black, and in the evenings port wine, gloved hands and glitter, and then the dark.

Yet he ate and slept well; he endured colds, rheumatism, and asthma—but seldom headaches. Recently Dr. Furnivall had offered him the whole Shelley Society and then arranged to have *The Cenci* performed on Browning's birthday. The world conspired to alleviate some of his tensions. Beneath an outer layer of contentment one detects Robert's almost confident feeling that he had not denied but assimilated Shelleyan radicalism at last, even as the old Rabbi who assimilates and transcends in "Jochanan Hakkodosh." Not that the world found him very radical. Denunciations of scientific positivism in his last three volumes tended to comfort the pious and bore the sophisticated.

Doomed to demolition by the Regent's Canal Bill, his house at last had to be abandoned. Finding the transition "no exhilarating business," Browning moved in the spring of 1887 to an ample, dignified slab of masonry behind iron railings at 29 DeVere Gardens, across the street from Henry James at No. 32. Weekend traffic resumed in the new vestibule. "Come in," Sarianna chirped as briskly as ever. "Not into the dining-room," she told Anne Thackeray Ritchie, "there are some ladies waiting there; and there are some members of the Browning Society in the drawing-room. Robert is in the study, with some Americans who have come by appointment."[8]

What did worry him specifically—now and then—was that Elizabeth's "unhappy letters which concern spiritualism" might some day be published. The public would be entertained richly "by the aberrations of a soul so immeasurably superior in general intelligence," he groaned to George.[9] The problem was complicated by Elizabeth's loquacity and his own sentimentality: he could hardly get his hands on *all* her letters, nor mutilate some of the precious but incriminating ones he had. The laughter of the future reached his ears—as distinctly as Gandolf's reached the bishop's.

Challenging J. H. Ingram in *The Athenaeum* about Elizabeth's very birthdate, Robert floated above real vicissitudes of the present like a grand old galleon in a moderate sea. If Fannie Coddington had been an unknown quantity, he thundered at Pen, in the happiest conditional mode, "—or one of the innumerable pleasant parties to a flirtation and utterly useless for anything else, I should have given you up for lost."[10] Fortunately Browning had approved of the Coddingtons even before they made Fannie into a very far from penniless orphan. Now thirty-eight, Pen combed and trimmed a Gargantuan wiry moustache and married blond Fannie at Hawkwell Place in Pembury near London, on October 4, 1887. There was a short honeymoon in Venice, then a longer one in America. Pen telegraphed sadly to his parent about Fannie's miscarriage. He also purchased a live alligator which he sent his father.

Pen and Fannie were back in Venice in the fall of 1888, and so were Robert and Sarianna. The great topic of conversation was the Palazzo Rezzonico, and, as relatives of a negotiating purchaser, father and aunt were permitted to inspect the interior. Repeatedly they gazed from without at the colossal baroque façade with its river gods and fluted pillars. Carlo, who became Pope Clement XIII, had once dwelt soberly within. Later Emperor Joseph II of Austria had paced under the floating Tiepolo ceilings, and quaffed champagne in a golden salon. Certainly, the palace was now in a deplorable state: its chapel brutally desecrated, its ceilings white-washed, its upper floors inhabited by art students who had wandered in from *Pippa Passes.* Yet the unbelievable fact was that Fannie's inheritance was to rescue the whole moldering temple for her husband, who was to make inviolately permanent the honeymoon abandonment of his easel. Pen "will occupy the Pope's old apartment," Browning wrote Pen's uncle with perfect restraint in December, "and quietly wait till, bit by bit, he 'furnishes' the whole of his domain—which he does not find at all too vast. He reminds me of the mouse (in a poem of Donne's) who got into the trunk of an elephant."

But by February 1889, parental uneasiness gave way to ebullience. The costliest restorations in Venice had progressed to everyone's satisfaction; surely Pen's success with plaster and marble would send him back to paint and canvas. A nephew of Pope Clement's significantly had been christened "Widmann." George Barrett now heard from Pen's father that "my mother's maiden name was 'Wiedemann' —and Pen was named after her."[11]

Numerous people in London as a matter of fact had begun to note unmistakable signs of decline in Robert Browning, despite his gayety On April 7, a month before his seventy-seventh birthday, he stumbled in the familiar opening of "How They Brought the Good News." A wax cylinder recording made that evening at the Lehmanns' survives today.

I sprang to the saddle [stirrup], and Joris, and he,

Browning shouts into the scientific future, trilling his 'r's' with theatrical gusto,

> I galloped, Dirck galloped, we galloped all three;
> "Speed!" echoed the wall to us galloping through;
> "Speed!" echoed the—
> I forget it! [followed by a few indistinct syllables] . . . I'm most terribly sorry that I can't remember my own verses. . .![12]

Edmund Gosse was not surprised by the poet's weariness two months later, or when, inevitably, in the shadowy precincts of a Trinity College tree, Browning sat down without a word, and then slowly divulged "early loves and hatreds, Italian memories of the forties, stories with names in them that meant nothing to his ignorant listener."[13]

One Sunday, Robert sat in a pleasant garden chair with the *Letters and Literary Remains of Edward FitzGerald,* recently edited by W. Aldis Wright. The book fell open to some private words of 1861:

> Mrs. Browning's Death is rather a relief to me, I must say: no more Aurora Leighs, thank God! A woman of real Genius, I know: but what is the upshot of it all?[14]

Never having met the misogynist who scribbled the *Rubáiyát,* Browning confronted in white heat a faceless ghost. He composed a poem Monday, sent it off to *The Athenaeum* Tuesday, tried to retract it by telegram Wednesday or Thursday, and saw it again—now in irrevocable print—on Saturday, July 13, 1889:

TO EDWARD FITZGERALD.

I CHANCED upon a new book yesterday:
I opened it, and, where my finger lay
  'Twixt page and uncut page, these words I read
—Some six or seven at most—and learned thereby
That you, Fitzgerald, whom by ear and eye
  She never knew, "thanked God my wife was dead."

Ay dead! and were yourself alive, good Fitz,
How to return you thanks would task my wits:
  Kicking you seems the common lot of curs—
While more appropriate greeting lends you grace:
Surely to spit there glorifies your face—
  Spitting—from lips once sanctified by Hers.[15]

"Like all impulsive actions," Robert explained to Furnivall early the next week, "I believe I might preferably have left the thing to its proper contempt." Yet there the poem was. Aldis Wright's apology in the *Athenaeum*—and some louder cacophony elsewhere—underlined the fact that Browning had called attention to a slight insult by most violently compounding it. With tactful, dignified, and sometimes excruciating letters of apology and self-defense, he managed to console almost everyone mortally offended by his savagery except himself. He had shown to the public a raw, brutal reaction, he had humiliated himself, and probably he knew that in doing so he had humiliated Elizabeth in a way FitzGerald never could.[16]

"Your papa," Sarianna wrote Pen, has been "quite ill." Early in August, Robert promised to let William G. Kingsland see some manuscripts, "if I live," and "repeated more than once— *'If I live.'* " But optimism returned—and "weariness and indisposition" fled—as he thought of a rejuvenating working holiday at Asolo, "my old attraction," followed by a visit with Pen and Fannie in a rejuvenated palace. Smith and Elder's grand, climactic sixteen-volume edition had been steadily appearing. An appropriately slim volume of his new lyrics was almost ready. "Your papa is in good health now," Sarianna wrote Pen with normal economy on August 16, "—but he may change."[17]

Browning and his sister were on their way to Italy a fortnight later.

The plump benignity of Mrs. Katharine Bronson's round face greeted them at Asolo. She had taken rooms for them at Signora Tabacchi's—opposite La Mura, her own villa in the town's ramparts. "The pure and the severe did not appeal to her," Lady Paget remembers of this American hostess,[18] and indeed Mrs. Bronson usually surrounded herself with Chinese lap dogs and pepperminted chocolates. Yet she had watched maternally over Henry James, and listened affectionately even when Browning read the Venetian police reports. She kept an eye on him now—alarmed by Robert's "very apparent" wheezing as he climbed stairs. The worst of his asthma disappeared, "either under the influence of the pure, invigorating air," as she wavered later, "or the small globules of arsenicum which he took daily."

Signing herself "Caterina," after that deposed Cyprian queen who ruled Asolo once with Cardinal Bembo, Mrs. Bronson was nevertheless an unobtrusive potentate. She noticed that Browning was very busy, that he planned his days with "precision and regularity." She waited with eager passivity for his appearance on her loggia at three each afternoon. "Here you can see all this beauty without fatigue," Robert remarked, admiring the crenelated white city rising on one side, vineyards and plains billowing on the other. After tea, Queen Caterina would summon a carriage, and presently smother his knees for no reason at all. "One would think we were going to Siberia," Browning told her. As they rolled out past orchards and hedgerows, he talked incessantly and gaily. Mrs. Bronson wondered—perhaps with perfectly normal Protestant alarm—why he doffed his hat to priests. "I always salute the church," Browning enlightened her.[19]

What struck him was the evanescence of a marvelous shimmering abundance: "the sea of fertility all round our height, which a month ago showed pomegranates and figs and chestnuts—walnuts and apples all rioting together in full glory—all this is daily disappearing," he notes philosophically on October 8. "Shall I ever see them again?"[20]

Pen came for a short visit, and saw no reason in his father's health to prolong his stay. There were morning rambles on green knolls with Sarianna, evening sessions at a muted spinet with Caterina. He took both ladies to watch a "decent" theatrical troupe as it mimed and ranted within crumbling castle walls. Boasting that he was "good for ten years," Robert outlined delicious plans to renovate a roofless schoolhouse nearby, and applied to purchase the property. "I shall call it 'Pippa's Tower,' " he explained to Mrs. Bronson. "We will have

flag-signals. . . . The telephone is too modern; don't you think so?"
Perhaps he needed to symbolize that lost Asolo when

natural objects seemed to stand
Palpably fire-clothed!

But he knew that little had changed in fifty years except the beholder:

earth, sky,
Hill, vale, tree, flower,—Italia's rare
O'er-running beauty crowds the eye—
But flame? The Bush is bare.[21]

Wordsworthian visions did not deeply depress him. He contemplated writing a great tragedy soon. On October 15, Browning dispatched to Murray Smith thirty vigorous little poems for *Asolando*—"some few written here, all revised."[22]

Real rain, looming rheumatism, and a conceivable need to prod a publisher of Elizabeth's works made him vaguely restless. Besides, every idyll must end. Just before this one did, the Storys arrived with bright gossip and nostalgic chatter. As they were about to depart, Robert ran back to the carriage and stuck his ivory face in the window: "Friends for forty years," William heard him exclaim, "and with never a break!"[23]

At Venice with Sarianna on October 31, Robert found miracles and enchantments in the Palazzo Rezzonico. The desolation of a "dingy cavern" had appalled him the year before; Pen and Fannie now led him over gleaming marble floors, among gigantic pedestals, through brightly damasked silken rooms. And crowning miracle of all, the great palace was "warmed throughout by a furnace and pipes." Surprised at Pen's achievement in turning a cavern into a habitable museum, Browning kept repeating for Evelyn Barclay's diary: "I never thought it was in him!"[24]

Not that a cozy mezzanine, nor even the chapel dedicated to Elizabeth, made him linger much. Browning rose at six now, read for two hours, breakfasted, and then promptly floated away to the Lido for chatter and exercise. Hiram Corson labored "to keep pace" with an inquisitive sightseer who scattered the pigeons at St. Mark's—and seemed to know the metropolis "*par coeur.*"[25] Swarms of admirers called at the Palazzo; Robert returned the calls and saw Venice by night. Instinctively at this time, he pushed himself to the limit to achieve the illusion of his own contentment. Several poems in *Asolando* suggest not so much a conscience haunted by guilt, as the difficulty of maintaining determined attitudes and of disciplining one's deepest feelings. The dreamer in "Bad Dreams. III" is at the mercy of his nightmare—in which "Perfidious snake-plants" strangle a pavilion, and in a stream-of-consciousness style, upper pavements are cracked and split by powerful thrusts of Nature from below:

each oak
Held on his horns some spoil he broke
By surreptitiously beneath
Upthrusting: pavements, as with teeth,
Griped huge weed widening crack and split
In squares and circles stone-work. . . .[26]

It is difficult not to see Robert as the terrified dreamer, and again, as the speaker in "Reverie" who seeks protection from what obscurely "thwarts, what irks, what grieves."[27]

Browning had become less candid about the true state of his health. He had told Mrs. FitzGerald about his "spasmodic asthma," and also about tiring himself "thoroughly with quantities of pleasant things enough—had they presented themselves in moderation."[28] But he would not recognize his own foolishness now. He threw himself immoderately into the social life of an unreal city. He exercised too rapidly and too often, retired late and rose early, and with conspicuous gallantry accepted a round of invitations. Probably, he feared the emotion-laden memories of the past and his own responsibility for the behavior of a son who seemed likely to abandon a profession. Clearly, Pen's easels were not much in evidence. As Evelyn Barclay's diary for this season shows, Browning regarded Pen's achievements in interior decoration with some irony and condescension. And yet in forcing his mind away from the old, old problem of his betrayal of Elizabeth's trust, Browning undoubtedly escaped the weight of other problems as well. Though not bent on self-destruction, he was wearing himself out for the sake of a moderately good conscience. . . . No other place better suited his "bodily and intellectual needs," he declared on November 9; "I am *quite* well, every breathing inconvenience gone."

Seventy-two steps divided Robert's stratospheric bedroom from the ground floor. Repeatedly he ascended them to point to one painting of Pen's on the ceiling: "a most vigorous conception," as Mrs. Corson happily judged, "an eagle struggling with a serpent, illustrative of

Shelley's Revolt of Islam." Browning also corrected proofs for *Asolando,* looked quizzically at the photographer who snapped him with his son on palatial steps, chatted with Pen's gondoliers and even—in the "Pope's Room"—with Jocko the parrot. On November 19, while fogs descended, he began to recite poetry for friends at 4:30 "and read standing with one short interval till 6:30."[29]

With boastful exuberance at a party one evening, he held out his arm under medical eyes. Dr. Bird, who felt his pulse, looked back expressionlessly. Coughing several days later, Browning diagnosed liver trouble and prescribed for himself a reduced diet. The days were now cold and thick with fog; the late Adriatic sirocco kept everything, indoors and outdoors, saturated. Robert hailed gondoliers, kept coughing, refused wraps and medical advice: "My dear boy, I never catch cold." When Miss Barclay's suitor, G. D. Giles, sketched him one evening, he seized the drawing and returned it with an instructive "unpublished work":

Here I'm gazing, wide awake,
Robert Browning, no mistake!

Only ropes and chains would have kept him from rushing off to meet a German admiral at the Layards'. But, "too ill to stay longer," he was forced to return after dinner. The next evening he attended a performance of *Carmen* and nearly fainted on the alpine climb to bed. In the foothills of the mezzanine on November 29, he confessed frankly to a cold—and even hedged on plans to start for England—but would not stay in bed. Pen defied parental injunctions. Dr. Cini, physician ordinary to the English colony, diagnosed bronchitis, complicated by "irregular" heart action.[30] Having stayed up all night to minister poultices, Pen and Fannie were relieved by a Venetian nurse.

By then, Browning was desperately ill. The whole palace knew it. He probably knew it. Through the siege of poultices, Miss Barclay wrote, "he was most patient, always saying 'How good you are to me. Thank you.' " His bladder was affected, and he suffered "dreadful attacks of coughing." To satisfy the curiosity of the world, bulletins blandly ignoring the facts were posted outside the porter's lodge to report that the poet was not worse and not in pain.

On Tuesday, December 10, there was "a syncopy [*sic*] of the heart and . . . they thought it was the end." Miss Barclay ran for brandy, Dr. Cini's assistant remained to inject ether in the event of "collapse."

That night Robert shouted deliriously. The next day, in lucid intervals, he remembered to speak in Italian to three consulting physicians—who could soften their report to the family only to the extent of saying recovery was "still possible." By now, Mrs. Orr had boarded an express train in France; telegrams were arriving from all parts. Copies of *Asolando* also had arrived. The poet weakly fingered one of them, declared its binding a "pretty colour." On Thursday, December 12, Browning recovered from a syncope long enough to order everyone out of his room and then lapsed into incoherence. But late in the afternoon, a nurse heard him declare: "I feel much worse. I know now that I must die."[31]

Pen came softly to his father's bedside at 6:30 and read aloud a telegram from Murray Smith. *Asolando,* published that day, had met with "most favourable" reviews, and the edition was "nearly exhausted."[32]

"More than satisfied," murmured Browning, and then, "I am dying. My dear boy. My dear boy."[33]

His condition changed perceptibly at about ten o'clock. Half an hour later the poet's forty-year-old son informed Mrs. Bronson, "Our Beloved breathed his last as San Marco's clock struck ten,—without pain—unconsciously,"[34] and then Pen stayed up until 2:30 A.M. to inform a few friends in Italy, and all of England, that Browning was dead.

Murray Smith in London received a telegram before midnight, and took it over to the editor of *The Times.*

The death of Robert Browning surprised rather few people. Having been alerted by a series of portentous bulletins, obituary writers had reams of material and somber, dignified phrases at hand. "Carlyle, George Eliot, Matthew Arnold; and now Robert Browning, a greater name than all these, has passed into silence," *The Athenaeum* ventured, and *The Saturday Review* almost swallowed its wrath after a single allusion to "unintelligent BROWNING-worship."[35] Elegies appeared with almost equal promptitude:

World-wide the grief for Robert Browning dead!

hymned Maria S. Porter of Boston.[36] Arthur Symons had nine stanzas ready by December 15. In one of seven commemorative sonnets, Swinburne was quite polished:

Venice and winter, hand in deadly hand,

Have slain the lover of her lovely strand
And singer of a storm-bright Christmas Eve.[37]

Julia Ward Howe jotted unsteadily in a pullman on the way to Fresno,

Open your gates, Westminster high!
Where should the minstrel sovereigns lie?[38]

Unhappily the question of where a minstrel sovereign *would* lie was "painful and urgent," as Mrs. Orr could plainly see when she reached a sorrowing Palazzo on December 13. With common sense, Sarianna had suggested that her brother ought to be buried in Florence next to his wife. Mrs. Orr herself reported the poet's explicit wish to be interred approximately wherever he happened to drop. Lady Layard told her diary: "Pen has telegraphed ab[t] his fathers death & to see if it is wished that he should be buried in West[r] Abbey,"[39] but the only information that day from London was that a memorial service in the Abbey would be unobjectionable. Florentine authorities were mute, distressed friends interceded, but on Saturday Pen learned that only an act of the Italian Parliament could open the closed Protestant cemetery to his father. Resigned to the urgency, Mrs. Orr wired her brother Leighton to move heaven and earth at Westminster. Apparently Murray Smith got to the Dean first. Hearing the Dean's decision from his father's old publisher, Pen instantly accepted the offer of a tomb in England's grandest abbey.

Venetians themselves offered a public funeral when they learned, one day late, that Browning was dead. Shortly before noon on Sunday, Fannie helped carry the body to the coffin. Pen placed a wreath of bay leaves on his father's head, and another when the coffin was sealed and transferred to the Sala, on the mauve silk pall. After a gloomy, perfunctory English service, eight blue-uniformed pompieres from the small attending troop carried the coffin down the steps to the canal, placing it on a canopied black-and-gold barge. Gondoliers in velvet heaped wreaths and crosses. Then Pen, Fannie, and Sarianna boarded Admiral Noce's launch, a tow-line snapped tight, and the cortege moved languorously down the Grand Canal in a red-and-orange evening.

For several days the coffin rested in purgatorial solitude at San Michele, the Island of the Dead, and then an English servant accompanied it all the way to the iron railings of 29 DeVere Gardens.

In Venice the poet's sister seemed to Lady Layard pale, weary, unrealistic, and defiant. Sarianna, in fact, "talked of her brother always in the present tense—& said she was going home to destroy all unpublished M.S. he may have left." But soon after loyally rummaging in her brother's desk, this caretaker of three generations of Brownings returned to live in a watery palace. The Michael Field ladies—able to imply whole worlds in a mere glance—would presently consider Sarianna a tedious octogenarian. Henriette Corkran would find "something of the old Trojan about her," admire her handwriting (it was like "copperplate"), and discover a new picturesqueness in an old friend.[40]

Fannie's marital happiness was short-lived. Seeking the consolations of Marienbad and Mrs. FitzGerald, then the more dubious ones of a lonely apartment on Fifth Avenue in New York, she would finally leave Pen altogether: "he was a pervert, he was degenerate, he had mistresses in the very same house, . . . he kept large snakes in the cellar."[41] Fannie, observes Paul Landis, "belonged to a society which in its idealizing sought to ignore the flesh. . . . Granted that Pen's wife would have needed more than ordinary forbearance, whatever that is, she might have benefited if she could have heard her mother-in-law say, as she wrote to Isa Blagden: 'I am afraid you don't sufficiently realize to yourself the physical tendencies of the sexes.' "[42] Fannie was destined to become a blameless and charitable Anglican nun and to live until 1935.

Pen Browning tried honorably to understand all that had happened to him. He bought Casa Guidi, erected Pippa's Tower, edited some famous love letters, and employed Ferdinando and Wilson in their dotage in the echoing Palazzo Rezzonico. Forced by his creditors to sell his Venetian home, he managed a yapping "Palazzo Pigstye" at Asolo, and even established a silk mill nearby. In 1906, three years after his aunt died, he acquired the pleasant Torre all' Antella near Florence. Pen "thinks about life till he is on the road to madness," agreed the Michael Fields, who found him red and bald as an apple, "and escapes with jocund instinctive habits . . . like those of a squire."[43] In his final illness at sixty-three, Pen must have reverted often to the intense sensations and melting impressions of the very last day in his father's life.

Robert Browning was buried in a thick London fog on December 31, 1889. Ticket holders waited in long, cold, indistinct queues for their chance to mourn him. Inside Westminster Abbey the upper arches were swallowed in dark haze, and the choir candles and long-chained lamps were surrounded by eery copper mist. Six hundred people tried to keep warm during an eventless morning. A bell tolled until about 12:30, when the sudden relief of organ strains indicated "that the procession from DeVere Gardens had arrived."[44] George Meredith whispered in Edmund Gosse's ear: "The presence of Bulwer in Poet's Corner so defiled it that no Real Man should wish to be there! Nevertheless our dear Browning doubtless did wish it, so all is well!"[45]

Sarianna was too ill to attend the funeral. Pen, alone, led the procession into the Abbey and down the central aisle. People stared sympathetically, but he found even familiar faces unrecognizable through his tears. The *Times* correspondent gazed with proper curiosity: the coffin seemed of un-English make, and the pall bearers, representative of "art, music, law, literature, philosophy, and the two Universities."[46] Hallam Tennyson, Murray Smith, Leighton, and the others lowered their burden in the south transept.

The burial ceremony ended at last with a benediction and the Dead March. In the interval, fog in the Abbey lifted a little, and Mrs. Browning's lines, "What would we give our beloved?" were sung in a limpid boy's treble and answered by the full choir. Michael Field remembered the practical tick of a workman's hammer, the crunch of sod under a carpet, and a significant blue flash of violets "as we pressed quietly to the spot."[47]

. . . Let it be.
Life has ebbed from me—I am on dry ground—
All sounds of life I held so thunderous sweet
Shade off to silence—
—all the motions drawn
From Beauty in action which spun audibly
My brain round in a rapture, have grown still.

References

CHAPTER 1 ***Childhood 1812–24*** (pp. 1–12)

1 See Henry James's preface as well as his short story, "The Private Life," in *The Altar of the Dead . . . and Other Tales* (New York, 1909), and, in a milder vein, his "Browning in Westminster Abbey" in *Robert Browning: A Collection of Critical Essays*, ed. Philip Drew (London, 1966). As S. E. Lind and Leon Edel point out, James often seems to be writing about himself when he writes of Browning. See also Richard D. Altick, "The Private Life of Robert Browning," *Yale Review*, XLI (1951), 247–62, and Miller, *Portrait, passim.* Three earlier psychoanalytic studies are pertinent: F. R. G. Duckworth's *Browning: Background and Conflict* (London, 1931), and Stewart W. Holmes's "Browning's *Sordello* and Jung: Browning's *Sordello* in the Light of Jung's Theory of Types," *PMLA*, LVI (1941), 758–96, and Holmes's "Browning: Semantic Stutterer," *PMLA*, LX (1945), 231–55.

2 Orr, *Life*, pp. 3–4.

3 *RB and EBB*, II, 1005–1006 [August 26, 1846].

4 Miller, *Portrait*, p. 7.

5 *RB and EBB*, II, 1011 [August 27, 1846].

6 Quoted by Griffin and Minchin, p. 12.

7 Mr. Browning wrote about sixty lines in 1842, *e.g.*,

> 'Tis Hammelin (but you had better perhaps
> Turn over your atlas and look at the maps)
> Which, without flattery,
> Seem'd one vast rattery . . . !

before hearing of Robert's "The Pied Piper of Hamelin," composed in April or May of that year; see Griffin and Minchin, p. 21.

8 Hood, p. 106 (to Kirkup, February 19, 1867).

9 Orr, *Life*, p. 25.

10 Domett, *Diary*, p. 212.

11 Orr, *Life*, p. 18.

12 "Mr. Browning's Religious History," *The British Weekly*, December 20, 1889, p. 117.

13 *A Course of Sermons on Faith and Practice Delivered at York Street Chapel, Walworth, 1838–39* (London, 1839), p. 213.

14 Hood, p. 106.

15 Quoted by Miller, *Portrait*, p. 8.

16 *Ibid.*, p. 7.

17 *Ibid.*, p. 13.

18 Only a sample survives of the doggerel Browning wrote in his class when "first there":

We boys are privates in our Regiment's ranks—
'Tis to our Captain that we all owe thanks!

Later, Mr. Ready and his Peckham school with its glass greenhouse were banished to epigrams, e.g.:

Within these walls and near that house of glass,
Did I, three years of hapless childhood pass—
Damned undiluted misery it was!

See Domett, *Diary*, pp. 73–74; also "The Texts of Fifteen Fugitives by Robert Browning," *Victorian Poetry*, V (1967), 158–59.

19 Domett, *Diary*, p. 73.

20 "Development," lines 1–15.

21 Griffin and Minchin, p. 26.

22 *Ibid.*, p. 22.

23 *De' Simboli Trasportati al Morale.*

24 W. C. DeVane, *Browning's Parleyings: The Autobiography of a Mind* (New Haven, 1927), pp. 56–57.

25 *Life*, pp. 30–31.

26 "Fra Lippo Lippi," line 284.

27 "A Toccata of Galuppi's," line 19.

28 See "Parleying with Charles Avison," lines 137–252.

29 "Abt Vogler," line 49.

30 *Browning's Parleyings*, p. 252.

31 "Parleying with Charles Avison," lines 70–78.

32 For Browning's musical training see his letter of 1887 to Henry Spaulding in H. E. Greene, "Browning's Knowledge of Music," *PMLA*, LXII (1947), 1095–99; also comments in Griffin and Minchin, pp. 15–17; DeVane, *Browning's Parleyings*, pp. 252–82; and G. M. Ridenour, "Browning's Music Poems: Fancy and Fact," *PMLA*, LXXVIII (1963), 369–77.

33 "Parleying with Charles Avison," lines 81–82; DeVane, *Browning's Parleyings*, pp. 254–55.

34 *Browning's Parleyings*, pp. 257–58.

35 Griffin and Minchin, p. 11.

36 William Hazlitt, "The Dulwich Picture Gallery," *The Picture Galleries of England, The Complete Works*, ed. P. P. Howe (London, 1930), X, 18 ff.

37 *The Ring and the Book*, III, 59.

38 D. G. Rossetti, quoted by Griffin and Minchin, p. 12.

39 *RB and EBB,* I, 509 [March 3, 1846].

40 "Parleying with Gerard de Lairesse," line 33.

41 The 1778 English edition, translated from the Dutch by the painter John Frederick Fritsch.

42 Quoted in DeVane, *Browning's Parleyings,* p. 221.

43 *Ibid.*, pp. 223, 225.

44 Hood, p. 217 (to Furnivall, April 15, 1883); DeVane, *Handbook*, pp. 172–73.

CHAPTER 2 *To Shelley's School 1824–29* (pp. 13–29)

1 Orr, *Life,* p. 96 (to Fanny Haworth [August 1, 1837]); the letter is dated by DeVane, *Handbook,* p. 132, n. 1.

2 See *New Poems by Robert Browning and Elizabeth Barrett Browning,* ed. F. G. Kenyon (London, 1914), pp. 3–12.

3 *RB and EBB,* II, 986 [August 22, 1846].

4 See Frederick A. Pottle, *Shelley and Browning: A Myth and Some Facts,* with a foreword by W. L. Phelps (Chicago, 1923).

5 See C. G. Jung, *Psychologische Typen* (Zürich, 1921), pp. 552 ff.

6 Griffin and Minchin, p. 53.

7 Pottle, *Shelley and Browning,* p. 27.

8 Griffin and Minchin, p. 52.

9 Pottle, *Shelley and Browning,* pp. 42 ff.

10 See Shelley's footnotes to lines V, 189; VII, 135,136; VII, 13; VIII, 211, 212.

11 Orr, *Life,* p. 43.

12 *A Course of Sermons on Faith and Practice Delivered at York Street Chapel, Walworth, 1838–39* (London, 1839), p. 247.

13 Quoted in Orr, *Life,* p. 45.

14 Correspondence No. 655, University College Library, London. Mr. Browning misspelled the name as "Coatts."

15 Correspondence No. 1252, University College Library, London.

16 Miller, *Portrait,* pp. 17–18.

17 See *ibid.*, p. 5.

18 *Paracelsus,* I, 238–46.

19 *Ibid.*, II, 144–49.

20 Harriet Martineau, *Five Years of Youth; or, Sense and Sentiment* (London, 1831), p. 132.

21 Quoted by Mrs. F. L. Bridell-Fox, "Memoir," in Sarah Flower Adams, *Vivia Perpetua: A Dramatic Poem in Five Acts, With a Memoir of the Author, and Her Hymns* (privately printed, 1893), p. x.

22 Quoted by Richard and Edward Garnett, *The Life of W. J. Fox, Public Teacher and Social Reformer, 1786–1864* (London, 1910), p. 71.

23 Macready, I, 325 (June 7, 1836).

24 R. and E. Garnett, *Life of Fox* (London, 1910), pp. 66–67.

25 *Five Years of Youth; or, Sense and Sentiment* (London, 1831), p. 132.

26 *Ibid.*, p. 184.

27 R. and E. Garnett, *Life of Fox* (London, 1910), pp. 68–70.

28 Moncure D. Conway, *Centenary History of the South Place Society* (London, 1894), pp. 46–47.

29 Miller, *Portrait*, p. 30.

30 *Ibid.*, p. 34, n. 2.

31 *New Letters*, p. 176 (to Mrs. Bridell-Fox, July 21, 1866).

32 Hood, p. 20 (to Horne, December 3, 1848).

33 *Pauline; A Fragment of a Confession*, lines 1–9. In 1888 Browning clarified punctuation and phrasing in sections of the poem cited in this and following chapters; our citations are to the text of that year.

34 *Ibid.*, lines 33–35.

35 Hood, p. 20 (December 3, 1848).

36 R. and E. Garnett, *Life of Fox* (London, 1910), p. 23.

37 *Ibid.*, pp. 32–33.

38 W. J. Fox, *A Course of Lectures on Subjects Connected with the Corruption, Revival, and Future Influence of Genuine Christianity* (2nd edn.; London, 1819), p. 52.

39 *Ibid.*, p. 103.

CHAPTER 3 *Crisis and Confession 1829–33* (pp. 30–45)

1 "The Texts of Fifteen Fugitives by Robert Browning," *Victorian Poetry*, V (1967), 158–59.

2 Serjeant Talfourd, *The New Monthly Magazine*, March 1831, cited in H. N. Hillebrand, *Edmund Kean* (New York, 1933), p. 320.

3 William Hazlitt, "Mr. Kean's Richard," *A View of the English Stage, The Complete Works*, ed. P. P. Howe (London, 1930), V, 182.

4 Dr. Doran, quoted in Hillebrand, *Edmund Kean* (New York, 1933), p. 320.

5 Hazlitt, "Mr. Kean's Richard," *A View, Works,* V, 182.

6 DeVane, *Handbook,* p. 41.

7 *Pauline; A Fragment of a Confession,* lines 764–67.

8 She is, like Eliza, a musician; see line 46.

9 But the poem imitates technical features of Shelley's "Alastor" and "Epipsychidion" throughout.

10 Lines 23, 30, 80–81.

11 "Browning's *Sordello* and Jung: Browning's *Sordello* in the Light of Jung's Theory of Types," *PMLA,* LVI (1941), 772.

12 See *Pauline,* lines 89–123.

13 W. S. Swisher interprets these dreams from the Freudian point of view. In the first, the watery cave is the mother's womb; the swan, with its long neck, the masculine organ, and as a common symbol both of masculinity and poetry, to be identified with Robert's father and with Shelley. The dream embodies for Robert a fancied prenatal memory of coitus between his parents and a desire to be reborn—freed from the guilt and trouble in which he finds himself. It also indicates a passionate projection on his father and on Shelley, whom indeed he addresses several times in images suggestive of sexual love. ("A Psychoanalysis of Browning's 'Pauline,'" *The Psycho-Analytic Review,* VII [1920], 126–30. See *Pauline,* lines 192–200, 209–225.) Hence the singular lack of emotion—in an otherwise emotional poem—about Pauline. The second dream, even more patently homoerotic, expands and explains the first. Here Browning is clearly identifying with the feminine. "But all the time," says Jung, "the symbol is developing which is fitted to resolve the conflict." (C. G. Jung, *Psychological Types* [London, 1926], p. 327). Such a symbol is often a woman—part goddess, part mother, part maid. Mr. Holmes suggests that in Browning's poem Pauline is the reconciling symbol.

14 *Pauline,* Lines 260, 268–70.

15 Line 575.

16 See note 13 above.

17 Line 351.

18 Lines 403, 415–16, 418–19, 424–29.

19 Lines 458–64, 466–67.

20 Line 469.

21 Lines 557–59.

22 Lines 628–29.

23 Line 686.

24 Line 937.

25 Lines 839–40.

26 Lines 1020–28.

27 *RB and EBB,* I, 17 [February 11, 1845].

28 *Ibid.,* II, 725 [May 24, 1846].

29 Orr, *Life,* p. 53 (to Fox [March 1833]).

30 Richard and Edward Garnett, *The Life of W. J. Fox, Public Teacher and Social Reformer, 1786–1864* (London, 1910), p. 193.

31 *Ibid.,* p. 194.

32 J. A. Froude, *Thomas Carlyle: A History of the First Forty Years of His Life, 1795–1835* (New York, 1882), II, 370.

33 R. and E. Garnett, *Life of Fox* (London, 1910), p. 160.

34 The Mill-Taylor Collection, XXVII, No. 27, Library of the London School of Economics.

35 Mill-Taylor Collection, XXVII, No. 23, London School of Economics.

36 Froude, *Thomas Carlyle* (New York, 1882), II, 356, 362, 376.

37 F. A. Hayek, *John Stuart Mill and Harriet Taylor: Their Correspondence and Subsequent Marriage* (Chicago, 1951), pp. 79–80.

38 March 23, 1833, p. 183.

39 N.S. VII (1833), 252–62.

40 Mill's actual article is lost.

41 *John Stuart Mill and Harriet Taylor* (Chicago, 1951), p. 43.

42 *Robert Browning: A Collection of Critical Essays,* ed. Philip Drew (London, 1966), p. 176.

43 *John Stuart Mill and Harriet Taylor,* p. 43.

44 See page 32 above.

45 See "Mill and *Pauline*: the Myth and Some Facts," *Victorian Studies,* IX (1965), 154–63.

46 DeVane, *Handbook,* p. 48.

47 *Ibid.*

48 Preface of 1868.

49 Preface of 1888.

50 *Colombe's Birthday,* I, 15–16.

51 "Incident of the French Camp."

52 Lines 17–31.

53 Griffin and Minchin, p. 62; *RB and EBB,* I, 149 [August 10, 1845].

54 Katharine DeKay Bronson, "Browning in Venice," *The Century Illustrated Monthly Magazine*, LXIII (1902), 577.

55 Line 441.

56 "The Making of the Dramatic Lyric," *Bulletin of the John Rylands Library*, XXXV (1953), 367.

57 *Ibid.*, p. 364.

CHAPTER 4 ***The Promise of Paracelsus 1834–37*** (pp. 46–67)

1 Orr, *Life*, p. 67; they first met on August 1, 1834; at least eight letters of Browning's to him, of 1834–41 and 1854, survive.

2 Griffin and Minchin, p. 71.

3 Mrs. F. L. Bridell-Fox, "Browning," *The Argosy*, XLIX (1890), 112.

4 Lines 620–21.

5 Part II, line 220.

6 Miller, *Portrait*, pp. 4–5.

7 I, 37.

8 I, 507 ff.

9 I, 460–61.

10 I, 276–77.

11 I, 341–43.

12 I, 784.

13 I, 728–29.

14 II, 634–37.

15 III, 833–36.

16 See *The Alien Vision of Victorian Poetry: Sources of the Poetic Imagination in Tennyson, Browning, and Arnold* (Princeton, 1952).

17 See DeVane, *Handbook*, p. 55.

18 V, 696–98.

19 Orr, *Life*, p. 65 (to Fox, April 16, 1835).

20 August 2, 1835, p. 640.

21 Pp. 563–65.

22 In *The Collected Works* (London, 1867), VI, 299–312.

23 April 16, 1836, pp. 19–20.

24 "Evidences of a New Genius for Dramatic Poetry," *New Monthly Magazine and Literary Journal*, XLVI (1836), 289–308.

25 *RB and EBB*, I, 312 [December 9, 1845].

26 Richard and Edward Garnett, *The Life of W. J. Fox* (London, 1910), p. 166.

27 *Ibid.*, p. 212.

28 *Ibid.*, p. 180.

29 *Ibid.*, p. 177.

30 *Ibid.*

31 Mrs. F. L. Bridell-Fox, "Browning," *The Argosy*, XLIX (1890), 112.

32 *Ibid.*, p. 114 (RB to Fox, January 1857).

33 Macready, I, 264 (November 27, [1835]).

34 *Ibid.*, I, 258 [1835].

35 Quoted by J. C. Trewin, *Mr. Macready: A Nineteenth-Century Tragedian and His Theatre* (London, 1955), p. 113. The Macready sketch owes much to this book.

36 Macready, I, 265 [1835].

37 Orr, *Life*, p. 80.

38 Macready, I, 267 (December 31, [1835]).

39 Gordon N. Ray, *Thackeray: The Uses of Adversity, 1811–1846* (New York, 1955), p. 288.

40 *John Forster* By One of His Friends [Percy H. Fitzgerald] (London, 1903), p. 48.

41 Douglas Jerrold, *Georgian Adventure* (New York, 1938), p. 26.

42 Macready, I, 226, n. 5.

43 Griffin and Minchin, p. 76.

44 *Ibid.*, p. 53.

45 Blanchard Jerrold, "Memoir," *The Poetical Works of Laman Blanchard* (London, 1876), p. 7.

46 Macready, I, 277 (February 16, [1836]).

47 Quoted in Trewin, *Mr. Macready*, p. 118.

48 *Ibid.*, p.119.

49 Macready, I, 313 (May 11, [1836]).

50 "'This Happy Evening:' the Story of Ion," *The Twentieth Century*, CLIV (1953), 53–61.

51 Macready, I, 318 (May 26, [1836]).

52 *Ibid.*, I, 320.

53 *Ibid.*, I, 319.

54 A. G. K. L'Estrange, ed., *The Life of Mary Russell Mitford, Told by Herself in Letters to Her Friends* (New York, 1870), II, 174.

55 Extract from MS. letter (Yale University Library), quoted in *EB to Miss Mitford*, p. xiii.

56 Orr, *Life*, p. 82.

57 *Paracelsus*, II, 148–49.

58 Griffin and Minchin, p. 77.

59 "'This Happy Evening,'" *The Twentieth Century*, CLIV (1953), 57.

60 Orr, *Life*, p. 82.

61 *New Letters*, p. 12 (May 28, 1836).

62 Macready, I, 361 (November 20 and 21, [1836]).

63 *Ibid.*, I, 362 (November 23, [1836]).

64 *Ibid.*, I, 382 (March 29, [1837]).

65 *Ibid.*, I, 387 [1837].

66 *Ibid.*

CHAPTER 5 *Macready's Boards 1837* (pp. 68–75)

1 Bernard Shaw, "Preface," *Ellen Terry and Bernard Shaw: A Correspondence*, ed. Christopher St. John (New York, 1931), p. x.

2 *Ibid.*, p. xvii.

3 Of the nine plays, *Strafford* (1837), *King Victor and King Charles* (1842), *The Return of the Druses* (1843), and *A Blot in the 'Scutcheon* (1843) were intended for Macready's theater; *Colombe's Birthday* (1844) was written for Charles Kean and his wife to act; and *Pippa Passes* (1841), *Luria* (1846), *A Soul's Tragedy* (1846), and "In a Balcony" (1855) were intendedly closet dramas. Most of the nine have been performed by Browning societies and student groups; a producer such as Arthur Kincaid at Oxford has found actable qualities even in "In a Balcony" (*Browning Society Notes*, 1972). Perhaps the least readily intelligible play is *King Victor*, and the most stageworthy, that for the Keans—as Helen Faucit discovered in 1853.

4 *Strafford: An Historical Tragedy* (London, 1837), p. iii.

5 *Ibid.*

6 *Poet-Lore*, V (1893), 517–19.

7 Harold Orel, "Browning's Use of Historical Sources in *Strafford*," *Six Studies in Nineteenth-Century English Literature and Thought*, ed. H. Orel and G. J. Worth (Lawrence, Kansas, 1962); Gordon Pitts, in Variorum, II (1970), 339–60.

8 Text of 1837.

9 I, ii, 20–31.

10 I, ii, 146–53.

11 IV, ii, 1–2.

12 *Browning's Characters: A Study in Poetic Technique* (New Haven, 1961), pp. 47–57; D. C. Somervell, "An Early Victorian Tragedy," *London Mercury*, XVI (1927), 170–78.

13 Orr, *Life*, p. 84 (May 1, [1837]).

14 Edmund Gosse, *Robert Browning, Personalia* (Boston and New York, 1890), p. 44.

15 Griffin and Minchin, p. 108.

16 Gosse, p. 45.

17 Griffin and Minchin, p. 110.

18 Macready, I, 392 (May 4, [1837]).

19 *Ibid.*, I, 392–93 (May 9, [1837]).

20 *Ibid.*, I, 394 [1837].

CHAPTER 6 *Sordello 1837 and 1833–40* (pp. 76–92)

1 Orr, *Life*, p. 66.

2 V, 998.

3 Consider David Duff's note on Naddo, which is almost a definition of Forster's character: "He is a common-sense critic, with a devotion to men of genius and great desire to 'run' them successfully." *An Exposition of Browning's 'Sordello,' With Historical and Other Notes* (Edinburgh, 1906), p. 25, line 693. See also such lines as II, 788–801, 821.

4 DeVane, *Handbook*, pp. 75–76.

5 See *ibid.*, p. 76.

6 See Stewart W. Holmes, "The Sources of Browning's *Sordello*," *Studies in Philology*, XXXIV (1937), 467–96.

7 See his letter of April 16, 1835, to Fox, in Orr, *Life*, p. 66.

8 Griffin and Minchin, pp. 92–93.

9 *RB and EBB*, I, 336 [December 21, 1845].

10 *Handbook*, p. 79.

11 *Autobiography*, ed. Maria W. Chapman (Boston, 1877), II, 325.

12 Orr, *Life*, p. 88 (to Robertson, "Good Friday, 1838").

13 *Ibid.*, p. 95.

14 Hood, pp. 1–3 [July 24, 1838].

15 III, 676–81.

16 III, 689–91.

17 III, 696–98.

18 III, 717–18.

19 III, 741–44.

20 III, 747–50.

21 See S. W. Holmes, "Browning's *Sordello* and Jung: Browning's *Sordello* in the Light of Jung's Theory of Types," *PMLA*, LVI (1941), 758–96.

22 VI, 775–81.

23 VI, 790.

24 Hood, p. 3.

25 Griffin and Minchin, p. 112.

26 Orr, *Life*, p. 96 [August 1, 1837].

27 Mrs. F. L. Bridell-Fox, "Robert Browning," *The Argosy*, XLIX (1890), 112.

28 Griffin and Minchin, pp. 47, 49.

29 *Ibid.*, p. 135; quoted from Gavan Duffy, *Conversations with Carlyle* (London, 1892), pp. 56–57.

30 D. A. Wilson, *Carlyle on Cromwell and Others* (New York, 1925), III, 122.

31 Hood, p. 7 [c. December 30, 1841].

32 Orr, *Life*, p. 97.

33 *Ibid.* [August 1, 1937].

34 In vol. 8 of Ludovico Antonio Muratori's *Rerum Italicarum Scriptores*.

35 See Browning's dedication of *Sordello* to "J. Milsand, of Dijon," in *Works*, 1863, III.

36 Macready, II, 64 (June 17, [1840]).

37 March 14, 1840, p. 257.

38 May 30, 1840, pp. 431–32.

39 "Browning: Semantic Stutterer," *PMLA*, LX (1945), 231–55.

40 V, 635–37.

41 "*Zum Formproblem in Brownings* Sordello," *Englische Studien*, LXVII (1933), 352.

42 II, 581–601.

43 Browning's aim and techniques were conceivably influenced by the popular Victorian diorama, in which transparent painted screens were arranged one behind another and lit so as to produce stereoscopic effects. As frequently in *Sordello*, the beholder experienced two or three "viewpoints" simultaneously. See Daniel Stempel, "Browning's *Sordello*: The Art of the Makers-See," *PMLA*, LXXX (1965), 554–561.

44 Heuer, "*Zum Formproblem*," *Englische Studien*, LXVII (1933), 367.

45 II, 600–601.

46 Compare the discussion of Browning's imitation of the Deity, in J. Hillis Miller, *The Disappearance of God: Five Nineteenth-Century Writers* (Cambridge, Mass., 1963).

47 Ezra Pound, *Cantos, I, Lustra with Earlier Poems* (New York, 1917).

48 I, 1–11.

49 See F. A. Pottle, *Shelley and Browning: A Myth and Some Facts* (Chicago, 1923).

50 III, 85–93.

51 V, 84–97.

52 In the *Essay on Man.* See Hoxie N. Fairchild, "Browning's 'Whatever Is, Is Right,'" *College English,* XII (1951), 377–82.

53 See VI, 850–70.

CHAPTER 7 *Mass Attack on the Theater 1837–44* (pp. 93–111)

1 Orr, *Life,* pp. 96–97.

2 Macready, II, 22.

3 *Ibid.,* II, 23 (September 5, [1839]).

4 Mrs. Sutherland Orr, *A Handbook to the Works of Robert Browning* (London, 1885), p. 54.

5 VI, 854, 856.

6 See Griffin and Minchin, p. 126.

7 Introduction, lines 163–64.

8 Introduction, lines 89–90.

9 I, 217–18.

10 I, 227–28.

11 I, 282.

12 See J. M. Ariail, "Is 'Pippa Passes' a Dramatic Failure?" *Studies in Philology,* XXXVII (1940), 122; and Margaret E. Glen, "The Meaning and Structure of *Pippa Passes,*" *University of Toronto Quarterly,* XXIV (1955), 410–26.

13 Introduction, line 190.

14 *The Philosophy of Literary Form: Studies in Symbolic Action* (1941).

15 Introduction, lines 163–64.

16 G. K. Chesterton, *Robert Browning* (London, 1951), p. 45.

17 Quoted by DeVane, *Handbook,* p. 92.

18 July 10, 1841.

19 December 11, 1841, p. 952.

20 Orr, *Life,* p. 103 (March 9, [probably 1840]).

21 *Ibid.,* p. 97 [August 1, 1937].

22 Morse Peckham, in Variorum, III (1971), 387–90.

23 II, 1, 42.

24 II, 286–91, 296–97.

25 Macready, II, 72.

26 *Ibid.*

27 *New Letters,* p. 20 [August 23, 1840].

28 Macready, II, 76 (August 27, [1840]).

29 *Ibid.*

30 *Ibid.,* II, 80 (September 15, [1840]).

31 Quoted in Miller, *Portrait,* p. 52, n.l.

32 Hood, p. 5.

33 J. C. Trewin, *Mr. Macready* (London, 1955), p. 186.

34 John Forster, *The Life of Charles Dickens* (London, 1873), II, 25.

35 *RB and AD,* p. 48 (December 13, 1842).

36 *The Early Literary Career of Robert Browning* (New York, 1911), pp. 113 ff.

37 See Edmund Gosse, *Robert Browning, Personalia* (Boston and New York, 1890), p. 62; and Joseph W. Reed, Jr., "Browning and Macready: The Final Quarrel," *PMLA,* LXXV (1960), 598.

38 Orr, *Life,* p. 117.

39 Gosse, *Personalia* (Boston and New York, 1890), p. 62.

40 The manuscript shows that Macready substituted words, cut 310 lines, or nearly a quarter of the play, and penciled in new lines for continuity; Reed, "Browning and Macready," *PMLA,* LXXV (1960), 597–603.

41 *RB and AD,* p. 63.

42 Macready, II, 195 (February 6, [1843]).

43 Orr, *Life,* p. 112 (RB to Hill, December 15, 1884).

44 Gosse, *Personalia* (Boston and New York, 1890), p. 66.

45 Macready, II, 196 (February 10, [1843]).

46 Orr, *Life,* p. 112 (to Hill, December 15, 1884).

47 Hood, pp. 295–96 (June 29, 1888).

48 In I, iii.

49 *Personalia* (Boston and New York, 1890), p. 68.

50 *The Early Literary Career of Robert Browning* (New York, 1911), p. 131.

51 *RB and AD*, pp. 65–66.

52 February 18, 1843, p. 166.

53 Hood, p. 9 (to Dowson, March 10, [1844]).

54 Notes to "Colombe's Birthday," Variorum, IV.

55 II, 263–71.

56 III, 163–64.

57 *The Examiner*, June 22, 1844, p. 389.

58 *RB and EBB*, I, 236 [October 15, 1845].

CHAPTER 8 *Impressionism* (pp. 112–126)

1 Donald Smalley, "Joseph Arnould and Robert Browning: New Letters (1842–50) and a Verse Epistle," *PMLA*, LXXX (1965), 90.

2 *Ibid.*, pp. 92–93. On occasion Arnould took Pope as his model.

> Forgive me, Browning, that I can't dispose
> My rebel thoughts to wear the garb of prose,

he wrote for example on November 27, 1842, in a lengthy verse epistle, prefaced with an explanatory letter in prose.

> Friend you have triumphed, with imperious skill,
> And a strong energy of Stoic will,
> Sage Lord of wealth unbounded you have taught
> Language to be the *minister* of Thought. . . .

This was his loyal reaction to the *Dramatic Lyrics*. He was an equally "fierce advocate" of *A Blot in the 'Scutcheon.*

3 *RB and AD*, pp. 33–34 (May 22, 1842).

4 *Ibid.*, pp. 95–96 (November 8, 1843).

5 *Ibid.*, pp. 40 (July 13, 1842); 54 (May 15, 1843).

6 *Ibid.*, p. 51 (March 5, 1843).

7 *Ibid.*, pp. 51–52.

8 *Ibid.*, p. 56 (May 15, 1843).

9 *Ibid.*, pp. 92–93 (October 9, 1843).

10 *Ibid.*, p. 86 [n.d.].

11 *Ibid.*, p. 104 (July 28, 1844).

12 *Ibid.*

13 *Dearest Isa*, p. 377 (March 30, 1872).

14 Quoted by Edmund Gosse, "Browning, Robert" in *D.N.B.*

15 See W. J. Bate, *From Classic to Romantic* (Cambridge, Mass., 1946).

16 Lines 5–8.

17 Lines 24, 25, 57, 68–70.

18 "Marching Along," lines 13–16.

19 *Letters, 1848–1888*, ed. George W. E. Russell (New York, 1895), I, 70 (February 9, 1858).

20 Lines 37–42.

21 Lines 10–20.

22 Lines 5–12, 19–21.

23 "Burns' 'Holy Willie's Prayer' and Browning's 'Soliloquy of the Spanish Cloister,'" *Notes and Queries*, CXCVI (1951), 252.

24 Dedication of *Sordello* to "J. Milsand, of Dijon," *Works* (1863), III.

25 Preface to *Lyrical Ballads* (1800).

26 Elizabeth F. Boyd, *Byron's Don Juan: A Critical Study* (New York, 1958), pp. 53–54.

27 André Gide, in his Introduction (trans. Dorothy Bussy) to this remarkable novel (London, 1947, p. xii), proposes that it may have inspired Browning's "Johannes Agricola in Meditation." It suggests both "Johannes" and the "Spanish Cloister," except that neither of Browning's works makes much of the Devil.

28 Benjamin Willis Fuson, *Browning and His English Predecessors in the Dramatic Monolog* (Iowa City, 1948), pp. 69–71.

CHAPTER 9 *Friends 1842–45* (pp. 127–133)

1 *Works and Days, From the Journal of Michael Field*, eds., T. and D. C. Sturge Moore (London, 1933), p. 208.

2 Donald Smalley, ed., "Essay on Chatterton," Variorum, III (1971), 364–65.

3 *Ibid.*, III, 165.

4 *Ibid.*, III, 168.

5 *Ibid.*, III, 176.

6 *Ibid.*, III, 177.

7 Mrs. Newton Crossland (Camilla Toulmin), *Landmarks of a Literary Life, 1820–1892* (London, 1893), pp. 149–150.

8 *The Complete Poetical Works and Letters of John Keats*, ed., Horace E. Scudder (New York, 1899), p. 343.

9 Edmund Blunden, *Leigh Hunt, A Biography* (London, 1930), pp. 75–77.

10 *Bleak House*, chap. 6.

11 Luther A. Brewer, *My Leigh Hunt Library, The Holograph Letters* (Iowa City, 1938), p. 361 (August 15, 1856).

12 R. H. Horne, ed., *A New Spirit of the Age* (2nd edn.; London, 1844), II, 155.

13 *Ibid.*, II, 181–82.

14 *RB and AD*, p. 102 (July 28, 1844).

15 In 1849 retitled "The Bishop Orders his Tomb at St. Praxed's Church [Rome, 15—]."

CHAPTER 10 ***To a Third-floor Chamber 1844–45*** (pp. 134–150)

1 DeVane, *Handbook*, pp. 154, 165.

2 *RB and AD*, p. 106 (July 31, 1844).

3 Mazzini, quoted by Henry W. Redman, *Italian Nationalism and English Letters: Figures of the Risorgimento and English Men of Letters* (London, 1940), p. 26.

4 Jane Welsh Carlyle, *Letters to Her Family, 1839–1863*, ed. Leonard Huxley (New York, 1924), p. 129.

5 Charles Gavan Duffy, *Conversations with Carlyle* (New York, 1892), p. 109.

6 *Dearest Isa*, p. 136 (November 19, 1862).

7 See DeVane, *Handbook*, pp. 156–57.

8 Orr, *Life*, pp. 126–27 [late in 1844].

9 *Handbook*, pp. 166–67.

10 See Roma A. King, Jr., *The Bow and the Lyre: The Art of Robert Browning* (Ann Arbor, 1957), pp. 52–75.

11 *New Letters*, pp. 35–36 (February 18, 1845).

12 *RB and EBB*, I, 271 [November 16, 1845]; the word "England" is conjectural and is perhaps overwritten by the word "Strafford".

13 R. H. Horne, ed., *A New Spirit of the Age* (2nd edn.; London, 1844), II, 132–33.

14 Elizabeth Barrett Browning, *Letters Addressed to Richard Hengist Horne, with Comments on Contemporaries*, ed. S. R. Townshend Mayer (London, 1879), II, 132–33.

15 *RB and EBB*, I, 61 [May 12, 1845].

16 *Blackwood's Edinburgh Magazine*, LVI (1844), 621.

17 *RB and EBB*, I, 271 [November 16, 1845].

18 *Ibid.*, I, 3.

19 *Ibid.*

20 *Ibid.*, I, 5 (January 11, 1845).

21 *Ibid.*, I, 7 (January 13, 1845).

22 *Ibid.*, I, 9 (January 15, 1845).

23 *Ibid.*, I, 15 (February 3, 1845).

24 *Ibid.*, I, 13.

25 *Ibid.*, I, 17–18 [February 11, 1845].

26 *Ibid.*, I, 18.

27 *Ibid.*, I, 25 [February 26, 1845].

28 *Ibid.*, I, 32 (March 1, [1845]).

29 *Elizabeth Barrett Browning* (London, 1953), p. 135.

30 *RB and EBB*, I, 57 [May 5–6, 1845].

31 *Ibid.*, I, 41 (March 20, 1845).

32 *Ibid.*, I, 65 [May 15, 1845].

33 *Ibid.*, I, 68 [May 16, 1845].

34 *Ibid.*, I, 69 [May 17, 1845].

CHAPTER 11 ***Chronicle of an Invalid 1806–45*** (pp. 151–171)

1 *Flush, A Biography* (New York, 1933), pp. 24–25.

2 *EB to Miss Mitford*, p. 178 (May 4, [1843]).

3 *Letters*, ed., Kenyon, I, 125 (to Boyd, February 21, 1843).

4 Mary Russell Mitford, *Recollections of a Literary Life; or, Books, Places, and People* (London, 1852), I, 268.

5 *EB to Miss Mitford*, p. 138 (October 27, 1842).

6 *RB and EBB*, I, 422 [January 26, 1846].

7 *Letters*, ed., Kenyon, I, 202 (to Mrs. Martin, October 5, 1844).

8 *Ibid.*, I, 158 (to Westwood, October 1843).

9 *Ibid.*, I, 218 (to Mrs. Martin, po. November 26, 1844).

10 *EB to Miss Mitford*, p. 109 (March 16, 1842).

11 *Letters to George*, p. 105 (July 13, 1843).

12 *EB to Miss Mitford*, p. 50 (August 11, 1839).

13 *Ibid.*, p. ix.

14 *Letters*, ed., Kenyon, I, 233 (to Chorley, January 7, 1845).

15 *EB to Miss Mitford*, p. 126 (July 22, [1842]).

16 *Ibid.*, p. 147 (November 27, 1842).

17 *Ibid.*, p. 145 (November 21, 1842).

18 *Ibid.*, p. 144.

19 *Ibid.*, pp. 147–48 (November 27, 1842).

20 *Ibid.*, p. 145 (November 21, 1842).

21 *Ibid.*, p. 212 (January 11, 1844).

22 University of Texas Library MS., EB to Miss Mitford ("Tuesday" [c. 1844]).

23 "Glimpses into My Own Life and Literary Character, Written by Elizabeth Barrett in the Year 1820 when Fourteen Years Old," *Elizabeth Barrett Browning: Hitherto Unpublished Poems and Stories with an Inedited Autobiography* (Boston, 1914), I, 6.

24 *RB and EBB*, I, 326 [December 19, 1845].

25 "Glimpses" *Inedited Autobiography* (Boston, 1914), I, 13.

26 *Ibid.*, I, 15.

27 *EB to Miss Mitford*, p. 125 (July 22, [1842]).

28 *Ibid.*, pp. 161–62 (January 4, 1843).

29 "Glimpses," *Inedited Autobiography* (Boston, 1914), I, 10–11.

30 *Ibid.*, I, 12.

31 *EB to Miss Mitford*, p. 139 (October 31, 1842).

32 *Ibid.*, p. 196 (August 17, 1843).

33 "Glimpses," *Inedited Autobiography* (Boston, 1914), I, 13–14.

34 *Ibid.*, I, 26–27.

35 *Ibid.*, I, 23.

36 *Ibid.*, I, 16–17.

37 *Ibid.*, I, 18–19.

38 *Ibid.*, I, 22–23.

39 *Aurora Leigh*, Book II.

40 *Letters to George*, Appendix II, pp. 343–44 (June 24, 1821).

41 *Ibid.*, p. 341.

42 *EB to Mr. Boyd*, p. 46 (June 6, 1828).

43 *Diary by E.B.B.: The Unpublished Diary of Elizabeth Barrett Barrett, 1831–1832*, eds. Philip Kelley and Ronald Hudson (Athens, Ohio, 1969), p. 164.

44 *EB to Mr. Boyd*, pp. 106 [October 8, 1830]; 63 (Saturday [1828]).

45 *EB to Miss Mitford*, p. 150 (December 6, 1842).

46 *EB to Mr. Boyd*, p. 124 [1831].

47 *EB to Miss Mitford*, p. 151 (December 6, 1842).

48 *EB to Mr. Boyd*, p. 185 (July 10, 1832).

49 Wellesley College Library MS., EB to Miss Mitford, July 4, 1842.

50 Bennett Weaver, ed., "Twenty Unpublished Letters of Elizabeth Barrett to Hugh Stuart Boyd," *PMLA*, LXV (1950), 408–409, (po. November 3, 1832).

51 *RB and EBB*, II, 804 [June 21, 1846].

52 *Ibid.*, II, 951 [August 10, 1846].

53 "To G. B. H., November 2, 1844," *Hitherto Unpublished Poems* (Boston, 1914), II, 234; see also *RB and EBB*, II, 951–52.

54 Folger Library MS., EB to Miss Mitford, n.d.

55 *EB to Miss Mitford*, p. 141 (November 8, 1842).

56 *Letters*, ed., Kenyon, I, 35 (January 1, 1836).

57 *Ibid.*, I, 141 (to Mrs. Martin, December 7, 1836); *EB to Miss Mitford*, p. 73 (June 14, 1841); *RB and EBB*, I, 169 [August 22, 1845].

58 *RB and EBB*, I, 170.

59 Gardner B. Taplin, *The Life of Elizabeth Barrett Browning* (New Haven, 1957), p. 78.

60 *Letters to George*, p. 47.

61 *RB and EBB*, I, 422 [January 26, 1846].

62 *Ibid.*, I, 170–71 [August 22, 1845].

63 Gardner B. Taplin, *The Life of Elizabeth Barrett Browning* (New Haven, 1957), p. 79.

64 *RB and EBB*, I, 171 [August 22, 1845].

65 *Letters*, ed., Kenyon, II, 174 (to Miss Mitford, September 4, 1854).

66 *Ibid.*, I, 60 (to Boyd, May 1838).

67 *Ibid.*, I, 82–83 (July 8, 1840).

68 *RB and EBB*, I, 169–170 [August 22, 1845].

69 *Ibid.*, II, 687 (May 7, 1846).

70 *Letters*, ed., Kenyon, I, 87 (to Mrs. Martin, March 29, 1841).

71 *Ibid.*, I, 87–88.

72 *EB to Miss Mitford*, p. 76 (June 23, 1841).

73 *Ibid.*, p. 74 (June 14, 1841).

74 *Letters to George*, p. 70 [July 24, 1841].

75 Yale University Library MS., Miss Mitford to Miss Anderdon (October 4, 1841).

76 *EB to Miss Mitford*, p. 219 (September 1, 1844).

77 *RB and EBB*, I, 152 (po. August 11, 1845).

78 EB to Miss Mitford, p. 126 (July 26, 1842).

CHAPTER 12 *"Not Death, but Love" 1845* (pp. 172–187)

1 *RB and EBB,* I, 69 [May 17, 1845].

2 *Ibid.,* I, 489 [February 23, 1846].

3 *Ibid,* I, 491 [February 25, 1846].

4 *Ibid.,* II, 764 [June 7, 1846].

5 *Ibid.,* I, 70 [May 20, 1845]. The deaf relative was his uncle, Reuben Browning, whose hearing had been damaged when he was struck by a cricket ball.

6 *Ibid.,* I, 488–89 [February 23, 1846].

7 *EB to Miss Mitford,* p. 244 [May 26, 1845].

8 *RB and EBB,* I, 70–71 [May 21, 1845].

9 *Ibid.,* I, 72–73 [May 23, 1845].

10 *Ibid.,* I, 74 [May 24, 1845].

11 *Ibid.,* I, 75–76.

12 *Ibid.,* I, 78–79 [May 25, 1845].

13 *Ibid.,* I, 130–31 [July 21, 1845].

14 *Ibid.,* I, 95 (June 14, 1845).

15 *Ibid.,* I, 86 [June 6, 1845].

16 *Ibid.,* I, 168 [August 22, 1845].

17 *Ibid.,* I, 99–100 [June 19, 1845].

18 *Ibid.,* I, 125 [July 16–17, 1845].

19 *Elizabeth Barrett Browning* (London, 1953), p. 142.

20 *RB and EBB,* I, 206 [September 18, 1845].

21 *Ibid.,* I, 135 [July 25, 1845].

22 *Ibid.,* I, 145 (po. August 8, 1845).

23 *Ibid.,* I, 146–47 [August 8, 1845].

24 *Ibid.,* I, 131 [July 21, 1845].

25 *Ibid.,* I, 139 [July 31, 1845].

26 *Ibid.,* I, 141 [July 31, 1845].

27 *Ibid.,* I, 144 [August 3, 1845].

28 *Ibid.,* I, 173 [August 27, 1845].

29 *Ibid.,* I, 174 [August 27, 1845].

30 *Ibid.,* I, 176 [August 30, 1845].

31 *Ibid.,* I, 178 [August 31, 1845].

32 *Ibid.*, I, 196 (po. September 16, 1845).

33 *Ibid.*, I, 192–93 [September 13, 1845].

34 *Ibid.*, I, 195, 196 (po. September 16, 1845).

35 *Ibid.*, I, 184 [September 6, 1845].

36 *Ibid.*, I, 119 [July 11, 1845].

37 *Ibid.*, I, 211 (po. September 25, 1845).

38 *Ibid.*

39 *Ibid.*, I, 212–13 (po. September 25, 1845).

40 *Ibid.*, I, 214.

41 *Ibid.*, I, 216 [September 26, 1845].

42 *Ibid.*, I, 233 [October 13, 1845].

43 *Ibid.*, I, 244 [October 21–22, 1845].

44 *Ibid.*, I, 245 [October 23, 1845].

45 *Ibid.*, I, 265 [November 12, 1845].

46 *Ibid.*, I, 261 [November 9, 1845].

47 *Ibid.*, I, 270 [November 16, 1845].

48 *Ibid.*, I, 275 [November 17, 1845].

49 See Edward Snyder and Frederic Palmer, Jr., "New Light on the Brownings," *Quarterly Review*, CCLXIX (1937), 50.

50 *RB and EBB*, I, 135.

51 Hood, p. 217 (April 15, 1883).

52 See DeVane, *Handbook*, pp. 171–76; and Fred Manning Smith, "Elizabeth Barrett and Browning's 'The Flight of the Duchess,'" *Studies in Philology*, XXXIX (1942), 102–17.

53 "New Light," *Quarterly Review*, CCLXIX (1937), 51.

54 *RB and EBB*, I, 117 [July 7, 1845].

55 *Ibid.*, I, 233; Elvan Kintner dates this portion October 13, 1845; see also Smith, "'The Flight of the Duchess,'" *Studies in Philology*, XXXIX (1942), 116.

56 *RB and EBB*, I, 257–58 [November 5, 1845].

57 See DeVane, *Handbook*, pp. 150–84.

58 For a more elaborate relation of this story to "The Glove," as well as of "The Glove" to "Parleying with Daniel Bartoli," see W. C. DeVane, *Browning's Parleyings: The Autobiography of a Mind* (New Haven, 1927), pp. 50–91.

59 *RB and EBB*, I, 239 [October 17, 1845].

60 *Ibid.*, I, 241 [October 18, 1845].

61 *Ibid.*, I, 244 [October 21–22, 1845].

62 *The Eclectic Review*, 4th Ser. XIX (1846), 413, 421–26; *The Athenaeum*, January 17, 1846, pp. 58–59; *The Examiner*, November 15, 1845, pp. 723–24.

63 *New Letters*, p. 37 (to Moxon, [November 19, 1845]).

64 *RB and EBB*, I, 288 [November 23, 1845]. See also *Browning: The Critical Heritage*, eds., Boyd Litzinger and Donald Smalley (London, 1970), p. 108.

65 *Ibid.*, I, 268 [November 14, 1845].

66 *Ibid.*, I, 18.

67 *Ibid.*, I, 26 [February 26, 1845].

68 See *ibid.*, I, 411.

69 Act IV.

70 Act V.

71 *RB and EBB*, I, 451–52.

72 April 25, 1846, pp. 259–60; LXVI (1848), 357–400.

CHAPTER 13 *Into the Light 1845–46* (pp. 188–214)

1 See Dorothy Hewlett, *Elizabeth Barrett Browning* (London, 1953), p. 160.

2 *RB and EBB*, I, 317 [December 12, 1845].

3 *Ibid.*, I, 318–19, 320 [December 12, 1845].

4 *Ibid.*, I, 324 [December 18, 1845].

5 *Ibid.*, I, 331 [December 20, 1845].

6 *Ibid.*, I, 388 [January 15, 1846].

7 *Ibid.*, I, 408–409 [January 21, 1846].

8 *Ibid.*, I, 394 [January 16, 1846].

9 *Ibid.*, I, 417 [January 24–25, 1846].

10 *Ibid.*, I, 421, 422 [January 26, 1846].

11 *Ibid.*, I, 433 [January 31, 1846].

12 *Ibid.*, I, 436 (po. February 4, 1846).

13 *Letters*, ed., Kenyon, I, 277 [February or March 1846].

14 *RB and EBB*, I, 340 [December 22, 1845].

15 *Ibid.*, I, 315 [December 9, 1845].

16 *Ibid.*, I, 257 [November 5, 1845].

17 *Ibid.*, I, 348–49 [December 30, 1845].

18 *Ibid.*, I, 437 [February 4, 1846].

19 *Ibid.*, I, 449 [February 11, 1846].

20 *Ibid.*, I, 430 [January 30, 1846].

21 *Ibid.*, I, 435 (po. February 4, 1846).

22 *Ibid.*, I, 487–88 [February 23, 1846].

23 *Ibid.*, I, 463–64 [February 15, 1846].

24 *Ibid.*, I, 469 [February "15" for 16, 1846].

25 *Ibid.*, I, 474 [February 19, 1846].

26 *Ibid.*, I, 492 [February 25, 1846].

27 *Ibid.*, I, 494 (po. February 26, 1846).

28 *Ibid.*, I, 496 [February 26, 1846].

29 *Ibid.*, II, 595–96 [April 7, 1846].

30 *Ibid.*, II, 601 [April 8, 1846].

31 *Ibid.*, II, 607 [April 8, 1846].

32 *Ibid.*, II, 608 [April 9, 1846].

33 *Ibid.*, II, 610 [April 9, 1846].

34 *Ibid.*, II, 611 [April 10, 1846].

35 *Ibid.*, II, 719 [May 21, 1846].

36 *Ibid.*, I, 536 [March 15, 1846].

37 *Ibid.*, I, 484 [February 21, 1846].

38 *Ibid.*, II, 727 [May 24, 1846].

39 *Ibid.*, I, 503 [March 1, 1846].

40 *Ibid.*, I, 511 [March 3, 1846].

41 *Ibid.*, I, 514 [March 3, 1846].

42 *Ibid.*, I, 515–16 [March 4, 1846].

43 *Ibid.*, I, 518, 517 [March 5, 1846].

44 *Ibid.*, I, 268 [November 14, 1845].

45 *Ibid.*, I, 438 [February 6, 1846].

46 *Ibid.*, I, 491 [February 24, 1846].

47 *Ibid.*, II, 628 [April 16, 1846].

48 *Ibid.*, II, 624 [April 16, 1846].

49 *Ibid.*, II, 695–96 [May 11, 1846].

50 *Ibid.*, II, 728 [May 24, 1846].

51 *Ibid.*, II, 747–48 [June 2, 1846].

52 *Ibid.*, II, 793 [June 17, 1846].

53 *Ibid.*, II, 720 [May 21, 1846].

54 *Ibid.*, II, 615 [April 12, 1846].

55 *Ibid.*, II, 836 [July 2, 1846].

56 *Ibid.*, II, 839 [July 3, 1846].

57 *Ibid.*, II, 827 [June 30, 1846].

58 *Ibid.*, II, 893 [July 22, 1846].

59 *Ibid.*, II, 894.

60 *Ibid.*, II, 906 [July 27, 1846].

61 *Ibid.*

62 *Ibid.*, II, 855 [July 7, 1846].

63 *Ibid.*, II, 892.

64 See Gardner B. Taplin, *The Life of Elizabeth Barrett Browning* (New Haven, 1957), p. 88. Elizabeth's room was up three flights: in British usage, of course, the "third" floor, in American, the "fourth."

65 *RB and EBB*, II, 948 [August 9,1846].

66 *Ibid.*, II, 989 [August 23, 1846].

67 *Ibid.*, II, 909 [July 28, 1846].

68 *Ibid.*, II, 911 [July 29, 1846].

69 *Ibid.*, II, 987–88 [August 22, 1846].

70 *Ibid.*, II, 873 [July 13, 1846].

71 *Ibid.*, II, 875–76 [July 15, 1846].

72 *Ibid.*, II, 880 [July 16, 1846].

73 *Ibid.*, II, 881–82 [July 16, 1846].

74 *Ibid.*, II, 885 [July 17, 1846].

75 *Ibid.*, II, 888 [July 19, 1846].

76 *Ibid.*, II, 892 [July 22, 1846].

77 *Ibid.*, II, 922 [August 2, 1846].

78 *Ibid.*, II, 926 [August 3, 1846].

79 *Ibid.*, II, 923 [August 2, 1846].

80 *Ibid.*, II, 927 [August 3, 1846].

81 *Ibid.*, II, 1023 [August 30, 1846].

82 *Ibid.*, II, 924 [August 2, 1846].

83 *Ibid.*, II, 927 [August 3, 1846].

84 *Ibid.*, II, 950 [August 10, 1846].

85 *Ibid.*, II, 992 [August 23, 1846].

86 *Ibid.*, II, 879 [July 15, 1846].

87 *Ibid.*, II, 1021 [August 30, 1846].

88 *Ibid.*, II, 1022, 1023 [August 30, 1846].

89 *Ibid.*, II, 1059 [September 10, 1846].

90 *Ibid.*, II, 1061 [September 10, 1846].

91 *Ibid.*, II, 1062 [September 12, 1846].

92 *Ibid.*, II, 1063 (September 12, [1846]).

93 See *ibid.*, II, 1061–62; actually their ninety-second meeting.

94 *Ibid.*, II, 1064–65 [September 13, 1846].

95 *Ibid.*, II, 1063 (September 12, [1846]).

96 *Ibid.*, II, 1065 [September 13, 1846].

97 *Ibid.*, II, 1071 [September 14, 1846].

98 *Ibid.*, II, 1066 [September 13, 1846].

99 *Ibid.*, II, 1068 [September 13, 1846].

100 *Elizabeth Barrett Browning* (London, 1953), p. 196.

101 *RB and EBB*, II, 1073.

102 *Ibid.*, II, 1072–73 [September 14, 1846].

103 *Ibid.*, II, 1081 [September 16, 1846].

104 *Ibid.*, II, 1087.

105 *Letters to George*, pp. 149–52 [September 17–18, 1846].

106 Dorothy Hewlett, *Elizabeth Barrett Browning*, pp. 195–96.

107 *RB and EBB*, II, 1072 [September 14, 1846].

CHAPTER 14 ***Pisa to Florence 1846–47*** (pp. 215–234)

1 Quoted by Dorothy Hewlett, *Elizabeth Barrett Browning* (London, 1953), p. 196.

2 Berg MS., Paris [September 26, 1846].

3 Gerardine Macpherson, *Memoirs of the Life of Anna Jameson* (Boston, 1878), p. 230.

4 George K. Boyce, "From Paris to Pisa with the Brownings," *The New Colophon*, III (1950), 112, 114, 115.

5 Berg MS., Paris [September 26, 1846].

6 *Twenty-Two Unpublished Letters of Elizabeth Barrett Browning and Robert Browning, Addressed to Henrietta and Arabella Moulton-Barrett* (New York, 1935), pp. 1–12

(October 2, 1846). Quotations in the five preceding paragraphs, also, are taken from this source.

7 Boyce, "From Paris to Pisa," *The New Colophon*, III (1950), 115, 116, 117.

8 Berg MS., EBB to Arabel, Pisa [October–November 1846].

9 Boyce, "From Paris to Pisa," *The New Colophon*, III (1950), 117.

10 Mrs. Macpherson, *Anna Jameson* (Boston, 1878), p. 231.

11 *Letters*, ed., Kenyon, I, 324 (to Westwood, March 10, 1847).

12 Berg MS., EBB to Arabel, Pisa [October–November 1846].

13 *Twenty-Two Letters* (New York, 1935), p. 15 (November 24, 1846).

14 Berg MS., EBB to Arabel, Pisa [October–November 1846].

15 Boyce, "From Paris to Pisa," *The New Colophon*, III (1950), 118, 119.

16 *Letters*, ed., Kenyon, I, 301 (November 5, [1846]).

17 *Twenty-Two Letters* (New York, 1935), p. 14 (November 24, 1846).

18 *Letters*, ed., Huxley, pp. 4 (November 24, 1846); 11 (December 19, 1846).

19 *Twenty-Two Letters* (New York, 1935), pp. 28–29 (January 23–29, 1847); 11, 5 (October 2, 1846); 17 (January 7, [1847]).

20 *Letters*, ed., Huxley, p. 5 (November 24, 1846).

21 *Letters*, ed., Kenyon, I, 318–19 (to Miss Mitford, February 8, 1847).

22 *Twenty-Two Letters* (New York, 1935), p. 19 (November 24, 1846).

23 *Ibid.*, pp. 15–24 (November 24, 1846; January 7, [1847]).

24 Berg MS., EBB to Arabel, December 24–25, [1846].

25 *Twenty-Two Letters* (New York, 1935), pp. 15 (November 24, 1846); 37–38 (January 27, [1847].

26 Thomas Moore, ed., *The Works of Lord Byron: With His Letters and Journals, and His Life* (London, 1839), V, 291 (to Murray, December 4, 1821).

27 *Letters*, ed., Kenyon, I, 321–22 [c. February 1847].

28 *Twenty-Two Letters* (New York, 1935), pp. 22, 21 (January 7, [1847]); *Letters*, ed., Kenyon, I, 310 (to Mrs. Jameson, po. November 23, 1846).

29 "A Defense of Mrs. Browning's Father," *The Literary Digest*, May 20, 1899, p. 578.

30 Houghton MS., EBB to Henrietta, December 19, [1846].

31 *Twenty-Two Letters* (New York, 1935), pp. 22–33 (January 7, [1847]); [January 23–27, 1847].

32 *Letters*, ed., Kenyon, I, 319–20 (February 8, 1847).

33 *Twenty-Two Letters* (New York, 1935), pp. 40–43 [March 26, 1847].

34 *Letters*, ed., Huxley, pp. 14–15 (March 31, 1847).

35 *Twenty-Two Letters* (New York, 1935), pp. 44 [March 26, 1847]; 47–48 (May 6, 1847).

36 "A Woman's Last Word," *Men and Women* (1855).

37 *Letters*, ed., Huxley, pp. 19–20 (April 1847).

CHAPTER 15 *"O Bella Liberta, O Bella!" 1847–49* (pp. 235–257)

1 T. Adolphus Trollope, *Tuscany in 1849 and in 1859* (London, 1859), p. 6.

2 *The Greville Memoirs, A Journal of the Reigns of King George IV and King William IV* (London, 1875), I, 302.

3 T. A. Trollope, *What I Remember* (London, 1887), II, 101.

4 No. 4222, according to Gardner B. Taplin, *The Life of Elizabeth Barrett Browning* (New Haven, 1957), p. 195.

5 *Letters*, ed., Huxley, pp. 23, 20 (April 1847).

6 "The Light of Love"; *Letters*, ed., Kenyon, I, 327 (to Mrs. Martin, April 24, 1847).

7 *Letters*, ed., Huxley, p. 22 (April 30, 1847); *Letters*, ed., Kenyon, I, 327 (to Mrs. Martin, April 24, 1847).

8 T. Wemyss Reid, *The Life, Letters and Friendships of Richard Monckton Milnes, First Lord Houghton* (New York, 1891), I, 384.

9 *Letters*, ed., Huxley, pp. 62–63 (November 23 and 24, 1847).

10 *Letters*, ed., Kenyon, I, 329 (to Mrs. Jameson, May 12, [1847]); 331 (May 26, 1847).

11 *Letters*, ed., Huxley, p. 39 (July 9, 1847).

12 Taplin, *The Life of Elizabeth Barrett Browning* (New Haven, 1957), p. 200.

13 Berg MS., EBB to Arabel, June 22–25, [1847].

14 *Letters*, ed., Huxley, p. 29 (May 19, 1847).

15 *Ibid.*, pp. 25–27 (May 16, 1847).

16 *Letters*, ed., Kenyon, I, 336 (to Mrs. Martin, August 7, 1847).

17 Berg MS., EBB to Arabel (May 10, 11 [1848], and July 26, [1847]).

18 *Twenty-Two Letters* (New York, 1935), p. 54 (November 25, [1847]).

19 *Letters*, ed., Kenyon, I, 350 (to Miss Mitford, December 8, 1847).

20 *Twenty-Two Letters* (New York, 1935), p. 54.

21 Mary Boyle, *Her Book*, ed., Sir Courtenay Boyle (London, 1902), pp. 219–20.

22 *Twenty-Two Letters* (New York, 1935), pp. 50 (October 4, 1847); 56 (April 2, [1848]).

23 Huntington MS., April 6, 1848.

24 *Letters*, ed., Huxley, pp. 43–44 (September 13, 1847).

25 Griffin and Minchin, p. 162.

26 *Letters*, ed., Huxley, pp. 76–77 (February 21, March 2–4, 1848).

27 *Letters*, ed., Kenyon, I, 357, 359 (to Miss Mitford, February 22, [1848] and April 15, [1848]).

28 *Letters*, ed., Huxley, pp. 83 (April 22, 1848), 81 (March 7–April 1, 1848).

29 *Letters*, ed., Kenyon, I, 370 (to Sarianna Browning [c. June 1848]).

30 *Letters*, ed., Huxley, pp. 84 (April 22, 1848), 87 (June 24, 1848), 92 (November 19, 1848).

31 *Letters*, ed., Kenyon, I, 448 (May 4, [1850]).

32 *Letters*, ed., Huxley, p. 97 (November 19, 1848).

33 *Letters*, ed., Kenyon, I, 378–80 (to Mrs. Jameson, July 15, [1848]); 381 (to Miss Mitford, August 24, 1848).

34 Miller, *Portrait*, p. 156.

35 Hood, pp. 20–21 (to Horne, December 3, 1848).

36 *Letters*, ed., Huxley, pp. 29 (May 16, 1847), 60 (November 23 and 24, 1847).

37 *Letters*, ed., Kenyon, I, 385 (October 10, 1848).

38 *Letters*, ed., Huxley, pp. 92–93 (November 19, 1848).

39 *Ibid.*, p. 87 (1848).

40 *Letters*, ed., Kenyon, I, 374 (July 4, [1848]); 386 (October 10, 1848).

41 *Letters*, ed., Huxley, p. 101 (February 10, 19, 20, 1849).

42 *Letters*, ed., Kenyon, I, 392 (to Miss Mitford, December 16, [1848]).

43 *Letters*, ed., Kenyon, I, 401 (to Miss Mitford, April 30, 1849).

44 *Tuscany in 1849 and 1859* (London, 1859), p. 217.

45 *Letters*, ed., Huxley, p. 105 (May 2, 3, 4, 5, 1849).

46 *Letters*, ed., Kenyon, I, 383 (August 24, 1848).

47 *Letters*, ed., Huxley, p. 107 (May 2, 3, 4, 5, 1849).

48 *Letters*, ed., Kenyon, I, 389 (December 3, 1848).

49 *Letters*, ed., Huxley, p. 105 (May 2, 3, 4, 5, 1849).

50 *Ibid.*, p. 100 (February 10, 19, 20, 1849).

51 *Twenty-Two Letters* (New York, 1935), pp. 63–64, 65, 66 [March 9, 1849].

CHAPTER 16 ***Sober Questions 1849–51*** (pp. 258–277)

1 *Letters*, ed., Kenyon, I, 399 (to Miss Mitford, April 30, 1849).

2 *Ibid.*, 396, 398, (to Sarianna Browning: po. April 1, 1849 and [April 1849]; 400 (to Miss Mitford, April 30, 1849).

3 *Ibid.*, 410–11 (to Miss Mitford [c. July 1849]); 403 (to Sarianna Browning, May 2, 1849).

4 Hood, p. 23 (July 2, 1849).

5 *Ibid.*, p. 25.

6 *RB and JW*, pp. 114–15 [November 11, 1864].

7 *Letters*, ed., Kenyon, I, 418 (to Miss Mitford, August 31, 1849).

8 *Letters*, ed., Huxley, pp. 111 (September 19, 1849), 114 (October 19, 1849); *Letters*, ed., Kenyon, I, 421 (to Mrs. Jameson, October 1, [1849]).

9 *Letters*, ed., Kenyon, I, 417, 413 (to Miss Mitford, August 31,1849, and [July, 1849]).

10 *Letters*, ed., Huxley, pp. 112–13 (September 19, 1849).

11 *Letters*, ed., Kenyon, I, 353 (to Miss Mitford, December 8, 1847); 422 (to Mrs. Jameson, October 1, [1849]).

12 See *RB and EBB*, II, 678 [May 5, 1846].

13 *Ibid.*, I, 7 (January 13, 1845); 17 [February 11, 1845].

14 See DeVane, *Handbook*, pp. 194–205; also C. R. Tracy, "Browning's Heresies," *Studies in Philology*, XXXIII (1936), 616.

15 *Letters*, ed., Kenyon, I, 429.

16 "Christmas-Eve," line 464.

17 Lines 1322–27.

18 *Handbook*, p. 198.

19 *Letters*, ed., Kenyon, I, 449 (May 4, [1850]).

20 *The Athenaeum*, June 1, 1850, p. 585.

21 *Letters*, ed., Kenyon, I, 443 n.; 445 (to Miss Mitford, April 1850); 440 (to Mrs. Jameson, April 2, [1850]).

22 *Letters*, ed., Hudson, p. 242 (Story to Lowell, March 21, 1849).

23 Henry James, *William Wetmore Story and His Friends, from Letters, Diaries, and Recollections* (Boston, 1903), I, 130–31.

24 Quoted in Katherine Anthony, *Margaret Fuller: A Psychological Biography* (London, 1922), p. 11.

25 *Ibid.*, pp. 146–47.

26 *Letters*, ed., Kenyon, I, 428, 459–60 (to Miss Mitford, December 1, 1849, and September 24, 1850).

27 Hood, p. 28 (July 29, 1850).

28 *Ibid.*, pp. 28, 30.

29 *Letters*, ed., Kenyon, I, 459 (to Miss Mitford, September 24, 1850).

30 Gardner B. Taplin, *The Life of Elizabeth Barrett Browning* (New Haven, 1957), p. 254.

31 *Letters*, ed., Huxley, p. 123 (May 25, 1850).

32 *Letters*, ed., Kenyon, I, 466 (to Miss Mitford, po. November 13, 1850); 469 (to Westwood, December 12, 1850); 478 (to Sarianna Browning, po. April 23, 1851).

33 *Dearest Isa*, p. 232 (March 19, 1866).

34 Berg MS., EBB to Arabel, June 5, [1851].

35 Berg MS., EBB to Arabel, June 26, [1851].

36 *Letters*, ed., Kenyon, II, 11 (to John Kenyon, July 7, [1851]); I, 470 (to Westwood, December 12, 1850); 472 (to Miss Mitford, December 13, 1850).

37 *Letters*, ed., Huxley, pp. 136–37 (July 21, 1851).

38 *Alfred Lord Tennyson, a Memoir by His Son* (London, 1897), I, 341.

39 *Letters*, ed., Kenyon, II, 14 (to Mrs. Martin [c. August 1851]).

40 See Miller, *Portrait*, pp. 157–58.

41 *Letters*, ed., Kenyon, II, 17, 15 (to Mrs. Martin, "Saturday" and "Wednesday" [c. August 1851]).

42 Quoted in Miller, *Portrait*, p. 157.

43 *Letters*, ed., Huxley, p. 138 (July [31?], 1851).

44 *Letters*, ed., Kenyon, II, 16 (to Mrs. Martin [c. August 1851]).

45 *Letters*, ed., Huxley, p. 138 (July [31?], 1851).

46 Sara Coleridge, *Memoir and Letters, Edited by Her Daughter* (London, 1873), II, 447.

47 Bayard Taylor, *Prose Writings: At Home and Abroad,* 2nd ser. (New York, 1862), pp. 412–13, 415.

48 Hood, p. 32 [July 28, 1851].

49 See *RB and EBB,* I, 187 [September 9, 1845].

50 *Letters of Thomas Carlyle to John Stuart Mill, John Sterling and Robert Browning,* ed., Alexander Carlyle (New York, 1923), p. 281.

51 *Letters*, ed. Kenyon, II, 20 [September 1851].

CHAPTER 17 ***Paris: Excursions and Alarums 1851–52*** (pp. 278–300)

1 *Letters*, ed., Kenyon, II, 23, 27, 25 (October 21, [1851]); *Last Words of Thomas Carlyle* (London, 1892), p. 152.

2 *Last Words* (London, 1892), pp. 151–53, 158, 161, 183–84.

3 Berg MS., EBB to Arabel, po. October 14, 1851.

4 *Letters*, ed., Huxley, p. 145 (October 29, 1851).

5 *Ibid.*, p. 148 (December 1, 1851).

6 *Ibid.*, p. 158 (April 1, 1852).

7 N.S. XI (August 1851), 661–89.

8 Griffin and Minchin, pp. 182–83; Orr, *Life*, p. 176.

9 *Letters*, ed., Kenyon, II, 40 (to Miss Mitford, December 24, [1851]).

10 *Ibid.*, II, 50 (to Miss Mitford, February 15, [1852]).

11 *Ibid.*, II, 56, 57 (to John Kenyon, February 15, 1852).

12 *Letters to George*, p. 174 [February 28, 1852].

13 *Letters*, ed., Kenyon, II, 63 (to Miss Mitford, April 7, 1852); 59, 60 (to Mrs. Jameson, February 26, [1852]).

14 Orr, *Life*, p. 171; *Letters*, ed., Kenyon, II, 63 (to Miss Mitford, April 7, 1852). See also *Learned Lady*, p. 112.

15 *Letters to George*, p. 159 [December 4–5, 1851].

16 London *Times*, July 2, 1852.

17 "Browning and the Harriet Westbrook Shelley Letters," *University of Toronto Quarterly*, XXXII (January 1963), 184–92.

18 Leigh Hunt, *Lord Byron and Some of His Contemporaries* (London, 1828), I, 312, 313.

19 Hood, p. 223 (October 12, 1883).

20 *Ibid.*, pp. 223–24.

21 Thomas Love Peacock, *Memoirs of Shelley*, ed., H. F. B. Brett-Smith (London, 1900), p. 48.

22 Hood, pp. 223 (to Furnivall, September 29, 1883); 371 n. (Swinburne to D. G. Rossetti, June 24, [1869]).

23 Admittedly, his faith remained ambiguous. "I am sadly unsettled in my feelings about Shelley, or rather confirmed in my secret apprehensions, by the recent books," he wrote Isa Blagden, on November 19, 1862, by which time he could have read Hogg's *Life* (1858), Middleton's *Shelley* (1858), Trelawny's *Recollections* (1858), Lady Jane Shelley's *Memorials* (1859), and Garnett's *Relics* (1862). Still, Browning's admiration for Shelley survived his perusal of any or all of these, as comments in his later correspondence and in his testimony when under oath at a public trial in 1879 suggest. A cautious attitude toward poetry societies, and some disillusionment with honorary offices, were involved in his refusal of the presidency of the Shelley Society in 1885. See *Dearest Isa*, pp. 137 and 140 n.; also "Browning's Testimony on His Essay on Shelley in 'Shepherd v. Francis,'" *English Language Notes*, II (1964), 27–31; and the last chapters of this biography.

24 Griffin and Minchin, pp. 184–85.

25 See J. M. Baker, *Henry Crabb Robinson* (London, 1937), pp. 210–11.

26 Hood, p. 36.

27 *Portrait*, pp. 178–79.

28 See Albert Léon Guérard, *Napoleon III* (Cambridge, Mass., 1943), pp. 113–24.

29 *Letters*, ed., Kenyon, II, 28 (to Miss Mitford, October 22, [1851]).

30 Pierre Labracherie, *Le Second Empire* (Paris, 1962), I, 130.

31 *Letters to George*, p. 154 [December 4–5, 1851].

32 *Letters*, ed., Kenyon, II, 37 (to Mrs. Martin, December 11, [1851]).

33 *Letters to George*, p. 157 [December 4–5, 1851].

34 See p. 155 above.

35 *Letters*, ed., Kenyon, II, 36 (December 11, [1851]).

36 *Letters to George*, pp. 168–69 (February 4, 1852).

37 *Ibid.*, p. 169 (February 4, 1852).

38 *Letters*, ed., Huxley, p. 146 (December 13 and 14, 1851).

39 See "An Address Delivered by Edward R. Moulton-Barrett on the Opening of the Elizabeth Barrett Browning Centenary Exhibition on 30th May 1961," *Catalogue of the Centenary Exhibition held at St. Marylebone Central Public Library May 31st–July 8th 1961*, introd., L. P. Kelley.

40 *Letters*, ed., Kenyon, II, 24 (October 21, [1851]).

41 Brit. Mus. typescript, EBB to Mrs. Jameson, August 23, 1853.

42 Quoted in Miller, *Portrait*, p. 167.

43 Berg MS., EBB to Arabel, May 25, [1852].

44 See John Huebenthal, "The Dating of Browning's 'Love Among the Ruins,' 'Women and Roses,' and 'Childe Roland,'" *Victorian Poetry*, IV (1966), 51–54.

45 DeVane, *Handbook*, p. 259.

46 Johnstone Parr, "The Site and Ancient City of Browning's 'Love Among the Ruins,'" *PMLA*, LXVIII (1953), 128–37.

47 Lines 73–78.

48 *The Poetry of Experience: The Dramatic Monologue in Modern Literary Tradition* (London, 1957), p. 192.

49 George Arms, "'Childe Roland' and 'Sir Galahad,'" *College English*, VI (1945), 258–61.

50 Quoted by Lilian Whiting, *The Brownings: Their Life and Art* (London, 1911), p. 261.

51 *Handbook*, p. 231.

52 Lines 131–33.

53 "Browning's 'Childe Roland,'" *PMLA*, XXXIX (1924), 963–78.

54 Lines 1026–27.

55 II, ii, 155–56.

56 "Browning's 'Childe Roland' and Wordsworth," *Tennessee Studies in Literature*, VI (1961), 121.

57 Line 103.

58 Lines 176–77.

59 Lines 179–80.

60 Line 182.

61 Lines 189–92.

62 Lines 193–95, 198.

63 Line 203.

64 Lines 29–35.

65 Lines 43–49.

66 Lines 99–105.

67 London *Times*, July 2, 1852.

68 Houghton MS., EBB to Henrietta, po. July 24, 1852.

69 Houghton MS., EBB to Henrietta, po. September 16, 1852.

70 Quoted by Gardner B. Taplin, *The Life of Elizabeth Barrett Browning* (New Haven, 1957), p. 264.

71 *New Letters and Memorials of Jane Welsh Carlyle*, ed., Alexander Carlyle (London, 1903), p. 39.

72 Berg MS., EBB to Arabel, po. October 17, 1852.

CHAPTER 18 *"Two Souls, and Not a Third" 1852–55* (pp. 301–327)

1 *Letters*, ed., Kenyon, II, 95, 96 (to John Kenyon, November 23, 1852); 93 (to Sarianna Browning, po. November 14, 1852).

2 "By the Fire-Side," 113–115.

3 *New Letters*, pp. 66 (to Forster, November 13, 1853); 59 (to Chapman, March 5, 1853).

4 *Letters*, ed., Kenyon, II, 107 (to Mrs. Jameson, March 17, [1853]).

5 *Letters*, ed., Huxley, pp. 177–78 (March 4, 1853).

6 "Pictor Ignotus," line 15.

7 *Letters*, ed., Huxley, p. 185 (May 14, 1853).

8 *Letters*, ed., Kenyon, II, 102, 106 (to Miss Mitford: February and March 15, [1853]).

9 *New Letters*, p. 61 (to Forster, April 12, 1853).

10 *Letters*, ed., Kenyon, II, 112–13 (April 12, [1853]).

11 *Letters to George*, p. 183.

12 *New Letters*, p. 63 (July 18, 1853).

13 *Letters*, ed., Kenyon, II, 99 (to Miss Blagden [Winter, 1852–53]).

14 Hood, p. 38 (January 16, 1853).

15 *Letters*, ed., Kenyon, II, 123 (to Miss Mitford, July 15, 1853).

16 Hugh J. Schonfield, ed., *Letters to Frederick Tennyson* (London, 1930), p. 99.

17 Ernest Thompson, *The History of Modern Spiritualism* (Manchester, 1948), p. 21.

18 *Ibid.*, pp. 21–31.

19 *Letters*, ed., Huxley, p. 190.

20 Brit. Mus. Kenyon typescript, EBB to Miss Mitford, May 20, 1853.

21 Quoted by Jeannette Marks, *The Family of the Barretts: A Colonial Romance* (New York, 1938), p. 626.

22 *Celebrities and I* (London, 1902), pp. 31–33.

23 *Letters*, ed., Kenyon, II, 137 (to Miss Haworth, August 30, [1853]).

24 *Letters*, ed., Huxley, p. 179 (March 4, 1853).

25 *Letters*, ed., Kenyon, II, 117 (EBB to John Kenyon, May 16, [1853]).

26 *Letters to George*, p. 190 (July 16, 17, 18, [1853]).

27 *Letters*, ed., Huxley, p. 184 (May 14, 1853).

28 *Letters to George*, p. 192 (July 16, 17, 18 [1853]).

29 *Ibid.*, pp. 188, 189–90.

30 *Letters*, ed., Kenyon, II, 125 (to Miss Blagden, July 26, [1853]).

31 *Letters to George*, pp. 190, 189 (July 16, 17, 18, [1853]).

32 *Letters*, ed., Kenyon, II, 121 (to Miss Haworth, July 3, [1853]).

33 Brit. Mus. Kenyon typescript, July 26, 1853.

34 Henry James, *William Wetmore Story and His Friends* (Boston, 1903), I, 274, 273.

35 *Letters to George*, p. 189 (July 16, 17, 18, [1853]).

36 *Letters*, ed., Kenyon, II, 142 (to Mrs. Martin, October 5, [1853]).

37 James, *William Wetmore Story* (Boston, 1903), I, 273.

38 Lines 136–140.

39 *Letters*, ed., Huxley, p. 185 (May 14, 1853).

40 Quoted in Miller, *Portrait*, p. 177.

41 *Letters*, ed., Huxley, p. 198 (December 30, 1853).

42 See Elmer Edgar Stoll, "Browning's 'In a Balcony,'" *Modern Language Quarterly*, III (1942), 407–17.

43 *Ibid.*, p. 407.

44 *Letters to George*, p. 201 (October 7, [1853]).

45 *Letters*, ed., Kenyon, II, 152 (to Miss Mitford, January 7, [1854]).

46 *Ibid.*, II, 168 (to Sarianna Browning [May 1854]).

47 *Ibid.*, II, 152 (to Miss Mitford, January 7, [1854]).

48 *Ibid.*, II, 153.

49 *Ibid.*, II, 149, 147 (to Mrs. Jameson, December 21, 1853); 153–54 (to Miss Mitford, January 7, [1854]).

50 *New Letters*, p. 69 (December 19, 1853).

51 *Letters*, ed., Huxley, p. 203 (March 4, 1854).

52 *New Letters*, p. 68 (to Sarianna Browning, December 19, 1853).

53 *Letters*, ed., Huxley, p. 196 (December 30, 1853).

54 *The Letters and Private Papers of William Makepeace Thackeray*, ed., G. N. Ray (Cambridge, Mass., 1945–46), III, 24.

55 *New Letters*, p. 69 (to Sarianna Browning, December 19, 1853).

56 *Letters*, ed., Kenyon, II, 157 (to Westwood, February 2, [1854]).

57 *Ibid.*, II, 148 (to Mrs. Jameson, December 21, 1853); 166 (to Miss Mitford, May 10, 1854).

58 *Letters*, ed., Hudson, p. 33 (RB to Story, June 11, 1854).

59 *Letters*, ed., Kenyon, II, 170–71, 160 (to Miss Mitford: June 6 and March 19, 1854).

60 *New Letters*, p. 73 (April 2, 1854).

61 Brit. Mus. Kenyon typescript, December 21, 1853.

62 *Letters*, ed., Kenyon, II, 167 (to Sarianna Browning [May 1854]); 159 (to Miss Mitford, March 19, 1854); 147 (to Mrs. Jameson, December 21, 1853).

63 Anne Thackeray Ritchie, *Records of Tennyson, Ruskin, Browning* (New York, 1892), pp. 194–95.

64 *Letters*, ed., Kenyon, II, 159, 154 (to Miss Mitford, March 19, 1854, and January 7, [1854]); 163 (to Sarianna Browning [March 1854]).

65 *Letters to George*, pp. 209–210 (January 10, [1854]).

66 *Letters*, ed., Kenyon, II, 163 (EBB to Sarianna Browning [March 1854]).

67 *Letters*, ed., Huxley, p. 202 (March 4, 1854).

68 Miller, *Portrait*, p. 182.

69 Lines 46–55.

70 Ritchie, *Records* (New York, 1892), pp. 191–92.

71 *Letters*, ed., Huxley, p. 196 (December 30, 1853).

72 *Letters to George*, pp. 212–13 (January 10, [1854]).

73 *Ibid.*, p. 210.

74 *Letters*, ed., Kenyon, II, 153 (to Miss Mitford, January 7, [1854]).

75 James, *William Wetmore Story* (Boston, 1903), I, 284–85.

76 *New Letters*, p. 73 (to Forster, April 2, 1854).

77 Berg MS., EBB to Arabel, April 3, [1854].

78 *Letters*, ed., Huxley, p. 198 (December 30, 1853).

79 *New Letters*, pp. 73 (April 2, 1854); 77 (June 5, 1854).

80 *Letters*, ed., Kenyon, II, 187 (February 24, 1855).

81 *New Letters*, p. 78 (July 1, 1854).

82 *Letters*, ed., Huxley, pp. 211 (February 12, 1855); 216 (April 27, 1855).

83 *Ibid.*, p. 212 (February 12, 1855).

84 Orr, *Life*, p. 212.

85 *Letters*, ed., Kenyon, II, 253 (po. February 2, 1857).

86 *Letters*, ed., Huxley, p. 208 (November 6, 1854).

87 *Letters*, ed., Kenyon, II, 203–204 (po. June 12, 1855).

88 *Ibid.*, II, 189 (to Mrs. Jameson, February 24, 1855); 193 (to Mrs. Martin, April 20, 1855).

89 *Ibid.*, II, 189.

90 *Ibid.*, II, 187.

91 *Letters*, ed., Huxley, p. 210 (February 12, 1855).

92 *Letters*, ed., Kenyon, II, 196 (to Mrs. Braun, May 13, [1855]).

93 According to DeVane and Knickerbocker's demonstration, "it is fair to assume that only about half the lines which eventually were to make up *Men and Women* were composed before August, 1854." Browning's two volumes in 1855 contain 7167 lines. Most of these were composed in the period 1853–1855; it is very possible that about half of them were composed in the ten months between August 1854 and June 1855—when, according to Elizabeth, Browning had 8000 lines on hand. *Men and Women* was published five months later, on November 17, 1855. See Taplin, *The Life of Elizabeth Barrett Browning* (New Haven, 1957), pp. 285, 288; and *New Letters*, p. 78, n. 2.

94 Berg MS., EBB to Arabel, June 25, [1855].

CHAPTER 19 *Publications 1855–58* (pp. 328–359)

1 Berg MS., EBB to Arabel, May 15, [1855], and June 25, [1855].

2 Houghton MS., September 6, [1855].

3 *Letters*, ed., Kenyon, II, 229 (to Mrs. Jameson, po. May 2, 1856); Berg MS., EBB to Arabel, June 30, [1855].

4 Quoted by Miller, *Portrait*, p. 184.

5 *Letters*, ed., Kenyon, II, 206 (to Mrs. Martin [July or August 1855]).

6 *Letters,* ed., Huxley, p. 222 (August 21, 1855).

7 Quoted by Miller, *Portrait,* p. 187.

8 Aurelia B. Harlan and J. Lee Harlan, Jr., eds., *Letters from Owen Meredith (Robert, First Earl of Lytton) to Robert and Elizabeth Barrett Browning* (Waco, Texas [1936]), p. 79.

9 Frederick Locker-Lampson, *My Confidences, An Autobiographical Sketch Addressed to My Descendants* (London, 1896), p. 158.

10 *Letters,* ed., Kenyon, II, 213 (to Mrs. Martin [October 1855]); 209 (to Mrs. Jameson [July or August 1855]).

11 *Letters,* ed., Huxley, p. 230 (October 3, 1855).

12 *Letters,* ed., Kenyon, II, 196 (to Mrs. Braun, May 13, [1855]).

13 *Letters,* ed., Huxley, p. 218 (July 13, 1855).

14 W. L. Phelps, "Robert Browning on Spiritualism," *Yale Review,* n.s. XXIII (1933), 129.

15 *Ibid.,* p. 130.

16 *Letters,* ed., Huxley, p. 220 (August 17, 1855).

17 Phelps, "Browning on Spiritualism," pp. 131–34.

18 *Portrait,* p. 198.

19 *TLS,* November 28, 1902, p. 356 (to Miss de Gaudrion, August 30, 1855).

20 D. D. Home, *Incidents in My Life,* Second Series (London, 1872), pp. 106–8.

21 *Letters,* ed., Huxley, pp. 232 (November 15, 1855), 236 (December 6, 1855).

22 *Letters,* ed., Kenyon, II, 221 (to Mrs. Jameson, posted December 17, 1855); 219, 218 (to Ruskin, November 5, [1855]).

23 *New Letters,* p. 59 (March 5, 1853).

24 "Deux lettres inédites de Robert Browning à Joseph Milsand," *Revue Germanique,* XII (1921), 251, letter of February 24, 1853.

25 *Letters,* ed., Huxley, p. 233 (November 15, 1855).

26 See "Notes," *Browning: Men and Women,* ed., Paul Turner (London, 1972).

27 See *Browning's Characters* (New Haven, 1961), pp. 132 ff.

28 Lines 50–61.

29 Lines 98–101.

30 Lines 154–57.

31 Walter Pater, *The Renaissance: Studies in Art and Poetry* (London, 1920), p. 237. Not Lippo's doctrines, or his normal behavior, but his temperament itself might seem to violate the desiderata of Pater; Roy E. Gridley calls attention to the significance of his anger (*Browning* [London and Boston, 1972], pp. 94–95), which is reminiscent of the poet's own. Yet Pater refers to Browning's poems with the

highest praise, and Browning's influence upon Pre-Raphaelitism and the later Victorian Aestheticism of Pater is clear.

32 John Henry Cardinal Newman, "The Tamworth Reading Room," *Essays and Sketches*, ed., Charles Frederick Harrold (New York, 1948), II, 206.

33 Lines 568–73.

34 See Sir Charles Gavan Duffy, *My Life in Two Hemispheres* (London, 1898), II, 157; and Isobel Armstrong (ed.), in *The Major Victorian Poets: Reconsiderations* (London, 1969), p. 117.

35 "Irony and Tension in Browning's 'Karshish,'" *Victorian Poetry*, I (1963), 132–39.

36 Lines 97–100.

37 See "Robert Browning's Pluralistic Universe: A Reading of *The Ring and the Book*," *University of Toronto Quarterly*, XXXI (1961), 20–41.

38 "Browning's 'Cleon,'" *Journal of English and Germanic Philology*, XXVI (1927), 485–90.

39 *The Athenaeum*, November 17, 1855, pp. 1327–28.

40 *Fraser's Magazine*, LIII (1856), 105–14.

41 VI (1856), 493–501.

42 LX (1856), 139–40.

43 December 22, 1855, pp. 1346–47.

44 LXV (1856), 291.

45 See Esther Rhoads Houghton, "Reviewer of Browning's *Men and Women* in the *Rambler* Identified," *Victorian Newsletter*, No. 33 (1968), 46.

46 V (1856), 54–71.

47 *New Letters*, p. 85 (December 17, 1855).

48 *Ibid.*, pp. 89 (to Chapman, February 6, 1856); 81, n. 2.

49 *Ibid.*, p. 89 (February 6).

50 David J. DeLaura finds the lengthiest letter, that of December 2, 1855, "full of good-natured but perversely imperceptive bewilderment": Ruskin discovers much "power" in *Men and Women*, but is baffled even by "porridge" in the last line of "Popularity" ("What porridge had John Keats?"). See DeLaura, "Ruskin and the Brownings: Twenty-Five Unpublished Letters," *Bulletin of the John Rylands Library*, LIV (1972), 314–56.

51 *Letters of Thomas Carlyle to John Stuart Mill, John Sterling and Robert Browning*, ed., Alexander Carlyle (New York, 1923), pp. 297–99.

52 *Letters*, ed., Kenyon, II, 230 (to Mrs. Jameson, posted May 2, 1856).

53 *Letters*, ed., Huxley, p. 249 (June 12, 1856).

54 *Ibid.*, pp. 248, 249.

55 *Ibid.*, p. 243 (April 11, 1856).

56 *Letters,* ed., Kenyon, II, 232 (posted May 6, 1856).

57 *Letters,* ed., Huxley, p. 246 (May 7, 1856).

58 *Letters,* ed., Kenyon, II, 229 (to Mrs. Jameson, posted May 2, 1856).

59 Nathaniel Hawthorne, *The English Notebooks* (New York, 1941), pp. 381–82.

60 *Letters,* ed., Kenyon, II, 237 (to Mrs. Martin, posted September 9, 1856).

61 Houghton MS., EBB to Henrietta, October 19, [1856].

62 *Letters,* ed., Kenyon, II, 238 (to Mrs. Martin, posted September 9, 1856); 239 (to Sarianna Browning, posted September 13, 1856).

63 *Letters,* ed., Huxley, p. 255 (September 8, 1856).

64 *Ibid.,* p. 240 (March 4, 1856).

65 *Ibid.,* pp. 257, 256 (1856).

66 *Ibid.,* pp. 259 (October 17, 1856); 258 (October 11, 1856).

67 *Ibid.,* p. 262 (November 18, 1856).

68 Alethea Hayter (in *Mrs. Browning: A Poet's Work and Its Setting,* London, 1962, pp. 159–74) traces borrowings in detail.

69 Quoted by Taplin, *Elizabeth Barrett Browning* (New Haven, 1957), p. 311.

70 *Letters,* ed., Kenyon, II, 249 (December 29, 1856).

71 *Ibid.,* II, 242 [November 1856].

72 *New Letters,* pp. 96–97 (December 2, 1856).

73 *Letters,* ed., Kenyon, II, 246–47 (to Mrs. Jameson, posted December 26, 1856); 248, 249 (to Mrs. Martin, December 29, 1856).

74 *Letters,* ed., Huxley, p. 265 (January 10, 1857).

75 *Ibid.,* p. 277 (August 4, 1857).

76 *Ibid.,* p. 269 (March 4, 1857).

77 *Letters,* ed., Kenyon, II, 242 (to Sarianna Browning [November 1856]).

78 Brit. Mus. typescript, c. July 1857.

79 Miller, *Portrait,* p. 200.

80 Quoted by Taplin, *Elizabeth Barrett Browning,* p. 350.

81 Quoted by Miller, *Portrait,* p. 201.

82 *Letters,* ed., Huxley, p. 272 (May 13, 1857).

83 *Letters,* ed., Kenyon, II, 263–64 (RB to Mrs. Martin, May 3, 1857).

84 *Harriet Hosmer: Letters and Memories,* ed. Cornelia Carr (London, 1913), p. 80.

85 Quoted by Leonard Huxley, "Mrs. Browning and Her Father's Forgiveness," *Cornhill Magazine,* n.s. LXXIV (1933), 335–36.

86 Brit. Mus. typescript, February 1858.

87 See *Letters to George*, p. 223, n. 1.

88 Brit. Mus. typescript, EBB to Mrs. Martin, May 14, 1857.

89 *Letters*, ed., Huxley, p. 277 (August 4, 1857).

90 *Letters*, ed., Kenyon, II, 268 (August 18, [1857]).

91 Brit. Mus. Kenyon typescript, October 1857.

92 *Letters*, ed., Huxley, p. 282 (October 12, 1857).

93 Berg MS., October 28, [1857].

94 *Letters*, ed., Kenyon, II, 274 (to Miss Haworth, September 28, [1857]).

95 *Ibid.*, II, 275.

96 *Letters*, ed., Huxley, p. 285 (October 28, 1857).

97 *Ibid.*

98 Berg MS., EBB to Arabel, November 22, [1857], and April 12, [1858].

99 *Letters*, ed., Kenyon, II, 277 (to Mrs. Martin, March 27, [1858]).

100 *Letters*, ed., Huxley, p. 289 (April 3, 1858).

101 Berg MS., EBB to Arabel, posted March 24, 1858, and March 12, 1858.

102 *Letters*, ed., Huxley, p. 287 (December 30, 1857).

103 Brit. Mus. transcript, May 1858.

104 Berg MS., posted March 24, 1858.

105 Brit. Mus. transcript, February 1858.

106 *Letters*, ed., Kenyon, II, 279 (to Mrs. Martin, March 27, [1858]).

107 *Passages from the French and Italian Notebooks* (Boston, 1899), pp. 293–96.

108 Berg MS., EBB to Arabel, posted November 13, 1858.

109 *Letters*, ed., Kenyon, II, 284 (to Miss Blagden [July 8, 1858]).

110 *Ibid.*, II, 282 (to Miss Haworth, posted July 8, 1858); 283 (to Miss Blagden [July 8, 1858]; 286 (to Miss Haworth, posted July 23, 1858).

111 *Ibid.*, II, 287 (to Mrs. Jameson, posted July 24, 1858).

112 *New Letters*, p. 108 (to Chapman, August [1858]).

113 *Dearest Isa*, p. 17 (September 4, 1858).

114 *Letters*, ed., Kenyon, II, 293 (to Miss Haworth [October 1858]).

CHAPTER 20 *"The Cycle is Complete" 1858–61* (pp. 360–383)

1 Berg MS., EBB to Arabel, po. November 26, 1858.

2 *Letters*, ed., Kenyon, II, 298 (to Sarianna Browning, po. November 26, 1858).

3 *Dearest Isa*, p. 25 (January 7, 1859).

4 *Letters*, ed., Kenyon, II, 303 (to Miss Blagden, January 7, [1859]); 311 (to Sarianna Browning [April 1859]).

5 *Letters*, ed., Huxley, p. 310 (March 4, 1859).

6 *Letters*, ed., Kenyon, II, 309 (to Miss Blagden, March 27, [1859]).

7 *Letters*, ed., Huxley, p. 311 (March 4, 1859).

8 *Letters*, ed., Kenyon, II, 309 (to Miss Blagden, March 27, [1859]).

9 *Letters*, ed., Huxley, p. 314 (May 27, 1859).

10 *Letters*, ed., Kenyon, II, 308 (March 27, [1859]).

11 *Letters*, ed., Huxley, p. 315 (May 27, 1859).

12 Berg MS., EBB to Arabel, po. March 3, 1859.

13 See *Dearest Isa*, p. 30, n. 36.

14 *Ibid.*, p. 25.

15 Berg MS., EBB to Arabel, June 2, [1859]).

16 *Letters*, ed., Huxley, p. 316 (May 27, 1859).

17 Betty Miller, "The Child of Casa Guidi," *Cornhill Magazine*, CLXIII (1949), 419.

18 Henry James, *William Wetmore Story and His Friends* (Boston, 1903), II, 54, 53.

19 Berg MS., EBB to Arabel, June 2, [1859].

20 *Letters*, ed., Kenyon, II, 325 (to Mrs. Jameson, August 26, [1859]); 321, 322 (to Miss Blagden [July–August 1859]).

21 *Ibid.*, II, 323 (to Miss Haworth, po. August 24, 1859).

22 Quoted by Miller, *Portrait*, p. 209.

23 *New Letters*, p. 122 (August 7, 1859).

24 *Dearest Isa*, p. 41 [August 2, 1859].

25 *Letters*, ed., Kenyon, II, 334 (to Chorley, September 12, [1859]).

26 *Ibid.*, II, 343 (to Sarianna Browning [September–October 1859]).

27 *Ibid.*, II, 354 (to Sarianna Browning [December 1859]); 343.

28 The Marchesa Peruzzi de' Medici [née Edith Story], "Walter Savage Landor," *Cornhill Magazine*, n.s. XXXVIII (1915), 492.

29 Quoted by James, *William Wetmore Story* (Boston, 1903), II, 15–16.

30 Mrs. Story's "Recollections of Walter Savage Landor; with After-Dinner Talk at Siena," in James, *Story* (Boston, 1903), II, 20.

31 Marchesa Peruzzi, "Landor," *Cornhill Magazine*, n.s. XXXVIII (1915), 494.

32 *Letters*, ed., Kenyon, II, 351 (November 25, [1859]).

33 *Ibid.*, II, 345 (to Sarianna Browning [September–October 1859]); 345 (to Mrs. Jameson [October 1859]); 353 (to Sarianna Browning [December 1859]).

34 Quoted by John Forster, *Walter Savage Landor* (London, 1869), II, 569.

35 *Dearest Isa*, p. 48 (November 30, 1859).

36 See *New Letters*, pp. 108, 111 (August 8, [1858,] and September 19, 1858).

37 Brit. Mus. Kenyon typescript, December 7, 1859.

38 *Letters*, ed., Kenyon, II, 355 [Winter 1859].

39 H. C. Minchin, *Walter Savage Landor: Last Days, Letters and Conversations* (London, 1934), pp. 39–40.

40 *Dearest Isa*, p. 51 (January 1, 1860).

41 Quoted by John Weiss, *Life and Correspondence of Theodore Parker* (New York, 1864), II, 410.

42 "*Caliban upon Setebos,*" *Studies in Philology*, XXXV (1938), 487–99.

43 Lines 98–103.

44 Lines 55–56.

45 See "Belial upon Setebos," *Tennessee Studies in Literature*, IX (1964), 87–98, for the poem's relation to *Paradise Lost*.

46 *Letters*, ed., Kenyon, II, 376 (EBB to Miss Blagden [April 1860]).

47 *Dearest Isa*, p. 61 (April 19, 1860).

48 *Letters*, ed., Kenyon, II, 382 (May 2, [1860]).

49 *Ibid.*, II, 385 (to Forster [May 1860]).

50 *Ibid.*, II, 368–69 (to Sarianna Browning [March 1860]).

51 *Letters*, ed., Hudson, p. 167.

52 *Letters*, ed., Kenyon, II, 370 (to Sarianna Browning [March 1860]).

53 Brit. Mus. Kenyon typescript, EBB to Fanny Haworth, August 25, 1860.

54 *Letters*, ed., Kenyon, II, 388 (to Miss Haworth, po. May 18, 1860).

55 See *Dearest Isa*, p. 314 (April 19, 1869).

56 Orr, *Life*, pp. 225–26.

57 *Letters*, ed., Kenyon, II, 395 (to Miss Haworth, po. June 16, 1860).

58 *Ibid.*, II, 397 (to Sarianna Browning [June 1860]).

59 *Letters to George*, p. 244 (October 12, [1860]).

60 Quoted by John Forster, *Walter Savage Landor* (London, 1869), II, 570.

61 *Letters*, ed., Kenyon, II, 398 (to Sarianna Browning [June 1860]).

62 *Letters to George*, p. 235 (September [6], [1860]).

63 *Letters,* ed., Kenyon, II, 405 (to Miss Haworth, August 25, [1860]).

64 *Letters to George,* pp. 251, 252 (December 3, 1860).

65 *Dearest Isa,* p. 66 (December 3, 1860).

66 *Letters to George,* p. 252 (December 3, 1860).

67 Brit. Mus. typescript [December ?, 1860], EBB to W. Surtees Cook.

68 *Dearest Isa,* p. 68 [December 8, 1860].

69 *Letters,* ed., Kenyon, II, 411 [Winter 1860]. Internal evidence indicates this letter was not written before December.

70 *Ibid.,* II, 415 [November or December 1860].

71 *Ibid.,* II, 415, 416 (to Mrs. Martin [December 1860]).

72 *Dearest Isa,* p. 70.

73 *Letters,* ed., Kenyon, II, 411 (to Miss Haworth [Autumn 1860]).

74 *Ibid.,* II, 418 (to Miss Blagden [January 1861]).

75 *Ibid.,* II, 434 (to Sarianna Browning [March 1861]).

76 *Letters to George,* p. 249 (November 1, [1860]).

77 *Ibid.,* p. 253 (April 2, [1861]).

78 *Letters,* ed., Kenyon, II, 434–35 [March 1861].

79 *Ibid.,* II, 436.

80 *Ibid.,* II, 370 (to Sarianna Browning [March 1860]).

81 *Ibid.,* II, 449 (po. June 7, 1861).

82 *Ibid.,* II, 439 [April 1861].

83 *Ibid.,* II, 423 [January 1861].

84 *Ibid.,* II, 448–49 (to Sarianna Browning, po. June 7, 1861).

85 Hood, p. 59 (to Sarianna Browning, June 30, 1861).

86 Story to C. E. Norton, August 15, 1861, quoted by James, *William Wetmore Story* (Boston, 1903), II, 65.

87 *Letters,* ed., Hudson, p. 68.

88 Hood, p. 60 (to Sarianna Browning, June 30, 1861).

89 *Ibid.,* p. 61.

90 Hood, *loc. cit.,* and *New Letters,* p. 138 (to Forster, [July 1861]).

91 Hood, p. 62.

92 Story to C. E. Norton, August 15, 1861, quoted by James, *Story* (Boston, 1903), II, 64.

93 *Ibid.,* II, 62.

94 *Ibid.*, II, 65–66.

95 Hood, p. 63.

96 James, *Story* (Boston, 1903), II, 66.

97 *Letters to George*, p. 271 (July 2, [1861]).

CHAPTER 21 *Booths at the Fair 1861–62* (pp. 384–392)

1 *Letters*, ed., Hudson, p. 80.

2 Hood, p. 63.

3 *Ibid.*, p. 65 (July 20, 1861).

4 *Letters to George*, p. 271 (July 2, [1861]).

5 *New Letters*, p. 133 (July 5, [1861]).

6 *Ibid.*, p. 136 (to Sarianna Browning, July 13, 1861).

7 *Ibid.*, p. 140 [July 1861].

8 *Letters*, ed., Hudson, p. 76 (August 20, 1861).

9 "The Child of Casa Guidi," *Cornhill Magazine*, CLXIII (1949), 420.

10 *Dearest Isa*, pp. 86 (August 31, 1861); 88 (September 9, 1861).

11 *Letters*, ed., Hudson, p. 83 (November 10, 1861).

12 *Dearest Isa*, p. 114 (July 26, 1862).

13 *Ibid.*, p. 100 (March 7, [1862]).

14 *Ibid.*, p. 107 (June 19, 1862).

15 *Letters*, ed., Hudson, p. 94 (January 21, 1862); *Dearest Isa*, p. 104 (March 25, 1862).

16 *Dearest Isa*, p. 98 (February 15, 1862).

17 *Letters*, ed., Hudson, p. 85 (November 10, 1861).

18 *Dearest Isa*, p. 88 (September 9, 1861).

19 *Ibid.*, p. 94 (February 6, 1862).

20 *Ibid.*, p. 112 (July 19, 1862).

21 *Ibid.*, p. 105 (March 25, 1862).

22 *Ibid.*, p. 127 (October 18, 1862).

23 *Letters*, ed., Hudson, pp. 100–1 (March 19, 1862).

24 *Dearest Isa*, p. 104 (March 25, 1862).

25 *Ibid.*, p. 111 (July 19, 1862).

26 *Ibid.*, p. 106 (June 19, 1862).

27 *Ibid.*, p. 165 (May 19–21, 1863).

28 *Ibid.*, p. 148 (January 19, 1863).

29 *Ibid.*, pp. 194, 195 (October 19, 1864).

30 *Ibid.*, p. 175 (September 19, 1863).

31 *Ibid.*, p. 149 (January 19, 1863).

32 *Ibid.*, p. 133 (November 19, 1862).

33 *Ibid.*, p. 182 (December 19, 1863).

34 *Ibid.*, p. 201 (December 19, 1864).

35 "Gold Hair: A Legend of Pornic," lines 141–45.

36 *Dearest Isa*, p. 180 (November 19, 1863).

37 *Ibid.*, p. 128 (October 18, 1862).

CHAPTER 22 *A Sunning Hawk 1862 and 1860–65* (pp. 393–412)

1 *Letters to George*, p. 283 (December 22, 1862).

2 D. G. Rossetti to RB, January 5, 1863, quoted in the catalogue of R. H. Dodd, *An Important Collection of MSS and Autograph Letters of R. and E. B. Browning, with Presentation Copies of Books* (New York, 1916), p. 37.

3 February 7, 1863, pp. 91–95.

4 May 30, 1863, pp. 523–24.

5 *Letters*, ed., Hudson, p. 136 (November 26, 1863).

6 *Ibid.*; also see Moncure D. Conway, *Autobiography: Memories and Experiences* (London, 1904), I, 367–68, II, 28.

7 *Dearest Isa*, pp. 130 (October 18, 1862); 156 (March 19, 1863).

8 Stephen Coleridge, *Memories* (London, 1913), p. 96.

9 See Geoffrey Faber, *Benjamin Jowett: A Portrait with a Background* (Cambridge, Mass., 1957), p. 175; and G. Faber, "Benjamin Jowett" in *Ideas and Beliefs of the Victorians: An Historic Revaluation of the Victorian Age*, foreword by Harman Grisewood (New York, 1966), p. 404.

10 *Letters*, ed., Hudson, p. 134 (November 26, 1863).

11 *Ibid.*, p. 146 [August 22, 1864]; also historical notes by Annette Brosais, in "Ste.-Marie-sur-Mer," *Courrier de Paimboeuf*, Loire-Atlantique, February 13, 1965.

12 *Dearest Isa*, p. 125 (September 19, 1862).

13 *Ibid.*, p. 126; *Letters*, ed., Hudson, p. 111 (October 1, 1862).

14 *Dearest Isa*, p. 172 (August 19, 1863).

15 *Letters*, ed., Hudson, pp. 142 (May 3, 1864); 134 (November 26, 1863); 125 (July 17, 1863).

16 *Ibid.*, pp. 134; 120 (March 17, 1863).

17 *Ibid.*, p. 123 (May 2, 1863).

18 *Dearest Isa*, p. 159 (April 19, 1863).

19 See *Browning Society's Papers* (London, 1890), III, 37–38.

20 June 4, 1864, pp. 765–67.

21 June 18, 1864, pp. 711–12.

22 *Eclectic and Congregational Review*, 6th Series, VII (July 1864), 61–72.

23 See *The Edinburgh Review*, CXX (October 1864), 537–565.

24 See "Wordsworth, Tennyson, and Browning; or Pure, Ornate, and Grotesque Art in English Poetry," *The National Review*, NS 1, XIX (November 1864), 27–67.

25 Lines 23–28, 15–16. However, as Charlotte Crawford Watkins notes, "Prospice" elicited little attention in 1864 and 1865 from reviewers of *Dramatis Personae*. ("Browning's 'Fame Within These Four Years,' " *Modern Language Review*, LIII [1958], 492–500.) But the poem became a favorite among Victorians; see DeVane, *Handbook*, p. 304, as well as Hood, p. 372, n. 85: 5–1.

26 Line 24.

27 See " 'Rabbi Ben Ezra', 49–72: A New Key to an Old Crux," *Victorian Poetry*, I (1963), 46–52.

28 Lines 64–72.

29 *Handbook*, p. 293.

30 *The Life of Robert Browning* (London and Toronto, 1927), p. 233.

31 *Portrait*, p. 227.

32 See C. H. Herford, "Frances Julia Wedgwood, A Memoir," in *The Personal Life of Josiah Wedgwood, The Potter, by His Great-Grand-Daughter, the Late Julia Wedgwood* (London, 1915), pp. xi–xxx.

33 *The Moral Ideal: A Historic Study* (London, 1888), p. vi.

34 In her Preface to a one-shilling edition (London, 1866) of *An Old Debt*, Miss Wedgwood quotes and then replies to this reviewer.

35 Anon. [Julia Wedgwood], *Framleigh Hall. A Novel* (London, 1858), III, 4.

36 *RB and JW*, p. 23.

37 *Dearest Isa*, p. 187 [February 8, 1864].

38 *RB and JW*, pp. 26–28 (June 25, 1864); 133 (March 1, 1865).

39 *Ibid.*, p. 28.

40 *Ibid.*

41 *Ibid.*, pp. 29–30.

42 *Ibid.*, p. 32 (June 27, [1864]).

43 *Ibid.*, pp. 52 (July 28, 1864); 42, 43 (July 23, 1864).

44 *Ibid.*, p. 53 (July 28, 1864).

45 *Ibid.*, pp. 100 (October 14, 1864); 98 (October 10, 1864).

46 *Ibid.*, pp. 53 (July 28, 1864); 74 (September 2, 1864).

47 *Letters*, ed., Hudson, pp. 145–46 [August 22, 1864].

48 *RB and JW*, pp. 60–61, 63 (August 19–20, 1864). For Sarianna's sketch see the plate in Hood, facing p. 80.

49 October 13, 1864, quoted in *Alfred Lord Tennyson, a Memoir, by His Son* (London, 1897), II, 16.

50 W. M. Rossetti, *Rossetti Papers, 1862 to 1870* (London, 1903), p. 302.

51 See "The Dating of Browning's Conception of the Plan of *The Ring and the Book*," *Studies in Philology*, XXXVIII (1941), 543–51.

52 *Dearest Isa*, p. 193 (September 19, 1864).

53 *RB and JW*, p. 86 (September 19, 1864).

54 *Ibid.*, p. 92 (October 3, 1864).

55 *Ibid.*, p. 94.

56 *Letters of Thomas Carlyle to John Stuart Mill, John Sterling and Robert Browning*, ed., Alexander Carlyle (London, 1923), p. 300.

57 *The Ring and the Book*, I, 52, 53, 55, 57.

58 I, 83, 39.

59 I, 100–1, 105–7, 110–12, 114.

60 I, 115–117.

61 See Rudolf Lehmann, *An Artist's Reminiscences* (London, 1894), p. 224.

62 See *The Ring and the Book*, I, 425; XII, 775–87.

63 See Griffin and Minchin, p. 234; A. K. Cook, *A Commentary upon Browning's "The Ring and the Book"* (London, 1920), p. 277, especially n. 1; *Letters*, ed., Kenyon, II, 150–51; and William Allingham, *A Diary*, ed., H. Allingham and D. Radford (London, 1907), pp. 326, 180.

64 Allingham, *Diary*, ed., H. Allingham and D. Radford (London, 1907), pp. 181, 180.

65 *RB and JW*, p. 168 (January 21, 1869).

66 "The Dating of Browning's Conception of the Plan of *The Ring and the Book*," *Studies in Philology*, XXXVIII (1941), 551.

67 *Dearest Isa*, p. 128 (October 18, 1862).

68 *RB and JW*, p. 95 (October 3, 1864).

69 Book I, lines 774, 776–78; and *Dearest Isa*, pp. 196 (October 19, 1864); 212 (March 18, 1865).

70 *Letters*, ed., Hudson, p. 151 (April 11, 1865).

71 *Ibid.*, pp. 154, 155 (July 8 and July 26, 1865).

72 *Dearest Isa*, pp. 199, 202 (November 19 and December 19, 1864); Evelyn Abbott and L. Campbell, *Life and Letters of Benjamin Jowett* (London, 1897), I, 400–1, June 12, 1865.

73 *Dearest Isa*, p. 220 (August 19, 1865).

74 *Ibid.*, p. 216 (May 19, 1865).

75 *RB and JW*, p. 132 (March 1, 1865).

76 *Ibid.*, pp. 135, 136 [early in March 1865].

CHAPTER 23 ***The Muse in Her Strength 1865–69*** (pp. 413–442)

1 *Dearest Isa*, pp. 218, 219 (August 19, 1865); 224 (September 19, 1865).

2 *Ibid.*, pp. 223 (September 19, 1865); 227–28 (October 19, 1865).

3 *Ibid.*, p. 226.

4 *Letters*, ed., Hudson, p. 158 (October 21, 1865); *Dearest Isa*, pp. 231 (March 19, 1866), 229 (December 19, [1865]); *New Letters*, p. 169 (to Milnes, December 20, 1865).

5 *Dearest Isa*, p. 235 (April 22, 1866).

6 *Ibid.*

7 Thomas Woolner, quoted in David Alec Wilson and David Wilson Alexander, *Carlyle in Old Age (1865–1881)* (New York, 1934), p. 116.

8 *Dearest Isa*, pp. 227 (October 19, 1865); 238, 239 (May 19, 1866); William Allingham, *A Diary*, ed., H. Allingham and D. Radford (London, 1907), pp. 127–28.

9 Hood, pp. 94–95, 96 (to Pen Browning, [June 13, 1866,] and June 14, 1866).

10 Browning's father's dossier—either on Pope Formosus or, more likely, on Pope Innocent XII—does not survive; it certainly reached the poet's hands before he completed the Pope's soliloquy for *The Ring and the Book*. See Hood, pp. 105–6 (to Kirkup, February 19, 1867).

11 *Dearest Isa*, p. 241 (June 20, 1866).

12 *Ibid.*

13 See Kenneth Leslie Knickerbocker, "Why Browning Severed Relations with Chapman and Hall," *New Letters*, Appendix C, p. 397.

14 *Dearest Isa*, p. 243 (August 7, 1866); Hood, p. 106 (to Kirkup, February 19, 1867).

15 *Dearest Isa*, p. 247 (September 24, 1866).

16 *The Immortal Lovers: Elizabeth Barrett and Robert Browning* (London, 1950), p. 306. Mrs. Winwar's report is not included in the New York edition (1950) of her book; possibly its source is an unpublished letter now in the United States. If they existed and the poet heard of them, Pen's Croisic daughters would help to explain much in

the late spring and summer of 1869: Browning's unusual dissatisfaction with Pen, his repugnance for Pen's summer companion Willy Bracken, his sudden cancellation of a Breton holiday, his nervous exhaustion, pallor, forgetfulness, refusal to see his old friends, and, early in September, his extraordinary behavior at Loch Luichart, which had considerable consequences for his poetry. In 1869, Pen's academic failures in themselves were no longer a novelty. See Chap. 24, and also: Miller, *Portrait,* p. 248; *Letters to George,* p. 296, n. 2; and M. L. G. De Courten, "Pen, il figlio di Browning," *English Miscellany,* VIII (1957), 125–42.

17 *Dearest Isa,* p. 247 (September 24, 1866).

18 *Ibid.,* pp. 249 (October 19, 1866); 253–54 (February 19, 1867).

19 *Ibid.,* p. 269 (June 19, 1867).

20 Baylor MS., December 6, 1887.

21 Henriette Corkran, *Celebrities and I* (London, 1902), p. 15.

22 *The Letters of John Stuart Blackie to His Wife,* ed., Archibald Stodart Walker (Edinburgh and London, 1909), p. 160.

23 *RB and JW,* p. 141 (May 17, 1867).

24 *Ibid.,* p. 142 (May 17, 1867).

25 *Dearest Isa,* pp. 258, 259 (March 21, 1867); 261 (April 23, 1867).

26 *Ibid.,* p. 300 (August 28, [1868]).

27 See DeVane, *Handbook,* p. 408.

28 "Hervé Riel," lines 119–25.

29 *The Browning Box, or, The Life and Works of Thomas Lovell Beddoes As Reflected in Letters by His Friends and Admirers,* ed., H. W. Donner (London, 1935), p. 101, RB to Kelsall, May 15, 1868.

30 Hood, p. 123 (to Dowden, October 16, 1867); *Dearest Isa,* p. 285 (November 19, 1867).

31 See Gertrude Reese, "Robert Browning and his Son," *PMLA,* LXI (1946), 790.

32 *Ibid.,* p. 793.

33 Balliol MS., RB to Major Gillum, June 17, 1863.

34 Brit. Mus. MS., RB to George Murray Smith, July 30, 1868.

35 *Dearest Isa,* p. 298 (June 19, 1868).

36 *Ibid.,* pp. 297 (June 16, 1868); 298, 299 (June 19, 1868).

37 *Ibid.,* p. 291 (February 20, 1868); *The Browning Box,* ed., H. W. Donner (London, 1935), p. 101.

38 *Dearest Isa,* pp. 299, 300 (August 28, [1868]).

39 Gertrude Reese, "Robert Browning and his Son," *PMLA,* LXI (1946), 791.

40 *RB and JW,* p. 148 (November 5, 1868).

41 See *Intimate Glimpses from Browning's Letter File*, ed., A. J. Armstrong, Baylor University's Browning Interests Series Eight (Waco, 1934), p. 5.

42 J. E. T. Rogers, *Education in Oxford: Its Method, Its Aids, and Its Rewards* (London, 1861), p. 128.

43 *Dearest Isa*, p. 308 [late January 1869].

44 William Allingham, *A Diary*, ed., H. Allingham and D. Radford (London, 1907), p. 181.

45 Baylor MS., RB to Fields, July 12, 1868; also W. S. Tryon, *Parnassus Corner: A Life of James T. Fields, Publisher to Victorians* (Boston, 1963), p. 325.

46 Brit. Mus. MS., RB to George Murray Smith, July 30, 1868.

47 See *RB and EBB*, I, 17 [February 11, 1845].

48 *RB and JW*, pp. 144–45 (October 30, 1868).

49 *Ibid.*, pp. 150 (November 5, 1868); 152, 154 (November 15, 1868).

50 *Ibid.*, pp. 158, 159.

51 *Ibid.*, pp. 162, 163.

52 See *Alfred Lord Tennyson, a Memoir, by His Son* (London, 1897), II, 59.

53 "Browning talked about [Alfred Austin's] article in the *Temple Bar*, saying that he, as shown in the *Ring and Book*, is an analyst, not creator, of character. This, [Browning] very truly says, is not applicable; because he has had to create, out of the mass of almost equally balanced evidence, the characters of the book as he conceives them, and it is only after that process that the analysing method can come into play." See W. M. Rossetti's diary entry of July 4, 1869, in *Rossetti Papers, 1862 to 1870* (London, 1903), p. 401.

54 See *RB and JW*, pp. 158–59 (November 19, 1868).

55 Allingham, *Diary*, ed., H. Allingham and D. Radford (London, 1907), p. 207.

56 See *Curious Annals: New Documents Relating to Browning's Roman Murder Story* (Toronto, 1956), pp. xxx–xlviii.

57 *The Ring and the Book*, VI, 167–69.

58 See page 382 above.

59 See William Clyde DeVane, "The Virgin and the Dragon," *Yale Review*, n.s. XXXVII (1947), 33–46.

60 I, 33–35.

61 See *RB and JW*, p. 188 [February 22, 1869]; and Robert Langbaum, "The Importance of Fact in *The Ring and the Book*," *Victorian Newsletter*, No. 17 (1960), 11–17.

62 I, 1.

63 See "The Clarity of Browning's Ring Metaphor," *PMLA*, LXIII (1948), 1276–82.

64 I, 33.

65 I, 1364–78.

66 RB to Furnivall, February 20, 1883, quoted in *Frederick James Furnivall, A Volume of Personal Record,* ed., John Munro (London, 1911), p. lxxi.

67 See Richard D. Altick and James F. Loucks, II, *Browning's Roman Murder Story: A Reading of "The Ring and the Book,"* (Chicago and London, 1968), pp. 26–28.

68 See Thomas Carlyle, "On History," *Critical and Miscellaneous Essays* (New York, 1900), II, 87–88.

69 See Henry James, "The Novel in 'The Ring and the Book'," *Notes on Novelists with Some Other Notes* (London, 1914), p. 319.

70 I, 847, 883, 920.

71 See Allingham, *Diary,* ed., H. Allingham and D. Radford (London, 1907), p. 221.

72 V, 89.

73 XI, 444–51.

74 *RB and JW,* p. 188 [February 22, 1869].

75 *Ibid.*, pp. 176–77 (February 1, 1869); D. G. Rossetti to RB, March 1869, quoted in Sotheby, Wilkinson, and Hodge's *The Browning Collections. Catalogue of Oil Paintings, Drawings & Prints; Autograph Letters and Manuscripts; . . . the Property of R. W. Barrett, Esq. . . .* (London, 1913), p. 58, lot 272.

76 See "Robert Browning's Pluralistic Universe: A Reading of *The Ring and the Book,*" *University of Toronto Quarterly,* XXXI (1961), 20–41.

77 X, 1790.

78 Leslie Stephen on Browning's *La Saisiaz,* quoted in A. K. Cook, *A Commentary upon Browning's "The Ring and the Book"* (London, 1920), p. 221.

79 X, 348–53.

80 XII, 831–36.

81 VIII, 222–31.

82 I, 1391–93.

83 II, 96–105.

84 III, 1–7.

85 James, "The Novel in 'The Ring and the Book'," *Notes on Novelists* (London, 1914), pp. 306, 312.

86 See Cook, *A Commentary* (London, 1920), p. 8; Browning strongly objected to having the Old Yellow Book published, as he told Furnivall in a three-page letter devoted to the subject (Huntington MS., January 29, 1884).

87 March 20, 1869, p. 399.

88 See Harriet Jay, *Robert Buchanan: Some Account of His Life, His Life's Work and His Literary Friendships* (London, 1903), p. 110.

89 *The London Quarterly Review*, XXXII (July 1869), 356.

90 July 24, 1869, p. 474.

91 *The Edinburgh Review,* CXXX (July 1869), 185–86.

92 LI (October 1869), 125.

93 XIX (January 1869), 262.

94 See *RB and JW,* p. 193 (March 5, 1869).

95 *The Fortnightly Review,* March 1, 1869, pp. 331–43.

96 NS XXV (July 1869), 61.

97 *The British Quarterly Review,* XLIX (March 1869), 456–57.

98 See B. R. McElderry, Jr., "Browning and the Victorian Public in 1868–69" and "Victorian Evaluation of *The Ring and the Book,*" in *Research Studies of the State College of Washington,* V (1937), 193–203; VII (1939), 75–89.

99 *The Cornhill Magazine,* XIX (February 1869), 253.

100 *New Letters of Thomas Carlyle,* ed., Alexander Carlyle (London, 1904), II, 253–54.

101 *The Letters of Queen Victoria, Second Series,* ed., G. E. Buckle (London, 1926), I, 586–87.

102 *RB and JW,* p. 195 (March 8, 1869).

CHAPTER 24 *"Some Faint Show of Bigamy" 1869–72* (pp. 443–470)

1 *Letters,* ed., Hudson, p. 101 (March 19, 1862).

2 *Dearest Isa,* pp. 315, 314 (April "19" for 20, 1869).

3 See Norton B. Crowell, *Alfred Austin, Victorian* (Albuquerque, N.M., 1953), p. 110, n. 20.

4 *The Browning Box, or, The Life and Works of Thomas Lovell Beddoes,* ed., H. W. Donner (London, 1953), p. 126, RB to Kelsall, September 22, 1869.

5 *Dearest Isa,* p. 323 (August 28, [1869]).

6 Rudolf Chambers Lehmann, *Memories of Half a Century: A Record of Friendships* (London, 1908), p. 119, RB to Mrs. Lehmann, July 27, 1869.

7 *Dearest Isa,* pp. 323, 322 (August 28, [1869]).

8 See Henry James, *William Wetmore Story and His Friends* (Boston, 1903), II, 198.

9 Baylor MS., Sarianna Browning to Miss Egerton Smith, August 27, [1869].

10 See *Harriet Hosmer: Letters and Memories,* ed., Cornelia Carr (London, 1913), pp. 355, 97.

11 *Ibid.,* p. 355.

12 *Letters,* ed., Hudson, p. 106 (April 10, 1862).

13 James, *Story* (Boston, 1903), II, 200.

14 *Ibid.,* II, 197.

15 Walburga, Lady Paget, *Embassies of Other Days, and Further Recollections* (London, 1923), I, 280–81.

16 James, *Story* (Boston, 1903), II, 196.

17 Augustus J. C. Hare, *The Story of My Life* (London, 1896), V, 73; see also Adolphus G. C. Liddell, *Notes from the Life of an Ordinary Mortal* (London, 1911), pp. 205–6.

18 *Dearest Isa,* p. 322 (August 28, [1869]).

19 Baylor MS., Sarianna Browning to Miss Egerton Smith, August 27, [1869].

20 *Dearest Isa,* pp. 322, 323 (August 28, [1869]).

21 See *Harriet Hosmer,* ed., Cornelia Carr (London, 1913), pp. 275–76.

22 Hood, pp. 325–38; Miller, *Portrait,* chap. 4; *Letters,* ed., Hudson, pp. 108–87. A detailed discussion of the evidence appears in William Whitla, "Browning and the Ashburton Affair," *Browning Society Notes,* II (July 1972), 12–41. The theory that a marriage proposal dates from October 1871 is ruled out by Browning's statement on April 4, 1872, that Louisa wanted to "get . . . done with it all" "after nine or ten months' teazing": October 1871 was then six months ago, and he notes his "six months' stay in town." There were "two years" of her "cajoleries and pathetic appeals" for a *rapprochement* (Hudson, p. 186, RB to Story, June 19, 1886) between September 1869 and October 1871; Browning says it was "fourteen years since" (i.e., in 1872) that he copied letters, stretching over two years, that proved he had not "been making endeavours to renew a relation of even ordinary acquaintance" with Louisa. There are many other indications that an unsuccessful proposal occurred in September 1869, when, as we know, Browning was in an exceptional frame of mind with Louisa at Loch Luichart; the fact that all of the Storys (who were with Browning and Louisa in September 1869) knew of the proposal; the poet's behavior after the visit; his friends' unusual concern for him; his innuendoes of the "'left off' it all is, I very sincerely assure you" kind (November 16, 1869) are pertinent. "So far as we know Browning's 'stumble' into disloyalty," as Gordon S. Haight points out (*TLS,* July 2, 1971, p. 784), "was never repeated" with another woman, as indeed his placid and friendly relations with Mrs. Benzon during and after the gossip of 1873, and again his comparatively guilt-free relationships with women such as Mrs. Bloomfield-Moore, Mrs. Bronson, Mrs. Skirrow, and Mrs. Orr, might indicate. Difficult as guilt is to document and demonstrate, there are too many indications of Browning's strong sense of regret over the Lady Ashburton affair (let alone of disorientation and anxiety) to leave room for the theory that she proposed, rather than he. Unless and until more evidence comes to light, the primary documents will remain his two letters to Edith Story about the proposal and related gossip: that of January 1, 1872 ("Two years ago, *just* before we went to Scotland . . . but this last year, Lady A[shburton] began upon me one day about the 'utter falseness of Miss G[abriel]'") and the more revealing one of April 4, 1872.

23 *Letters,* ed., Hudson, pp. 170–71 (to Edith Story, April 4, 1872).

24 Baylor MS., November 19, 1863.

25 Quoted by Iris Origo, "The Carlyles and the Ashburtons: A Victorian Friendship," *The Cornhill Magazine,* No. 984 (1950), 479.

26 *Dearest Isa,* pp. 322 (August 28, [1869]); 281 (September 19, 1867).

27 *Letters*, ed., Hudson, p. 142 (May 3, 1864).

28 *Ibid.*, pp. 170–71 (to Edith Story, April 4, 1872).

29 *Dearest Isa*, p. 324 (September 19, 1869).

30 *Letters*, ed., Hudson, pp. 190 (April 4, 1887); 175 (June 9, 1874).

31 See *Parleyings with Certain People of Importance in Their Day*, "With Daniel Bartoli," XVII, XVIII.

32 Sir Sidney Colvin, *Memories & Notes of Persons & Places, 1852–1912* (London, 1921), pp. 84, 79.

33 *Letters*, ed., Hudson, p. 160 [September 28, 1869].

34 *Ibid.*, p. 162 (November 16, 1869).

35 *Ibid.*, p. 186 (to Story, June 19, 1886).

36 *Ibid.*, pp. 170–71; 187 (June 19, 1886).

37 *Dearest Isa*, p. 328 (January 19, 1870).

38 *Letters to George*, pp. 292–93 (June 17, 1870); 295–296 (July 1, 1870); 297 ("Monday," [probably July 4 or 11, 1870]).

39 Michael Howard, *The Franco-Prussian War: The German Invasion of France, 1870–1871* (New York, 1962), p. 116.

40 *Dearest Isa*, pp. 340, 341 (July 19, 1870); 342 (August 9, 1870).

41 *Ibid.*, pp. 342 (August 19, 1870); 344 (August 22, 1870).

42 *Ibid.*, pp. 343 (August 22, 1870); 346, 345 (September 19, 1870).

43 Griffin and Minchin report that Browning was mistaken for a spy before Milsand led the way to Honfleur; Mrs. Orr writes that "it only needed some unusually thickheaded Maire for Mr. Browning to be arrested," but does not say that he was detained or questioned (Griffin and Minchin, p. 243; Orr, *Life*, p. 277).

44 Baylor MS., "Mettle and Metal: written at the end of January, 1871."

45 See the dedication to *Balaustion's Adventure* and also *Dearest Isa*, p. 364.

46 *Mythology and the Romantic Tradition in English Poetry* (Cambridge, Mass., 1937), p. 366.

47 Line 307.

48 Lines 265–74.

49 Lines 804–6.

50 Lines 830–35.

51 See William Allingham, *A Diary*, ed., H. Allingham and D. Radford (London, 1907), p. 240.

52 See "Euripides Browningized: The Meaning of *Balaustion's Adventure*," *Victorian Poetry*, II (1964), 179–186.

53 *Dearest Isa,* pp. 362 (July 19, 1871); 363 (August 19, 1871).

54 Edwin Harrison, quoted in Evelyn Abbott and Lewis Campbell, *The Life and Letters of Benjamin Jowett* (London, 1897), II, 13.

55 *Dearest Isa,* p. 365 (August 19, 1871).

56 See Abbott and Campbell, *Jowett* (London, 1897), II, 13.

57 See *Prince Hohenstiel-Schwangau, Saviour of Society,* lines 2 and 1200.

58 *Dearest Isa,* p. 372 (January 25, 1872).

59 See *The Focusing Artifice: The Poetry of Robert Browning* (Athens, Ohio, 1968), p. 171.

60 *Dearest Isa,* p. 365 (August 19, 1871).

61 *Letters,* ed., Hudson, p. 170 (April 4, 1872).

62 See DeVane, *Handbook,* pp. 364–65.

63 Orr, *Life,* p. 282.

64 Domett, *Diary,* pp. 52–53.

65 *Fifine at the Fair,* line 507.

66 Lines 2286, 2306, 2310–12, 2338–40.

67 Lines 2352–55.

68 "Prologue, Amphibian," lines 13–20.

69 *Ibid.,* line 61.

70 "Epilogue, The Householder," lines 1–4.

71 *Ibid.,* lines 7–8.

72 *Ibid.,* lines 9–11.

73 *Ibid.,* lines 17–24.

74 See Barbara Melchiori, *Browning's Poetry of Reticence* (London, 1968), chap. 8.

75 *Fifine at the Fair,* lines 43–45.

76 See lines 512–551.

77 Lines 628–630.

78 See Charlotte Crawford Watkins, "The 'Abstruser Themes' of Browning's *Fifine at the Fair,*" *PMLA,* LXXIV (1959), 430.

79 *Fifine at the Fair,* lines 1058, 1065–67.

80 William O. Raymond, "Browning's Dark Mood: A Study of 'Fifine at the Fair'," *The Infinite Moment* (2nd edn.; Toronto, 1965), p. 115.

81 See Oswald Doughty, *A Victorian Romantic: Dante Gabriel Rossetti* (London, 1960), pp. 516–18; and Helen Rossetti Angeli, *Dante Gabriel Rossetti: His Friends and Enemies* (London, 1949), pp. 164–70.

82 See "The Harlot and the Thoughtful Young Man: A Study of the Relation between Rossetti's *Jenny* and Browning's *Fifine at the Fair*," *Studies in Philology*, XXIX (1932), 463–84.

83 Quoted by Doughty, *Rossetti* (London, 1960), p. 517.

84 October 1, 1872, pp. 545–46.

85 July 12, 19, 1872, pp. 17–18, 42–43; September 25, 1872, pp. 1215–16; XIV (August 1872), 277–79.

86 XVIII (July 1872), 118–120.

87 DeVane, *Handbook*, p. 370.

88 Domett, *Diary*, p. 45.

89 The preface is dated May 14, 1872.

CHAPTER 25 ***Murder, Natural Death, and the Greeks 1872–80*** (pp. 471–498)

1 See William Lyon Phelps, "As I Like It," *Scribner's Magazine*, LXXVI (1924), 442–43.

2 Anne Thackeray Ritchie, *Records of Tennyson, Ruskin, Browning* (New York, 1892), pp. 175, 177.

3 Hood, p. 309 (to Nettleship, May 16, 1889).

4 *Red Cotton Night-cap Country*, lines 844–49.

5 See M. E. G. Duff, *Notes from a Diary* (London, 1901), I, 208–9, and *Dearest Isa*, p. 385 (September 19, 1872).

6 *Dearest Isa*, p. 385.

7 *New Letters*, pp. 212 (March 15, 1873), 214 (to George Smith [March 26, 1873]); and Domett, *Diary*, p. 78. For clarity in the chapters of this biography, when only two of his names appear, George Murray Smith is "Murray Smith." Browning addressed the publisher as "George."

8 Lines 1796–1803.

9 See Charlotte Crawford Watkins, "Browning's 'Red Cotton Night-cap Country' and Carlyle," *Victorian Studies*, VII (1964), 359–74.

10 P. 5.

11 *New Letters*, p. 216; and Ritchie, *Records* (New York, 1892), p. 181. Mrs. Orr's review appeared in the June *Contemporary Review* (XXII [1873], 87–105).

12 *Diary*, p. 105.

13 Lines 600–3, 608–17.

14 Lines 2167–72, 2125.

15 See "A Parleying with Aristophanes," *PMLA*, LV (1940), 833.

16 *Aristophanes' Apology*, lines 5206–11, 5224–29.

17 Baylor MS., RB to Sarianna, August 28, 1875; and DeVane, *Handbook*, pp. 384, 385.

18 *The Inn Album*, lines 11, 17–18, 3015–16, 3042–44, 3079.

19 Henry James, *Views and Reviews* (Boston, 1908), p. 42; *The Academy*, November 27, 1875, pp. 543–44; *Macmillan's Magazine*, XXXIII (1876), 347–54.

20 On December 9, 1875. See Domett, *Diary*, p. 162.

21 See Norton B. Crowell, *Alfred Austin: Victorian* (Albuquerque, 1953), and *Temple Bar*, XXVI (1869), 316–33.

22 *Dearest Isa*, pp. 332 (March 22, 1870); 359 (May 21, 1871); xxvi–xxvii (to Mme. Mazini, June 5, 1873).

23 Griffin and Minchin, p. 260, and *Aristophanes' Apology*, line 1674.

24 "Of Pacchiarotto," lines 530–32, 541–44, 554–70.

25 James Thomson, *Biographical and Critical Studies* (London, 1896), p. 483, and Edward Dowden in *The Academy*, July 29, 1876, p. 100.

26 *Portrait*, pp. 259–61.

27 See Kenneth Leslie Knickerbocker, "An Echo from Browning's Second Courtship," *Studies in Philology*, XXXII (1935), 120–24.

28 *The Examiner*, June 10, 1876, and August 5, 1876, quoted in Hood, pp. 359–60.

29 August 12, 1876, pp. 904–5.

30 *Letters to George*, p. 303.

31 See *Handbook*, pp. 415–19.

32 Matthew Arnold to RB, November 26, 1877, in John Drinkwater, *A Book for Bookmen: Being Edited Manuscripts and Marginalia, with Essays* (New York, 1927), p. 231.

33 See *A Diary*, ed., H. Allingham and D. Radford (London, 1907), pp. 257–60.

34 Paul F. Mattheisen, ed., "Gosse's Candid Snapshots," *Victorian Studies*, VIII (1965), 344–45. The luncheon occurred on July 25, 1876.

35 *Letters*, ed., Hudson, p. 174 (June 9, 1874).

36 See Baylor MS., September 9, 1875, and *Letters to George*, p. 299 (January 20, 1875). Pen's chief portraits of his father are illustrated in Grace Elizabeth Wilson, *Robert Browning's Portraits, Photographs and Other Likenesses and Their Makers*, ed., A. J. Armstrong (Waco, Texas, 1943).

37 *Celebrities and I* (London, 1902), p. 163.

38 See R. C. Lehmann, *Memories of Half a Century: A Record of Friendships* (London, 1908), p. 122; and Domett, *Diary*, p. 169.

39 Florence Compton, *A Literary Friendship: Letters to Lady Alwyne Compton, 1869–1881, from Thomas Westwood* (London, 1914), p. 195.

40 See *The Academy*, April 6, 1878; *The Athenaeum*, May 4, 1878; *The Times*, May 31, 1878.

41 See Brit. Mus. Ashley 5719, a notebook of newspaper cuttings about Pen.

42 *Learned Lady*, p. 49 (June 9, 1878); *The Athenaeum*, January 4, 1890; *Letters*, ed., Hudson, p. 180 (Pen to Waldo Story, December 26, 1881); RB to Tennyson, March 26, 1878, MS courtesy of Thomas J. Collins; and William Allingham, *A Diary*, ed., H. Allingham and D. Radford (London, 1907), pp. 263–64.

43 Rudolf Lehmann, *An Artist's Reminiscences* (London, 1894), p. 230; Wilfred Meynell, "The 'Detachment' of Browning," *The Athenaeum*, January 4, 1890; and Lady Laura Troubridge, *Memories and Reflections* (London, 1925), pp. 44–45.

44 Gertrude Reese, "Robert Browning and His Son," *PMLA*, LXI (1946), 796.

45 Hood, p. 247 (May 12, 1886).

46 *New Letters*, p. 235 (to Mrs. Skirrow, August 3, [1876]); *Learned Lady*, pp. 46–47 (August 30, 1877), and pp. 44–45 (August 17, 1877).

Dr. Roussel, owner and builder of the chalet, held that *la saisiaz* means *rock-cleft* or *fissure*; Mrs. Orr declares that it means *the sun*.

47 *The Nineteenth Century* had been launched in March 1877 to perpetuate the aims of the Metaphysical Society; a sonnet by Tennyson in the first issue images the search for faith as a mountain ascent. September's issue carries a symposium on eschatology (R. H. Hutton writes from an Anglo-Catholic, T. H. Huxley from an agnostic and anti-Comtian, and Roden Noel from a pantheistic viewpoint, for example). Browning and Miss Smith discussed the issue's contents "lightly" as they strolled (*La Saisiaz*, 162–63), and it is probable that the essays helped him to assemble his ideas for the poem later; see Hoxie N. Fairchild, "*La Saisiaz* and *The Nineteenth Century*," *Modern Philology*, XLVIII (1950), 104–11; and E. C. McAleer, "Browning's 'Cleon' and Auguste Comte," *Comparative Literature*, VIII (1956), 142–45.

48 *New Letters*, pp. 240–41 (to Mrs. Skirrow, September 15, 1877); Domett, *Diary*, p. 210.

49 Harriet Jay, *Robert Buchanan: Some Account of His Life, His Life's Work and His Literary Friendships* (London, 1903), pp. 112–13.

50 Lines 1–4.

51 Line 144.

52 "Bishop Blougram's Apology," lines 990–91.

53 *La Saisiaz*, lines 615–17.

54 Lines 210–16.

55 Lines 266–67, 269, 333–34.

56 See F. E. L. Priestley, "A Reading of *La Saisiaz*," *University of Toronto Quarterly*, XXV (1955), 47–59.

57 Lines 349–50, 355.

58 Lines 612–14, 608.

59 Harriet Jay, *Buchanan* (London, 1903), p. 112.

60 It is difficult to find a year, between 1865 and 1889, when Browning was not about to marry someone—according to Victorian gossip. In 1873 letter-writers excelled

themselves, and the widow of Ernest Leopold Schlesinger Benzon, the steel magnate, almost became the new Mrs. Browning; see Gordon S. Haight, "Robert Browning's Widows," *TLS* (1971), 783–84. In the 1880s, Browning's kissing of ladies surprised his valet; Mrs. Bloomfield-Moore believed that the poet's love for her was not platonic, and Mrs. Orr and Browning were sometimes thought to be having an affair.

61 Julian Hawthorne, *Shapes That Pass* (London, 1928), p. 144; Michael Field, *Works and Days* (London, 1933), pp. 216–17.

62 W. B. Maxwell, *Time Gathered: Autobiography* (London, 1937), pp. 113–15; *New Letters*, p. 204 (to Mrs. Skirrow, January 2, 1872).

63 Mary Gladstone Drew, *Diaries and Letters*, ed., Lucy Masterman (London, 1930), pp. 116–17; *The Journals of Lady Knightley of Fawsley, 1856–1884*, ed., Julia Cartwright (London, 1915), p. 251.

64 *Learned Lady*, p. 54; *New Letters*, p. 248 (to Mrs. Skirrow, September 12, 1878).

65 "Pheidippides," line 116.

66 "Clive," lines 199–200.

67 See C. R. Tracy, "Tray," *PMLA*, LV (1940), 615–16. DeVane (*Handbook*, p. 420) summarizes Victorians on *La Saisiaz.*

68 *Letters*, ed., Hudson, p. 193 (September 30, [1878 not 1889]); *Learned Lady*, p. 68 (September 28, 1878).

69 Flooded roads and rheumatism kept Browning from reaching Venice in 1882; an Italian border quarantine and Mrs. Bronson's travel plans, in 1884; work on the *Parleyings*, and another invitation, in 1886; and plans for his son's fall wedding, in 1887. He was fond enough of Venice to attempt in 1885 and 1886 to buy the Manzoni Palace. See Katherine Bronson, "Browning in Venice, with a Prefatory Note by Henry James," *Cornhill Magazine*, LXXXV (1902), 145–71, and also Orr, *Life*, p. 311, and *Learned Lady*, p. 71 (October 12, 1878).

70 See "Browning's Testimony on His Essay on Shelley in 'Shepherd v. Francis,'" *English Language Notes*, II (1964), 27–31.

71 *The Daily Telegraph*, June 16, 1879, p. 2.

72 Eveline M. Forbes, "A Visit to Balliol, 1879," *Nineteenth Century*, XC (1921), 862–63.

73 *Learned Lady*, pp. 85 (August 17, 1880); 102 (October 23, 1880).

74 *New Letters*, pp. 262–63 (March 18, 1881).

CHAPTER 26 *Lion and Sage 1881–85* (pp. 499–508)

1 See "The Study of Poetry," *Essays in Criticism: Second Series* (London, 1888), p. 1. The essay was first published in 1880.

2 Folger Shakespeare Library MS., RB to Dr. Ingleby, February 25, 1881.

3 *Frederick James Furnivall: A Volume of Personal Record*, ed. John Munro (London, 1911), p. lxxv.

4 *The Browning Society's Papers* (London, 1881–91), I, 1*.

5 See F. J. Furnivall, "The Late George Smith," *The Athenaeum*, May 4, 1901. Demand soon increased. Exclusive of income from American editions, Browning earned about £436 in 1886, £756 in 1887, £1252 in 1888, and £1013 in 1889 from the sale of his poetry (*Robert Browning's Finances from His Own Account Book*, ed., Roma A. King, Jr. [Waco, 1947]).

6 *Papers* (London, 1881–91), I, 19; the prospectus is dated July 27, 1881.

7 "It seems to me that that sort of thing borders on the ridiculous," Curtis heard Browning say, in French, when the prospectus arrived in the post at Warwick Crescent; MS. notebook by D. S. Curtis, quoted by William S. Peterson, *Interrogating the Oracle: A History of the London Browning Society* (Athens, Ohio, 1969), p. 181. The sketch of the Browning societies owes much to this book.

8 See *Learned Lady*, p. 124 (September 6, 1881), and *Papers* (London, 1881–91), I, 1*–2*, 186, 175.

9 *Nation*, November 24, 1881, p. 415; *Cambridge Review*, November 30, 1881, p. 103; *Echo*, October 29, 1881, p. 1, and October 31, 1881, p. 1.

10 Hood, pp. 202 (to Miss Dickinson West, November 12, 1881); 212 (to Edmund Yates [late in 1881]).

11 Baylor MS., RB to Furnivall, April 25, 1882.

12 Hood, pp. 207–8 (to Furnivall, January 12, 1882).

13 William S. Peterson, *Interrogating the Oracle* (Athens, Ohio, 1969), p. 109.

14 See Richard D. Altick, "Robert Browning Rides the Chicago and Alton," *The New Colophon*, III (1950), 78–81.

15 Brit. Mus. typescript Ashley 5768, RB to Mr. Williams, September 24, 1886.

16 See *The Academy*, March 20, 1886, p. 200; *Journal of Education*, n.s. VIII (1886), 207–8; and Robert Sidney, "Some Browning Memories," *Saturday Review*, May 11, 1912, p. 584.

17 *Learned Lady*, pp. 185–86 (November 4, 1884).

18 See *The Times*, June 15, 1882, p. 8; Rosaline O. Masson, "Robert Browning in Edinburgh," *Cornhill Magazine*, XCIX, n.s. XXVI (1909), 229; and William Lyon Phelps, "A Conversation with Browning," *ELH*, XI (1944), 155–56.

19 Masson "Browning in Edinburgh," *Cornhill Magazine*, XCIX (1909), 237; and *Poet-Lore*, II (1890), 102–3.

20 *Learned Lady*, pp. 147 (August 16, 1882); 152 (September 3, 1882).

21 "Pambo," lines 51, 53–54.

22 Hood, p. 218 (April 17, 1883).

23 See "The Texts of Fifteen Fugitives," *Victorian Poetry*, V (1967), 160.

24 See "Replies to Challenges to Rhyme" in *New Poems*, ed., F. G. Kenyon (London, 1914).

25 *Ferishtah's Fancies*, "Prologue," lines 1–4, 29–32.

26 Thomas Jones, *The Divine Order and Other Sermons and Addresses* (London, 1884), p. 13; and see Philip Drew, "Henry Jones on Browning's Optimism," *Victorian Poetry*, II (1964), 29–41.

27 "A Pillar at Sebzevah," lines 25–30.

28 *Ferishtah's Fancies*, "Epilogue," lines 25–28.

29 "Browning As I Knew Him," by his Valet [William Grove], *The Sunday Express*, December 4, 1927, p. 9.

30 See R. C. Lehmann, *Memories of Half a Century* (London, 1908), p. 114. Browning told William Allingham in June 1888: "The acting of my four plays ["In a Balcony," *A Blot, Colombe*, and *Strafford*] by professionals, *unpaid*, for the Browning Society, is surely one of the greatest and most wonderful honours ever paid to a dramatic writer" (*Diary*, ed. H. Allingham and D. Radford [London, 1907], p. 373).

CHAPTER 27 ***The Summit Attained 1886–89*** (pp. 509–522)

1 L. C. Collins, *Life and Memoirs of John Churton Collins* (London, 1912), p. 83; Sir Theodore Martin, *Helena Faucit* (Edinburgh and London, 1900), p. 389.

2 Orr, *Life*, p. 347.

3 *Parleyings*, "With Bernard de Mandeville," lines 72–74.

4 *Parleyings*, "With Francis Furini," lines 601–3. See William Clyde DeVane, *Browning's Parleyings: The Autobiography of a Mind* (New Haven, 1927), pp. 210–12; and for a defense of the *Parleyings* as an associational structure, Roma A. King, Jr., *The Focusing Artifice* (Athens, Ohio, 1968), chap. 7.

5 Thomas James Wise, *A Browning Library: A Catalogue of Printed Books, Manuscripts, and Autograph Letters by Robert Browning and Elizabeth Barrett Browning* (London, 1929), p. xxvi—a work which includes falsified information. Though irritated by his requests and astonished by the first-edition mania of "unwise Wise," and initially suspicious of the fabricated "Runaway Slave," Browning was fooled by Wise's painstaking forgeries. In 1934, Wise was undone by John Carter and Graham Pollard's microscopic examination of paper and exhaustive study of the datable evolution of type *(An Enquiry into the Nature of Certain Nineteenth Century Pamphlets* [London and New York]). Also see RB to Tennyson, December 13, 1885.

6 "Browning As I Knew Him," by his Valet, *Sunday Express*, December 4, 1927, p. 9.

7 William Lyon Phelps, "Robert Browning as Seen by His Son: A Talk with Barrett Browning," *Century Magazine*, LXXXV, n.s. LXIII (1913), 419.

8 Brit. Mus. MS. Ashley 5768, RB to Mr. Williams, June 7, 1887; Anne Thackeray Ritchie, *Records of Tennyson, Ruskin, Browning* (New York, 1892), p. 187. No. 19 Warwick Crescent was not demolished until 1960.

9 *Letters to George*, pp. 320 (January 21, 1889); 309 (November 5, 1887).

10 Hood, pp. 265–66 (August 19, 1887).

11 *Letters to George*, pp. 318 (December 21, 1888); 322–23 (February 24, 1889).

12 "The public loudness, stridency and even violence of Browning's late voice are all

evident in the recording—even if one makes allowance for the degree of shouting that was necessary to make any voice register clearly on the early cylinders," comment Michael Hancher and Jerrold Moore, in " 'The Sound of a Voice That is Still': Browning's Edison Cylinder," *The Browning Newsletter*, No. 4 (Spring 1970), pp. 21–33; see p. 27, and the second part of the article in issue No. 5. Browning pronounces "my" as "me," and speaks his signature with force at the close: RrOB-ət! BRrOWN-ing! Some words are conjectural: "that" may be "but." The date of the recording (April 7, 1889) is established by H. R. Haweis in *The Times*, December 13, 1890, p. 10.

13 Edmund Gosse, *Robert Browning, Personalia* (London, 1890), p. 85.

14 *Letters and Literary Remains of Edward FitzGerald*, ed. William Aldis Wright (London, 1889), I, 280 (Edward FitzGerald to W. H. Thompson, July 15, 1861).

15 See *The Athenaeum*, July 13, 1889, p. 64, and Hood, *Letters*, p. 378n.

16 Hood, p. 313 (to Furnivall, July 16, 1889). Compounding Browning's anxiety was, undoubtedly, the feeling that he had offended Lady Tennyson and Tennyson himself, "one of FitzGerald's oldest friends"; see Christopher Ricks, "Two Letters by Browning," *TLS*, June 3, 1965.

17 William G. Kingsland, "Robert Browning: Some Personal Reminiscences," *Baylor Bulletin*, XXXIV (1931), 40; and Hood, pp. 315 (July 17, 1889); 316, 318 (August 16, 1889).

18 Walburga, Lady Paget, *In My Tower* (London, 1924), II, 349.

19 Katherine C. Bronson, "Browning's Asolo, with Sketches by Clara Montalba," *Century Magazine*, LIX, n.s. XXXVII (1900), 925, 922, 923.

20 *Learned Lady*, p. 202.

21 *New Letters*, p. 384 (to Mrs. Skirrow, October 15, 1889); Mrs. Bronson, "Browning's Asolo," *Century Magazine*, LIX (1900), 925; and *Asolando*, "Prologue," lines 24–25, 32–35.

22 *New Letters*, p. 384.

23 Huntington MS., Story to Dana Estes, April 21, 1891; and *Letters*, ed., Hudson, p. 197 (Story to Pen, December 13, 1889).

24 Orr, *Life*, p. 398; Miller, *Portrait*, p. 280; and "Diary of Miss Evelyn Barclay," *Baylor Bulletin*, XXXV (1932), 5.

25 Quoted by Lilian Whiting, *The Brownings* (Boston, 1911), p. 290.

26 Lines 29–34.

27 Line 140.

28 *Learned Lady*, pp. 192 (December 4, 1886); 195 (April 2, 1887).

29 See Orr, *Life*, p. 398, and B. R. Jerman, "The Death of Robert Browning," *University of Toronto Quarterly*, XXXV (1965), 55–56.

30 "Diary," *Baylor Bulletin*, XXXV (1932), 7–8; Orr, *Life*, p. 400.

31 "Diary," *Baylor Bulletin,* XXXV, 8–9; Jerman, "The Death," *University of Toronto Quarterly,* XXXV, 58; Orr, *Life,* p. 401.

32 L. P. Kelley, "Robert Browning and George Smith: Selections from an Unpublished Correspondence," *Quarterly Review,* CCXCIX (1961), 334.

33 See Jerman, "The Death," *University of Toronto Quarterly,* XXXV (1965), 59–60, 73 n. 46.

34 See Lilian Whiting, *The Brownings* (Boston, 1911), p. 294.

35 December 21, 1889, p. 858; December 14, 1889, p. 665.

36 *Recollections of Louisa May Alcott, John Greenleaf Whittier, and Robert Browning, Together with Several Memorial Poems* (Boston, 1893), p. 57.

37 A. C. Swinburne, *A Sequence of Sonnets on the Death of Robert Browning* (London, privately printed, 1890), III.

38 See "My First Thought," in *More Homage to Browning,* ed., John Richter, with a preface by A. Joseph Armstrong (Waco, 1939).

39 Orr, *Life,* p. 401; and Lady Layard, quoted by Jerman, "The Death," *University of Toronto Quarterly,* XXXV (1965), 61.

40 Lady Layard, quoted, *op. cit.,* p. 63; and Henriette Corkran, *Celebrities and I* (London, 1902), pp. 16–17.

41 See Mabel Dodge Luhan, *European Experiences* (New York, 1935), pp. 115–16.

42 Introduction, *Letters to George,* p. 18.

43 *Works and Days* (London, 1933), p. 215.

44 Elizabeth Rachel Chapman, "Browning's Funeral," *The Scots Magazine,* n.s. V (1890), 219–20.

45 Brit. Mus. Add. MS., A. 2562, Edmund Gosse, December 31, 1889.

46 *The Times,* January 1, 1890.

47 *Works and Days* (London, 1933), pp. 39, 40.

The lines "Let it be" are from Browning's unfinished and untitled draft of a soliloquy for Aeschylus.

Cue Titles

Cue titles have been used in the References (on pages 523 to 585) for citations to the following printed sources and manuscript collections:

Balliol	Letters in the Balliol College Library at Oxford.
Baylor	Letters and other documents in the Armstrong Browning Library at Baylor University in Waco, Texas.
Berg	Letters in the Henry W. and Albert A. Berg Collection of the New York Public Library. Astor, Lenox and Tilden Foundations.
Brit. Mus.	Documents in the Manuscript Collection of the British Museum in London.
Dearest Isa	*Dearest Isa: Robert Browning's Letters to Isabella Blagden,* ed., Edward C. McAleer (University of Texas Press: Austin, 1951).
DeVane, *Handbook*	William Clyde DeVane, *A Browning Handbook* (2nd edn.; Appleton-Century-Crofts: New York, 1955).
Domett, *Diary*	*The Diary of Alfred Domett, 1872–1885,* ed., E. A. Horsman (Oxford University Press: London, 1953).
EB to Miss Mitford	*Elizabeth Barrett to Miss Mitford: The Unpublished Letters of Elizabeth Barrett Barrett to Mary Russell Mitford,* ed., Betty Miller (John Murray: London, 1954).
EB to Mr. Boyd	*Elizabeth Barrett to Mr. Boyd: Unpublished Letters of Elizabeth Barrett Browning to Hugh Stuart Boyd,* ed., Barbara P. McCarthy (Yale University Press: New Haven, 1955).
Griffin and Minchin	W. Hall Griffin and Harry Christopher Minchin, *The Life of Robert Browning with Notices of his Writings, His Family, & His Friends* (Methuen and Company: London, 1938).
Hood	*Letters of Robert Browning Collected by Thomas J. Wise,* ed., Thurman L. Hood (Yale University Press: New Haven, 1933).
Houghton	Letters in the Houghton Library of Harvard University.
Huntington	Letters in the Henry E. Huntington Library and Art Gallery at San Marino, California.
Learned Lady	*Learned Lady: Letters from Robert Browning to Mrs. Thomas FitzGerald, 1876–1889,* ed., Edward C. McAleer (Harvard University Press: Cambridge, Mass., 1966).
Letters, ed., Hudson	*Browning to his American Friends: Letters between the Brownings, the Storys and James Russell Lowell, 1841–1890,* ed., Gertrude Reese Hudson (Barnes and Noble: New York, 1965).
Letters, ed., Huxley	*Elizabeth Barrett Browning: Letters to her Sister, 1846–1859,* ed., Leonard Huxley (John Murray: London, 1929).
Letters, ed., Kenyon	*The Letters of Elizabeth Barrett Browning,* ed., Frederic G. Kenyon (Macmillan and Company: New York, 1897), 2 vols.

Letters to George	*Letters of the Brownings to George Barrett*, eds., Paul Landis and Ronald E. Freeman (University of Illinois Press: Urbana, 1958).
Macready	*The Diaries of William Charles Macready, 1833–1851*, ed., William Toynbee (G. P. Putnam's Sons: New York, 1912), 2 vols.
Miller, *Portrait*	Betty Miller, *Robert Browning: A Portrait* (John Murray: London, 1952).
New Letters	*New Letters of Robert Browning*, eds., William Clyde DeVane and Kenneth Leslie Knickerbocker (Yale University Press: New Haven, 1950).
Orr, *Life*	Mrs. Sutherland Orr, *Life and Letters of Robert Browning*, new edition, revised by Frederic G. Kenyon (Smith, Elder and Company: London, 1908).
RB and AD	*Robert Browning and Alfred Domett*, ed., Frederic G. Kenyon (Smith, Elder and Company: London, 1906).
RB and EBB	*The Letters of Robert Browning and Elizabeth Barrett Barrett, 1845–1846*, ed., Elvan Kintner (The Belknap Press of Harvard University Press: Cambridge, Mass., 1969), 2 vols.
RB and JW	*Robert Browning and Julia Wedgwood: A Broken Friendship as revealed in their Letters*, ed., Richard Curle (John Murray and Jonathan Cape: London, 1937).
Variorum	*The Complete Works of Robert Browning, With Variant Readings & Annotations*, ed., Roma A. King, Jr., *et al.* (Ohio University Press: Athens, Ohio, 1969, *et seq.*), notes.

INDEX

Titles are indexed or included under author.